The Second World War
Asia and the Pacific

The
Second World War
Asia and the Pacific

John H. Bradley

Jack W. Dice
Contributing Author

Thomas E. Griess
Series Editor

DEPARTMENT OF HISTORY
UNITED STATES MILITARY ACADEMY
WEST POINT, NEW YORK

SQUAREONE
PUBLISHERS

Illustration Credits

Page

11 General Hideki Tojo. Photo: Picture used by permission of Professor Alvin D. Coox.

84 Lieutenant General Masaharu Homma. Photo: Reproduced with the permission of the Controller of Her Britannic Majesty's Stationery Office.

220 Lieutenant General William Slim. Photo: Reproduced with the permission of the controller of Her Britannic Majesty's Stationery Office.

222 Lieutenant General M. Kawabe. Photo: Reproduced with the permission of the controller of Her Britannic Majesty's Stationery Office.

222 Lieutenant General R. Mutaguchi. Photo: Reproduced with the permission of the controller of Her Britannic Majesty's Stationery Office.

227 Jungle Road During 1944 Monsoon. Photo: Reproduced with the permission of the controller of Her Britannic Majesty's Stationery Office.

All other illustrations are reprinted courtesy of the U.S. Armed Forces.

Series Editor, Thomas E. Griess
In-House Editor, Joanne Abrams
Cover design by Phaedra Mastrocola

Library of Congress Cataloging-in-Publication Data
The Second World War.
   p. cm.
   "Department of History, United States Military Academy, West Point, New York."
   Originally published: Wayne, N.J. : Avery, 1984. (The West Point military history series)
   Includes bibliographical references and index.
   Contents: [1] Europe and the Mediterranean / Thomas B. Buell ... [et al.] — v. [2] Asia and the Pacific / John H. Bradley ; Jack W. Dice, contributing author.
   ISBN 0-7570-0160-2 (pbk.) — ISBN 0-7570-0162-9 (pbk.)
   1. World War, 1939–1945—Campaigns. I. Buell, Thomas B. II. Bradley, John H.
III. Dice, Jack W. IV. United States Military Academy. Dept. of History. V. West Point
military history series.

D743 .S384 2002
940.54'1—dc21

2002026672

Contents

To the Corps of Cadets at the United States Military Academy,
whose preparation for the military profession
is enhanced by the study of military history.

Illustrations

Acknowledgements

This work like all of this type is the product of many people, all of whom deserve our thanks for their help and counsel. They in large part were our co-authors.

To Colonel Thomas Griess, Professor and Head of the Department of History, we owe the chance to try our hands at writing history, and to him we owe a great deal of thanks for his careful and painstaking editing, scholarly criticism, and helpful suggestions. Few will ever understand the interest and time he put into this history.

To Professors Frank Vandiver of Rice University, Theodore Ropp of Duke University, Jay Luvaas of Allegheny College, and Alvin Coox of the State University of California, San Diego, we are indebted for our historical training and for much specific counsel. We wish to acknowledge the special help given by Professor Coox—he read the manuscript and provided much original material and professional advice on the history of the Imperial Japanese Army.

To General Albert Wedemeyer, Major General William Chase, Brigadier General Bradford Chynoweth, Colonel (MC) John Hall, Colonel Edward Lobit, Captain Charles Keyes, USN, Lieutenant Colonel John Brownewell and the many other officers and men who shared their experience and knowledge about World War II with us, we acknowledge our grateful appreciation.

To Mr. Edward Krasnoborski, Mr. John Cerillo, and Mrs. Deanne Beckwith, the cartographers of the Department of History, we owe a large debt—they produced the final drawings of all maps and sketches, items which have always distinguished the texts produced by the department.

To the administrative staff of the department we gladly extend our thanks. Mrs. Dorothy Waterfield and Mrs. Sally French provided invaluable administrative supervision, and remained helpful even in the face of impossible requests. Sylvia Smith, now the bride of a graduated cadet, spent nearly a year typing most of the original manuscript. The balance of the work fell to Sharon and Judy Pacenza, two stalwarts in typing history texts.

To all the officers of the department—particularly Lieutenant Colonel Robert Ackerson, Lieutenant Colonel Sidney Britt, Lieutenant Colonel Edward Turek, Lieutenant Colonel David Mets, Lieutenant Colonel James Agnew, Commander Jay O'Connell, Major John Votaw, Major James Evetts, Major Alonzo Coose, and Major John Hixson—we profer our thanks for their interest, criticism, and light-hearted comments about our working habits.

To the Library staff, especially Mrs. Marie Capps, Mrs. Ruth Murphy, Mrs. Ruth Donato, and Mr. Robert Schnare, our thanks for their help and support.

Finally, to our wives Ann and Marga, our thanks for living with us for several years in the jungles, atolls, and seas of the Pacific and in the vastness of Asia, Burma and India.

We would be remiss, however, if we did not acknowledge that the mistakes—they seem to be an inevitable part of history—are ours.

John H. Bradley
Jack W. Dice

West Point, New York

Foreword

Cadets at the United States Military Academy have studied military campaigns and institutions for almost a century in a course entitled History of the Military Art. Beginning in 1938, that study of history was supported by texts and maps which were prepared by departmental faculty under the direction of T. Dodson Stamps, then Head of the Department of Military Art and Engineering. The first integrated treatment of the Second World War under this scheme was introduced in 1953 with the publication of *A Military History of World War II*, a departmental text which was jointly edited by Stamps and Vincent J. Esposito. That work, with an accompanying atlas which depicted the military operations described in the text, served cadets until 1959, when Esposito adopted the commercially published *The West Point Atlas of American Wars*. Departmentally prepared and edited by Esposito, *The West Point Atlas of American Wars* included coverage of World War II.

New texts and supporting atlases were required when I modified the scope of the course in the History of Military Art in 1967. Two years later the course came under the direction of a newly created Department of History, wherein it was structured around themes which broadened the coverage of the course in order to accommodate new events and the need to teach more than purely operational military history. Cadets were urged to:

> study military history in depth to get beneath the historian's necessarily imposed pattern of seeming orderliness and to try to understand what war is really like; in breadth to understand the flow of events and the existence of continuity or discontinuity therein; and in context to appreciate the political, social and economic factors that exercise important influences on the military part of the equation.[1]

To help the cadets organize their inquiries and study of the military art, the department proposed that they use a device called the "threads of continuity."

While the threads of continuity have no inherent worth, they can provide students with a way of getting at information, and serve as a lens through which they can examine events and place them in perspective. The military past can be envisioned as a carpet of mankind's activities, ideas, and discoveries, which is woven from strands representing major factors or themes. The carpet is a complex one, and it is in a constant state of subtle change. Focusing on these factors, which are the threads of continuity, can help students understand the meaning of the past and why changes have occurred. The importance of individual factors will vary from one era to another, for the strands in the tapestry of the military past fluctuate in size as their importance to the tapestry as a whole dictates. The threads which the Department of History adopted are: military thought and doctrine, strategy, tactics, generalship, logistics and administration, military professionalism, political factors, social factors, economic factors, and technology.[2]

Participating in a project which extended over a decade and a half, faculty members of the Department of History researched and wrote the texts which support the 1967 instructional concept just described. They also devised the maps which depict the military campaigns described in the texts. Although occasionally resorting to primary source materials, for documentation they relied largely upon sound secondary sources, particularly the excellent official histories of the various wars. Working under my guidance, the authors took pains to emphasize pertinent threads of continuity; in this endeavor, they were guided by a departmentally constructed blueprint of

---

[1]Thomas E. Griess, "A Perspective on Military History" in John E. Jessup and Robert W. Coakley (eds.), *A Guide to the Study and Use of Military History* (Government Printing Office: Washington, D.C., 1979), p. 39. The author is indebted to Michael Howard for the conceptualization regarding the study of military history.

[2]For a more detailed discussion of the threads of continuity see: John F. Votaw, "An Approach to the Study of Military History" in Jessup and Coakley (eds.), *Guide to Military History*, pp. 47-48; John I. Alger, *Definitions and Doctrine of the Military Art: Past and Present* (Department of History: West Point, New York, 1979), pp. 5-11.

the evolution of the art of war, which was collectively discussed and carefully structured and revised before writing commenced. The authors tried to bring breadth and context to their narratives by developing strategic and political themes and by emphasizing institutional factors; they sought to achieve depth of coverage by periodically examining a particular military operation in some detail.

The reader of *The Second World War* will quickly perceive that the text is essentially a narrative of the military campaigns of the war. In the text devoted to the war in Europe, ground operations are emphasized; in the text which narrates events pertaining to the war between Japan and the Allies, naval operations predominate, but there is still considerable coverage of ground actions. In both works, the vital role played by airpower is stressed, and the political aspect of the war is highlighted in appropriate places. With regard to the latter, Chapter 8, "The Grand Alliance," in *The Second World War: Europe and the Mediterranean,* is particularly important; the reader should refer to it repeatedly in order to understand the subtle nuances associated with the higher direction of the war. Also, for its background on the United States military services, Chapter 2, "From Versailles to Pearl Harbor," in *The Second World War: Asia and the Pacific,* is recommended for frequent reference. Finally, the maps which depict operations should be studied as carefully as the narrative. They illustrate the importance of terrain, the vastness of space in some of the campaigns, the ebb and flow of battle, and the crucial importance of mobility in fighting forces. At the same time, the reader should recognize that maps can depict military operations too neatly. It must not be assumed that as the battle raged, any military leader saw things as clearly as the maps now represent them—and, lest the reader forget, the small red and blue arrows depict flesh and blood men, who were usually tired, hungry, dirty, scared, and unaware of the larger human drama which was unfolding around them.

Nine faculty members of the Department of History shared in the writing of this military history of the Second World War. Thousands of graduated cadets and the department are indebted to them for their efforts, which were performed under the pressure of time and with minimal resources. They pioneered in the development of unique texts which were designed to be used in the teaching of an unusual course in military history. Their work contributes to the literature on the history of World War II. In the text on the European and Mediterranean Theaters of Operation, John A. Hixson sets the stage in the opening chapters by relating how far-reaching German thinkers harnessed technology so as to unleash mobile elements which spearheaded the early German conquests. David R. Mets and Thomas B. Buell respectively treat the important roles air and sea

power played, particularly in the pivotal battles. Bruce R. Pirnie describes the events which took place in the vast eastern theater and shows how Russia, just barely able to absorb the German onslaught, recovered and developed her own form of *blitzkrieg*. Clifton R. Franks recounts the story of the entry of the United States into the war in North Africa, and then illustrates how the vagaries of coalition strategy influenced the course of the war in Italy. Commencing with the highly complex invasion of Normandy, Thomas R. Stone surveys the advance of the western Allies into Germany, highlighting the importance of logistics and the running argument over campaign strategy. James F. Ransone, Jr., describes how the most successful coalition in history planned the war at the highest levels, and coincidentally illustrates the global nature of the Second World War. John H. Bradley was the primary author of *The Second World War: Asia and the Pacific.* His sweeping narrative captures the essence of the war which was fought over the vast reaches of the Pacific Ocean, stressing the interrelationship between land, sea, and air forces. Jack W. Dice prepared the chapter on the war in the "forgotten theater" of China-Burma-India, emphasizing China's difficult role, the importance of logistics, and how critical the proper training of military forces can be when war comes. Each of these authors also conceptually contributed to the design of supporting maps. The project would have faltered, however, but for the work of Edward J. Krasnoborski and his assistant, George Giddings. An unusually gifted cartographer, Mr. Krasnoborski made innumerable suggestions regarding the depiction of operations, supervised the drafting effort, and personally drew most of the maps. His skill is imprinted everywhere upon the finished product.

This present edition of *The Second World War* is essentially the text which was produced at the Military Academy as described above. As editor, however, I have attempted to clarify certain passages for the general reader, amplify purely military terminology, and improve the evenness of the narrative. Also, in an occasional instance, I have added material which was not available when the original text was written. The best example of this aspect of editing is the inclusion of the Allied intelligence effort known by its product as ULTRA. The editor is grateful for the advice and suggestions which were tendered by Rudy Shur and Joanne Abrams of Square One Publishers. Their assistance was timely and helpful. Ms. Abrams immeasurably improved the narrative through her painstaking editing, corrections of lapses in syntax, and penetrating questions related to clarity of expression.

Thomas E. Griess
Series Editor

Introduction

War, Japanese style, swept like a scythe through the Far East and Pacific in 1941 and 1942. Everywhere the Japanese were successful. For the most part, Allied reaction was brief and ineffectual; and surrender followed surrender, as the Japanese crushed all resistance. It seemed as if a modern horde had swept out of Asia, unleashing the dreaded four horsemen upon the beautiful Pacific and the somnolent islands and peninsulas of south and Southeast Asia, which had languished for so many years under the control of European colonial powers and the United States. (*See Atlas Map No. 1.*)

First, and most shockingly, the Japanese had followed their own precedents by making a surprise raid not only on the United States Pacific Fleet anchored in Pearl Harbor, but also on surrounding military installations on Sunday, December 7, 1941. They did it to destroy the American fleet, especially the aircraft carriers, so that the rest of their audacious plan could be executed without interruption. Soon thereafter Japanese air forces struck Luzon, destroying the major part of the newly formed American air forces in the Philippines in a debacle similar to Pearl Harbor. Concurrently, in the central Pacific, Guam fell immediately, while Wake's garrison resisted heroically but was soon overwhelmed. Could the Americans do anything right? In 1941, they could not.

The British could do little better. Hong Kong's defenses, recently reinforced to insure that the Empire's prestige could be upheld, cracked easily when the Japanese slipped around the colorfully named Gin Drinker's Line. A greater disaster occurred when with remarkable speed the Japanese taught the British a lesson in tactics, swiftly driving them down the Malayan peninsula, through Johore, into the modern but largely unprepared fortress of Singapore. The final fight was desperate, but with guns pointing seaward, the British surrendered to a foe who had found an Achilles heel by attacking the rear and undefended side of Singapore.

There was a semblance of a battle on Luzon. After the first few days of war in the Philippines, the Japanese landed at several locations on Luzon and drove the largely Filipino forces before them, much to the dismay of Douglas MacArthur who had placed so much confidence in the untried Philippine Army. Retreating—it seemed that the Allies always retreated at this early stage of the war—the Americans and Filipinos pulled back into Bataan, where they fought the Japanese to a standstill. Then, facing fresh, healthy, and well supplied Japanese troops, the defenders of Bataan finally collapsed. Only Corregidor remained in Allied hands. One month later, when the Japanese crossed the ramparts of the fortress, it fell. Within hours, official resistance in the Philippines ended. It was not long before Americans and Filipinos began dismal lives as prisoners of war.

The struggle on Bataan hardly held up the Japanese drive into Borneo and the Netherlands East Indies. The Borneo oil fields were seized intact; Amboina fell; Timor was assaulted by amphibious and parachute troops, and soon resistance stopped; the island of Celebes was attacked; Sumatra was occupied; and, in the culminating stroke, the Japanese gained their strategic goal, the incredibly rich island of Java. These victories brought under Japan's control the oil she so desperately required.

In actions elsewhere, the Japanese sought to expand the area under their dominance. Moving southwest into the Bismarcks, they captured Rabaul, which possessed the finest natural harbor in the area, and crossed the Vitiaz Straits to enter the Markham Valley of New Guinea. These movements threatened Australia, which had already lost a substantial number of its few but first-line troops in Malaya, Singapore, Timor, and Amboina. The advances also secured the left flank. Now the right flank—Burma—had to be secured; victory there would isolate Japan's great enemy, China, against whom a bitter but inconclusive war had been raging since 1937. The end of the story was the same there as everywhere else. Driving relentlessly north, the Japanese routed British and Chinese troops and threatened the very safety of India.

Only guerrillas were left behind the lines to carry on the Allied fight against Japan. Theirs was an impossible task.

The Japanese had cried "Asia for the Asiatics," and by early May 1942 they had driven the white man from the control of the western Pacific and south and Southeast Asia; they had also humiliated him, and destroyed the myth of white superiority. If the Japanese were supreme, however, that supremacy did not mean that Asia was now to be turned over to the Asians; it merely gave emphasis to the fact that for the immediate future Japan had established her "new order" in the Orient in lieu of that of other imperial powers—the Americans, British, Dutch, and French.

There was little the Allies could say or do to salve their wounded pride. Caught unprepared and having under-estimated Japan, they were stunned. The British, expelled from their colonies and worried about holding India in case of a national uprising for independence, could only hope to turn "defeat into victory." Americans could elevate the defense of Wake, Bataan, and Corregidor to national legend, but MacArthur in his imperious way could only promise to return. He set no date. For the Dutch, the bravery of ship crews in the Java Sea was the only memory. For the isolated Australians, Japanese invasion was the immediate fear.

The Japanese offensive exploded across the East to open a long and bitter war. The intricate planning, timing, and coordination were remarkable. Japanese soldiers, sailors, and airmen had done the improbable in record time and high style. They were not lucky; they were good! They had outplanned, outgeneralled, and outfought the Allies. The opening rounds of the new war went to the Japanese. They had made war look simple. To them belonged the glory; the Allies monopolized the agony.

Toward a New Order in the Far East

1

If I am told to fight regardless of the circumstances, I shall run wild for the first six months or a year, but I have utterly no confidence for the second or third year.

Admiral Isoroku Yamamoto

The first and last scenes in the tragedy of modern Imperial Japan were played in Yedo Bay. Commodore Matthew Perry, United States Navy, sailed his famous smoke-belching "black ships" into the bay in 1853. With a mailed fist, Perry pried open the doors of isolation which had closed off the Empire of the Rising Sun from Asia and the rest of the world during the 267 years of the Tokugawa Shogunate. This act, followed by the Meiji Restoration in 1868, thrust Japan into the modern world. Until 1931, the dominant western powers in the Far East watched the accomplishments of the "Yankees" of the Orient with awe and some satisfaction. But the Japanese learned to copy their imperial friends too well, moving year by year against the outposts of Russia, Germany, and China to gain new territories and greater control in Asia. Western admiration turned to dislike, satisfaction to fear, and pacifism to mobilization. By 1937, Japan was fully at war with China, and she was a power to be reckoned with throughout Asia and the Pacific.

War with the West came in 1941 and ended 46 months later in Yedo Bay. Americans were involved again, but this time their ships were gray. Now they would accept the surrender of a proud people who had never lost a war, and would once again place Japan into the hands of a *shogun*, albeit this time an American *shogun*.*

*In pre-Meiji times, the *shogun* was the actual ruler of Japan. He was invested by the Emperor, and succession was hereditary as long as a family could remain in power.

Roots of War: China, Japan, and the United States

Long before Commodore Perry opened up Japan, Americans had been trading with China. Enterprising New York merchants dispatched the small *Empress of China* to Canton in 1784.[1] While China's relations with other western nations were often tumultuous, its relationship with the United States was for the most part placid and amicable. The American government meant to develop the same atmosphere *vis-a-vis* Japan after Perry's historic visit, and for many years the intercouse between the United States and Japan was quite friendly, as was its continued relationship with China.[2]

Early American interests in the Far East were based upon trade, and Perry's mission to Japan was designed to support the American trade route to the Orient. Once trade was established, however, it had to be protected, and the United States Navy began urging that the nation obtain bases throughout the Pacific Ocean for coaling stations and anchorages. The acquisition in the nineteenth century of Midway Island (1867), Alaska (1867), the Hawaiian Islands (1898), the Philippine Islands (1898), and Samoa (1900) accented this need for naval bases and supported the maritime policy of the United States.[3] (*See Atlas Map No. 2.*) With the annexation of the Philippines, the United States became overnight a major power in the Pacific Ocean and an influential one in the Far East. The next year, Secretary of State John Hay set the stage for unseen future trouble in the Orient when he proclaimed a policy of an Open Door in China. This policy merely restated the earlier desires of the United States for establishment of equal trade rights in China, coupled with the recognition by all foreign imperial powers of the territorial and administrative integrity of China. This had always been advantageous to the Americans, latecomers to the race for Chinese markets; but, at the same time, it illustrated the altruistic difference between the policies of the United States and the other land-grabbing imperial powers trading with China. For the others, carving up China had few limitations.

By 1899, a new and modernized Japan had also blossomed into a major Pacific power and was fast becoming a rival of the United States and the other western powers in the Far East. Under the Emperor Meiji, Japan had industrialized, reformed her government, and armed in modern fashion. She had also decided to emulate occidental policies toward China. In 1874, Japan sent a punitive expedition to Formosa to chastise the natives for their actions against sailors from the Ryukyu Islands. In this first display of forceful diplomacy, the Japanese gained an indemnity from China along with suzerainty over the Ryukyus. Two years later, the Japanese opened up Korea, and then, in 1894, Japan challenged China over Korea. After the ensuing successful war, Korea was declared independent, and China ceded Formosa and the nearby Pescadore Islands to Japan. Four years later, when the Americans annexed the Philippines, the two young maritime powers were inextricably drawn together as probably opponents on the chessboard of the vast Pacific.

While United States territorial expansion ended in the Philippines, the Japanese continued to seek new lands and political and economic control in the Orient. Collision with European rivals was inevitable. In 1904, without a declaration of war, Japan launched a surprise attack which destroyed the Russian fleet at Port Arthur. (*See Atlas Map No. 3.*) In due time, the Japanese Army captured Port Arthur and Mukden, forcing the Russians out of southern Manchuria; then, in one of the grand acts of the drama, Admiral Heihachiro Togo annihilated the Russian Baltic Fleet in the Straits of Tsushima in 1905.

Defeated on land and sea and wracked by dissension at home, the Russians had had enough. Japan, much more exhausted than her people realized, was also ready to negotiate a peace. Having engineered the Treaty of Portsmouth, President Theodore Roosevelt brought the Russo-Japanese War to a conclusion in 1905. Russia lost heavily in the settlement: she gave up her railroads in southern Manchuria, ceded the southern half of Sakhalin Island, and transferred her lease of the Liaotung Peninsula. From the fires of war, Japan, ally of Great Britain, victor over the Russians, and possessor of new dominions, emerged a great power.

The Japanese continued to expand their interests in the Chinese province of Manchuria and established better relations with Tsarist Russia, meanwhile, however, coming with each step more and more into conflict with the American policy of the Open Door. By 1909, the Japanese so controlled the area that even the American railroad magnate, E. H. Harriman, could not wedge his way into the rail business there.[4]

On the eve of World War I, the Japanese had replaced the Russians as the main threat to American policy in the Far East. In an attempt to pacify the Orient and cement good feelings, the United States and Japan in 1907 agreed to maintain the status quo: they would recognize each other's positions in the Philippines, Hawaii, Formosa, and Korea, and would uphold the Open Door. It was apparent to all that policies would be effective only if backed by power. In 1910, Japan annexed Korea.[5] Continued Japanese aggrandizement in the Orient would clash further with American policy and interests unless the United States abandoned the Open Door. This would not happen. The Open Door had become as much a part of the American heritage as the Monroe Doctrine.[6] In 1914, within a few days after war began in Europe, Japan (England's ally) declared war against Germany and seized and retained her possessions in the coveted Shantung Peninsula. The same year, the Japanese took possession of the German-controlled Mariana, Caroline, and Marshall Islands in the central Pacific. (*See Atlas Map No. 2.*) They then presented Twenty-One Demands to the revolutionary government of China in 1915, attempting through diplomacy to make the new Chinese republic a vassal of the Japanese Empire.

These acts upset the Americans. Seizure of the island groups isolated the Philippines and made its defense difficult. While seizure of Shantung violated the Open Door, the Twenty-One Demands made a mockery of the policy. The United States pressured the Japanese to moderate their demands, but such action was only partly successful, and unless the Americans were prepared to fight, the fate of China was in Japanese hands. Since the Japanese had received the tacit approval of the preoccupied European powers for their moves, and since everyone wanted Japan to be a participant in the war, the United States was forced to accept the situation. Accordingly, in the Lansing-Ishii Agreement of November 1917, the United States recognized that Japan had "special interests" in China although such interests were not to impinge on the territorial sovereignty of China or the policy of the Open Door. The Japanese, in this diplomatic coup, established their new doctrine of "special interests" to combat the Open Door.[7]

By 1914, Americans had also angered the Japanese. Perry's original act, of course, could be considered an insult and not the most convivial way to begin relations between two sovereign nations. More importantly, the annexation of the Philippines placed the United States in a position to influence affairs in China, Formosa, the Ryukyus, and Japan strongly. As a maritime power, Japan could not easily accept the presence of an occidental naval power in such a strategic position—one which could challenge her expansion in the Far East and hinder her penetration of Southeast Asia and the East Indies. There were other sore points. The Japanese people were upset after the Russo-Japanese War because the nation did not gain enough in the peace treaty to offset its wartime sacrifices. They blamed this failure on President Theodore Roosevelt. In 1906, when the San Francisco School Board denied Japanese immigrant children entrance to the regular school system, the Japanese were insulted. Restricted American immigration policies also displeased them, and even after a gentleman's agreement was signed at Japanese expense in 1908, the cancer of racial discord could not be eradicated. In addition, the Japanese could never understand why the United States could have favored positions in Central and South America while Japan could not have such a position in nearby China.[8]

By 1919, there was a growing rift between Japan and the United States. The most serious conflicts involved: Open Door versus "special interests" in China; the American possession of the Philippines and the Japanese control of the Marianas, Carolines, and Marshalls; the animosities of racial discrimination; and the normal troubles associated with competitive trade interests of major world powers. Each would play an important role in the next 20 years. It was obvious by this time that the two nations could not remain real friends while the Japanese continued to expand at the expense of China, America's older Asian friend. Furthermore, because of the Twenty-One Demands, Japan so angered the Chinese, who were then experiencing revolutionary change, that the island empire became the symbol for detested foreign rapacity against China.

The end of World War I did not ease the problems in the Far East. China, having entered the war on the Allied side, failed to regain Shantung and reverse Japanese wartime gains. Japan failed to gain a clause in the settlements which proclaimed racial and national equality. The United States failed to dislodge the Japanese from the central Pacific and was dismayed to see the islands there mandated to Japan by the League of Nations. Furthermore, Japanese bullying during American actions in Siberia from 1918 to 1921 proved to many observers that Japan was bent on continued military expansion.[9]

A new issue between Japan and the United States developed from 1921 to 1922, when the American Secretary of State proposed massive naval disarmament, the scrapping of major naval vessels, and the abstinence from naval construction for 10 years. The proposal caught the imagination of a war weary and armament-burdened world. Based upon fleets in being, a naval limitation treaty was hammered out which gave the primacy in naval power to Great Britain and the United States, secondary rank to

Japan, and tertiary positions to France and Italy. Japanese naval officers were horrified by the legislated inferiority of the resultant 5–5–3 ratio of capital ships, but the country was in the hands of liberal administrators and the agreement was accepted. To ensure her security, however, Japan demanded that the status quo be recognized in the Far East and that all powers refrain from building new bases or improving the ones presently established in the Orient. The occidental powers agreed to this. By this stroke Japan guaranteed herself a position of dominant naval strength in the western Pacific.

Other agreements were reached in Washington. Japan returned Shantung to China, but retained her economic rights in the area. It was a paper concession. Japan kept her mandated islands in the Pacific. Two other treaties were important in the Far East. One, the Nine Power Treaty, guaranteed the Open Door policy in China. The other, the Four Power Treaty between Japan, France, Great Britain, and the United States, replaced the Anglo-Japanese Alliance of 1902 and guaranteed that the four powers would respect each other's possessions in the Far East and would work out their problems peacefully in case of difficulties. All in all, the move toward disarmament was a diplomatic victory for the United States. In Japan, liberal governments desired China more as a market than as an expensive colony, and since they were also uninterested in military or naval expansion, these agreements would insure more peaceful relations in the Pacific and Asia.[10] For a time following the Washington Conference, the China problem was relegated to the background on the international scene.

For the Japanese and American military and naval leaders, the problems associated with the central Pacific intensified after World War I. American planners, becoming more and more concerned about the strategic position of the Philippines, argued for years about whether the islands should or could be held. Both Army and Navy officers knew that defending them would be nearly impossible if Japan moved against the islands in force, but they hoped that the Philippines could be retained until reinforcements arrived from the United States. With the Carolines, Marianas, and Marshalls in Japanese hands, such action would be even more dangerous and difficult. At the same time, Japanese strategists appreciated the value of their own possessions and recognized the problem created by having a major American base within their own sphere of influence. As war neared and the United States flew strategic bombers into the Philippines, their apprehensions grew. Still, the Japanese knew they had the upper hand in the western Pacific because they had the naval power to make the defense or reinforcement of the Philippines tenuous for the United States.[11]

Until 1941, all Japanese plans regarding America were

defensive in nature. The Japanese hoped to lure the American fleet into nearby waters where it could be destroyed in the manner of Tsushima. American strategy remained offensive: get to the Philippines, reinforce it, and gain control of the western Pacific.[12] Obviously the two fleets would clash.

By the late 1920s, Americans were deeply involved in the Great Depression. The Japanese, similarly involved, were nearly ready to abandon their experiment with democratic government. The Chinese, trying desperately to bring an end to the state of chaos existing across the country, were slowly establishing a modern national state. As the United States turned more and more inward, it became more and more impotent militarily. At the same time, the slumbering nationalistic sentiments of the Japanese were being awakened by right-wing militants who were dissatisfied with corruption in government, decadent westernism, and the continuing surrender in diplomacy to white occidental powers. Not comfortable with democracy, capitalism, and internationalism, many Japanese, led by some very radical young Army officers, yearned to rid the nation of its bureaucrats, its monied *Zaibatsu* class, and its politicians in order to "purify" the Emperor system and return to more ancient and traditional Japanese ways. Revolution was urged by the Right; assassinations began. Thus, by the early 1930s Japan had turned away from democracy.[13]

Rightest leaders yearned to bring more direction to the Japanese government and goals. Interested in a strong monarchy, they also favored a return to the old traditions of the *samurai*,* the elimination of capitalism in favor of some form of corporate state, the destruction of communism, and the expansion of the Japanese Empire. Expansion would allow migration from the home islands and relieve the population explosion; it would also give the nation new sources of raw materials, add markets, and help solve the national depression. Such expansion, moreover, would find a ready object on mainland China.

Militarism grew rapidly under such conditions. After many assassinations, the Government found that it could do little against the offenders; the public supported their actions, while the Army and Navy would not police their own ranks for fear of greater problems. Government by assassination destroyed the power of the Government to act in crisis. In 1931, the Army in Manchuria, confident of its own power and no longer subservient to the civil government, took things into its own hands. In the infamous "Manchurian Incident," it moved to take over the Chinese province on

the alleged provocation that the Chinese had tried to blow up the Japanese-controlled Southern Manchurian Railroad. Manchuria was overrun while a stunned Japanese Government acceded to the *fait accompli* rather than admit that it did not control its own Army. (*See Atlas Map No. 3.*)

The Manchurian aggression brought the United States and Japan into immediate diplomatic conflict. When the United States demanded that the Japanese withdraw, Japan refused, feeling that she had acted within her treaty rights to protect her "special interests." The world and the League of Nations disagreed. Japan defiantly withdrew from that international body in 1932, and in that same year Manchuria became Manchukuo, officially independent but really a Japanese puppet. The prospects for many more peaceful years in the Orient dimmed.

In Manchuria the Japanese Army thrived. Its leaders used it as a base of power and fostered the growth of the Kwantung Army, thereby becoming a real threat to the stability of the home government. The province became all that the Army desired: a major industrial base for the support of Japan and its armed forces, one which proved the Army's contention that further expansion was required to make the nation self-sufficient.[14] Soon the Army began to covet the northern provinces of China and to infiltrate into Jehol and other areas which were not yet under the firm control of the government of Chiang Kai-shek. It seemed just a matter of time before the Japanese Army found an excuse to continue its aggrandizement. Near the Marco Polo Bridge in Peking in 1937, Chinese troops allegedly fired upon nearby Japanese forces, giving the Japanese garrison an excuse. Immediately, the latter attacked, again without governmental approval.[15] This time, however, China did not succumb, and a full-scale war resulted. Although the Japanese called it merely "The China Incident," they ultimately found the going as rough in China as Napoleon had in Russia in 1812. Japan's act did not improve relations with the United States, and while that country was not prepared to fight in China's defense in 1932, it had elected a President who would soon take the first steps toward naval rearmament; and its armed forces more and more considered that war with Japan was on the horizon.

Other problems aggravated relations between the United States and Japan. Racial tensions flared again in 1934, perhaps heightened by the fact that cheap Japanese goods were flooding the world market. Continual changes in the disarmment treaties failed to give the Japanese Navy the 10-10-7 parity it desired, leading to a renewal of the naval building race in 1934 with Japan's renouncement of the Washington Conference agreements. In 1936, Japan signed an Anti-Comintern Pact with Italy and Germany, placing

---

*In feudal times, the *samurai* were the warriors. They were noted for being particularly adept swordsmen. Farmers and merchants were subservient to them.

herself in the orbit of the fascist powers. In the following year feelings grew more tense when the Japanese local forces attacked the American gunboat, *Panay*, on the Yangtze River. Only because the Japanese Government accepted responsibility for the act and made immediate reparations did the hostile feelings subside.

War in China brought little glory to Japanese arms. The amorphous giant simply would not capitulate. Japanese troops captured key ports, cities, and railroads, but they could not eliminate the new government of Chiang Kai-shek, which retreated into the interior, taking much of the critical industry and even its universities with it. Protracted war began, frustrating the Japanese militarists.[16]

As the war in China continued, the Japanese were faced with two problems: possible war with the Soviets on the Manchurian-Siberian border and an inability to isolate China from outside aid. Japan had always been apprehensive that Russia might attack, and for 30 years she had oriented her military plans on the Eurasian colossus. (Russia had been active in China for years, initially helping Sun Yat-sen, then Chiang, and finally Mao Tse-tung after Chiang expelled his Russian advisors.) From 1937 to 1939, the two nations clashed on their common border, and the Russians ultimately smashed the Japanese forces on the eve of war in Europe. Not surprisingly, considering national interests and the international situation, within a year and a half a Russo-Japanese neutrality pact was signed. In coping with the other problem of isolating China, Japan was more successful. Amphibious expeditions secured most of the important coastal towns. Canton, adjacent to Hong Kong, was seized in 1938; the next year the Japanese landed at Hainan Island and turned it into a valuable base, which could control the northern reaches of the South China Sea.

The world situation in the 1930s grew more and more troubled until it seemed that war was inevitable. In Japan in 1932, air raid drills were held at night as the Japanese practiced defense against hypothetical enemies. In Manila,* people kept to peaceful ways, trying to push the thoughts of war with Japan forever out of their minds.[17] In China, there was no change because the Japanese had been bombing for years, had raped Nanking in 1937, and by late 1939 were pounding at the inland city of Chungking in an effort to crush the government of Chiang. Developments in Europe added to the woes in the Far East. Fascist Germany was ready to march, and when she did her acts reverberated in the Orient where the Japanese watched carefully as Hitler destroyed France and pushed England to the brink. German victories left the great European colonies helpless in the Far East, ripe for a "new order" to establish its suzerainty.

*Conversations with Amelia Bradley. Amelia Bradley lived in Japan from 1933 to 1934, and witnessed air raid practices. She also lived in Manila from 1932 to 1933 and from 1935 to 1945.

Japan saw her opportunities and moved early. She demanded from the Netherlands government in the East Indies access to oil and improved trade relationships. The Dutch refused. Then the Japanese persuaded a harassed Great Britain to close the Burmese border, thus preventing outside aid from reaching Chiang from that source. The embattled British complied, but three months later, with pressure in Europe having lessened, reneged on the earlier agreement. After signing the Tripartite Alliance in 1940, Japan openly joined the Axis, directing the major thrust of her alliance against the United States. With German assistance, the Japanese gained agreements with the Vichy French government, which allowed occupation of certain areas in northern Indochina, thereby sealing off a major supply route to China through Hanoi.

These Japanese acts were looked upon disapprovingly in the United States. Businessmen who had previously admired the Japanese had to admit that their actions were provocative and warlike. Americans began to perceive Japan as the Germany of the Orient: a militaristic and aggressive state—bent upon continental expansion and aggrandizement—which threatened China and the colonies and possessions of the occidental powers in the Far East. They were particularly worried about the alliance which the Japanese had concluded with the European Axis. It could lead to a world war of vaster proportions than The Great War.

A slowly rearming America, however, was more oriented toward Europe, as the Japanese inched closer and closer to an open break with the western powers. As the war intensified in Europe, Japanese belligerence increased. Allied leaders knew that Japan would have to be stopped, but the overwhelming problem of Nazi aggression had primacy. Everyone hoped that the Philippines, Singapore, and the other western bastions could be reinforced.

The German attack on Russia in June 1941 served as something of a catalyst for affairs in the Far East. With commitments to both countries, Japan decided to do nothing. Distressed as she was with the German action, she was relieved that Russia could no longer threaten her in the Far East. Now she was free to move south to obtain the coveted resources in the Indies and to threaten the British position in Singapore. On July 24, 1941, Japan made a crucial move by entering southern Indochina. American reaction was quick and unexpected. By executive order, President Roosevelt froze all Japanese assets in the United States and placed oil exports to Japan under restrictive licensing, thus creating an economic blockade of Japan which could not be broken short of war or the reversal of Japanese policy. The Japanese were shocked. Roosevelt's drastic action would paralyze Japan financially, and its war machine would only be able to operate for about 18 months on reserve oil stocks. Hard decisions were demanded. If the

Japanese wished to work for their own self-interests, they could withdraw from Indochina and China and reject their alliance with the Axis. Following that, they could then act as they did in World War I when they expanded their trade at the expense of the western nations who were locked in fights to the finish.[18] They could also try to break the blockade. With the Dutch and the British lined up squarely behind the Americans, however, the blockade could only be cracked in battle. By the summer of 1941, Japan was on the verge of declaring war.

Through diplomacy, one tenuous hope for peace remained. Since early March 1941, negotiations had been proceeding in Washington between Ambassador Kichisaburu Nomura and Secretary of State Cordell Hull in an attempt to reach a reasonable settlement in the Far East. So far these had proved fruitless. Unofficial personal diplomacy had failed, and President Roosevelt rejected a summit meeting with the Japanese Prime Minister. At one time, the Japanese thought that Americans had accepted their ideas in principle, but it turned out that the Japanese negotiator had misunderstood the American Secretary of State. Misunderstandings abounded, resulted in increased bad feelings on both sides of the Pacific.[19] In Japan, the Government was being pressured by the military either to gain a diplomatic settlement without sacrificing Japanese interests or to step down so that a new government could prepare for war. Such pressure was growing too strong for the moderates, who were willing to compromise with the United States. Finally, in October 1941, the civilian Prime Minister resigned; General Hideki Tojo, Minister of War, accepted the Imperial request to head the government. Tojo's cabinet "reeked of gunpowder."[20]

The basic differences between the two nations can be summarized by comparing the first official proposal made by the United States in April 1941 to the last Japanese proposal made by the Tojo Government in November 1941. The American Secretary of State proclaimed four principles for negotiations:

1. Respect for the territorial integrity and the sovereignty of each and all nations.
2. Support the principle of non-interference in the internal affairs of other countries.
3. Support the principle of equality, including equality of commercial opportunity.
4. Non-disturbance of the status quo in the Pacific except as the status quo may be altered by peaceful means.[21]

Japan opposed this set of principles. She wanted to end American aid to China, restore normal trade, gain economic independence, and establish a commanding position in the Orient. Secretary Hull's doctinaire proposal reiterated the substance of the Open Door policy which was anathema to the Japanese who had step-by-step occupied the lucrative territory of China. They could not accede to the American principles without withdrawing from China; but such a reaction would be impossible because Japan would lose face, and no Japanese leader could survive such a dishonorable act. Still, as time would prove, the Americans would not budge. Time and time again they would come back to their four points, points which the Japanese could neither circumscribe nor accept.[22]

On November 20, 1941, Admiral Nomura presented Secretary Hull with the following proposal:

1. Both the Government of Japan and the United States undertake not to make any armed advancement into any of the regions in the South-eastern Asia and the Southern Pacific area excepting the part of French Indo-China where the Japanese troops are stationed at present.
2. The Japanese Government undertakes to withdraw its troops now stationed in French Indo-China upon either the restoration of peace between Japan and China or the establishment of an equitable peace in the Pacific area.
   In the meantime the Government of Japan declares that it is prepared to remove its troops now stationed in the southern part of French Indo-China to the northern part of the said territory upon the conclusion of the present agreement which shall be embodied in the final agreement.
3. The Government of Japan and the United States shall cooperate with a view to securing the acquisition of those goods and commodities which the two countries need in the Netherlands East Indies.
4. The Government of Japan and the United States mutually undertake to restore their commerical relations to those prevailing prior to the freezing of the assets.
5. The Government of the United States undertakes to refrain from such measures and actions as will be prejudicial to the endeavors for the restoration of general peace between Japan and China.[23]

In other words, Nomura proposed that the United States help Japan gain her goals in China. Hull was concerned that Japan did not mention an abrogation of her treaty with Germany, because in case of a German declaration of war against America, Japan could or would become an active belligerent against the United States. Furthermore, by remaining in southern Indochina, Japan threatened the dominions of the British and the Dutch to the south and virtually isolated the Philippines with bases to the west, north, and east of the islands. To Hull it seemed that the Japanese wanted American aid in establishing their hegemony of the western Pacific and eastern Asia.[24] (*See Atlas Map No. 2.*)

The United States Government essentially rejected the

Japanese proposal on November 26. By then, war orders conditional on the progress of negotiations had gone out from Tokyo to the Pearl Harbor Striking Force. War would begin December 8, 1941.

All the Japanese diplomatic moves during this period were known, because the American cryptographers had broken the secret Japanese diplomatic (PURPLE) codes. Therefore, the final Japanese proposal was not rejected with the hope of improved future negotiations. To the insiders, Japan obviously had decided on war. It was just a matter of time and place. Secretary of War Henry Stimson wanted to make sure, however, that the Japanese fired the first shot. He spoke of maneuvering the Japanese into war.[25] Roosevelt felt that war was imminent; so did the service chiefs. War alert messages went out on November 26. The President told the Chinese Ambassador that he expected "foul play" by the Japanese in Malaya, Thailand, the Indies, or possibly the Philippines.[26] Hawaii was never mentioned.

The Japanese had decided to strike everywhere almost simultaneously, but first the Imperial Navy had to destroy the American fleet at Pearl Harbor. They would take the bold step, attacking not only the weakened European powers, but the United States as well. It was a momentous decision—and a fatal one.

Japanese leaders explained the goals to the nation's soldiers:

> The New Restoration of the thirties has come about in response to the Imperial desire for peace in the Far East. Its task is the rescue of Asia from white aggression, the restoration of Asia to the Asians, and —when peace in Asia has been won—the firm establishment of peace throughout the whole world.[27]

The situation had evolved slowly, seemingly inexorably from the peaceful relationship which had once been the order of the day between the United States and Japan. This relationship foundered when Japan went to war against China, America's oldest friend in the Far East, and when Japan moved more and more aggressively to establish her "new order" in the Far East, thereby violating the Open Door.

The Dagger: The Imperial Japanese Army

The Japanese soldier was probably the most hated opponent United States soldiers have faced in combat. Biased by barely concealed dislike and racism, media reports described the Japanese soldier as a slant-eyed, buck-toothed, yellow-bellied, bandy-legged, or *banzai*-yelling son of Nippon. Because of these reports, he was despised for his alleged treachery, cruelty, and savagery; ridiculed for his devotion to his Emperor; and abhorred for his supposed penchant for suicide and disregard of human life.[28]

Unlike his occidental foes, the conscripted Japanese soldier was raised in a society which glorified "the way of the warrior" (*Bushido*) and respected the individual soldiers, the *samurai*, who had for centuries served the great *shoguns* and *daimyos** of Japan as combination knights, soldiers, and policemen. The Emperor Meiji abolished the *samurai* class, but the traditions of the men who carried a sword and dagger as a badge of office in Japan did not die. Defrocked *samurai* entered the new Imperial Japanese Army where they implanted their old traditions of superb self-discipline, unshakable loyalty, and great valor.†[29] As the Army matured, it reflected these ideals; even after absorbing new ideals from Europe it nurtured the "way of the warrior" and kept deep in its soul the tradition of the *samurai*.

Not a soldier in the western mold, the Japanese soldier who fought in World War II was first, last, and always a warrior. So were his officers. While the spirit of the warrior made the Japanese incredibly brave and willing to die at the slightest whim of his Emperor or his officers, it made him fight too often with his heart and his body and unnecessarily pit flesh against steel. He found quickly that individual warriors could not defeat armies.

Warriors, however, made superb infantrymen who fought cunningly on all the battlefields of Asia and the Pacific. The Japanese infantryman was so good that he became a myth. In Burma, the British Tommy believed him to be the most expert of jungle fighters, assuming that he had been trained long and hard for such actions.[30] In fact, the opposite was true. The Japanese soldier had been trained mostly for cold-weather fighting in the isolated wastes of Manchuria and Siberia where the Japanese High Command had always felt the main land war would occur. Many Japanese suffered more in the humid jungles of the tropics than did those Americans who were raised in the hot regions of the United States. Because of their peasant life in Japan, however, the soldiers of the Emperor were more able to bear the privation

---

*A *daimyo* was a feudal lord.
†The *Imperial Precepts for Soldiers and Sailors* emphasized the following characteristics:
1. Loyalty (the essential duty) coupled with spirit.
2. Propriety (the respectful conduct of officers and men towards each other).
3. Valor.
4. Faithfulness (keeping one's word) and righteousness (fulfilling one's duty).
5. Simplicity.
6. Sincerity.

and hardship in the isolated and debilitating tropics. The hard peasant life also brought with it an unusual tolerance for authority and discipline. In the Japanese Army, discipline flowed downhill: senior officers slapped junior officers, junior officers slapped non commissioned officers, and so on down the line until the lowliest of privates, with no subordinates to chastise, often vent his wrath on unfortunate prisoners of war.[31] Japanese officers had to be careful, however, not to shame a man, because under that circumstance a subordinate would often commit *hara-kiri* to expunge his error or regain his honor in the face of unjust punishment.[32]

This *samurai* tradition made the Japanese soldier unusually well trained for combat. General Robert Eichelberger, reminiscing about his service in Siberia after World War I, commented in 1952 about the Japanese soldier:

> In contrast to the Thirty-First Infantry [USA] in marching, discipline, their flankers, etc., I found the Japanese much better soldiers. In marching down a valley one would receive signals from the ridge tops and various places indicating the way was clear. Soldiers marched at suitable intervals and march discipline was perfect. . . .

> These lessons of half trained American troops as compared with Japanese troops remained with me and into the heavy jungle fighting of World War II. I still feel that the Japanese soldiers were a commander's dream, e.g., they never exposed themselves unnecessarily, they never fired until they had a good target, and they obeyed the orders of their officers while taking perfect cover.[33]

It was a pity that Allied soldiers were not as impressed with Japanese soldiers prior to the war as Eichelberger was in retirement. It might have prevented the superior attitude of the Allies which clouded military judgment.

At the start of the war, Japan was a militarized, totalitarian state bent on expanding in Asia to gain living room and resources while ejecting the white colonial powers. The military services, primarily the Army, had brought on this transformation from the democratic regimes of the 1920s because they had become upset by the state of the country under the liberal governments. Disarmament followed by the reduction of the Army had angered most Japanese soldiers. Most of the soldiery and their officers were from the rural areas of Japan—the ones which had been hit the hardest in the depression, and ones in which traditional Japanese culture dominated. Thus, westernism, internationalism, and capitalism were causes of great discontent. When radical solutions were proposed to reform Japan, the younger officers from the country moved to the front of

activist groups in order to improve the lives of their soldiers and their families. Out of this internal ferment came the assassinations of Japanese leaders. Out of it grew also the power of the Army.

Even as these changes created military strength, they brought problems to the Army. For instance, once the younger officers showed a willingness to kill to gain their ends, senior commanders, sympathizing with the objectives of their subordinates, often failed to discipline them. To make matters worse, the commanders were often afraid to anger the younger men because their own lives would be in danger. Discipline was virtually destroyed in the officer corps. Furthermore, factionalism grew as officers took sides on how to reform the government. Advocating rapid change was the *Kodo Ha* (Benevolent Way Rule), or Imperial Clique, which supported terror tactics. More gradual change, albeit with the same ultimate objectives, was the position of the *Tosei-Ha*, or Control Group. Insubordination, however, persisted. Young officers, defying tradition, took their political ideas into the public forum to oppose the Government's policies. A meeting in Tokyo in 1936 was the turning point; after stormy and armed confrontations, the Control Group, led by men like Hideki Tojo, gained control of the Army.

Once the Army moved into active politics it destroyed the delicate balance between the civilians and the military in Japanese government. In the end, the militarists gained complete control. The Meiji Constitution made this possible by dictating that the Army and Navy Ministers had to be active duty officers and, moreover, that no cabinet could be formed without the ministers. At the slightest whim, a service minister could resign, toppling a government. Since the ministers had to come from the active Army, the high command of the Army could influence government by their selections and by their actions.

Militarism in Japan was enhanced by the tradition of allowing field commanders nearly complete independence in local affairs. In military affairs, the general staff was as reluctant to exert its influence over such commanders as the Japanese Cabinet was to exert its influence over the Army. Thus, an ambitious general could easily use a portion of the Army as he saw fit, even if his action contradicted Army or governmental policy. This actually occurred in Manchuria and China when the Kwantung Army and sister units marched without having received orders.[34]

By 1941, the Army was the dominant service in national affairs, even though the Navy was perhaps the better known and more respected of the two forces. Closer to the people, more traditional, and definitely pro-Japanese, anti-American, and anti-British, the Imperial Army was a strange blend of the *samurai* and the Prussian-oriented *Wehrmacht*. When the Japanese after the Meiji Restoration sought new ideas in

Europe for their Army, they had intended to copy the French Army. However, German victory in the Franco-Prussian War convinced them to study the German Army too, and they returned to Japan prepared to build an army in the latter mold. This was particularly noticeable in the command system, which copied the German General Staff. While the Emperor was the theoretical commander-in-chief, and while there was a special but unofficial Liaison Council, which established state policy between the Cabinet and the military and naval leaders, the wartime Imperial General Headquarters was supposedly the locus of supreme command. In practice, however, the Army and Navy Sections worked independently of each other. Orders or plans which concerned both services had to be agreed upon by the Chief of the General Staff and the Chief of the Naval General Staff before they could be disseminated to each service. Without agreement, no program could be accepted. The headquarters depended on the direction of an active monarch, or at least a dominant chief of staff; but without either it was no headquarters at all. Under such a regime, there were never any subordinate joint commands. The Army and Navy "cooperated" to execute agreed programs. Throughout the war, the Japanese never had unified command at any level. Advisory bodies also existed, but they were cosmetic at best.

High command in the Army was divided among five powerful agencies. Eight bureaus, headed by the Minister of War, handled administration, personnel, supply, and mobilization. The general staff formulated strategy and war plans; its First Bureau (Operations) dominated the Second (Intelligence) and Third (Logistics) Bureaus. An Inspectorate General of Military Education handled all training except aviation training, which came under the Inspectorate of Aviation. The latter office also supervised the air forces of the Army. A fifth agency, National Defense Headquarters, was established in 1941 to protect the homeland.[35]

The Japanese Army had still other characteristics that were peculiar to it. Senior officers gave orders but seldom supervised their implementation, feeling it to be beneath their dignity to do so. This led to serious breaches of discipline.[36] If high commanders failed, they resorted to the grisly rite of *Bushido*—ceremonial suicide or *hara-kiri*. Surrender was considered dishonorable, so much so that death in any form was preferred. Loyalty to the Emperor was absolute, and was never to be shaken in the war. On more mundane levels, the Japanese Army had no corps organization, but had armies which equalled western corps and area armies which equalled western armies. Special Japanese units abounded, being named for every possible commander or area associated with a locality of war.

Infantry was considered the pivotal force in the Army. Transportation was heavily dependent on horses due to the expectation of fighting in Siberia. Infantry weapons were light. Soldiers were equipped with the barest of necessities. Medical service was abominable by western standards: a wounded Japanese soldier often could not count on seeing a doctor or getting even rudimentary medical care.[37] The Army had its own air force, but it was inferior to the air arm of the Imperial Japanese Navy. Tactically oriented, Japan had no strategic bomber comparable to the American B-17.

The basic Japanese triangular infantry division was built around three regiments of infantry. Each regiment normally had three battalions, each of which in turn was made up of three companies. Companies were about 150 men in strength. Divisions averaged 15,000 men. A cavalry, an engineer, and a field artillery regiment were part of divisions, along with smaller signal, transportation, and medical units. In 1941, many Japanese divisions were old "square" divisions with brigade organization.[38]

Japanese tactics stressed the primacy of the infantry. As the ultimate weapon of decision, that arm was charged with fighting alone to achieve desired goals if this became necessary. Rugged training emphasized stealth, infiltration, and close combat. The offensive spirit was applauded, and valor was demanded, becoming nearly an obsession with the officers who were expected to lead from the van of their units. The *samurai* tradition highlighted personal valor rather than leadership. Envelopments (movements around flanks) were emphasized. Night attacks, a traditional feature of Japanese tactics, remained in vogue. In such attacks soldiers were expected to crawl, avoid the use of firearms, and assault with bayonets to destroy the enemy. Shock action, rather than fire, was the backbone of infantry action. Army manuals exhorted the Japanese infantrymen to "have implicit faith in the superiority of friendly forces in hand-to-hand combat, charge the enemy with intrepidity at the risk of their lives, and overwhelm and annihilate the hostile force."

When on the defensive, the Japanese soldier was trained to stop the enemy at the front line of strongpoints or to die in place. Defense in depth was not advocated, even though the Japanese studied its use by the Russians with great interest. All positions were improved with wire, obstacles, fire, and fortified emplacements. The Russian *tochka*, or pillbox, impressed the Japanese who adopted the Russian word as their name for a pillbox. As in the attack, they relied on the spirit of the soldier to make up for any deficiences in men or materiel when they met the enemy in hand-to-hand combat on defensive positions.[39]

The Army was also experienced in landing operations, but it did not have a special corps for such actions. Although doctrine on on this subject appeared in 1924, it was not as sophisticated as that developed by the United States Marine Corps. Surprise was emphasized; naval bombardment was slighted. Generally, Japanese operations were simply landings rather than amphibious assaults.[40]

As alluded to earlier, for many years Japanese strategic planning was geared for warfare with Russia; tactics, training, and equipment followed this strategical focus. Even when the war in China usurped much of the attention of Japan, the high command always kept one eye cocked on the Russian colossus. Russian victories on the Siberian and Mongolian borders in 1938 and 1939 shocked the Japanese, and proved to them that the Russian menace was real. While the neutrality pact with the Soviet Union ultimately released some of the pressure in the north, 13 divisions were still kept in Manchuria, ready to meet a Russian invasion.

The attention of the Army turned southward when it became apparent that China would have to be surrounded before she could be defeated. Such a movement meant that Japan would probably come into conflict with the colonial powers, especially Great Britain and France. War plans had existed which envisioned war against each power, but the situation in the Far East grew more critical as Japan began to move southward, and new problems had to be faced. Movement into northern Indochina was relatively successful, having occurred without battle because of German pressure on the Vichy Government. Closing Burma meant war with the British, and such a war meant attacking Malaya and securing Singapore. To do this, Japan needed bases in southern Indochina. When she gained these facilities, the United States entered the picture forcefully. The key American threat was the strategic air force at Clark Field, Luzon, but the American position in the Philippines also endangered any Japanese move into the Indies. Oil restrictions and embargoes implemented by the Americans and the Dutch had caused Japan's fuel reserves to dwindle. The Japanese Army, facing prolonged war in China and possible war in Manchuria, needed fuel for its vehicles and aircraft. The Army's need, however, was less than that of the Navy, which by 1941 was placing additional pressure on the soldiers to move into the Netherlands East Indies to secure oil for the fleet.[41]

Four alternative plans were considered. One, the most risky, advocated striking straight into the Indies. Neither service liked it. A second, supported by the Army, considered advancing into Malaya, then across to Sumatra and Java, northward to Borneo, and lastly to the Philippines; this plan seemed to ensure capturing the resource areas quickly while avoiding early war with the United States. The Navy wanted to go the other way, starting with the Philippines and ending with Malaya, because the islands threatened the Japanese line of communications to the Indies. A fourth plan, a compromise, incorporated the second and third proposals as simultaneous operations. Because of the nature of Japanese decision making (i.e., mutual agreement),

the compromise was adopted in August 1941—before Admiral Yamamoto advocated his plan for attacking Pearl Harbor.[42]

The final Japanese war plan was daring and complex. It hit everywhere simultaneously. Timing was critical; cooperation was essential; good and steady troops were required; and intelligence had to be outstanding. While the Japanese had fewer numbers of men and aircraft than the Allies, they really had superior forces because of their training and experience. Moreover, surprise would add divisions to the Japanese cause, as would Allied unpreparedness; myths would add still more power, sapping the morale of the opposing Allied forces. (*See Atlas Map No. 4.*)

The Japanese plan outlined three major phases: a "centrifugal offensive"; a period of consolidation; and a defensive phase.[43] During the first phase, Japanese air, land, and naval forces would strike throughout the Pacific, the Far East, and the Netherlands East Indies to destroy Allied forces and gain all desired objectives. In the second phase, the Japanese would continue offensive operations in Burma, but would devote most of their time and energy to the consolidation and security of their captured empire. During the third phase, Japanese forces would defend the territories.

Detailed plans were made for only the first phase, which was broken down into three separate parts. The first of these parts concerned the attack on Pearl Harbor; the seizure of Thailand; and the initial landings and attacks against Malaya, Hong Kong, the Philippines, Guam, Wake Island, and the Gilbert Islands. The second part concentrated on the capture of Singapore, operations in the Netherlands East Indies, the seizure of the Bismarck Archipelago, and the initial capture of the British air fields in southern Burma. In the final part of the first phase, Japanese forces would capture Java, occupy Sumatra, and launch a major offensive into Burma.

Army planners concentrated first on the reduction of British power in Malaya and the capture of the largest of the Allied bases—Singapore.[44] The Twenty-Fifth Army, Lieutenant General Tomoyuki Yamashita commanding, was assigned to make the main attack against the British. (*See Appendix 1.*) The secondary Japanese drive into the Philippines, to be made by Lieutenant General Masaharu Homma's Fourteenth Army, would not begin until the Japanese had gained air superiority over Luzon. Lieutenant General Hitoshi Imamura, commanding the Sixteenth Army, would control the army and naval landing forces, which would drive through the various islands of the Netherlands East Indies (Dutch Borneo, the Celebes, Amboina, Timor, Bali, and Sumatra) to seize Java. Lieutenant General Shojiro Iida, the Fifteenth Army commander, would begin the offensive into Burma after the other three armies were committed to action. In the Philippines and the

Indies, small, battalion-sized naval landing forces would assist the army units. These four numbered armies would be controlled by General Count Hisaichi Terauchi, commanding Southern Army in Saigon.

Smaller forces would operate elsewhere. The 38th Division (South China Army) would capture Hong Kong. Forces under Southern Army would land in British Borneo to protect Japanese forces in Malaya. East of the Philippines and the Indies, Army troops from the South Seas Detachment or naval landing forces would assault a variety of small objectives: Rabaul and Kavieng in the Bismarcks, Guam, Wake, and the Gilberts, as well as several towns on the coast of New Guinea.

An Army air corps (about 430 planes) was assigned to General Yamashita while another group (about 150 planes) would assist Homma. Ground-based aircraft were to support all landings.

The Japanese undertook an ambitious program, considering the fact that only 11 divisions, 9 tank regiments, and 2 air groups were assigned to the Southern Army for the centrifugal offensive. Their chances for success were enhanced by the careful consideration given to the use of airpower and the proximity of major air and logistical bases in Indochina, Formosa, the Pescadore Islands, the Ryukyus, and the mandated islands in the central Pacific. From Indochina and Formosa, Japanese aircraft could reach Malaya and Luzon; Camranh Bay, Indochina was a vital logistical base; and the Japanese mandates provided a variety of important bases astride the American line of communications from Hawaii to the Philippines.

Japanese planners, however, did not concentrate on these operations only. Indochina would have to be stabilized. War would continue unbated in China with the 28 divisions deployed there. In Manchuria, 13 divisions would be alert for a Russian strike, although the Japanese were most concerned about destroying the Soviet air elements in case of war on that front.

War came after the Japanese Army, under General Hideki Tojo, had virtually assumed control of the Japanese nation. Tojo, to western observers, was the epitome of the Japanese militarist. Born in 1884, the son of a former *samurai* who had become a general in the Japanese Army, Tojo had impressive military credentials. He had attended the War College; served in Germany; commanded the Military Academy, a regiment and brigade of infantry, the military police of the Kwantung Army, and then the Kwantung Army itself; served as Inspector General of Army Aviation; and, finally, served as the War Minister. A top flight administrator and disciplinarian, he was a man both to avoid and respect. Sharp—hence the nickname, "The Razor"—Tojo became the nation's best War Minister. Absolutely devoted to the Army and to the cause of

General Hideki Tojo

expansion advocated by the Army, Tojo moved his nation toward war. Feeling diplomacy alone could bring dishonor, he was convinced that Japan could win.[45]

While few westerners will ever change their censorious view of Tojo, one of his friends and subordinates, General Yamashita, earned the respect of many of his opponents for his military skill. Next to Tojo, he is perhaps the best know Japanese Army officer. Like Tojo, Yamashita was a German-oriented infantry officer, who served on the general staff and graduated from the War College. Before commanding the Malayan invasion force, he had fought in China and served as the Commander of the Kwantung Army Defense Forces. His reputation was to be marred with charges of atrocities committed by his troops in China, Malaya, and the Philippines, although his combat actions in each area were admired.[46] A large, stern appearing man, Yamashita was probably Japan's greatest general. He thought of himself as a "Great Cedar," but is remembered as the "Tiger of Malaya." All warrior, after being sentenced to death for war crimes, he wrote:

> The world I knew is now a shameful place
> There will never be a better time
> For me to die.[47]

When the Japanese Army launched its attack on the western Allies, it was a well-trained force, much better than its adversaries had estimated. Its officers had been carefully and professionally trained at home and abroad. Built on Japanese and German tradition, it would fight either with brilliance or with blind fury throughout the war. Light, mobile, and tough, it would give an excellent account of itself wherever it fought. Cunning, valor, and dedication to the Emperor were its hallmarks; cruelty and savagery were its curses. Observing the "way of the warrior," the Imperial Japanese Army was a collection of *samurai* and like the dagger of the *samurai* it was an instrument of spirited, close-in, bloody fighting.

The Sword: The Imperial Japanese Navy

When Horatio Nelson signalled "England expects that every man will do his duty" prior to engaging Napoleon's fleet off Cape Trafalgar in 1805, little could he guess that a century later Admiral Heihachiro Togo would emulate him before engaging the Russian fleet in the straits of Tsushima by hoisting the following signal to the masthead of the *Mikasa*: "On this battle rests the fate of our nation. Let every man do his utmost."[48] Togo's victory over the Russians was the most impressive victory at sea since Trafalgar, and it is no wonder that the Japanese considered the admiral their Nelson. At Tsushima, aboard the *Nisshin*, young Ensign Isoroku Yamamoto was wounded in his first combat. For the remainder of his life, he would serve in the Imperial Japanese Navy, gaining a reputation to rival that of Togo but not the glory of Nelson.[49]

Japan owed her victory at Tsushima in great part to the Royal Navy, which had been used as a model by the Imperial Japanese Navy.[50] Great Britain had given Japan some of her first ships in the latter part of the Nineteenth Century, established her Naval College at Eta Jima, and had even exported the red bricks to build the college in the image of Dartmouth. In the first years of the Meiji period, Japan bought many of her ships from the British. Tactics were British. Togo's crossing of the "T" at Tsushima was done in the best style of British ships-of-the-line. When the Japanese developed their naval air forces, they continued to follow the British lead. In 1921, a special air mission was sent from England to train the infant Japanese naval air service and develop new aircraft for it. The Japanese officer corps adopted the traditions and customs of the Royal Navy, emphasizing, for example, the British concern for gentlemanliness, which was the mark of the gentry who served in the Royal Navy. This was a mistake. Instead of adopting the hard discipline upon which the Royal Navy officer's gentlemanliness was based, the Japanese took only the form. When war came in 1941, Japanese admirals were often brilliant, but too gentle, lacking the salty leadership needed to direct a battle fleet in a tough fight. The only non-British part of the Imperial Navy was its German-like general staff system which resembled the organization of the Imperial Japanese Army.

Because their service took them abroad, the Japanese Navy, unlike the Imperial Army, contained many internationalists. Furthermore, their interest in Great Britain, world trade, and developments in other navies mean that they had to be more world-oriented than the men of the Army. While the naval officer was theoretically as much a *samurai* by tradition as the ground officer, his attitudes were softened by his constant exposure to the western world. This exposure made most naval officers quite realistic when they contemplated war with the United States and Great Britain. While there were a few zealots in the naval service, most of the older admirals, in particular, and the officer corps, in general, opposed war. To them, it was obvious that the Allies had the preponderance of naval power. The United States Pacific Fleet, once built up to a capacity desired by the Roosevelt Administration, would alone be superior to the Japanese fleet. Furthermore, the officers recognized that Japan had neither the industrial base nor the raw materials, especially oil, to challenge the Allies in a long war. In the final test, however, the naval officers were patriots who believed that if war were necessary, they would have to do their utmost to win it for Japan.[51]

Until 1909, Japanese naval policy and strategy concentrated on China and Russia. That year the United States became the prime theoretical enemy in the minds of the navalists, thereby creating a dualism in strategic planning which hurt Japanese policy for years to come because the Army continued to concentrate on Russia. Naval strategists assumed that Japan would have to fight a defensive war, and that the United States Pacific Fleet would advance toward Japan or her possessions once war was declared.[52] The Japanese planned to react by deploying submarines to harass the American fleet in distant waters while massing their own battle fleet near the Bonins and the Marianas, where it was anticipated a decisive sea battle would occur. (*See Atlas Map No. 1*) This decisive battle was the supreme goal of the Japanese naval strategists, one which remained so throughout most of the war. In it, the battleship would play the key role.

In the 1920s and 1930s, Naval strategists assumed that an attacking fleet would have to be 50 percent larger than the defending fleet if victory were to be assured. This meant that the Japanese Navy would have to be at least 70 percent as large as the American force if Japan were to survive an American attack.[53] Japanese building programs were designed to achieve this goal. In 1922, the Imperial Japanese Navy, with 547,000 tons of war-shipping, ranked third behind the British (1,400,000 tons) and American (1,100,000 tons) multi-ocean navies.[54]

At the time of the disarmament conference in Washington in 1921, Japan was still expanding her naval forces at a rapid rate. As early as 1919, 30 percent of the Japanese national budget was allocated for naval expenditures.[55] Accordingly, the conference proposal for a 5–5–3 ratio between the three leading maritime powers, which gave the United States the theoretical strength to overcome the Imperial fleet, was opposed by Japan. The Japanese representative protested the proposal, but the Americans and British, desirous of maintaining their primacy, stood firm. Under the approved ratios, the United States received a 67 percent advantage in capital ships over Japan, enough to be victorious in a head-to-head engagement. The Japanese were also very worried about their allowed submarine tonnage. Feeling that they needed a minimum of 78,000 tons regardless of established ratios, they were upset with the 52,700 tons allowed in the 1930 conference, although it gave Japan parity with Great Britain and America. In this later conference, Japan did get a 10–10–7 ratio in cruisers, an accomodation which, if attained in capital ships earlier, would have satisfied even her most ardent naval expansionists. By this time, however, the militaristic revival in Japan had nearly ordained the end of naval disarmament agreements.

Japan, however, was not at such a disadvantage in naval strength as it appeared. Holding the mandates in the central Pacific gave the Imperial Navy dominance in the western Pacific. Also, some American strength would always be deployed in the Atlantic and Caribbean, further reducing the theoretical disparity between the two nations. In one way, however, Japan was weaker. By planning for a defensive war in nearby waters, she designed ships with short ranges and a navy with a small fleet train. As a result, Japan could not project her naval power as well as the United States by the time war came.

After Franklin D. Roosevelt was elected President and it became obvious that the United States intended to increase its Navy to the size authorized by treaty, Japan began a series of "Replenishment Programs" to increase her fleet battle tonnage. To gain superiority at sea, the Japanese Naval General Staff ordered four super battleships of 63,700 tons in 1937. When the first two, the *Musashi* and the *Yamato*, were completed, they appeared to be the most impressive warships in the world. Carrying 18.1-inch main batteries and displacing 75,500 tons when fully loaded (double the American standard), they were the greatest battleships of their time. Their 18.1-inch guns could fire armor piercing rounds through a destroyer or thin-skinned aircraft carrier.

The Japanese designed their new warships for combat only; crew comfort was not a consideration. While earlier Japanese shipwrights had copied European warships, the vessels of the 1930s were of original Japanese design. Everything was done to give the ships an advantage over American or British warships in speed, armor, and arma-

ment. Combat quality was stressed. In light cruisers, for instance, the Japanese achieved exceptional 30-knot speeds after designing huge 152,000 horsepower engines; and Japanese *Fubuki* class destroyers, built from 1928 to 1932, were the best of their kind in the world. Opponents described these ships as "wolves of the sea," in admiration of their battle-designed qualities. In submarines, the Japanese were also inventive, designing fleet boats, midgets, and even aircraft-carrying boats. These craft, however, suffered from the lack of creature comfort associated with Japanese warships. Life aboard these submarines was abominable. The crews needed extensive rest and relaxation to fight effectively; when in the course of war Japan could not provide such luxuries, morale in the undersea forces sagged, dragging down combat efficiency.

The Japanese Navy also excelled in their construction of aircraft. Their Mitsubishi Type O (the Zero or Zeke) naval fighter aircraft was the world's best. Although many had been used in China during 1940 and 1941, American air experts did not know that this fighter existed. The Japanese torpedo bomber, the Kate, was better than its American counterpart and far superior to the British torpedo bombers. The Japanese Val dive bomber was equal to the American Dauntless.[56]

Foreign observers tended to criticize Japanese equipment, claiming that their items were merely poor imitations of western equipment. In some areas they were right, but in naval aircraft and warships they were totally wrong. In retrospect, its seems strange that the British and Americans could have been so myopic. Japanese ships had been observed for years. War in China had given reasonable testimony to the expertise of Japanese air forces, even though propaganda obscured the real facts from the public.

The Japanese Zero Fighter

Japan, of course, went out of her way to keep her developments secret in the last years before the war. This helped to dupe the Allies.

It is equally ironic that Japan in 1941 could be considered behind the times, when the "advanced" British Navy fought the first years of the war with lumbering bi-planes. The Japanese were superior in optics, and their pyrotechnics were equally good. But it was in torpedoes that they had an extraordinary advantage. Having developed an oxygen-fueled torpedo with a speed of 32 knots and an incredible range of 40,000 meters (or 49 knots and 20,000 meters), the Japanese had a weapon which the Americans could not match for years. Because they had practiced extensively with the weapon, had eliminated its major technical deficiencies, and had kept torpedo tubes on their cruisers, the Japanese had a distinct advantage in close-surface combat, which would bear fruit in the early naval engagements of the war.[57]

There are two areas, however, in which Japanese naval construction can be criticized: the weak industrial base and the small merchant marine. The first of these was critical. Japanese shipyards turned out essentially piece work, never gaining the ability to mass produce warships or merchantmen. Because of this, Japan could never compete in a building race with the United States. This became more and more evident as the war continued. The second weakenss was recognized by the Japanese themselves before the war. Japan estimated that its approximate 6,000,000 tons of cargo shipping would support its war effort only if there were no substantial losses. With great losses, Japan could not transport the raw materials of Manchuria and the Southern Resources Area to her industrial base. Consequently, shipbuilding would suffer, as would other heavy industries. Without adequate ship-building, the merchant losses could not be replaced. It was a vicious interrelated circle.

One type of vessel has not yet been discussed. When war began, the Imperial Japanese Navy had 10 fleet carriers in commission—3 more than the United States possessed and 7 more than the United States had in the Pacific. Possessing this superiority, Japanese admirals could roam the Pacific and Indian Oceans with impunity. Japanese interest in carriers grew early, following the lead of the Royal Navy. The first carrier (the *Hosho*), a small 7,470-ton vessel, was commissioned in 1922. It was the first carrier in the world to be built from its keel up. In 1928, the 34,000-ton *Agaki* was built, and in the following year the 33,000-ton *Kaga* was finished. The 11,700-ton *Ryujo* (1933), 18,800-ton *Soryu* (1937), the 20,500-ton *Hiryu* (1939), and the 13,950-ton *Zuiho* (1940) followed. They showed the penchant of the Japanese for a large number of small carriers. In 1941, the 25,675-ton sisters, the *Shokaku* and *Zuikaku*, were com-

missioned. Considering the design of their other surface warships, it is surprising that the Japanese carriers, although excellent vessels, lacked the speed of the American carriers.[58] Only the original *Hosho* survived the war.

Japanese naval aviation doctrine and procedures were quite advanced. Displaying early interest in air operations at sea, men such as Admiral Isoroku Yamamato helped the air service to develop. Yamamoto, an unorthodox sailor, felt that the carrier would be the key weapon of any future war. While not an aviator himself, although he was a naval air administrator who directed the Kasumigaura Air Training Center and commanded the First Air Fleet, Yamamoto became a hard taskmaster for the men who joined the Naval Air Corps. Training under him was thorough and demanding. In the early days, pilots did not live very long; but regardless of the dangers, Yamamoto required them to fly at night and work in all sorts of difficult areas.[59]

Four distinct specialities grew in the naval air service: dive bombing, torpedo bombing, fighter escort, and long-range patrol bombing. In each, the navy had excellent aircraft and well-trained air crews, many of whom had seen combat in China. By 1941, leading Japanese naval aviators included Admiral Takijiro Onishi, who would plan the Pearl Harbor attack with Yamamoto, and Commander Minoru Genda, a combat leader and leading aviation staff officer, who would be a key figure in the Pearl Harbor and Midway battles. Genda won his laurels in China where his squadron was known as "the Genda Circus." Later in the war, his tactics would be known as "Gendaism." As a fighter pilot, Genda believed in using large formations of fighters to gain air superiority and in massing carriers in a single tactical theater.[60]

The Imperial Japanese Navy differed from the United States Navy and the Royal Navy in that it never organized a marine corps to act as infantry in naval campaigns. It did

Estimated Annual Needs

Army	5.7
Navy	17.6
Civilian Economy	12.6
Total	35.9

Annual Production

Home Crude	1.6
Synthetic	1.6
Total	3.2
Deficit	32.7
Stocks on Hand, 1941	42.7
Available Annually in Netherlands East Indies	65.1

Note: Data expressed in millions of U.S. barrels.

The Japanese Oil Situation in 1942

form Special Naval Landing Forces which began spear-heading landings on the China coast as early as 1932, but such forces never gained the stature of a large marine force. These Japanese formations, comprised of sailors and naval officers, were best suited for unopposed landings. In opposed landings, the sailors were unable to fight effectively as infantry. Still the units performed satisfactorily in China; in the drives into the Philippines, Netherlands East Indies, New Britain and New Ireland; and at Wake Island and the British Gilberts. Moreover, as the war progressed, the Special Naval Landing Forces became defensive experts in the Pacific.[61]

As war approached in 1940 to 1941, Japanese naval strategists considered seizing the vital resource areas in Southeast Asia and the Netherlands East Indies.* With about an 18-month supply of reserve oil stocks, the Navy could fight a limited war with some success, but a long war would prove disastrous for the fleet. Hence, it is understandable that the loss of oil imports was a major problem. Without oil, Japan would become militarily impotent.[62]

Any drive into the Southern Resources Area would, however, be threatened by American strategic bombers in the Philippines and by the United States Pacific Fleet, which had been moved from San Diego to Pearl Harbor. Orthodox Japanese planners believed that the objective could be captured before the Americans could react. Then, in line with their old strategic assumption, they could react to any attack by the American fleet in the Pacific, perhaps even attaining victory in the decisive sea battle they had always desired.

Early in 1941, Yamamoto, now the Commander-in-Chief of the Combined Fleet, began to develop an adjunct to Japanese strategic plans. Believing strongly that any Japanese move to the south could not be accomplished unless the American fleet was neutralized, the admiral proposed to attack the United States Fleet at Pearl Harbor. The daring plan had precedents. In 1596, Shogun Hideyoshi destroyed the Korean fleet in Inchon while peace negotiations were underway with the Korean Emperor; Admiral Togo had neutralized the Russian Asiatic Squadron in Port Arthur when he attacked without a declaration of war in 1904; and in November of 1940, Italian airplanes had tried to sink the British cruiser *HMS Gloucester* in Alexandria, while the Royal Navy, in a night attack, destroyed the major portion of the Italian Navy with torpedo bombers in Taranto Bay.[63] In addition, the concept of a surprise attack

against Pearl Harbor was not new. The British naval commentator, Hector Bywater, in his novel *The Great Pacific War*, had prophesied the attack on the American fleet, much as Homer Lea, the American general of China and associate of Sun Yat-sen, had prophesied the Japanese invasion of the Philippines in *The Valor of Ignorance*. Bywater's and Lea's works were required reading in Japanese war colleges.[64]

Working with Admiral Onishi and Commander Genda, Yamamoto devised his plan.[65] Six fleet carriers would form the heart of the attack. Moving across the bleak north Pacific, they would approach Hawaii from the northwest in order to launch their aircraft about 230 miles from the objective. Total secrecy was required, because to carry out the audacious plan the force would have to reach Hawaii without being discovered. Radio silence would be maintained. Because of their limited ranges, ships would have to refuel at sea, with destroyers having to do so three times. It would be ticklish business in the rough autumn weather. A submarine force would surround Pearl Harbor to pick off ships outside the target. Even midget submarines, literally human-directed torpedoes, would be used to slip inside the harbor and cause havoc.

Yamamoto fully appreciated his difficulties, but he felt that the operation had to be executed if Japan had any hope of success. In it he demonstrated his belief in naval air power, placing his reliance first on torpedo bombers and then on dive bombers. His use of submarines was a concession to his more conservative associates.

The Navy General Staff did not like Yamamoto's plan. The Chief of Staff, Osami Nagano, was reluctant, and the First Bureau (Operations) Chief, Shigeru Fukudome, thought it only had a 40 percent chance of success. Even after war games had been conducted, the staff officers were skeptical. They objected for several reasons. First, the whole operation was dependent upon surprise; second, it was not so indispensable that it had to be executed regardless of risk; third, vessels would have to be refueled at sea in less than optimum conditions; fourth, there was a high probability that the task force would be spotted and interdicted; lastly, knowledge of it would break down negotiations, which would be going on while the force was enroute.

By virtue of a persuasive personality, Yamamoto overrode his critics, but he gained Admiral Nagano's acceptance of the plan in early November only after threatening to resign his post as Commander-in-Chief. Even so, many naval officers (including Yamamoto's old chief of staff, Admiral Fukudome, and the assigned task force commander, Vice Admiral Chuichi Nagumo) feared that it was an unwise move. Only the air zealots, Onishi, Genda, and Commander Mitsuo Fuchida, the appointed air strike commander,

---

*Yamamoto developed his Pearl Harbor plan independently of the Army. As earlier mentioned, Army planners had always concentrated on Russia, while the Navy focused on the United States. Because of this separatism, Yamamoto's plan is presented here rather than with the total war plan discussed earlier, which had been hammered out between the two services in August 1941. When executed in December, Yamamoto's plan meshed beautifully with the rest of the Japanese scheme.

really approved of the action. But even Onishi wavered.

With its final acceptance by the Army and the Government, Yamamoto went about final preparations for the operation. Ships were moved into the isolated Kuriles to anchor at Hitokappu Bay. (*See Atlas Map No. 1.*) Dummy radio stations were kept operational in the Inland Sea. Security was tightened. No one obtained information about the plan if he did not need it. Torpedo experts developed wooden fins to install on weapons so that they would not strike bottom in the shallow waters of Pearl Harbor. Special armor-piercing bombs made from naval shells were readied for the dive bombers. Pilots practiced their air strikes, presumably for service with the Army; but they flew at unusually low levels for dry-run torpedo strikes, in an area similar to Pearl Harbor. The Imperial Navy spared no effort to train the crews of the 60 odd ships and the 360 or so aircraft which would make the attack on Pearl Harbor.[66]

When Admiral Nagumo led the Pearl Harbor Striking Force out of Hitokappu Bay on November 26, he had the cream of the Imperial Japanese Navy with him. Aboard the six carriers were the finest flyers in Japan; many were combat veterans of China. The officers were professionals of first rank. Unlike the Army, which had lost many of its exceptional officers in combat in China, the Navy was fielding its first team.[67] Sailors, volunteers, and conscripts were admirably trained. For years, the fleet had maneuvered for long periods in the isolated northern Pacific. Often 20 to 100 sailors were lost in this inhospitable area as the Navy went through its realistic exercises. Safety always played a secondary role to combat readiness in the fleet.[68] By 1941, officers and seamen, flyers and engineers, deck hands and submariners, were prepared to do their duty for their Emperor. The Japanese Combined Fleet would be a tough opponent.

Five hundred miles from Hawaii, ships' captains, after reading the Emperor's message of war to their crews, relayed the final words of Admiral Yamamoto: "The rise and fall of the Empire depends upon this battle. Every man will do his duty." The next day, the Admiral penned this short verse:

> What does the world think?
> I do not care
> Nor for my life
> For I am the sword
> Of my Emperor.[69]

The man who had opposed the alliance with Germany and Italy, who had been sent to sea to prevent his assassination by right-wing militants, who had argued that war with the United States was folly, and who had predicted that he could "run wild" for six months, had to brood aboard his flagship *Nagato* in the Inland Sea, while the fleet he had ordered to war sailed to unexpected infamy at Pearl Harbor.

A Questionable Decision

The Imperial Rescript declared war on the 8th day of the 12th month of the 16th year of *Showa*:*

> . . . Our Empire for its existence and self-defense has no other recourse but to appeal to arms and to crush every obstacle in its path.
>
> The hallowed spirits of our Imperial Ancestors guarding Us from above, We rely upon the loyalty and courage of Our subjects in Our confident expectation that the task bequeathed by Our Forefathers will be carried forward, and the sources of evil will be speedily eradicated and an enduring peace immutably established in East Asia, preserving thereby the glory of Our Empire.[70]

The evoking of ancestral assistance through spiritual intercession was not a shallow, war-inspired gesture.

Long before the attack on Pearl Harbor, Japanese leaders had proclaimed their faith in the dominance of spirit over material things. Of course, material things were important to them, and the Japanese did worry about preparations for war. Accordingly, by 1941 the nation was devoting nearly half of its annual income to military purposes. If those expenditures for armaments were carefully made, however, they were also envisioned as symbols of an all-conquering Japanese spirit. Such a view was—and is—generally misunderstood by, and foreign to, westerners. The spirit was everlasting, the Japanese believed, but there were limits to material resources. This reliance upon spirit so deeply permeated the Japanese culture that it could evoke from military leaders slogans such as: "To match our training against their numbers and our flesh against their steel."

Among civilians the situation was the same. Under the pressure of 12-hour work-days and, later, terrible all-night bombings, factory workers were exhorted by the authorities: "The heavier our bodies, the higher our will, our spirit, rises above them . . . The wearier we are, the more splendid the training." This deeply engrained concept of the triumph of

---

*Showa is the reign of the Emperor—in this case Hirohito. The formal declaration of war came at 4:00 P.M., December 7, 1941, Washington time, when the Japanese Imperial Headquarters proclaimed that a state of war existed between Japan, the United States, and Great Britain. The 14-part Japanese note received in Washington on December 7 did not contain a declaration of war; without breaking off diplomatic relations, it simply terminated the lengthy discussions between the two countries.[71]

spirit over matter was not apparent only in the latter years of the war when it might be viewed as an alibi for Japanese defeats; it was also emphasized during those early months when Japan was victorious. The most significant revelation about spirit, however, is associated with the way in which the Japanese would explain their loss of the war. After 1945, while acknowledging that "spirit was not enough and defending positions with bamboo spears was a fantasy," they contended that "*their* spirit was insufficient and that it was matched . . . by the spirit of the American people." Apparently, material means were not conclusive in the outcome.[72]

In the war which began on December 7, Japanese spirit would not be wanting, but it would not prove capable of coping with the material might of Japan's enemies when her own material strength was inadequate. Without a superior industrial base, Japan could not build warships, merchantmen, and aircraft which were required for a long war. Without sufficient raw materials, particularly oil and iron, she could neither manufacture nor operate her machines of war. Without adequate manpower she could not train the pilots, officers, and other men required to defend her new Empire when the losses mounted. Without a German victory over Great Britain and Russia and without her own triumph in China, Japan could not expect to defeat her main adversary, the United States.

Japan misgauged the type of war she would have to fight, commencing in 1941. Entering that war with limited objectives, the Japanese hoped that it would be short and end in a negotiated peace when the Americans reached the point of discouragement. Quite to the contrary, Japan would find herself engaged in a sanguinary struggle as severe as any she had ever faced. The Americans were in a vengeful mood, incited principally by what they viewed to have been a sneak attack on Pearl Harbor; accordingly, they were determined to bring overwhelming strength to bear on Japan and to demand unconditional surrender. Under this script, the Japanese decision to opt for war was questionable in its wisdom.

Notes

[1]Thomas A. Bailey, *A Diplomatic History of the American People* (New York, 1955), p. 320, and Franz H. Michael and George E. Taylor, *The Far East in the Modern World* (New York, 1956) pp. 125-126.

[2]This section is a synthesis of several sources: Michael and Taylor, *The Far East*, pp. 141-177, 236-277, 472-540, and 615-648; Edwin O. Reischauer, *Japan, Past and Present* (New York, 1969), pp. 108-200; Herbert Feis, *The Road to Pearl Harbor, The Coming of the War Between the United States and Japan* (Princeton, 1950); A. Russell Buchanan, *The United States and World War II*, (2 Vols.:New York, 1964), I, 28-86; and Baily, *Diplomatic History*.

Also useful were: Joseph W. Ballantine, "Japan: Foreign Relations (1931-1945)," *The Encyclopedia Americana* (New York, 1958), Volume XV, pp. 715-719; Hugh Borton, "Japan: Development of the Modern State (1850-1945)," *The Encyclopedia Americana* (New York, 1958), Volume XV, pp. 710-714; Henry Steele Commager, *Documents of American History* (2 Vols.:New York, 1968), II, 9-11, 45, 52-53, 133-134, 181-185, and 411-413; Richard N. Current, "How Stimson Meant to 'Maneuver' the Japanese," *The Mississippi Valley Historical Review*, XI (June 1953), 67-74; Marius B. Jansen, et al., "Japan: History," *Encyclopaedia Britannica* (Chicago, 1964), Volume XII, pp. 905-936; and Louis Morton, "The Japanese Decision for War," The United States Naval Institute *Proceedings*, LXXX (December 1954), 1325-1335.

[3]Michael and Taylor, *The Far East*, p. 160.

[4]Bailey, *Diplomatic History*, fn p. 580, and Michael and Taylor, *The Far East*, pp. 168-171.

[5]Bailey, *Diplomatic History*, pp. 564-576; Michael and Taylor, *The Far East*, pp. 168-169; and Commager, *Documents*, II, 52-53.

[6]Fred Greene, "The Military View of American National Policy, 1904-1940," *American Historical Review*, LVXI (January 1961), 354-377, highlights the importance of the two doctrines.

[7]Michael and Taylor, *The Far East*, pp. 174-175, and Commager, *Documents*, II, 133-134.

[8]Courtney Browne, *Tojo: The Last Banzai* (New York, 1972), pp. 91-92.

[9]General Robert L. Eichelberger, "Dictations" (February 21, 1955), pp. E108-E118 and (July 26, 1961), pp. E1-E6, comments on Japanese actions in Siberia ("Dictations" are available at Duke University Library); Jansen, "Japan: History," 927; and Michael and Taylor, *The Far East*, pp. 339-342.

[10]Reischauer, *Japan*, pp. 149-150; Borton, "Japan: Development of the Modern State," 713.

[11]Masanori Ito with Roger Pineau, *The End of the Imperial Japanese Navy*, translated by Andrew Y. Kuroda and Roger Pineau (New York, 1962), pp. 12-17; Louis Morton, *Strategy and Command: The First Two Years* (Washington, 1962), pp. 21-44 and 67-91; and Greene, "The Military View of American National Policy," 354-377.

[12]John Deane Potter, *Yamamoto, the Man Who Menaced America* (New York, 1971), pp. 61-63; Morton, *Strategy and Command*, pp. 21-32.

[13]Reischauer, *Japan*, pp. 157-185; Michael and Taylor, *The Far East*, pp. 501-504; and John Toland, *The Rising Sun, The*

Decline and Fall of the Japanese Empire, 1936-1945 (New York, 1971), pp. 1-36.

[14]Michael and Taylor, *The Far East*, pp. 506-513; Reischauer, *Japan*, pp. 170-171.

[15]Reischauer, *Japan*, pp. 186-187.

[16]Theodore H. White and Annalee Jacoby, *Thunder Out of China* (New York, 1961), pp. 48-67.

[17]"Conversations" with Amelia M. Bradley, San Diego, California, August 1972.

[18]Reischauer, *Japan*, pp. 191-192, presents these two ideas.

[19]Robert J. C. Butow, "The Hull-Nomura Conversations: A Fundamental Misconception," *American Historical Review*, LXV (July 1960), 822-836.

[20]"Conversations" with Professor Alvin D. Coox, San Diego, California, August 21, 1972. The description of Tojo's Cabinet comes from Professor Coox. He states that it was a description which many Japanese knew was applicable to the group.

[21]Feis, *Road to Pearl Harbor*, p. 178.

[22]*Ibid.*

[23]Feis, *Road to Pearl Harbor*, p. 309, quoting from *Papers Relating to the Foreign Relations of the United States: Japan, 1931-1941* (Washington, 1943), Volume II, pp. 755-756.

[24]Feis, *Road to Pearl Harbor*, p. 310, quoting from *The Memoirs of Cordell Hull* (2 Vols.:New York, 1948), II, 1069-1070.

[25]Current, "How Stimson Mean to 'Maneuver' the Japanese," 67-74.

[26]Feis, *Road to Pearl Harbor*, p. 340.

[27]Colonel Masanobu Tsuji, *Singapore, The Japanese Version*, translated by Margaret E. Lake (New York, 1962), p. 304. This quote is from a Japanese pamphlet entitled *Read this Alone—And the War Can be Won*, translated by G. W. Sargent. It is found in Appendix 1 of Tsuji's book.

[28]Most of this section is based upon Saburo Hayashi (In collaboration with Alvin D. Coox), *Kogun, The Japanese Army in the Pacific War* (Quantico, Va, 1959), pp. 1-46; Coox, "Conversations"; Michael and Taylor, *The Far East*, pp. 501-532; Reischauer, *Japan*, pp. 109-193; Morton, *Strategy and Command*, 234-239; Browne, *Tojo*; and Ruth Benedict, *The Chrysanthemum and the Sword, Patterns of Japanese Culture* (Boston, 1946), pp. 20-43.

[29]The Foreign Affairs Association of Japan, *The Japan Year Book, 1940-1941* (Tokyo, 1941), pp. 210-212.

[30]Field Marshall Sir William Slim, *Defeat into Victory* (New York, 1961), pp. 25-26, 29, 123, 154-166, comments on British morale.

[31]Stanley L. Falk, *Bataan: The March of Death* (New York, 1962), pp. 221-237, explains the reasons for Japanese severity.

[32]Benedict, *Chrysanthemum and Sword*, pp. 145-176 and 199-206. See also Alvin D. Coox, "Chrysanthemum and Star: Army and Society in Modern Japan" (Unpublished Manuscript), pp. 11-12.

[33]Eichelberger, "Dictations" (July 25, 1952), p. III-53.

[34]For the rise of militarism see: Hayashi and Coox, *Kogun*, pp. 4-7; Michael and Taylor, *The Far East*, pp. 501-518; and Reischauer, *Japan*, pp. 157-185.

[35]Hayashi and Coox, *Kogun*, p. 27 and fn 197, p. 199; Morton, *Strategy and Command*, pp. 234-239; and Major Ben Bruce

Blakeney, "The Japanese High Command," *Military Affairs*, IX (Summer 1945), 95-101, cover the Japanese command and staff systems.

[36]Coox, "Conversations," and Falk, *Bataan*, pp. 221-239.

[37]Benedict, *Chrysanthemum and Sword*, pp. 30-35 (loyalty to Emperor), 36-38 (medical service), and 38-41 (death and surrender).

[38]Lionel Wigmore, *The Japanese Thrust* (Canberra, 1957), pp. 109-117, and Foreign Affairs Association of Japan, *Japan Year Book, 1940-1941*, p. 217.

[39]Headquarters, United States Army Forces, Far East, and Eighth United States Army Military History Section, Japanese Research Division, "Japanese Night Combat" (n.p., May 10, 1955) discusses all aspects of Japanese tactics with special attention to night attacks. Quote is from page 219. Comment on envelopments is from Wigmore, *Japanese Thrust*, p. 116. Slim, *Defeat into Victory*, pp. 96-97, also talks about "hooks" or envelopments. See also: General Headquarters, India, Military Intelligence Directorate, *Japanese in Battle* (Delhi, 1944), pp. 1-5, for later wartime evaluations.

[40]Headquarters, Army Forces Far East, "Japanese Memorandum Number 156, Historical Review of Landing Operations of the Japanese Forces" (n.p., 30 April 1952), and Robert B. Merrifield, "Japan's Amphibious Bid," *Marine Corps Gazette XXXVIII* (May 1954), 40-47.

[41]For Japanese planning see: Hayashi and Coox, *Kogun*, pp. 20-25 and 29-35. Also of interest is Tsuji, *Singapore*, pp. 14-23.

[42]Morton, *Strategy and Command*, pp. 95-96.

[43]The term "centrifugal offensive" seems to have been coined by the Department of Military Art and Engineering, U.S. Military Academy, after World War II.

[44]Hayashi and Coox, *Kogun*, pp. 29-35, describes the Army's war plan in detail.

[45]Hayashi and Coox, *Kogun*, pp. 27 and p. 237; Browne, *Tojo*, pp. 100-102 and 117-120; and Coox, "Conversations."

[46]Hayashi and Coox, *Kogun*, p. 240, and Blakeney, "Japanese High Command," 110-111.

[47]John Deane Potter, *A Soldier Must Hang, The Biography of an Oriental General* (London, 1963), pp. 194-197 and p. 206.

[48]Toland, *The Rising Sun*, p. 177. There are several versions of Admiral Togo's remark.

[49]This section is a synthesis of the following sources: Mitsuo Fuchida and Masatke Okumiya, *Midway, The Battle that Doomed Japan, The Japanese Navy's Story* (New York, 1955), pp. 24-54; Samuel Eliot Morison, *The Rising Sun in the Pacific, 1931-April 1942* (Boston, 1948), pp. 19-27; Potter, *Yamamoto*, pp. 11-113; and Donald Macintyre, *Aircraft Carrier, The Majestic Weapon* (London, 1972), pp. 8-78.

[50]For British influence see: Potter, *Yamamoto*, pp. 23-37; Macintyre, *Aircraft Carrier*, pp. 20-34; 36-39, and 72-77; and Morison, *Rising Sun in the Pacific*, p. 21.

[51]Ito and Pineau, *End of the Japanese Navy*, pp. 15-20; Fuchida and Okumiya, *Midway*, pp. 28-31; and Potter, *Yamamoto*, pp. 55-60.

[52]Fuchida and Okumiya, *Midway*, pp. 24-44 give the best view of Japanese naval strategy.

[53]Fuchida and Okumiya, *Midway*, p. 27.

[54]Morison, *Rising Sun in the Pacific*, p. 18.

[55]Japanese Foreign Affairs Association, *Japan Year Book, 1940-1941*, p. 219.

[56]Ito and Pineau, *End of the Japanese Navy*, pp. 15-17, 20-29, and 51 and Morison, *Rising Sun in the Pacific*, pp. 21-24 discuss Japanese ships, aircraft, and equipment.

[57]Morison, *Rising Sun in the Pacific*, p. 23 and Ito and Pineau, *End of the Japanese Navy*, pp. 25 and 51.

[58]Masatake Okumiya and Jiro Horikoshi, with Martin Caidin, *Zero!* (New York, 1956), p. 176. Data about aircraft carriers vary with every source. This is the most complete Japanese source found.

[59]Potter, *Yamamoto*, pp. 32-34, 37, and 52-55, and Toland, *Rising Sun*, pp. 183-185.

[60]Fuchida and Okumiya, *Midway*, pp. 33-34, and Toland, *Rising Sun*, p. 173.

[61]United States War Department, *War Department Technical Manual TM E30-480, Handbook on Japanese Military Forces* (Washington, October 1, 1944), pp. 56-58, and Merrifield, "Japan's Amphibious Bid," 40-47.

[62]Morison, *Rising Sun in the Pacific*, pp. 62-64; Hayashi and Coox, *Kogun*, pp. 24-25; and Feis, *Pearl Harbor*, pp. 88-94 and 267-270 cover the subject of oil.

[63]Macintyre, *Aircraft Carrier*, pp. 48-52, and A.J. Barker, *Pearl Harbor* (New York, 1970), p. 19.

[64]Toland, *Rising Sun*, fn p. 172; Clare Booth, "The Valor of Homer Lea," an introduction to Homer Lea, *The Valor of Ignorance* (New York, 1934), p. xxxi. Also see Richard O'Connor, *Pacific Destiny* (Boston, 1969), p. 321.

[65]Shigeru Fukudome, "Hawaii Operation," in United States Naval Institute, *The Japanese Navy in World War II* (Annapolis, 1969), pp. 1-15. See also: Potter, *Yamamoto*, pp. 68-85; Toland, *Rising sun*, pp. 177-178; and Morison, *Rising Sun in the Pacific*, pp. 80-84.

[66]Potter, *Yamamoto*, p. 80 and pp. 92-95; Barker, *Pearl Harbor*, pp. 65-76; Morison, *Rising Sun in the Pacific*, pp. 80-86.

[67]Alvin D. Coox, "Effects of Attrition on National War Effort: The Japanese Army Experience in China, 1937-1938," *Military Affairs*, XXXII (October 1968), 57, 62, discusses the impact of attrition on the Japanese Army officer corps.

[68]Morison, *Rising Sun in the Pacific*, pp. 24-25.

[69]Gordon W. Prange, *At Dawn We Slept: The Untold Story of Pearl Harbor*. Penguin Books Edition (New York, 1982), p. 472 (quote of message); Potter, *Yamamoto*, pp. 49-50, 58, 63, and 339 (quote of verse).

[70]*Reports of General MacArthur*, Volume II-Part I, *Japanese Operations in the Southwest Pacific Area*, compiled from Japanese Demobilization Bureaux Records, (Washington, 1966), p. xiv.

[71]Prange, *At Dawn We Slept*, pp. 485, 558.

[72]Benedict, *Chrysanthemum and Sword*, pp. 22-28; quotations appear on pp. 24 and 26.

From Versailles to   2
Pearl Harbor:
Development of the
American Armed Forces

In many cases there is but one officer on duty with an entire battalion; this lack of officers has brought Regular Army training in the continental United States to a virtual standstill.

Douglas MacArthur, 1932

World War I was a watershed in American history, and from Versailles to Pearl Habor the nation and its armed forces developed with the legacies of the last great war clearly in mind. For soldiers, sailors, airmen, and marines, the 20 years of peace were ones of boredom and indifference, punctuated by crises and an occasional new development. The Army and the Navy managed to survive the buffeting by the antimilitarists, the limitations of the disarmament conferences, and the stagnation brought about by insufficient annual budgets; but much of the time the United States was militarily impotent. Nevertheless, in the two services there were men who thought about fighting the next war and tried to prepare for it. They developed innovative ideas about strategic bombing and amphibious warfare. There were also leaders who tried to train themselves to assume responsibility for organizations larger than their experience had ever permitted them to know. Concurrently, planners in Washington were able to develop world-encompassing strategic plans for wartime eventualities. In both the areas of procurement of equipment and field training, however, there was generally stagnation, largely due to budgetary restrictions and a national isolationist attitude. While this situation eased somewhat for the Navy by 1935, thereby permitting construction of aircraft carriers and submarines in particular, the Army could neither equip nor train mechanized formations of the type the Germans were developing. For an appreciation of how Americans envisioned fighting World War II, as well as the degree to which they were prepared, it is necessary to examine the activities of the military services during the interwar years.

The Regeneration of the United States Army

June days at West Point are cheerful ones for the graduating class. After the Class of 1927 had heard General Charles Summerall's graduation address they were anxious to receive their diplomas from the Secretary of War and get on with things. In the true tradition of all graduates, "their future was a cloudless sky."[1]

Little did the 204 new lieutenants realize what was in store for them. Most had been born just after the turn of the century and were in elementary school during the First World War. They had entered the Military Academy just after General of the Armies John Pershing had "sent" the dashing superintendent, Brigadier General Douglas MacArthur, to the Philippines. During their diverse careers, the men of '27 would absorb the lessons of World War I, suffer through the Great Depression, fight in the Second World War, and rise to high office in the Korean War. About one fourth of the class would fight against Japan; 11 members would die in the war.

The Class of 1927 served during the years when the Japanese Empire expanded and fell, when the United States Army nearly died but then arose phoenix-like from its ashes. When Lieutenant Thomas J.H. Trapnell, United States Cavalry, reported to his first troop in Brownsville, Texas, the commander explained to him his policy that troop officers alternate in supervising Sunday morning stables. Because the captain had been the only officer in the troop for the last six years, Trapnell would have the privilege of taking Sunday stables for the next six years.[2]

This story, most likely apocryphal, tells something of the stagnation of the Army during the halcyon days of the "Roaring Twenties." In those years there was little to do in many of the troop units: the duty day was short, first sergeants ran the units, polo was the cavalryman's avocation, and there was time to read and study tactics and strategy. At West Point, first lieutenants lived in the spacious new quarters on Lee Road, poverty stricken probably, but with a room and bath for a maid. Such were the good old days of the prewar Army.

By the time the new second lieutenants graduated from West Point, the United States had returned to normalcy after the First World War. The horrors of the war had created a deep aversion to militarism among western nations, and their leaders had tried in 1922 to lessen the chances of war by naval disarmament. In 1928, most nations would ratify the idealistic and pacifistic Peace of Paris, which outlawed war as a means of settling international disputes. During the late 1920s and into the 1930s, self-defense was the only rationale for armaments and armed forces in the United States; appropriations for offensive weapons like B-17 bombers would not be approved. The impact of this mood was pervasive. As one result, Congress became more and more miserly in allocating funds for the Army and the Navy. This policy was by far the Army's worst handicap during the interwar years; without adequate funds it could not gain and maintain the men and equipment needed to defend the United States and its possessions against a foreign enemy.

Until 1921 it appeared that the Army could maintain a reasonably large and effective force under the provisions of the newly enacted National Defense Act of 1920. This act encompassed the ideas of a thoughtful officer, Colonel John McAuley Palmer, and was supported by General Pershing. When their proposals were accepted by the important Wadsworth Committee of the Senate, the bill quickly became law, remaining the governing legislation of the Army until 1950.

Palmer's ideas were not those of the majority of the Army's general staff officers, who were disciples of the pensive Emory Upton, the Army's most influential nineteenth century theorist. These modern Uptonians drafted a plan which proposed a 500,000 man force, universal military training for 11 months, a skeletonized field army of 5 corps, and a relegation of the National Guard to a tertiary position in the national defense pecking order. In an emergency, the previously trained Reserves would fill up the Army, and regular officers would rise to the major command positions. The staff had updated the "expansible army" of John Calhoun and modernized Upton; but while it had convinced a reluctant Chief of Staff, Peyton March, to support the plan, it could not sell the program to Congress.

Palmer recommended a citizen-based army, which he felt was more appropriate for a democracy. In his plan, while the Regular Army would be the vanguard of the ground forces, the National Guard and the Organized Reserves would provide the bulk of the wartime Army. Citizen officers would command most of the citizen soldiers. In peacetime, the Regulars would train their associates in the Guard and Reserves. While Palmer also hoped for universal military service, this unpalatable provision was not acceptable in peacetime.

The old Hamilton-Jefferson controversy between a purely professional and a militia-based defensive force had been resolved in favor, once again, of the militia. Palmer had proposed an Army in the American tradition. Politically feasible, the proposal was favored and accepted by the Wadsworth Committee. The Army's official program was discarded because it was too un-American, as was so much of the philosophy of the Germanophile, Emory Upton. In giving the nation what Palmer and Peshing wanted, the Act of 1920 also established the Air Service as a separate arm, gave the fledgling Tank Corps to the Infantry, and established nine corps areas in the United States for the administration and control of the peacetime Army. One Regular, two Guard, and three Reserve divisions were allocated to each corps.[3]

All this looked good on paper, but unfortunately Congress did not provide sufficient funds to implement the National Defense Act fully until 1940. Money was so scarce that training centers were closed. In order to keep the maximum number of officers and men on duty, new equipment was not purchased; and during the depression salaries were reduced to such a low level that officers and soldiers alike were barely earning enough to live. The Act authorized 280,000 men and 17,726 officers. Immediately after it was passed, the Army was reduced from 228,650 to 147,335 men and women. In 1932, at lowest ebb, it had a strength of 134,024. After struggling for many years to prove its worth, the Army grew to 267,767 in 1940 because of the threat of war in Europe. By mid-1941, after the first peacetime draft had been implemented and peacetime restrictions had been lifted, the strength stood at 1,460,998 men and women on active duty. From that point on, growth was phenomenal.[4]

During the stultifying interwar period, the Army did its most productive work in procuring and educating the officer corps. West Point continued to provide a small annual complement for the active officer corps; but, very importantly, the expanded Reserve Officer Training Corps commissioned additional officers who would man many of the formations of the 1940s. These ROTC graduates proved indispensible during mobilization. Active duty officers were exposed to a thoroughly professional education. Garrisons established officer schools which became important requirements for young officers; and branch schools, particularly the Infantry School under Colonel George C. Marshall's regime as Assistant Commandant, became centers for professional study and growth. Many officers who would serve in future high command positions gravitated to Fort Benning during Marshall's tenure; all spoke highly of the training which they received there. At the Command and General Staff College, Fort Leavenworth, Kansas, student officers gained the background necessary for future work as division staff officers and commanders of major tactical units. When the school was closed in 1940, the faculty remained to write and publish the 250 field manuals which became doctrinal bibles in World War II, establishing the norms and the basics so desperately needed by the Reserve and Guard officers and their men.[5] The Army War College in Washington was the "finishing school" for the top commanders and staff officers of the war, until it too was closed in 1940. The new Army Industrial College, established in Washington in 1923, taught a limited number of military and civilian leaders the intricacies of industrial mobilization based upon World War I experiences. With little field activity and without extensive combat experience in World War I, the Regular officer had to rely upon schoolwork and private study to gain knowledge of his profession during peacetime.

Training in the field, however, was difficult. With only about half the soldiers in the Army in the troop units in the United States, there were seldom enough officers or soldiers in any of those units to train in realistic situations. Marching, drill, and marksmanship, boring at best, were the staples of the day; maneuvers were uncommon. Night attacks were nearly unknown; in fact, two regimental commanders in the prewar Army later stated that they did not remember having participated in any. At Leavenworth, according to one of these officers, night attacks were not even suggested as a preferred solution to any tactical problem.[6] In Panama, the Philippines, and China, the troops were reputed to be better trained. Lieutenant Colonel George Marshall trained the men of the 15th Infantry well during the three years he was in Tientsin; but Major Robert Eichelberger reported that from 1920 to 1921 the officers in that regiment were more interested in tennis, the races, and shopping than working. Sloth and boredom destroyed the tactical worth of many units. Eichelberger complained constantly about the great number of officers who were totally uninterested in their profession.[7] Boredom brought frustration. Many officers got out; soldiers bought out. Brigadier General Bradford Chynoweth, Class of 1912 at West Point, resigned after World War I but returned for two reasons: "in a Depression Year, [he] did not gain a foothold outside; and . . . as an army-brat [he] truly loved

the army."[8] His decision brought him unknowingly to the Philippines and capture in 1942. Lieutenant Charles Jackson, Class of 1919, resigned too. Joining the United States Marine Corps in 1927 as a private, he served later as a non commissioned officer in the 4th Marines on Corregidor.[9] Even Pershing was bored as the Chief of Staff. He took extended vacations in Europe and left his aide, Marshall, behind to mind the shop. One of his vacations lasted nearly six months.[10] For the soldier, drinking, gambling, and whoring were the main distractions from the dullness of Army life.[11] At least the officer could study—and, of course, some could play polo.

Infantry tactics evolved from the World War I experience but remained traditionally American, emphasizing open warfare rather than trench warfare. In 1939, the rifle company assaulted in the familiar "two up and one back" deployment, but the trailing unit was designated a support platoon rather than a reserve. Wave assaults, reminiscent of 1918, still appeared in tactical diagrams; the line of skirmishers used in World War II was not yet employed. The World War I concept of "defense in depth" was adopted by the American tacticians. This deployment of irregular and scattered strong points throughout a regimental zone was to give way to a neater and shallower system of area or perimeter defense.[12] The common description of proposed fighting based on such "defense in depth" echoed the instructions given to German soldiers when they occupied the Hindenberg Line in 1917.

The creation of a mechanized force of combined arms was delayed until the eve of the American entry into World War II. There were several reasons for this shortcoming. In the first place, there were not sufficient funds available to buy the equipment needed, even if the Army had been able to establish a clear-cut priority. Second, many horse cavalrymen, flying in the face of twentieth century technology and historical precendent, believed that horse-mounted units could play an important role on the modern battlefield.[13] As late as 1941, Major General Robert Richardson, the eventual commander of Army forces in the Central Pacific theater, spoke for a number of them:

> Horse cavalry must be judged today by its perfected organization, by the power of its arms, and by its battlefield mobility. If there is one lesson that the actual battle experiences of the present war [in Europe] has clearly shown, *it is the rebirth of the Cavalry as a powerful combat force.*[14]

Another debilitating influence was the lack of a driving interest at the highest levels of leadership. Pershing, whose prestige and influence through former subordinates was enormous, had never been conspicuously interested in tanks. Nevertheless, in 1929 and 1930, Major Adna Chaffee, a vociferous advocate of a combined-arms armored force, began to make some progress through his reports about a force which had been assembled as an experiment. Then, the new Chief of Staff, Douglas MacArthur, ordered the staff to restudy the question of mechanization, which resulted in a decision to allow each branch to develop such mechanized forces as it saw fit. Infantry and cavalry went their separate ways, neither accomplishing much. As a result, it would be 1940 before the Army organized an armored division comparable to the German *panzer* division. The 1st Cavalry Division, which would fight in the Pacific as infantry, was still a horse-mounted unit in 1941.[15]

Tactics and training suffered during this era because of inadequate weapons and equipment. While better small arms, artillery, and tanks had been developed, they were not issued until the late 1930s or until war broke out. Even then, few items were available. This serious problem, caused by the lack of funds during the interwar period, restricted purchase of the new items; then, when they were ordered in quantity, industry was not prepared to build them. As a result of this industrial lag, fewer divisions could be equipped than could be mobilized, and the Chief of Staff could only fully equip two million of the four million combat troops needed in 1942. Equipping the Army was further hindered by the priority which the President gave to building ships for the Navy, fabricating ten thousand airplanes for the Air Force, and distributing huge quantities of tanks, trucks, and airplanes to the British and Russians under lend-lease. Foreign armies were equipped before the United States Army, indicating that the President hoped to avoid war by giving the Allies the material they needed to win the war without American intervention.

The American soldier in the Pacific, moreover, would fight initially with outdated equipment. The M1 (Garand) rifle, the M1 carbine, the 81-mm mortar and the 105-mm howitzer came later. The new small arms replaced World War I standards as did the mortars and howitzer, but World War I Browning machineguns and the Browning Automatic Rifle remained World War II issue.

A basic change in the organization of the infantry division supported the tactical doctrine while incorporating the new weapons. A flexible and more mobile triangular division of 15,000 men replaced the 28,000-man square division of World War I. The older division had been designed for powerful, sustained assaults using two brigades of two regiments each. Each regiment had three battalions; the battalions had four rifle companies, and each company had four rifle platoons. In the triangular division, the brigades were abolished, one regiment was dropped, a

heavy weapons company replaced a rifle company in each battalion, and a weapons platoon replaced a rifle platoon in each company.[16]

During the initial planning for war, 213 divisions were proposed for mobilization. Of these, only 89 would be organized, and all but two would see combat. A serious flaw in actual mobilization was that the service and support forces of the Army absorbed too much manpower. As a result, the Pacific theater received no new divisions after the last strategic reserves were sent to Europe in December 1944. There was abundant manpower in the United States, but the Navy, Air Force, service forces, and American industry drained off the men who were needed in the ground divisions. With only one quarter of its men in its divisions, the United States was fortunate to be allied with Russia, a country with immense manpower resources. Accordingly, the United States could allocate an unusual number of men to the Navy and air forces, take better than average care of its ground troops, and organize only about 40 percent of its planned ground divisions.[17]

By 1941, many of the coming war's top leaders had risen to command the combat forces. Highest in rank was George C. Marshall, who had learned his profession at the knee of Pershing. Marshall was an exemplary staff officer and trainer of officers and men. He had learned to deal with civilian leaders of state, and was touted throughout the period as probably *the* "comer" among all of his contemporaries. Assuming the position of Chief of Staff officially on September 1, 1939, barely three years after being promoted to brigadier general, Marshall would become

General of the Army, George C. Marshall, 1945

a rock of strength for the Army and, in the eyes of many observers, the most influential military advisor of President Roosevelt. The major field command of the Army in the Pacific would go to Douglas MacArthur, the former Chief of Staff who had become the Military Advisor to the President of the Commonwealth of the Philippines in 1935, instead of retiring at 55 years of age or accepting a corps command. When he did retire two years later, MacArthur had spent 19 of his 34 years in the Army as a general officer. Recalled to active duty in 1941, he began a second career which would overshadow his first. Both these generals were powerful, talented men, but in different ways: Marshall—the team player, calm, retiring, diplomatic, and a coordinator of programs—was an exceptional choice for Chief of Staff; MacArthur—dramatic, aloof, imperious, brilliant—was much more at home in an environment where he was the ultimate autocrat.

Pershing, MacArthur, and Marshall had placed their stamps on the Army, and the legion of officers who had grown up under them would serve in the war against Japan. These men included "Vinegar" Joe Stilwell, a China expert, rival of Claire Chennault, British baiter, long associate of Marshall, *the* American in Admiral Louis Mountbatten's Southeast Asian Command, and, after his relief, commander of Tenth Army under MacArthur; German-born Walter Krueger, a private in the Spanish-American War, translator of German texts on tactics, general staff plans officer, and commander, first of Third Army in the Louisiana Maneuvers and later of MacArthur's Sixth Army; Robert Eichelberger, an infantry officer who served in Siberia in 1918 and later as an intelligence officer in the Far East, member of the Adjutant General's Department and the Secretary of the General Staff for MacArthur and his successor, and I Corps and Eighth Army Commander under his old chief; George Kenney, one of the imaginative airmen of the Army, admirer of the flamboyant MacArthur, the general's air chief; and Simon Bolivar Buckner, Jr., scion of the old, old Army, perhaps star-crossed in the tradition of Forts Henry and Donelson, commander of Tenth Army under Admiral Chester Nimitz until he was killed on Okinawa, and the only American field army commander to die in combat. There were many more, too numerous to mention. In addition to the famous generals, however, there were many professional colonels who would become the commanders of the regiments which fought the war. They were the steady heads, the leaders of the combat troops, and the ones who executed the strategies of the "name" commanders. One of these colonels, William Verbeck, was from the Class of 1927, and his 21st Infantry would fight throughout the Philippines in 1944 and 1945. Without these officers there would have been few successful generals.

Marshall would direct the Army during the war through a General Staff which had evolved slowly from its World War I organization. In 1921 it was reshaped in the image of Pershing's staff in France. The now familiar G1 (Personnel), G2 (Intelligence), G3 (Operations and Training), and G4 (Supply) became the Army standard. Pershing's G5 Section (Training) at Chaumont was combined with the G3 in the War Department, and a fifth section, the War Plans Division, was formed. This appendage was to provide the operations staff for the appointed American commander of any future expeditionary force. Although it was expected that the incumbent Chief of Staff would take command of such a force in time of war, this was not to happen in World War II, greatly disappointing Marshall who had always desired high field command.

Marshall was more than just a staff officer. By 1939, the Chief of Staff was by "rank and precedent," position, and presidential desire the chief military executive of the Army; his preeminent position was never challenged. This had not been true of all previous Chiefs of Staff. In World War I, Pershing had defied the Chief of Staff's authority because he felt that he worked directly for the President, and because he was senior to the Chief, Peyton March. In World War II, with MacArthur the senior Army officer on active duty by date of rank, the same situation could have developed again. President Roosevelt would insure that it did not. Unlike his friend, Winston Churchill, he would depend upon his Joint Chiefs of Staff to deal with his field commanders.

The General Staff, originally formed in 1903 as a planning and policy agency, did not command subordinate units and agencies. In 1917, however, General March began to centralize his control of the Army, and this trend continued into Marshall's administration. By 1942, Marshall had made the War Plans Division (later renamed the Operations Division) the Army's command post in Washington. This was done with the expectation of running the war out of this inner sanctum, while the administrative and support functions of the Army in the United States would be handled by the "G" sections of the staff. As it developed, however, Marshall reorganized his headquarters just prior to the outbreak of hostilities, forming three commands which absorbed much of the General Staff's old functions. These commands were: Army Field Forces, commanded by Major General Leslie McNair; Army Air Forces, commanded by Major General Henry Arnold; and the Services of Supply (later the Army Service Forces) commanded by Major General Brehon Somervell. McNair and Arnold were concerned primarily with the training of ground and air forces for deployment overseas and for the defense of the continental United States. Somervell had complex duties involving planning and operations, which required close coordination throughout the war with the Army G4 or the War Plans Division. Logistical planning, originally a G4 function, later would become the province of War Plans, because the staff officers soon realized that they could not develop strategy without concurrent and integrated logistical planning. This reorganization allowed Marshall to devote his attention to high-level policy, strategy, and world-wide operations in lieu of everyday administrative and training tasks.[18]

From 1903 to 1942, the General Staff worked closely with the Navy through the Joint Army-Navy Board. Most of the serious strategical study and planning was done by a Joint Planning Committee under the supervision of the Board. In 1942, the Board became the foundation of the Joint Chiefs of Staff committee, whose members included the Army's Chief of Staff, the Army Air Forces' Commanding General, the Navy's Chief of Naval Operations and fleet commander, and the President's Representative or Chief of Staff. The latter officer, Admiral William Leahy, a former Chief of Naval Operations, was the logical head of the committee, but he never assumed that position because he felt that he was more of a liaison officer or "legman" than a supervisor.[19] For most of the war, Leahy's associates were Marshall, Arnold, and Admiral Ernest King.

By 1942, the command and staff of the Army had been modernized, enabling Marshall to direct the war effort from a central command post in Washington where the Army's missions could be coordinated at the highest level with the Navy, Marine Corps, and Army Air Forces, and, most importantly, the British and the President. An active director of strategy, President Roosevelt would insure unity of effort and, in effect, unity of command.

Between the two wars, the major mission of the General Staff was to develop plans for mobilization and deployment of personnel and materiel for the next war. Problems associated with mobilization have been touched on, and no further elaboration will be attempted. Of unusual interest and importance, however, are the war plans. As early as 1904, Army officers had begun to think about war with Japan and other nations. Under the instigation of Lieutenant General Adna Chaffee, the Chief of Staff, they developed before 1914 a series of "color" war plans in conjunction with the Navy. At first these were merely statements of intention, but by 1924 more detailed and sophisticated outlines had been written. In preparation for a possible attack by the British, war plan RED was developed; for the Germans, there was war plan BLACK; the Japanese were the enemy in war plan ORANGE; and even Mexico assumed the position of the enemy in war plan GREEN. Hybrid war plan RED-ORANGE, hypothesizing a war

with the two great seapowers, Great Britain and Japan, was highly theoretical; but it made the Army and Navy planners think out the problems associated with a two-ocean war. This would later be useful.

From 1924 to 1938, with Great Britain a firm friend and Germany defeated, American strategic thought concentrated on war with Japan. War plan ORANGE predicated a war with Japan only, and posited that the Philippines had to be held as an advanced naval base for the fleet. Almost from the first, Americans believed that this would be a difficult task and would require a defensive war in the Philippines before a fleet could arrive from Hawaii or the United States with reinforcements. When Japan was given the mandated islands in the central Pacific, and later when the status quo on American bases west of Hawaii was frozen at the Washington Conference, the ability of the United States to defend the islands became highly questionable. As the years went by, the Army became less and less interested in the defense of the Philippines, although General Leonard Wood and his great admirer, MacArthur, would insist that the archipelago be held. Army planners did not think that the islands could be held without massive reinforcements; they accepted their capture in order to defend in strength the "strategic triangle" of Alaska, Hawaii, and Panama. The Navy, however, remained offensively minded in the Pacific right up to 1940, when it appeared that the Royal Navy would not be able to survive in the Atlantic. What is interesting about war plan ORANGE is that the United States never had the forces available to implement it, making the defense of the Philippines theoretical at best.

With the threat of a two-front war apparent in 1939, the Joint Board ordered new plans to meet the situation, discarding the color plans. That year, five Joint Army-Navy War Plans were formulated and designated RAIN-BOW 1 through 5. Of key importance in the plans was the defense of the continental United States, the Western Hemisphere, American territories and possessions, and American trade routes. As events unfolded in Europe, the first four RAINBOW plans were cancelled. RAINBOW 5 evolved slowly into the basic American war plan, and after conversations with the British it grew into the basic Allied plan for coalition warfare against the Axis.[20]

RAINBOW 5, as approved in 1939, tasked the Army and Navy to:

a. Prevent the violation of the letter or spirit of the Monroe Doctrine by protecting that territory of the Western Hemisphere from which the vital interests of the United States can be threatened, while protecting the United States, its possessions and its seaborne trade. This territory is assumed to be any part of the Western Hemisphere north of the approximate latitude ten degrees south.

This plan will not provide for projecting U.S. Army Forces farther south than the approximate latitude ten degrees south or outside of the Western Hemisphere.

b. Project the armed forces of the United States to the Eastern Atlantic and to either or both of the African and European Continents, as rapidly as possible consistent with carrying out the missions in *a* above, in order to effect the decisive defeat of Germany, or Italy, or both. This plan will assume concerted action between the United States, Great Britain, and France.[21]

There were many interesting aspects of the ORANGE and RAINBOW 5 plans. Every ORANGE plan, for instance, was based upon the assumption that Japan would begin a war with a surprise attack. Time and again Pearl Harbor was mentioned as a likely spot for such an attack. Many planners believed that the Japanese would strike the United States Pacific Fleet. The Philippines became a "prestige" objective as well as a pragmatic one because America's honor was at stake and Manila Bay was important as a major naval base. Holding the bay was a central feature of all plans. To make this possible, Corregidor and the small islands adjacent to it were fortified. The fight for the control of the Japanese mandates through which the fleet had to steam to get to the Philippines was expected to be a difficult two to three year struggle. A substantial role for airpower was foreseen, but this made the Philippines even less defensible because of their proximity to Japanese land-based aircraft on Formosa and the Japanese carrier fleet assembled in the nearby home islands. As war approached on two fronts, nearly everyone agreed that the United States would have to concentrate first against Germany before turning against Japan. Throughout the war, this basic premise of Allied coalition strategy fitted perfectly with assumptions in RAINBOW 5. Thus, when war came, the United States implemented a revised RAINBOW 5 and immediately went on the defensive in the Pacific. There was no other choice, because there were too few troops to defeat the Japanese Army in the Far East. Preoccupation with Germany doomed American positions west of Wake Island.

By June 1941, the Army had come a long way from its nadir in 1932. It had evolved into a modern bureaucratic institution, and it was being reforged into a modern field force capable of fighting on extended fronts against three major nations. But it was not yet prepared to fight a war. Only one new division out of the 36 in the United States was ready for combat. It would be mid-1942 before there would be enough divisions to form an effective fighting arm.

In the Philippines, the most exposed position, MacArthur hoped he would have until 1942 to complete preparations for war. He planned to wage an aggressive defense of all the islands with the enlarged Philippine Army. Unfortunately, the Filipino conscriptees lacked satisfactory leadership and were untrained and poorly equipped.

While American officers advised Philippine Army units and commanded the crack Philippine Scouts, there were few totally American units in the islands. The largest American maneuver unit was the 31st Infantry Regiment, "Manila's Own," the American regiment of the Philippine Division. With 120,000 Filipinos inducted and 1,500,000 Americans under arms, the United States would not deploy one full American division to its most threatened possession.[23] (*See Atlas Map 5.*)

The first American soldiers to feel the brunt of battle on the ground would be the troops of MacArthur in the Philippines. Eleven members of the Class of 1927 were among them: Thomas J.H. Trapnell, Maurice F. Daly, Stanley B. Bonner, Harold J. Coyle, Theodore Kalakuka, Mark K. Lewis, Jr., Joseph Ganahl, Stuart Wood, Dudley G. Strickler, Montgomery McKee, and Martin Moses. Lewis would be killed in an air crash on December 9; two months later, Strickler would fall while leading the battalion of Philippine Scouts. By the fall of Corregidor, Coyle would have been executed by the Japanese on Cebu and the eight remaining classmates would be prisoners of war. Moses would be executed in November after escaping and becoming a guerrilla leader on Luzon, and Kàlakuka would die on a special mission on Luzon before the end of the year. Daly, ex-Army football coach, Bonner, Ganahl, and McKee would perish on Japanese prisoner-of-war ships before the end of the war, leaving Wood and Trapnell the only survivors of the eleven men. Trapnell, the last commander of the 26th Cavalry (Philippine Scouts), and winner of a Distinguished Service Cross, would live through the march of death across Bataan, survive the sinking of two prisoner-of-war ships, and suffer for the duration of the war the privations of extended captivity in the Philippines, Japan, and Manchuria. By 1945, he could look back a long way to Brownsville, Texas.

It was in great part for the American prisoners of war and their fallen comrades that Douglas MacArthur would promise to return to the Philippines. His promise was to shape much of the ensuing strategy against Japan, provide the spirit for the drive through the southwest Pacific to the Philippines, and keep the Army in the Pacific War. It was under MacArthur that the United States Army would make its major contribution to the fight against Japan.

Mitchell, Independence, and Strategic Bombardment: The United States Army Air Forces

When the young, flying "Hotspurs" of the fledgling Army Air Service returned to the United States after World War I most were convinced that airpower had unique potential, and were dedicated to founding an independent air force. During the interwar years, the history of the Army's air force revolved around demands for independence, development of doctrine, design of a heavy bomber, and preparations for war. Led initially by the flamboyant Brigadier General William "Billy" Mitchell, the most prominent of the World War I air officers, and supported by a legion of airmen in and out of the Army,* the Army aviators struggled with their problems and clashed with the doughboy generals and the battleship admirals. Their struggle was a bitter one—the arguments were full of polemics, blinding zeal, or obstinate orthodoxy—and it destroyed more than one career of a dedicated airpower enthusiast in the Army.[24]

The fight for independence was in many ways a bureaucratic one. Time and time again, bills were introduced in Congress to establish a separate service; but due to pressure from the Army and Navy, from Congress, and from most of the Presidents, the bills never passed. Airmen saw their service grow in stages. Right after the war, in 1920, the Air Service was made a branch of the Army, similar to the traditional arms of Infantry, Field Artillery, and Coast Artillery. Although six years later the service had been renamed the Air Corps† and had representation on the General Staff, as well as a promise of more men and equipment in the future, the airman's status had not essentially changed. A second stage was reached in 1935 when a General Headquarters Air Force was established to control all combat aviation. This headquarters was not under the control of the Chief of the Air Corps; thus, a dualism entered air organization and remained for some time. In 1939, the Chief of the Air Corps regained control of the GHQ Air Force, but the following year he lost control of the headquarters when it became a coequal command with the newly designated Army Field Forces and Services of Supply. The last prewar reorganization took place just

*Among them were Fiorella LaGuardia, James Doolittle, Alexander Seversky, Frank Andrews, Oscar Westover, Lawrence Kuter, George Kenney, and Henry Arnold.

†The name of the air arm of the Army changed often. It was the Air Service in 1920, the Air Corps in 1926, the Air Corps and Air Force in 1935, and the Army Air Forces in 1941. Each name will be used in the appropriate time frame, but in describing World War II, Army Air Forces or air force(s) will be used for the Army's air arm.

six months before Pearl Harbor. The new Army Air Forces took control of the GHQ Air Force and the Office of the Chief of the Air Corps; the former became the Air Force Combat Command and was charged with controlling combat aviation, while the latter retained its name and continued to supervise the administration, service, support, and individual training of the air forces. Dualism was eradicated. Another reorganization took place during the war, making the United States Army Air Forces nearly independent of the Army.

Billy Mitchell never commanded the Air Service during his career. Immediately after World War I, command of the airmen went to two non-flying officers, and by the time their tours were up, Mitchell had resigned from the Army. Prominent air officers from World War I filled the top billets after that, but the man most associated with command of World War II air forces, General Henry Arnold, did not become the Chief of the Air Corps until 1939, after Major General Oscar Westover died in an air accident. "Hap" Arnold then rose to be the Deputy Chief of Staff to General Marshall, and when the Army Air Forces was established he became its commanding general. Arnold remained the air commander for the duration of the war.

The fight for acceptable air power doctrine was a curious and interesting one. It was curious because the doctrine which was found in the publications of the day did not

Billy Mitchell Poses in the Cockpit of a Thomas Morse Scout

represent the advanced thinking of the Army's airmen, but rather the ideas acceptable to the Army General Staff. As a result, it did not emphasize strategic airpower. To discover what airmen thought about airpower, one has to read the books, articles, and speeches of Billy Mitchell and his associates, or investigate what was being taught at the Air Corps Tactical School. The Tactical School promulgated what could be considered "official" doctrine for airmen in the late 1930s. This doctrine, showing Mitchell's heavy influence, was a synthesis of the more radical ideas proposed after World War I.

A detailed review of what Mitchell and other air theorists said during the various stages of air force development is beyond the scope of this section, but its final synthesis can be described. Essentially, American airmen supported the theory of strategic airpower which could strike across long distances against an enemy's entire national structure, destroying the will of that enemy to resist. There were many philosophies associated with such a theory: strategic airpower was an offensive, not a defensive weapon; it could be used as a threat against an opponent to gain national objectives in lieu of war; it could be used against field armies, naval fleets, or air forces to destroy them in battle, but more importantly it could be directed against the enemy's industrial fabric to destroy the enemy's physical capacity to resist; and it could also be employed against the enemy population to shatter a nation's morale. While the airmen acknowledged that their forces should be employed in conjunction with the Army and Navy, they claimed that they were really first among equals because only their forces could fight effectively on land, air, and sea while the other services could not do so. Air theorists, particularly the combative Mitchell, stated that surface fleets were obsolete and that the new carrier forces would not survive against a first-class enemy.* Furthermore, he said that airpower could defend the United States with the help from only submarines, thus denying the Navy's traditional role as the nation's first line of defense. In the eyes of the true believer, airpower could do everything, especially make wars short, cheap, and victorious. The only hitch in the concept of strategic airpower before the war was the range of the heavy bomber; but to make up for this, the air *philosophes* changed their old idea of striking from homeland bases to one of demanding intermediate bases from the Allies for the heavy bombers. All in all, the American airman had a powerful theory, which by 1941 had become dogma.[25]

B-17 Bomber: The Flying Fortress

In their overwhelming enthusiasm for strategic airpower, the Army airmen unfairly dismissed many conflicting theories.† The Army's insistence upon using airpower to support the ground forces in battle and to protect them from opposing air forces, once primary in Mitchell's mind, was relegated to a secondary role, with strategic bombardment coming first.[26] The bitter attack on the Navy nearly emasculated the development of carrier forces, because it did not objectively analyze the great striking power which carrier aviation could provide the fleet and the nation.[27] Moreover, before World War II, the airmen ignored other forms of airpower which would make strategic bombing more effective and less costly: they neglected to develop a suitable long-range escort fighter for the bombers; they refused to build adequate interceptors to defend their own bases; and they neglected to develop a modern air transport fleet which could supply deployed forces, ferry troops long distances, and drop paratroops. This lack of appreciation for alternative ideas was understandable since airmen's ideas were attacked tooth and nail by many intransigent soldiers and sailors; but World War II demonstrated that the airmen had wagered too much money on one horse.

Strategic bombing was only a theory until the Boeing Aircraft Company built the B-17 bomber in 1935. It was a radical departure from earlier bombers. With four engines, a 2100-mile range, a combat bomb load of 2,400 pounds, a service ceiling of 35,000 feet, a speed of 258 mph, and five

---

*Mitchell attempted to prove his theory by sinking a moored World War I German battleship, *Ostfreisland*, in static tests in 1921. He even violated the ground rules for the test by continuing to bomb the ship until it was severely damaged instead of stopping to evaluate each strike. The Navy objected because the ships could not move and fight back, but Mitchell's claim stood in the public's mind.

†Most Army officers after World War I insisted that the true function of the airplane was to support the advance of the land armies, because the airplane was just another useful infantry support weapon. Officers were more impressed with close support, air superiority, observation, and reconnaissance than they were with strategic bombardment. Their view was both practical and shortsighted. Lack of Air Corps interest in Army missions never gave the ground troops the close air support which the *Luftwaffe* gave to the *panzer* division and which marine aviators eventually gave to the marines and soldiers whom they supported.

machineguns for self-defense, the B-17 was not quite the "Flying Fortress" it was called, but it was a truly remarkable airplane. When the first production models rolled off the line in 1937, the airmen had the world's finest heavy bomber. With constant improvements, the B-17 would be employed throughout the war and would become the backbone of the American strategic air forces in Europe.* While airmen wanted an aircraft with a 4,000 to 5,000-mile range and a heavier payload of bombs, the B-17 was all that a bomber enthusiast could expect before 1940.[28]

The production of the B-17 was opposed by the Army because in the General Staff's opinion it was a superfluous weapon during peacetime. The posture of the United States during peace was defensive, and offensive weapons were generally opposed on that ground. The Army's mission included the defense of the nation's coastline; this, however, could be done with the current twin-engine medium bomber. Furthermore, Army interest in aviation still centered on the application of airpower to the direct support of the land forces and to the securing of aerial supremacy. The B-17 was not built for such restrictive missions. It also placed the Army in competition with the Navy, and it cost more than other needed aircraft. For these reasons, only the 13 original B-17s were in service in 1938. With the threat of war, the President ordered increased bomber production in 1938, and the B-17, still the only heavy bomber in production, was immediately ordered in quantity. Nearly 300 were delivered by December 1941.[29]

While Boeing was building its magnificent new bomber, no aircraft company in the United States had yet produced a fighter airplane of similar excellence. However, it appears that Army desires influenced fighter production. When the P-39 (Airacobra) and P-40 (Warhawk) were built, the Army got what it wanted: good, strong, low-level fighters which were excellent close-support aircraft that could be used effectively to repel invading forces. But no outstanding interceptor was built. As a result, there was no pursuit plane available in 1941 which could fight one-on-one with the Japanese Zero, to say nothing of competing with a British Spitfire or a German Messerschmitt 109.[30]

When war came in Europe in 1939, the Army's air arm did not have the combat crews or airplanes necessary to wage a world-wide campaign. Perhaps more than any other service, it suffered the most from its rapid expansion. From a corps of 20,503 in 1939, requiring 1,200 new pilots and 5,500 airplanes a year, the Air Force would soon have over 150,000 men, and would be requesting 30,000 pilots and 50,000 new aircraft a year by 1941. Pilots, planes, and

crews had to be mass produced. So did barracks, airfields, and flying schools. These were hectic days for the officers of the small peacetime Air Force, but they did everything humanly possible to organize and train 24 combat air groups by 1941.[31] This, however, they were unable to accomplish. As a result, the Air Force was not prepared to fulfill its assigned missions in the Pacific or within the United States when the Japanese struck. Expansion and mobilization had come too late.

The United States Army Air Forces' missions in 1941 were subordinated to the strategies which the Army and Navy had developed together since 1935. Although RAIN-BOW 5 gave official priority to the European theater, on their own, air strategists were inclined to be more concerned with Europe than they were with either hemispheric defense or the Pacific; the *Luftwaffe* was a most formidable air opponent, and Germany offered the most difficult problems for an air war. It was quite clear to airmen that Germany would be the tougher enemy.

The bomber-conscious air planners applied the doctrines of Mitchell in their initial plans for an air war against Germany. Deciding that a primary target had to be the German air industry, they were determined to destroy it, thereby limiting the *Luftwaffe's* ability to conduct sustained and effective counter air operations. Tactically, the airmen had adopted procedures which were radically different from those the British had advised them to use. Foremost, American bomber experts decided to attack during daylight because they believed in precision rather than area bombardment. The British felt that this was foolhardy, that it went against their experiences in World War I and World War II, and that it would be too costly in men and planes. The Americans persisted. The planners also decided to fly into target areas without fighter escort, believing that the B-17 could survive, at least for the time being. They did, however, begin looking for an escort fighter† to be employed later in the war, when German interceptor procedures could be expected to improve.[32] Large numbers of heavy bombers were to be used. They were to approach at high speed and high altitude, and their formations were designed to give the attackers a good defense.[33]

Fighter tactics before the war seemed to be based upon one-on-one engagements or "dogfights." Even during the Battle of Britain, pilots scrambled when enemy ships were sighted, climbed up to altitude, and engaged the incoming bombers on an individual basis. Such tactics required a superior air-to-air fighter, one which could outclimb,

---

*In the Pacific, General George Kenney and his bomber commanders preferred the B-24 Liberator.

† Failure to develop an escort fighter before the war was a great blunder. Daylight strategic bombing over Germany was nearly stopped in 1944 because the unescorted American heavy bombers were being shot down at an excessive rate by the *Luftwaffe.*

outmaneuver, outrun, and outdive the enemy's fighters which protected their bombers. Often it meant fighting at high altitudes—over 15,000 feet—and required high overall speeds. First-line American pursuit planes, the P-39 and the P-40, were unable to match the Japanese Zero fighter in most of these critical categories. The Zero could easily outclimb and outturn either American aircraft, and therefore could destroy the American planes in dogfights. Older American fighters were so outclassed that fighting Zeros in them was tantamount to suicide. Not until Americans absorbed the lessons learned by Major General Claire Chennault's "Flying Tigers" did they stand a chance against the superior Japanese fighter.[34]

During the late 1930s, the American airman's involvement in the Germany-first strategy and the prospective air war in Europe distracted him from many of the developments in the Far East. In fact, airmen nearly forgot the Pacific, particularly the Philippines, where in mid-1940 only 26 obsolete fighters were available for the defense of the islands. This pathetic posture was as sad as that of the ground forces, if not worse; but as interest in the American possession increased, more and more fighters and bombers were dispatched to the Philippines. The first P-40s arrived in October 1940, along with other older fighters and bombers. More came the following year. Finally, Army Air Forces Headquarters, alarmed at the situation in the Pacific, ordered 265 B-17s along with 240 newer models of the P-40 for the islands. The first B-17s arrived in September 1941, but there were only 35 when the war began. By the time the war erupted, fighter strength had reached 107 P-40s of various models and some inadequate P-26s, which were flown by Filipino pilots. The total force was insufficient to oppose a determined Japanese attack.

Many of the problems confronting airmen in the Philippines were not solved prior to December 7, 1941. There was only one ferry route for bombers to the islands, and it passed over the Japanese-mandated islands in the central Pacific. No usable fighter ferry route existed. Only two airfields in the Philippines could handle the heavy B-17. All airfields lacked sufficient protective "blast pens," hangers, and control facilities. There was no satisfactory air warning and interceptor system in operation, although radar sets had been received and two were installed. Nor was there adequate antiaircraft artillery deployed to defend the operating strips. All strips were sod, and could not be used in wet weather. Most important, more airplanes, crews, training, and maintenance were needed to make the Far Eastern Air Force an effective combat force. While equipment was arriving every day and a substantial convoy was enroute in late November, time was running out, and it was the most critical ingredient for increased preparedness.

P-40 Fighter: Hawk

Across the Pacific in Hawaii, air preparations had suffered because of the recent emphasis on bolstering the Philippines. By December 7, 1941, there were 231 Army aircraft in Hawaii, only half of which were considered modern. These included 97 P-40s, 12 B-17s, and 12 A-20s (Havocs, essentially light attack, ground support bombers). Although there was a degree of cooperation among the military services in Hawaii, there was no centralized command under any one headquarters. The Navy took care of long-range reconnaissance, while the Army was charged with the defense of Hawaii itself. Army air forces were thus tied to the Army's basic mission: the defense of the Navy's great base at Pearl Harbor. Although the need for aircraft at the outlying islands of Wake and Midway as well as the dispatch of many aircraft to the Philippines complicated the problem, Hawaii's air defenses were better than those of the Philippines; Navy and Marine squadrons, including those on the aircraft carriers of the Pacific Fleet, gave the islands more airplanes to defend the territory, and there were radar stations operating on a part-time basis. In December of 1941, however, most air officers in the islands believed that the first Japanese strike would come in the Philippines. (*See Atlas Map No. 5.*)

So it was that when war came in the Pacific, the Army's air forces were unprepared to fight a modern enemy air force. In application of the RAINBOW 5 war plan, Americans in the Pacific would commence the war in a defensive stance, a stance which in the air required a first-line pursuit aircraft to destroy the opposing Japanese air forces.* Neither American fighters nor the B-17s could accomplish this. Strategic bombardment, an offensive

---

*Chennault seemed to be one of the few prominent airmen who believed in pursuit aviation. He said that fighters could defeat enemy bombers and that they were needed to escort bombers.

concept, was a useless doctrine in the Philippines in 1941 because the limited number of available B-17s could not survive against the overwhelming number of enemy fighters. At Hickman, Wheeler, and Clark Fields, on December 7 and 8 of 1941, the 20-year emphasis on strategic bombardment paid no dividends.

Disarmament, Carriers, and Submarines: The United States Navy

Ensign Charles Keyes left Annapolis in June 1932 and joined the United States Fleet when the Navy, like the Army, was struggling for survival.[35] During the administration of President Herbert Hoover not a single warship had been laid down. This condition boded ill for the Navy, which foresaw the inevitability of war with maritime Japan.[36] Nonetheless, it was still in better shape than the Army in 1932. There were 5,377 line officers and 79,700 sailors in service; they manned 373 warships, including 3 carriers and 15 battleships.[37] More powerful than its probable adversary on a form sheet, the United States Navy was strong enough to protect the nation from Japan or from any other single naval power, but it could not protect the outlying possessions like the Philippines, nor could it fight in the Atlantic *and* the Pacific, as had been hypothesized in war plan RED-ORANGE.

President Hoover's political demise was imminent when Chuck Keyes graduated and was commissioned. In Franklin Roosevelt the Navy gained a staunch friend and advocate. Like his older relative, Theodore Roosevelt, the new President had been an Assistant Secretary of the Navy and was deeply interested in naval affairs. Carl Vinson, Georgia Congressman and Chairman of the Naval Affairs Committee in the House of Representatives, was also a powerful supporter of expanding naval expenditures and new naval construction. Vinson proposed legislation in 1933 which began the rebuilding of the Navy; then, in 1938, he introduced additional legislation which insured the steady growth of the fleet through the next decade.

For Ensign Keyes and all the members of the Navy, the main political problem of the post World War I years was the international stress on naval disarmament.[38] As a result of the various diplomatic ententes, several problems were evident to naval officers in the 1920s. First, the Philippines were extraordinarily vulnerable to Japanese attack, especially from nearby Formosa and even from Japan itself; moreover, the westward route across the Pacific to the islands was flanked by the Japanese mandates. Second,

Manila Bay was not yet the fleet base it should have been, and the plans for its development or the establishment of an alternate anchorage at Subic Bay, just to the north, had to be abandoned. Guam was surrounded by Japanese mandates, and its development was useless and prohibited. Thus, the only suitable fleet anchorage in the Pacific remained Pearl Harbor in Hawaii. Third, to operate in the western Pacific, all American ships would have to be "long-legged,"* that is, capable of extended cruises.[39] Fourth, given the parsimonious attitude of Congress, the Navy would have to scramble for every dollar necessary to maintain the fleet at the strength authorized by the disarmament treaties, something which would not be done. Lastly, the Navy could not be sure that the various treaty nations would abide by the provisions of the Washington Conference. In fact, the British objected to parity with the United States in cruisers and built over treaty limits; the French decided to build more submarines for similar reasons.[40]

While these exterior influences greatly affected the Navy in the 1920s, internal forces were also at work. Primary among them was the move to harness aviation to the fleet. As early as 1914, Congress had recognized the Navy's need for an air arm, and land-based naval aviators had served in Europe during World War I, performing admirably in anti-submarine patrols and in the bombings of German submarine bases in Belgium.[41] Most importantly, they had learned firsthand about the innovations the British devised relative to their airplane-carrying ships. Seaplanes were assigned to capital ships for scouting, and seaplane carriers were developed,† one, the *Ark Royal*, being used in the Dardanelles-Gallipoli Campaign with some success. The first flight deck was built on the forward half of the light battle cruiser, *Furious*, in 1917, and the next year another deck was built on the rear of the ship. It was from the *Furious* that Squadron Commander E.H. Dunning made the first takeoff from a decked ship in August 1917. Dunning also made the first landings, but his death in a landing trial caused the abandonment of landings on the *Furious*. Until landing problems could be solved, the British naval aviators had to ditch next to their ships at sea or fly back to land fields. By 1918, sea-based aircraft had fought effectively against Zepplins, and Admiral David Beatty, of Jutland fame, was considering a carrier-based air strike against the penned-up German High Seas Fleet, which was out of range of land-based aircraft. Beatty's

---

*The "long-legged" capacity would be a real asset by the time of the Okinawa Campaign in 1945. Royal Navy ships were not so designed, and were less useful on extended operations in that campaign.

† While the Allies did not continue to develop and use seaplane carriers in World War II, the Japanese used such vessels extensively to support their initial amphibious operations from 1941 to 1942.

concept was disapproved, so no precursor of World War II carrier strikes took place during The Great War; but the seed of carrier warfare had been planted.[42]

When in mid-1918 the Royal Navy commissioned its first full-decked aircraft carrier, the *Argus*, perceptive officers of all navies recognized that aviation had found a place with fleets. Construction of the *Argus* forced the United States to build its first carrier, and in 1922 a converted collier, the *Jupiter*, joined the United States fleet as the aircraft carrier *Langley*. For six years, the *Langley* would be the test ship for American naval aviators. On her, the pioneer flyers would master the fundamentals of taking off, landing, navigating, gunfire spotting, and aerial gunnery, which then would be passed on to the men who followed. Like Army air operations, initial carrier air operations stressed reconnaissance as a primary task, while gunfire spotting was accorded secondary priority. When it became clear that some aircraft would have to defend the pilots performing the basic missions, new fighter aircraft were built to protect the other airplanes. There was some experimenting with aerial bombing and torpedo strikes in these early days, but naval aviators did not consider these roles to be major missions for naval airpower.[43]

The *Langley* was an inadequate substitute for a large, fast, seagoing carrier. Fortunately, during the Washington Conference the United States was granted the right to convert two battle cruisers under construction to aircraft carriers; and in 1928, the sleek 33,000 ton sisters, the *Lexington* and the *Saratoga*, were commissioned. (The "Sara" was destined to survive the war after seeing some of the grimmest naval combat of the era, but the "Lady Lex"

was not to be as fortunate. She was the first American carrier lost in combat, going down after the Battle of the Coral Sea in May 1942 near the Great Barrier Reef off Australia.*) With the construction of the two large carriers, naval aviation had come to stay; it was only a matter of time before the carriers would become the primary capital ships of the fleet.

While the giant ships were being built, the Morrow Board, appointed by President Coolidge to study the role of military aviation from a national perspective, ruled that the Navy should be built around both ships and planes. This 1925 decision was the Magna Carta for naval aviation, for it negated Billy Mitchell's argument that all aviation should be under one command, as it was in England. Thereafter, the Navy, unlike the Royal Navy, was free to develop its air arm fully prior to World War II.[44]

Much could be made of the controversy in the Navy between the battleship admirals and the naval aviators, but even the most general review of naval history during the 1920s shows that many officers were thinking realistically about the role of naval aviation in the future. Carriers were used in war games at the Naval War College as early as 1921. Two years later, maneuvers against the Panama Canal illustrated that ship-launched aircraft could bomb the canal. When the *Langley* joined the fleet maneuvers in 1925, her performance was so excellent that the Fleet Commander immediately requested that the *Saratoga* and *Lexington* be rushed into service. Rear Admiral W.A. Moffett, the father of naval aviation, had lobbied throughout

*The *Langley* was sunk off Java in March 1942, but she was no longer an active carrier.

USS Lexington

the period for the gradual replacement of battleships with carriers, feeling that the carriers were the capital ships of the future. Even on the General Board, the Navy's highest policy-making body, officers believed that carriers would be necessary, especially if the fleet had to operate in Philippine waters. The importance of the vessel, however, still revolved around the use of aircraft for reconnaissance, spotting, and self-defense, and it would be too optimistic to say that by 1932 the Navy recognized the future of its surface fleet as resting on the carrier.[45] In fact, as late as July 1940, Rear Admiral J.K. Taussig won an Honorable Mention award for his article in the United States Naval Institute *Proceedings* about the primacy of the large fighting ships—implicitly, the battleships.[46]

While sailors and aviators were wrestling with the problems associated with battleships and aircraft carriers, another group in the Navy was grappling with the problems associated with the submarine. Rejecting for the most part the experience of World War I, which highlighted the submarine as a commerce destroyer, American submariners concentrated on developing boats for two distinct purposes—coast defense and fleet support. The first mission presented few difficulties. Short-ranged, comfortable, and moderately well-armed boats could be built to operate around the coastlines of the United States. Technical problems, however, frustrated the officers who were dedicated to building submarines which had the range and speed to operate with the fleet as both reconnaissance and attack boats during extended operation in the Pacific.

During the years before 1932, extremely large submarines were built, but these V-Boats, which had many of the desired characteristics of a fleet submarine, proved to be too large and unwieldy. One problem was obvious: no diesel engine could be designed which was small and powerful enough to propel a small submarine at high speeds on the surface, while giving it reasonable living and working room and adequate torpedo power. Surface speed was a necessity because the submarines had to be able to stay with the fleet. Furthermore, most traveling was done on the surface; boats submerged only to attack or avoid detection. A second major problem was range of operation; to operate from the base at Pearl Harbor, great amounts of fuel had to be carried on fleet boats. When in 1938 submarines were built with the desired surface speeds and extended ranges, American submariners had the ability to strike Japan from Hawaii. The lack of intermediate naval bases west of Pearl Habor had proved to be a blessing in disguise for the submariner.[47]

One might ask why the United States Navy avoided the doctrine of unrestricted submarine warfare. Public objection was a major factor. Another was that treaty limitations barred the use of submarines against a merchantman unless the vessel was stopped, the crew evacuated, and the ship's papers salvaged. Such limitations, accepted as international law, were duly impressed upon all submarine commanders. Violations would make submariners pirates, subject to immediate destruction. Also influential was the opinion of the officers of the Royal Navy, who remembered the precarious position into which the U-Boats had forced Britain in World War I, and who tried as early as the Washington Conference to outlaw the use of submarines. Lastly, American sailors felt that the greatest value of the submarine was its ability to destroy capital ships.[48]

Chuck Keyes was lucky when he began his service in 1932, because the Navy was about to experience a renaissance. With President Roosevelt's support, the service expanded energetically, doing many things which should have been done years earlier. At the same time, the situation in the Far East had grown steadily worse since 1931, when the Japanese Army invaded Manchuria and began aggressive moves into other parts of China. Soon after graduation, Ensign Keyes could see that the Navy's interests were more than ever centered on the Pacific. It is evident to a reader of the 1933 *Proceedings*[49] of the Naval Institute that the officers in the Navy, expecting war with Japan, were concerned with the disparity between the potent Imperial Japanese Navy and their own service, which was below treaty strength. It is interesting to see that in the *Proceedings* the observant naval officers, young and old alike, were exposed to current thinking about Japan's war potential, her modern fleet, her lack of oil, her need for controlling the vast oil deposits in the Netherlands East Indies, her valuable strategical position in the mandated islands, her developing naval air forces, and, most importantly, the problems which the United States Navy would face in combatting Japan in the western Pacific and in reinforcing the Philippines. The 1933 *Proceedings* was a primer in naval strategy. Whether or not the junior officer in the Navy knew about the current war plan ORANGE, the most important naval journal in the United States clearly outlined all its parameters.

If the Far Eastern situation challenged the naval officers, the funds which the new administration poured into the Navy gave them the ships which would be their fighting instruments in case of war. The first funds, permitting the construction of new cruisers and smaller vessels, were appropriated in 1933. In 1934, an eight-year building program was approved and another 102 ships of all types were provided for. By 1936, when treaty limitations were due to expire, the nation was rapidly trying to build up to authorized treaty strength.

A 20 percent addition to overall ship tonnage was

approved in 1938, when Congressman Vinson sponsored another construction bill. After France fell, money was no longer a limit, since the Navy could grow only as fast as shipyards could produce ships. This was a difficult situation because many American shipyards had been shut down prior to the construction boom, and skilled workmen and usable yards were hard to find. Fortunately, since the major construction had begun much earlier than had similar work in the Army, the Navy did not have to depend on the ships laid down after 1940 to fight the first years of the war.[50] A late start in naval rebuilding would have been disastrous.

As new construction began, the Navy modernized older ships and placed more emphasis on naval aviation, carriers, submarines, and the building of new bases. Improvements in submarine construction gave the Navy a chance to build and test new boats. After 1931, the two-type submarine program was abandoned in favor of a single, all-purpose submarine. Added funds gave impetus to the program, and when a new diesel engine which could give the American submarine the speed and range desired was finally developed in 1938, an all-purpose *Tautog* class submarine was accepted as standard by the Navy Board. These submarines were constantly improved; the newer classes became the mainstays of the force which roamed the Pacific from 1942 to 1945. In December 1941, the silent service had 131 submarines of all types in commission, while 73 more were being built.[51]

Major ship construction provided the new 14,500-ton carrier *Ranger*, in 1934, followed by the stalwarts of the early war against Japan: the 19,800-ton twins the *Yorktown* (1937) and the *Enterprise* (1938), the 14,700-ton *Wasp* (1940), and the 19,800-ton *Hornet* (1941). The first of over 70 escort carriers, the 7886-ton *Long Island*, joined the fleet in 1941. When war came, the United States had

seven fleet carriers in operation, the largest and oldest of which were the *Saratoga* and the *Lexington*. Each ship carried between 85 and 90 aircraft of various types.[52] The keels also had been laid for most of the large carriers and escort carriers which would be commissioned by 1943. This great increase of American carrier forces showed how much naval aviation had developed in the previous decade. It was a major part of the Navy in 1941. But while some officers would prophesy that the carrier task force would be the backbone of the war fleet,[53] there were still many officers who were reluctant to assume that the battleship had been replaced. It would take a war to settle the issue.

Newer surface vessels were also built at a furious rate with the additional funds. The number of battleships was nearly doubled, cruiser forces tripled, and destroyer forces doubled. The Navy had 17 battleships, 37 cruisers, and 171 destroyers in commission when war began.[54]

Unlike the Army and the Army air forces, the Navy was a reasonably effective force in 1941, if not as powerful as the number of ships might indicate. The surface paradox lies in the exigencies of the period from 1939 to 1941 in Europe which had created the need for two separate fleets, each able to fight independently of the other. This change in fundamental American naval policy came about when the resurgent U-Boats seemed about to wrest control of the Atlantic from the Royal Navy. The United States Navy had always assumed that the Royal Navy could take care of the Atlantic, thus allowing the Americans to employ most of their ships in the Pacific.[55] When the U-Boats threatened to invalidate this assumption, major elements of the fleet were dispatched to the Atlantic, giving the Japanese superiority in naval forces in the Pacific.

Naval aviation profited by the new funds because the Navy was finally able to buy new aircraft for use at sea. The rearmament of the United States helped all the aircraft companies, and the ones long associated with the Navy began producing the first all-metal monoplanes, which would be the standard aircraft in 1941. Fortunately, standardization came late, and the Navy was able to pick the aircraft which it needed from the best available models. The basic carrier fighter became the Grumman Wildcat.

The new carrier fighter was a quantum jump ahead of the obsolete Brewster Buffalo; but, although well armed and protected, the Wildcat was still no match for the Japanese Zero. Like their cousins flying P-40s, Wildcat pilots would learn quickly to avoid dogfights with Zeros; to survive in combat they had to depend on improved tactics rather than the flying characteristics of their aircraft. The Douglas Dauntless became the standard dive bomber when it came into the naval service in 1940, along with the Wildcat. A sister ship, the Douglas Devastator, became the primary

USS Archerfish (1943)

torpedo bomber, but unfortunately it would prove to be more destructive to its crews than would their Japanese opponents. Perhaps the finest of all the prewar Navy aircraft was the large, ungainly amphibian (PBY or Catalina) made by Consolidated, which served with distinction as a patrol, reconnaissance, and bomber aircraft throughout the war.[56]

The mention of dive and torpedo bombers indicates the extent to which naval aviation had changed since the first planes flew off the *Langley*. With the addition of the new aircraft, the fleet became a true air-sea striking force; airpower was no longer a defensive or peripheral complement to the surface fleets. Dive bombing had developed as a result of marine glide bombing experiments in 1919; experience gained with the Army Air Service at Kelly Field, Texas in 1923; and the 1927 exploits of the marine airmen in combat in Nicaragua. Finding that high altitude bombers were not satisfactory against moving targets, the Navy decided that more precise attacks would be necessary to sink a fighting ship. Since dive bombers and torpedo bombers could attack ships more effectively than high flying bombers, they became the Navy's standard attack aircraft. Early Devastator torpedo bombers, however, proved unsatisfactory against the Japanese, largely due to their slow attack speed which allowed either defending fighters to shoot them down with impunity or antiaircraft and main batteries on enemy ships to destroy them before they could launch torpedoes. Dive bombers would become the primary naval attack aircraft, carrying the air battle to the Japanese on land and sea. In time, the bombers would attack the home islands of Japan.[57] The aircraft carrier and its dive bombers gave the Navy a strategic air capability which in many ways was superior to that of the Army air forces in the Pacific, because naval fliers were able to strike many targets before these targets could be attacked by land-based bombers whose bases were too far away. Billy Mitchell would have been embarrassed by the strategic nature of the Navy's air arm. He also would have been chagrined to find out how inadequate high altitude bombing would prove to be against maneuvering fleets. In the long run, it was a fortunate thing that the Navy fought so doggedly to develop its own air force, even though there was much duplication of effort and unnecessary bitterness between the Army and Navy air services.

In modern warfare, technology and a nation's industrial base can critically influence strategy and planning. If not always obvious, the impact of these factors upon the Navy's preparations for the fighting of World War II was crucial. Carriers needed tremendous new engines to operate in the vast expanses of the Pacific, and fleet submarines were hindered by the early limitations of diesel engines. We have

also noted how aircraft were restricted by the requirements to fly off carriers. But if in some cases American products were inferior to the Japanese,[58] American technology produced its share of breakthroughs. Americans overcame the extended range requirement by designing high pressure, high temperature steam engines which propelled American fleet carriers through the seas at 33 knots or more, and allowed them to remain at sea for 100,000 miles before shipyard maintenance was needed. They built efficient diesel engines to power the long-range fleet submarines and helped develop the radar which would overcome the Japanese night optical devices. Perhaps most important, although often overlooked, was the capacity of American industry to build great numbers of warships and merchantmen. In this area, the Japanese were critically inferior; in no way were they ever able to match American industry in new ship construction.[59] All the major ships and most of the aircraft which would be used by the Navy in the war were designed and, in many instances, were in some stage of construction by 1941; all that was needed to build the fleet up to overwhelming strength was money, manpower, and time. President Roosevelt's rebuilding program largely provided the Navy the money and the time.

In addition to the development and construction of new weapons systems, the Navy's interwar efforts included the training of its corps of officers and petty officers. During these lean years, many of the future war leaders developed their skills and sharpened their minds. Annual fleet maneuvers tested new tactics and ideas, forcing naval officers to practice their art on the high seas. In this arena, the sailors were years ahead of the soldiers, who had too few forces at their disposal to practice much of anything until after 1939. Activities at the Naval War College at Newport, Rhode Island, kept the brightest naval officers thinking about the problems of strategy and logistics associated with war against Japan and the important problem of Philippine defense. Veteran sailors and petty officers spent many of these years at sea. For most, the Navy was a family in which the officers and non commissioned officers knew each other by name or reputation.[60] This reservoir of talent went a long way when the Navy had to stock its ships with new sailors and partially trained officers. While the Navy would have its share of Ensign Pulvers, immortalized in the novel and, later, the Broadway play *Mr. Roberts*, great numbers of such officers would have ruined a combat fleet. Competition in training was a tradition in the prewar Navy. There was much interest and effort lavished on such activities for many years, but in the end the means became the end—instead of competing to improve combat readiness and proficiency, crews competed simply for the sake of competition.[61] Still, by 1941, the officers and the men who

Admiral Ernest King

manned the ships of the United States could be considered well trained. When the first rounds went off, they knew enough of the basics to form a first-class combat force overnight.

The most influential sailor of World War II would be Admiral Ernest King. A senior naval aviator, he had commanded a submarine division (four boats) in 1922 and the Navy's Aircraft, Battle Force (five aircraft carriers) in 1938; as Commander of the Atlantic Fleet in 1941 he had been in charge of the amphibious exercises in which marine and army forces participated. Considered by Samuel Eliot Morison, the Navy's distinguished historian, to be the most brilliant American strategist, King was not everybody's friend. Disliked by many Army and Navy officers, American and British alike, and irritating to Winston Churchill, King was a man whom even admirers learned to avoid, for "Jesus" King would break a man in a minute. Officers said he was incredibly tough, yet fair. Pro-Navy all the way, King looked upon the Pacific as the Navy's preserve, and accordingly, he would tangle with MacArthur over just about anything. At the top, King would rule the Navy with an iron hand throughout the war.[62] Perhaps it was an error not to have had him in command of the Pacific Fleet when war broke out.

Unlike the Army, the surface Navy fought against Germany before hostilities began with Japan. American vessels operating in the Atlantic in the period just before the war saw combat on October 17, 1941 and again on October 31. While escorting a convoy, the destroyer *USS Rueben James* was sunk by a U-Boat. Because of these problems in the Atlantic, the attention of the Navy shifted more to a balance between the Pacific and the Atlantic than ever before. But while pressures mounted in the Atlantic, Japan's overt actions brought more and more pressure to bear on the Navy in the Pacific, especially on the forces assigned to the Philippines and the outlying islands of Guam, Wake, and Midway. The small Asiatic Fleet was stationed in the Philippines for prestige; but with its heaviest ship a cruiser, it was incapable of combating the air and sea power of Japan, whether in the northern waters of the Philippines or in the China Sea.

Regardless of the reinforcement of the Philippines by small land and air forces, the major power of the United States in the Pacific Ocean in 1941 rested on the Pacific Fleet, which had been recently moved from San Diego to Pearl Habor to deter Japanese advances into the Netherlands East Indies and Southeast Asia. (*See Atlas Map No. 5.*) Because he opposed this movement, the incumbent fleet commander was replaced by Admiral Husband Kimmel. Kimmel was a fine officer with an excellent reputation, but he faced those same vexing problems about which his predecessor had complained. Pearl Harbor had neither the physical facilities for the nearly 100 ships of the force nor the recreational facilities for the sailors. Furthermore, it was a trap, one which could not be cleared in under three hours, even in an emergency.

Kimmel brought his fleet into port on weekends because in the peacetime Navy it had become necessary to have reasonably light duty and plentiful recreational opportunities in order to induce the men of the day to enlist and then remain in the Navy. Pacifist ideology in the previous decades had bred many men who were not prepared for the rigors normally associated with service on a ship of the line.[63] While the Navy and the Army prepared for war, and while all Pacific commands had received the "war message" of November 27 from Washington, Kimmel persisted in bringing the fleet into port on weekends. It was natural, therefore, that when Japanese aircraft flew over the mountains of Oahu on December 7, they would find 94 warships of the United States Navy lying at anchor in Pearl Harbor.[64]

On that fateful day, Lieutenant Charles Keyes was on duty at the Naval Academy at Annapolis. For over nine years, he had watched his service expand to meet the growing power of the Japanese. As a traditional sailor—

neither airman, submariner, nor amphibious expert—Keyes had spent eight years on sea duty, serving primarily on destroyers. He had served first on the *USS Detroit*, a light cruiser which was the flagship of the Battle Force, Destroyers; then, he had successively been assigned to the destroyer *Smith*, the submarine tender *Holland*, and the destroyer *Philip*. He had gained experience in the hard-nosed part of the Navy which he would put to good use first as a ship's officer and then as a captain aboard destroyers during the war. World War II would illustrate how much the Navy had changed since 1919, because while Keyes would serve on the workhorses of the fleet, he and those officers like him were being superseded in importance in the naval service by the airmen on the carriers, the mariners beneath the sea, and the experts of the amphibious assault forces. As the age of the battleship drew to a close, so too did the prestige of the old-line sailors who manned the cruisers and destroyers which made up the bulk of the surface fleet. In the greatest war in its history, the United States Navy would be remembered for its amphibious assaults, its submarines, and its fast carrier task forces.

America's Australians: The United States Marine Corps

John Michael Langley, age eight, proclaimed most proudly in 1945 that the Australians had won World War II all by themselves.[65] His youthful opinion reflected the unlimited pride which the Australians had in their armed forces as well as the faith associated with such pride. Not unlike John Langley, United States Marines of all ages express unlimited pride in the accomplishments of their corps in all wars, and when they are talking about the war in the Pacific their opinions are so strong that one often wonders what happened to the other forces which fought with the marines during the war.[66] Whether in reading the memoirs of the caustic marine general, Holland ("Howlin' Mad") Smith, the more subdued official histories of the Marine Corps, or the popular histories about marine exploits, one finds that marines believed their newly developed amphibious techniques revolutionized warfare in World War II. Most sources rely for proof on that provocative historian, J.F.C. Fuller, who like many Englishmen has always been enamored of the Corps.

If such contentiousness gives rise to violent arguments, it is an established fact that the United States Marine Corps specialized in the amphibious assault, thereby playing an essential role in the Pacific War. In carving out their new specialty, the marines moved away from the traditional functions of their corps and those of the Royal Marines of Great Britain whom they had emulated for so many years. In the age of sail, marines had normally served as guards aboard ships, engaged in close combat on the high seas, and acted as the infantry of landing parties. With the coming of steam-powered navies shortly after the American Civil War and the attendant emasculation of their traditional role, marines began to serve as the police force of the Navy, as gunners on larger ships, and, in the American service, as the small force which intervened in many countries to protect national interests. United States Marines became interested in landing operations at the turn of the century when the Navy, their parent service, began to expand its interest in the Pacific Ocean. In emulation of the British Royal Navy, the United States sought to establish distant coaling stations throughout the area so that its fleet could operate efficiently in the far reaches of the western Pacific. Initial strategical thinking clearly indicated that American advanced naval bases would have to be held in time of war. It seemed logical that the men to defend those bases were the sea soldiers of the Marine Corps. Therefore, prior to World War I, the Navy organized a small, 1750-man force of marines, called the Advanced Base Force, for the task of holding such bases.

Naval landing forces, however, had not been confined to defensive operations before World War I. In 1898, the Navy seized Guantanamo Bay in Cuba with a small marine force. Marines also envisioned offensive action with landing parties, and one young staff officer, Major Earl "Pete" Ellis,* considered their employment in a future war which, Ellis anticipated, would match Japan against the United States.[67] The marines, however, emerged from World War I tied to orthodox ground combat in support of the Army, and to their traditional missions aboard ships and naval installations.

Japanese expansion in the central Pacific stirred American interest in amphibious operations. Knowledgeable naval strategists expected that in case of war the Japanese mandates would have to be taken, but such action would require more than landing parties or advanced base forces—it would demand amphibious assaults. In 1921, the imaginative Ellis drew up a plan entitled "Advanced Base Operations in Micronesia," which stressed the need for assault operations

---

*Major Ellis seems to be the key individual in the development of early marine plans involving the central Pacific. All basic works cite his contributions in some detail. Ellis died mysteriously on Kokor Island in the Palau Group in 1923 while on a leave of absence from the Marine Corps, granted as a result of poor health. He probably was spying against the Japanese. The exact cause of Ellis's death and the circumstances surrounding it are not known.

and gave the Marine Corps a blueprint for its future actions. Ellis's document became the cornerstone of prewar marine plans for possible operations in the central Pacific. The major was not alone in his concern, having been joined by John A. Lejeune, the Major General Commandant. In 1923, Lejeune, an instructor at the Naval War College, emphasized the importance of landing-force operations.[68] Thus was planted the seed of the marine assault doctrine which would soon germinate and replace the older concept of advance-base defensive forces.

As with the other armed services, skimpy appropriations in the 1920s limited the ability of the Marine Corps to form new units, conduct extended training, and buy new equipment. Small battalion or regimental exercises, however, did take place in 1921, 1922, and 1923, in both the Caribbean and the Atlantic. In 1924, the Marine Corps began to experiment seriously with landing craft and to examine landing procedures carefully. The next year, exercises with the Army in Hawaii indicated that the marines were able to direct and conduct amphibious operations with units larger than a brigade, although no such unit existed in the Corps until 1941.[69] In 1925, maneuvers were held in the Caribbean, but these were to be the last landing exercises for six years, as shortly afterwards the Marine Corps became deeply enmeshed in armed interventions in the Caribbean area.

While the legendary Eugene "Chesty" Puller and other marines won their laurels in Central America, the Joint Army-Navy Board in 1927 gave the Marine Corps its new mission:

> [to conduct] land operations in support of the fleet for the initial seizure and defense of advanced bases and for such limited auxiliary land operations as are essential to the prosecution of the naval campaign.[70]

Furthermore, the marines were told to execute the same task in support of the Army. While the Army was not prohibited from performing amphibious operations, it was clear that the marines were being designated the primary service for such actions. The Board further directed that the marines conduct special training in landing operations. Although marines were now the official American amphibious specialists, they had neither doctrine nor procedures with which to work.

In order to devote full attention to developing doctrine and skills in the new specialty, the Marine Corps turned away from conventional (long-term) land operations which lay in the Army's province. In a historical sense, there were useful precedents to study: Winfield Scott at Vera Cruz; the seizure of Guantanamo Bay in 1898; and the British fiasco

at the Dardanelles in 1916. The marines gleaned the most from the last affair.[71] As an initial step, the Corps adopted a new organization, establishing the Fleet Marine Force in 1933.* This force was an administrative one, much like Battleships, Pacific Fleet or Submarines, Atlantic Fleet. It was an integral part of the United States Fleet, subordinate to the fleet's commander-in-chief.† The relationship insured unified command in amphibious assaults. The Commandant of the Marine Corps provided the Fleet Marine Force with troops, but controlled them only when they were not embarked or were not involved in naval operations. In turn, the Fleet Marine Force commander provided all or part of his force to the fleet commander for specific missions as required.

At the same time, the Marine Corps Schools at Quantico developed the necessary doctrine. This requirement was so pressing that the Assistant Commandant closed the schools in November 1933, and told the faculty members and students to develop optimum doctrine and procedures. For a while, no brilliant lights led the way; in January 1934 however, the officers presented the first *Tentative Manual for Landing Operations.*[72] Approved for issue a few months later, it was mimeographed and immediately sent to the fleet for testing. By 1938, a revised manual was approved as official Navy doctrine, and in 1941 the Army accepted most of the same doctrine, publishing it as its *Field Manual 31-5.*

Although the doctrine was not perfect, its essential concepts stood up for the duration of the war. Commanders modified procedures as experience was gained in training exercises and ultimately in actual combat. Two officers were involved in much of the crucial testing. The marines' amphibious expert was Holland Smith. The man for whom Smith worked was the irascible "sundowner," Rear Admiral Ernest King, the eventual World War II Chief of Naval Operations. Both would play important roles in the Pacific War—Smith in battle and King in planning.[73] The *Tentative Manual* concentrated on command relationships; naval gunfire support; air support; ship-to-shore movement; combat unit loading; and the organization and duties of shore parties. By the time the marines went into combat, the greatest deficiencies remaining in these procedures were in the logistical areas.

---

*Fleet Marine Force was an administrative command of marine units which were embarked for possible landing operations. When necessary, all or part of the force could be employed in an amphibious task force to conduct such operations. This force did not control marine detachments stationed on various ships of the fleet.

†The Navy preferred to have marine landing forces because they were under full naval command at all times. Command problems were easily solved, and interservice squabbles were avoided.

During the tests in the 1935-1941 period it was evident that the marines did not have suitable landing craft for men or vehicles. In 1939, after war began in Europe and was imminent in the Pacific, the need for beaching craft became acute. Fortunately, help came from a New Orleans boat designer, Alexander Higgins. In 1926, Higgins had built a 36 foot boat with a "tunnel stern" to protect the propeller and flat "spoonbill" bow for easy beaching and retracting from shorelines. Vice Admiral Daniel Barbey, MacArthur's amphibious commander during the war, insists that the boat was built for rum running during Prohibition; but regardless of the admiral's story,[74] Higgins' boat performed excellently in swamps, on inland lakes, and on ocean beaches. After first evaluating the boat in 1934 the marines wanted to purchase it, but lack of funds made this impossible. Higgins persisted. He modified the boat by adding a movable ramp on the bow after a marine equipment officer mentioned that the Japanese had successfully used a drop-ramp landing craft for years. His persistence paid off in 1941 when the Navy finally accepted the "Higgins Boat." The 36-foot craft was the forerunner of the LCVP (Landing Craft, Vehicle, Personnel), which was used throughout the war as the basic assault landing craft. Higgins also designed the 50-foot prototype tank lighter, which became the LCM (Landing Craft, Mechanized). He merely stretched his earlier design to the desired length for the new boat. When his competitor, a Navy-designed lighter, nearly overturned in trials, the Navy ordered Higgins's larger boat in 1942.

After a battleship admiral had seen a photograph of an amphibious tractor in a 1937 issue of *LIFE* magazine, the marines ordered the unusual civilian vehicle for landing purposes. Passed to the Marine Equipment Board, the photograph and article stirred interest. Ultimately accepting

the vehicle for combat use, the Board insisted that its aluminum hull be changed to steel before it was manufactured for the Corps. Designated the LVT (1) (Landing Vehicle, Tracked), this vehicle was called the "Alligator." Armored versions with a light tank turret and a 37-mm gun soon appeared.

Larger seagoing landing craft were not available at the start of the war. While capital ships proved useless for the movement of large landing forces, the Navy was able to convert some of its old four-stack World War I destroyers to transports before 1941.[75] These destroyer transports, APDs, were useful as high speed transports, particularly in the Admiralties in 1944. The LST (Landing Ship, Tank), sarcastically called a "Large Slow, Target" by her sailors, was not yet on the scene. It was a British-designed vessel, but had to be constructed in American shipyards for both the British and the Americans. At the beginning of the war, LSTs had a low construction priority because destroyers were needed to fight the U-Boats in the Atlantic.[76]

Because it was the only American amphibious force in being in 1941, the Marine Corps was assigned the mission of training Army landing forces. It trained three divisions in the early 1940s, and four additional ones during the war. Ironically, the United States Army made more and larger amphibious landings during the war than the marines, but the Marine Corps must be credited with unique contributions to amphibious doctrine and procedures.

Just before Pearl Harbor the marines mobilized air and ground reserves and had 65,881 men on active duty. Over 25,000 of these troops were in the Fleet Marine Force, which for the first time had organized two triangular divisions and had two air wings in operation. This enlarged force was sparsely distributed across the Pacific, the Atlantic, and the United States. Part of it, the 4th Marines and the 1st Special Battalion, would fight in the Philippines, while several defense battalions and scattered marine air groups were to taste combat early in the central Pacific.[77] (*See Atas Map No. 5.*) It was in that latter vast region that the United States Marines would play their largest role, fulfilling in a large measure the prophetic plans of Major Ellis, and employing the doctrine, techniques, and equipment developed before the war.

In 1941, of the American armed services, the United States Navy was probably the best prepared for war, while the United States Army was the least prepared. War would be the crucible in which the developments and preparations of the interwar years would be tested. Armed with new doctrines of war, equipped with ever increasing numbers of guns, airplanes, and ships, and led by the many professionals who had risen to the top in each service, the Army, Navy, Army Air Forces, and Marine Corps stood by to execute

An LVT (A), 1943

the missions assigned to them in war plan RAINBOW 5.

Initially, the American forces were found wanting in the Pacific. Partly a result of military error, the tragedy which followed was also a logical outcome of the moribund interwar years. The legacies of Versailles gave way to those of Pearl Harbor.

Notes

[1]Most of the institutional history of the Army is taken from Russell F. Weigley, *History of the United States Army* (New York, 1967), pp. 395-450 and from Maurice Matloff, *American Military History* (Washington, 1969), pp. 405-422. For additional details on the office of the Chief of Staff, see Mark S. Watson, *Chief of Staff, Prewar Plans and Preparations* (Washington, 1950), pp. 1-240; for information on strategy, see Louis Morton, *Strategy and Command: The First Two Years* (Washington, 1962), pp. 21-44; and for information on the War Plans Division, Ray S. Cline, *Washington Command Post: The Operations Division* (Washington, 1951), pp. 1-106, is an excellent source. Other Army official histories were consulted as needed.

Detailed information concerning Generals John J. Pershing and George C. Marshall comes from Forrest C. Pogue, *George C. Marshall: Education of a General, 1880-1939* (New York, 1964), pp. 221-366; that on General Douglas MacArthur from D. Clayton James, *The Years of MacArthur, 1880-1941* (Boston, 1970), pp. 259-294, 351-476, and 577-619; and the comments by General Robert L. Eichelberger are from his "Dictations", a series of transcribed recordings deposited in the Duke University Library.

Information about the Class of 1927, United States Military Academy, comes from *The Register of Graduates and Former Cadets* (West Point Alumni Association, Inc., 1971), pp. 392-396. It can be found in any edition of the *Register*.

These are the main sources for this section. Specific references to these works is used sparingly, primarily for clarity.

[2]Personal knowledge of author. Story often told by Lieutenant General T.J.H. Trapnell, USA, Commanding General, Strategic Army Corps (STRAC), XVIII Airborne Corp and Fort Bragg to various civilian and military groups, 1960-1961.

[3]Weigley, *United States Army*, pp. 396-400, discusses Palmer's role in detail. See also: Russell F. Weigley, *Towards an American Army: Military Thought from Washington to Marshall* (New York, 1962), pp. 226-239, and Matloff, *American Military History*, pp. 407-409.

[4]Strength figures are from Watson, *Chief of Staff*, p. 16. They include Philippine Scouts and are those of June 30 of each year mentioned.

[5]Watson, *Chief of Staff*, p. 187.

[6]Letter, Brigadier General Bradford G. Chynoweth, USA, Ret., to author, July 22, 1972 and Letter, Major General Frank B. Mallon, USA, Ret., to author, July 24, 1972. Letters concern night operations in the Army in the 1920-1940 period and were replies to a query made by the author to General Chynoweth.

[7]Pogue, *Marshall, Education of a General*, pp. 246-264, describes Marshall's activities in China. Eichelberger's comments are in his "Dictations", (August 29, 1960), p. III-53. Throughout his "Dictations" (about July 1954), p. E72; (July 26, 1961), pp. E26-E27; (March 25, 1955), p. III-04; and (August 25, 1958), pp. III/II-25-27, Eichelberger continually harps on the lack of interest, and implicitly the lack of bravery, of his brother officers.

[8]Letter, Brigadier General Bradford G. Chynoweth, USA, Ret., to author, July 31, 1972.

[9]Alexander D. Kirby, "Charles Ream Jackson," *Assembly*, XXXI (West Point Alumni Foundation, Inc., Spring 1972), 103-104.

[10]Pogue, *Marshall, Education of a General*, p. 236.

[11]Pogue, *Marshall, Education of a General*, p. 258, explains Marshall's problems with venereal disease, liquor, and cheap women in the 15th Infantry in China. Eichelberger throughout his "Dictations" often mentions troop problems associated with drinking, gambling, and prostitution. See "Dictations" (March 25, 1955), p. III-2; (June 26, 1959), p. III-13; (August 1, 1960), p. E-137; and (August 29, 1960), p. III-53. Perhaps the most famous story or "expose" of the prewar Army and the problems that soldiers had with drinking, gambling, and women is James Jones' novel, *From Here to Eternity* (New York, c. 1951). It is considered a credible source.

[12]The Military Service Publishing Company, *Tactics and Techniques of Infantry, Advanced*, 9th ed. (Harrisburg, Pa, 1939), pp. 414-421 (The Rifle Company in Attack) and pp. 423-428 (The Rifle Company in Defense).

[13]The Military Service Publishing Company, *Tactics and Techniques of Cavalry, Advanced*, 9th ed. (Harrisburg, Pa, 1939), pp. 315-330, and 345-360. For various pleas for cavalry see: Brigadier General H.S. Hawkins, "The Missions of Cavalry in Modern War," *The Cavalry Journal*, L. (September-October 1941), 38-41, and Colonel Albert E. Philipps, "U.S. Horse Cavalry Girds for War," *The Cavalry Journal*, L. (May-June 1941), 9. Watson, *Chief of Staff*, pp. 238-239, relates the demise of cavalry for deployment overseas.

[14]Major General Robert C. Richardson, Jr., "The Wider Role of Cavalry," *The Cavalry Journal*, L (January-February 1941), 8.

[15]Weigley, *United States Army*, pp. 409-411; James, *MacArthur*, p. 358.

[16]Virgil Ney, *Evolution of the US Army Division, 1939-1968* (Fort Belvior, Va, 1969), pp. 18-56; and Weigley, *United States Army*, pp. 461-471.

[17]Weigley, *United States Army*, pp. 436-440, describes the personnel situation excellently. See also: Maurice Matloff, "The 90-Division Gamble" in Kent R. Greenfield (ed.), *Command Decisions* (Washington, 1960), pp. 365-381.

[18]Watson, *Chief of Staff*, pp. 56-83; Pogue, *Marshall, Education of a General*, p. 236, and pp. 348-350; Weigley, *United States Army*, p. 405, and pp. 444-450; and Cline, *Washington Command Post*, pp. 1-49, all present excellent information on the general staff. For Marshall's disappointment at not being selected to command the Normandy invasion see Forrest C. Pogue, *George C. Marshall: Organizer of Victory, 1943-1945* (New York, 1973), pp. 320-322.

[19]Forrest C. Pogue, "Commander in Chief—Commander Relationships: Roosevelt and Marshall" (Paper read for American Historical Association, December 30, 1968), p. 7. Also, "Conversations" with Forrest C. Pogue, West Point, New York, April 1972, by author.

[20]Strategic planning is adequately presented in Morton, *Strategy and Command*, pp. 21-44, and 67-91.

[21]Maurice Matloff and Edwin M. Snell, *Strategic Planning for Coalition Warfare* (Washington, 1953), pp. 7-8.

[22]Weigley, *United States Army*, pp. 435-436, gives these data. Matloff, *American Military History*, p. 420, says there were 27 infantry, 5 armored, and 2 cavalry divisions available in the Autumn of 1941.

[23]Louis Morton, *The Fall of the Philippines* (Washington, 1953), p. 27.

[24]This section is based primarily on Wesley Frank Craven and James Lea Cate (eds.), *The Army Air Forces in World War II*, Volume I, *Plans and Early Operations, January 1939 to August 1942* (Chicago, 1948), pp. 3-193, and 591-611. Special sections cover: Organization, pp. 18-33; Air Doctrine, pp. 33-54; the Long Range Bomber, pp. 54-71; Hawaii, pp. 170-175; the Philippines, pp. 175-193; and Tactics, pp. 591-611.

[25]An excellent summary of air war theory is found in Craven and Cate, *Plans and Early Operations*, pp. 51-52.

[26]Craven and Cate, *Plans and Early Operations*, p. 19. For an Army view of tactical air deficiency see Weigley, *United States Army*, pp. 411-414. Colonel John H. Parker, USA, Ret., "The National Defense-1938," (an unpublished manuscript), p. 6, states that the true mission of the air force is observation, information, and control.

[27]Commodore Dudley W. Knox, "Introduction: The United States Navy Between World Wars," in Samuel Eliot Morison, *The Battle of the Atlantic September 1939-May 1943* (Boston, 1948), p. xliii-xlvii, blames Mitchell for weakening the Navy which was to fight in World War II. Knox vehemently opposed Mitchell's ideas as "unsound" and "fallacious."

[28]B-17 specifications vary according to source. Most are from Wesley Frank Craven and James Lea Cate (eds.), *The Army Air Forces in World War II*, Volume VI, *Men and Planes* (Chicago, 1955), p. 205. See also: Ray Wagner, *American Combat Planes* (Garden City, NY, 1960), pp. 115-118 for other technical data; and Martin Caidin, *Flying Forts, The B-17 in World War II* (New York, 1972), pp. 33-68, for interesting details on the bomber's development.

[29]Craven and Cate, *Men and Planes*, pp. 202-205.

[30]Craven and Cate, *Men and Planes*, pp. 212-215. For other comments on the Japanese Zero's superiority see: Martin Caidin, *The Rugged, Ragged Warriors* (New York, 1972), pp. 36-37; Ron Heiferman, *Flying Tigers, Chennault in China* (New York, 1971), pp. 26-33; and Wagner, *Combat Planes*, p. 393.

[31]Craven and Cate, *Plans and Early Operations*, pp. 107-111.

[32]Many sources mention the failure to develop an escort fighter. See: Craven and Cate, *Men and Planes*, p. 212; Noble Frankland, "Some Reflections on the Strategic Air Offensive, 1939-1945," *Royal United Service Institution Journal*, CVII (May 1962), 94-110; and William R. Emerson, "Operation Pointblank" (Harmon Memorial Lecture, U.S. Air Force Academy, May 27, 1962).

[33]Bomber tactics are mentioned in Craven and Cate, *Plans and Early Operations*, pp. 597-599; Frankland, "Reflections on the Strategic Air Offensive," 94-107; and Emerson, "Operation Pointblank."

[34]See Note 30. See also Edward Warner, "Douhet, Mitchell and Seversky: Theories of Air Warfare," in Edward Mead Earle (ed.), *Makers of Modern Strategy, Military Thought from Machiavelli to Hitler* (Princeton, 1941), pp. 485-503, for strategic air theory which overlooked the need for escort fighters.

[35]General naval history is based upon E.B. Potter (ed.), *The United States and World Sea Power* (Englewood Cliffs, NJ, 1955), pp. 560-594; Knox, "The United States Navy Between Wars," pp. xxi-1x; and Samuel Eliot Morison, *Two-Ocean War* (New York, 1963), pp. 1-38. Morison updates Knox's earlier essay.

For specific subjects the following sources were used: Norman Polmar, *et. al.*, *Aircraft Carriers, A Graphic History of Carrier Aviation and Its Influence on World Events* (Garden City, NY, 1969), pp. 1-77; Donald Macintyre, *Aircraft Carrier, The Majestic Weapon* (New York, 1972), pp. 8-47; Director of Naval History, *Dictionary of American Fighting Ships* (Washington, 1963), Volume II, pp. 460-486; Theodore Roscoe, *United States Submarine Operations in World War II* (Annapolis, 1949), pp. 3-23; Wagner, *American Combat Planes*, pp. 295-300, 334-345, and 389-393.

Information about Captain Charles M. Keyes, USN. Ret., is from United States Naval Academy, *Lucky Bag* (Annapolis, 1932); Bureau of Navigation, *Navy Directory* (Washington, 1932-1940); Department of the Navy, *Register of Commissioned and Warrant Officers of the United States Navy and Marine Corps* (Washington, 1932-1945); and "Dictations" (Upper Marlboro, MD, 1973).

[36]Morison, *Two-Ocean Navy*, p. 5.

[37]United States Naval Institute *Proceedings*, LVIII (1932), 124, 176, and 460.

[38]See Naval Institute *Proceedings*, LVIII (1932), 150-171 for detailed provisions of the various naval and disarmament treaties in effect in 1932.

[39]Morison, *Two-Ocean Navy*, p. 458.

[40]Potter, *World Sea Power*, pp. 564-588, and Knox, "United States Navy Between Wars," pp. xxv-xxxvi.

[41]Potter, *World Sea Power*, pp. 587-588, and Knox, "United States Navy Between Wars," p. xlvii.

[42]British naval air developments are explained in Polmar, *Aircraft Carriers*, pp. 23-34, and are summarized in Macintyre, *Aircraft Carrier*, pp. 8-19.

[43]Potter, *World Sea Power*, pp. 590-593.

[44]Most military histories stress the importance of the Morrow Board.

[45]Knox, "United States Navy Between Wars," pp. xlix-1i, and Potter, *World Sea Power*, pp. 590-591.

[46]Rear Admiral J.K. Taussig, "The Case for the Big Capital Ship," United States Naval Institute *Proceedings*, LXVI (July 1940), 929-940.

[47]Ernest J. Andrade, Jr., "Submarine Policy in the United States Navy, 1919-1941," *Military Affairs*, XXXII (April 1971). 50-53.

[48]Andrade, "Submarine Policy," 55-56, and Roscoe, *US Submarine Operations*, pp. 18-19.

[49]United States Naval Institute *Proceedings*, LIX (1933), 124-125, 132-135, 293-295, 301-302, 310, 596, 600-605, 612, 751-752, 759-762, 905-908, 1070-1072, 1216-1217, 1223-1224, 1276-1280, 1340-1342, 1366-1368, 1504-1507, 1639, 1650-1653, 1789-1790, 1794-1795, 1798-1799, and 1806-1808.

[50]Potter, *World Sea Power*, p. 569—see table.

[51]Potter, *World Sea Power*, pp. 568-569; Morison, *Two-Ocean War*, p. 15; *Dictionary of American Ships*, II, 468-471; and Andrade, "Submarine Policy," 53-55.

[52]*Dictionary of American Ships*, II, 462-465. Difference sources have different technical information about American carriers.

[53]*Dictionary of American Ships*, II, 468-471, and 477-478; Potter, *World Sea Power*, p. 591.

[54]Potter, *World Sea Power*, p. 569.

[55]Louis Morton, *Strategy and Command*, pp. 68, and 79-86.

[56]American naval aircraft are discussed in Wagner, *American*

Combat Planes, pp. 295-300 (patrol bombers), 334-345 (dive and torpedo bombers), and 389-393 (fighters). Comparative statistics for Japanese planes can be found in Macintyre, *Aircraft Carriers*, pp. 37-40 and in Samuel Eliot Morison, *The Rising Sun in the Pacific, 1931-April 1942* (Boston, 1948), fn p. 94.

[57]Potter, *World Sea Power*, pp. 591-592; Polmar, *Aircraft Carriers*, pp. 44-47; and Wagner, *American Combat Planes*, pp. 334-35.

[58]For the superiority of Japanese equipment see: Masanori Ito and Roger Pineau, *The End of the Imperial Japanese Navy*, translated by Andrew Y. Kuroda and Roger Pineau (New York, 1962), pp. 20-22, 25, and 51; and Morison, *Rising Sun in the Pacific*, pp. 31-34.

[59]Morison, *Two-Ocean War*, pp. 17-18; Ito and Pineau, *End of the Japanese Navy*, pp. 25-26; and Potter, *World Sea Power*, p. 569.

[60]Walter Lord, *Day of Infamy* (New York, 1965), pp. 51-52.

[61]Morison, *Two-Ocean War*, pp. 8-9.

[62]Morison, *Two-Ocean War*, pp. 28-29. See also: Admiral J.J. Clark, "Sundowner Par Excellence," United States Naval Institute *Proceedings*, XCVII (June 1971), 54-59; E.G. Potter, "The Command Personality," United States Naval Institute *Proceedings*, XCV (January 1969), 19-21; and General H.M. Smith and Percy Finch, *Coral and Brass* (New York, 1949), pp. 75-80. In these works King is lauded.

[63]Morison, *Two-Ocean War*, pp. 31-32.

[64]The number of ships vary with the source. This figure is from Morison, *Rising Run in the Pacific*, p. 100.

[65]Personal knowledge. "Conversations" of author with John Michael Langley, Melbourne, Australia, April 1945.

[66]This section is based upon the most recent official history of the United States Marine Corps: Lieutenant Colonel Frank O. Hough, Major Verle E. Ludwig, and Henry I. Shaw, Jr., *Pearl Harbor to Guadalcanal* (Washington, 1958), pp. 3-34, and 47-56. Unless specified it is the source of all material used. Other useful works consulted are: Vice Admiral Daniel E. Barbey, *MacArthur's Amphibious Navy* (Annapolis, 1969), pp. 11-20,

and 359-363; Jeter A. Isely and Philip A. Crowl, *The United States Marines and Amphibious War* (Princeton, 1951), pp. 3-71; Potter, *World Sea Power*, pp. 576-587; and Smith, *Coral and Brass*, pp. 43-85. In case of differing opinions—and there are some—Hough, et al. is used.

[67]Lynn Montross, "They Mystery of Pete Ellis," *Marine Corps Gazette*, XXXVIII (July 1954), 30-33.

[68]Hough, et al., *Pearl Harbor to Guadalcanal*, p. 10.

[69]Hough, et al., *Pearl Harbor to Guadalcanal*, p. 10. Potter, *World Sea Power*, p. 582, stresses that this maneuver was a test of British "combined operations" doctrine which said that land and naval force commanders merely coordinated their actions during an amphibious operation in lieu of having a single overall commander. British techniques were not adopted as a result of the test. Hough, et al., *Pearl Harbor to Guadalcanal*, p. 11, makes the point used in the text.

[70]Hough, et al., *Pearl Harbor to Guadalcanal*, p. 11. Other sources vary in their implications.

[71]Potter, *World Sea Power*, p. 582, mentions the impact of the study of the Dardanelles-Gallipoli Campaign by Colonel Robert H. Dunlap, USMC.

[72]The best account is in Isely and Crowl, *Marines and Amphibious War*, pp. 34-36.

[73]Smith, *Coral and Brass*, pp. 64-85, has interesting comments on this testing. "Sundowner" is Navy slang for martinet.

[74]Barbey, *MacArthur's Amphibious Navy*, p. 17.

[75]For boat development see Hough, et. al., *Pearl Harbor to Guadalcanal*, pp. 23-24; Barbey, *MacArthur's Amphibious Navy*, pp. 11-20, and 359-363; and Smith, *Coral and Brass*, pp. 88-99.

[76]For the training of Army divisions see: Smith, *Coral and Brass*, pp. 73-85, and Kent Roberts Greenfield and Robert R. Palmer, "Origins of the Army Ground Forces: General Headquarters, United States Army, 1940-1942," in Kent Roberts Greenfield, et al., *The Organization of Ground Combat Troops* (Washington, 1947), pp. 84-92.

[77]Hough, et al., *Pearl Harbor to Guadalcanal*, p. 56.

"East Wind, Rain": Japan Strikes 3

I believe that a surprise attack on Pearl Harbor is a possibility.

Admiral Husband Kimmel to
Admiral Harold Stark
February 18, 1941

Quietly the ships of the Pearl Harbor Striking Force slipped into bleak Hitokappu Bay in the Kuriles for the final rendezvous.[1] Behind them, the rest of the Combined Fleet, anchored at Kure Naval Station, increased its radio chatter to deceive American eavesdroppers who tracked the courses of the Japanese warships by their radio traffic. Vice Admiral Chuichi Nagumo, the reluctant commander of the Striking Force, took no chances on being detected; crystals were removed from radios, and even garbage was not thrown overboard. On November 23, 1941, after the admiral held his last meeting with his key officers aboard his flagship the aircraft carrier *Akagi*,[2] pilots learned for the first time that they would bomb Pearl Harbor. Later, Admiral Yamamoto ordered Nagumo to depart for Hawaii on the morning of November 26.

Snow was on the nearby hills as the *Akagi* slipped her moorings and followed the lead ships into the desolate reaches of the North Pacific. As the armada gained the open sea, destroyers fanned out to form the screening force while three submarines patrolled 200 miles out in front of the screen. In the center, moving in two columns, were the six carriers which had been selected for the attack: *Akagi* ("Red Castle"), *Kaga* ("Increased Happiness"), *Hiryu* ("Flying Dragon"), *Soryu* ("Green Dragon"), *Shokaku* ("Soaring Crane"), and *Zuikaku* ("Happy Crane"). On the flanks cruised the modernized battleships and the heavy cruisers, and trailing in the wake of the warships were the

---

AIR ATTACK FORCE (Vice Admiral C. Nagumo)*	**SUPPORT FORCE** (Rear Admiral G. Mikawa)	**SCREEN** (Rear Admiral S. Imori in CL *Abukuma*)
Carrier Division 1: CV *Akagi* CV *Kaga*	**Battleship Division 3:** BB *Hiei* BB *Kirishima*	**Destroyer Squadron 1:** DD *Tanikaze* DD *Urikaze* DD *Isokaze*
Carrier Division 2: CV *Hiryu* CV *Soryu*	**Cruiser Division 8:** CA *Tone* CA *Chikuma*	DD *Hamakaze* DD *Kasumi* DD *Arare* DD *Kagero*
Carrier Division 5: CV *Shokaku* CV *Zuikaku*		DD *Shiranuhi* DD *Akiguma*
SHIP LANE PATROL (Captain I. Imaizumi) SS *I-19* SS *I-21* SS *I-23*	**MIDWAY NEUTRALIZATION UNIT** (Captain K. Konishi) DD *Akebono* DD *Ushio*	**TRAIN** 8 tankers and supply ships

*Note: Vice Admiral Nagumo, in CV *Akagi*, commanded the entire force.

The Pearl Harbor Striking Force

sluggish oilers, riding low in the water with their precious cargo of fuel. Within a day, the great circular formation was lost in the ocean and rain, and fog engulfed the ships as they plowed eastward through the heavy seas. The voyage was a tense one. The maintenance of radio silence in the heavy fog made collisions a distinct possibility. On some ships, captains slept nervously on their bridges. Everyone feared detection. Refueling was expected to be difficult, there being a distinct possibility that sailors would be swept overboard in the rough weather when the huge hoses from the tankers broke loose and uncoiled across the decks like giant snakes.

Because negotiations were still going on in Washington between Ambassadors Nomura and Kurusu and Secretary of State Hull, there was a slight chance that the Striking Force would be recalled. Admiral Nagumo, never an enthusiast about the impending attack, waited anxiously to learn if he must continue to Hawaii. All the confident predictions of his chief of staff and the air officers, Minoru Genda and Mitsuo Fuchida, could not convince him that there was not a high chance of failure. Finally, on December 2, Nagumo received the critical signal from Yamamoto: "Climb Mount Niitaka" (Proceed with the attack).* A later

*The following is a list of Japanese code words associated with the early war:
1. East Wind, Rain: Severance of Japanese-American relations.
2. North Wind, Cloudy: Severance of Japanese-Russian relations.
3. West Wind, Clear: Severance of Japanese-British relations.
4. Climb Mt. Niitaka: Proceed with attack on Pearl Harbor.
5. Tora, Tora, Tora: Successful, surprise attack, Pearl Harbor.

message designated the date of the attack, X-Day, as December 8, Tokyo time. War was at hand unless the force was discovered. If sighted before X-Day minus two, Nagumo was to turn back. If discovered on X-Day minus one or later, Nagumo could turn back or proceed, as he saw fit.[3]

When the sailors were finally told of their objective, excitement grew in the fleet.[4] Officers and men drank toasts, boasted, and pampered the pilots. Still the admiral worried about detection. On December 3, Hawaii time, when due north of Midway, the Striking Force turned southeast; three days later at 9:00 P.M., still undetected, Nagumo turned south toward his prescribed launch point, 230 miles north of Hawaii.

Rough seas greeted the aviators when they awoke early in the morning of December 7. At 5:30 A.M., two float planes left cruisers to reconnoiter Pearl Harbor. On the carriers, Commander Fuchida, the commander of all air striking elements, took off at 6:00 A.M., as scheduled. In training, takeoffs would have been delayed until dawn; but on this day, safety would be sacrificed for the fate of the Empire. Fuchida asked only that launchings be coordinated with the upward pitch of the flight decks. As the six carriers swung into the wind, green lanterns waved. Zero fighters, their exhausts shooting red sparks in the dark, rolled down the spray-wetted flight decks, pulled up hard, and were airborne as the deck crews cheered. Within 15 minutes the 183 fighters, bombers, and torpedo planes of the First Air Fleet headed for Hawaii.[5]

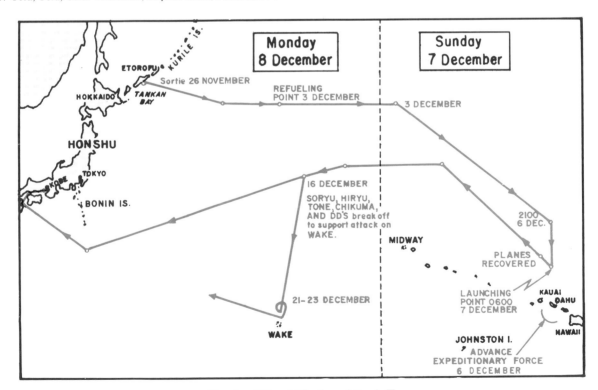

Route of Pearl Harbor Attack Force

In Washington, the Japanese Embassy code clerks were busy completing the transcription of a long message, the fourteenth and last part of which announced:

> The Japanese Government regrets to have to notify hereby the American Government that, in view of the attitude of the American Government, it cannot but consider that it is impossible to reach an agreement through further negotiations.[6]

The message, which was Japan's answer to Secretary Hull's November 26 communication, was to be delivered at 1:00 P.M. Washington time, one half hour before Fuchida's flyers were to attack.[7]

Business as Usual

While Admiral Yamamoto had been preparing his plan for the attack on Pearl Harbor (OPERATION Z), his two major opponents had assumed command of their respective forces in Hawaii.[8] Admiral Husband Kimmel, a Kentuckian, had graduated from Annapolis in 1904, and then progressed through a series of assignments to command Cruisers, Battle Force, United States Fleet in 1940 before being appointed Commander-in-Chief, Pacific Fleet. Promoted to the rank of admiral on February 1, 1941, Kimmel assumed the additional duty of Commander-in-Chief, United States Fleet. On the same day, Ernest King became a full admiral and assumed command of the Atlantic Fleet. Kimmel, considered one of the Navy's ablest strategists, was selected for his new command over 46 senior officers. With over 19 years of sea duty, he was an accomplished officer.[9] His Army associate was 61-year old Lieutenant General Walter Short, who assumed command of the Hawaiian Department on February 7 after tours in the United States commanding IV Corps (Fort Benning, Georgia) and I Corps (Columbia, South Carolina). Short was the junior of six lieutenant generals on active duty. An infantryman, he was a 1901 graduate of the University of Illinois.[10]

Both officers were eager to improve conditions in Hawaii; but unfortunately, neither was appointed overall commander. Even Admiral Kimmel could not be considered by his rank to be the de facto commander, because an even more senior admiral, Claude Bloch, a former fleet commander, was the Commandant of the 14th Naval District in Hawaii.[11] To make a matters worse, there was no single air commander for the forces which were assigned to Kimmel and Short. In an attempt to insure that Hawaii was properly defended, the two commanders tried very hard both to cooperate but not to interfere with each other. However, each also tried to protect his own prerogatives. Although friendly, trusting, and well-meaning, neither man really knew what the other

one was doing. From their perspectives, the cooperative command appeared sound; more surprising, even from Washington's viewpoint, the system seemed effective.[12]

At the working level there is nothing to suggest that the Army and the Navy fully integrated their efforts. Army antiaircraft batteries placed around Pearl Harbor were not manned during the Japanese attack. There was no central air directory unit to control the service aircraft operating in Hawaii, especially those flying from bases on Oahu. Joint air searches around the islands were not initiated. Each service did its work in its own specialties, ignorant for the most part of the requirements and problems of the other. Moreover, even in the months immediately before Pearl Harbor, inter-service relations suffered from the continual fights for funds, the normal service jealousies, and the hard feelings which followed such affairs as the attacks of Billy Mitchell on the Navy.[13]

When Admiral Kimmel and General Short arrived in Hawaii, the basic United States war plan was RAINBOW 5. While focusing on a primary effort in Europe against Germany, the plan still called for the Pacific Fleet to advance into the Marshalls and Carolines upon the outbreak of war, to secure bases there, and then to be prepared to drive into the Philippines. This offensive mission was Kimmel's primary concern. Equally important, of course, was the protection of the Pacific Fleet from enemy attack. Under RAINBOW 5, General Short was charged with the defense of Hawaii, particularly the Navy's main base at Pearl Harbor. His involvement with operations in the Pacific included assisting in the deployment of incoming B-17s to the Philippines and developing an adequate bomber ferry route from Hawaii to Australia to the Philippines.

When Kimmel and Short assumed command, both felt that local plans for the defense of Hawaii were totally inadequate. General Short immediately began working on improved plans, and by the end of March he had completed his revision, gained the admiral's acceptance, and published the plan for his forces.[14] The central assumptions of the Joint Coastal Frontier Defense Plan (Hawaiian Department and the 14th Naval District) approved by Short, Kimmel, and Bloch, on April 11, 1941 were:

1. Relations between the United States and [Japan] are strained, uncertain, and varying.
2. In the past [Japan] has never preceded hostile actions by a declaration of war.
3. A successful sudden raid against our ships and naval installations on Oahu might prevent offensive action by our forces in the Western Pacific for a long period.
4. A strong part of our fleet is now constantly at sea in the operating areas organized to take strong offensive action against any surface or submarine force which initiates hostile action.

5. It appears that Japanese submarines and/or a Japanese fast raiding force might arrive in Hawaiian waters with no prior warning from our intelligence service. . . .[15]

An agreement between the local air commanders, Major General Frederick Martin and Rear Admiral Patrick Bellinger, signed on March 31, outlined the steps which the Hawaiian Air Force and the Naval Base Defense Air Force would take to implement the Joint Defense Plan. Martin and Bellinger based their agreement on a most interesting estimate. They assumed that:

(a) A declaration of war might be preceded by:
    (1) A surprise submarine attack on ships in the operating area.
    (2) A surprise attack on Oahu including ships and installations in Pearl Harbor.
    (3) A combination of these two.

(b) It appears that the most likely and dangerous form of attack on Oahu would be an air attack. It is believed that at present such an attack would most likely be launched from one or more carriers which would probably approach inside three hundred miles.[16]

Martin concluded that the Japanese would probably make a dawn attack, launching their aircraft from a point 233 nautical miles due north of Oahu.[17]

Throughout this period, Kimmel worked on fleet plans. The Chief of Naval Operations, Admiral Harold Stark, kept him advised on strategic developments, especially the outcome of the ABC-1 talks with the British and the problems associated with American national strategy. Kimmel adjusted his planning, developing by July 21, 1941 his own Fleet Operations Plan to implement RAINBOW 5. He sent it to Admiral Stark who approved it on September 9. Kimmel's confidential letter to his commanders on October 14 further spelled out the security measures necessary to protect the fleet. These emphasized patrolling and defense against air and submarine attack.[18]

The actions of Short and Kimmel pleased Washington. The Joint Coastal Frontier Defense Plan was considered a model, and Admiral Stark sent it to his other commands for emulation. The admiral was also pleased with Kimmel's plan for the Pacific Fleet. In fact, it appeared that the officers in Hawaii had so well considered all contingencies that further implementation of these plans could be left up to their good judgment.[19]

There is no doubt that in the early months of 1941 the Army and the Navy commands in Hawaii, as well as officials in Washington, believed that the Japanese would strike at Pearl Harbor, doing so with a surprise attack.

Officers were familiar with the 1904 Japanese actions at Port Arthur, and the undeclared wars in Manchuria and China were too fresh for men to forget. Martin and Bellinger were not clairvoyant; they merely analyzed the obvious based upon their knowledge of Japan and her capabilities. Before he was relieved of duty, Kimmel's predecessor wrote Stark that "Japanese attacks may be expected against shipping, outlying possessions or naval units."[20] In Washington, at the same time, Secretary of the Navy Frank Knox, fretting about the inability of the Army to defend Pearl Harbor, said essentially the same thing, adding that bombing and torpedo attacks against the fleet were highly probable.[21]

While everyone was concerned with a surprise attack against Hawaii in early 1941, while the planners worked out the concepts for the defense of the islands and the action of the Army, Navy and their air forces, and while the War and Navy Departments believed that they now only had to get the supplies to the Hawaii to do the job, the training of men and units became a major problem for Kimmel and Short.[22] Both officers had to prepare their commands for their wartime missions, but training could not be accomplished if the commands were kept in a state of high readiness to repel attacks. At the same time, the state of readiness would decline if the forces trained.

The Navy's problems developed because the fleet was expanding daily as new ships were commissioned. Kimmel had to strip experienced officers and men from trained crews to form the skeleton ones needed to man the new ships and to train the incoming replacements. Materiel shortages in planes, fuel oil, bombs, and antiaircraft guns, plagued the fleet. If Kimmel went to sea for training, he could only be assured of having a nine-day war reserve of oil in Hawaii when he returned; if he deployed all his available planes on a thorough 360 degree search around Hawaii, the air crews could not train sufficiently to support the fleet in its wartime mission of advancing into the Marshalls. In effect, to perform his wartime offensive mission, Admiral Kimmel had to train his units away from home base, thereby leaving Pearl Harbor without the protection of the fleet.[23]

Complicating all of his plans was the requirement to keep the sailors and the crews contented. Kimmel's predecessor, Admiral James Richardson, had kept the fleet in Laihana Roads, where it could reach the open sea in a hurry; he felt that Pearl Harbor had inadequate anchorage, repair and liberty facilities, and that in an emergency the port could easily be blocked. Richardson had angered the Navy wives and the Honolulu merchants by refusing to bring the fleet into Pearl Harbor; he had also upset the President by arguing that the fleet belonged on the West Coast where it had greater freedom of action and better facilities.[24] Caught in a dilemma, Admiral Kimmel brought the fleet into Pearl Harbor, knowing the disadvantages which Richardson had abhorred. Morale went up with an attendant decline in security since, once in port, the Pacific Fleet set dangerous patterns. Normally, the fleet went to sea on Tuesday and came back into port on Fridays. When the training mission was longer, the Fleet went out Friday and came in Saturday of the next week.[25] This clockwork schedule was known to the Japanese.

On land, General Short acted similarly to Admiral Kimmel, placing his emphasis on training. But soldiers, like sailors, can not be kept on alert for long periods of time without morale and discipline breaking down. The general quickly discovered that during actual alerts his ammunition was destroyed and his training was interrupted. Since nothing happened in the early turnouts in May, July, and October, Short decided to modify his alert conditions to save equipment and to insure that training was not interrupted unnecessarily. For years, the Army had had just one alert condition—all-out alert. Short developed a three-phase system, starting with a condition to prevent sabotage and subversion, going to an immediate posture to defend against air attack, and ending with an all-out alert against invasion. Unfortunately, when the new system was implemented in November, Short did not explain it to Admiral Kimmel. While the Navy also had a three-phase alert system, the system's numbered conditions were in the reverse order of the Army's. Short's new action did little to simplify matters for the high command, although it definitely improved the training conditions for the Hawaiian Department.[26]

In one critical area, General Short made an unfortunate decision. In Hawaii, when the radar stations were finally installed, the daily drills for the operators were the responsibility of the Department Signal Officer. General Martin, Short's air commander, asked several times to have the radar sections placed under his control so that he could coordinate the efforts of the radar operators with his combat planes in the newly activated Interceptor Command. Martin felt that an adequate air defense system could not be established if the means of identification were under the Signal Corps while the means of interception were under the Air Corps. Short decided that the Signal Officer would control the radars until the operators were properly trained.[27]

Even more critical to the defense of Hawaii than the problems associated with command, strategic and defense planning, and readiness and training, was the intelligence mosaic which slowly evolved after the first of July. Central to the whole problem is the impact of the voluminous intelligence information upon Admiral Kimmel. Some of the information was "soft," or speculative, coming in great part from Admiral Stark in Washington; but part of it was "hard" data which apprised Kimmel of Japanese actions or messages.

On the first day of July, the Imperial Japanese Navy changed its call signs, as it habitually did every six months,

and for a few days, American radio analysts "lost" the Japanese fleet. Two days later, Admiral Stark wrote Kimmel stating that deductions of Japanese actions showed that future policy "probably involves war in the near future."[28] For the next two weeks or so the Chief of Naval Operations sent his subordinates transcripts of the intercepted Japanese diplomatic messages.* These messages contained information concerning impending military occupation of southern Indochina. The intercepted Japanese message of July 14 was quite specific: "We will endeavor to the last to occupy French Indo-China peacefully but, if resistance is offered, we will crush it by force, occupy the country and set up martial law." It was also noted that the Japanese would use the area " . . . to launch therefrom a rapid attack when the international situation is suitable."[29] After talking with Ambassador Nomura about the prospective Japanese move into southern Indochina, Admiral Stark conjectured that the Japanese would move to cut off the Burma Road and invade Borneo. The Chief told Kimmel, however, that he did not think the Burma and Borneo actions would take place soon.[30]

On July 25, Stark warned his commanders that full economic sanctions would be imposed against Japan the next day. Commenting that war was not likely, he still urged his admirals to take precautionary measures.[31] In Hawaii, Admiral Kimmel began reconnaissance flights to the north, and General Short put the Army on full alert. These activities lasted less than a week.[32]

The rest of July and August saw an impasse develop in negotiations as Secretary Hull and Ambassador Nomura tried to find the formula for peace in Asia. In Japan, on September 6, the Imperial Conference decided to go to war if diplomacy failed. A deadline for successful negotiations was set as October 31. American intercepts gleaned little about the meeting, although diplomatic utterances indicated that something major was afoot. Because there were no indications whatsoever of military plans, Washington's analysts could only speculate about military details. They passed nothing to the field because there was nothing concrete to report.[33]

On September 22, Stark told Kimmel that "conversations with the Japs have practically reached an impasse."[34] In a letter dated September 29, he added:

> Admiral Nomura came in to see me this morning. . . .
> He usually comes in when he begins to feel near the
> end of his rope; there is not much to spare at the end

---

*The Japanese did not know that the Americans had broken their PURPLE diplomatic code. This feat was accomplished by an Army Signal Corps cryptanalyst, Colonel William F. Friedman; it enabled Americans to know the content of highly secret diplomatic messages. Cryptanalysts had also had some success in reading codes used by Japanese agents in major American cities. Like the comparable ULTRA employed by the British, MAGIC was the name given by the United States to the intercepts of Japanese messages.

now. . . . Conversations without results cannot last forever. If they fall through, and it looks like they might, the situation could only grow more tense.[35]

On October 14, Admiral Kimmel, upon receipt of this letter, issued to his commanders a Confidential Letter of Instructions which emphasized that a surprise attack without a declaration of war was possible, and outlined the security measures to be taken by the Navy in case of imminent attack.

When General Tojo assumed effective control of the Japanese Government two days later, Admiral Stark reacted swiftly, warning his commanders to take precautions and begin preparatory deployments. In extension, the admiral also ordered the rerouting of all American shipping south, away from the mandates in the central Pacific. Convoys to the Philippines would have to detour through Torres Strait, passing south of New Guinea and then up to the islands.[36] On October 17, Stark seemed less worried, telling Kimmel that "I do not believe the Japs are going to sail into us and the message I sent you merely stated the 'possibility'."[37] Still the tension was growing. Admiral Kimmel had already ordered war patrols out to Midway, Wake, and Guam, but he then dispatched additional reinforcements to Johnston, Wake, and Palmyra Islands and ordered out submarine patrols. (*See Atlas Map No. 5.*) General Short, interpreting the latest outburst of messages to mean that Russia and Japan were close to war, increased Army precautions against sabotage and subversion.[38]

November brought added problems. Breaking their pattern, the Japanese changed the call signs of the Combined Fleet on November 1. Three days later, Admiral Stark reported to all navy commands that the Japanese were withdrawing their ships from the Western Hemisphere.[39] Intercepted messages early in the month kept mentioning that time was critical, although these diplomatic messages were not sent to the operating forces. On November 5, General Short changed his alert system. By November 7, Admiral Stark was wondering what would happen next. He could only see things getting "worser and worser." In fact, he felt that anything might happen the next month. He communicated his thoughts to Kimmel.[40]

At about the time the Pearl Harbor Striking Force began moving into the Kuriles on November 14, radar warning units, one of which went in at Kahuku Point on northern Oahu, became operational in Hawaii under the command of the Signal Corps. On the diplomatic scene, the Japanese sent two last proposals to Washington for discussion: the first assumed a complete solution to the Asian question, while the second assumed some sort of truce. MAGIC intercepts gave the Americans the text of these diplomatic moves before they could be presented formally. In addition, a virtual flood of information arrived on the intended Japanese operations in the south. Analysts concluded that the Japanese could move south after November 25; Dutch officials reported Japanese deployment into the Palaus; and American observers told of Japanese air and sea reconnaissance of shipping routes to Australia. A Japanese dispatch to Washington warned that if negotiations were not successful by November 29, "things were automatically going to happen."[41] Most of this information reached Hawaii.

Admiral Stark wired Admiral Kimmel on November 24:

Chances of favorable outcome of negotiations with Japan very doubtful. This situation, coupled with statements of Japanese Government and movements their naval and military forces indicate in our opinion that a surprise aggressive movement in any direction including attack on Philippines or Guam is a possibility. Chief of Staff has seen this dispatch, concurs, and requests action addresses to inform senior Army officers their areas. Utmost secrecy necessary in order not to complicate an already tense situation or precipitate Japanese action. . . .[42]

In Hawaii, after discussing the Chief's message with his staff, Kimmel decided to wait out events. General Short, also, took no action.[43] The next day, Stark told Kimmel that the President and Secretary Hull would not be surprised if the Japanese launched a surprise attack. Concluding that an attack on the Philippines would be the most embarrassing, Stark reiterated his belief that the Japanese would probably go after the Burma Road.[44] About this time, the radio analysts in Hawaii announced that one Japanese carrier was in the Marshall Islands. The message was treated as routine.

Unknown to Stark, Kimmel, and Short, November 26 was a highly critical day. On that date, the Pearl Harbor Striking Force left the Kuriles, and Secretary Hull presented the American answer to the last Japanese diplomatic proposal. Disregarding the possibility of a truce or a *modus vivendi*, Hull reaffirmed the longstanding American principles which demanded that Japan give up her military conquests in China and Indochina. It was so tough a note that it shocked the Japanese Ambassadors, who dared not send it immediately to Tokyo. Even Americans were taken by surprise. Army and Navy officers were still working on compromise provisions for the President. Stark was worried.[45]

The next day, Washington officials alerted field commanders. The Chief of Naval Operations sent the following message:

This dispatch is to be considered a war warning. Negotiations with Japan looking toward stabilization of conditions in the Pacific have ceased and an aggressive move by Japan is expected within the next few days. The number and equipment of Japanese troops and the organization of Naval task forces indicates an amphibious expedition against either the

Philippines, Thai, or Kra Peninsula or possibly Borneo. Execute an appropriate defensive deployment preparatory to carrying out the tasks assigned in WPL46 [RAINBOW 5]. Inform district and Army authorities. A similar warning is being sent by the War Department.... Continental districts Guam Samoa directed take appropriate measures against sabotage.[46]

Secretary of War Henry Stimson's message to General Short was much milder.[47] Although not announcing a "war warning," the Secretary did note that "hostile action was possible at any moment." Follow-up messages to Generals Short and Martin emphasized the need to prevent sabotage and subversion.[48] Army commanders were required to report their actions. General Short did so immediately. The Army staff, however, did not recognize at the time that the general had not put his command on all-out alert. They also overlooked Short's emphasis on sabotage. His comments about liaison with the Navy were taken to mean that all the local defensive measures designed to counter an enemy attack were being implemented.[49]

On November 28, a sudden "hush" fell over the Pacific. The final estimates of Stark and Marshall indicated that the Japanese would probably strike south. At a White House council the same day, Secretary Hull announced that on the twenty-seventh he had told his colleague Stimson that the matter of national security was in the hands of the Army and the Navy.[50] On that same day, in the Pacific, the cruiser USS Helena spotted an unidentified submarine off Pearl Harbor. After Vice Admiral William Halsey had seen the "war warning" and been told to use his own discretion in case of Japanese attack, Halsey's Task Force 8 also left Pearl Harbor to deliver planes to Wake Island.[51]

More and more, American officials believed war to be imminent. On December 1, the Combined Fleet changed call signs again. There was no trace of the fast Japanese carriers, and the Japanese submarines could not be found. When he received this information, Admiral Kimmel noted the gravity of the situation, which to even the most casual intelligence analyst implied that military action was probable.[52] Three days of talks with General Short followed, during which the attention of the two commanders was focused on Southeast Asia, the locus of all the most recent military information. Following the talks, Kimmel ordered Rear Admiral John Newton to depart with Task Force 12 on December 5 to reinforce Midway Island, but he did not tell Newton about the "war warning" of November 26. At this time, Admiral Kimmel knew that General Short had placed his units on alert, although he did not know the details of the general's new system. The admiral believed the Army to be on full war alert. General Short, in turn, assumed that the Navy would be conducting long-range reconnaissance as was prescribed in the joint defense plans.[53] Both commanders were wrong.

Meanwhile, other significant information had continued to filter into Hawaii. On December 2, an unidentified submarine had been sighted in the Pearl Harbor Restricted Sea Area, and the next day Washington had passed on the word that the Japanese had ordered their embassies and missions to destroy their secret codes, ciphers, and machines. On December 4, the Chief of Naval Operations had informed his outlying commands that they too could destroy their secret material, including codes. Two days later, Admiral Kimmel received authority to permit his subordinates to destroy secret material, including codes, while Admiral Bloch reported to Admiral Stark that the Japanese in the embassy in Honolulu were destroying their codes.[54]

It seems clear today that by the first of December everyone had all the information needed to understand that Japan was ready to march. In the Philippines, MacArthur had alerted his entire command. Other outposts were equally prepared. Only in Hawaii did business continue as usual. On December 5, the Navy's War Plan Division in Washington decided that future prodding of subordinate commands was not needed. Too much had already been said. More warnings were unnecessary.[55]

On December 6, two important events occurred. On that date, the lengthy Japanese reply to Cordell Hull's proposals arrived in Washington, in several parts. American code clerks, through MAGIC intercept, deciphered the message at the same time as Nomura's staff was working on it. That evening, the first 13 parts of the message were distributed to responsible officials in the Roosevelt Administration. (Nomura would submit the official version the next day.) At about 10:00 P.M., Lieutenant Lester R. Schulz, an assistant naval aide, presented the message to President Roosevelt, who was in conference with Harry Hopkins. The President carefully read the long message and then passed it to Hopkins, who also read it. Then, "the President turned to him [Hopkins] and said, 'This means war.' Schulz was 'not sure of the exact words' but had no doubt about the meaning." Hopkins agreed and observed that since war was surely coming at Japanese convenience, it was too bad that the United States could not strike first and prevent surprise. Roosevelt nodded but said that since Americans were a peaceful people such a move was an impossibility. He added, "But we have a good record." The President wanted to talk to Admiral Stark, but decided not to call him out of a theater, lest such action cause undue alarm. Shortly before midnight, the two men talked, but no call for action followed the conversation.[56]

The other event occurred in Honolulu at about the same time. There, the head of the office of the Federal Bureau of Investigation notified intelligence officers at Kimmel's and Short's headquarters of a lengthy telephone conversation which had taken place on December 3 between a Tokyo newspaperman and a Honolulu dentist's wife, Mrs. Motokazu

Mori. The FBI had a transcript of the conversation as a result of a tap on overseas telephone lines. The FBI, which already had Dr. Mori on its list of Japanese agent suspects, was suspicious of the conversation and thought that it might be of military significance. Short's staff officer agreed, suspecting that the conversation evolved around coded information dealing with conditions at Pearl Harbor and the surrounding area. Accordingly, he met with the G-2 of the Hawaiian Department and General Short; the three men agreed that the conversation seemed very fishy, but they could not pin down anything specific.* No action was taken.[57]

Early the morning of December 7, the fourteenth part† of the Japanese message was distributed to Washington authorities through MAGIC channels. The President's reaction to it was milder than his response had been to the first parts of the message the previous evening. The most involved War Department intelligence officer, Colonel Rufus S. Bratton, reacted similarly. Upon seeing the intercept of a much shorter message from Tokyo to Nomura, however, Bratton was shocked into action; the message instructed the Ambassador to submit the 14-part note to Secretary Hull at 1:00 P.M. on December 7. Convinced that Japan intended to attack some American installation in the Pacific, and that the time and date in the message were significant, he wanted to warn field commanders. Having no authority to send such a message, at about 9:00 A.M. Bratton tried to reach General Marshall. The Chief of Staff had gone horseback riding and did not return Bratton's call until 10:30 A.M. Bratton then told Marshall that he had a most important message, but the Chief of Staff declined having it delivered, saying that he would shortly be coming to his office.**

Marshall arrived at his office at 11:25 A.M. and Bratton promptly went to see him, but had to wait while the Chief digested the 14-part reply to Hull. Fretting because the minutes were slipping by, Bratton finally presented the message he considered so important. Following a brief consultation with several staff officers, Marshall decided to send a warning to Army outposts, after informing Stark of his intent. When contacted, the Admiral said that he thought the overseas commands had already been badgered with enough warnings. Marshall decided to send the message anyway. He was reassured when Stark called back, concurred in sending the warning, and asked Marshall to include instructions for Army commanders to inform their naval

opposites. The Chief of Staff then told Bratton to have the message dispatched by "the fastest safe means." By then it was almost noon.

Because atmospheric conditions had blocked the radio channel to Honolulu, at 12:17 P.M. the War Department Signal Center sent the message through Western Union channels. Marshall's communication advised commanders that Japan would be presenting what amounted to an ultimatum at 1:00 P.M. Washington time, and that her consulates were under orders to destroy their code machines at once. It further said that the significance of the hour set was not known, and directed the commanders to be on the alert. This warning message reached Honolulu at 7:33 A.M., but the messenger making the delivery to the Hawaiian Department was caught in the rain of Japanese bombs. The message finally reached Short at 3:00 P.M.

We shall never know whether a more expedient dispatch of the final warning message might have blunted the Japanese strike on Pearl Harbor. It is clear, however, that no one in Washington seems to have considered using the telephone, which might have given Short and Kimmel about an hour's preparation time—if it is assumed that they would have taken the message seriously and gone to full alert status at once. Likewise, the Washington authorities, including those who were most concerned about the Japanese 1:00 P.M. message, seem to have considered Pearl Harbor an unlikely point of Japanese attack. Marshall later testified that "even if he had used the phone, he would have first called MacArthur, then Panama."[59]

Saturday night was a beautiful night in Pearl Harbor, one which reflected the serenity of the American armed forces. Admiral Kimmel's ships were berthed throughout the harbor. The battleships were tied up around Ford Island. No torpedo nets were out, because the admiral had decided months before that such nets would restrict the ships if they had to clear the congested bay in an emergency. Even so, it would take three hours to move the fleet into the open sea. Naval air searches had been employed during daylight to the west and south; however, none were flown this night, and none went due north into the area from which General Martin and Admiral Bellinger had suggested that the Japanese would launch their surprise strike against Hawaii. Few search aircraft went out beyond 200 miles, even though Martin and Bellinger had said that the most probable launch point was 233 miles out. Close in to Pearl Harbor and around the entrance to it, PBY Catalina patrol bombers were aloft before dawn, but there were no close-in air searches by the Army. On the sea below, destroyers and minesweepers patrolled the restricted sea area. There was no complacency here. The Navy was patrolling; security appeared adequate.[60]

On land, General Short had moved to prevent sabotage and subversion, his lowest alert priority. Soldiers were

---

*No direct evidence has been found to indicate that the Mori call contained coded information. It is known that the Japanese received information telephonically from Honolulu about the Pacific Fleet, and that they also knew that Oahu Island was calm, a fact which Mrs. Mori had stressed in her telephone conversation.[58]

†For the content of the message, see p. 47.

**While Marshall later did not recall this conversation, Bratton clearly remembered it.

pulled back from the field, congesting the garrisons and inadvertently lessening the security of the island. Gunners were even pulled off the antiaircraft batteries scattered around Oahu. Aircraft were parked close together on the airfields to increase their security. Arms rooms were under lock and key, and ammunition was closely guarded. Only a few men could even *get* into the caches. From noon on, only the weekend duty personnel manned the critical centers of the Hawaiian Department. Even the air information center and radar sections would only operate Sunday morning for four hours. There were no Army air patrols overhead, but a few pilots were on alert at each of the major fields, Wheeler and Hickam. Security was adequate for sabotage and, like the Navy, the Army was not complacent. Neither was it alert.[61]

Things began to happen early in the morning on December 7. At 3:42 A.M., Ensign R.C. McCloy, on the minesweeper *USS Condor*, spotted what appeared to be the periscope of a small midget submarine. McCloy signalled his discovery to the destroyer, *USS Ward*, which was patrolling nearby. The *Ward*, commanded by Lieutenant William Outerbridge, Annapolis 1927, came over, went immediately to general quarters, and then searched the area. Neither ship sighted any hostile craft. Outerbridge returned to his cabin after sending his off-duty sailors back to sleep at 4:43 A.M. Neither McCloy nor Outerbridge reported the incident, and a shore station, overhearing chatter between the *Condor* and the *Ward*, also failed to pass on the word.

Less than two hours later, Ensign William Tanner and his co-pilot, Ensign Clark Greevey, spotted what looked like a submarine in the restricted area near the mouth of Pearl Harbor. It was about 6:30 A.M. Thinking at first that it was an American boat in trouble, the officers dropped two smoke pots from their "Catalina" patrol bomber to alert the submariners. Within a few minutes they were amazed to see one of their destroyers race toward the submarine, fire on it, and then depth-bomb it. The flyers, the lookouts on the *Ward,* and the crew of the supply ship *Antares* had simultaneously spotted the submarine as it trailed the *Antares*. The *Antares'* watch officer had then called Lieutenant Outerbridge on the *Ward*. After ordering general quarters for the second time, Outerbridge increased speed to attack. His first gun fired at 6:45 A.M. It missed, but his second gun hit the conning tower of the little green submarine. Depth charges followed, and the submarine disappeared.

At 6:51 A.M., Outerbridge reported his attack to the 14th Naval District Headquarters. Two minutes later, he sent a stronger message: "Attacked, fired on, depth-bombed, and sunk, submarine operating in defensive sea area."[62] The watch officer did not receive the message until 7:12 A.M. By 7:25 A.M. Admiral Bloch was notified. A

few minutes later the staff duty officer at Kimmel's headquarters was called.

There was a good deal of confusion in the various duty sections on this fatal day. With few people on duty, there were not enough hands to man all the telephones, receive the messages, and pass on information. Lieutenant Commander Harold Kaminsky at 14th Naval District was particularly plagued. Messages from the *Ward* came in code. The code clerk was slow. As the message went forward, it became distorted. Seniors called for clarification. Orders had to be issued to the alert and standby destroyers to sortie or prepare to do so. New reports from the *Ward* and the Naval Air Station had to be processed. To make matters worse, the telephone circuits to each duty officer were jammed. The friction of war began to disrupt simple procedures.

Back at sea, the *Ward* was in action again. At 6:48 A.M., she sighted a white sampan in the restricted area. When approached by the destroyer, the Japanese captain raised a white flag, a rather strange procedure. While engaged in towing the sampan back to the Coast Guard Station, the *Ward's* sound equipment discovered another submarine. The *Ward* raced to the attack. Her five depth charges produced an instant oil slick. Outerbridge notified 14th Naval District, and proceeded to pick up the sampan again. His information reached Admiral Kimmel, but this time the sampan was more interesting news at Kimmel's headquarters than was the second sinking.

By 7:00 A.M., the Catalina pilots had notified the naval air station at Kaneohe of their earlier experience with the *Ward*. Their message did not reach the fleet duty officer for one half hour, however, delayed once again by the need to decode it and the incredulous reaction of air officers who, like everyone else, wanted it verified. Although the airmen's report verified the first report by Outerbridge, somehow the importance of the events did not make a strong impression on Admiral Kimmel. With one or possibly two unidentified submarines sunk and a suspicious sampan in tow, the only reaction by the Navy's higher commanders was to dispatch an alert destroyer to aid the *Ward* and to order the standby ship to build up steam.[63]

At the Army's Opana radar station on Kahuku Point, the northernmost point on Oahu, Privates Joseph Lockard and George Elliott were on duty early. At 7:02 A.M. they noticed that a large flight of aircraft was approaching Oahu from three degrees north at a range of 127 miles. This was an unusually large sighting, and even on a busy morning it would have attracted notice, but on this morning few aircraft had been identified. The last sighting had occurred at 6:45 A.M. when two single aircraft had been spotted coming in from the northeast at a range of 130 miles. The Opana station operated every morning from 4:00 A.M. to 7:00 A.M., General Short having established these hours after receiving the "war warning" on November 27. On this Sunday, Lockard and Elliott were playing with the equipment rather than searching for enemy aircraft; since the breakfast truck was late, Elliott had asked his buddy to teach him to operate the radar. Thus, at two minutes after the set normally closed down, the novice Elliott made the large sighting.

The huge blob on the radar screen excited the two privates. They tried to radio the Air Operations Center at Fort Shafter, but were unable to make contact. When the telephone finally worked, Elliott reported his findings to the phone operator, who said that he was the only man left in the center. After hanging up, however, the operator noticed that Lieutenant Kermit Tyler, the pursuit officer on duty, was still in the center; he promptly reported the radar sighting to the lieutenant, who was not impressed. Upon calling Opana back to tell Elliott not to worry, the operator got hold of an even more excited Lockard. The young soldier wanted to speak to the lieutenant. Tyler came to the phone, heard the radarman out, told him not to be concerned about things, and hung up. At 7:39 A.M., Lockard had noted that the aircraft were only 22 miles out before he lost them in the radar's sweep, blocked by the mountains. Lieutenant Tyler went back to his desk, confident that there was nothing to worry about. He knew that several B-17s were due in Hawaii from the west coast, and also that U.S. carriers might be sending their planes home; the radar sightings, accordingly, were understandable. At Opana, the privates closed up shop for the day, hopped on the breakfast truck at 7:45 A.M., and began the bumpy ride back to camp. No one reported the incident to higher Army headquarters or to the Navy.[64]

During all the activity just described, the United States Pacific Fleet was preparing for Sunday colors. It was the custom in the fleet each Sunday for the ships to raise their colors simultaneously at 8:00 A.M. Officers and sailors on all ships were preparing for the ceremony as Lockard and Elliott drove home. At 7:55 A.M., the blue signal flag went up on a water tower in the Navy yard, and on this cue color parties moved fore and aft on all ships to stand by to raise the jack and the national color. Aboard the battleship *Nevada*, the ship's band stood in place to play the national anthem. The officer of the deck, Ensign Joseph Taussig, fresh out of Annapolis, was not as calm as the bandsmen, because he did not know which size flag to use. With everyone standing by, he took no chances and sent a sailor over to the nearby *Arizona* to see what flag his counterpart on that battleship would use. While all these last-minute arrangements were proceeding, some men noticed strange planes in the sky. Some planes had fixed landing gear, unlike American aircraft; others approached from directions never taken by American pilots; and some appeared to be diving. Suspecting a practice alert, the deck officer on one

ship broke out his guns to practice with the pilots. On the *Nevada*, the bandmaster prepared to give the downbeat.[65]

"Air Raid. Pearl Harbor. This is No Drill"

Commander Mitsuo Fuchida led the first wave of aircraft away from Admiral Nagumo's carriers toward Hawaii. He flew with the 49 bombers he comanded at approximately 2,000 meters. To his right and slightly below were the 40 torpedo planes under command of Lieutenant Commander Shigeharu Murata, and off to the left at about the same range, but flying higher, were 51 dive bombers under Lieutenant Commander Kakuichi Takahashi. Forty-three fighters, commanded by Lieutenant Commander Shigeru Itaya, provided cover above the entire air armada.[66]

As the Japanese pilots winged their way southward, only the clouds worried Fuchida. They blotted out the ocean, making navigation more difficult, but more importantly to the commander they could hinder the attack on the Pacific Fleet by obscuring the targets. Luckily, two local radio stations provided assistance; one allowed Fuchida to adjust his course using his radio detection finder, and the other announced the weather for the day. It was partly cloudy in Honolulu; a cloud base would form at 3,500 feet, mostly over the mountains. Visibility was good. Fuchida was pleased. Adjusting his route slightly to avoid approaching over the northeastern mountains, he decided to fly west of the island and attack from the south.

As the striking force approached Kahuku Point, Fuchida ordered it to deploy. Believing that he had achieved complete surprise, the commander signalled his pilots that the torpedo bombers would attack first, the high-level bombers would follow, and then the dive bombers would attack. The first groups would concentrate on the fleet; but the dive bombers were to attack the many airfields in the area: the naval air field at Ford Island which serviced the carrier aircraft; the Army's nearby Hickam Field where interceptors were stationed; the Kaneohe Naval Air Station where patrol bombers were located; the Marine field at Ewa; and the Army's bases at Wheeler and Bellows Fields. Seeing the "Black Dragon" flare which Fuchida fired, the bombers adjusted their formations for the attack, but the fighters took no action. To insure that Itaya knew what was happening, Fuchida fired a second "Black Dragon." Seeing the signal, the fighters sped to Pearl Harbor to provide the critical air cover for the incoming bombers. Unfortunately, Lieutenant Commander Takahashi thought that the second flare was part of the two-flare signal which was to be fired if surprise was not possible. He, therefore, deployed his dive bombers to attack first, the planned action in case surprise

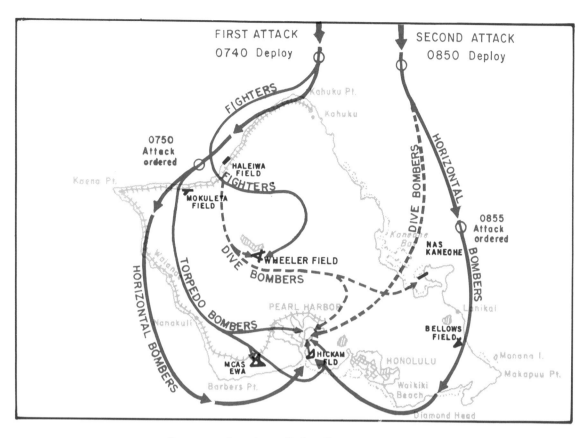

Japanese Attack on Oahu, December 7, 1941

could not be achieved. His action changed all Japanese plans. As a result of it, both the dive bombers and the torpedo bombers would attack simultaneously.

At the last moment, the float plane from the *Chikuma* reported the location of the American battleships. Along Ford Island, facing southwest, stood the *California*; then the *Maryland* and *Oklahoma*, moored together; the *Tennessee* and the *West Virginia*, side-by-side; the *Arizona*, with a smaller ship alongside; and, standing alone in the rear, the *Nevada*. The battleship *Pennsylvania*, flagship of the Pacific Fleet, was in dry dock across the channel, nearly opposite the *California*. The target battleship *Utah* was anchored on the north side of Ford Island. Cruisers and destroyers were distributed randomly in small groups around the rest of the harbor. The *Tone's* float plane reported in also, verifying that the fleet was not in the Lahaina anchorage. Based upon these reports, Fuchida knew that there were no American carriers in the area. The choicest targets could not be destroyed.

After inspecting the area around Ford Island through binoculars, Commander Fuchida ordered his pilots to attack at 7:49 A.M. The coded signal was sent to the air leaders: "To . . . to . . . to. . . . " Within minutes the Japanese aircraft were in position to attack.

Lieutenant Commander Takahashi divided his dive bombers

into two groups. The main part under his command would bomb Ford Island and nearby Hickam Field to the south, while the other, under Lieutenant Akira Sakamoto, would strike Wheeler Field inland. At 7:55 A.M., Takahashi's dive bombers attacked their targets. Strafers from Itaya's group followed. Within minutes, the Japanese wrecked the majority of the first-line American aircraft corps in Hawaii. Thirty-three of the Navy's best planes, nearly half of the total, were heavily damaged or destroyed at Ford Island. Of the 36 Catalinas at Kaneohe, 27 were destroyed and 6 were heavily damaged. The marines at Ewa lost 9 of their 11 Wildcats, 18 of their 32 scout bombers, and all 6 of their auxiliaries. At Wheeler, Bellows, and Hickam Fields, the Army fared no better. Only the practice field at Haleiwa was not bombed. The Japanese pilots had an easy time destroying the aircraft, which in most cases were parked wing tip to wing tip to prevent sabotage. The only bright spot at these places was that the Americans reacted quickly and soon were firing madly at all aircraft in the vicinity. Much of the fire was haphazard, but it prevented succeeding Japanese attacks from being as successful as the first ones. Some aircraft took off, but they could not really challenge the Japanese.

Within seconds of Takahashi's attacks, the torpedo planes under Lieutenant Commander Murata swept in from the south to launch their torpedoes against the exposed port sides of the anchored battleships. The outboard ships received the brunt of the attack. At 7:56 A.M., the first torpedoes struck the *West Virginia* in the middle of the battleship row; six or seven eventually hit her, sinking the battleship in place. Just behind her, the *Arizona* received several lethal torpedoes in the first minutes. In front of the *West Virginia*, the exposed *Oklahoma*, torpedoed five times, capsized quickly, stopping when her masts stuck in the mud. At the rear of the line, the old *Nevada* got underway immediately because she was not berthed with any other ship, but she still absorbed one hit in the forward structure from an aerial torpedo. At the front of the line, the *California* was hit at 8:04 A.M. by two deep-running torpedoes. With six manhole covers removed from her double bottom, the *California* could not be saved. She settled quickly to the bottom, leaving only her superstructure showing.

Bombs also damaged the battleships. The inside vessels, the *Tennessee* and the lucky *Maryland*, were hit, but did not sink. The *California* absorbed two hits which created serious damage, numerous bombs splashed all around the *Oklahoma* as she was capsizing, the *West Virginia* was hit twice, and even the *Nevada* took five strikes while underway. It was the *Arizona*, however, which absorbed the real punishment. At 7:56 A.M., a heavy armor-piercing bomb struck her second gun turret, plunged all the way down into one of her forward magazines, and exploded. Flames shot 500 feet into the air. The forward part of the *Arizona* was totally ruined. Within minutes, another bomb went down her stack into the bowels of the ship; six more hit the aft of the bridge before the great battleship rolled over. Four fifths of her complement were lost: 47 of 100 officers and 1,056 of 1,411 sailors were killed or missing. Hundreds were trapped below decks for hours before rising water or fouled air killed them.

Most of the damage to the battleships was done by the first group of attacking aircraft, which had come in under Commander Fuchida's direction. After a short lull, the second wave of 181 Japanese aircraft arrived under the command of Lieutenant Commander Shigekazu Shimazaki. Coming over Kahuku Point at approximately 8:50 A.M., the formations deployed; 54 high-level bombers went to Hickam and Kaneohe airfields again, 81 dive bombers continued south toward the fleet, and the fighters broke off to strafe around the area. While Shimazaki's pilots inflicted

Battleship Row, Pearl Harbor, December 7, 1941

some major damage, the Americans, alerted now, held off many attackers. Ammunition had been resupplied to anti-aircraft guns, new weapons had been set up, and some ships were moving from the harbor. Without torpedo bombers, the Japanese second wave was not as effective against the warships. Still the high-level bombers which crisscrossed over Pearl Harbor did considerable damage with their armor-piercing bombs.

By the time the second Japanese wave withdrew at 9:45 A.M., the damage to American installations and forces was considerable. As fires raged on ships and on shore, the guts of the United States Pacific Fleet lay in ruin around Ford Island. The giant battleships, ripped apart like tin cans in a bathtub, had been destroyed or immobilized, just as Billy Mitchell had sunk the German battleship *Ostfriesland* in the 1921 tests. In addition, the defenseless target battleship *Utah* had been sunk, and the *Pennsylvania*, in dry dock, had taken one hit from an armor-piercing bomb which went through her deck and exploded in a five-inch gun casement. The minelayer *Oglala* was sunk, and the two destroyers in dry dock with the *Pennsylvania* were wrecks. The cruiser *Helena*, badly hit, miraculously was still afloat. Two other cruisers had taken heavy beatings, a third destroyer was sunk, and everywhere there was minor damage. It had been the most embarrassing day ever for the United States Navy; only the valiant reaction of the officers and men in manning all available guns and executing damage control procedures prevented more damage and loss.

Mitsuo Fuchida, watching all the attacks from his bomber, saw most of the damage through the smoke below.[67] When he turned for home he was sure that his pilots had destroyed at least four American battleships, heavily damaged three more, and destroyed at least half of the American aircraft on Oahu. He had lost 9 fighters, 14 dive bombers, and 5 torpedo planes in the attack, while one aircraft had crashed upon takeoff earlier that morning. Even in his wildest dreams, the commander could not have hoped for greater success for such minimal costs. His code signal "Tora . . . Tora . . . Tora. . . ," meaning that a successful surprise attack had occurred, was sent before his aircraft had struck. He would not have to correct it.

When he arrived back on the *Agaki*, Fuchida reported to Admiral Nagumo and requested permission to make a follow-up attack to destroy the remaining American power in Hawaii. The planes were armed and ready to go. All that was needed was for Nagumo to say "go." But the admiral refused Fuchida's request, believing that he had accomplished his mission by inflicting the required damage on the United States Pacific Fleet. Fearing attacks by surviving land-based American aircraft, anticipating larger Japanese losses from more alert interceptors and antiaircraft gun crews, and

not knowing the whereabouts of the American carriers, Admiral Nagumo would not strike again. There would be no *coup de grace*. Fuchida was dissatisfied with the decision.[68]

As Nagumo turned his task force north at high speed, Americans in Hawaii prepared for another attack. Nerves were frayed, gunners were jumpy, and rumors flew. Some people reported that Japanese paratroopers had landed; other said that amphibious troops were coming ashore; and some talked of an uprising by local Japanese. In the confusion, Army units began to deploy to stop an invasion, while order was restored at the many airfields and ships got under way to gain the open sea. As the news of the disaster spread through the island, service families began to wonder about their men. For the Navy families, the news was grim.

Within minutes after the first bombs had dropped, the word had gone out to the world: "Air raid, Pearl Harbor. This is no drill."[69] In Manila, Admiral Thomas Hart, commander of the Asiatic Fleet, was awakened at 3:00 A.M. December 8, with the informal news. The Navy passed the word to MacArthur. In New York, many people found out while they were at the Dodger-Giant football game. In Malaya, Hong Kong, Wake, Midway, Luzon, and Guam, the Japanese delivered more personal messages.[70] In Washington, President Roosevelt learned of the attack while at lunch.[71] Secretary of the Navy, Frank Knox, could not believe the report. "My God!" he said to Admiral Stark, "This can't be true; this must mean the Philippines."[72] Stark confirmed that it was Hawaii. Secretary Hull was told shortly after 2:00 P.M.

The Japanese Ambassadors, delayed in getting their Government's message properly prepared because of difficulties in decoding, typing, and a plethora of changes, arrived at Hull's office at 2:00 P.M., an hour late for their scheduled appointment. Twenty minutes later, ushered in to see the angry Secretary of State, the Japanese handed over the 14-part message, which concluded that the problems between the United States and Japan could no longer be resolved through negotiations. It was to have been delivered 30 minutes before the bombs fell; but, unluckily for Japan, the ambassadors were late and Fuchida was early. Nomura was shocked at Hull's cold and contemptuous reaction, for he had not been privy to the significance of the 1:00 P.M. timing. Nor was he aware that Pearl Harbor had been attacked.[73] To most Americans the delay appeared to be a treacherous ruse, designed to allow Fuchida's pilots to attack without warning. An incensed President Roosevelt would say as much the following day when he called the Japanese attack "dastardly" and proclaimed that December 7, 1941 was a day "which will live in infamy."[74] Shortly thereafter, the United States Congress declared war against the Japanese Empire.

"The Whole World Upside Down"

In Washington, Secretary Knox told the President that he had to go to Honolulu to see for himself what had happened.[75] When he arrived hours later, he found the Battle Force of the Pacific Fleet in shambles. Seven of the eight battleships in port were badly damaged; two, the *Arizona* and *Oklahoma*, would never rejoin the fleet. The others, repaired by the time the Navy began its 1944 offensive, would reappear like ghosts to pound away at the Japanese positions throughout the Pacific. While the battleships were badly hit, the rest of the fleet was in good shape. The few cruiser and destroyer losses were not serious. The submarines, except for some light damage, were ready to sortie. Five were already on war patrol off of Oahu, Midway, and Wake. The aircraft carriers were undamaged. On shore, the major repair facilities had not been bombed, the dry docks were usable, and the important oil storage facilities were intact. The other major damage had been suffered by the air forces on Oahu. While there were some aircraft available for local defense, the bulk of the first-line aircraft in the Army and Navy air forces had been destroyed. Personnel losses were the most grievous. The Navy suffered 2,008 killed or missing and 710 wounded; the Army, 218 killed or missing and 364 wounded; and the Marine Corps, 109 killed or missing and 69 wounded. In addition, 68 civilians lost their lives and another 35 were wounded.[76]

The Japanese raid shocked the American public and the world by destroying the great battleships of the Pacific Fleet. But the time of Trafalgars and Jutlands had passed; battleships were no longer the capital ships of the fleet. Pearl Harbor forced the United States Navy to follow the lead of the Imperial Japanese Navy and place its reliance on the airpower of the carriers. Ironically, disaster pushed the American Navy into the modern era faster than any other event could have.[77]

Following the Pearl Harbor attack, it became clear that the United States Navy did not have the power to challenge the Japanese in the central Pacific because American carrier strength was less than that of the Japanese. Moreover, it was divided between the Atlantic and the Pacific. For the first months of the war, American carriers would shuttle back and forth across the ocean to block or impede Japanese advances. It was to be a shoestring operation. One or two losses would have given the Japanese a preponderance of strength which could have overwhelmed the American surface forces.

Still, the Pacific Fleet had an ace in the hole in its submarine force. Conceived primarily as a fleet-support weapon, the submarine was the only type of vessel which could operate anywhere in the Pacific after December 7. The new fleet boats had the range to engage the Japanese in their homewaters, off the Philippines, or in the Java Sea. Within hours after Pearl Harbor, the unexpected happened as the Chief of Naval Operations ordered the Navy to begin unrestricted submarine warfare. Nine days later the *USS Swordfish* made the first kill of the war, sending the 8,662-ton cargo vessel, *Atsutasan Maru*, to the bottom of the ocean. On December 22, the older *S-38* sank the *Hayo Maru*, a 5,445-ton cargo ship, in Lingayen Gulf. In January 1942, the number would grow as Allied submarines began to pick off Japanese ships here and there, beginning the ravaging of the Japanese merchant fleet. In these early days, however, the American submarines were plagued with poor torpedoes which ran deeper than set or had defective warheads. With better ordnance, the silent service would have posted even more impressive early victories.[78]

When Secretary Knox arrived, Admiral Kimmel had his fleet actively patrolling against the enemy. The initial searches of December 7 had been ineffective because confusing intelligence had sent the ships southward instead of to the north. It was, perhaps, a fortuitous error. Halsey's small Task Force 8 was not strong enough to deal with the six carriers under Admiral Nagumo's command. While patrolling between Oahu and California, Halsey's fliers sank one Japanese submarine, the *I-170*, on December 10. There were other contacts, but no additional sinkings. After five days of hectic patrolling for submarines, things quieted down around Hawaii, and by December 15 Halsey was able to return to Pearl Harbor to refuel.[79]

By this time Nagumo had escaped without a scratch. On the fifteenth, he dispatched the carriers *Soryu* and *Hiryu*, two heavy cruisers, and two destroyers from his force so that they could assist in the invasion of Wake Island, scheduled for December 22. Except for the loss of 29 airplanes, the major Japanese losses at Pearl Harbor were taken by the submarine force which had been assigned to penetrate and to blockade the harbor. One I-Boat was lost, and all five midget submarines were sunk or disappeared. Nine of the ten men who manned the midgets were immortalized as national heroes for their futile and unproductive actions, much to the disgust of the Japanese naval aviators who had done so much more. This glorification of suicide missions was a precursor of things to come. The surviving midget submarine officer became the first prisoner of war when he was captured on an Oahu beach.[80]

After the Japanese attacked Pearl Harbor, the Americans drastically modified their strategy. The old plan of advancing into the central Pacific, securing a base at Truk, and then driving into the Philippines was just not feasible. On December 8, Admiral Stark issued new instructions. First, the Navy would support the Army in defending Hawaii, Wake, Johnston, and Palmyra. Second, to keep open the sea routes to Australia and New Zealand, the Navy would escort Allied shipping going to those countries between the American possessions and the International Date Line. Third, the Navy would prevent the Japanese from attacking further into the Western Hemisphere and against Samoa and Figi. Fourth, American carriers and submarines were to begin tactical offensives against the Japanese, raiding advanced bases and sea communications wherever possible. Lastly, Guam and the Philippines would not be reinforced.

Stark's orders made sense. The new American posture had to be defensive; the Navy could only attempt the possible. It was important to keep the sea routes open—to protect Hawaii and other areas which would be vital advanced bases or support areas for continuing the war against Japan—and to protect American shipping moving from the West Coast to Hawaii from enemy attack. In all cases, the Navy would have to be careful to operate under an air umbrella.

Kimmel's estimate of the situation after Pearl Harbor was realistic, and his initial actions were sensible. He drew up defensive plans immediately to support the new goals, but he would not have the opportunity to implement them. On December 31, Admiral Chester Nimitz, the quiet, restrained officer who had been the Chief of the Bureau of Navigation when war started, arrived in Hawaii and became the new Commander-in-Chief of the United States Pacific Fleet. Three days later, Admiral Ernest King assumed the position of Commander-in-Chief, United States Fleet.* For the rest of the war, King would guide the destiny of the Navy, while Nimitz would control the majority of the Navy's forces in the Pacific.[81]

While there is much to criticize about the performance of American commanders, the Japanese had planned and executed OPERATION Z with consummate skill and daring. Planning had been thorough, and training had insured success. By using the most isolated part of the Pacific to approach Hawaii, by attacking with carrier aircraft at dawn from an unexpected direction, and by keeping the operation a total secret, the Japanese had nearly guaranteed success. Still, American errors helped the Japanese, at the very least making the operation less expensive in men and ships. Originally, the Japanese had expected to lose up to a third of their attacking force, but Americans underestimated their capabilities. Americans were even surprised by the damage inflicted by Japanese torpedoes, which were not expected to function well in shallow waters, and by the penetrating power of the Japanese bombs which split battleship armor open easily.

American errors were numerous. There were institutional deficiencies: no unity of command in Hawaii, no centralized air control center and interceptor command, no central intelligence agency, and no central command in Washington. There were also errors of judgment: Admiral Stark's interesting but highly speculative comments to Admiral Kimmel; Kimmel's decision not to go on full war alert after receiving Stark's "war warning"; General Short's obsessive concern with sabotage; the constant urging of Army officials in Washington to prevent sabotage and subversion, when war was imminent; the decision by the Navy Staff in Washington not to send any more warnings to Hawaii because enough alerts had already been sent; and the compounding of delays in the transmission of Marshall's last warning. There were others: Short's control and operation of the radars, his changing the Army's alert system without coordinating it with the Navy, his failure to conduct close-in air reconnaissance after receiving the "war warning," Kimmel's failure to institute long-range air reconnaissance after November 27 (especially in the area from which General Martin and Admiral Bellinger had predicted that a Japanese attack probably would be launched), his decision not to use torpedo nets after the Italian experience at Taranto, and his policy of keeping the fleet in port en masse when war was possible.

While errors in judgment, faulty command relationships, operational deficiencies, and even the dulling experience of 20 years of peace followed by hectic mobilization and training were all important reasons for the Pearl Harbor debacle, the central failure was that of American intelligence. It was a failure that started at the White House and transcended every important agency. By the time negotiations were about to fail, the key figures in Washington and Hawaii had all hypothesized that the Japanese would attack southward from Indochina. It was a false premise based upon what the observers thought that the Japanese would do, rather than an intelligent analysis of what they had the capability of doing. Like Napoleon, who thought that the Austrians would never attack him at Marengo, the American leaders assumed that the Japanese would not attack American forces at Pearl Harbor. This was a fatal mistake.

A possible explanation for the intelligence failure was the volume of information coming in about the Japanese plans for the southern area. Such volume overly impressed American observers. Furthermore, because of the size of the Japanese effort, Americans did not believe that the Japanese could have enough aircraft to support another major action. Another problem was rooted in the intelligence agencies themselves. In the Navy Department, for example, information was collected, but seldom was it analyzed and then disseminated to the field. Much information, even in

---

*Admiral King did not become the Chief of Naval Operations until March 18, 1942.

raw form, never left Washington. One piece, the so-called "ships in harbor" report by the Japanese Embassy in Honolulu, was not considered important enough to send forward. In later years, Kimmel and Short said that it would have been the key to the attack, and that they would have reacted differently had they seen it.[82]

While there is no doubt that the strategic intelligence picture was not the clearest and that Washington did not provide Kimmel and Short with the most incisive intelligence analyses, the two commanders received several signals which should have alerted them to the fact that war was imminent and that an attack could strike Hawaii. These included:

1. The increasing frequency of code changes by the Combined Fleet. (November 1, December 1)
2. The withdrawal of all Japanese shipping from the Western Hemisphere. (November 4)
3. The inexplicable "loss" of the Japanese carriers, starting in late November.
4. The "war warning" and the imminent breaking of diplomatic relations. (November 27)
5. The reported destruction of codes, ciphers, and cryptographic machinery by Japanese diplomats. (December 3)

Two or more of these should have motivated the Army and Navy commanders to go on a full war footing. At a minimum, thorough, long-range reconnaissance was demanded, twenty-four hours a day, all around Hawaii. Nothing this drastic happened in Hawaii. All other American overseas commanders went on full war alert on November 27.

Admiral Kimmel and General Short were like two sentinels on duty, charged with the defense of Hawaii.[83] Like sentinels, they should have taken complete charge of their posts, remaining always on the alert and observing everything which took place within sight or hearing; they should have been especially watchful at night and during critical times, challenging all air and sea vessels which attempted to come near their posts. While there were many reasons for their failure, there were no excuses, because as commanders they were responsible for everything their commands did and failed to do. On them fell the onus of failure at Pearl Harbor.

Short was relieved soon after Kimmel. Then Stark was relieved, but not Marshall. In the ensuing months, recrimination and counter-recrimination flowed as investigators began to fix the responsibility for the disaster. Congress ultimately surveyed the entire matter in 1945 and published 49 volumes of testimony and findings. The Joint Congressional Committee Investigating the Pearl Harbor Attack developed 25 conclusions (*See Appendix 2*) which in the final analysis laid the blame for failure squarely on Kimmel and Short, but tainted the reputation of key military and naval officials in Washington.

No Quarter

Admiral Yamamoto sent the Pearl Harbor Striking Force to battle to protect the left flank of the Japanese forces which were to seize the Southern Resources Area.[84] At the same time, the admiral hoped to be able to destroy the major combat power of the United States Pacific Fleet, specifically its carriers, so that the Imperial Japanese Army would have the time to secure the captured areas before the United States would be powerful enough to threaten Japan again. Convinced that the United States was preparing to reduce Japan to the status of a second class power, the Japanese Government hoped that the attack would be the opening act of a limited war, one in which American resolve could be quickly shattered by Japanese victories, which when coupled with German victories over Great Britain and the Soviet Union in Europe, would force the United States to negotiate a peace. It is doubtful if Admiral Yamamoto ever believed that the United States would collapse so easily; on the other hand, General Tojo believed that Japan had to take the gamble.[85]

On December 7, the Japanese gained their military goals at Pearl Harbor, but from that day on a limited war and a negotiated peace were impossible dreams. The attack on Hawaii struck the emotional trigger in the American people; shocked, humiliated, and infuriated, Americans rose nearly as one to demand revenge. American war spirit soared, shattering the Japanese myth that the Americans could be spiritually dominated on the battlefield.[86] This phenomenon made up for the physical losses of Pearl Harbor; and, when coupled with the material superiority which American industry could provide, it would give the United States the long-term superiority needed to destroy the armies, navies, and air forces of the Japanese Empire.

American historians highlight the "strategic imbecility" and the "folly" of the Pearl Harbor attack, basing their arguments upon the strategic impact of the action, not its tactical success.[87] Admiral Morison's comment—"One can search military history in vain for an operation more fatal to the aggressor. . . . On the strategic level it was idiotic. On the higher political level it was disastrous."— sets the tone for the basic American historical evaluation of the operation.[88] Louis Morton agrees with Morison, concluding that he is at loss to explain why the Japanese attacked the United States when they might have secured their economic goals in the East Indies without bringing the

Americans into war.[89] Many commentators remind their readers that if war had opened in an orthodox manner, the United States Fleet would have steamed into the central Pacific, following exactly that course of action for which the Japanese had planned. The two fleets probably would have clashed, and in 1941 or early 1942, the Combined Fleet, being bigger, stronger, and better trained than the Pacific Fleet, probably would have won a decisive victory.[90] Pearl Harbor was a poor substitute.

The Chief of the First Bureau (Operations) of the Imperial Japanese Navy, Vice Admiral Shigeru Fukudome, disagrees with Morison's thesis.[91] Believing that American reaction would have been the same regardless of how the war began, he declares that it was to Japan's advantage to gain as much as possible in the opening battles. In his view, Pearl Harbor was a strategic necessity; what is more, it kept the United States at bay in the Pacific for nearly two years, the time required for the fleet to be built up to support operations in the central Pacific. Still, in retrospect, the emotional impact of the attack created the mood which drove the United States nearly to obliterate Japan as a nation, giving "no quarter" in the Pacific.

The gravity of war descended on the United States on December 7. Within hours the nation faced a declared war with Japan, Germany, and Italy, one which for many months would bring little but defeat. Victory in the future could not be assumed. The situation was bleak.

Many Japanese, never expecting war with the United States, were shocked by the news of Pearl Harbor; but at the same time they were invigorated by the tremendous victory which fanned the spirit of the proud nation. Japan was no longer a second class power; no longer would it be strangled by the economic sanctions of the Americans and their allies. Newspapers gloated over the new Japanese dominance in the Far East, but Admiral Yamamoto was pessimistic.[92] Just after the great event he wrote:

This war will give us much trouble in the future. The fact that we have had a small success at Pearl Harbor is nothing. The fact that we have succeeded so easily has pleased people. Personally I do not think it is a good thing to whip up propaganda to encourage the nation. People should think things over and realize how serious the situation is.[93]

Shortly thereafter, the Pearl Harbor Striking Force returned to Japan, and the Emperor asked to see Admiral Nagumo, Commander Fuchida, and Lieutenant Commander Shimazaki.[94] It was their greatest hour, but while they basked in the glory accorded to national heroes, Isoroku Yamamoto, architect of the victory, could not enjoy his masterpiece.

Admiral Isoroku Yamamoto

Notes

[1]This section is based upon: Mitsuo Fuchida, "The Attack on Pearl Harbor," in the United States Naval Institute, *The Japanese Navy in World War II* (Annapolis, 1969), pp. 16-27; Walter Lord, *Day of Infamy* (New York, 1965); Samuel Eliot Morison, *The Rising Sun in the Pacific, 1931–April 1942* (Boston, 1948), pp. 88-95; and John Toland, *The Rising Sun, The Decline and Fall of the Japanese Empire 1939-1945* (New York, 1971), pp. 193-240.

[2]Date from Lord, *Day of Infamy*, p. 16. Toland, *Rising Sun*, p. 197, says it was the 25th.

[3]Fuchida, "Attack on Pearl Harbor," p. 19.

[4]Sources vary on dates that the Japanese sailors were told of mission. Time used is from Toland, *Rising Sun*, p. 211. He places it after reception of "Climb Mt. Niitaka" message.

[5]Fuchida, "Attack on Pearl Harbor," pp. 21-22.

[6]United States Congress, Joint Committee on the Investigation of the Pearl Harbor Attack, *Pearl Harbor Attack Hearings*, Part 12, p. 245. See: Message, Tokyo to Washington, #902, Part 14 of 14, December 7, 1941.

[7]John Deane Potter, *Yamamoto, the Man Who Menaced America* (New York, 1971), pp. 97-98; Shigeru Fukudome, "Hawaii Operation," in United States Naval Institute, *The Japanese Navy in World War II* (Annapolis, 1969), p. 10; and Toland, *Rising Run*, p. 215, all stress the plan for the 30-minute warning.

[8]This section is based upon three excellent studies: T.B. Kittredge, "United States Defense Policy and Strategy; 1941," *U.S. News & World Report* (December 3, 1954), 53-63, 111-139; Roberta Wohlstetter, *Pearl Harbor, Warning and Decision* (Stanford, 1962); and extracts of United States Army Command and General Staff College, "Pearl Harbor," in Walter Scott Dillard, (ed.), *Readings in the History of United States Foreign Relations*, Volume II, (West Point, 1970-71), pp. 61-106. Also consulted were the original sources found in the congressional hearings on the Pearl Harbor attack.

[9]Department of Military Art and Engineering, United States Military Academy, [*Biographies of World War II Leaders*], *Supplementary Material Subcourse VI* (West Point, 1957-1958), pp. IV-SM-I-147-148.

[10]United States War Department, *Official Army Register, 1 January 1941* (Washington, 1941), p. 772; and the United States War Department, *Army List and Directory* (Washington, 1939-1941).

[11]Morison, *Rising Sun in the Pacific*, fn p. 134; United States Department of the Navy, *Register of Commissioned and Warrant Officers of the United States Navy and Marine Corps* (Washington, July 1, 1941), p. 14. Bloch and Kimmel were both permanent rear admirals. Bloch was the senior, having a signal number of 7 (DOR: July 1, 1931). Kimmel had a signal number of 40 (DOR: November 1, 1937), but was given the rank of admiral on February 1, 1941).

[12]For comments on command see: T. Dodson Stamps and Vincent J. Esposito, (eds.), *A Military History of World War II*, Volume II, *Operations in the Mediterranean and Pacific Theaters* (West Point, 1956), p. 213; Kittredge, "Policy and Strategy," 137-138; Morison, *Rising Sun in the Pacific*, p. 134; USACGSC, "Pearl Harbor," pp. 62-63; and conclusions number 1, 21, 25 of the Joint Committee Investigating the Pearl Harbor Attack

found in USACGC, "Pearl Harbor," pp. 93, 104-106.

[13]Brigadier General Elliot R. Thorpe, *East Wind, Rain* (Boston, 1969), p. 17; Kittredge, "Policy and Strategy," 58.

[14]USACGSC, "Pearl Harbor," p. 62, and Joint Committee, *Pearl Harbor Attack Hearings*, Part II, pp. 5471-5472. See Admiral Kimmel's confidential letter to his commanders, February 4, 1941.

[15]Joint Committee, *Pearl Harbor Attack Hearings*, Part 15, p. 1436. See Major General F.L. Martin and Rear Admiral P.L.N. Bellinger, "Joint Estimate Covering Joint Army and Navy Air Action in the Event of Sudden Hostile Action Against Oahu or Fleet Units in the Hawaiian Area, 13 March 1941," paragraph 1, "Summary of the Situation," for the listed assumptions. Kittredge, "Policy and Strategy," 61, gives the identical information but cites the Joint Coastal Defense Plan as his source.

[16]Joint Committee, *Pearl Harbor Attack Hearings*, Part 15, p. 1437. See Martin and Bellinger, "Joint Estimate . . . ," paragraph III, "Possible Enemy Action."

[17]Joint Committee, *Pearl Harbor Attack Hearings*, Part 14, p. 1029. See Major General F.L. Martin, "Study of the Air Situation in Hawaii, 20 August 1941," paragraph V, "Conclusion."

[18]Kittredge, "Policy and Strategy," 62.

[20]Joint Committee, *Pearl Harbor Attack Hearings*, Part 14, pp. 994-1002. See "Letter from Commander-in-Chief, U.S. Fleet (Admiral J.O. Richardson) to The Chief of Naval Operations, Subject: ' . . . Plan Dog,' " 25 January 1941, paragraph 4 (f).

[21]From Kittredge, "Policy and Strategy," 58. See Letter from Secretary of the Navy to Secretary of War, January 24, 1941.

[22]Kittredge, "Policy and Strategy," p. 62.

[23]Morison, *Rising Sun in the Pacific*, pp. 132-133. See also: Joint Committee, *Pearl Harbor Attack Hearings*, Part 33, pp. 691-698, for Admiral Kimmel's comments on his problems of command.

[24]Morison, *Rising Sun in the Pacific*, pp. 46-47, and Thorpe, *East, Wind, Rain*, pp. 14-16.

[25]Fuchida, "Attack on Pearl Harbor," p. 20.

[26]Morison, *rising Sun in the Pacific*, pp. 133-134; Joint Committee, *Pearl Harbor Attack Hearings*, Part 33, p. 707, statement of Admiral Kimmel; and Joint Committee, *Pearl Harbor Attack Hearings*, Part 39, pp. 113-116, and 124-127. See also Joint Committee, *Pearl Harbor Attack Hearings*, Part 15, pp. 1440-1443 for Hawaiian Department, "Standing Operating Procedure," November 5, 1941.

[27]Joint Committee, *Pearl Harbor Attack Hearings*, Part 39, pp. 105-111, and Joint Committee, *Pearl Harbor Attack Hearings*, Part 29, pp. 1983-1995, testimony of Colonel C.A. Powell, Signal Officer.

[28]Joint Committee, *Pearl Harbor Attack Hearings*, Part 14, p. 1396. See Top Secret Message, CNO to CINCAF, CINCPAC . . . , July 3, 1941.

[29]Joint Committee, *Pearl Harbor Attack Hearings*, Part 12, p. 2. See Message Canton to Tokyo, #95, July 14, 1941.

[30]Joint Committee, *Pearl Harbor Attack Hearings*, Part 16, p. 2173. See Letter from Admiral Stark to Admiral Hart, July 24, 1941.

[31]Joint Committee, *Pearl Harbor Attack Hearings*, Part 14, pp. 1400-1401. See Top Secret Message, CNO to CINCPAC, July 25, 1941.

³²Joint Committee, *Pearl Harbor Attack Hearings*, Part 27, pp. 138-141, testimony of Major General Philip Hayes, and Part 36, p. 408, testimony of Rear Admiral C.C. Bloch.

³³Kittredge, "Policy and Strategy," 125.

³⁴Joint Committee, *Pearl Harbor Attack Hearings*, Part 16, p. 2213. See Letter from Admiral Stark to Admiral Kimmel, September 22, 1941, postscript #1.

³⁵Joint Committee, *Pearl Harbor Attack Hearings*, Part 16, p. 2213. See Letter from Admiral Stark to Admiral Kimmel, September 22, 1941, postscript #2, September 29.

³⁶Joint Committee, *Pearl Harbor Attack Hearings*, Part 14, p. 1403. See Top Secret Message, OPNAV to CINCPAC, COM 12 (INFO: CINCPAC), October 17, 1941.

³⁷Joint Committee, *Pearl Harbor Attack Hearings*, Part 6, p. 2214. See Letter from Admiral Stark to Admiral Kimmel, October 17, 1941.

³⁸Joint Committee, *Pearl Harbor Attack Hearings*, Part 16, p. 2516, Admiral Kimmel's testimony, and Part 32, p. 191, testimony of General Short.

³⁹Joint Committee, *Pearl Harbor Attack Hearings*, Part 14, p. 1403. See Top Secret Message from OPNAV to CINCPAC, CINCAF . . . , November 4, 1941.

⁴⁰For the best summary of the Japanese messages which emphasize the criticality of time see the compilation in Wohlstetter, *Pearl Harbor*, pp. 194-196. See also Joint Committee, *Pearl Harbor Attack Hearings*, Part 16, p. 2219, Letter from Admiral Stark to Admiral Kimmel, November 7, 1941.

⁴¹Joint Committee, *Pearl Harbor Attack Hearings*, Part 12, p. 165. See Secret Message #812, Tokyo to Washington, November 22, 1941.

⁴²Joint Committee, *Pearl Harbor Attack Hearings*, Part 14, p. 1405. See Top Secret Message, CNO to CINCAF, CINCPAC . . . , November 24, 1941.

⁴³Joint Committee, *Pearl Harbor Attack Hearings*, Part 32, pp. 231-234. See testimony of Rear Admiral Kimmel. USACGSC, "Pearl Harbor," p. 67.

⁴⁴Joint Committee, *Pearl Harbor Attack Hearings*, Part 6, p. 2517. See testimony of Admiral Kimmel. See also Part 16, p. 2226, Letter from Admiral Stark to Admiral Kimmel, November 25, 1941, postscript.

⁴⁵Kittredge, "Policy and Strategy," 116; Feis, *Road to Pearl Harbor*, p. 322; and Wohlstetter, *Pearl Harbor*, p. 246.

⁴⁶Joint Committee, *Pearl Harbor Attack Hearings*, Part 14, p. 1406. See Top Secret Message, CNO to CINCAF, CINCPAC, November 27, 1941. My italics.

⁴⁷Joint Committee, *Pearl Harbor Attack Hearings*, Part 14, p. 1328. See Secret Message, Marshall to CG, Hawaiian Department, November 27, 1941. Secretary Stimson sent the message in Marshall's name, according to Kittredge, "Policy and Strategy," 116-117, and Wohlstetter, *Pearl Harbor*, pp. 258-260.

⁴⁸Joint Committee, *Pearl Harbor Attack Hearings*, Part 14, p. 1330. See messages to CG, Hawaiian Department from Adams. Kittredge, "Policy and Strategy," 117.

⁴⁹Joint Committee, *Pearl Harbor Attack Hearings*, Part 14, p. 1330. See Secret Message, General Short to Chief of Staff, November 28, 1941. Text reads: "Report department alerted to prevent sabotage period Liaison with Navy reurad four seven two twenty seventh."

⁵⁰Kittredge, "Policy and Strategy," 117.

⁵¹Joint Committee, *Pearl Harbor Attack Hearings*, Part 26, pp. 52-53, and 322-323.

⁵²USACGSC, "Pearl Harbor," p. 69.

⁵³USACGSC, "Pearl Harbor," p. 68; Joint Committee, *Pearl Harbor Attack Hearings*, Part 6, pp. 2583-2584, testimoney of Admiral Kimmel; and Kittredge, "Policy and Strategy," 118.

⁵⁴For information about code destruction see various messages, Joint Committee, *Pearl Harbor Attack Hearings*, Part 14, pp. 1407-1409. Admiral Bloch's message is in Kittredge, "Policy and Strategy," 120.

⁵⁵Kittredge, "Policy and Strategy," 119-120; USACGSC, "Pearl Harbor," p. 70 and 73; and Joint Committee, *Pearl Harbor Attack Hearings*, Part 29, p. 2313. Marshall believed enough warnings had been sent.

⁵⁶Feis, *Road to Pearl Harbor*, p. 339; USACGSC, "Pearl Harbor," p. 70. Quotation is from Gordon W. Prange, *At Dawn We Slept* (New York, 1982), pp. 474-475.

⁵⁷Joint Committee, *Pearl Harbor Attack Hearings*, Part 15, p. 1867 (Mori telephone conversations); also see Prange, *At Dawn We Slept*, pp. 477-478.

⁵⁸Prange, *At Dawn We Slept*, pp. 478-479.

⁵⁹USACGSC, "Pearl Harbor," pp. 72-73; Kittredge, "Policy and Strategy," 133; Lord, *Day of Infamy*, pp. 175-176; and Prange, *At Dawn We Slept*, pp. 485-486, 493-495 (Quotations appear on pg. 494.)

⁶⁰Morison, *Rising Sun in the Pacific*, pp. 95-98 and 133-139.

⁶¹Morison, *Rising Sun in the Pacific*, pp. 125, 132 and 137-138; and Joint Committee, *Pearl Harbor Attack Hearings*, Part 39, pp. 118-122, "Status of Defense. . . . December 7, 1941."

⁶²Lord, *Day of Infamy*, p. 39.

⁶³Lord, *Day of Infamy*, pp. 27-29, 35-39, 58-61, and Morison, *Rising Sun in the Pacific*, pp. 95-98.

⁶⁴Description of the actions at Opana are based on Lord, *Day of Infamy*, pp. 41-45; Morison, *Rising Sun in the Pacific*, pp. 137-138; and Wohlstetter, *Pearl Harbor*, pp. 6-12.

⁶⁵Lord, *Day of Infamy*, pp. 62-63; and Captain Joseph K. Tassig, Jr., "I Remember Pearl Harbor," United States Naval Institute *Proceedings*, LCVIII (December 1972), 18-19.

⁶⁶Japanese information in this section is based upon Fuchida, "Attack on Pearl Harbor," pp. 21-27; American information is from Morison, *Rising Sun in the Pacific*, pp. 98-127.

⁶⁷Fuchida and Morison differ somewhat on times and actions. Fuchida, "Attack on Pearl Harbor," pp. 23 and 26, reports the following times/actions:

1st Wave:	7:55 A.M.	Dive bombers attack Hickam and Wheeler
	7:57 A.M.	Torpedo bombers attack battleships
	8:00 A.M.	Fighters strafe airfields
	8:05 A.M.	High-level bombers attack battleships
2nd Wave:	8:40 A.M.	Arrive off Kahuku Point
	8:45 A.M.	Ordered to attack

Morison, *Rising Sun in the Pacific*, fn, p. 102, gives the following information:

1st Wave:	7:55-8:25 A.M.	(Phase I) Torpedo and dive bombers attack battleships, strafers attack Ford Island, Ewa, Kaneohe, Wheeler, Hickam, and Bellows fields
	8:25-8:40 A.M.	(Phase II) Lull
2nd Wave:	8:40-9:15 A.M.	(Phase III) High level bombing of Pearl Harbor
	9:15-9:45 A.M.	(Phase IV) Dive bombers attack Pearl Harbor
	9:45 A.M.	(Phase V) Withdrawal

No attempt has been made to rectify the times.

[68]Nagumo, not an air admiral, was a reluctant commander of the force from the beginning. His decision was the safe, correct one, but one which has been criticized. See Fuchida, "Attack on Pearl Harbor," p. 27; Fukudome, "Hawaii Operation," p. 15; Lord, *Day of Infamy*, pp. 180-182; and Potter, *Yamamoto*, p. 142.

[69]Generally credited to Commander Logan C. Ramsey.

[70]Morison, *Rising Sun in the Pacific*, pp. 168-169 and Lord, *Day of Infamy*, p. ix.

[71]Feis, *Road to Pearl Harbor*, p. 340.

[72]Morison, *Rising Sun in the Pacific*, fn p. 101, quoted in many sources. See also Kittredge, "Policy and Strategy," 133-134.

[73]Feis, *Road to Pearl Harbor*, p. 341; Prange, *At Dawn We Slept*, pg. 554.

[74]Henry Steele Commager, *Documents of American History*, Volume II, p. 451.

[75]This section is based primarily on Morison, *Rising Sun in the Pacific*, pp. 120-146 and 209-222.

[76]Morison, *Rising Sun in the Pacific*, pp. 124-126 and 209-214, and Ernest Andrade, Jr., "Submarine Policy in the United States Navy, 1919-1941," *Military Affairs*, XXXII (April 1971), 55-56. Casualty figures are from Prange, *At Dawn We Slept*, pg. 539.

[77]Morison, *Rising Sun in the Pacific*, pp. 213-214 and 220. Potter, *Yamamoto*, pp. 136-137.

[78]Andrade, "Submarine Policy," 55-56. Theodore Roscoe, *United States Submarine Operations in World War II* (Annapolis, 1949), pp. 4-5, 18-22, 31-39, and 527-563.

[79]Morison, *Rising Sun in the Pacific*, pp. 214-218.

[80]Fukudome, "Hawaii Operation," pp. 13-14; Fuchida, "Attack on Pearl Harbor," p. 25; Fuchida and Okumiya, *Midway*, pp. 21-22; and Lord, *Day of Infamy*, pp. 210-213.

[81]Morison, *Rising Sun in the Pacific*, pp. 209-222, 249-250, and 255-257, provide details on post attack actions, new plans, and Kimmel's relief.

[82]Morison, *rising Sun in the Pacific*, p. 134, and Kittredge, "Policy and Strategy," 131-132.

[83]Idea of Secretary of War Henry L. Stimson: "The outpost commander is like a sentinel on duty . . . " in Joint Committee, *Pearl Harbor Attack Hearings*, Part 11, p. 5428.

[84]This section is based primarily on Morison, *Rising Sun in the Pacific*, pp. 125 and 132; Fukudome, "Hawaii Operation," pp. 13-15; and Louis Morton, "The Japanese Decision for War," United States Naval Institute *Proceedings*, LXXX (December 1954), 1333-1335.

[85]Morton, "Japanese Decision," 1334-1335.

[86]The Japanese expected to overcome American materiel strength with greater spirit or moral strength. See pp. 16-17. The American reaction to Pearl Harbor is common knowledge.

[87]Morison, *Rising Sun in the Pacific*, pp. 125 and 132, and Morton, "Japanese Decision," 1333-1335.

[88]Morison, *Rising Sun in the Pacific*, p. 132.

[89]Morton, "Japanese Decision," 1334.

[90]A.J. Barker, *Pearl Harbor* (New York, 1970), p. 153.

[91]Fukudome, "Hawaii Operation," pp. 13-15.

[92]Barker, *Pearl Harbor*, p. 150.

[93]Potter, *Yamamoto*, p. 149.

[94]Barker, *Pearl Harbor*, pp. 151-152.

Centrifugal Offensive: Japan Victorious

4

I claim we got a hell of a beating, . . . it is humiliating as hell.

Major General Joseph W. Stilwell

When the news of Pearl Habor spread across the Pacific on the morning of December 7–8, the garrisons at Midway, Wake, Guam, and the other small American-held islands stood like lonely outguards waiting for imminent attacks. At 9:30 P.M. on the seventh, two destroyers bombarded Midway, but after laying down an accurate 30-minute barrage they withdrew without landing ground forces. At Wake Island, the most remote of the outposts and an ideal permanent aircraft carrier on the main lines of communications across the Pacific, the garrison was alerted at 6:50 A.M., December 8 (Tokyo time); but it failed to detect the incoming Japanese bombers which arrived at 11:58 A.M. and heavily damaged the facilities around the atoll. Three days later, Japanese troops began to land without air support, and as a consequence of their oversight were driven off by the fire of the American shore batteries and the attacks of the four remaining Wildcat fighters. Embarrassed by their only unsuccessful landing of the centrifugal offensive, the Japanese returned to their nearby bases, marshalled their strength, and returned on December 23 to overwhelm the Wake defenders. By that time, Guam had also fallen. Without coastal defense guns, aircraft, and antiaircraft artillery, the garrison on Guam could not defend itself against the regimental-sized force which attacked the island on December 10.[1] (*See Atlas Maps No. 4 and No. 12.*) After Wake and Guam fell they were replaced by the mobile outguards of the early Pacific war, the aircraft carriers *Saratoga, Enterprise,* and *Lexington.* For many months to come, these vessels alone could project American power into the central Pacific.

End of a Myth: Malaya

In 1941, Hong Kong, Singapore, and Manila formed the corners of an impressive looking triangle of Anglo-Saxon power in the Far East. However, each was much weaker than it appeared, especially the tiny Crown Colony off the coast of southern China.[2] Hong Kong was militarily unimportant; in fact, it was a strategic liability, being surrounded by the Japanese bastions in Formosa, Canton, Hainan Island, and French Indochina. During the prewar years the British could have demilitarized the colony with little fanfare, but they decided that Hong Kong was a politically prestigious outpost which, unlike Wake or Guam, could not be sacrificed without great loss of face. In order to maintain their prestige throughout the eastern world, the British planned to hold Hong Kong as long as possible in the face of a probable Japanese attack.

Japanese strategists knew the British situation in Hong Kong. They knew that defeat of the British would shatter Anglo-Saxon prestige in the Orient, and that Hong Kong would be the easiest place to gain a rapid victory. In addition, the Japanese wanted the valuable port to aid in their planned drive to the south. To gain the prize, the Imperial Japanese Army assigned the veteran 38th Division, part of the Twenty-Third (South China) Army, to attack Hong Kong from the north. (*See Atlas Map No. 6.*) Early on December 8, the assault began, ending 18 days later with British capitulation. The Japanese had badly mauled the Allies and gained a propaganda victory of giant proportions, one which was a serious blow to British morale, pride, and influence. By Christmas, one part of the Anglo-Saxon triangle had been wrenched from Allied control.

Even before the Japanese attacked Hong Kong, the land and air forces of the Imperial Army had struck Malaya and Singapore. In a startling 70-day campaign the Japanese would improve on their Hong Kong performance, gaining the greatest land victory every achieved by Japanese arms. For England, Malaya was perhaps the most humiliating campaign ever fought by the Army, including Yorktown; on that distant peninsula, Lieutenant General Arthur Percival surrendered the largest number of British troops ever forced to capitulate as a result of a single campaign.

Japanese planning for Malaya began when the Taiwan Army Research Unit was formed in Taipei, Formosa in 1941. This unit was:

> . . . allotted the task of collecting, in approximately six months all conceivable data connected with tropical warfare—the organization of army corps, equipment, campaign direction, management and treatment of weapons, sanitation, supply, administration of occupied territory, and military strategy, tactics, and geography.[3]

Since Japanese attention heretofore had been focused on warfare in Manchuria and China, this was no mean task. The Japanese officers assigned to the project worked with zeal to gather the information which would be needed for a possible campaign in the southern regions. Information came from diverse sources: Japanese merchants and sailors were particularly helpful; professors gave vital information; and, in many cases, Army officers infiltrated different areas to obtain data which was needed.

Among the officers assigned to the Research Unit was the enigmatic and controversial Colonel Masanobu Tsuji, who was studying Malaya and who would in time become the staff officer in charge of Operations and Planning for General Tomoyuki Yamashita. Tsuji applied himself diligently to the task at hand. A zealot in every sense, he went out of his way to gain what was needed and to impress both peers and seniors with his plans for the invasion of Malaya from the north. Tsuji concluded from his studies that Singapore was defenseless from the rear, that British fighter strength was much weaker than announced in Malaya, that the British land and air forces in northern Malaya had only recently been reinforced, and that the British had 80,000 troops in the country, but only about half were European.[4]

As the Research Unit collected its information, the strategists in Japan began considering an advance into the southern regions. When the United States froze Japanese assets in July 1941, the move south became more and more urgent to both the Imperial Army and the Imperial Navy. Key to any such move was the capture of Singapore, because, even more than Manila, it could prevent the Japanese from moving into the Netherlands East Indies. From Singapore, British air forces could interdict the Japanese line of communication south, if not disrupt

operations in Java and Sumatra. If the fortress were held, reinforcements could be sent across the Indian Ocean to expand the British garrison; but if the fortress fell, the Japanese could jump into Burma, the Indian Ocean, Sumatra, and Java and perhaps sever the umbilical cord of power from England and India to Australia. As a by-product they would gain the valuable tin and rubber resources of Malaya. Therefore, the Japanese decided to direct their main forces into Malaya with the intention of capturing Singapore within 100 days.

Singapore was the center of all British plans because it always had been the key to British power in the Far East. Large enough to hold a good-sized battle fleet, the port had been slowly fortified so that in case of war it would be impregnable against sea attack. Its strength was so well advertized that everyone believed Singapore was impregnable, even though another highly reputed position, the Maginot Line, had fallen earlier in the war. To the residents of the city, and to men of the stature of Winston Churchill, the strength of Singapore became an article of faith.

By late 1941, the British port was not a powerful base because the bulk of the Royal Navy was tied up fighting the Axis in the Atlantic and the Mediterranean. When Churchill did send naval reinforcements to the Far East Fleet, they were not sufficiently large to make the fleet competitive with the Japanese. Although one can criticize the British for failing to send naval air forces with the battleship, *HMS Prince of Wales*, and the battle cruiser, *HMS Repulse*, practically it would have made little difference, since the obsolete British bi-wing naval aircraft (Albacores and Swordfish) would have been no match for the modern Japanese fighters.[5] Moreover, without adequate sea power, the British planners had decided months earlier to rely upon airpower to defend Singapore. Then, although they built air bases throughout the northern and eastern areas of Malaya to protect against the Japanese in Indochina, the British showed an inconsistency by failing to send first-line fighter aircraft to these bases. Consequently, their squadrons remained equipped with the totally-obsolete American Brewster Buffalo and the sturdy Hurricanes of Battle-of-Britain fame. Both models were inferior to Japanese aircraft in air-to-air combat. The British needed the Spitfire in Malaya, although it too would have been inferior in many ways to the Zero.

The idea of defending the naval base at Singapore with air power was not unsound, but it required massive air formations and up-to-date fighters which were not available in 1941. This emphasis on airpower put British army forces in Malaya in a precarious position. These units were given the primary mission of defending the many airdromes in Malaya, causing the three assigned divisions to be so scattered over the peninsula that they could not support each other. Moreover, they could not hold the northern border, the eastern coast, Singapore, and all the airfields, and still conduct mobile operations throughout Malaya if the Japanese attacked in force. Concentrated at any single defensive position, the British ground forces could have waged a vicious, static, defensive war; but spread as they were all over Malaya, they invited piecemeal destruction.[6] (*See Atlas Map No. 7a.*)

There were several other complicating issues. First, was the British MATADOR plan, which called for an advance into Thailand to seize Singora, its adjacent airfields, the railroad, and the dominant terrain in the vicinity of the Kra Peninsula to forestall any Japanese advance. This mission was assigned the Indian 11th Division; but as so often happens when units are few, the division was also ordered to defend the airfields in northern Malaya and to construct a defensive line at Jitra to block any Japanese attack southwestward. Nor was MATADOR politically feasible, because the British did not want to push Thailand into the Japanese orbit by violating her neutrality. Nevertheless, the British retained the plan as a primary concept right up until war was declared, although it had little chance for success. (Only after Japanese troops had landed did the British commander order the 11th Division to defend, thus cancelling MATADOR.)[7]

The unique geography of Malaya greatly influenced military operations. The 600-mile-long peninsula is divided from north to south by a central mountain range, which has few east-west corridors to facilitate movement from one coast to the other. (*See Atlas Map No. 7b.*) For the most part, the country is covered with heavy and deep jungle which impedes defense but allows an attacker to infiltrate with impunity. Many of the deep rivers run parallel to the coast, making them less than desirable military obstacles to north-south movement. The long coast lines give an enemy an excellent chance to land where he will, and in doing so to attack a vulnerable strategic flank. Malaya was a difficult area in which to defend because the terrain did not favor a defense from north to south, certainly not with the eastern coast exposed to Japanese attacks at any point.

Perhaps the most important British deficiency was mental—a preconception that the Japanese would probably not attack Malaya, but that if they did they could not possibly be successful. Many military men, like the Far East Commander, Air Chief Marshal Sir Robert Brooke-Popham, did not believe that Japan would strike during the monsoon season of November through April, or until a German victory in Russia eliminated the Soviet threat from Japan's northern flank.* Coupled with the complete faith in the

strength of Singapore, such attitudes blinded the British to the fact that all recent information pointed to an imminent Japanese attack into Malaya in late November 1941.[8]

The Japanese planned a three-pronged invasion of the Malayan Peninsula. Two forces would strike southern Thailand to seize the tiny airfields at Singora and Pantani, while a third would drive into British territory to gain the valuable airfield at Kota Bharu. The Japanese 5th Division † was to go ashore in Thailand, while one regiment from the *18th Division* was to land at Kota Bharu. To support the invasion, aircraft from the *Third Air Army* would attack from Indochina to gain air superiority as rapidly as possible, while a strong naval force, the *Second Fleet*, commanded by Vice Admiral Jisaburo Ozawa, would escort the amphibious forces and provide surface support. No aircraft carriers were to be used. (*See Atlas Map No. 6.*)

To assist the invading forces which formed the *Twenty-Fifth Army* under Lieutenant General Tomoyuki Yamashita, the *Fifteenth Army* (Lieutenant General Shojiro Iida) would relinquish control of the *Imperial Guards Division*. That unit would move down the railroad from the Indochinese border to Bangkok to threaten the Thai Government, stabilize the country politically, and finally turn southwest down the Kra Peninsula to link up with the Japanese forces already established in the Singora position. Small battalion-sized landing forces from the *Fifteenth Army* would land on the Kra Peninsula on December 8, both to secure the route of march for the *Imperial Guards Division* and to seize the major British airdrome at Victoria Point on the western side of the narrow isthmus. Seizure of this airfield would prevent the British from ferrying fighters from Burma or India to Singapore, forcing them to depend on aircraft carriers or slow surface shipping. Ultimately, the *Fifteenth Army* would move into southern Burma. By cowing Thailand, the Japanese gained access to two major theaters while isolating the British forces in Malaya.[9]

Colonel Tsuji was responsible for a change in the original plan, which had disregarded the importance of Kota Bharu. Before war broke out, he had made an aerial reconnaissance of northern Malaya in an unmarked aircraft, and had noticed that the terrain cannalized movements along the roads and that the well-built British airfields were, in reality, large patches cut out of heavy jungle. (*See Atlas Map No. 7a.*) Moreover, he observed that the central mountain spine caused the weather on the east to differ from that on the west. Seeing Kota Bharu, the colonel decided after his inspection that the airfield there would have to be taken during the initial attacks because it would threaten the planned Japanese assaults into Patani and Singora. Further-

---

*Brooke-Popham did not command all British forces in Malaya. The Far East Fleet was not under his command.

† Hereafter Japanese units are italicized to ensure clarity in descriptions of tactical situations.

more, since Thai airfields were very poorly developed, the British airfield at Kota Bharu would be needed to support the ensuing land operations. On Colonel Tsuji's insistence, the high command changed the plan and decided to send one of the three invasion forces to Kota Bharu.[10]

Cooperation between the various Japanese services was exemplary prior to the execution of the invasion. The Army built forward air strips for its flyers, flyers went out of their way to do what the Army wanted, and the Navy agreed to give the Army total support. There was, of course, no centralized command. The overall commander of the southern land operations was General Count Hisaichi Terauchi, whose headquarters was in Saigon. The overall naval leader was Vice Admiral Nobutake Kondo, *Second Fleet* commander.[11]

On December 4, the Japanese invasion forces began moving from their various ports of embarkation. As the majority of the invasion force steamed around the southern point of the Indochinese peninsula, a British aircraft sighted one convoy at 12:12 P.M. on December 6, while another reconnaissance aircraft picked up the larger convoy from Camranh Bay at 12:45 P.M. the same day. In Malaya, Air Marshal Brooke-Popham was authorized to implement MATADOR; he did not do so because of political warnings from the British consul in Bangkok and because of restrictions from London. Within a few hours the weather in the Gulf of Siam grew worse and the Japanese ships found refuge in the storms at sea.[12]

The seas were still running high when the invasion forces arrived off their assigned area on the night of December 7. Off Singora, Colonel Tsuji waited to go ashore with the lead battalion. While many felt that the invasion might be delayed, there appeared to be no doubt that Yamashita was determined to land on schedule. Signals were soon passed between the ships, and after 2:00 A.M. on the eighth, the first troops went down the sides of the transports into their landing craft. Soon the first boats headed for Singora, and the lead troops landed on their assigned beaches by 4:00 A.M., one and a half hours before Commander Fuchida's airmen attacked Pearl Harbor. At Patani, the Japanese went ashore before dawn. Both of these landings were unopposed by local Thai troops, although there was some firing later on as the invaders began to move through the area toward the Malayan border. Once ashore at Singora and Patani, the Japanese planned to make their main thrust with the *5th Division* from Singora to the southwest, across the border to Jitra, down the main western road net to Alor Star, and across the Perak River obstacle to Kuala Lampur. (*See Atlas Map No. 7b.*) Elements of the division would assist the main movement by following the lesser road net from Patani to Kroh to threaten the right flank of the defenders.

The *Takumi Detachment** (the reinforced *56th Infantry Regiment* from the *18th Division*), assigned to land at Kota Bharu, was to attack down the east coast of Malaya. Unlike the other Japanese forces, this regiment came under intense fire when it began to land. Coastal guns and Royal Air Force fighters set two of the three Japanese transports afire, but the invasion troops made it ashore. Pinned down for some time by small arms fire, the Japanese soldiers worked their way forward in the sand, burrowing down to protect themselves until they finally got to the British wire. In the close combat that followed they broke through the forward defenses and went on to launch a night attack, capturing the airdrome by midnight. Having established its base in British Malaya, the detachment began moving southward along the east coast.[13]

Throughout the entire campaign, the Japanese sought to capture airfields in order to displace their supporting Army air forces forward to cover land operations. To oppose this ploy, once his air force was destroyed, Percival sought to defend the fields to prevent such displacement by the Japanese.

On December 10, the lead elements of the *5th Division* met British forces at the border, but they were not stopped. (*See Atlas Map No. 7b.*) Pushing on with one battalion, the Japanese were able to disrupt the British plans for delay along the road to Jitra. In action, the rather ill-trained troops of the 11th Division became easily confused and demoralized. Caught between planning for an offensive into Thailand and a defensive at Jitra, the troops were victimized also by constantly changing orders and emphasis. Nothing was done well and nothing received total concentration and effort. In both the meeting engagements and the rear guard actions, the Indians did poorly. Japanese tanks shattered their confidence and broke up many of their units; even traditionally stalwart Ghurka units failed. As a result, when the Japanese hit the first prepared position at Jitra, the British division commander had already lost most of his forward brigade.

At Jitra, a British division was defeated by about two Japanese battalions. It was a sordid show, one which definitely did not live up to the tradition of Mons where expert British riflemen in defensive positions shattered a German division in 1914. Errors abounded: units were fired on by their own men; reports to the division commander were totally erroneous; units in excellent positions were withdrawn to poorer positions when there was no necessity to do so; gaps were not closed rapidly; communication was inadequate between units; and actions seemed to be ordered

---

*Japanese forces were often organized as detachments built around an infantry battalion, regiment, or infantry group (two or more regiments). Each detachment was named either for its commander or area of operation.

piecemeal. When it appeared that the other elements of the *5th Division* moving toward Kroh would cut off the 11th Division from the east, the division commander ordered a withdrawal. It was a mess. Some units were still at Jitra when the dawn broke. Others had stumbled back to new positions at Gurun, just in front of the Alor Star airfield, the position which the British had hoped to protect by their defense of Jitra.[14]

Before the Jitra battle began in earnest, the Japanese air forces had overwhelmed the Royal Air Force in northern Malaya, and from that point on the defenders were subjected to constant air attack. While not always effective in terms of casualties, the constant air harrassment lowered morale and made movement in daylight hours difficult.

More embarrassing to Great Britain than the loss of airpower, however, was the victory of the Japanese air forces over the *Prince of Wales* and the *Repulse* on December 10. In the great tradition of the Royal Navy, confirmed so recently at Dunkirk and Crete, Vice Admiral Thomas (Tom Thumb) Phillips decided to sortie on December 8 to destroy the Japanese invasion force. He asked for air cover, but the air disaster in northern Malaya prevented such support. Still the admiral decided to sail. Moving into the Gulf of Siam, the two capital ships managed to avoid Japanese detection for some time; but after receiving false information that the enemy was landing at Kuantan, Admiral Phillips turned northward and accidentally moved into an area where he was quickly sighted. (*See Atlas Map No. 6.*) Japanese pilots had been scouting for the ships all morning, and some had turned for Indochina convinced that their prey had eluded them for the time being. But when a Japanese submarine sighted the *Prince of Wales* and the *Repulse*, all aircraft in the vicinity immediately attacked. The British ships fought back with all they had, but each soon received a lethal, aircraft-launched torpedo hit, followed by similar strikes and bomb hits. In a few minutes the two capital ships were sinking, and their captains began ordering their crews to abandon ship. Officers pulled the *Repulse's* captain off with them, but Admiral Phillips and the captain of the *Prince of Wales* stayed with their battleship. For the first time in war, aircraft alone had sunk battleships on the high seas, and the ships were fighting back with everything they had.[15]

The British position in Malaya was doomed. In addition to the successful invasion of northern Malaya, the neutralization of forward British air fields, and the loss of the *Prince of Wales* and the *Repulse*, the Thai Government submitted quickly to the Japanese, isolating Malaya from Burma. The Army might have made a fight for it if it had been able to withdraw to a central defensive position where it could have concentrated its strength and combat power. Instead,

Lieutenant General Percival* had to spread his troops thinly to delay the three prongs of the Japanese advance while he tried to gain time to build up the defenses of Singapore, prepared to receive additional reinforcements, and deployed to protect Malaya from invasion in the Mersing area. His three and a half divisions, strung out over 600 miles, were not defensive shields, but rather crusts, which when broke would allow the Japanese to run amuck in Malaya. (*See Atlas Map No. 7a.*) Percival ordered his commanders to delay as long as possible, but at the same time he told them not to take risks because there were no other troops to take the places of lost units.

The repetitive delaying actions hurt the 11th Division. Failure at Jitra on December 11–12, at Gurun on December 14–15, and then the long withdrawal to Kuala Kangsar, exhausted the division by December 22, leaving it in a weakened state for the remainder of the campaign. By the time the 11th Division had retreated to the Perak River, the finest natural defensive line in northern Malaya, it did not have the combat power to stop the *5th Division*. Abandoning the obstacle to gain time, the British III Corps commander, Lieutenant General Sir Lewis Heath, decided to make a strong stand on the main and trunk roads just to the south of Kampar.[16]

While the bitter fighting was taking place on the western plain, the small British column, KROHCOL, which had been ordered to advance into Thailand along the Kroh-Patani Road, was also forced to retreat rapidly in the face of the aggressive advance of the Japanese *42nd Infantry Regiment*. (*See Atlas Map No. 7b.*) It held just north of Kroh on December 13, but the next day it pulled back to a position just west of Kroh. By moving to the west of the small town, the British commander uncovered the Kroh-Grik Road which the Japanese could use to envelop the 11th Division farther south. As KROHCOL withdrew under pressure toward Sungei-Patani and a link-up with the 11th Division, a small force from the 12th Brigade was sent north to block the Japanese advance toward Grik. By the sixteenth, KROHCOL was absorbed into the main body of the 11th Division. The other blocking force joined the division when it arrived in the vicinity of Kuala Kangsar on December 22.[17]

On the east coast, the elements of the Indian 9th Division were faring little better than Allied units on the other fronts. Pressed southward by the *Takumi Detachment*, the British retreated to Kuantan; but rather than risk the destruction of more troops in close engagements, the high command ordered the defending brigade to withdraw westward to

*General Percival commanded the British land forces only. Like the Royal Air Force commander, he was subordinated to Air Marshal Brooke-Popham.

preserve itself. It did so on January 3, but not before a series of tough, costly combats were fought with the advancing Japanese. When the brigade moved west to join other retreating British forces at Jerantut, the Japanese were able to advance down the coast to near Mersing without opposition. Events in the east were developing so favorably that General Yamashita cancelled plans for an amphibious envelopment of Kuantan by the *55th Regiment* of the *18th Division*. He then reinforced the attacking formations with this unused regiment.[18]

At Kampar, the British fought their best battle of the campaign. The battered 11th Division had an excellent position; swamps in the west and a large mountain complex in the east restricted maneuver, while the roads through Kampar traversed ground which the division could reasonably defend. Additionally, open ground to the north and west gave the defenders good fields of fire. Essentially a defile, Kampar was the strongest natural position occupied during the campaign. It had to be held to prevent the capture of the airfield at Kuala Lampur and, at the same time, to allow enough time for the 9th Division to extract itself from the east coast through the only east-west highway in British hands (running through Jerantut and Kuala Lipis).

The British occupied the Kampar position on the night of December 27, and the Japanese attacked on the thirtieth. Initially attacking on the flanks and then infiltrating, they were repeatedly repulsed. While British reserves were being chewed up restoring the inland position, the Japanese landed small forces in barges to the west on January 1, turning the British position. Without adequate reserves and without the air and naval forces to contest the landings, the British commander ordered a withdrawal to the Slim River area. The 11th Division began to pull back on January 3. Once again, Japanese tactics—tank-led spearheads, night attacks, infiltrations, flanking maneuvers, and amphibious envelopments—had frustrated the British.[19]

After Kampar the situation deteriorated rapidly. At the Slim River, the Japanese cracked the British position by driving tank-led spearheads down the main roads against the tired defenders. At about this same time, the Allies formed the ABDA Command to coordinate all operations in the southwestern Pacific, and by the agreement of President Roosevelt, Prime Minister Churchill, and their chiefs of staff at the Arcadia Conference, General Sir Archibald Wavell was appointed the ABDA Commander.* One of his first acts was to visit Malaya.

Seeing the situation firsthand, the general ordered Percival to stop the costly delaying actions, to withdraw all his forces into northern Johore where he could fight a major action, and to prepare Singapore for defense if further withdrawal became necessary.[20] Wavell was not happy with what he saw, and was particularly displeased by the inadequacy of the Singapore defense against land attack from Johore. He notified Churchill that Singapore was not impregnable, which shocked the Prime Minister. Churchill then ordered Wavell—and Wavell instructed Percival—not to surrender until there had been "protracted fighting in the ruins of Singapore."[21]

When Percival got all his troops into Johore in mid-January, he was finally able to use his fresh Australian 8th Division and some of the reinforcements which had just arrived. With good plans, reasonable control, and inspired leadership, the British could have given a good account of themselves in Johore. But such was not to be the case. Command relationships were sadly deficient: the Australian division commander was given a command which he could not control with his limited staff; units were broken down into bits and pieces and were distributed all over the battlefield (even the Australians did not fight as an integral division); and the leadership was uninspiring (Percival gave no vitality to the senior commanders or to his troops.) In the ensuing fights the Japanese won again, forcing the British to retire into the fortress of Singapore.

After the last British troops closed onto the island, General Percival had approximately 80,000 troops under his command, most of whom were in reasonably good health. He had ample ammunition and a fair stock of food. His critical problem was water. The general also had to worry about the civilians who were still living in the city and its environs.

Percival deployed his men around the perimeter of Singapore island to await the inevitable Japanese assault. In doing so he ignored the most probable landing site to the northwest, even though Wavell and Heath advised him that the Japanese would attack there. Percival desired to stop the Japanese at the water's edge because the terrain inland was not suitable for defense, but by spreading his troops all over the island he developed a static defense without a mobile reserve.

When Yamashita attacked the northwest coast of Singapore with three divisions on the nights of February 8 and 9, 1942, the Australians took the brunt of the attack.

---

*On January 4, General Wavell was appointed the Supreme Commander, Southwest Pacific Area or ABDA (America, British, Dutch, and Australian) area. He assumed command on January 15. His command included Burma, Andaman and Nicobar Islands, Malaya, Netherlands East Indies, the Philippines, and Christmas and Cocos Islands. This was one of the first attempts at a unified Allied command during the war. Similarly in China, Generalissimo Chiang Kai-shek assumed command of all Allied and air and land forces at the same time. Chiang, however, was not subordinate to the Combined Chiefs of Staff.

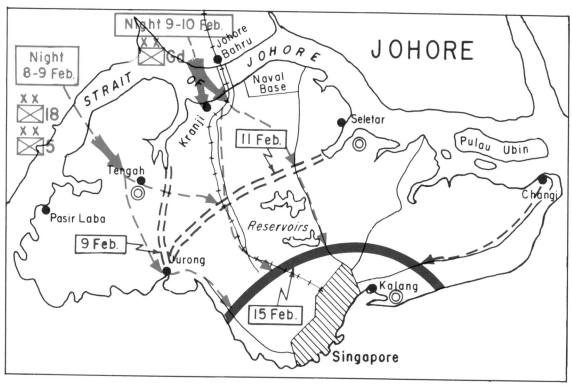

Japanese Seizure of Singapore Island, 1942

Few units were sent to their aid because the defensive preparations had placed so many units out of contact with each other. Counterattacks were essential, but there was no reserve. Percival then failed to strip the rest of his command of forces to engage the Japanese, believing that only one division had made the initial assault. Faulty judgment all along the line negated each British opportunity to hurt the Japanese. In more than one case, a brigade commander pulled his unit out of line without orders, and in doing so created other insurmountable problems. But in the front line, the Allied soldiers fought stubbornly. The Australians would not crack, so the Japanese shifted their assaults to other portions of the line. Unfortunately, a secret order from Percival authorizing a withdrawal reached some lower commanders, and as a result some units withdrew from their positions without pressure, breaking the continuity of the British line. By February 13, the defenders had regrouped around the city of Singapore to begin their last stand. Morale was down. Two division commanders recommended capitulation; Percival refused, arguing that he could still fight on because small arms ammunition was plentiful even if other ammunition was limited, that there were several days of military food stocks remaining, and that the civilian food stocks were adequate. Japanese aircraft continued to pummel the city, causing many casualties, but the civilian population remained calm. While putting off the inevitable capitulation, Percival kept

his engineers busy destroying the useful works in the city. The final straw was the loss of the water supply, which threatened the population of Singapore with a major epidemic. [22]

Facing a water shortage, fearing excessive civilian casualties, and having finally received permission to surrender from General Wavell, Percival sent a delegation forward at 11:30 A.M. on February 15 to seek terms from General Yamashita. Not interested in terms, the "Tiger of Malaya" demanded unconditional surrender. Yamashita wanted the fighting to end as quickly as possible because he feared an extended battle of attrition in the city of Singapore. Such a development would have been deleterious to both sides. With fewer troops and diminishing supplies of ammunition, Percival could not afford such a battle. From the Japanese viewpoint, another Bataan would have wrecked the time table of the centrifugal offensive. It was not surprising, therefore, that at 6:10 P.M. Percival signed the document of surrender; fighting ceased at 8:30 P.M. [23] His last message to General Wavell went out shortly thereafter:

Owing to losses from enemy action, water, petrol, food, and ammunition practically finished. Unable therefore to continue to fight any longer. All ranks have done their best and grateful for your help. [24]

Singapore fell silent. With it the myth of Anglo-Saxon

superiority died while a new myth of Japanese invincibility was born.

Yamashita's tank-led, veteran infantry would gain legendary fame as skilled tropical warriors and keen jungle fighters, although they had not had much training and experience in such operations. They had really beaten the British formations on the roads, in the towns, and along the coasts.[25] Japanese soldiers riding bicycles would become the symbol of British defeat in Malaya, and guns pointing aimlessly to sea would symbolize the impotence of Singapore. More important would be the impression gained throughout the world when the photos of surrender showed a frail and cowed Percival in the presence of a heavy-set, rather threatening Yamashita, giving outward credence, perhaps, to the impression that British leadership had been inadequate to the challenge of the Japanese.[26] After February 15, troops from the island empire could move at will into Burma, the Indian Ocean, and the Netherlands East Indies. Only in the Philippines was the offensive bogged down.

Debacle, Defeat, and a Promise: The Philippines

Manila, the third outpost of the Anglo-Saxon triangle in the Far East and the center of American power, was probably the strongest of the three Allied positions.[27] To defend on land, Lieutenant General Douglas MacArthur had one regular United States Army division and 10 newly mobilized Philippine Army divisions, along with an assortment of smaller infantry, cavalry, artillery, and engineer units. The Far East Air Force, commanded by Major General Lewis Brereton, with its 107 modern P-40s and 35 long-ranged B-17s, was expected to be a key element in the defense of the islands. At sea, Admiral Thomas Hart's small Asiatic Fleet was not powerful enough to challenge a major Japanese naval force, but its submarines were a threat to any invader.

Philippine defense began to improve after President Roosevelt recalled Douglas MacArthur to active duty as the Commander, United States Army Forces Far East (USAFFE) in July 1941, and after the forces of the Philippines were made part of the active United States Army.* MacArthur, long opposed to giving up the Philippines, immediately began to lobby for increased military preparedness in the islands. His enthusiasm, coupled with the view that strategic airpower could deter Japanese moves southward, helped to sway the Army staff in Washington toward a more positive stand in the Philippines.[28] MacArthur began immediately to ask for more men and equipment. While M1 (Garand) rifles were denied him, new guns, aircraft, and tanks arrived before war began. Marshall even offered the general a national guard division, but MacArthur declined it because he felt that he had sufficient American infantry. Philippine defense would rest on the performance of his trusted Filipinos.

---

*MacArthur was recalled as a major general on July 26, 1941. The next day he was appointed a lieutenant general, the first time he had ever held the grade. In December, he became a full general with a date of rank of September 16, 1936.

Filipino Troops in Training, 1941 (Probably Philippine Scouts)

While the numbers of troops and airplanes seemed impressive in late 1941, the Allied garrison in the Philippines was not as strong as it appeared. Most of the Philippine divisions were untrained, had uneven leadership, and were not equipped with adequate artillery or any tanks. The first regiments were called to the colors on September 1, the second regiments were called up in early November, and the third regiments were activated after war began. Filipino troops were issued only one field uniform, and the rifles which they were given—Springfields or Enfields—were too big for them. Filipino officers often were political appointees with little liking for soldiering, and many spoke a different dialect from that of their soldiers. In the breach, MacArthur would have to rely on his Philippine Division with its one American regiment and two Philippine Scout regiments, the separate 26th Cavalry Regiment (Philippine Scouts), and the better trained coast artillery units. His air squadrons were in much better shape than his divisions, but there were too few of them in number to combat the number of Japanese aircraft which would attack Luzon. Still, MacArthur's air force was the largest one outside the United States, it was well led, its American and Filipino pilots were well trained, and it had an operational radar intercept center at Nielson Field in Manila.

When he assumed command in the Philippines, MacArthur knew that War Plan ORANGE 3 was the basic document governing the Philippine Department's plans for war, although by that time RAINBOW 5 had replaced ORANGE as the standard United States war plan. Strategically, ORANGE 3 was out of date; but tactically, the plan was realistic and well thought out. Under it, the defenders would hold Manila Bay by defending Bataan Peninsula and the harbor forts (Forts Drum, Mills, Frank, and Hughes) which were built on Corregidor and the tiny islands near it. (*See Atlas Map No. 8.*) To assist in the extended defense, 180 days of supplies for 40,000 troops would be stockpiled on Bataan so that the defenders could hold out until the American fleet broke through to reinforce the islands.

Never satisfied with ORANGE 3, MacArthur was also displeased with RAINBOW 5, which accepted the loss of the islands without calling for an attempt to reinforce them. Therefore, when Marshall sent him the new RAINBOW 5 plan, MacArthur took the opportunity to recommend that he wage an active defense of all the islands with his new Philippine Army divisions and his additional air squadrons, rather than just hold Manila Bay. Marshall was impressed with the general's ideas, and because there was added emphasis in Washington on the defense of the archipelago, he submitted them to the Joint Army-Navy Board for consideration.

While the Joint Board decided what should be done in the Philippines, MacArthur, with the Chief of Staff's concurrence, began to adjust his plans to conform to his recommendations. Anticipating a favorable decision, MacArthur established five new commands: North Luzon Force (eventually to be commanded by Major General Jonathan Wainwright); South Luzon Force (Major General George Parker); the Mindanao-Visayas Force (Brigadier General William Sharp); the Harbor Defense Command (Major General George Moore); and the USAFFE Reserve. With the approval of his recommendations by the Joint Board on November 21, the general gave new missions to his commanders. Wainwright would defend the northern beaches at all costs and would protect the airfields in his sector with three Philippine Army Divisions, two Scout units, and assorted artillery. MacArthur gave the same basic mission to Parker in southern Luzon, but allocated him only two Philippine Army divisions and even less artillery. Sharp was ordered to defend the airfields in the Visayas, the B-17 base at Del Monte, Mindanao, and to protect the cities and utilities in the area; he got three Philippine Army divisions for this task. MacArthur charged General Moore with the defense of Manila Bay, giving him all the coast artillery available. MacArthur's reserve include the Philippine Division, two Philippine Army divisions, and Brereton's Far East Air Force.

Japanese planners decided that Luzon could be seized in 50 days, just half of the time they estimated the subjugation of Malaya would require. Then the rest of the islands would be seized leisurely. Although they erred in assuming that the major battle would take place around Manila, they were quite correct in evaluating the capacity of the Filipino and American forces. American units worried them; Filipino units did not. Therefore, the Japanese High Command allocated only two reinforced divisions to the Philippine Campaign—the *16th Division*, which had a poor reputation in combat in China, and the *48th Division*, which had never been in action. In addition, some naval landing troops were provided. Elements of the *Third Fleet* would transport, escort, and protect the invading forces. As the first major part of the campaign, the Japanese planned to gain immediate air superiority and simultaneously establish air bases in the islands from which they could extend the range of their aircraft. (*See Atlas Map No. 8.*) The Navy's Zero fighters were assigned targets below Lingayen Gulf because their range was greater than that of any Army fighter; Army aircraft would support the initial landings in northern Luzon, then be leapfrogged forward to new bases as they were developed. No aircraft carriers were to be used to support operations in northern and central Luzon; the three available were too slow, too small, and had too few aircraft.

Initial air attacks would be concentrated on Clark Field and Nichols Field; then the Japanese would strike Nielson, in Manila, and Clark's auxiliaries, Iba and Del Carmen.

The Japanese landing plan was very simple. Batan Island, north of Luzon, would be seized on December 8 to provide a forward airfield. (*See Atlas Map No. 6.*) Two days later, simultaneous landings would be made on Luzon by half regiment-sized detachments to seize airfields at Aparri on the northern coast and at Vigan on the western coast. All these forces would come from Formosa. On the twelfth, a regimental-sized Army force and a naval landing force would invade southern Luzon at Legaspi to seize the airfield there. Coming from the Palaus, these units would be supported by aircraft from the small carrier, *Ryujo*. About ten days after the first landings, another force from the Palaus was to land at Davao, Mindanao to capture the airfield and harbor as a forward base for the advance of the *16th Army* (from the Palaus) into the Sulu Archipelago (to seize airfields at Jolo), and then into Borneo and Java. Naval surface and air forces from the Palaus would support the Mindanao and Jolo operations.

The main Japanese landings were scheduled for December 20 and 22. The bulk of General Homma's *Fourteenth Army*, 43,110 men strong, would assault the eastern shoreline of Lingayen Gulf on the first date, while a 7000-man force would go ashore at Lamon Bay on the east coast of Luzon, across from Manila on the second date. These two forces would then converge on Manila for the decisive battle. The *Lingayen Force* would be supported by air units on Formosa, by air units deployed to the Philippines, and by the ships of the *Second* and *Third Fleets*. The *Lamon Bay Force*, staging in the Ryukyus, though supported by land-based air elements, would have much smaller naval surface and air forces in support.[29]

While the Japanese prepared for war throughout the Far East, Manila continued to be a festive city. Colonel Bradford Chynoweth, arriving in the capital on November 20, was amazed that he was encouraged to see the sights of Manila instead of being sent immediately to his division in the Visayas. John Michael Langley's father wrote his sister in Manila, urging her to return to Australia with her family because war was imminent; she chose to stay, believing her brother to be too anxious. Even after November 27, when American forces were alerted for war, it seemed that hostilities were still only a remote possibility. Plans for Christmas went on in most households. On the night of November 30, the rabid service football fans gathered as was customary on the lawn of the Army-Navy Club on Manila Bay to hear the early morning shortwave broadcast of the Army-Navy game. Even on the night of December 7, pilots from Nichols Field assembled at the officers club to celebrate the halfway point in many of their tours.[30]

As the American pilots enjoyed their party at Nichols Field, Japanese pilots began their preparations for the first attacks on Luzon. Late on the seventh, however, it seemed that Japanese plans would go astray as fog began to blanket Formosa; by midnight, it was obvious that the aircraft could not take off by 2:30 A.M. on the eighth, as planned. When the news of Pearl Harbor arrived at 2:20 A.M., the Japanese airmen knew that they would not gain strategic surprise with their attacks in the Philippines. Plans were changed. Clark and Iba Fields were designated the main targets; time could not be spared to fly all the way south to strike Nichols Field. While the flyers waited for the fog to lift, everyone was worried about an American strike against the congested airfields on Formosa. By 7:00 A.M. mist replaced the fog, enabling all the squadrons to head south for their first strikes by 8:45 A.M. Davao had already been bombed.[31]

In Manila, Admiral Hart and General MacArthur, after receiving the news of Pearl Harbor around 3:15 A.M., immediately alerted their forces. General Brereton arrived at MacArthur's quarters at 5:00 A.M. to get his orders. He wanted to bomb Formosa immediately, but was put off. At 7:30 A.M., Brereton received a call from General Arnold in Washington, warning him not to get caught in the same posture as had the air commander in Hawaii.[32]

When first reports of approaching Japanese aircraft reached the Nielson control center at 8:45 A.M., pursuit aircraft were ordered aloft.* Clark's fighters were sent north to intercept; Nichols' fighters went north to cover Clark; and, shortly thereafter, the B-17s which had not gone to Mindanao were ordered aloft to patrol in order to avoid being caught on the ground. By late morning there had been no contact, so the American aircraft returned to refuel and prepare for other missions. At 11:30 A.M. Clark's aircraft were home.

While his aircraft had been up, Brereton had continued trying to get permission to bomb Formosa.† Brigadier General Richard Sutherland, MacArthur's Chief of Staff, had initially evaded the request, recommending that a reconnaissance be flown before any attack was planned. But Brereton persisted. At 11:00 A.M., after MacArthur gave him permission to launch a late afternoon attack, Brereton recalled the B-17s.

---

*Allegedly, the P-40s at Iba had taken off shortly after 3:30 A.M. to intercept a formation of aircraft heading for Corregidor. According to Japanese accounts, no attacking aircraft left Formosa until dawn.

†This subject is the source of much controversy, MacArthur, Sutherland, and Brereton disagree on essential facts. Morton's logical conclusions have been accepted for this summation.

At 11:30 A.M., while the B-17s were being prepared for the attack on Formosa and the fighters were being serviced, radar plots, indicated that a large Japanese air formation was over northern Luzon. Telegraph and telephone reports from Filipino postmasters in the area confirmed the information. In the control center, Colonel Harold George, the Chief of Staff, Fifth Interceptor Command, decided that the main objective was Clark Field. Warnings were sent to Clark, but none got through to the bomber commander. A telephone call to an unknown lieutenant at Clark did little good. Nothing seemed to stir at Clark. Colonel George, however, took immediate action, ordering his fighter squadrons aloft. (*See Atlas Map No. 8.*) He sent the 17th Squadron from Nichols over Bataan, the 34th at Del Carmen to cover Clark, the 21st from Nichols to patrol over the Manila Area, and the 3rd at Iba to meet the threat over the South China Sea. The 20th Pursuit Squadron was ordered (presumably by Colonel George) to take off from Clark at 11:45 A.M. to intercept the Japanese aircraft. The P-40s at Nichols got off immediately, while the older P-35s at Del Carmen were held up by the dust on the runways. Iba's P-40s soon were up. At 12:15 P.M., as the lead fighters at Clark Field taxied to their takeoff positions, bombs hit the American field. In a matter of minutes, the Japanese bombers destroyed the major base facilities, including the communications center. Following the bombing, Zeros strafed the field, destroying most of the aircraft on the ground. Only three or four P-40s managed to take off in the holocaust, while five were blown to bits trying to get airborne.

Elsewhere, American airmen fared little better. At Iba, the fighters were attacked as they came home to refuel, but they prevented the strafing attacks which devastated Clark. Del Carmen's P-35s came into action over Clark and shot down three Japanese aircraft. They suffered so much damage, however, that the aircraft were nearly all ineffective when they returned to base after the attack. Over Bataan and Manila, the P-40 squadrons continued their patrols.[33] In the surprise attack, the Japanese destroyed half of the modern aircraft of the Far East Air Force—18 B-17s and 53 P-40s—and over 35 other types of aircraft, while heavily damaging many more. They lost only seven fighters. It was a debacle of the first magnitude. General Arnold could not believe it.

After the attacks, Admiral Hart, deciding that Manila was an untenable naval base, ordered the Asiatic Fleet to Borneo to assist in the defense of the Malay Barrier. Some days later, after more disasters, Hart ordered the remainder of his forces to withdraw, but he personally remained in Manila. So did the 4th Marines. In the capital, life went on almost as usual, although the bombings began to create problems. Even during the air raids, however, one American family moved across town to a new home, stopping occasionally when the Japanese air raids became too intense.[34]

Japanese air assaults continued in force for several days, whenever the weather over Formosa cleared to allow flight operations. Systematically they attacked all the airfields again and again, doing so with formations of 90 to 100 aircraft. By the night of the thirteenth, the Far East Air Force was shattered; only 22 P-40s remained, and they were directed to avoid combat in order to be available for reconnaissance. Two days later, the surviving B-17s were ordered to Batchelor Field at Darwin, Australia.[35]

Meanwhile, Japanese ground forces were carrying out operations according to plan and without meeting any initial ground resistance. (*See Atlas Map No. 9.*) Assault elements seized Batan Island on December 8. Two days later, the 2000-man *Tanaka Detachment* approached Aparri, but due to rough weather put only two companies ashore. The remainder of the force landed at Gonzaga on the east coast. To the west, in similar weather, a small portion of the 2000-man *Kanno Detachment* landed and took Vigan. The rest of the detachment went in the following day. Once ashore, troops were sent north to occupy the airfield at Laoag on Highway 3. With the Aparri airfield captured and facing no counterattack, Homma ordered Tanaka to take most of his force to join Kanno, and then move toward Lingayen Gulf. The only reaction to landings came from the air. Two B-17s hit Aparri, doing little damage; but at Vigan, USAFFE pilots sank a minesweeper, beached two transports, hit a destroyer, and even struck the flagship of the amphibious force.

At Legaspi, on December 12, the 2500-man *Kimura Detachment* landed without opposition, as supporting air forces pounded Luzon. As the Japanese advanced up the Bicol Peninsula on the seventeenth, they brushed aside a small party of Filipino engineers who were blowing up bridges. On December 22, however, they ran into a Filipino company which occupied an excellent position along the main highway. The Filipinos stopped the Japanese company cold, administered heavy losses, and drove it back six miles. Two companies of Filipino troops occupied another excellent position across the narrowest neck of the peninsula, but they had to withdraw on December 23 when Japanese forces landing at Lamon Bay threatened to cut them off. During these days, small air strikes against the Japanese in Legaspi were largely unsuccessful.

In the southern Philippines, the *Miura* and *Sakaguchi Detachments** from the Palaus (about 5,000 men in all)

---

*The *Miura Detachment* was part of the *16th Division*. The *Sakaguchi Detachment* was from the *Sixteenth Army*. The *Matsumoto Detachment*, part of the *Sakaguchi Detachment*, took Jolo along with elements of two special naval landing forces.

landed near Davao on December 20, met sporadic resistance, and captured the town and its airfield. (*See Atlas Map No. 6.*) B-17s from Darwin surprised the Japanese at sunset two days later, but the air attack did little damage. On the twenty-third, part of the *Sakaguchi Detachment* embarked for Jolo Island, which it captured the next day. With these easy victories, Japan opened the route to Borneo from the Philippines.

MacArthur noted all of these small operations, but he was not willing to react to them. He was waiting for the main landings at Lingayen Gulf, where Wainwright had deployed one division of the North Luzon Force across the head of the gulf to meet the Japanese assault, while another division had outposted the eastern coastline of the gulf as far north as San Fernando. In southern Luzon, Parker was prepared to repel landings in the east, south, or southwest. (*See Atlas Map No. 9.*) Only in the Bicol Peninsula had Allied troops been in contact with the initial Japanese forces.

General Masaharu Homma approached Lingayen Gulf with some trepidation. His units were scattered all over Luzon, and he knew that a determined Allied defense might be able to crush the three regiments which remained to make the main landings. Even with air supremacy, Homma knew that his task would not be easy. As he approached the gulf, a nearby typhoon threatened to disrupt his landings as rough seas pounded the gulf.

No Japanese regiment landed on its assigned beach on December 22, but all got ashore near their initial objectives. Homma's northernmost regiment, the *9th Infantry* (part of the *16th Division*), landed just south of the coastal town of Bauang which controlled the intersection of the coastal road (Highway 3) with the mountain road to Baguio. Filipino troops wreaked havoc on the leading elements with caliber .50 machineguns, but the Japanese troops pushed on, gained the beachhead, and then turned north to link up with the combined *Kanno* and *Tanaka Detachments* which were marching south from Vigan. This landing at Bauang disrupted the planned Allied attack on the *Kanno/Tanaka Detachment* and forced the defending forces (moving north, but now caught in flank) to retreat east toward Baguio. The second Japanese landing occurred at Aringay, where the *Formosan 1st Infantry Regiment (48th Division)* came ashore without meeting any resistance. Turning south along the coastal road, the *1st Infantry* reached Damortis by 4:00 P.M., linking up with its division's tank regiment and reconnaissance squadron. These two units had moved south from the landing beaches at Agoo, where they and the *47th Infantry Regiment* (*16th Division*) had gone ashore. The *47th Infantry*, rather than turning south immediately, moved due east to the Aringay-Rosario road, where it then turned south towards Rosario. Its movement, coupled with

that of the 1st Infantry, threatened Wainwright with a two-pronged attack down the coastal plain toward the road junction at Rosario. If Rosario fell, the Japanese would be able to move quickly into the northern portions of the Central Plain; at the same time, they would cut off the Allied forces which were retreating from Bauang through Baguio toward Rosario, and would secure the entire Japanese beachhead on the eastern side of Lingayen Gulf.

Wainwright's first crisis developed around Damortis and Rosario. Surprised by the Japanese landings on the east coast of the Gulf, the general had tried to disrupt them early on December 22, but the forces dispatched to Agoo broke and fell back. Wainwright immediately ordered up his 26th Cavalry Regiment to try to stem the Japanese advance. North of Damortis, the horse-mounted troopers and their scout elements came under intense ground fire and air attack around 1:00 P.M., but they stood firm for three hours until forced to withdraw to positions along the road to the southeast of Damortis. At 5:00 P.M., the exhausted cavalrymen were told to withdraw to Rosario.

As the two Japanese regiments converged on Rosario, the small town became the critical point on the battlefield. Wainwright's position became more difficult as the *47th Infantry* approached from Aringay, but then disaster nearly struck when Japanese tanks broke through the cavalry rear guard northwest of Rosario, creating panic everywhere. A possible rout was averted when Major Tom Trapnell blocked a bridge with a burning tank. Still the retreating cavalrymen barely cleared Rosario while their F Troop doggedly defended against the attacks of the *47th Infantry*.

While things had gone well for the Japanese on land, heavy seas had prevented General Homma from landing the remainder of his forces. He therefore ordered the ships to move to calmer anchorages closer to the head of the gulf. There they came under fire of American 155-mm guns at Dagupan, which while not doing much damage, nevertheless worried Homma. So did the low-level attack of B-17s from Darwin and the attacks of American submarines. In all these actions, only the submarine *S-38* was successful. She sank the 5,445-ton *Hayo Maru* on December 22 in the inner gulf.[36]

Homma continued to land supporting elements while his lead troops pushed south toward Pozorrubio on December 23. Wainwright tried to stem the Japanese attacks with fresh units, but the units broke under the attack of the Japanese armor. That night, the attackers knocked the last Filipino troops out of Pozorrubio. Wainwright then called MacArthur. He asked permission to withdraw behind the Agno River, which formed the first natural defensive line, 10 miles south of the gulf. At the same time he asked for the Philippine Division so that he could counterattack. Mac-

Arthur approved his withdrawal. He refused to give him the division, however, because he was now concerned about the ability of his forces to implement the plan to defend all of Luzon and also about the sighting of a Japanese convoy moving toward Lamon Bay. That night MacArthur ordered war plan ORANGE 3 executed. No longer would all the Philippines be defended, because it was clear that the Allied forces did not have the capability to stop the Japanese drives. The stand would be made on Bataan.

In southern Luzon, early on the morning of December 24 Japanese troops of the *16th Division* began landing at Lamon Bay. At dawn, more Japanese came ashore. Then, in good light, their main force landed. At each point, Filipino resistance varied. On one beach, elements of the newly mobilized 1st Regular Division (Philippine Army), supported by a few American planes, bloodied the Japanese attackers in a cross-fire, and by 2:30 P.M. had halted the Japanese advance. At another point, fighting was sporadic but intense, as Filipino troops fought well. Japanese reconnaissance elements, however, avoided fights and drove west as quickly as possible. In the Bicol Peninsula, Japanese troops moved to link up with the *Kimura Detachment* before turning northwest;* by late afternoon, they had cut off the Filipino battalion on the Bicol Peninsula. By nightfall, Lieutenant General Sasumu Morioka, the commander of the *16th Division* had put his 7000-man force ashore, had secured a difficult beachhead, and was in position to begin an immediate drive on Manila from the southeast. His success that day made Wainwright's position more critical than ever.

In the north, at 5:00 A.M. on December 24, the 26th Cavalry, fighting without antitank weapons, stopped attacking Japanese armor at its outposts near Binalonan. When the armor by-passed them to let the infantry close and attack, the cavalrymen stopped the Japanese assault again, counterattacked immediately, and forced the enemy to reinforce his infantry with more tanks. By midmorning, fighting a fresh regiment, the cavalrymen were so heavily engaged that they could not break off contact. When Wainwright found that the regiment was down to 450 men and saw its position, he ordered it to withdraw. Only then, in the late afternoon, did the Japanese finally gain access to the roads of the Central Plain.

Back in the United States, while many people demanded that more be done to defeat Japan, the chief planners in the War and Navy Departments accepted the ultimate loss of the islands until Marshall demanded that everything be done to reinforce the Philippines. He was supported by Secretary of War Henry Stimson and ultimately by the President; but the Navy was never enthusiastic about any

*Link-up occurred on December 27.

26th Cavalry Withdrawing through Pozorrubio

reinforcement because it would have to fight its way into the islands with the convoys of men and equipment. MacArthur argued for his cause: the Japanese were spread out and vulnerable; more fighters could turn the tide; a "master strike"—a carrier raid—against Japan would curtail Japanese expansion; and, most importantly, the islands could not be abandoned, because the respect of the Filipinos and the people of Asia would be lost. With Marshall's advocacy, his arguments finally fell on friendly ears in the War Department.

Marshall insured that a large convoy of troops, equipment, and aircraft was pushed through to Australia. Furthermore, he sent selected officers to Australia to insure that the convoy got to MacArthur. He transferred Brigadier General Dwight Eisenhower to the War Plans Group to handle Pacific affairs, knowing that Eisenhower understood the Philippine situation as well as any man, and had the trust and understanding of MacArthur. Marshall's actions, however, were futile. The Navy never vigorously supported the reinforcement of the Philippines, since both Admirals Stark and Hart were lukewarm to any such attempt. They were more interested in defending the Malay Barrier and Australia. Also, the Japanese advance into Borneo by New Year's Day cut the line of communications with MacArthur. When Hart left Manila on Christmas Day, the Navy wrote off the Philippines. MacArthur would never forget this.†

† For the rest of the war, MacArthur felt that the Navy had not done its best for him. He also never realized how hard Marshall had worked to support him, because all he saw were broken promises. Much of MacArthur's dislike of the Navy, Marshall, and the War Department stems from Bataan. Part of his criticism was open to question, but a great deal was justified.

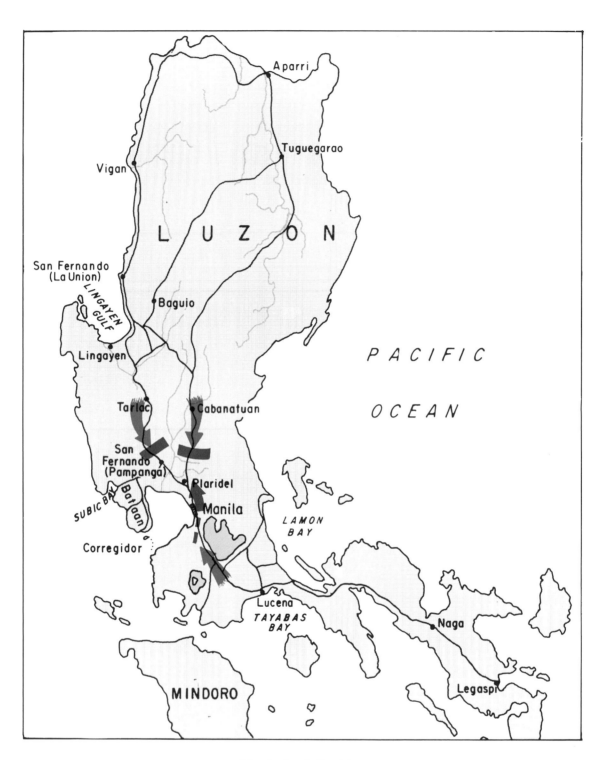

MacArthur's Problem:
Withdrawal Through Defile Into Bataan, December 1941

Moreover, in late December at the ARCADIA Conference, the United States confirmed that it would continue to support a Germany-first strategy, much to the relief of the British but eventually to the disgust of MacArthur.

Christmas Day found MacArthur in deep trouble on Luzon. His naval forces were gone except for small coastal craft, six PT boats, and the submarines, which were leaving shortly. With the Far Eastern Air Force impotent, he ordered General Brereton to Australia. Then he sent the remaining fighters to Bataan. Excess airmen who were not evacuated became infantrymen. On the ground he had to insure that his North Luzon Force held long enough for his

South Luzon Force to get into Bataan. (*See Atlas Map No. 9.*) To do this, Wainwright had to delay on five positions (D-1 through D-5) in the Central Plain, insuring that he held the important towns of San Fernando, Plaridel, and Calumpit which controlled the roads and bridges into Bataan. If San Fernando on Highway 3 fell, the Japanese could block any entrance into Bataan. If Plaridel or Calumpit were captured, the South Luzon Force would be unable to reach San Fernando. (*See Map, pg. 78.*) The withdrawal would depend on excellent timing and on Wainwright's delaying action.

On Christmas Eve, Wainwright was on the D-1 line (Aguilar-San Carlos-Urdaneta), just below the position where the 26th Cavalry had fought earlier that day. (*See Atlas Map No. 9.*) The next day he was on the D-2 line along the Agno River, with the 21st, 11th, and 91st Divisions (PA) on line from west to east. The Japanese attacked the left of this line on Christmas Day, forcing Wainwright back to the D-3 line (Paniqui-Guimba-San Jose) on December 27, after elements of the 11th Division and the two USAFFE tank battalions took heavy losses disengaging around Rosales on the Agno River. At the D-4 line (Tarlac-Licab-Cabanatuan), Wainwright decided to hold as long as possible, changing his original plan which had been to hold only the D-5 line in strength while using the forward positions to delay and disrupt the Japanese advance. General Homma played into Wainwright's hands by placing the bulk of his regrouped forces in the east, and ordering them to advance down Highway 5 to Cabanatuan on the Pampanga River. Only the *9th Infantry Regiment* moved along Highway 3 toward Tarlac-San Fernando.

Three Philippine Army divisions held the D-4 line: the 21st was at Tarlac, the remnants of the 11th at Licab, and the 91st at Cabanatuan. On December 29, the Japanese attacked the 91st at Cabanatuan, forcing it to withdraw after a tank column enveloped its right flank. The next day Japanese spearheads captured Gapan, shattering the 91st Division. At the same time, a Japanese battalion moved from Cabanatuan west to La Paz and towards the western highway, threatening to envelop Wainwright's left flank. To hold in the west, Wainwright ordered his left and center divisions back to a shortened D-5 line, which stretched from Bambam to Mount Arayat, the Pampanga River, and its adjoining swamps. In the east, Highway 5 to Baliuag and Plaridel lay open.

Facing collapse in the north, on December 30 MacArthur ordered Major General Albert Jones* to move the South Luzon Force to Bataan at once. Since the twenty-fourth, Jones had led two divisions against the two major Japanese

*Parker had gone to Bataan to organize the defensive position.

Japanese Tank Advancing on Luzon, 1941

columns which were advancing from Lamon Bay through the mountainous terrain below Laguna de Bay. On December 28, MacArthur had directed him to withdraw to Bataan, clearing the Calumpit bridges by early on January 1—an advance of one week over the original plan. Jones, occupying a good defensive position south of Laguna de Bay, had reluctantly pulled back and begun sending advance elements north, only to be told by an equivocating USAFFE headquarters early on the thirtieth to remain in position until driven back. Now, he quickly reinitiated the northern movement and began to withdraw to Bataan. Racing around Manila, which had been an open city since the twenty-sixth, most of the South Luzon Force cleared the Calumpit bridges by dawn on December 31.

About noon on the thirty-first, a new crisis developed at Plaridel, just south of Baliuag. (*See Atlas Map No. 9, Inset.*) Earlier that morning when the demoralized troops of the 91st Division reached Baliuag, Jones already had two battalions of Filipino infantry in Plaridel. Elements of the 71st Division moved up to support the forces in Baliuag. At 10:00 A.M., all the troops east of the Pampanga River— those in Plaridel and Baliuag—were placed under Jones's command so that he could coordinate the last withdrawals of his South Luzon Force through the Plaridel-Calumpit defile. Somehow Wainwright did not know of this development. He ordered the elements of the 71st Division and the remnants of the 91st Division to clear Calumpit by 6:00 A.M., January 1. At noon, the 91st began moving, and

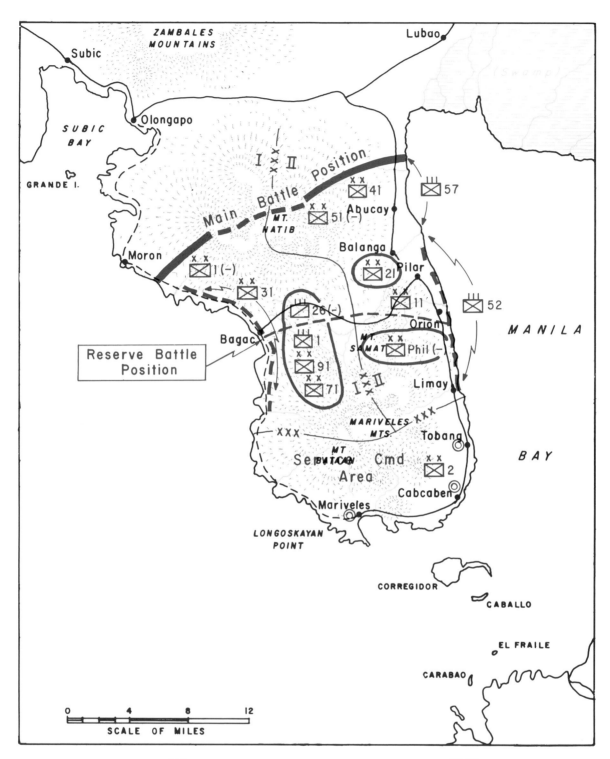

Allied Defensive Dispositions on Bataan, January 1942

shortly thereafter the troops of the 71st followed. Meanwhile, in Baliuag, the Japanese were massing for an attack, and General Jones was in a difficult predicament. After failing to stop the withdrawing units, at 5:00 P.M. the general ordered two tank platoons to make a spoiling attack into Baliuag. Totally stunning the Japanese, the tankers gained time for the remainder of the USAFFE troops to cross the Pampanga River. By 5:00 A.M., all but a few detachments were across the river headed for Bataan. At 6:15 A.M. with Wainwright watching, the bridges were blown.

On the west, Wainwright formed a new delaying position with his two western divisions, southwest from the D-5 line. Standing steady, these depleted divisions allowed the other forces to pass through San Fernando without difficulty. Wainwright then withdrew the two divisions to the Borac-Guagua line on January 1. There they beat off attacks by two Japanese regiments for three days. On the fourth, Wainwright ordered them into Bataan. One last blocking position was occupied, but the Japanese with heavy air support overwhelmed it, driving the last Filipino forces into Bataan on January 6. Here the Allies would make their last stand.

Bataan's great natural strength made it a defender's paradise. *(See Map, pg. 80.)* Three major mountain complexes, Mounts Natib, Samat, and Bataan, formed a central spur from north to south. Jungle covered the entire area except for the low rice and cane fields in the northeast. There was one perimeter road and one cross-peninsula road. The best landing beaches were on the Manila Bay shore, and the only port was Mariveles, across from Corregidor. MacArthur planned to hold Bataan in depth, deploying the I Corps (under Wainwright) from Moron to Mount Natib, and the II Corps (under Parker*) from Natib to just north of Abucay. He gave Wainwright four Philippine Army divisions (two of which had been badly mauled during the withdrawal from Lingayen) and the 26th Cavalry Regiment, while Parker received three divisions plus the 57th Regiment (PS) of the Philippine Division. The USAFFE Commander kept the bulk of the Philippine Division in reserve, and assigned the remaining units to the Service Command on Bataan and the Harbor Defense Command on Corregidor.

The main battle position was an unusual one. In the east, along the low ground, the troops had built excellent fortifications; but as the line approached Mount Natib, they had been unable to continue the construction because of inadequate tools, lack of time, and the extremely difficult terrain. Nor had Wainwright's sector been prepared prior to its occupation, although part of it had been surveyed before the war by officers of the Philippine Division which Wainwright had commanded. Wainwright's position weakened as it approached Mount Natib, just as Parker's did. In that area, patrols were assigned to protect the flanks of both corps. This inherent weakness worried most of the officers in the field as well as key men in USAFFE headquarters, but nothing was done about it.

Behind the main position, MacArthur feverishly worked on a reserve battle position, stretching from Bagac on the

west coast across the peninsula to the north of Mount Samat and on to the east coast near Orion. In prewar years this had been the planned main position, but the Commanding General had decided to defend foward of it to insure that it could be properly prepared as well as to protect the cross-peninsula road which paralleled it. Of the two locations, the Bagac-Mount Samat-Orion position was the stronger because it was placed on more mountainous terrain, its line could be held continuously, and it was shorter. Its main disadvantage was that it reduced the maneuver room of the defenders and subjected the rear installations to artillery fire.

Steeling themselves for the inevitable Japanese attack, Wainwright and Parker readied their troops on the main battle position. Each controlled about 22,000 men, but casualties, disease, and lack of supplies lessened their effectiveness. To make matters worse, the food ration was halved on January 6 because there were 80,000 soldiers on the peninsula instead of the planned 43,000, and there were also an additional 26,000 civilians.† On April 1, the ration would be halved again. Still the defenders of Bataan would fight grimly from their static positions and would surprise the Japanese, who underestimated their desire and capacity to fight.

The Japanese made a major mistake by concentrating on taking Manila rather than cutting off MacArthur's forces from Bataan. The city without the bay was useless.[37] They then compounded the error by withdrawing the *48th Division* a month early for the Java operation so that they could speed up their conquest of the Indies and turn their attention once more to the Soviet Union, still the major threat in the eyes of the Army's General Staff. When Homma did attack, he planned for pursuit-type operations against a weakened foe. To accomplish the task only four infantry regiments and one tank regiment were sent to Bataan. They were to prove inadequate.

On January 9, the Japanese attack came, with the major effort being made in the eastern sector. Parker's troops held reasonably well until the fifteenth. *(See Map, pg. 82)* But, by the end of the next week, the Japanese had pushed a regiment through the rugged ground around Mount Natib which had not been held in force, and in doing so threatened to envelop the left flank of II Corps. MacArthur ordered Parker to withdraw. By the same date, Wainwright also had to withdraw because a Japanese battalion had infiltrated through his undefended right flank, cutting the main road behind his position. Unable to destroy the Japanese battalion, Wainwright withdrew his forces along the coastal flats,

---

*General Parker had been assigned the mission of preparing positions on Bataan in December. The Philippine Division and two divisions from the South Luzon Force had been dispatched to do the bulk of the work.

† When MacArthur decided to defend all of the Philippines, prewar plans (ORANGE 3) to stock Bataan and Corregidor were scrapped. Supplies were moved to areas closer to the beaches. The responsibility for the lack of supplies must rest on MacArthur.

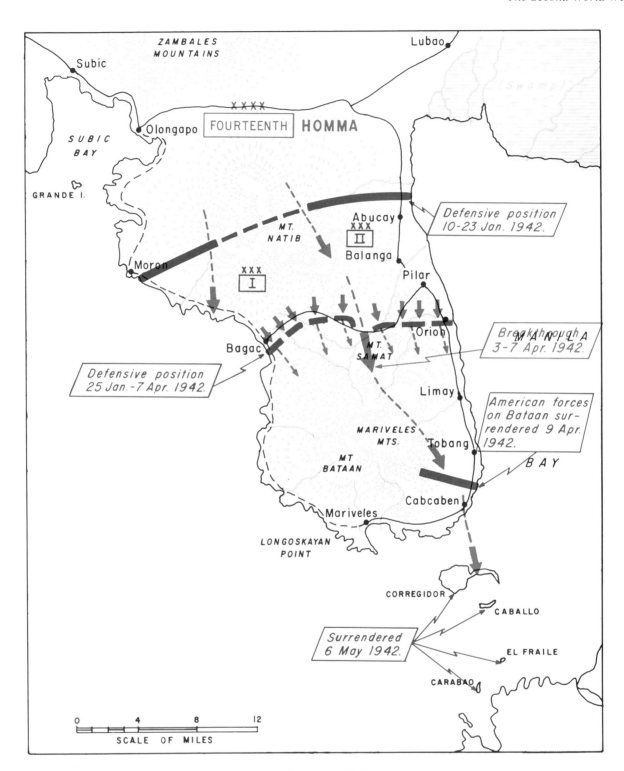

Battle of Bataan, 1942

leaving behind his artillery and transport. As predicted by many officers, Wainwright's and Parker's positions had fallen because the generals were unable to cover the rugged Mount Natib area with anything other than patrols.

Once the Allies occupied the reserve battle position there could be no further retreat. On January 22, the Japanese tried to envelop Wainwright's position with small amphibious forces, but were unsuccessful. Still I Corps had a hard time eliminating the pockets of enemy troops with the hodgepodge of units available. On January 26 and 27, the second series of major assaults struck the Allied line. By February 1, Parker had beaten off the attacks in his area. Wainwright, who had more difficulty destroying the penetration in the center of his zone, was not successful until February 15.

Homma's *Fourteenth Army* was now in bad shape. Instead of a quick victory, Homma had encountered World-War-I style operations, and his units had suffered greatly trying to batter the Allied defenders into submission. Many Japanese units had ceased to exit. On February 8, Homma reluctantly decided that he could not take MacArthur's position, and began withdrawing his forces to defensible terrain to the north. He would have to refit, re-equip, and reinforce his infantry before resuming the offensive.

Until April 3 the front was quiet. During this time the morale and health of the defenders dropped daily. Malnutrition and beriberi became common maladies. During the lull, few supplies reached Bataan even though three submarines arrived from Australia and ships were sent north from the Visayas with food.[38] On Bataan, hope for reinforcement dwindled. Nor was there much optimism in Washington, for on February 23 President Roosevelt ordered MacArthur to go to Australia. It was evident that the Philippine garrison was doomed, and that the talented soldier was needed to command the Allied forces in the southwest Pacific. On March 12, the general, his wife, his five-year old son, selected members of his staff (soon to be known as the "Bataan Gang"), and two naval officers boarded PT boats which took them to Mindanao. There, B-17s met them and flew them to Australia. General MacArthur arrived in Australia on March 17, and soon after landing issued a short statement to the press, concluding with the words: "I shall return." Those three words became the core of his strategic thought for the next three years.

Before leaving Corregidor, MacArthur reorganized his command. He set up a forward headquarters for USAFFE with his G-4 officer as the Deputy Chief of Staff, gave command on Bataan to Wainwright, and retained General Moore as the commander of the harbor forts. Sharp continued to command in Mindanao, and now all forces in the Visayas came under Brigadier General Bradford Chynowth. MacArthur left no one in overall command because he expected to direct operations from Australia. Unfortunately, the general did not inform the War Department of his arrangements, which led to some confusion in Washington where it was assumed that Wainwright was in command in the Philippines. Marshall objected to MacArthur's reorganization when he found out about it. While keeping Wainwright subordinate to MacArthur he ultimately made Wainwright the commander of all United States Forces in the Philippines (USFIP) with direct access to Washington. On Bataan, meanwhile, Wainwright

appointed Major General Edward King, the USAFFE Artillery Officer, to command Luzon Force. Marshall's decision would have unfortunate results.

MacArthur's dramatic escape and the changes in command did not overshadow the fact that the troops on Bataan were near collapse. When Homma's rejuvenated *Fourteenth Army* smashed into Parker's corps on Good Friday, April 3, it overwhelmed a dazed 41st Division on the left (the weakest part of the corps sector). (*See Map, pg. 82*) The intense air and artillery bombardment which preceded the attack guaranteed Japanese success. The next day, the Japanese continued to batter Parker's left flank. King used all available reserves to counterattack on the sixth, but the newly formed *4th Division* rolled eastward to the shore of Manila Bay. Withdrawal became useless and counterattacks impossible; the defenders were finished. With many of his units overrun and his hospitals and rear areas threatened, General King surrendered on April 9, even though I Corps was still in fairly good shape. He did so to avoid annihilation.

Since King had not surrendered all of the American forces, Homma immediately turned his attention to Corregidor, while subordinates began to round up and move the captured Americans and Filipinos to prisoner of war camps.* The journey of the captives—the Japanese considered them this rather than prisoners of war—became a march of death, one in which some officers deliberately planned to exterminate the captives.† For the Japanese Army, the Bataan Death March was a signal dishonor because during it the leadership, discipline, and every chivalric tradition of the Japanese warrior broke down. The grim story began early. On April 11, some 350 to 400 officers and noncommissioned officers of the 91st Division were bound together and executed *en masse* by Japanese officers wielding *samurai* swords and Japanese soldiers thrusting bayonets. Other men were bayonetted on the march by angry guards for seeking water or moving too slowly; a captain was beheaded on the spot for having some Japanese yen in his possession; and, on occasion, trucks

*Throughout the war, the Japanese treated their prisoners badly. Ruth Benedict probably sums up their attitude best when she relates that the Japanese considered prisoners to be "damaged goods." Ruth Benedict, *The Chrysanthemum and the Sword, Patterns of Japanese Culture* (Boston, 1946), p. 39.

†After the war, General Homma was executed by a firing squad for war crimes associated with the Bataan Death March. It is strange that he was so oblivious to such actions because he was probably the most western of all Japanese officers. In fact, because of his long association with England and his decent occupation policies in the Philippines, he was considered "too soft" by his superiors. According to John Toland, the ubiquitous Colonel Masanobu Tsuji was primarily responsible for issuing orders to kill prisoners in the name of Homma or Imperial General Headquarters. Tsuji was allegedly also responsible for the extermination of 5,000 Chinese in Malaya.

Lieutenant General Masaharu Homma

Sharp from his command so that only a minimum of troops would fall into Japanese hands. It was a wise move, because Sharp and his subordinates were capable of continued resistance, especially as guerrillas. While Sharp planned to concentrate around Del Monte airfield and defeat the attacking Japanese at the beaches, Chynoweth, the Visayan commander, had already begun moving supplies inland to mountain hide-outs to prepare for guerrilla warfare. When the Japanese landed on Cebu on April 10 and on Panay on April 16, Chynoweth had moved his forces to the hills.[41] By early May, Sharp had been forced to retreat to the mountains after two detachments from the north and part of the *Miura Detachment* from Davao had combined to defeat his small combat force. Both commanders, especially Chynoweth, were capable of carrying on, but they could not face the onslaught of regular Japanese units with their untrained and ill-equipped Filipino troops.

The American chain of command complicated Wainwright's problem. When he met Homma, Wainwright tendered the surrender of the troops on Corregidor and the adjacent islands, but the Japanese commander announced that he would not accept the capitulation unless Wainwright surrendered all American forces in the Philippines. Wainwright argued that Sharp was no longer under his command, but Homma countered this explanation by saying that American broadcasts had always indicated that Wainwright was the overall commander. Wainwright was caught in a dilemma. He fully believed that the Japanese would kill his Corregidor troops if the southern garrisons did not surrender, and he knew that his men could not fight on. In fact, while he was with Homma and during the temporary lull in fighting, Japanese troops had swarmed all over

drove into groups of marching prisoners, crushing the unaware and the slow-footed. Inexplicably, many groups were well treated by the Japanese guards along the entire route of the march. Approximately 600 Americans perished during the march, but Filipino casualties can only be estimated as having been between 5,000 and 10,000. For those who survived, Camp O'Donnell was an even greater trial. There, in not more than two months, over 1600 Americans and about 16,000 Filipinos died from malnutrition, beriberi, dysentery, and malaria because the Japanese failed to feed or care for the men properly.[39]

While the prisoners trudged northward, a determined Homma directed his artillery and air forces against the last American bastion, systematically destroying everything above ground. Most of the Corregidor garrison survived by remaining in Malinta Tunnel, but as the bombardment grew more and more severe, casualties mounted and the water supply dwindled. Still, Wainwright and his men and women hung on. Finally, on the night of May 5, a Japanese battalion landed between Cavalry and North Points on the tail end of the tadpole-like island. By noon, General Wainwright had begun negotiations for surrender.[40]

Prior to seeking terms with Homma, Wainwright released

General Wainwright Announces the Surrender of the Philippines, 1942

Corregidor and had even entered Malinta Tunnel. Reluctantly the American commander decided to surrender the Philippines; that night, on Corregidor, Wainwright signed the surrender document which promised that all other forces in the Philippines would surrender within four days. The following day, couriers were sent to active units on Luzon and to Sharp in Mindanao.*

Sharp also faced a difficult situation upon learning of Wainwright's surrender. He had been told by Wainwright that he was independent and had been advised by MacArthur to deal with the latter only. Now he had been informed by a captured Wainwright over Manila radio that he had surrendered all troops in the islands. Sharp too had released commanders from his control so that they could begin guerrilla operations. After Wainwright's courier convinced him that the safety of the Corregidor garrison was threatened, Sharp decided to surrender. He had a difficult time making his subordinates follow his lead, but ultimately they too capitulated when they heard that their intransigence could affect the survival of the men and women on Corregidor. By May 9, 1942, all organized units in the Philippines had officially surrendered. Those who did not choose to follow the lead of Wainwright and Sharp slipped quietly into the mountains to avoid capture.[42]

Throughout the islands in the following days, American and Filipino soldiers were assembled and moved into jails and camps where just like "the men who had survived the long march from Bataan and the bloody ramparts of Corregidor [they] found, at last, the bottom of the pit."[43]

Although the fight in the Philippines had finished on a more heroic note than had the one in Malaya, the final scenes were the same. It was the epilogue which would be different. Homma was relieved, and in the occupied Philippines, American and Filipino guerrillas remained to fight the war as best they could, longing as nearly everyone did for the day MacArthur promised to return.†

Loss of a Barrier: The East Indies

While battles raged in Malaya and the Philippines, the Japanese moved into British Borneo to seize the rich oil fields and useful airfields and to secure the flank of their forces operating in Malaya.[44] These small operations met little re-

*Lieutenant Colonel Theodore Kalakuka, USMA 1927, Wainwright's Assistant Quartermaster, was sent to contact a guerrilla leader in North Luzon. He was never seen again.

†It is hard to understand how much "I shall return" meant to Allied prisoners, internees, and Filipinos. For three long years it was a central belief of most who remained in the Philippines.

sistance on land because the British did not have the forces to spare to cover the primeval expanse which they governed, but Dutch aircraft and submarines managed to sink several Japanese ships (including two destroyers) during the various invasions. The Japanese landed at several places (Miri, Seria, Kuching, Jesselton, and Sandaken) during the period of December 15, 1941 to January 19, 1942 before the British dominions came under their nominal control. (*See Atlas Maps No. 6 and 10.*) These small actions were a sideshow to the more complex operations which the *Sixteenth Army* and supporting naval and air forces conducted in the Netherlands East Indies so that they could capture Java.

The pattern of Japanese operations in the Netherlands East Indies mirrored earlier exploits in Malaya and the Philippines. First, initial air strikes neutralized key areas and gained air superiority, after which landings were made to seize vital airfields and other important points. Then a new air umbrella was established to permit the leapfrogging of troops and aircraft forward in continuing operations. For the most part, British and Dutch reactions to the *Sixteenth Army's* attacks were similar to previous Allied operations. They relied first on their meager air forces to disrupt each Japanese landing. To assist, a stronger surface naval force husbanded from the remains of the various Allied squadrons in the area would contest the landings whenever possible, while submarines were sent out to interdict the amphibious convoys. Lastly, the Allies relied on their heterogenous ground forces to repulse landings or, if they failed to do that, to destroy the vital airfields as well as the great oil facilities before surrendering.

Once the initial objectives were taken in British Borneo, Malaya, and the Philippines, the Japanese strategists decided to launch a three-pronged attack southward to seize the oil resources in the Netherlands East Indies. (*See Atlas Map No. 10.*) Successful implementation of this plan would also cut the line of communications from Australia to the Philippines and Singapore so that Allied forces throughout the area could be isolated and destroyed. All operations pointed toward the final objective: Java.

The Japanese organized three major forces for the attack on the Indies. *Eastern Force** would stage in the southern Philippines at Jolo and Davao, then move southward to seize Celebes, Amboina, and Timor, to protect the flank of *Center Force** and to cut the line of Allied air reinforcement by seizing the airfield at Kupang, Dutch Timor. *Center Force** would strike from the same bases into Dutch Borneo to seize airfields and oil fields at Tarakan Island and Balikpapen and the airfield at Bandjermasin. These drives would be mutually supporting. *Western Force** would

** For clarity, the naval task force designations are used. Army elements came from the *Sixteenth Army.*

marshal at Camranh Bay (Indochina) and in Malaya, then would attack Palembang in southern Sumatra to capture the oil refineries and the large airfields. (*See Appendix 3.*)

On January 11, Lieutenant General Hitoshi Imamura's *Sixteenth Army* began its attacks. The *Sakaguchi Detachment* with the *Kure 2nd Special Naval Landing Force** landed at Tarakan after the small Dutch garrison had destroyed the oil fields. By the seventeenth, the Japanese were using the Tarakan airfield as a forward airbase, and a week later the mobile *Sakaguchi Detachment* took Balikpapen, only to find that the garrison had once again destroyed the oil fields. This time, Allied naval and air counterattacks were highly successful: a Dutch submarine sank a transport; a Dutch bomber sank another; and four combative American destroyers made a gun and torpedo attack at 3:00 A.M. on January 24, sinking four more transports in this foray. Although many ships were destroyed or damaged, the Japanese still easily overran the defending Dutch battalion, and by the twenty-eighth their air groups were operating from the Balikpapen airfields.[45]

By the time that *Center Force* reached Balikpapen, *Eastern Force* had advanced to Kendari in southern Celebes. On January 11, the *Sasebo Combined Special Naval Landing Force†* landed near Menado and Kema in northeastern Celebes, while the same day the Japanese dropped 334 paratroopers from the *Yokosuka 1st Naval Landing Force*** on the Menado airstrip. After the drop, the attackers were as confused as the defenders, and the battle did not swing toward the invaders until 185 more Japanese paratroopers landed on the twelfth. That day the airstrip was seized, and by January 24, aircraft were operating from it. The loss of Menado cut the line of communications with the Philippines for all but long-ranged aircraft and submarines. The *Sasebo Force* continued southeastward to take Kendari on January 24, gaining what the Japanese considered to be the finest airbase in the Indies, one which was within range of the air reinforcement route from Australia to Java. To protect their new gains, the Japanese sent the *228th Infantry Regiment (38th Division)* and the *Kure 1st Special Naval Landing Force* to capture Amboina on January 31. The small Dutch-Australian force succumbed to the attacks of the two fleet carriers and the invading force by February 4.

As the operations unfolded, General Sir Archibald Wavell, the newly appointed commander of the ABDA Command, was trying desperately to gain the time, the men, and the equipment to defend the Malay Barrier.†† Wavell hoped that Percival could hold Johore until he built up his air forces in Sumatra to contest Japanese airpower over Singapore. Reinforcements were on the way: 1,000 American planes were due within two months; an Australian corps would begin arriving at the end of February; even a tank brigade was slated for Malaya about the same time. Wavell knew that he was racing against time, and he well appreciated that the loss of Malaya, Sumatra, and Java would open up the Indian Ocean, Australia, New Guinea, and Melanesia to Japanese attack. Desperately he tried to coordinate Allied efforts so that he could hold the keystones for his planned defense: Singapore, the air bases in central and southern Sumatra, the Surabaja naval base in northeastern Java, and the Koepang airfield in western Dutch Timor. On paper, Wavell had adequate forces to execute his plan, but the ABDA units were no match for the Japanese, who could apply overwhelming air and naval power against any Allied position before assaulting it with small ground units.

The Japanese continued their advance in February, moving closer and closer to Java which was to be seized a month earlier than had been originally planned. *Eastern Force* sent the *Sasebo Combined Landing Force* into Makassar in southern Celebes on February 9 and the *228th Infantry Regiment* from Amboina to Timor on February 20, along with paratroops, who after marshalling at Kendari, dropped at the Koepang airfield. Only the sinking of a Japanese destroyer by an American submarine and the resistance of the Australians, who became instant guerrillas in Portugese Timor, marred the Japanese victories.[46] *Center Force* transported a battalion from the *Sakaguchi Detachment* to take Bandjermasin, but because of the loss of transports at Balikpapen, the Japanese landed far from their objective and attacked through 60 miles of mountainous jungles, capturing the oil center by February 10. In Sumatra, *Western Force* had the most difficult fight. On the fourteenth, 260 Japanese paratroopers from Malaya dropped on the main airfield near Palembang, while 100 more paratroopers jumped to capture the nearby oil refineries. In the bitter fight which followed, the defenders leveled their antiaircraft guns at the paratroopers to beat them off. In turn, the Japanese assaulted with grenades and small arms, suffering and inflicting heavy casualties. The paratroopers

---

*A Special Naval Landing Force (SNLF) was essentially a battalion with three rifle companies and a machinegun company. Its average strength was 800-820. The *Kure 2nd SNLF* also had an antiaircraft battery, increasing its strength to 1000. These units were not really equivalent to American Marine units, but were used for landing operations in naval spheres of influence.

† There were two 800-man landing forces in this combined unit.

**A battalion-sized unit of 1000 men with approximately 510 paratroopers.

†† Malay Barrier includes Malayan Peninsula, Sumatra, Java, Bali, Lombok and the other islands of the Lesser Sunda Group which stretch eastward to Timor. The anchors of the barrier are considered to be Burma and Australia.

took one refinery before it could be destroyed, but the Dutch were able to detonate their demolitions in the second facility. On February 15, 100 more paratroopers jumped to assist the airfield contingent, but it was not until that night that the troops of the *229th Infantry Regiment*, which had landed on Banka Island and crossed to Sumatra, linked up with the airborne soldiers, ensuring success. The battle for Sumatra ended when the Dutch commander decided to withdraw to the southwest.

By this time, Wavell had his hands full. His hastily organized, multi-national forces had failed to blunt the Japanese drives which had just about surrounded Java. Only an eternal optimist could fail to see that Java was doomed. On February 18, the day the Japanese invaded Bali and cut Wavell's line of communications to Australia, he told the Combined Chiefs of Staff that his air forces could only survive for two more weeks. Two days later, he declared that they could only last another week. On the nineteenth—that day the Japanese bombed Darwin—Wavell, deciding that the Dutch commander in Java could handle the affairs there, suggested to the Combined Chiefs that the ABDA Command be dissolved. The Combined Chiefs approved the recommendation, ordered Wavell to India, and made him Commander-in-Chief in India and Burma. When he left on February 25, Wavell predicted that the final Japanese attack on Java would come by the end of the month.

The Japanese planned a two-pronged attack on Java. In the east, the veteran *48th Division* and *Sakaguchi Detachment* would land near Surabaja to seize the town and the Dutch naval base there, clear the east coast, and capture the port of Tjilatjap on the southcentral coast. In the west, the fresh *2nd Division* and the accompanying *229th Infantry Regiment* would land on either side of Batavia, capture that port, and then drive into central Java to seize Bandoeng. To support the operation the Japanese had an estimated 400-500 fighters and 300-400 bombers as well as Vice Admiral Nobutake Kondo's entire fleet. The invaders would face about 25,000 Dutch regulars, 40,000 Home Guard troops, a small hybrid British unit called BLACKFORCE (3 Australian battalions, 25 light tanks, and some American artillery), not more than 100 operational aircraft, and a small fleet of 8 cruisers, 12 destroyers, and 32 submarines.

Landings began on the night of February 28, and within a week the Japanese had overrun Java. In the east, Surabaja fell on March 8, while Tjilatjap was occupied on the seventh. There was little resistance because the Dutch commander had deployed the majority of his forces in the west to protect Batavia, Bandoeng, and the airfields in the area. But even against the main ground forces the Japanese were extremely successful, capturing Batavia on March 5

and converging on Bandoeng two days later. The Dutch commander, Lieutenant General Hein ter Poorten, surrendered all forces on the eighth. He did not order his forces to resort to guerrilla warefare, because he was unsure of the Javanese loyalty to Europeans. The British commanders followed General ter Poorten's lead, surrendering on March 8 to avoid facing summary execution when captured.*

Of all the brutal fights of the campaigns, none were tougher than the two major naval engagements which preceded the invasion of Java. In the Battle of the Java Sea, fought in the afternoon and evening of February 27, the remaining five cruisers and nine destroyers of the Allies sortied under Rear Admiral K.W.F.M. Doorman, Royal Netherlands Navy, to intercept the Japanese transports headed for Java. In three separate engagements, the Japanese thoroughly defeated Doorman's force with little loss to themselves. Their aircraft and long-range torpedoes

---

*Throughout the war, the Japanese treated unsurrendered servicemen as bandits or outlaws rather than prisoners of war. Upon capture, these men were generally executed summarily. In 1945, some American officers dealt similarly with Japanese soldiers who contemplated resistance on Luzon after the Emperor surrendered his nation. Both actions were legal under the existing Rules of Land Warfare.

One of Japan's Young Warriors

made the difference. When the fight was over, Doorman had gone down with his flagship, the cruiser *De Ruyter*; furthermore, a Dutch cruiser, a Dutch destroyer, and two British destroyers had been sunk, while the surviving ships had scattered themselves throughout the Java Sea. All were eventually destroyed. In one succeeding fight, the Battle of Sunda Strait, the cruisers *USS Houston* and the *HMAS Perth* stumbled into the Japanese transports landing in western Java at Merak on the night of February 28. Opening fire, the Allied ships sank two transports and damaged several more at point blank range before the Japanese escorts (three cruisers and nine destroyers) arrived and sent the *Houston* and *Perth* under with extensive loss of life.[47]

The annihilation of the Allied fleet illustrated how powerful the Japanese actually were in March 1942, especially at sea and in the air. Throughout each campaign they had dominated Allied air and naval forces, making the outcome of the eventual land campaign painfully clear. Only in the Philippines had they failed. For the remainder of the war, there would only be minor opposition to Japanese rule in the Netherlands East Indies: SPARROW Force* in Timor would fight until evacuated in early 1943; American submarines would soon prowl the island waters; clandestine operations would occasionally disrupt the occupation when obsessed men like Captain Ivan Lyon† of the Gordon Highlanders would make their way back to the area; and finally, long-range American bombers would attack Balikpapen in late 1944 in a raid as daring as the one on Ploesti.[48] Except for these actions, the Indies remained an untouched Japanese oasis for the remainder of the war.

"Isn't That Burma Army Annihilated Yet?"

When General Wavell returned to India to become the Commander-in-Chief of British forces, he once again became intimate with the problems associated with the defense of Burma. For years, British officials had neglected the jungle fortress of Burma because they did not believe that any major campaign would be waged there. Even when war finally came, they paid more attention to the defense of Malaya, although they knew that Burma was the key to

India and the back door to China, and that on its soil were vital airbases which linked up to form part of the aircraft ferry route to General Percival in Malaya. For their lack of interest and concomitant lack of preparation, the British would suffer another extraordinary defeat at the hands of the Japanese, one which would shake more forcibly than ever the majesty and power of the British *Raj*.[49]

As the commander of the ABDA area, Wavell had been given control of all operations in Burma, and throughout his stay in Java he had tried to influence actions there.** He was too far away and too involved in the intimate details of the defense of the Indies, however, to command effectively on the continent. Still he was responsible for sending new commanders and new units to Burma, and when he returned to India as the Allied commander he was not totally ignorant of the situation facing him in Burma. Unfortunately, he never fully realized that his partially trained forces were no match for the Japanese. (*See Atlas Map No. 11.*)

By February 25, the day Wavell left Java, the first part of the Burma Campaign†† was drawing to a close and would end a few days later with the Japanese seizure of Rangoon. The first Japanese attacks went into southern Burma (Tenasserim) to capture the British airfields at Victoria Point (December 11) and Tavoy (January 19). The result of these small operations was the cutting of the British air line of communications to Malaya, the seizure of two airbases which could support Japanese movements into Malaya and Burma, and the British abandonment of a third airfield at Merjui (January 23) because it became untenable after Tavoy was seized. To protect Rangoon, the port through which all supplies entered Burma and through which lend-lease equipment was sent to China, the British command deployed its forces into Tenasserim, above Tavoy. This strategic move created a difficult tactical situation since the British troops were scattered and susceptible to piecemeal commitment, while at the same time they could be easily cut off by Japanese movement to the north toward Toungoo or even Pegu.

As the British deployed their forces to protect Rangoon, Lieutenant General Shojiro Iida, commander of the *Fifteenth Army*, having pacified Thailand and seized the southern airfields, began concentrating his two divisions, the *33rd* (-) and the *55th* (-),*** at Raheng, Thailand for the

---

*Once SPARROW Force was evacuated, no other Allied force ever survived after penetrating into Timor.

†On the night of September 26, 1942, Lyon and five other men sank five ships in Singapore harbor. They paddled in by canoes from a point nearly 20 miles away. This was Operation JAYWICK. A follow-up operation, RIMAU, failed. Lyon and all his men were killed, lost, executed, or died in captivity. Lyon's personal vendetta was one of the great adventures of the war.

** General Wavell was the British commander in India before being appointed the ABDA commander. As such he was responsible for the defense of Burma.

††Note the peculiarities of Burma: the long river valleys which dominate the country; the exposed border with Thailand; the lack of ports and overland routes to India; and the position of the country as a bridge or barrier between India and China.

***Both Japanese divisions fought with only two regiments during the initial campaign in Burma. After the fall of Rangoon, the *33rd Division* received its third regiment. The *55th* continued to fight with only two infantry regiments.

impending main invasion of Burma. Iida's aims in Burma were straightforward. He intended to protect the rear of the *Twenty-Fifth Army* in Malaya; secure the right flank of the *Southern Army* in Southeast Asia; threaten India; cut off the Burma Road, the last land route into China; and secure the vital oil, rice, tin, and tungsten resources of the country. To accomplish these goals, the Japanese first had to capture Rangoon, thereby isolating the Allied forces in Burma.

Japanese air forces began hammering Rangoon on December 23, and followed up their first attack on the city with a more intense raid on Christmas Day. Royal Air Force pilots in obsolete Brewster Buffaloes and "Flying Tigers" (American Volunteer Group) in P-40s challenged the Japanese and destroyed a substantial number of the attacking aircraft. During the ensuing raids, the Allied pilots, primarily those from the AVG, kept the Japanese from gaining air superiority over Rangoon. Accordingly, after costly raids on January 25 and 26, the Japanese gave up trying to gain air superiority over the port, resorting instead to spasmodic night attacks which proved ineffective. The primary value of the air raids was to drive away great numbers of the vitally needed Indian and Burmese laborers who unloaded the incoming ships.

Iida launched his invasion on January 20, and 10 days later Japanese forces captured the coastal town of Moulmein. The general then directed his two divisions to drive toward the Pegu, east of the Sittang River. There his divisions would split, one taking Rangoon, the other advancing north into the Sittang Valley toward Toungoo.

The Japanese advance rolled over the scattered units of the Indian 17th Division. By February 9, the *55th Division* had crossed the Salween River and cut off Martaban, while elements of the *33rd Division* infiltrated across the river further inland at Pa-an. Iida moved quickly in the north and kept the British from occupying their next prepared position, forcing them instead to withdraw to a poor position along the Bilin River. There the defenders were ordered to hold by the General Officer Commanding, Burma (Lieutenant General T.J. Hutton) so that reinforcements could continue to arrive in Rangoon and so that the Chinese could relieve the Burmese 1st Division in Toungoo, enabling it to join the 17th Division. The Japanese soon found that the British flanks on the Bilin were in the air, but they were unable to break the position for four days. On February 21, however, the defenders were ordered back to the Sittang River.

Unfortunately, the Japanese intercepted an order for the withdrawal, one which had been sent in the clear. At once the *33rd Division* commander sent a small force out to the Sittang to capture the only bridge across the unfordable river. The quick move failed to gain the prize, but it disrupted British plans to such an extent that the local

Lieutenant General Shojiro Iida

commander had to destroy the bridge prematurely on February 23 while two brigades were still east of the river.

The Sittang River obstacle broke the momentum of the Japanese attack where opposing forces had yet been unable to do so. While the British troops east of the river struggled to rejoin their mates in the west, the Japanese began to resupply their units for the first time in 34 days and to bring up bridging material. In the west, the British began moving their units into the area around Pegu to cover Rangoon and the southern entry to the Sittang Valley.

About this time, General Wavell, Commander-in-Chief in India and Burma, once again appeared on the scene. One of his first acts was to relieve General Hutton, who had consistently given accurate though pessimistic accounts of the situation in Burma, and who had just reported that it was unlikely that Rangoon could be held. Wavell, constantly urging the offensive, accepted General Sir Harold Alexander, one of the division commanders at Dunkirk, as the commander of the Burma Army. Alexander at first was as optimistic as Wavell, but after a few days in Burma he decided that the displaced Hutton, now his chief of staff, had been right when he said that Rangoon was untenable.

On February 27, Iida began probing west of the Sittang River with Japanese troops and with units of the renegade *Burma Independent Army*. On March 3, he crossed in strength, and moved to surround Pegu, block the road northeastward from Pegu, and drive toward the oil refineries east of Rangoon. By the fifth, Pegu was in Japanese hands. Iida then directed his *33rd Division* to take Rangoon while he sent the *55th Division* to take Toungoo. The *33rd* moved southwestward, crossed the Prome Road, left the road unguarded to enhance surprise, and then attacked Rangoon on March 8 from the northwest. The Japanese found an abandoned city. With the Prome Road open, the British had escaped the day before and were moving toward new positions near Prome.

With Rangoon in Japanese hands, the first part of the Burma campaign ended. General Iida finally had a port through which he could receive supplies, while the British and Chinese had lost their only major supply point. No road system existed yet between Burma and India, so all Allied supplies and reinforcements would have to be brought in by air. Allied success in Burma now depended upon the ability of the Burma Corps (Indian 17th Division, Burmese 1st Division, 7th Armoured Brigade, and supporting units) to hold in the vicinity of Prome in the Irrawaddy Valley while the Chinese Fifth Army* held in the Sittang Valley near Toungoo and the Chinese Sixth Army covered the eastern flank in the Shan States, the Karen Hills, and the Salween Valley.

In March 7 directives to General Iida, *Southern Army* ordered the general to destroy the Allied forces in Burma immediately, particularly the Chinese armies, and pursue them to the border of China. If possible a decisive battle would be fought near Mandalay. Iida was told to complete his mission by the end of May, the time when the monsoon would be in full force. To insure that the general could perform his tasks, *Southern Army* sent Iida the missing regiment from the *33rd Division*, the *18th Division* from Malaya, the *56th Division* from Java, two tank regiments, and enough squadrons to build the Japanese air forces up to 420 aircraft of all types.

The major Japanese attacks began in the east (near Toungoo) on March 19. The Chinese, now commanded by Lieutenant General Joseph Stilwell, fought well until they had to abandon their heavy equipment on the thirtieth and break out of the tightening Japanese cordon around Toungoo.† In the west, from March 28 to April 3, the Burma Corps, Lieutenant General William Slim commanding, withstood heavy Japanese attacks and tried to

support the Chinese by launching a counterattack to Okpo, 30 miles south of Prome. Unable to switch to the offensive, Burma Corps was forced to retire to save itself on April 3. Slim hoped to establish a new position to the north where he would be roughly in line with the new Chinese positions at Pyinmana, but he was unable to hold there. Falling back to the great oil fields around Yenangyaung, the British formations fought the Japanese in scorching temperatures, but once again the Japanese gained the upper hand. To assist, Stilwell dispatched his best division, the 38th, to Slim, and the Englishman and the Chinese division commander (a Virginia Military Institute graduate and the best Chinese commander of the war in Burma) pooled their forces and ejected the Japanese from Yenangyaung. The victory, however, was short-lived.[50] In the east, the Japanese had made contact with the Chinese at Pyinmana on April 16, and father east they had moved through sporadic resistance to surprise and decimate the Chinese 55th Division below Loikaw. Racing through the inept Chinese Sixth Army, the Japanese *56th Division* broke out into undefended country and moved quickly toward its goal: Lashio on the Burma Road. On April 23, Loilem fell, giving the Japanese a clear shot at Lashio. Stilwell recalled the 200th Division, which he had sent to reinforce Slim, and then personally led it east to retake Loilem and nearby towns.[51] He was too late. The *56th Division*, having replenished itself from captured stocks, was approaching Lashio, threatening the Burma Road and Mandalay with every march. The Allied flank had been turned; there were no fresh reserves to break the momentum of the Japanese attacks.

Before Lashio fell on April 28, General Alexander, now commander in Burma, decided to withdraw British forces into India and send the Chinese units back into China. From then on the Allied commanders fought essentially to extricate their units. Burma Corps, steadied by the indomitable Slim, retreated through Mandalay to Kalewa and then to Imphal. Most of the Chinese divisions returned to China as best they could, some leaving as masses of refugees. The Chinese 38th Division, however, retreated in good order into India. In the north, the irascible, 59-year-old "Vinegar Joe" Stilwell led 114 men and women over rugged mountain trails to safety in India. After this trek, his pithy conclusion to his first press conference summed up the Burma campaign for the Allies: "I claim we got a hell of a beating. We got run out of Burma and it is humiliating as hell. I think we ought to find out what caused it, go back and retake it."[52]

By May 20, General Iida had accomplished his mission in Burma, forcing the British to make the longest retreat in their history. The rains stopped him from continuing

---

*A Chinese army equalled a British division in combat power. Chinese units lacked artillery, tanks, and transport.

† General Stilwell was sent to China to be Chiang Kai-shek's Chief of Staff. In these early days he was appointed the commander of all Chinese forces in Burma, but such command was illusory. Chiang, in fact, was the commander; his subordinates would often not move unless he ordered them to do so. This difficult command situation constantly frustrated Stilwell as he tried to move his units quickly to counter probable and actual Japanese movements.

immediately into weakly defended India, and the gorge of the Salween River stopped him from moving quickly into western China. Nevertheless, Japanese forces were now in a position to bomb Calcutta. Moreover, as a result of a large Japanese naval raid into the Indian Ocean and the bombing of India (April 4–12), officials on the subcontinent feared an imminent invasion. Calcutta was nearly shut down as a port when the Japanese put forces ashore in the Andaman Islands in the Bay of Bengal and sank at least several merchant ships in their foray into the Indian Ocean. Many British warships had also been destroyed. Success in Burma and the Indian Ocean did seem to presage an early invasion of India. According to Wavell, it was "India's most dangerous hour."[53]

Japanese operations in Burma reflect once again thorough preparations, intelligent use of airpower, successful tactics, and aggressive generalship. Generals Slim and Stilwell agreed that Japanese airpower, the inadequate Allied preparation for war and paucity of troops and equipment, a hostile Burmese population, and fear of the Japanese soldier's expertness in the jungle played significant roles in the Allied defeat. Slim further noted that the Japanese had outclassed the Allies tactically, that British intelligence was inefficient, and that superior Japanese leadership undermined his campaign.[54] Stilwell, who was not as impressed with Japanese military prowess as Slim, put added blame on the vacillations of Chiang Kai-shek, the defeatist attitude of the British, and "stupid gutless command."*[55] Perhaps the fairest judgment is that the Allies were not prepared to fight in Burma, and once there they could have won only if they had used the massive reinforcements available from Chiang Kai-shek, who was both desirous and reluctant to engage the Japanese in decisive combat in Burma. The Allies did not do their best with what they had.

Burma also provides a laboratory for study of subjects other than military operations. Coalition warfare; integrated command; the use of foreign advisors and commanders; the reaction of Asian leaders to western strategy and postwar goals, as they involved the Chinese Communists; the use of Asian troops to fight western battles; and the impact of China on western strategy and operations are all subjects which, as sore points in the various Allied camps, strongly affected the early war in Burma. Most would complicate the war effort for the duration. In addition, two Allied generals are worthy of study: William Slim, the man who led the armies to victory in Burma in 1945 and who gained the respect of almost all who worked with him during the war;

*Stilwell's comments were made in his report to the War Department. They were so caustic that all copies were supposedly destroyed. Stilwell's comment on command probably applied as much to the British as it did to the Chinese. Slim was the only Britisher whom Stilwell really seemed to respect and trust.

and the remarkable Joseph Stilwell, who fought to build and lead a Chinese army into battle to destroy the Japanese, but who would find that final victory was denied to him. Both were fighters, both were leaders of extraordinary courage, and both were inextricably linked to the forgotten theater of the war—Burma. Through their eyes, the Allied defeat is seen in bitter perspective.

Victory

As Japanese forces swarmed over Malaya, the Philippines, the Indies, and Burma, the Army's *South Seas Detachment* and naval landing forces quietly occupied the Gilbert Islands and moved into New Guinea, the Bismarcks, and the Solomons, gaining important advance bases for naval and air forces at Tarawa, Hollandia, Lae, Salamaua, Rabaul, Kavieng, and Kieta. These actions completed the operations outlined for the first phase of the original Japanese war plan. Now the captured territories had to be assimilated into the Greater East Asia Co-Prosperity

The Victors

Sphere and garrisoned. Then the Japanese could ward off the expected Allied counterattacks. (*See Atlas Map No. 12.*)

By May 1942, the Southern Resources Area was a Japanese fief, its adjacent seas a Japanese lake, and the skies overhead a friendly haven. Yamashita, Homma, Imamura, and Iida, with the help of the air forces and navy, had conducted operations every bit as daring and successful as Yamamoto's attack on Pearl Harbor, defeating numerically stronger opponents with forces which were better trained, led, and supported. The value of tactical airpower had been proven over and over again, and amphibious operations had been used skillfully to flank Allied positions or to land at weak and vulnerable spots. While the land forces had been small, the overwhelming Japanese air and naval forces gave the generals their margin for victory. With such strength, the unorthodox centrifugal offensive had succeeded. Only on Bataan, in the air over Rangoon, off Balikpapen, and in the mountains of Timor, had the Allies put up a good fight; but even these actions came to naught against the Japanese juggernaut.

In victory, the hardest task is to keep one's edge and avoid overconfidence. By the summer of 1942, Japanese forces were beginning to relax after their six months of unparalleled activity, but in the Pacific the Americans were awakening from their stupor and beginning to fight back with more daring and determination. Before General Iida achieved victory in Burma, Lieutenant Colonel James Doolittle had led a group of B-25 bombers on a raid on Tokyo, while in the Coral Sea off Australia, an American carrier task force had fought a Japanese one to a draw. Elsewhere in the Pacific, Allied naval raids began; and behind Japanese lines guerrillas began to harass the victors.

As the Japanese forces relaxed in their new domains and began to savor their swift victories, the strategists in Japan began to refocus their attention on the war in China and the plans for a joint attack with Germany on the Soviet Union. The Pacific was relegated to its original position as an appendage to the China War, a dangerous move considering that the most powerful enemy the Japanese faced was the United States. It would be demonstrated later that the same ingenuity, leadership, and technology which had brought Japan victory could be applied more massively against the island empire by the rapidly mobilizing United States. Perhaps the high officials in Japan began to believe their own press clippings, succumbing slowly but surely to the dreaded malady of all conquerors—complacency.

Notes

[1]This section is based primarily on T. Dodson Stamps and Vincent J. Esposito (eds.), *A Military History of World War II*, Volume II, *Operations in the Mediterranean and Pacific Theaters* (West Point, 1956), p. 215 (Midway), pp. 215–216 (Wake Island), p. 216 (Guam) and Samuel Eliot Morison, *The Rising Sun in the Pacific, 1931–April 1942* (Boston, 1948), pp. 222–254 (Wake).

[2]This section is based primarily on Major General S. Woodburn Kirby, *et. al.*, *The War Against Japan*, Volume I, *The Loss of Singapore* (London, 1957); Brigadier General Vincent J. Esposito (ed.), *The West Point Atlas of American Wars*, Volume II (New York, 1959), Maps 116–118; Saburo Hayashi (In collaboration with Alvin D. Coox), *Kōgun, The Japanese Army in the Pacific War* (Quantico, 1959), pp. 29–36; and Masanobu Tsuji, *Singapore, the Japanese Version*, Trans. by Margaret Lake (New York, 1961).

[3]Tsuji, *Singapore*, p. 4.

[4]*Ibid.*, pp. 1–33.

[5]Donald Macintyre, *Aircraft Carrier, The Majestic Weapon* (New York, 1972), photos on p. 63, and pp. 78–79; Kirby, *Loss of Singapore*, pp. 506–509.

[6]For British plans see: Kirby, *Loss of Singapore*, pp. 169–176 and Paul Kennedy, *Pacific Onslaught, 7th December 1941/7th February 1943* (New York, 1972).

[7]For MATADOR see: Kirby, *Loss of Singapore*, pp. 76–77, 78, 170, 173–175, 180–182, 184–186, and 462.

[8]Kirby, *Loss of Singapore*, pp. 172–173 and 456–457.

[9]Tsuji, *Singapore*, pp. 61–67.

[10]*Ibid.*, pp. 41–56.

Ibid., pp. 52–67.

[12]Kirby, *Loss of Singapore*, Map 7, pp. 180-182 and Tsujii, *Singapore*, pp. 73–82.

[13]For the details of the Japanese plans, landings, and initial actions see: Tsuji, *Singapore*, pp. 61–96.

[14]Kirby, *Loss of Singapore*, pp. 203–213 and Tsuji, *Singapore*, pp. 111–118.

[15]Cecil Brown, "Tragedy in the China Sea," in Don Congdon (ed.), *Combat, The War Against Japan* (New York, 1969), pp. 9–42; Kirby, *Loss of Singapore*, pp. 193–199; and Tsuji, *Singapore*, pp. 96–103.

[16]Kirby, *Loss of Singapore*, pp. 238 and 245.

[17]Data on KROHCOL is found in Kirby, *Loss of Singapore*, pp. 170, 184–187, 207, 209, 212–214, and 229.

[18]Kirby, *Loss of Singapore*, pp. 269–272.

[19]For Kampar see: Lieutenant General A.E. Percival, *The War in Malaya* (London, 1949), pp. 194–199 and Kirby, *Loss of Singapore*, pp. 242–248.

[20]Kirby, *Loss of Singapore*, pp. 283–285.

[21]*Ibid.*, pp. 316–318, 403–404, and 410; Kennedy, *Pacific Onslaught*, pp. 50–51; and John Toland, *The Rising Sun, The Decline and Fall of the Japanese Empire, 1936–1945* (New York, 1971), p. 312.

[22]Kirby, *Loss of Singapore*, pp. 403–415.

[23]For the surrender see: Kirby, *Loss of Singapore*, pp. 414–415; Tsuji, *Singapore*, pp. 265–269; Toland, *Rising Sun*, pp. 312–317; Kennedy, *Pacific Onslaught*, p. 53; and Kenneth Attiwill, *Fortress, The Story of the Siege and Fall of Singapore*

(Garden City, 1960), pp. 221–226.

[24]Kirby, *Loss of Singapore*, p. 415.

[25]Tsuji, *Singapore*, p. 161, comments on Japanese jungle training:

> Mr. Churchill says in his memoirs that the Japanese Army had become expert in jungle warfare . . . this is high praise. But his comment is surprising. The 5th and 18th divisions had had abundant experience on the Chinese Front, but they did not even know the meaning of the word "jungle." The soldiers first saw jungle when they commenced the landings in Malaya.

Tsuji, pp. 56–57, also comments that he gave the *5th Division* its orders in Shanghai on October 28, 1941, and the *18th Division* its orders on October 29 in Canton. In retrospect, it is hardly possible for the Japanese soldiers to have been thoroughly trained in jungle operations in the time remaining before their assaults. According to Tsuji, pp. 32–33, the *Imperial Guards Division* was a typical palace guard outfit which had little expertise in field operations. Western commentators continue to speak about the excellent jungle training the Japanese troops received. I conclude that these claims are questionable. The Japanese units performed well because they were trained thoroughly and were combat veterans for the most part.

[26]Failure of British leadership is an interesting theme. See Kirby, *Loss of Singapore*, p. 468, for comments on leadership on Singapore; Stamps and Esposito, *Military History*, II, 230–231, for general comments; and Kennedy, *Pacific Onslaught*, p. 43, for comments about Percival.

[27]This section is based primarily on Louis Morton, *The Fall of the Philippines* (Washington, 1953).

[28]Morton, *Fall of the Philippines*, p. 30. For early use of the B-17 in Europe in July 1941, see Wesley Frank Craven and James Lea Cate, (eds.), *The Army Air Forces in World War II*, Volume I (Chicago, 1948), pp. 600–602.

[29]For Japanese plans see: Morton, *Fall of the Philippines*, pp. 51–61 and Koichi Shimada, "Air Operations in the Philippines," in *The Japanese Navy in World War II* (Annapolis, 1969), pp. 29–39. See also Saburo Sakai, with Martin Caidin and Fred Saito, *Samurai* (New York, 1967), pp. 46–50 and Morison, *Rising Sun in the Pacific*, pp. 46–52.

[30]Brigadier General Bradford G. Chynoweth, "Visayan Castaways" (unpublished manuscript), pp. 5–10; "Conversations" with Amelia M. Bradley (August 1972); and Lieutenant Colonel John L. Brownewell, "Dictations" (February 11, 1970).

[31]Shimada, "Air Operations," pp. 35–36 and Sakai, *Samurai*, pp. 48–56.

[32]For Clark Field action see: Morton, *Fall of the Philippines*, pp. 77–90; Craven and Cate, *Army Air Forces*, I, 201–212; and Shimada, "Air Operations," pp. 35–36.

[33]Brownewell, "Dictations," talks about his quiet afternoon over Manila Bay.

[34]Author's personal knowledge.

[35]Morton, *Fall of the Philippines*, pp. 92–97 and Shimada, "Air Operations," pp. 36–39.

[36]Theodore Roscoe, *United States Submarine Operations in*

World War II (Annapolis, 1949), pp. 34–39.

[37]Morton, *Fall of the Philippines*, pp. 58–59, discusses the Japanese decision. The American decision to withdraw to Bataan is analyzed in Louis Morton, "The Decision to Withdraw to Bataan" in Kent Roberts Greenfield (ed.), *Command Decisions* (Washington, 1960), pp. 151–172.

[38]Chynoweth, "Visayan Castaways," pp. 44–53, discusses his actions to send food to Bataan and Corregidor.

[39]For the Bataan Death March see: Stanley L. Falk, *Bataan: The March of Death* (New York, 1962), pp. 102–237; Lieutenant Colonel Wm. E. Dyess, *The Dyess Story* (New York, 1944), pp. 68–120; and Toland, *The Rising Sun*, pp. 335–344, 362–367, and endnotes, pp. 1025–1026.

[40]General Jonathan M. Wainwright, *General Wainwright's Story* (Garden City, 1946), pp. 104–127.

[41]Chynoweth, "Visayan Castaways," pp. 99–110.

[42]Wainwright, *Story*, pp. 128–156; Morton, *Fall of the Philippines*, pp. 562–584; and Toland, *The Rising Sun*, pp. 355–362.

[43]Charles Brown, *Bars from Bilibid Prison* (San Antonio, 1947), p. 34.

[44]This section is based primarily on Kirby, *Loss of Singapore*, pp. 221–227 (British Borneo), 291–299 (Celebes and Dutch Borneo), and 347–358, 417–449 (Sumatra, Timor, Bali, and Java). Also useful is Morison, *Rising Sun in the Pacific*, pp. 271–380.

[45]Morison, *Rising Sun in the Pacific*, pp. 285–291 and Kirby, *Loss of Singapore*, pp. 297–298.

[46]For detailed allied actions on Timor see: Lionel Wigmore, *The Japanese Thrust* (Canberra, 1957), pp. 446–494; Dudley McCarthy, *South-West Pacific Area—First Year, Kokoda to Wau* (Canberra, 1957), pp. 598–624; and Bernard J. Callinan, *Independent Company, The 2/2 and 2/4 Australian Independent Companies in Portuguese Timor* (Melbourne, 1954).

[47]For the battle in the Java Sea and the Sunda Strait see: Kirby, *Loss of Singapore*, pp. 435–442 and Morison, *Rising Sun in the Pacific*, pp. 343–358 and 363–370.

[48]For the exploits of Ivan Lyon see: Ronald McKie, *The Heroes* (New York, 1961) and Brian Connell, *Return of the Tiger* (New York, 1962). For the Balikpapen raid see: Captain Elliott Arnold and Captain David Hough, "Raid on Balikpapen," in Congdon, *Combat, the War with Japan*, pp. 218–233.

[49]This section is based primarily upon Major General S. Woodburn Kirby, *The War Against Japan*, Volume II, *India's Most Dangerous Hour* (London, 1958), pp. 1–22 (Plans), 23–46 (Early Operations), 59–78 (Bilin and Sittang Rivers), 79–114 (Rangoon), 145–186 (Central Burma), and 199–220 (Withdrawal). Also useful are: General Joseph W. Stilwell, *The Stilwell Papers* (New York, 1948), pp. 13–109; Field Marshal the Viscount Slim, *Defeat into Victory* (New York, 1961), pp. 3–99; and Barbara Tuchman, *Stilwell and the American Experience in China, 1911–45* (New York, 1972), pp. 328–385.

[50]Slim, *Defeat into Victory*, pp. 20–67, adds many pungent details.

[51]Stilwell, *Papers*, pp. 87–95.

[52]*Ibid.*, p. 108.

[53]Kirby, *India's Dangerous Hour*, pp. 115–131.

[54]Slim, *Defeat into Victory*, pp. 88–99.

[55]Tuchman, *Stilwell*, pp. 383–385 and D.D. Rooney, *Stilwell* (New York, 1971), p. 52.

Waltzing Matilda   5
The Early
Carrier War

I am still the sword
Of my Emperor
I will not be sheathed
Until I die

       Admiral Isoroku Yamamoto

Her sailors called the *Yorktown* the "Waltzing Matilda of the Pacific Fleet" because the great ship danced across the eastern and southern Pacific at a hectic pace during the first half of 1942, striking Japanese forces at one place after another and trying to blunt or divert new offensives. The irregular chart of the *Yorktown's* voyages typified the action of all the carriers of the Pacific Fleet in the early carrier war.[1]

American carrier task forces began their wartime operations immediately after Pearl Harbor when Rear Admiral Frank Jack Fletcher sortied with Rear Admiral Aubrey Fitch's *Saratoga* group to support the besieged garrison at Wake Island. Unfortunately, due to vacillation in the Navy's high command and indecisive action at sea, Fletcher never came to Wake's support even though on December 23, 1941, the day that the Japanese finally landed on the island, he was within 425 miles of the American outpost. In eight more hours Fletcher could have launched his aircraft, but instead he followed orders from Hawaii and turned back. Two other available carrier forces, Vice Admiral Wilson Brown's *Lexington* group and Vice Admiral William Halsey's *Enterprise* group, were operating west of Hawaii, but neither admiral was able to support Wake either. Many old salts could not understand the Navy's timidity at this time. The carrier task forces had little to brag about for their first sortie.

A more offensive attitude soon developed in the Pacific after testy Ernest King was appointed the Commander-in-Chief of the United States Fleet on December 20, 1941, and quiet Chester Nimitz became the Commander-in-Chief of the Pacific Fleet on December 17, 1941.* Assuming his new post, Admiral King directed Nimitz to guard the vital Midway-Johnston Island-Hawaii triangle in the eastern Pacific and to protect the sea route (Line Islands-Samoa-Fiji) of communications to New Zealand and Australia. (*See Atlas Map No. 13.*) Furthermore, King hoped that Nimitz would begin striking the Japanese as quickly as possible. This could not be done, however, until the small surviving garrisons in the Pacific were reinforced under the protection of the available carriers.

American offensive operations in the Pacific began in January 1942. The first carrier raid was planned for late January against the Japanese outpost at Wake, but after the Japanese torpedoed the oiler assigned to Admiral Brown's *Lexington* group, the mission was scrubbed. On January 25, however, Admiral Halsey, commanding the *Enterprise* group, was ordered to move northwest from Samoa, rendezvous with the *Yorktown* group, which was then south of him, and strike Japanese bases in the Gilberts and the Marshalls. It was hoped that this would stop any Japanese move from the mandated islands to Samoa.

Halsey, the overall commander, sailed in the *Enterprise* for the Marshalls while Rear Admiral Fletcher with the *Yorktown* moved into the Gilberts. (*See Atlas Map No. 13.*) While both commanders surprised the Japanese in their respective objective areas, neither of their air or surface forces did much damage, although their pilots claimed huge successes. About the best that could be said for the raids was that they were good training for the inexperienced American pilots and that they drew the bulk of the Japanese fast carriers into the central Pacific and back to Japan, away from the Bismarcks, Solomons, New Guinea, and the Netherlands East Indies.

*The admirals were all graduates of the United States Naval Academy: King, 1901; Nimitz, 1905; Brown, 1902; Halsey, 1904; F.J. Fletcher, 1906; and Fitch, 1906. Admiral King was not yet the Chief of Naval Operations.

Type	Commissioned	Tonnage	Speed In Knots	Aircraft
Lexington Class				
Lexington (CV-2)	1927	33,000	34	90
Saratoga (CV-3)	1927	33,000	34	90
Yorktown Class				
Yorktown (CV-5)	1937	19,800	32.5	81–85
Enterprise (CV-6)	1938	19,800	32.5	81–85
Hornet Class				
Hornet (CV-8)	1941	19,800	32.5	81–85

American Carriers in the Pacific, 1942

While these American raids had been going on, Japanese forces seized the small port and airfield at Rabaul, New Britain, and began building it into a major staging base, making it into the Truk of the southwest Pacific. The build-up at Rabaul threatened the Australian positions in New Guinea (especially the key base at Port Moresby), the Solomon Islands, and the Free French-controlled islands of the New Hebrides and New Caledonia, where Allied forces were being deployed. Rabaul also dominated the Coral Sea.

In late February, the United States Navy joined with land-based Allied air forces to raid Rabaul, after Admiral King placed Admiral Brown's _Lexington_ group under the temporary command of Vice Admiral Herbert Leary, the commander of the recently organized ANZAC force.* Charged with the defense of the eastern approaches to Australia and New Zealand in case of a Japanese thrust to the southeast against either country, Leary was overjoyed when Brown suggested that his group be used to attack Rabaul. On February 25, 1942, the _Lexington_ task force was within 225 miles of Rabaul when Japanese scout aircraft spotted the American ships. Soon Japanese bombers attacked.

Aboard the ships, fascinated sailors watched their pilots intercept the enemy bombers. In one amazing performance, Lieutenant (JG) Edward "Butch" O'Hare won a Medal of Honor and a two-grade promotion by destroying five out of the first group of nine bombers which attacked the American ships. Regardless of O'Hare's heroics and the remarkable performances of other Wildcat pilots, Admiral Brown had lost the element of surprise, and he could not take the chance of attacking an alerted Rabaul. Accordingly, late in

the afternoon, he reversed course and sailed for the Coral Sea.

Four days after the air battle over the _Lexington_, Halsey and the _Enterprise_ group were back in action. This time the target was Wake Island. Trying to divert Japanese attention from the southwest Pacific, Admiral Nimitz, at King's urging, ordered Halsey to strike Marcus Island, which was barely a thousand miles from the Japanese home islands. Halsey's pilots bombed Wake on February 24, moving on to attack Marcus on March 4. Neither attack accomplished much, although the officers and men of the task forces were improving their skills as they maneuvered across the vast expanse of the Pacific.

While Halsey was sailing from Marcus Island to Pearl Harbor, Brown and his _Lexington_ group rendezvoused with Fletcher's _Yorktown_ group off the New Hebrides in preparation for another attack on Rabaul. The Japanese landings at Lae and Salamaua changed the admirals' plans, however, and they decided to take advantage of the exposed Japanese positions in the Huon Gulf by immediately attacking the landing areas. (_See Atlas Map No. 13._) To do so quickly and at the same time to protect the carriers, the admirals decided to launch their aircraft south of Papua and have them fly across the rugged Owen Stanley Mountains to the targets, rather than to steam around the southeastern tip of New Guinea into poorly charted waters where their ships would be perfect targets for Rabaul-based aircraft. On the morning of March 10, the air raiders left the _Lexington_ and _Yorktown_, maneuvered through a 7,500-foot gap in the Owen Stanleys, and emerged undetected on the far side to find the unprotected Japanese ships unloading troops and supplies at Salamaua and Lae. In the ensuing attacks, the American pilots sank a converted light cruiser, a converted minelayer, a large minesweeper, and a freighter, although they claimed greater success.[2] It was the greatest victory the carrier pilots had yet achieved, but they failed to gain greater rewards because the Japanese ship captains weighed anchor quickly and headed for the open sea.

The most dramatic American carrier raid of the period came on April 18. Sixteen Army Air Force B-25 bombers,

*ANZAC Force was a combined American and Australian naval command organized by the Combined Chiefs of Staff. It included three heavy cruisers (_HMAS Australia, HMAS Canberra,_ and _USS Chicago_), a light cruiser (_HMAS Hobart_), two American and two Australian destroyers, and several Australian corvettes. It was under Admiral King's strategic direction. The ANZAC area was established on January 26 and abolished on April 22, 1942. It corresponded to the ABDA Area but covered the Australian, British, and French possessions east of the ABDA area; eastern Australia; and New Zealand.

*Wake Island Relief: December 1941 Rear Admiral F.J. Fletcher CV *Yorktown*	**Marcus Island Raid**: March 4, 1942 Vice Admiral W. Halsey CV *Enterprise*
*Wake Island Raid: January 1942 Vice Admiral W. Halsey CV *Enterprise*	**Lae-Salamaua Raid**: March 10, 1942 Vice Admiral W. Brown CV *Lexington*, CV *Yorktown*
Marshalls Raid: February 1, 1942 Vice Admiral W. Halsey CV *Enterprise*, CV *Yorktown*	**Tokyo Raid**: April 18, 1942 Vice Admiral W. Halsey CV *Enterprise*, CV *Hornet* (with 16 B-25s)
*Rabaul Raid: February 20, 1942 Vice Admiral W. Brown CV *Lexington*	**Battle of the Coral Sea**: May 7–8, 1942 Rear Admiral F.J. Fletcher CV *Yorktown*, CV *Lexington*
Wake Island Raid: February 24, 1942 Vice Admiral W. Halsey CV *Enterprise*	**Battle of Midway**: June 4, 1942 Rear Admiral F.J. Fletcher CV *Yorktown*, CV *Enterprise*, CV *Hornet*
	*Operations cancelled/aborted enroute.

United States Fleet Carrier Operations, December 1941 - June 1942

under the command of Lieutenant Colonel James Doolittle, USA, took off from the pitching deck of Captain Marc Mitcher's *Hornet* (part of Admiral Halsey's Task Force 16 which included his own *Enterprise*) and flew to Japan where they bombed Tokyo, Nagoya, Osaka, and Kobe.* After the attack, the Army pilots few toward designated landing fields in China, but because they had been forced to take off earlier than expected from the *Hornet* after the discovery of the task force by a Japanese picket boat, the Americans were unable to reach the fields. All but one of the crews crashed or had to bail out before the bombers reached their planned destinations. One plane landed in Vladivostok, and the Russians interned the crew. Most of the men—71 out of 80—survived the raid; one was killed when he jumped, three were executed by the Japanese, and one of the captured airmen died in his cell.[3]

President Roosevelt announced that the raid on Japan had come from "Shangri-La." His facetious comment amused a delighted nation which savored the success of the bombing in reparation for Pearl Harbor. The Japanese High Command, however, was stunned and unnerved by the raid. Fearing similar actions in the future, the Japanese leaders

---

*General MacArthur suggested such a raid while he was in the Philippines. President Roosevelt is often credited with the basic idea. Colonel (later Lieutenant General) Doolittle was awarded the Medal of Honor for his part in the raid.

B-25 Bomber

made several crucial decisions. First, four Army air groups needed in the Solomons were withdrawn to defend the homeland.[4] Also, the Army urged that the major Chinese airbases be captured immediately, and consequently Imperial General Headquarters issued orders on April 21 for such a campaign to begin very promptly.[5] The most momentous decisions, however, were made by the senior officers in the Imperial Navy. Deciding that something had to be done about the American carrier threat, they now supported Admiral Yamamoto's previously unpopular plan to attack Midway.[6] In addition, they suspended operations in the southeastern region* of the defensive perimeter pending the completion of the Midway action. A tactically ineffective raid, designed primarily to buoy American morale, had produced sizeable strategic results: it forced the Japanese to take the poisoned American pawn at Midway on their next move on the Pacific chessboard.

No Contact

While the American carriers were acting like gnats in the east, the Japanese carriers which had attacked Pearl Harbor maneuvered across even more imposing distances to support the movements of their ground forces. Enroute home from Hawaii, *Carrier Division 2* (*Hiryu* and *Soryu*), commanded by the brilliant, Princeton-educated Rear Admiral Tamon Yamaguchi, pulled out of the *First Air Fleet's* formation and headed south toward Wake Island. There the fast carriers supported the successful invasion of the American outpost and provided distant cover for all the forces involved. Ironically, if the *Yorktown* and *Lexington* had come to the support of Wake, the Japanese carriers would have welcomed the intervention. The central core of the Japanese air fleet's philosophy was the destruction of the American carriers, and no man supported it more than Admiral Yamaguchi, Yamamoto's possible successor. But the carriers did not make contact. This would be the scenario for many more weeks—until they finally met in May in the Coral Sea.[7]

Admiral Chuichi Nagumo's *First Air Fleet* went back into action during the period of January 20 to 23, 1942, when four large carriers moved south from Truk to support the invasion of the Bismarcks and the northern Solomons, and to harass the Australian positions at Lae and Salamaua. (*See Atlas Map No. 14.*) Once again the air groups of the *Agaki, Kaga, Shokaku,* and *Zuikaku* attacked their objectives under veteran commanders. There was really little for the air groups to do in the area, however, because the

Allies had withdrawn most of their forces. In fact, Commander Mitsuo Fuchida, was upset that the carriers were diverted from the central task of destroying the American carriers. In his eyes "a sledge hammer had been used to crack an egg. . . . "[8]

After returning to Truk, the carriers swung about their anchors as the Japanese admirals prepared to steam southwestward to support the continuing operations in the Celebes. When news arrived that Halsey had attacked the Marshalls, Nagumo's force was dispatched eastward to combat the threat; but after the Americans retired and nothing could be done, the admiral turned about. Enroute to Palau, *Carrier Division 5* (*Shokaku* and *Zuikaku*) was recalled to Japan by Admiral Yamamoto to patrol east of the home islands and thwart any future American attacks in that area. Yamamoto was obsessed with the fear that the Americans would bomb Tokyo. He particularly feared an attack against the Emperor himself.[9]

Admiral Yamaguchi, in the meanwhile, had sortied with his carrier division from Japan to the Banda Sea between the Celebes and New Guinea. There, on January 24 and 25, his aircraft attacked Amboina to soften up the objective for the troops who were scheduled to land on January 31. After other operations in the area, Yamaguchi rejoined Admiral Nagumo in Palau.

Vice Admiral Chuichi Nagumo

---

*The southeastern region included the Bismarcks, Solomons, eastern New Guinea, Papua, New Caledonia, Fiji, and Samoa.

Type	Completed	Tonnage	Speed In Knots	Aircraft
CVs				
Akagi	1927	26,900	31.0	66
Kaga	1928	26,900	27.5	72
Soryu	1937	15,900	34.5	57
Hiryu	1938	17,300	34.3	57
Shokaku	1941	25.675	34.2	72
Zuikaku	1941	25.675	34.2	72
Junyo	1942	24.140	25.5	48
CVLs				
Hosho	1922	7,470	25.0	15
Ryujo	1933	8,000	29.0	36
Shoho	1942	11,200	28.0	27
Zuiho	1940	11,200	28.0	27

Japanese Carriers

By February 19, Nagumo had brought four of the fast carriers into the Banda Sea in order to launch an attack on the Allied base at Darwin, Australia. The airmen of the *First Air Fleet*, including Commander Mitsuo Fuchida, flew 188 aircraft off the *Agaki, Kaga, Hiryu,* and *Soryu* early on the nineteenth. At 9:58 A.M., the Japanese flyers began a devastating raid on the Australian city, destroying 24 aircraft on the ground, sinking 10 ships, and damaging 13 more. At a time when the Allies were desperately trying to stock war supplies and deploy them from Darwin to the Netherlands East Indies, the losses were disheartening. A second attack launched from Kendari, Celebes added to the woe of the Allies, although it did not do the damage that the naval air attack had done.[10]

Following the Darwin attack, Nagumo's force moved to Staring (Teluk) Bay, below Kendari in the Celebes, from which it supported operations in the area, especially the Japanese invasion of Java. On March 3, in one significant raid, Nagumo's pilots bombed Tjilatjap, Java. Finding the harbor crammed with Allied ships, the 180-plane force destroyed an estimated 20 Allied vessels.

Until the fall of Java, Admiral Nagumo had had few losses among the pilots and air crews of his carrier divisions. Even more remarkably, the admiral had not had one of his ships damaged or sunk by enemy action. In his next two engagements, the admiral's luck would not hold. In the first, the Indian Ocean Raid, he would lose the first large group of experienced airmen; in the second, Midway, he would lose four carriers.

The Indian Ocean Raid had two major purposes: "to

Pearl Harbor Raid: December 7, 1941
Vice Admiral C. Nagumo
CV *Akagi*, CV *Kaga*, CV *Hiryu*, CV *Soryu*, CV *Shokaku*, CV *Zuikaku*

Wake Island Support: December 23, 1941
Rear Admiral T. Yamaguchi
CV *Hiryu*, CV *Soryu*

Bismarcks and New Guinea Support: January 20–22, 1942
Vice Admiral C. Nagumo
CV *Akagi*, CV *Kaga*, CV *Shokaku*, CV *Zuikaku*

Sortie to Intercept Halsey in the Marshalls: February 1, 1942
Vice Admiral C. Nagumo
CV *Akagi*, CV *Kaga*, CV *Shokaku*, CV *Zuikaku*

Raid on Amboina: February 24–25, 1942
Rear Admiral T. Yamaguchi
CV *Hiryu*, CV *Soryu*

Raids on Darwin: February 19, 1942, **Tjilatjap, Java**: March 3, 1942, **and Support of Java Operations**
Vice Admiral C. Nagumo
CV *Akagi*, CV *Kaga*, CV *Hiryu*, CV *Soryu*, CV *Shokaku*, CV *Zuikaku*

Indian Ocean Raid: March 8–12, 1942
Vice Admiral C. Nagumo
CV *Akagi*, CV *Hiryu*, CV *Soryu*, CV *Shokaku*, CV *Zuikaku*

Battle of the Coral Sea: May 7–8, 1942
Rear Admiral R. Hara
CV *Shokaku*, CV *Zuikaku*, CVL *Shoho* (under separate command)

Battle of Midway: June 4, 1942
Vice Admiral C. Nagumo
CV *Akagi*, CV *Kaga*, CV *Hiryu*, CV *Soryu*
Under Separate Command and Not Engaged:
CV *Junyo*, CVL *Ryujo*, CVL *Hosho*, CVL *Zuiho*

Japanese First Air Fleet Operations, December 1941-June 1942

impress the people of India with Japanese might and foment trouble in India at a time when Anglo-Indian political relations were particularly delicate"; and to secure the supply lines through the Straits of Malacca and the Bay of Bengal to Rangoon.[11] Admiral Kondo, the Commander-in-Chief of the *Second Fleet* and the naval commander of southern operations, directed the huge operation, which sent Vice Admiral Jisaburo Ozawa's *Malaya Force* into the Bay of Bengal to raid shipping and bomb India, a pack of submarines to the west coast of India to destroy merchant-men, and Admiral Nagumo's *First Air Fleet* to Ceylon to neutralize the British naval forces in the area—the major threat to the Japanese line of communications to Rangoon.

Sortying from Staring Bay on March 26, Admiral Nagumo led the *Agaki, Hiryu,* and *Soryu*, and the rejoined *Shokaku* and *Zuikaku*, into the Indian Ocean. (*See Atlas Maps No. 11 and No. 14.*) On Easter Sunday, April 5, he sent 180 aircraft under Fuchida against Colombo on the west coast of Ceylon; then, on April 9, he sent a similar force against Trincomalee on the east coast of the island. Japanese fliers destroyed many of the ground facilities at each target, while sinking a destroyer and a half dozen merchant vessels. In both these raids, however, the Royal Air Force challenged the attackers, and as a result the veteran Japanese air groups suffered their first serious casualties to enemy interceptors. At sea, Nagumo's fliers were even more successful. On the fifth, they sank two cruisers, and on the ninth they caught and overwhelmed the small fleet-carrier *Hermes* and her escorting destroyer.[12]

Once the carriers had entered the Indian Ocean, Admiral Ozawa's six cruisers and the Japanese submarines went to work on British shipping. Ozawa's force sank 92,000 tons of shipping (19 vessels) while the submarines destroyed 32,000 tons more off the west coast of India. Air strikes from the light carrier *Ryujo** began on March 5 against the east coast of the subcontinent, causing great alarm among the native population. When the Japanese forces withdrew through the Straits of Malacca, the British were expecting an invasion of India momentarily.

Admiral Kondo's massive raid was the first and last major Japanese sortie into the Indian Ocean. For the remainder of the war, those waters would remain under Allied control. A determined push in 1942 probably would have driven all the way to the coast of Africa and to the Persian Gulf with little difficulty; coupled with a German conquest of the Suez Canal, it could have been a disastrous development for the Allies, because India would have been completely isolated. Moreover, without sufficient numbers of carriers, the Royal Navy was impotent against the *First Air Fleet*; it had become abundantly clear in 1942 that only

carriers could stop Admiral Nagumo.

Enroute home, the Japanese carriers divided. The *Agaki, Hiryu,* and *Soryu* joined the *Kaga* for much needed maintenance and resting of crews in Japan. The *Shokaku* and the *Zuikaku*, under Rear Admiral Tadaichi Hara, steamed for Truk, where they would prepare for immediate operations in the Coral Sea.

The Japanese carriers had performed remarkably in the first months of 1942. Admiral Nagumo could be proud of their achievements. These ships had travelled over 50,000 miles; fought in two oceans and several seas; destroyed hundreds of Allied aircraft on the ground and in the air; sunk one British aircraft carrier, five American battleships, two British cruisers, and several Allied destroyers; and damaged or destroyed many other major vessels, merchantmen, and small fighting ships. Nagumo's veteran team was good, but the long campaign had thinned its ranks by 40 skilled airmen, the equivalent of the fighter pilots on the *Hiryu* and *Soryu*.[13] Thus began the debilitating attrition of the Japanese forces. Soon to be intensified by action in the Coral Sea, this continuing depletion raised the crucial question of Japan's staying power.

Japanese Strategical Arguments

During the time when the American and Japanese carrier forces were maneuvering across the Pacific and Indian Oceans, Japanese Army and Navy officers were trying to determine what should be done once the first phase (centrifugal offensive) of the inital war plan had been successfully completed and the second phase (consolidation) began. Opinions were divided along three separate lines: the Army General Staff,† the Naval General Staff,† and the staff of the *Combined Fleet*.[14] As a result, the Japanese war effort suffered, because the total resources available were committed to three different areas at times when they were needed at one major point of decision.

In early 1942, Army planners on the general staff were most interested in regrouping their combat forces on the Asian mainland to prepare for decisive action against the Chinese, while preparing for possible offensives against the Soviets in case the Germans smashed the Russians later in the year. As a result, several divisions were to be redeployed from the southern regions, leaving only token forces behind to pacify the conquered areas and to maintain law and order. Many Army planners insisted that no future operations be conducted in the southern areas because the Army

---

*Sometimes erroneously identified as the *Ryuho*.

† The Army and Naval General Staffs formed the Army and Navy Sections of Imperial General Headquarters in wartime. The staff desig-nation rather than the section designation is used in this text.

needed to construct defenses* to repel the British and American counterattacks, which were expected in early 1943. Navy pressure and changing conditions, however, forced the Army to consider expanded operations on the outer perimeter. Finally, the Army General Staff asked to deploy ground forces into the Aleutians, and agreed to assist at Midway as well as to move into the southeastern region of the planned perimeter (the Solomons, eastern New Guinea, Papua, New Caledonia, Fiji, and Samoa).[15] (*See Atlas Map No. 4.*)

More desirous of expansion than the Army planners, officers of the Naval General Staff, encouraged by recommendations from the staff of the *Fourth Fleet* at Truk, began to focus their attention on added operations in the southeastern region around the newly-captured base at Rabaul. The Navy had originally insisted that Rabaul be captured to safeguard Truk, but even in the prewar planning conferences, the *Fourth Fleet* commander had recommended that he seize key points in New Guinea and the Solomons to prevent enemy air attacks on Rabaul. These operations were included as possible actions in the *Combined Fleet* Operations Order of November 5, 1941, along with possible actions to seize other outlying areas such as Fiji, Samoa, the New Hebrides, New Caledonia, parts of northern Australia, Midway, and the Aleutians.[16]

After the Japanese captured Rabaul and Kavieng with ease, Naval General Staff officers urged immediate expansion to New Guinea, the Solomons, and other nearby areas, while the most aggressive of the group talked of invading Australia. When the Army rejected Australia on the grounds that it had insufficient troops and that there was inadequate transportation, the Navy planners looked for a less demanding task. (*See Atlas Map No. 12.*) On January 29, the Navy got the Army to agree to: a joint invasion of Lae and Salamaua in New Guinea; a naval invasion of the Solomons to seize Tulagi, possibly with the aid of army units; and the capture of Port Moresby in Papua, if possible.

By the middle of February, *Fourth Fleet* and the Army's *South Seas Detachment* had worked out the details for the operations, but a few days later the *Fourth Fleet* commander, Admiral Inouye, decided against executing the Tulagi or Port Moresby invasions because American carriers had entered the Coral Sea and the Japanese carriers, which had aided in the conquest of the Bismarcks, had returned to Truk. Admiral Inouye believed that the two operations were too risky; he would wait until the fleet carriers could be assigned to support the actions. While he was waiting for

the carriers, the admiral sent his forces into New Guinea (March 8) and then took the Shortlands (March 30), Buka Island (March 30), Kieta, Bougainville (March 31), the Hermit Islands (April 7), the Admiralties (April 8), and Talesea, New Britain (April 7–8)—all to secure his position at Rabaul.[17]

In early April 1942, the attention of the Naval General Staff was focused fully on the southeastern region where their air, ground, and sea forces were engaged, and where they planned to deploy two fast carriers upon their return from the Indian Ocean. In addition, the increased Allied naval and air actions in and around Port Moresby and the Coral Sea drew their attention. What really concerned the naval planners, however, was the necessity for an extension of the Japanese defensive perimeter to the southeast so that the Allies in Australia could not interrupt the consolidation of the Japanese gains. At the same time they were looking forward to isolating Australia from the United States by moving rapidly into the southern Solomons and Papua, and then into New Caledonia, Fiji, and Samoa. In essence, the Japanese had completed the first part of their plan to isolate Australia; when the carriers returned to the Pacific, they would begin the next step: the seizure of Tulagi and Port Moresby.

As Admiral Nagumo steamed for the Indian Ocean in early April, the staff of *Combined Fleet* presented a new plan of operations to the Naval General Staff for approval. This plan would change the whole course of the war.[18] The plan had evolved slowly from the analysis of several different propositions. The staff's premise was that it was unwise for Japan to sit back during the second phase of her war plan and mark time. Rather, it was imperative that the Japanese armed forces continue expanded offensive operations against the Allies, who were not expected to be capable of offensive action at sea for at least another year.

Admiral Matome Ukagi, Yamamoto's chief of staff, had begun considering three major alternatives in January 1942: an advance to the east to take Hawaii, an advance to the west toward India, and an advance to the south to take Australia. Ukagi personally desired to seize Hawaii so that the *Combined Fleet* could precipitate a battle which would allow it to destroy the carrier forces of the United States Pacific Fleet and shatter the American will to resist, always an important Japanese goal. When Ukagi's staff officers rejected his concept as too risky, however, the plan died. Another staff officer immediately proposed an attack on Ceylon, the destruction of the British Fleet, and a link-up with the Germans in the vicinity of the Suez. This proposal was studied for some time, gaining the general approval of the Navy; but the Army rejected it at a joint meeting in the middle of March because it would take too many troops.

After toying with such grandiose plans, the *Combined*

---

*The Navy at this time was responsible for defense of the areas east of Borneo and the Lesser Sundas. These areas inside the defensive perimeter had been secured with naval troops, and for the most part came under the control of the *Fourth Fleet* at Truk. (*See Atlas Map No. 4.*)

Fleet staff settled on a lesser scheme which involved the invasion and capture of Midway. The Japanese naval officers hoped that this would precipitate the desired decisive fleet battle which had been central to all Imperial Navy thinking since plans had been made years before to fight a hypothetical enemy fleet in the western Pacific. After gaining Admiral Yamamoto's approval of their scheme, the planners drafted a tentative Midway plan by March 29. On April 2, Yamamoto's representative began debating the merits of the plan with a representative of the Naval General Staff. General staff opposition centered on the questionable strategic value of Midway as part of the defensive perimeter, the problem of guaranteeing a decisive naval engagement, the inability of the Navy to resupply the carriers with new aircraft, and the belief that the Japanese Navy could probably get its desired naval battle in the southeast once the movement toward Fiji and Samoa began. The *Combined Fleet* representative heard the general staff officer out, and then asked for instructions from *Combined Fleet* Headquarters aboard the battleship *Yamato*. Admiral Yamamoto's reply was unflinching—if the Japanese were to succeed they had to destroy the United States Pacific Fleet, particularly its carriers. Faced with such a reply, the Naval General Staff officers capitulated. Midway was on. Once again, as before Pearl Harbor, Yamamoto's immense prestige overruled his theoretically higher headquarters. All that had to be ironed out then were the operational details. For some days thereafter, the two staffs haggled without much success, trying to resolve the various problems. Resolution came after Doolittle raided Japan. From that point forward, the Naval General Staff could not argue that their southeastern operations were more important than the elimination of the carrier threat. Still, something had to be done about the southeastern operations because the *Shokaku* and *Zuikaku* were enroute to Truk, and a few days later the invasion of the Solomons and Tulagi was scheduled to take place. By the end of the month, everything had been worked out. The Army and Navy agreed to conduct the drive into New Caledonia, Fiji, and Samoa after the Midway operation.[19] The Tulagi and Port Moresby invasions, however, would begin as scheduled.

On May 5, on the even of the Battle of the Coral Sea, Imperial General Headquarters issued Order Number 18, directing that the Midway operation be executed in June after Admiral Osami Nagano, the Chief of the Naval Staff, formally had given his approval for the action in the name of the Emperor.[20] Thirteen days later, after the Battle of the Coral Sea, the Imperial General Headquarters issued orders for the capture of key points in New Caledonia, Fiji, and Samoa.[21] In each case, the Army had supported the plans because it had so few troops involved.

Thus, by the middle of May, the three headquarters had resolved their differences and had fallen in line with the decision to expand the defensive perimeter by continuing offensive operations. The Army turned its attention to new campaigns in China while the Navy compromised and accepted two major tasks—the seizure of Midway, including the destruction of the United States Pacific Fleet, and the isolation of Australia.

American Arguments Over Strategy

On March 17, 1942, the United States assumed the responsibility for the defense of the Pacific while the British assumed the responsibility for the defense of the Indian Ocean and the Middle East, thereby changing the earlier concepts of RAINBOW 5. That same day, General MacArthur and his party landed at Darwin from Del Monte Field, Mindanao. Barely a fortnight later, the Joint Chiefs of Staff unofficially assigned MacArthur a new command. As a result, on April 18, the general officially became the Supreme Commander of the newly designated Southwest Pacific Area, a theater which included all of the Netherlands East Indies except Sumatra, the Philippines, New Guinea, the Bismarks, the Solomons, Australia, and the waters surrounding the various islands. For the remainder of the war, MacArthur dominated the area.[22]

The Joint Chiefs of Staff assigned the rest of the Pacific to naval commanders. In Hawaii, Admiral Nimitz, Commander-in-Chief of the Pacific Fleet, assumed command of the Pacific Ocean Area* and its three subordinate theaters —North Pacific Area, Central Pacific Area, and South Pacific Area. They also designated a separate Southeast Pacific Area to control the waters off Central and South American and Antarctica, but they did not place it under Nimitz.

While a single unified command was considered—both President Roosevelt and General Marshall strongly desired it—none was formed in the Pacific. The Navy vigorously resisted entrusting its fleet to an Army officer, particularly to MacArthur, who some naval officers felt did not understand how to employ air and naval forces properly. The Army, however, had virtually guaranteed their most famous and most senior officer the command in the southwest Pacific. Some command, therefore, had to be found for the general. To prevent unnecessary discord, the Joint Chiefs of Staff designated two huge theaters. They then appointed

*Later it became the Pacific Ocean Areas.

MacArthur to head the theater in which the Army had a dominant interest, while Nimitz gained command of the Navy's area of dominant interest. In essence, the Joint Chiefs acted as the overall Pacific commander, with Marshall directing MacArthur, and King directing Nimitz.[23]

American strategy in the Pacific in early 1942 revolved around the interests of both the Army and Navy, even though the announced policy of the United States Government was to defeat Germany first. However, as the Japanese moved toward Australia, New Caledonia, Fiji, and Samoa, and as General MacArthur, the Australian Government, and Admiral King began to make their ideas and demands felt, RAINBOW 5, which assumed that the United States would defend in the Pacific, was nearly abandoned.

From the beginning of the war, the Navy felt that the Japanese must be stopped quickly in the Pacific. To men like King, Australia, Hawaii, Midway, and the island and sea routes between them were positions which had to be secured immediately; they could not be lost, because they were defensive bastions as well as advanced naval bases. If they were all lost the fleet could not operate in the Pacific. Furthermore, having always considered the Pacific their domain, naval strategists tended to treat its defense as their primary task. Even more important, the threat of a continued Japanese advance brought an urgency to the situation in the Pacific which the admirals, especially King, believed had to be dealt with before Europe could be reinforced. As early as February 18, 1942, King—still the Commander-in-Chief of the United States Fleet—proposed an offensive against Guadalcanal in the Solomons. He even urged the establishment of a new base at Efate Island, New Hebrides to support the proposed Guadalcanal venture, and a further step-by-set advance up the Solomons to the Bismarcks. By March 5, the admiral's idea reached the President.[24] But King's ideas were a bit too audacious in February 1942, for the Allies were in trouble all over the world, and if Japan attacked India, Australia, or the Soviet Union, the situation would worsen. Much worse would be German victories in Russia or the Mediterranean. The Joint and Combined Chiefs had to consider the main threat.

For these reasons, King's idea did not sit well with the Army planners who were most interested in Europe.* While General Marshall agreed to send troops and aircraft to Australia and the islands along the line of communication in January and February, he did so to defend those areas

against further attack—not to build up the areas as bases for immediate offensive actions. He never deviated from his original concern for Europe, although he was buffetted from many sides. His staff stood by him, and in some cases was less forbearing. Brigadier General Eisenhower, Chief of War Plans, for example, became irritated with the drain of men and material to the Pacific, stating as early as January 22, 1942: "We've got to go to Europe to fight, we've got to quit wasting resources all over the world—and still worse—wasting time."[25]

General MacArthur proved to be an unexpected ally for the Navy. The general wanted to push hard against the Japanese, and even interpreted his "defend" orders to include an active defense in New Guinea, which had all the implications of a limited offensive. He put great pressure on General Marshall to support his strategy, and when frustrated in American channels asked Prime Minister John Curtin of Australia to pressure the American command through the British Government in London.[26]

In early May 1942, the American strategic problem reached an impasse as the American and Japanese commanders were beginning their actions in the Coral Sea. Marshall requested that the President rule on the priority between the planned build-up in England (BOLERO) and the reinforcement of the Pacific. The President replied in part on May 8: "I don't want 'BOLERO' slowed down."[27] His decision, however, did not end all problems, and it did not stop the flow of men and materiel to the Pacific, even after the scheduled deployments were completed.[28]

By the end of April, the Army, like the Navy, had sent large forces into the Pacific war zone and was preparing to send more. Reinforcements had built the Hawaiian garrison up to three divisions and 62,700 men. There were 16,900 ground troops in Australia and 30,400 were enroute, including the bulk of the 32nd and 41st Infantry Divisions. Sixteen thousand Army troops had arrived at New Caledonia, and they would soon be organized into the Americal Division. At Christmas, Bora Bora, Canton, Fiji, and the New Hebrides each, there were smaller garrisons and generally one pursuit squadron for air defense. Furthermore, there were over a thousand new aircraft throughout the zone, most of which were fighters based in Australia. Additional Marine Corps and Navy units were also on station at Palmyra, Midway, and Johnston Islands, complementing the Army ground and air deployments.

Within a few weeks the Army would have 140,620 air and ground troops in the Pacific. After the President made his decision on May 8, Army staff officers would break their backs to rush additional forces westward to bring the total up to the projected strength of 415,720 so that they could finally concentrate on the war in Europe.[29] Nevertheless, although the Army planners seemed glad to turn their

---

*At the London Conference of April 1942, the Allies decided to limit the resources to be committed to the war against Japan; reconfirmed their view that Europe had priority among theaters; decided to keep the Soviet Union in the war; and began planning for an invasion of Europe in 1943 (ROUNDUP) and an emergency landing on the French coast to assist the USSR (SLEDGEHAMMER).

American Troops Arrive at Noumea, New Caledonia in 1942

attention away from the war against the Japanese, they would find that the war in the Pacific and Asia would not go away.

First Contact: Scratch Two Flattops

The newly honed Japanese and American strategies clashed for the first time in May 1942, when contesting naval forces met in the Coral Sea. That beautiful sea became the battleground for evenly matched carrier forces which thrashed around in its placid waters for several days before making contact with each other.[30]

The Japanese plan to seize Port Moresby and Tulagi was as detailed and complex as most Japanese plans were during the war. (*See Atlas Map No. 15a.*) Admiral Shigeyoshi Inouye, commanding *Fourth Fleet* from Rabaul, broke his forces into five groups to fulfill the primary tasks of Operation MO. Two invasion groups of transports, destroyers, and smaller craft were formed to land army and naval forces at Tulagi and Port Moresby. A *Support Group* organized around a seaplane carrier group was to establish a seaplane base in the Louisiade Archipelago off the southeastern tip of New Guinea to assist the landings at Port Moresby. Also in support was a small *Covering Group* (the light carrier *Shoho*, four heavy cruisers, and a destroyer) and the main *Striking Force* (the two carriers *Shokaku* and *Zuikaku*, two heavy cruisers, and six destroyers). The latter would support both landings as necessary and protect the whole force from American carriers, which were expected to attack the Japanese during the operation. In addition, Admiral Inouye could count on, but did not command, land-based naval aircraft at Rabaul and subsidiary

bases in the area, which provided long-range reconnaissance, additional air strikes, and local protection. (*See Appendix 4.*) The Japanese landing forces would stage from Rabaul; the attack and support forces would move down at the last minute from Truk. The Tulagi invasion would begin on May 4. (*See Atlas Map No. 15a.*)

Before the Japanese assembled their forces for the encirclement of the Coral Sea, Admiral Nimitz learned through decoded radio intercepts, that the Japanese invasion force, supported by three carriers, would enter the Coral Sea.[31] By April 20, he had concluded that the Japanese would most likely attack Port Moresby on May 3. With his forces scattered all over the Pacific, and with little time for planning, Nimitz decided to send two carriers into the Coral Sea to stop the Japanese attack. On April 29, he ordered Rear Admiral Frank Jack Fletcher to "operate in the Coral Sea starting 1 May" with his *Yorktown* group. Nimitz then placed under Fletcher's command both Rear Admiral Aubrey Fitch's *Lexington* group and the American and Australian ships of "MacArthur's Navy," which Rear Admiral John Crace, Royal Navy, commanded.* Nimitz gave Fletcher no tactical instructions; battle dispositions and actions were left to him as the officer in tactical command. While this battle force would be the main Allied organization in the Coral Sea, Allied air forces, submarines from Australia, and smaller forces scattered around the nearby islands were also available to assist Fletcher. (*See Appendix 5.*)

On May 1, Fletcher met Fitch about 250 miles off Espiritu Santo Island (New Hebrides), and the admirals began immediately to refuel their carrier groups. The

*Admiral Crace was an Australian, but an officer of the Royal Navy. His group included two Australian cruisers, the American heavy cruiser *Chicago*, and two American destroyers.

following day, while Fitch continued to refuel, Fletcher moved slowly north to reconnoiter because MacArthur was reporting the approach of the Japanese naval forces. The two groups were to rendezvous farther west at daylight on May 4.

As the American carrier groups were leisurely refueling in the southern portion of the Coral Sea, the *Tulagi Invasion Group* (Rear Admiral Kiyohide Shima) began landing its forces on May 3 at 8:00 A.M. There was no opposition. The *Covering Force* (Rear Admiral Arimoto Goto) with the *Shoho* and the *Support Group* (Rear Admiral Kuninori Marumo) with the seaplane carrier *Kamikawa Maru* were waiting off the west coast of New Georgia in the central Solomons, in case of trouble. As soon as Admiral Fletcher heard about the landing at Tulagi from MacArthur, he changed all of his plans. Without waiting for the *Lexington* to join him, he decided to strike Tulagi the next morning. Before turning northeast, however, Fletcher sent his fleet oiler and her escort to join the forces under Fitch and Crace—to announce his change of plans and to direct the two admirals to rendezvous with him at daybreak on the fifth at a point 300 miles south of Guadalcanal.

Fletcher moved close to Tulagi without being discovered, and then, with the aid of a 100-mile wide cold front stretching across the Coral Sea, was able to send his aircraft undetected to their targets. Three strikes were launched throughout the day. The inexperienced American pilots met little interference in the various sorties, but their individual attacks against the small ships and boats in the harbor were not particularly effective. Only a destroyer, two small minesweepers, four landing barges, and some grounded aircraft were destroyed, although the jubilant *Yorktown* pilots claimed that they had sunk most of the Japanese fleet in the area. The American aviators were still not as proficient as their Japanese counterparts.

Withdrawing southward, Fletcher rejoined Fitch and Crace as scheduled on the fifth, and immediately began to refuel. Shortly thereafter a *Yorktown* fighter shot down a four-engined Japanese flying boat from Rabaul. Inouye never learned of the incident. As a result, he sent his aircraft to bomb Port Moresby rather than the American carriers. By 7:30 P.M., when Fletcher turned to the northwest to cut off the Japanese force which he expected to sail from Rabaul toward the Louisiades, Vice Admiral Takeo Takagi's *Striking Force*, with Rear Admiral Tadaichi Hara's two fleet carriers, was rounding the southern tip of the Solomons enroute to the Coral Sea.

By all rights, the opposing naval forces should have made contact on May 6, because on that date all the Japanese vessels (except the *Tulagi Group*) were moving toward the Louisiades. The Japanese commanders were lax in search-ing for the Americans: on the fifth and sixth, Takagi did not launch any long-range searches. Fletcher did little better, relying instead on the land-based aircraft from the Southwest Pacific Area to perform distant reconnaissance. Without detailed coordination, this was useless.

There were sightings made, however, on the sixth by both Americans and Japanese. One one of these occurred at about 11:00 A.M., when a Japanese scout sighted the American carriers. At about 10:30 A.M., three American B-17s bombed the *Shoho* (part of the *Covering Force*) south of Bougainville. At noon, Allied pilots sighted the *Covering Force* again; an hour later, other Allied pilots spotted the *Port Moresby Invasion Force*, just south of Rabaul. Nothing of importance came of these sightings.

On the afternoon of the sixth, Fletcher's intelligence officers, evaluating the reports of enemy activities which had been reaching the flagship, confirmed the admiral's hunch that the Japanese would try to force the Jomard Passage on May 7 or 8. Accordingly, Fletcher turned his forces northwest to be in position to intercept the enemy the following day. In Rabaul, Inouye estimated that the American fleet was about 500 miles southeast of his position. He, too, expected contact the next day. In fact, it should have occurred earlier. Takagi had turned south at 9:30 A.M. on May 6, but American scout planes had not spotted his force. Thus, before dawn on the seventh, the opposing fleet carriers passed within 70 miles of each other.

On May 7 things began to happen. Early in the morning, Takagi's scout aircraft located two American ships south of his position. When these were identified as a carrier and a cruiser, Admiral Hara launched the bulk of his attack aircraft to pounce on the big ships. Upon locating the two American ships, disappointed Japanese pilots discovered that they were an oiler (*Neosho*) and a destroyer (*Sims*), not a carrier and a cruiser. This did not deter them. In a furious attack, Hara's airmen hit the *Sims* with three 500-pound bombs, buckling her, and severely mauled the *Neosho*. The first round betwen the opposing carriers went to Japanese.

At about 8:30 A.M., Japanese aircraft from Rabaul discovered Crace's Support Group. Fletcher had sent Crace's force west at about 6:45 A.M. to search for the *Port Moresby Invasion Group* as it debouched from the Jomard Passage, while the American carriers maneuvered to meet the Japanese carriers. Crace knew he was being tailed, but without carriers in his force there was little he could do about it. Early in the afternoon, three groups of Japanese aircraft from Rabaul attacked Crace's force, but the Allied skippers skillfully maneuvered their ships at high speeds and avoided all damage. The Japanese pilots, however, returned to Rabaul convinced that they had sunk a cruiser and a battleship, and had torpedoed another battleship. Just

An American Carrier Prepares to Launch its Aircraft

after the action ceased, three American B-17s mistakenly attacked the Support Group. Fortunately, the American airmen were as unsuccessful as the Japanese had been.

Long before Crace's difficulties began, and while the Japanese were pummelling the *Neosho* and *Sims*, the pilots from the *Yorktown* and *Lexington* won round two between the opposing carriers. At 8:15 A.M. on May 7, an American scout reported that there were two Japanese carriers and four heavy cruisers north of the Louisiades. Upon receipt of this information, Admiral Fitch began launching from the *Lexington* at 9:26 A.M. A half an hour later, Fletcher followed suit on the *Yorktown*.*

Fletcher soon found himself in a difficult position. After his aircraft had left, Fletcher learned that his scout had seen cruisers and destroyers, not cruisers and carriers. With his attack aircraft out on a wild goose chase, Fletcher also discovered that he had just been sighted by a Japanese reconnaissance aircraft, which continued to report his position over the radio to Rabaul and to the *Shoho*. There was nothing for Fletcher to do but sweat it out. Inouye, however, took immediate action—at 9:00 A.M. he ordered the *Port Moresby Invasion Force* to turn back to avoid the

impending battle. Aboard the *Shoho*, Japanese planes prepared to attack the American carriers.

The American pilots found the *Shoho* with her escorts at 11:00 A.M., before the Japanese airmen could fly toward the *Yorktown* and the *Lexington*. In a matter of minutes the 93 American aircraft swarmed over the Japanese carrier. A few minutes later, Lieutenant Commander R.E. Dixon, a dive-bomber leader, announced to the *Lexington* (as the crews of both carriers listened intently to the chatter of their pilots during the assault): "Scratch one flattop! Dixon to carrier. Scratch one flattop!"[32] Round two had gone to the Americans.[†] Admiral Fletcher had achieved his primary objective by stopping the *Port Moresby Invasion Force*; it would never again enter the Jomard Passage.

After Fletcher recovered his aircraft he considered, but did not launch, a second attack. Fletcher really was not interested in destroying the escorts to the *Shoho*. He was after the big carriers, and as yet he had not found them. He also decided against continuing to search for the Japanese carriers since flying conditions were deteriorating, and it would be dark very soon. Instead he chose to rely on land-based aircraft to search as he turned his forces westward toward the Jomard Passage once again.

---

*Neither admiral commanded the carriers. Captain Frederick Sherman, Annapolis 1918, was the skipper of the *Lexington*; Captain Elliott Buckmaster, Annapolis 1912, commanded the *Yorktown*.

[†] American pilots reported sinking the *Ryukaku*, *Shoho's* sister ship.

Takagi was more audacious than Fletcher. At 4:30 P.M., the *Striking Force* commander sent off 27 aircraft to make a sundown raid on the *Yorktown* and the *Lexington*, but the veteran pilots were unable to locate the two American carriers during the remaining light. As they turned for home, disaster struck them. First, American interceptors shot down nine in a surprise engagement. Then six pilots mistook the *Yorktown* for their own carrier and tried to land on the American flattop. One was shot down. Finally, even when Hara turned on his searchlights to guide the returning aircraft, 11 more were lost trying to land on the *Shokaku* and the *Zuikaku*.*

Late on the seventh, Admirals Fletcher, Inouye, and Takagi all considered making night surface attacks, but none took action. Inouye made another important decision that night. He postponed the Port Moresby operation for two days.

The carrier forces finally found each other early on May 8. The *Yorktown* and the *Lexington* were steaming in bright sunlight just below the cold front, which still stretched across the Coral Sea, and the Japanese carriers were about 100 miles to the north, just along the upper edge of the front and east of the tip of the Louisiade Archipelago. (*See Atlas Map No. 15a.*)

Beginning at about 9:15 A.M., attack pilots from the *Yorktown* and *Lexington* took off from their ships in search of the Japanese carriers. By 11:00 A.M. the *Yorktown's* 39 planes approached the *Shokaku* and *Zuikaku* at varying altitudes. When concentrated, the dive and torpedo bombers went after the *Shokaku*, because the *Zuikaku* neatly slipped out of danger into a nearby rain squall. The Americans hit the *Shokaku* with two bombs. The damage, however, was far from fatal. Only launch operations were deterred. The *Lexington's* planes did not come into full action as planned because many became lost enroute and had to return to the carrier. The ones which did get through attacked the burning *Shokaku*, registering one more non-fatal bomb hit. As the Americans withdrew, the crippled *Shokaku* turned north for Japan. Round three had gone to the Americans.

The final round of the Coral Sea engagement went to the Japanese when they managed to catch the American carriers in the open, with only a few fighters covering the force. Diving out of a rising sun, the first group of pilots headed for the *Lexington*. Torpedo pilots attacked the carrier on both bows, dropped their ordnance nearly simultaneously from altitudes as low as 50 feet and at a range of 1,300 yards, and hit the *Lexington* twice on the

port side. Dive bomber pilots then scored two minor hits.[33]

During the 19-minute attack on the *Lexington*, other air groups struck at the *Yorktown*. This attack, however, had minimal success. By failing to launch a simultaneous torpedo attack, the air groups allowed the *Yorktown* to maneuver violently and thereby avoid the dive bomber assaults. One 800-pound bomb did strike Fletcher's flagship, but although it went down to the fourth deck, it did not do any major damage.

Confident Japanese pilots withdrew around 11:45 A.M., believing they had sunk the *Saratoga* (the *Lexington's* sister ship) and either the *Yorktown* or her sister, the *Enterprise*. They were completely wrong. Both ships survived. A couple of hours later, however, the end of the "Lady Lex" began when a motor generator, which had been accidently left running, ignited gasoline vapors deep inside the carrier. Laboring feverishly in the afternoon, damage-control parties tried to save the ship, but it became evident to all that the efforts were in vain. Admiral Fitch advised the captain to abandon ship. Just after the last men got off, more internal explosions occurred, as the fires reached bombs and torpedoes in the lower decks. At 9:56 P.M. the *Lexington* was scuttled, while many sailors who had served on her since 1927 watched sadly.[34]

Both sides broke contact after the battle. Inouye did not believe there was much more to be gained, since his forces had reported sinking both American carriers. Yamamoto, however, felt differently, and immediately ordered Takagi to follow up his attacks. His orders came too late, for Fletcher, under Nimitz's orders, had left the Coral Sea. Inouye's forces then returned to Truk, and the admiral rescheduled the Port Moresby invasion for July 3.

United States	Japan
CV *Lexington*	CVL *Shoho*
AO *Neosho*	DD *Kikuzuki*
DD *Sims*	
66 Aircraft	77 Aircraft
543 Killed/Wounded	1074 Killed/Wounded

Losses in the Coral Sea

Propaganda mills on both sides began to exaggerate national successes in the Coral Sea, as each country tried to concoct a victory for its people. In fact, the Battle of the Coral Sea was a series of mistakes, miscalculations, missed opportunities, and confused sorties which cost both navies serious losses in pilots, aircraft, and carriers. In the world's first carrier-against-carrier battle, the Japanese did win a tactical victory, but they failed to achieve their strategic goal—Port Moresby. Moreover, the loss of at least 77 more veteran airmen and the severe damage to the *Shokaku*

---

*During the Battle of the Philippine Sea in 1944, Vice Admiral Marc Mitscher turned his lights on also to recover his aircraft, even though exposing himself to attacks by Japanese submarines.

would add to their problems in the next major engagement at Midway.[35]

While the Americans were hurt most by the loss of one of the largest of their carriers, May 8 was a happy day for them and all the Allied forces in the Pacific because a Japanese offensive thrust had finally been blunted. The action in the Coral Sea was pronounced a great Allied victory at a time when one was sadly needed. Only two days before, General Wainwright had surrendered on Corregidor.

Soon after the fires of battle cooled, the *Yorktown* hightailed it for Honolulu, the repair yard, and a refitting for her last battle.

"You Will be Governed by the Principle of Calculated Risk."

While Inouye and Fletcher were jockeying for position before the Battle of the Coral Sea, another naval battle took place aboard the 75,500 ton battleship, *Yamato*.[36] On the first of May, the staff of the *Combined Fleet* met to test the plan for the attack of Midway by playing a detailed war game. In these table top maneuvers, reminiscent of the ones played before the attack on Pearl Harbor, planners clearly saw the problems, but took no heed.[37]

Admiral Yamamoto's operation plan for Midway incorporated two major goals and a diversionary move. (*See Atlas Map No. 15b.*) First, the admiral planned to seize Midway in order to expand the defensive perimeter, thereby gaining greater protection for Japanese forces in the Pacific and ultimately greater protection at home. But, most importantly, Yamamoto wanted to meet the United States Pacific Fleet off Midway and defeat it in a decisive battle. The attack on the tiny island was to be the bait for the more important of the two actions. Lastly, the admiral added an invasion of the American-held Aleutian Islands to his plan, to divert attention away from his true objective. The whole concept was involved and complicated, reflecting the Japanese penchant for surprise, gambits, diversions, and massive double envelopments which materialized out of thin air.* Japanese sea engagements resembled land operations, but all seemed heavily dependent on traditional ideas extracted from the game of *GO* and from the study of German doctrine which glorified Tannenberg and repeatedly extolled Cannae as the most classic of all battles.[38] If

Hannibal was the ancient master of stratagem, Yamamoto and his staff were the modern masters.

The Japanese distribution of forces at Midway was terribly complex. Five major forces were organized. None were in reinforcing or supporting distance of each other and, therefore, when the battle was joined Admiral Yamamoto found that his 11 battleships, 8 carriers, 22 cruisers, 65 destroyers, 21 submarines, and over 700 airplanes were scattered so widely that they could not be concentrated rapidly enough to destroy the 3 carriers, 8 cruisers, 18 destroyers, and 25 submarines which faced him. The plan negated Japanese fleet superiority from the start, allowing the Americans a chance to make a fight of it against each group with their smaller and less powerful force. (*See Appendix 6.*)

Most of the strengths and weaknesses of the plan reflected the character of the admiral who directed that the operation be conducted. Yamamoto was known to his intimates as a strong-minded, unequivocal, bold commander who was not afraid to gamble for big stakes. He also had the unquestioned loyalty of the Japanese naval airmen because he had been a major air enthusiast for years, even though he was not a pilot. The courageous and confident commander, however, had some blind spots, most of which affected the Midway operation. Foremost among them was his obsession with protecting Tokyo and the Emperor, an obsession which was intensified by the Doolittle raid. To Commander Fuchida, the admiral also seemed to cherish the old dream of the battleship admirals: he always was looking for the single, decisive fleet battle. Moreover, Yamamoto brooked no opposition to his plan, not even from the experienced Admiral Kondo who felt that the Japanese could gain the desired battle more easily by attacking toward Fiji rather than going for Midway. Furthermore, he would not even consider delaying the operation for a month to allow time for his crews to rest and for new pilots to be trained. In retrospect, Yamamoto was as devoted to the idea of attacking Midway and destroying the Pacific Fleet according to a fixed plan as his old antagonist Admiral Kimmel had been devoted to the idea that Pearl Harbor could not be attacked. As it turned out, his stubbornness would lead to a stunning reverse for Japan.[39]

During the war game, the roll of the die dictated that while the Japanese aircraft from the *Agaki* and *Kaga* were off attacking Midway, American land-based aircraft were bombing and sinking the carriers. This so startled the *Combined Fleet's* chief of staff, who was the chief umpire, that he hedged the losses and then reversed them. Accordingly, the games appeared to show that the plan could work, when in reality they proved that the plan had major flaws in it. It was like cheating at solitaire; outwardly everything looked good, but nothing had been achieved. Such did not

---

*Japanese operations remained complex throughout the war. These characteristics are severely criticized by Admiral Samuel Eliot Morison, the distinguished naval historian; but, as it developed, even a veteran carrier commander like Halsey nearly failed because of a similar Japanese strategy at Leyte Gulf.

happen before Pearl Harbor. Then the possibilities had been judged realistically; then the officers had been intellectually honest.

Although more time was needed for preparation, the average officer believed that the *Combined Fleet* could defeat the Americans without difficulty. After all, the lightly regarded *5th Carrier Division* had managed to hold its own against the best the Americans could send at it in the Coral Sea. Admiral Yamamoto himself disregarded the need for further preparation. The Japanese Navy was overconfident; victory disease was endemic to it.

Then there was the problem of communication. The *Agaki* did not have the sophisticated gear that the *Yamato* had, because tall masts interfered with air operations and, as a result, the *Agaki* would not be able to monitor vital enemy transmissions necessary to adjust attack plans. To remedy this, the *Yamato* could have sailed with the carriers, but this was disapproved. This idea was also suggested by Rear Admiral Tamon Yamaguchi, commander of the *Hiryu* and *Soryu*, because he felt that independent and complete task groupings would make the fleet much more powerful and flexible. Yamaguchi believed that it was time to use the huge Japanese battleships to help screen and protect the carriers (particularly with antiaircraft fire) rather than to rely on the carriers to support the battleships. His ideas were accepted, but his plans were not implemented.* Even more ironically, the staff shrugged off the possibility of a flank attack by American carriers once the Japanese aircraft were attacking Midway.

So when the *Shokaku* and the *Zuikaku* limped home from the Coral Sea in late May, the plans were set, criticisms were ignored, and recent experiences were dismissed. For all intents, Yamamoto reigned supreme. Even the reverse in the Coral Sea made no difference; it was, after all, a mere sideshow, with Admiral Hara's less competent carrier group and Admiral Inouye's less powerful *Fourth Fleet* the principal actors.

On May 26 (Tokyo time; May 25, Midway time), the *Combined Fleet* began deploying from northern Japan, the Inland Sea, and the Marianas. From northern Honshu, Rear Admiral Kakuji Kakuta's carrier force, assigned to the Aleutians, weighed anchor and sailed into the north Pacific at noon on the twenty-sixth. The next day the carriers of the *First Air Fleet*, commanded by Vice Admiral Chuichi Nagumo, departed; on May 28 the bulk of the Aleutian force sailed. From Guam and Saipan, elements of Admiral Kondo's *Midway Invasion Force* also got underway on the

twenty-eighth; his main force sortied the next day. Finally, on May 29, the Commander-in-Chief led the *Main Body* from the Inland Sea into the central Pacific. Just as before the attack on Pearl Harbor, Japanese submarines were to be on station off Hawaii, and three were specially placed to refuel flying boats at French Frigate Shoals (500 miles west of Hawaii) so that the four-engined aircraft could reconnoiter Pearl Harbor while the naval forces were enroute to Midway.

No commander could have been more impressed with his command. Across the stormy Pacific, Admiral Yamamoto led over 200 vessels to battle aboard the mighty *Yamato*, the world's largest and most powerful battleship. Its 18.1-inch main batteries could sink any vessel in the world, and they represented the ultimate in Japanese industrial and professional pride. The *Combined Fleet* was ready for a fight; if handled properly, it might well be invincible.

Yamamoto, like Achilles, had a great weakness, but unlike the ancient Greek warrior the Japanese admiral did not know what it was. Chester Nimitz, however, like Troy's Paris, did know Yamamoto's weakness, and he exploited it fully to defeat his more powerful adversary in an inexplicable and humiliating manner. For many weeks in Hawaii, intelligence experts had been warning Nimitz that something was brewing in the Pacific besides a push toward Port Moresby and New Caledonia. It seemed that the Japanese were planning a move into the central Pacific area.

Commander Joseph Rochefort[†] of the Navy's Combat Intelligence Unit in Hawaii had been working feverishly for months to analyze the bits and pieces of the Japanese messages which his unit and others were able to intercept and translate. Only 10 to 15 percent of a message could be picked up by the best of the code breakers, but bit by bit they were pieced together to form an interesting mosaic of enemy plans and activities. By late April 1942, Rochefort and his men had predicted the impending action against Port Moreby, but it was some time before Midway became apparent in Japanese messages. Still, there were increasing references to a place designated as "AF," one which Rochefort could not identify. From earlier intercepts, Rochefort's group believed that "AF" referred to Midway, so in mid-May the commander asked Nimitz if Midway could send a message in the clear to see if the Japanese would slip and refer to it in their own messages. Nimitz agreed. Midway promptly sent out a message saying that its fresh water-making machinery had broken down. Two days later a Japanese message reported that "AF" was short of fresh water. Rochefort then knew that Midway was the next Japanese objective. Two days later, on May 14, Nimitz put

---

*At this point in the war, Yamaguchi was probably the most experienced Japanese carrier commander, having participated in the raids on Pearl Harbor, Darwin, and Ceylon as part of a large force, and having conducted two individual independent operations against Wake and Amboina.

[†] In late 1940, Rochefort had helped to crack the Japanese naval code JN-25.

the Hawaiian Sea Frontier on invasion alert, and the following day King told Nimitz that a Japanese force would leave Guam on May 24 for Midway. Nimitz then ordered all ships under Fletcher to return to Pearl Harbor.

While members of the various services got more and more excited about coming events around Hawaii, the intelligence unit continued to monitor its wires. On May 25, Rochefort's men picked up a message which gave units, ships, captains, courses, and times for the forthcoming operation. The Japanese attack on Midway would occur around June 3, 1942.[40]

With that information, Admiral Nimitz went to work. First, his three carriers—*Enterprise, Hornet,* and *York-town*—would have to be used. The *Yorktown,* coming in from the Coral Sea, needed repairs, probably about 90 days of them, but the ship could only be given two days in dry dock if the Americans were to meet the Japanese threat. To insure that the carrier could fight, airmen—primarily veterans of the *Saratoga**—were transferred to her so that she would have a full complement of rested flyers. The other two carriers were in good shape,† but their commander, "Bull" Halsey, was not. Suffering from nervous exhaustion and a damnable itch which would not allow him to eat or sleep, the combative Halsey was ordered to the hospital by Nimitz and replaced by the "black-shoe" admiral, Raymond Spruance (Annapolis, 1907), Halsey's cruiser commander. Spruance, as cool as Halsey was hot, an officer's officer, was destined to alternate command with Halsey in the Central Pacific Area later in the war.

Finally, on May 27, Nimitz issued orders to subordinates: "inflict maximum damage on enemy by employing strong attrition tactics" from an initial position northeast of Midway—out of range of the Japanese search aircraft.[41] It almost seemed as if Nimitz had studied Jackson's famous flanking position in the Shenandoah Valley in 1862.

Before his commanders departed, Nimitz urged that they "be governed by the principle of calculated risk" and avoid attacking a superior force unless there was a good chance of inflicting greater damage.[42] The advice fitted American policy to fight offensively while on the strategic defensive.

*The *Saratoga* was torpedoed on January 11, some 500 miles southwest of Oahu. This attack sent her to Bremerton, Washington for repair and modernization. Moreover, her air group was broken up; the airmen found other active carriers or went to training centers.

† The *Enterprise* was in top shape with seasoned fighters. The *Hornet's* air groups, however, had never been in combat. At this time, the United States carrier situation was so critical that the British were asked to loan the Pacific Fleet a carrier from the Indian Ocean. The request was turned down. Later in 1942, however, they did send a fleet carrier to bolster the Pacific Fleet.

Nimitz was fortunate to have an experienced and cautious Fletcher and a level-headed Spruance—the aggressive Halsey might have fouled the admiral's plans.

Spruance deployed first with the two carriers. Once the *Yorktown* was ready, Fletcher would join him and become the Officer in Tactical Command, as he had been in the Coral Sea. (*See Appendix 7.*)

Admiral Nimitz knew that Midway was the sentry protecting Hawaii, and that it had to be held to safeguard the American position in the Pacific. He rushed reinforcements onto the tiny island so that by the end of May there was little room to move, and the garrison was prepared to repel all invaders. The admiral also had to worry about Alaska and the exposed Aleutians, because intercepted messages indicated that the Japanese also were going to strike there. While the Aleutians were of little military use because of the extreme weather in the area, the commander-in-chief decided that at least a token force would have to go north. Therefore, on May 17 he dispatched a task force of 2 heavy cruisers, 3 light cruisers, and 10 destroyers there under the command of Rear Admiral Robert Theobald. Nimitz, however, refused to believe that the Japanese planned to make a main effort in the north. Furthermore, he decided against sending carrier forces with Theobald. Nimitz would not sacrifice Midway by securing the Aleutians. This decision emasculated Yamamoto's deceptive maneuver to the north.

As the days in May passed, the tension grew in Hawaii because the Americans were facing the gravest of crises. Admiral Yamamoto's *Combined Fleet* could easily over-whelm all of the remaining Pacific Fleet in a pitched battle at sea; there was just no way that the Americans could stop the Japanese if the Japanese commanders fought their fleets capably. The Japanese would have to make mistakes and the Americans would have to minimize their own if they were to stop the potent thrust at Midway. Admiral Nimitz and his commanders knew that if they failed, Hawaii and perhaps the West Coast of the United States would be at the mercy of the powerful Japanese armada. In fact, there were many military men in Hawaii and the United States who believed that the Japanese were going to attack Hawaii and not Midway, and they were perturbed at Nimitz's preparations which concentrated on Japanese intentions (i.e., Midway) and not Japanese capabilities (i.e., Hawaii).[43] The specter of Pearl Harbor loomed large in many minds; but the Americans knew where the *First Air Fleet* was in May 1942, and this made the difference as the forces approached each other off Midway. Intelligence was Admiral Nimitz's chief weapon, security was Admiral Yamamoto's Achilles' heel.

Second Contact: Scratch Five Flattops

There were bad omens present aboard the ships of the *Combined Fleet* as it pressed eastward toward Midway.[44] The Commander-in-Chief was not feeling well aboard the giant *Yamato*, and on the *Akagi* the three renowned veterans of the Pearl Harbor attack were also out of sorts. Vice Admiral Nagumo, the torpedo expert who somehow gained the command of Japan's air fleet, was complacent and passive. He had never liked the plan for the attack on December 7, and while he had not objected to the Midway operation, Nagumo was uneasy for much of the voyage. No longer the dynamo of his youth, the admiral was not keen for this operation, the greatest of his career. Also, the air officers, Minoru Genda and Mitsuo Fuchida, were below par. Fuchida was struck by an attack of appendicitis on May 27, and remained in sick bay after undergoing surgery aboard the *Akagi*. He was soon joined by his Naval Academy classmate, Genda, who had developed a high fever and was thought to have pneumonia. To make matters worse, the great fleet ran into fog almost immediately; throughout the journey, Japanese navigators were troubled by its effects, as the ships zig-zagged across the Pacific. Furthermore, on May 30, one of the submarines which had been sent to French Frigate Shoals to refuel the flying boats which were to reconnoiter Pearl Harbor, found the Shoals occupied by two American ships. After a delay of 24 hours, the reconnaissance operation had to be cancelled, depriving the attacking commanders of last-minute reports on the Pacific Fleet. By June 1, the officers on the *Yamato* knew that something was wrong: messages, spottings of American submarines, and chance encounters of long-range reconnaissance aircraft indicated that the Americans knew or suspected something was up around Midway. Unfortunately for Nagumo, Yamamoto did not relay the information to him, and on the *Akagi*, the admiral could not monitor the American stations because of inadequate communications. Nagumo sailed literally and figuratively in a fog.

By June 2, Nagumo's force was rapidly closing on Midway from the northwest while the *Midway Occupation Force* and its supporting vessels, commanded by Kondo, closed from the southwest. Nagumo's ships entered a weak weather front some 300 miles out from Midway, tried to refuel, but discontinued the difficult procedure due to poor visibility. Farther east, the Japanese submarine I-168 reconnoitered Midway.

To the east, by June 2 the American carrier task forces had left Pearl Harbor, refueled at sea, and rendezvoused some 325 miles northeast of Midway to await the expected Japanese attack. Fortunately, they were not spotted by the Japanese submarine screens because those craft were late getting to their assigned positions between Midway and Hawaii. (When they finally arrived on station, the American ships were already west of them.) Spruance commanded the *Enterprise* and *Hornet* groups (Task Force 16), which had two squadrons of Wildcat fighters (54), four of Dauntless dive bombers (75), and two of old Devastator torpedo bombers (29). Fletcher, the Officer in Tactical Command, led Task Force 17, which included the repaired *Yorktown*. Aboard the *Yorktown* were four squadrons of aircraft: 25 fighters, 37 dive bombers, and 13 torpedo bombers. The 112 Dauntlesses were the core of the carrier attack force.

As the fleets approached each other, the Naval Patrol Wing on Midway began flying 700-mile searches to the northwest and west with slow and dependable Catalinas. The first patrol of 22 of these planes was dispatched on May 30. On June 3, the searches paid off. At approximately 9:00 A.M., Ensign Jack Read sighted 11 ships of the *Midway Occupation Force*. That afternoon, nine Army Air Force B-17s attacked the force some 570 miles from Midway, beginning the Battle of Midway. The American pilots claimed two hits, but in actuality no Japanese ships were damaged in the engagement.

The battle had really begun earlier in the day when Japanese aircraft flying from the *Ryujo* and *Junyo* broke through the foggy weather to bomb and strafe Dutch Harbor in the Aleutians. While the attack was successful, it did not alter Nimitz's conviction that the main event was still to come in and around Midway. (*See Atlas Map No. 15b.*)

As the preliminary actions developed, the undetected *First Air Fleet* continued to zig-zag through extremely thick fog toward Midway. Searchlights were turned on, and on each vessel the captain and his deck officers strained their eyes to watch for others ships and prevent collisions. On the *Akagi*, Admiral Nagumo was ignorant of the developing situation near Midway. He had no idea that there were any American carriers in the area, and remained wedded to the planning assumption that the American carriers would sortie toward the island following his strike on the tiny American outpost. The admiral knew all too well that he had contradictory missions—bombard Midway to prepare for its invasion and destroy the enemy fleet—but without additional information he accepted the advice of his senior staff officer and decided to go ahead with the Midway operation first. Following the air attack, which was designed to destroy the American air forces at Midway, Nagumo would turn his attention to the United States Pacific Fleet and its precious carriers.

On Midway, the air commanders continued to react to

Ensign Read's first report and the reports of the B-17s which had attacked on the afternoon of June 3. Late that night, four Catalinas were sent out to engage the Japanese. At 1:15 A.M., they made radar contact with the *Midway Occupation Force*. Immediately, the big planes dropped to low altitudes to begin their torpedo attack. At 1:43 A.M., in bright moonlight, they struck, hitting the oiler *Akebono Maru* which, however, made repairs and continued on towards Midway.

Within an hour or so, the main events of June 4 began. By then Spruance and Fletcher had moved from positions 300 miles east-northeast of Midway to nearly 200 miles north of the island in order to be in position at dawn to attack the Japanese forces. At 4:30 A.M., thirty minutes after daybreak, Fletcher launched his first search: 10 Dauntlesses flew 100-mile patrols to the north. The action was welcomed by the pilots, who had breakfasted at 1:30 A.M. and twice before had been up and down, reacting to alerts.

The Japanese pilots had been similarly disturbed with false reports of attacking aircraft. Finally, at 4:30 A.M., Admiral Nagumo sent his air groups to attack Midway. Control officers waved their green lanterns on the four carriers and the leading Zeros rolled down the decks and lifted off into the early morning sky. Nine Zeros were ordered to cover the fleet; nine more were on standby on the carriers.

From 215 miles out, Lieutenant Joichi Tomonaga of the *Hiryu* led the 108 planes toward Midway. The planes included 36 level bombers from the *Hiryu* and *Soryu*, 99 dive bombers from the *Akagi* and *Kaga*, and 36 fighters from all carriers.[45] Each group was commanded by veterans who knew their business. For Tomonaga, this was his first mission in the Pacific. After his attack wave took off, Nagumo brought his second wave of aircraft up on deck to be ready for immediate launching against an American fleet. In addition, at about 4:35 A.M., the admiral launched search planes from the carriers and cruisers, but he used single-phase searches which would give each pilot only one change to reconnoiter a given patrol route.

Midway reconnaissance aircraft were also up early looking for the Japanese. About 40 minutes after sunrise, one of these hit the jackpot. Lieutenants Howard Ady and William Chase, copilots of a Catalina, reported sighting enemy carriers. Their report was monitored on the *Enterprise*. A few minutes later, at 5:45 A.M., the lieutenants reported that many Japanese planes were heading toward Midway; these planes were picked up by the Midway radar at 5:53 A.M. when they were 93 miles out. Finally, at 6:03 A.M., Ady and Chase announced that two Japanese carriers were 180 miles distant from the base of the Catalina.

The intervening minutes were busy ones for Americans, both ashore and at sea. Every flyable aircraft at Midway took off at approximately 6:00 A.M. The fighters climbed immediately for advantageous positions to engage the incoming raiders; the Catalinas, B-17s, and other aircraft simply got out of the way. At sea, Fletcher ordered Spruance to steam southwest immediately to attack; he would follow once he recovered his scout aircraft. Back at Midway, six new Avenger torpedo bombers flew off to strike the Japanese carrier force.

At about 6:16 A.M., the opposing fighters engaged over the sea near Midway when the Wildcat and Buffalo pilots tried to intercept the Japanese bombers. The Americans could not get to the bombers because the veteran Japanese pilots in their Zeros pounced on the Wildcats and obsolete Buffaloes, shooting down 17 of the 26 American fighters while the Japanese bomber pilots bored into their targets. From 6:30 A.M. to 6:50 A.M., the Japanese bombed Midway, destroying the Marine command post, mess, oil tanks, and seaplane hangers, and damaging the powerhouse, hospital, storehouses, and gasoline systems. During this attack, Americans managed to shoot down 5 Japanese planes—American sources say 36—but, more importantly, Lieutenant Tomonaga radioed the *Akagi* and recommended that a second attack be launched to neutralize Midway's air force completely. At 7:15 A.M., the "All Clear" siren sounded; the first and last air raid of the day was over.

While the air battle raged over Midway, Admiral Spruance made his first critical decision of the day—he decided to launch an all-out attack against the Japanese carriers two hours earlier than planned and at an extended range, hoping to catch the Japanese carriers refueling their strike aircraft. Captain Miles Browning, the admiral's chief of staff and an experienced carrier expert, recommended the action based upon his detailed analysis of the course of the Japanese carriers, their speed, and the anticipated recovery time for their aircraft.

Spruance knew the calculated risk he was taking. His aircraft would probably run very short of gas over the long distance. Furthermore, the admiral knew he had been sighted by a Japanese scout aircraft and that he was vulnerable to a counterattack, even though he kept 36 Wildcats behind to protect the task force. Launching began at 7:02 A.M., and because it was slow, Spruance ordered his squadrons to attack piecemeal.[46]

Before Lieutenant Tomonaga returned to the *Hiryu* and before Spruance could launch all his aircraft, the six Avengers and four Marauders from Midway found the *First Air Fleet*. All came in low for torpedo attacks. Aboard the *Akagi*, Fuchida noticed that it was a beautiful day, saw the battleship *Kirishima* fire her main batteries at the Americans, and then saw Zeros dive through antiaircraft fire to shoot down the bombers. Five of the Avengers fell; one hit the *Akagi*, but bounced off. Two Marauders fell also. There were no torpedo hits, although the Army flyers claimed three and the surviving Navy crew claimed one torpedo hit on the Japanese carriers.

Although futile, the attacks by the 10 American bombers changed the course of the battle, convincing Admiral Nagumo that Midway, indeed, did require another strike. At 7:15 A.M., the admiral accordingly ordered that the torpedo bombers of the second wave, which were spotted for takeoff on the *Akagi* and *Kaga*, be re-armed with bombs. The deck crews began their exhausting work. The aircraft were sent below, where the torpedoes were removed and carelessly strewn around the decks instead of being disarmed and returned to the magazines. Bombs went on and the planes were taken up to the flight deck. A few minutes later, at 7:28 A.M., the cruiser *Tone's* floatplane reported that he had spotted 10 enemy ships. This announcement upset all Japanese assumptions. According to their hypothesis, no American ships should be in the Midway area until after the island had been attacked. Nagumo, faced with the prospect of a fleet engagement, suspended his earlier decision to re-arm the torpedo planes with bombs and ordered his command to prepare for a possible attack on the American ships.

At the same time, the admiral demanded more precise information from his pilot, but before he received it he had to weather another series of attacks. At 7:55 A.M., 16 Marine dive bombers found the carriers. Led by Major Loften Henderson, the inexperienced flyers were unable to come in quickly. Instead, they glide-bombed. Eight were shot down. Only two of the returning bombers were serviceable, because they had been so badly damaged over the fleet. One marine aircraft had 259 hits on it. No Japanese ship was struck. Just as the marine attack died out, 15 Army Air Force B-17s attacked from 20,000 feet, but the bombadiers also failed to hit anything, although they scored some near misses on two carriers (particularly the *Soryu*), which they claimed as four hits. Finally, the critically sought information reached Nagumo—*Tone's* observer reported that the sighted ships were five cruisers and five destroyers. At 8:20 A.M., he added that there was one carrier trailing the formation. This electrified the Japanese, forcing Admiral Nagumo to reevaluate his suspended decision to attack Midway a second time.

The admiral could launch the 36 dive bombers which were ready on the *Hiryu* and *Soryu* and the torpedo bombers on the *Akagi* and *Kaga*, most of which had bombs on them; but if he did send them off immediately to attack the American carrier force, he could not send fighters to escort them. (Nagumo had sent his standby and second-wave fighters aloft to engage the American aircraft which had just attacked him, and they would have to be re-armed and possibly refueled before they could be used to escort the bombers.) Besides the launching of an immediate strike, Nagumo had two alternatives. First, he could launch all the planes on the flight decks, put them into orbit, and recover the second-wave fighters. Once re-armed and refueled, the Zeros could then join the circling bombers for the attack on the American force. Second, he could wait, recover all of his aircraft, reorganize his forces, re-arm and refuel, and then launch his strike. Both alternatives would take time, and time was becoming more and more critical because American carrier aircraft were enroute. Nagumo, however, did not know this.

As the admiral pondered his decision, Lieutenant Tomonaga's planes began to arrive from Midway. The crippled aircraft needed to be recovered immediately. To add to the pressure building on him, Nagumo's aggressive subordinate, Tamon Yamaguchi, called from the *Hiryu*, advising the admiral to attack immediately with his available bombers. Furthermore, 11 Marine dive bombers tried to attack the carriers again, but they never got in close enough to do so. Then the submarine *USS Nautilus* fired a torpedo at a Japanese battleship, but it also missed.

By the time the crippled planes began landing on their carriers, Nagumo had decided to clear all his flight decks, recover his second-wave fighters and the Midway aircraft, re-arm all torpedo bombers with torpedoes, reorganize his forces, and then launch his attack. The *Akagi's* Flight Officer could only exclaim: "here we go again!"[47] The conservative Nagumo ordered the *First Air Fleet* to change course ninety degrees just after he had recovered his last aircraft at 9:18 A.M. The force headed east-northeast as 102 aircraft were prepared for takeoff at 10:30 A.M. About 300 miles away, Admiral Yamamoto and his staff on the *Yamato* monitored the various transmissions of the *First Air Fleet* on their powerful receivers. All the officers were confident: Nagumo was going for the American fleet, and the long-awaited decisive battle was at hand.

At 8:38 A.M., Fletcher entered the picture. He decided to launch his aircraft, and at 9:06 A.M., 35 of his planes were airborne. As they flew off toward the Japanese fleet, another deckload of fighters and bombers was hoisted to the *Yorktown's* flight deck to stand by. Eight Wildcats flew air cover over Task Force 17.

Because of Nagumo's change in course, the first American planes to reach his position (the fighters and dive bombers from the *Hornet*) missed the *First Air Fleet* completely. They had to turn for Midway to refuel, but those that made it safely—all the fighters and two dive bombers crashed when they ran out of gas—never took part in the imminent battle. At 9:10 A.M., Lieutenant James Gray, leading the

Enterprise's Wildcats, sighted the Japanese carriers; but the lieutenant did not report the contact. Below him he saw Torpedo Squadron 8 (*Hornet*) disappear into a cloud, heading for the carriers. Thinking the *Hornet's* bombers were the ones he was escorting from the *Enterprise*, Gray waited for the call to come down to protect them, but it never came.

The first carrier planes to attack the Japanese fleet were the 16 Devastator torpedo bombers from the *Hornet*. Led by Lieutenant Commander John Waldron, who knew he was on a virtual suicide mission because of the short range of his aircraft, the pilots of the large, slow bombers dropped to sea level for their first and only run at 9:30 A.M. As they did so, 51 Japanese Zeros swarmed all over them. In a few minutes, Torpedo Squadron 8 vanished as it headed for the *Soryu*.* Only Ensign George Gay survived to tell the story, and for the remainder of the day he had a ringside seat floating in his Mae West in the middle of the *First Air Fleet*.[48]

Five minutes after the first torpedo planes lumbered in, Lieutenant Commander Eugene Lindsey led Torpedo Squadron 6 (*Enterprise*) in against the *Soryu*. Once again, the Americans were slaughtered, as 11 of the 14 bombers were shot out of the sky. A half hour later, Lieutenant Commander Eugene Massey, the commander of Torpedo Squadron 13 (*Yorktown*), led a third attack, once again against the *Soryu*. Twelve of his 13 bombers were destroyed, and again there were no hits.

Until now, Nagumo had won all the rounds. Five American squadron commanders had perished and their squadrons had been destroyed when they assaulted the Japanese air and naval forces. On the *Akagi* and other Japanese carriers, the veteran air officers were unimpressed by the amateurish performance of the American pilots. They appeared clearly inferior in skill to the Japanese naval aviators.

But in the confusion of battle, the tide was about to turn. At 9:35 A.M., Lieutenant Commander Clarence McClusky, the *Enterprise's* Air Group Commander, spotted a Japanese destroyer making high speed for the horizon, and he assumed that it was heading for the carriers. Already beyond the anticipated attack point, McClusky had gambled on finding the Japanese fleet once; now he decided to gamble again by following the destroyer. At 10:00 A.M., Lieutenant Gray finally reported his sighting of the carriers to McClusky. Admirals Spruance and Fletcher overheard the report, but before they could react, Captain Browning told McClusky to attack.

Within a few minutes the *Enterprise* air leader found the four Japanese carriers steaming in an extended diamond formation. Luckily, all the Zeros were at low altitudes, where they had helped to destroy the torpedo squadrons. For a moment Nagumo had dropped his guard; in a flash, the knockout punch would erase the admiral's early lead in points.

At 10:20 A.M., McClusky ordered one squadron of Dauntlesses to follow him toward the *Kaga*, and another to take on the *Akagi*. The bombers rolled over into 70 degree dives, heading for the large Japanese carriers at 280 knots. Below, on the proud Japanese flagship, Admiral Nagumo had just given the order to launch when ready. Four minutes later, as the first Zero left *Akagi's* deck, lookouts screamed "Hell Divers!" Within seconds, three bombs hit the *Akagi*. Then four smashed into the *Kaga*, killing its captain and most of the officers on the bridge. By 10:28 A.M., the Dauntlesses from the *Yorktown* had hit the *Soryu* three times. Few of the hits would have been lethal under normal circumstances. However, with refueled and re-armed aircraft on deck and armed bombs and torpedoes lying around, the Japanese carriers were fatally vulnerable. Damage-control parties could not isolate the raging fires or overcome the severe damage on any of the carriers. The backbone of the *First Air Fleet* had been broken in five startling minutes.

The rest of the Midway battle was anticlimactic. The stunned Nagumo left his flame-shrouded bridge by rope, followed closely by other members of his staff. Fuchida, who had left sick bay to observe the day's actions, broke both ankles dropping to the anchor deck during his escape. The captain of the *Soryu*, however, refused to leave his stricken carrier, preferring instead to go down with his ship in the tradition which had also taken Admiral Phillips and the captain of the *Prince of Wales* to their graves barely six months before. On the *Yamato*, Admiral Yamamoto gave orders for all of his forces to concentrate for a continued attack; so initially did Admiral Nagumo. With the light carriers *Ryujo*, *Junyo*, *Hosho*, and *Zuiho* available for action, the *Combined Fleet* could still fight.

In the last hours of June 4, Rear Admiral Tamon Yamaguchi showed the pugnaciousness that made him a feared opponent. He immediately launched 24 aircraft from the *Hiryu* at 11:00 A.M. to attack the known American carrier, while the *Akagi*, *Kaga*, and *Soryu* burned behind him. His planes attacked and hit the *Yorktown* as the American planes were returning, bringing the *Yorktown* to a virtual crawl. About the time Yamaguchi heard of this success, an air observer told him that there were three American carriers in the area. The admiral immediately launched his second wave at 12:45 P.M. to attack the carriers. Lieutenant Tomonaga, with enough fuel to attack but not to return, led the *Hiryu's* pilots on their last sortie.

---

*All the pilots in Torpedo Squadron 8 were awarded the Navy Cross. The crewmen were given Distinguished Flying Crosses.

The veteran air leader died when his plane exploded just short of the *Yorktown*, the ship which the Japanese believed to be a second American carrier. Although the *Yorktown* had shaken off the effects of the first attack and was making about 20 knots and launching aircraft, Tomonaga's men hit her with two torpedoes, bringing the "Waltzing Matilda" to a stop. At 3:00 P.M., the captain ordered "Abandon Ship."

To the north, Admiral Spruance's force had not been attacked, and at 2:45 P.M., when an American pilot reported the *Hiryu's* position to the admiral, he sent off 24 dive bombers without fighter escort to destroy the remaining fast carrier. The bomber pilots screamed down on the *Hiryu* at 5:00 P.M., just after the ship's crew had broken from General Quarters for a quick supper of sweet rice balls, preparatory to launching a sunset attack on the American carriers with the 15 remaining aircraft of the *First Air Fleet*. In seconds, four bombs fatally damaged Yamaguchi's flagship; an hour later Midway-based B-17s tried to add to the damage, but scored no hits. The *Hiryu* had to be scuttled, but like the *Yorktown* she went down hard. She took about 416 men with her, including her captain and Admiral Yamaguchi, who remained to atone for his failures. Both officers refused to leave, tying themselves to the bridge to insure that they went under with the carrier. Before this final act, Ensign Sandanori Kawakami, custodian of the Emperor's portrait, transferred the portrait to a waiting destroyer; that too was a tradition in the Imperial Japanese Navy.[49]

The last acts of June 4 were left to Spruance and Yamamoto. The American retired eastward at 7:07 P.M. rather than risk a night surface engagement with the still deadly *Combined Fleet*, which he knew had battleships and carriers and was well trained for night action. Spruance could ill afford to allow his small task force to be engulfed by his powerful opponent in a close engagement. A few minutes later, Yamamoto ordered Nagumo to continue the attack, but all the fight had gone out of the carrier commander, who had witnessed the destruction of his previously undamaged force. At 11:40 P.M., the Commander-in-Chief replaced the beaten Nagumo with the determined Admiral Kondo, who was steaming hard to assist the carrier force with the bulk of the *Second Fleet*. Aboard the cruiser, Nagumo and his staff contemplated suicide.[50] At 2:55 A.M. on June 5, Yamamoto changed his mind and ordered a general retirement. But he did not stop thinking of striking back. Not until two days later did he give up trying to bait Spruance into a trap. Thereupon he retired for good.

During those two days, the American fleet struck again. Turning westward on the fifth, Spruance's planes finally found and sank the new heavy cruiser *Mikuma*, which had been crippled in a collision with her sister ship *Mogami* during an attack by the American submarine *Tambor*. This was the last major American victory; it was fitting, although unknown, revenge for the *Perth* and the *Houston*, victims in Sunda Straight of the *Mikuma* and her sister.

The only Japanese victory of the battle came on June 6, when an attack finally sent the *Yorktown* to the bottom. The carrier had not sunk after being abandoned, and as a result a damage-control party had gone back aboard to try to save her. All was progressing satisfactorily when the Japanese submarine *I-168* slipped inside the destroyer screen and sent two torpedoes into the carrier at about 1:30 P.M. Two other torpedoes broke the escorting destroyer in two, sinking her in four minutes, with great loss of life.

At sunset on June 6, Spruance turned his task force eastward for Pearl Harbor. Fletcher joined him. As the admirals and their men sailed home, they knew that they had been in a fight. They had lost 99 carrier aircraft, 38 Midway-based aircraft, the *Yorktown*, and the destroyer *Hammann*. But compared to the Japanese losses of four fleet carriers, a heavy cruiser, an oiler, and an entire air group (over 250 aircraft and crews), the Americans had lost little.[51]

The airmen of the *Yorktown, Enterprise*, and *Hornet*, aided by those on Midway, had accomplished the seemingly impossible: they had stopped the Imperial Japanese Navy's *Combined Fleet* on the high seas. Only the Japanese invasion of the Aleutians marred the American victory, but that was a minor affair, because on June 4, 1942 the strategic initiative in the Pacific passed from Japanese to American hands. The Battle of Midway was a turning point in the war, one which predated El Alamein and Stalingrad, one which probably saved the Germany-first strategy, and one which belonged primarily to the aviators of the United States Pacific Fleet.

"Execute Unrestricted Submarine Warfare Against Japan."

Throughout the period of the early carrier war, Japanese and American submariners prowled the waters of the Pacific and Indian Oceans and the numerous adjoining seas looking for enemy ships to sink.[52] When the war began, both groups of undersea warriors held similar ideas about submarine warfare. In their eyes the submarine was designed to scout for the battle fleet and to attack the enemy's capital ships.

On December 7, 1941, however, the American Chief of Naval Operations ordered his commanders to begin unrestricted submarine warfare against Japan. As a result of

Admiral Stark's order, American submariners immediately deployed their available long-ranged fleet boats and their older S-Boats to attack Japanese merchantmen in lieu of Japanese warships.*

Admiral Nimitz dispatched his first submarine patrols both into the central Pacific (to cut the Japanese line of communications to Truk and to Rabaul) and to Japanese home waters (to intercept the coastal trade). His submariners found numerous targets in both places because the Japanese had assumed that their ships could cruise unmolested in these areas. Without adequate protection, the Japanese merchant ships were easy targets for the lurking American submarines. American submariners, however, had problems which decreased their overall effectiveness when they attacked Japanese vessels. First, their torpedoes tended to run 10 feet deeper than set. Second, the fuses on the torpedoes were defective; head-on hits often failed to detonate. The fuses seemed to work best when the torpedoes struck a ship at an angle.[53] These disheartening deficiencies lowered the morale of the raiders. When coupled with crowded conditions on most submarines, insufferable heat in the un-airconditioned boats, and extended patrols, they tended to lower the efficiency of even the bravest crew.

Navy	Submarines
U.S. Navy (in the Pacific, December 1941)	73
Japanese Navy (available December 1941)	60
German Navy (average number on duty in the Atlantic area, June 1942)	59.2

Comparative Submarine Strengths

By June 1942, American submarines, with some Allied assistance, had destroyed 215,198 tons of Japanese merchant shipping, approximately 57 percent of the 374,602 tons the Japanese had lost since Pearl Harbor.[54] As the war continued, the Americans would improve their score.

In contrast to the Americans, the Japanese submariners concentrated on attacking capital ships. They also were involved in special operations, such as refueling long-range reconnaissance aircraft. While Japanese submarines did attack merchantmen, they never made a sizeable, sustained impact. Immediately after the attack on Pearl Harbor, several ships were sunk off the west coast of the United

January	28,351	(7)
February	15,975	(5)
March	26,183	(7)
April	26,886	(5)
May	86,110	(20)
June	20,021	(6)

Note: Expressed in gross tons and numbers of vessels of over 500 tons.

Japanese Shipping Losses (Merchant Vessels) by Submarine Attack, January–June 1942[55]

States, but not until April did the Japanese submariners go after merchant shipping with a vengeance.† Then, off the west coast of India, the Japanese I-Boats** sank 32,000 tons of Allied shipping. At no time, during the carrier war, however, did the Japanese conduct a sustained submarine campaign against the Allied vessels plowing their way across the oceans to India, Hawaii, and Australia. In the Indian Ocean, the Japanese ignored the advice from the Germans to raid Allied shipping, and ultimately let the German U-Boats operate in Malaya and Java in lieu of their own forces.

The Japanese naval commanders failed to press as hard in the Pacific with their I-Boats as the Germans did with their U-Boats in the Atlantic. If the Japanese had coordinated their submarine efforts with the Germans, or had used their boats more effectively by themselves, they probably would have more deleteriously affected the Allied war effort in the Pacific in 1942 than their desperate fights-to-the-finish would do in 1944, when well supplied Allied forces would attack their outlying bastions.

As the war intensified in the Pacific, American submariners would improve and expand their operations as more and more boats became available. In future months they would remain committed to unrestricted submarine warfare. While American submariners would assist the fleet as they did at Midway, and while they would perform many special rescue, insertion, and supply missions throughout the war zone, they never varied from their primary task—the

---

*S-Boats ("pig boats") had the following general characteristics: length, 225 feet; beam, 21 feet; surface speed, 14½ knots; submerged speed, 11 knots; displacement, 906 tons; torpedo tubes, five 21-inch; and crew, 44. The *Gato* class submarine (a slightly modified *Tautog* class submarine) used throughout the war had the following characteristics: length, 307 feet; beam, 27 feet; surface speed, 20 knots; submerged speed, 9 or 10 knots; displacement, 1500 tons; torpedo tubes, ten 21-inch; and crew, 77. Like all aircraft and ship descriptions, these are approximations.

† The Japanese tried to use midget submarines in the early part of the war. Attacks on warships at Pearl Harbor (December 7, 1941) and Sydney, Australia (May 31–June 1, 1942) were unsuccessful. A midget attack on the British Fleet at Madagascar (May 31, 1942) sank a tanker and a battleship. Such operations were discontinued in 1942.

** The Japanese I-Boats were comparable to American fleet submarines. Generally they were larger (2,200 tons), had higher surface speeds (24 knots), similar cruising ranges (10,000 to 17,000 miles), and similar diving depths (300 feet). They had fewer torpedo tubes (6–8) and lacked radar, which the American boats had by late 1942. The I-Boats did not dive as well as American submarines, but their excellent torpedoes gave the Japanese boats a distinct advantage over American submarines. I-Boats incorporated some German designs.

	Atlantic Ocean	Indian Ocean	Pacific Ocean
January	270,348 (46)	31,081 (8)	19,481 (6)
February	427,733 (72)	13,072 (4)	29,331 (6)
March	507,502 (88)	25,583 (5)	913 (1)
April	388,182 (65)	32,404 (5)	1,435 (1)
May*	586,149 (120)	——— —	16,582 (3)
June	603,402 (115)	69,366 (15)	16,978 (4)

*Included 40 American ships—highest monthly American loss of the war.
Note: Expressed in gross tons and number of vessels.

**Allied Shipping Losses (Merchant Vessels) by
Submarine Attack, January–June 1942**

destruction of the Japanese merchant fleet, particularly the tankers. The Japanese submariner would not fare as well. While he would campaign against Allied merchant ships, other assignments would eventually override his attack function against both cargo and capital ships. As a result, the American submariner became the dominant undersea warrior in the Pacific. By 1945, his contributions would be astounding.

Lost Opportunities

Admiral Yamamoto probably lost the war for Japan in 1942 when he failed to use his overwhelming air and naval superiority to destroy the American carrier fleet. He had the time and the opportunity—the first six months of the war—but he frittered away his forces and his opportunities by sending his carriers all over the war zone striking less significant targets than the American carriers, which were allowed to roam unmolested in the central and south Pacific. Yamamoto had the Pacific Fleet on the ropes on December 7, but he never kept it there. When he released the direct pressure, the American carriers were able to regroup, obtain reinforcements, and sally forth to meet him another day.

At Midway, Yamamoto threw away his chance for a great victory by spreading his forces all over the central and north Pacific. In the battle, the *Combined Fleet* fought with one hand tied behind its back: only the *First Air Fleet* really engaged, while the bulk of the battle fleet remained hundreds of miles away. The admiral gave away all of his advantages in height, weight, size, reach, and experience, and at the critical moment of his career was too far away to influence the action. Sloppy planning, poor execution, overconfidence, and totally inadequate security allowed a few American dive bombers to gain a victory of opportunity in five minutes.

Admiral Yamamoto also threw away an opportunity to destroy the Allied merchant fleets in the Pacific and the Indian Oceans prior to June 1942. With his carriers and submarines he could have cut the lines of communications to India and Australia, perhaps even to Hawaii, and in doing so would have emasculated the Allied effort to build up forces in these major base areas for a future counterattack.

The *Combined Fleet* could not have gained victory for Japan. But if Admiral Yamamoto had properly employed, it, the *Combined Fleet* might have prevented the United States and her Allies from gaining victory in the Pacific, or at least delayed an Allied victory for some time. As the admiral sailed for Japan on the giant battleship *Yamato* he must have known this. He had had the opportunity to gain a Tsushima, had been given the chance to wage a Battle of the Pacific to complement the Battle of the Atlantic; and by his own previous actions he had gained complete domination of the Pacific for six full months. But for some inexplicable reason he had not exploited his opportunities successfully. Yamamoto must have wondered if he would be given another chance to be the Emperor's successful sword.

Notes

[1]This section is based primarily on Samuel Eliot Morison, *The Rising Sun in the Pacific, 1931-April 1942* (Boston, 1948), pp. 235-268 and 389-398.

[2]*Reports of General MacArthur, Volume II - Part I, Japanese Operations in the Southwest Pacific Area.* Compiled from Japanese Demobilization Bureaux Records. (Washington, 1967), p. 130. Footnote 23 gives these losses. Several other vessels were damaged. Morison, *Rising Sun in the Pacific*, p. 389, is less generous.

[3]James M. Merrill, *Target-Tokyo, The Halsey-Doolittle Raid* (New York, 1964), pp. 130-133.

[4]Morison, *Rising Sun in the Pacific*, p. 398.

[5]Saburo Hayashi (In collaboration with Alvin D. Coox), *Kogun, The Japanese Army in the Pacific War* (Quantico, Va, 1959), p. 49.

[6]Mitsuo Fuchida and Masatake Okumiya, *Midway, the Battle that Doomed Japan* (New York, 1955), pp. 68-73.

[7]This section is based primarily on Fuchida and Okumiya, *Midway*, pp. 44-54.

[8]Fuchida and Okumiya, *Midway*, p. 46.

[9]John Deane Potter, *Yamamoto, The Man Who Menaced America* (New York, 1971), pp. 172-173 and Fuchida and Okumiya, *Midway*, p. 67.

[10]For the Darwin attack see: Major General S. Woodburn Kirby, *The War Against Japan*, Volume I, *Loss of Singapore* (London, 1957), pp. 425-426; Dudley MacCarthy, *South-West Pacific—First Year, Kokoda to Wau* (Canberra, 1962), pp. 69-72; and Fuchida and Okumiya, *Midway*, p. 48.

[11]Major General S. Woodburn Kirby, *The War Against Japan*, Volume II, *India's Most Dangerous Hour* (London, 1958), p. 115.

[12]For the Indian Ocean Raid see: Kirby, *India's Most Dangerous Hour*, pp. 115-132; Fuchida and Okumiya, *Midway*, pp. 49-52; and Morison, *Rising Sun in the Pacific*, pp. 382-386.

[13]Andrieu D'Albas, *Death of a Navy, Japanese Naval Action in World War II* (New York, 1957), pp. 84-86.

[14]This section is based primarily on Fuchida and Okumiya, *Midway*, pp. 54-73; Hayashi and Coox, *Kogun*, pp. 41-57; and *Reports of MacArthur*, II-I, *Japanese Operations*, pp. 124-134.

[15]Hayashi and Coox, *Kogun*, pp. 41-46 and 56-57.

[16]*Reports of MacArthur*, II-I, *Japanese Operations*, p. 68 (fn 27) and pp. 126-127 (fn 13). See also Joint Committee on the Investigation of the Pearl Harbor Attack, *Pearl Harbor Attack Hearings* (Washington, 1946), Part 13, p. 438. Pages 431-486 contain the "Japanese Combined Fleet Top Secret Operation Order #1."

[17]*Reports of MacArthur*, II-I, *Japanese Operations*, pp. 126-134; Fuchida and Okumiya, *Midway*, pp. 59-61; Hayashi and Coox, *Kogun*, p. 43.

[18]Details of the discussion between the *Combined Fleet* and the Naval General Staff are found in Fuchida and Okumiya, *Midway*, pp. 56-66.

[19]*Reports of MacArthur*, II-I, *Japanese Operations*, p. 133.

[20]Fuchida and Okumiya, *Midway*, p. 72.

[21]*Reports of MacArthur*, II-I, *Japanese Operations*, p. 134.

[22]This section is based upon two main sources: Samuel Eliot Morison, *Coral Sea, Midway and Submarine Actions, May 1942-August 1942* (Boston, 1967), pp. 245-252 and Louis Morton, *Strategy and Command, The First Two Years* (Washington, 1962), pp. 198-224 and 240-263.

[23]Morton, *Strategy and Command*, pp. 241-263, covers the command problem.

[24]Morison, *Coral Sea, Midway and Submarine Actions*, pp. 245-249 and Morton, *Strategy and Command*, pp. 217-222. The authors differ on their emphasis in the development of American strategy. Morison leans toward the Navy's role; Morton leans toward the Army's.

[25]Morton, *Strategy and Command*, p. 218, quoting from "Eisenhower Notations," January 22, 1944.

[26]For MacArthur's ideas see Morton, *Strategy and Command*, pp. 221, 223, 225, and 251.

[27][Franklin D. Roosevelt] "Memorandum for General George Marshall: Chief of Staff," (May 6, 1942), paragraph 3. Found in Maurice Matloff and Edwin M. Snell, *Strategic Planning for Coalition Warfare, 1941-1942* (Washington, 1953), p. 220.

[28]For the Pacific versus BOLERO, see Matloff and Snell, *Strategic Planning*, pp. 217-221 and Morton, *Strategy and Command*, pp. 221-223.

[29]See Table 4 in Morton, *Strategy and Command*, p. 224.

[30]This section is based upon Morison, *Coral Sea, Midway and Submarine Actions*, pp. 3-64, unless otherwise indicated.

[31]The reference to the "encirclement" of the Coral Sea comes from the United States Strategic Bombing Survey (Pacific), *The Allied Campaign Against Rabaul* (Washington, 1946), p. 7. The information about American knowledge of Japanese movements is found in Morison, *Coral Sea, Midway, and Submarine Actions*, p. 13. See also: John Toland, *The Rising Sun, The Decline and Fall of the Japanese Empire, 1936-1945* (New York, 1971), p. 368.

[32]Stanley K. Johnston, *Queen of the Flat-tops, the U.S.S. Lexington and the Coral Sea Battle* (New York, 1968), pp. 178-229 describes the action as an eyewitness.

[33]Johnston, *Queen of the Flat-tops*, pp. 182-194 and Morison, *Coral Sea, Midway and Submarine Actions*, pp. 53-55.

[34]Johnston, *Queen of the Flat-tops*, pp. 229-233.

[35]Japanese casualty figures are from Fuchida and Okumiya, *Midway*, p. 99; American figures are from United States Strategic Bombing Survey (Pacific), *Campaigns of the Pacific War* (Washington, 1946), p. 55.

[36]This section is based primarily on Morison, *Coral Sea, Midway and Submarine Actions*, pp. 79-93 and Fuchida and Okumiya, *Midway*, pp. 77-94. Unless specified, American information comes from the first source and Japanese information from the second.

[37]Fuchida and Okumiya, *Midway*, pp. 90-94, cover the war games best. Also useful, but similar is Potter, *Yamamoto*, pp. 201-202.

[38]Morison, *Coral Sea, Midway and Submarine Actions*, p. 78, makes the comments on Cannae and Tannenberg based upon a CINPAC intelligence bulletin.

[39]Comments about Yamamoto are from Fuchida and Okumiya, *Midway*, pp. 74-77.

[40]The activities of Commander Rochefort are outlined in Walter Lord, *Incredible Victory* (New York, 1967), pp. 17-29.

Lord also provides much anecdotal material about the Midway action to highlight Morison's operational narrative. Other intelligence data are from Morison, *Coral Sea, Midway and Submarine Actions*, pp. 80-81.

[41]Morison, *Coral Sea, Midway and Submarine Actions*, p. 84. See also Lord, *Incredible Victory*, pp. 35-36, for more details on CINPAC Operation Plan Number 29-42.

[42]Morison, *Coral Sea, Midway and Submarine Actions*, p. 84.

[43]Lord, *Incredible Victory*, p. 28, highlights the point about intentions versus capabilities, implying in this case that Nimitz was right in reacting to intentions rather than Japanese capabilities.

[44]This section is based primarily on Morison, *Coral Sea, Midway and Submarine Actions*, pp. 93-159 and Fuchida and Okumiya, *Midway*, pp. 103-212. American actions are taken from Morison; Japanese actions are from Fuchida and Okumiya. Fuchida observed the battle from the bridge of the carrier *Akagi*.

[45]Fuchida and Okumiya, *Midway*, p. 136, gives these strengths; Morison, *Coral Sea, Midway and Submarine Actions*, p. 104, says that 108 aircraft were evenly divided between fighters, dive bombers, and torpedo planes loaded with bombs.

[46]Lord, *Incredible Victory*, pp. 136-138 and 140.

[47]Fuchida and Okumiya, *Midway*, p. 151.

[8]Lord, *Incredible Victory*, pp. 142-147, covers Waldron's attack and Gay's activities.

[49]Lord, *Incredible Victory*, pp. 248-249.

[50]Lord, *Incredible Victory*, pp. 251-252.

[51]USSBS, *Campaigns of the Pacific War*, p. 77, lists 150 American and 253 Japanese aircraft lost. Figures used are from Morison, *Coral Sea, Midway and Submarine Actions*, pp. 90-93.

[52]This section is based primarily on Morison, *Coral Sea, Midway and Submarine Actions*, pp. 65-68 and 187-234. Also useful is Theodore Roscoe, *Submarine Operations in World War II* (Annapolis, Md, 1949), pp. 12-19, 44-46, and 251-260.

[53]Morison, *Coral Sea, Midway and Submarine Actions*, p. 191 covers the problem of the torpedoes briefly and clearly. See also Roscoe, *Submarine Operations*, pp. 251-260.

[54]USSBS, *The War Against Japanese Transportation, 1941-1945* (Washington, 1947), p. 47.

[55]Data for charts which are referenced throughout the chapter come from Samuel Eliot Morison, *The Battle of the Atlantic, September 1939-May 1943* (Boston, 1948), pp. 410-411 (Allied losses) and from USSBS, *War Against Japanese Transportation*, p. 47.

Legacy of Midway: The Jungle War

6

Enemy forces overwhelming. We will defend our posts to the death, praying for eternal victory.

Tulagi Garrison to Rabaul

Upon hearing of the defeat of the *Combined Fleet* at Midway, General Hideki Tojo and other Japanese leaders decided to hide the results of the battle from their people because of the probable impact of the news on national morale. Accordingly, while stressing the success of the Aleutian operations, they falsified the reports of the battle off Midway and isolated the survivors of Nagumo's shattered force from the public[1]

Japanese naval leaders, however, were not prepared to halt all the operations on which they had been working for many months. Between the battles in the Coral Sea and Midway, Imperial General Headquaters had ordered the *Fourth Fleet* to invade New Caledonia, Fiji, and Samoa, and to seize Port Moresby with the Army's help when the Midway operation was completed. The stunning American victory in the central Pacific, however, initially forced the postponement of the invasion of New Caledonia, Fiji, and Samoa in June. Then in July, it was cancelled. But Imperial General Headquarters did not cancel the attack against Port Moresby; that piece of unfinished business needed to be completed as soon as possible.

As the Japanese made their adjustments to the fiasco at Midway, Admiral Nimitz cautiously proposed that the United States might be halfway to the goal of defeating Japan.[2] While the admiral and his associates could not claim at the time that the battle was the major turning point of the war, they did recognize that it had created new opportunities for Allied action in the Pacific. After reviewing these opportunities and enemy strengths and weaknesses in

the Pacific, American naval planners concluded that the Japanese would continue offensive action in only one place—the Southwest Pacific Area. It therefore became imperative for the United States to act promptly to blunt further Japanese offensives in the area in order to continue to protect the line of communications to Australia. Ultimately it would be necessary to neutralize the air and naval base at Rabaul. Not surprisingly, then, within six weeks after Midway, Allied and Japanese land forces were locked in combat in the mountains and jungles of New Guinea, and shortly thereafter in the primeval jungle of Guadalcanal. The jungle tried the patience, courage, and stamina of all the combatants: its green vegetation was armor for both sides; its insects and pests were universal scourges; and its humid climate sapped everyone's strength.

It was in the first six months of that jungle war that the United States seized the strategic initiative from the Japanese, thereby gaining the bases from which its forces could advance northwestward toward Rabaul. After winning the campaigns in Papua and Guadalcanal, however, it would take nearly 14 more months before the 1st Cavalry Division's Brewer Task Force completed the isolation of Rabaul by seizing the Admiralty Islands. In those long months between the beginning of the Papuan and Guadalcanal campaigns and the master stroke which captured the Admiralties, Allied and Japanese soldiers slugged it out, toe-to-toe, in some of the toughest and dirtiest fighting of the war.

No Margin for Error: The First American Offensive

On July 2, 1942, the American Joint Chiefs of Staff ordered Nimitz to seize Tulagi Harbor, Santa Cruz Island, and nearby areas in the southern Solomons on August 1. (*See Atlas Map No. 16.*) At the same time, they directed MacArthur to support the naval forces which would be employed under Nimitz. Concurrently, the Joint Chiefs gave the two theater commanders the blueprint for the future operations in the Southwest Pacific Area which were designed to capture the Japanese base at Rabaul.[3]

The directive outlined three tasks. Task One, just mentioned, would be conducted under naval command. Task Two, under MacArthur's strategic direction, specified the movement of Army and Navy forces northwestward from Guadalcanal and Papua to seize the remainder of the Solomons and strategic points along the New Guinea coast in preparation for the final operations. Task Three, also to be under MacArthur's control, would complete the two-pronged attack with the seizure and occupation of Rabaul and nearby positions. During all these operations the ultimate control of the American fleet carriers, which would be deployed to support the various actions, was to be vested in the Joint Chiefs, apparently to prevent their improper use.*

While the "Final Joint Directive for Offensive Action in the Southwest Pacific Area . . . " seemed to presage a straightforward integration of American power for the conquest of a major Japanese bastion, the Army and Navy had not readily reached agreement on the details of the offensive. First, the war in Europe and the Atlantic was not going well for the Allies: the ubiquitous General Erwin Rommel was gaining ground in the Libyan Desert and threatening the safety of the British position in Egypt; that master of undersea warfare, Admiral Karl Doenitz, was ravaging the Allied merchant fleet at sea with his efficient U-Boats; and on the far reaches of the Continent itself, the *Wehrmacht* was carving up Russian armies in a relentless advance eastward. Not surprisingly, therefore, Roosevelt and Marshall, in particular, were more concerned about the war in Europe than they were about the war with Japan. A reflection of this concern was the Allied decision at the Washington and London Conferences in June and July to invade North Africa in late 1942 in order to open a second front against Germany. Nevertheless, and in spite of the vexing problems in Europe, the Navy wanted to push ahead in the Pacific. King constantly pressured Marshall to

deploy more and more Army troops and aircraft to the Pacific to act as base forces so that the Navy could attack with its fleet and Marine forces.

The most important crisis concerning the decision to attack in the Southwest Pacific Area, however, revolved less around the European problem than around the two men who proposed similar strategies in the area—Admiral King and General MacArthur. King, as early as February, had urged offensive action in the Solomons. In March, he had even persuaded President Roosevelt to accept the Navy's view of how the war should be fought in the Pacific, although the President refused to accept King's view of the priority of the Pacific war, and insisted that nothing stand in the way of BOLERO.† Following Midway, however, King seized the opportunity to argue for quick implementation of his earlier scheme to occupy Tulagi and advance up the Solomons toward the ultimate objectives of New Britain and New Ireland. The admiral, now the Chief of Naval Operations as well as the Commander-in-Chief of the United States Fleet, projected a Navy-dominated operation in which the Army would follow in the wake of naval amphibious forces to care for the captured areas.

It was not in Douglas MacArthur's make-up to stand for such subordination, even though his strategic goals were substantially the same as King's. Boldly, therefore, on June 8 he proposed that with the support of fleet carriers and the loan of one amphibiously-trained marine division he could seize Rabaul in 14 days rather than move island-by-island up the Solomons. Army planners in Washington had developed a plan similar to MacArthur's, and they eventually persuaded their Navy associates to accept a quick advance on Rabaul rather than to continue planning for a slow advance through the Solomons.

At this critical point, King announced that he would have none of MacArthur's scheme, because the whole operation would be under MacArthur's command. Adamantly, he insisted that the aircraft carriers should never come under Army control. Furthermore, he believed that the Navy should control all amphibious operations; since the Solomons would be an amphibious campaign, it should be under naval command. King told Marshall that if the Army would not fall in line with his proposals for the offensive in the Solomons, he was prepared to initiate it without Southwest

---

*Throughout the war, Admiral King never would permit the Navy's fleet carriers to come under other than naval command. By keeping control of them at Joint Chiefs of Staff level, King, the executive agent for the Pacific, retained full control and command of the fleet carriers as Chief of Naval Operations and Commander-in-Chief of the United States Fleet. King really did not feel that an Army officer could command fleet carriers properly, particularly if that officer was MacArthur. Furthermore, if the carriers came under the Army's or MacArthur's command, the whole role and strategy of the Navy—and King's influence in the Pacific—would be diminished.

† Because of the British desire to attack North Africa and their reluctance to support an emergency landing to take the pressure off of the Soviet Union (SLEDGEHAMMER), General Marshall proposed to President Roosevelt that American efforts be redirected toward the Pacific in July 1942. Admiral King was amazed and pleased, but the President was not. While sympathizing with Marshall's desire to gain British support for SLEDGEHAMMER, the President scuttled all possibility of deserting the British, in favor of a big push in the Pacific. Roosevelt wanted Germany defeated first.

Pacific Area support. Marshall did not appreciate King's attitude and delayed answering the admiral's challenge. Meanwhile, MacArthur was outraged. He had no great love for the Navy to begin with; but King's approach, coupled with the admiral's habit of dealing directly with MacArthur's naval subordinates, did not ameliorate his feelings toward the naval service. Regardless of Army reaction, on June 26 the Chief of Naval Operations went so far as to order Admiral Nimitz to begin planning for the Tulagi operation before the Joint Chiefs had approved it. Marshall's patience in doing everything possible to prevent a head-on clash with his colleague finally paid dividends when, during private talks, King suggested a compromise solution—give command of Task One to Nimitz, and then allow MacArthur to control Tasks Two and Three. To further this compromise, the South Pacific Area boundary was shifted west to include Tulagi and Guadalcanal.[4]

By the time the plan had been agreed on in Washington, MacArthur had backtracked from his original plan for a bold advance on Rabaul and was talking of a more deliberate movement. Although he never approached King's slower timing schedule, the general grew more and more cautious as time wore on. After discussing the tasks with Vice Admiral Robert Ghormley, the newly appointed commander of the South Pacific Area and the commander of Operation WATCHTOWER (Task One), MacArthur decided with Ghormley that the American plan as outlined in the July 2 directive was not acceptable, given their present forces. The two commanders wanted to wait until they had the forces on hand to execute the three assigned tasks in a continuous campaign. Two days after they had wired their comments to Washington and Hawaii, the Joint Chiefs replied. Task One would be executed on August 1, as directed. Information received on July 5 that the Japanese were building an airstrip on Guadalcanal probably tipped the scales against the theater commanders.[5]

Even before the Joint Chiefs confirmed their previous decision, the Navy had been hard at work in the Pacific trying to get its forces prepared to strike the lower Solomons. The 1st Marine Division and aircraft carriers were key elements in the planning. The marines were enroute from the United States to New Zealand where the division commander, Major General Alexander Vandegrift, hoped to be able to train his division for another year before committing it to combat. The luxury of such a schedule could not be accommodated, however, and on June 26, Vandegrift learned that his division was to land at Tulagi and Guadalcanal in less than 40 days.[6]

Vandegrift faced other problems in addition to his division's deficiency in training. First, since the division had been moved administratively organized to new Zealand,

it now had to be combat-loaded. This required that all the vessels be unloaded and then immediately reloaded. While normally a herculean task with trained stevedores, Vandegrift had to assign his men to the task because labor difficulties in New Zealand prevented the use of the local stevedores. Working in 300-man groups on each ship, the sea-soldiers performed the laborious task in good style. Then, as his ships were being unloaded, the general began working on his plans only to find that there was a dearth of information about the objective area, although the British had had an administrative center in Tulagi for years. Former residents of the area reported all they knew, but their information proved inadequate when the marines finally landed. Vandegrift completed plans and then embarked with his command to sail to the vicinity of the Fiji Islands for a rehearsal on July 28 to 30. In the tense and rushed atmosphere of the day, the rehearsal was a "complete bust." Vandegrift, in retrospect, believed that it was a waste of time and effort—quite an admission for a man who was known as a stickler for such practice landings.[7] There were two other major problems which involved the Navy's command system and the deployment of aircraft carriers. (*See Appendix 8.*) Admiral Ghormley, the overall commander, had broken down the forces into three main groups: the Amphibious Force, under Rear Admiral Richmond Turner; the land-based air elements, under Rear Admiral John McCain; and the carrier forces, under Rear Admiral Leigh Noyes. But Vice Admiral Frank Jack Fletcher commanded the Expeditionary Force which controlled the carriers, and, in an unusual arrangement, he would also direct the overall operation, at least initially. The line of command passed through Fletcher to Turner and then to Vandegrift, and throughout the campaign Vandegrift would remain subordinate to an admiral afloat. This did not please the Marine general, but his arguments were in vain.*

The most critical problem concerned the use of the carriers. Fletcher was not enthusiastic about maneuvering his carriers in the close waters of the Solomons. This was understandable, if exasperating, since he had lost two carriers already in the war and was reluctant to place his ships in any position where they could be easily sunk. Therefore, on July 26 he told Turner and Vandegrift, when the commanders met for their first conference on his flagship *Saratoga*, that he would cover the landing for two days; then he would withdraw.[8] Turner demanded that he remain to protect his forces for the four days needed to unload the troops and their supplies. Fletcher refused. Vandegrift could do nothing, but he knew the danger that

---

*Later in the war, the Navy agreed to let Marine commanders command operations on land once the invasion force was firmly established ashore.

Until New Ships Joined the Fleet, Nimitz Could Ill-Afford Losing Scarce Aircraft Carriers Such as the *Lexington*, Shown Here Being Abandoned in May 1942 After the Coral Sea Engagement.

his troops would be in without adequate air cover. In a strategic sense, Fletcher was probably right, because even though the Americans had won at Midway, they did not have an abundance of carriers to squander in amphibious operations. Only four (the *Enterprise*, the repaired *Saratoga*, the *Hornet*, and the newly arrived *Wasp*) were in the Pacific, and they would have to carry the bulk of the naval war for some time* Nimitz sent all of them, except the *Hornet*, south to support Ghormley. If Fletcher got into difficulty, as the Japanese had at Midway, he could lose more in a few minutes than the marines could gain during a lengthy campaign in the Solomons.

The various problems delayed the planned invasion by seven days, but did not dampen the spirits of the men who were to make the first American amphibious landing of the war. Aboard the various transports, the Marine commanders briefed their men. General Vandegrift divided his division into two main forces: Group Yoke, led by his assistant division commander, Brigadier General William Rupertus, would assault Tulagi and its environs; Group X-Ray, under his command, would land at Red Beach, Guadalcanal, to establish a beachhead in the weakly defended Lunga Point area. Rupertus' initial objectives included the Tulagi seaplane anchorage and the nearby islands of Gavutu and Tanambogo, while Vandegrift's were Mount Austen, believed to be just two miles away, and the nearly completed Japanese airfield. (*See Atlas Map No. 17a.*) Because Rupertus' forces were expected to meet the most resistance, Vandegrift assigned his most experienced troops to his assistant—the 1st Marine Raider Battalion, the 1st Parachute Battalion, and a battalion of the 5th Marines, all with reinforcing units. The 1st Marines and the balance of the 5th Marines remained under Vandegrift's direct command. The 2nd Marines were in reserve.

When the 19,000 marines departed from the rehearsal area for the Solomons, the American commanders knew that the operation was being launched on a shoestring and that there could be little margin for error. Nevertheless, with the landing on August 7, regardless of the future tactical situation, the Japanese lost the strategic initiative in the Solomons. What the Americans did not know, moreover, was that the Japanese in the objective area would be in even more desperate straits. The 3,730 defenders, however, would fight fanatically; and, when reinforced, they would prevent the Americans from winning a quick victory.[9]

*During the Guadalcanal Campaign the *Wasp* and *Hornet* were sunk; the *Enterprise* and *Saratoga* were hit.

Coincident Interests: Buna and Port Moresby

While the Japanese leaders and planners paid scant attention to the lower Solomons, they coveted the forward Allied base at Port Moresby from which Allied air forces could threaten their southeastern positions and from which Allied counterattacks could be mounted. Even after the advance into New Caledonia, Fiji, and Samoa was canceled, Port Moresby remained a key objective. Because of the naval losses at Midway, however, Imperial General Headquarters decreed on June 12 that Port Moresby would have to be taken by an overland attack across the Owen Stanley Mountains, which divided the southeastern part of the island into two coastal strips.[10]

On July 11, Imperial Headquarters ordered Lieutenant General Haruyoshi Hyakutake, the newly appointed *Seventeenth Army* Commander, to seize strategic points along the New Guinea Coast and capture Port Moresby. (*See Atlas Map No. 16.*) One of the strategic points was Buna, a small coastal village 200 miles southeast of Salamaua, which was ideal for locating a forward air base to cover the proposed actions against Port Moresby.

General Hyakutake did not have a large army to perform his assigned tasks. In fact, when activated the *Seventeenth Army* was only a paper unit; but by July the general had a force of approximately nine infantry battalions, which formed the backbone of the *South Seas Detachment* at Rabaul, the *Aoba and Yazawa Detachments* at Davao, and the *Kawaguchi Detachment* at Palau. (*See Appendix 9.*) In addition, an engineer regiment was assigned. It eventually became the *Yokoyama Force* and included one infantry battalion. Hyakutake could count on the support of the *Eighth Fleet* at Rabaul (organized July 14), its air forces, other naval forces, and elements of the *Sasebo 5th Special Naval Landing Force*, which was at Rabaul.

Although the second advance on Port Moresby was to be an overland one, the Japanese did not possess maps of the area and had to rely on recent aerial photographs to guide their troops through the jungled mountains. Planned to start at Buna, the troops would move southwest toward Wairopi at the head of the Kokoda Trail, then to Kokoda on the plateau west of Wairopi, and lastly southwest along the rugged Kokoda Trail to the environs of Port Moresby. To insure that the main force would succeed, Imperial General Headquarters ordered that a reconnaissance force inspect the route before any major action was undertaken. As it turned out, however, the emphasis on a reconnaissance would diminish, with the designated reconnaissance force becoming an advanced party which would prepare the route

for future use, secure key areas, and begin developing roads.

General Hyakutake issued his final orders for the attack against Port Moresby on July 18, when he was still in Davao. The *Yokoyama Force* would land near Buna on July 21 with elements of naval landing and base forces; almost immediately it would push inland to begin the trek along the Kokoda Trail. The *South Seas Detachment*, commanded by Major General Tomitaro Horii and assisted by the small *Yazawa Detachment*, was to take Port Moresby. The *Aoba Detachment*, still at Davao, would be the general's reserve. To assist the overall advance, the *Eighth Fleet*, with the *Kawaguchi Detachment*, was ordered to secure Samarai Island off the southeastern tip of New Guinea so that it could be developed as a seaplane base. Meanwhile, the Japanese naval forces at Lae and Salamaua would divert Allied attention to the Bulolo Valley by attacking the forward outposts of KANGA Force.* In a supporting role, Japanese submarines would step up their attacks on Allied shipping off Australia. Finally, naval landing forces were to be prepared to land near Port Moresby as the Army forces debouched from the mountains to take the Allied base.[11]

As the Japanese were developing their plans for an attack on Port Moresby, General MacArthur was putting the final touches on his plans to support the attack in the lower Solomons and to begin his own operations under Task Two, which would bring his forces into position to take Rabaul. Key to his moves were the development and security of Port Moresby as a forward base, the building of airfields in northern Australia to advance his bomber line by 500 miles, and the training of the American 32nd and 41st Infantry Divisions, which had closed into their camps in Australia in May.

Believing that Australia could best be defended from positions in New Guinea, MacArthur was eager to take the offensive. He would later claim that this had been his view from the time of his arrival in Australia in March 1942.[12] Although he detested sitting still, without the necessary resources he could do little except send his growing air squadrons against the Japanese outposts. With the decision of July 2, however, the general was hopeful that he could implement Task Two without much delay. For this reason, he was interested in the same places as were the Japanese: Port Moresby, the southeastern tip of New Guinea, the Kokoda Trail, and Buna.

When the Japanese failed to capture Port Moresby

---

*KANGA Force was formed around the nucleus of the local militia, the New Guinea Volunteer Rifles, and a recently arrived Australian commando-type unit, the 5th Independent Company.

during the Battle of the Coral Sea, MacArthur had been relieved, but he had little doubt that they would attempt again to secure that base. Therefore, in May, he had begun sending Australian infantry units to New Guinea and had started the construction of new bases from which he could both defend Port Moresby and cover his projected movements north toward Rabaul.

After the first major Australian reinforcements arrived at Port Moresby in May, MacArthur authorized General Sir Thomas Blamey, his Allied Land Force Commander and also the commander of the Australian Army, to reinforce KANGA force in the Bulolo Valley with the Australian 5th Independent Company (a commando-type unit). (*See Appendix 8.*) Both men hoped that KANGA Force could protect the airfield at Wau and, even more importantly, that it would be able to retake the airfields at Lae and Salamaua. The guerrillas could not get close to Lae, but they managed to damage the Japanese facilities at Salamaua in late June. When they proved incapable of retaking any airfield, however, MacArthur had to abandon plans for the deployment of fighters to the forward strips.[13]

MacArthur took more concrete action to secure Port Moresby. (*See Atlas Map No. 16.*) In May and June, he directed the construction of airfield complexes to protect the flanks of the Allied base. To the east, at a Lever Brothers' coconut plantation near Milne Bay, work began on new airfields when troops arrived late in June. Australian P-40s flew in a month later. The Milne Bay fields not only protected Port Moresby, but also gave the Allies a place from which they could better patrol the Coral Sea and cover northern Australia. In the west, the Allies also began building airfields at Merauke in Netherlands new Guinea. In addition to constructing new airfields, MacArthur ordered the Australian commander in Papua to cover the Kokoda Trail to prevent the Japanese from attacking Port Moresby through its back door. This took some time to accomplish, but on July 7 a single Australian infantry company, reinforced by a 300-man Papuan Infantry Battalion, left the coast on a five-day march across the Owen Stanleys to its new home at Kokoda.

To better prepare for his expected advance toward Rabaul (Task Two), MacArthur needed forward airbases north of the Owen Stanleys to neutralize the Japanese positions at Lae and Salamaua. The obvious place for such an advanced position was Buna. On July 10 and 11, Allied officers reconnoitered the Buna area, but they did not like the marshy ground there, and recommended instead that the Allied fields be built nearby at Dobodura. MacArthur accepted the recommendation, and on July 15 he issued orders for the seizure of the Buna-Gona-Dobodura area by a small force which would march over the Kokoda Trail to

reach Buna between August 10 and 12. The operation was named PROVIDENCE.

Fate undid PROVIDENCE, however, when Japanese naval forces, managing to avoid heavy American air attacks, landed the first elements of the *Yokoyama Force* near Buna on the night of July 21. By nightfall of the next day, the lead Japanese forces were approaching Wairopi and the outposts of the MAROUBA Force which guarded the Kokoda Trail.[14]

The possibility of a Japanese attack in southeastern New Guinea had not been totally unexpected, since American aircraft had reported large shipping concentrations around Rabaul and nearby harbors for some time. But the sudden arrival of the Japanese forces at Buna precipitated the long battle for Papua and negated MacArthur's optimistic preparations for an immediate offensive. Now the general would be forced to defend New Guinea while his air and naval forces assisted the Navy in the Solomons. For the time being, the Japanese would maintain the initiative in the Southwest Pacific Area.

To Stop the Japanese Advance: Guadalcanal

As Rear Admiral Victor Crutchley, Royal Navy, a red-bearded Victoria Cross winner at Jutland,[15] led the van of the American task force toward Guadalcanal in the cruiser *HMAS Australia*, many officers wondered if Operation WATCHTOWER could possibly succeed. It seemed full of flaws: tactical plans were hastily prepared; the green troops had not had a good landing rehearsal; there were no plans for follow-up logistical support; no Army units had been alerted to prepare to reinforce the marines who were to land; command arrangements were tenuous; air cover would be problematical; and intelligence was lacking. The operation was obviously a gamble because it was to be undertaken with insufficient combat power and inadequate logistics, and would strike a Japanese dominated area. Nevertheless, the marines aboard the transports were eager to fight. Old hands, such as Colonel LeRoy Hunt, commander of the 5th Marines, knew that the beach assaults would be tough going, but that did not deter them from telling their troops that they expected the operation to be a complete success.[16]

The Marine commanders were surprised on August 7 when there was no resistance on Guadalcanal and no casualties on Red Beach. Colonel Hunt's 5th Marines and Colonel Clifton Cates' 1st Marines secured the beachhead by late afternoon, but because of the difficult terrain and the heat, the regiments were unable to push all the way to the west to seize Lunga Point or Mount Austen, their assigned objectives. Throughout the campaign on Guadalcanal—indeed, in all of the Solomons—the terrain as well as the hot and extremely humid climate would bedevil all combatants. On Guadalcanal there were no roads—just a few inland trails and a rough track which passed through two coconut plantations on the northeast coast. The central feature of the island—and all the Solomons—was a rugged interior mountain complex, covered with dense jungle and drained by many streams which flowed to the sea and formed many unpleasant swamps. To make life even more difficult, the anopheles and aedes mosquitos were present everywhere, and were an instant source of malaria and dengue fever. Skin diseases, too, were endemic to the entire area.

The next day, however, both units moved into the Lunga Point area, secured the unfinished Japanese airfield, established a rudimentary defense perimeter, and set up a main line of resistance along the beach to repel any Japanese counterlanding.[17] (*See Atlas Map No. 17b.*)

General Rupertus' marines were not quite as fortunate when they landed across Sealark Channel on Tulagi, Gavutu, and Tanambogo Islands. There, determined Japanese fought from caves and other dug-in positions until they were annihilated by the Americans on August 8. Flank attacks on Florida Island succeeded without difficulty.

General Vandegrift could not have asked for a more auspicious start to the campaign, but his luck did not hold for long. Rear Admiral Gunichi Mikawa, the *Eighth Fleet* commander at Rabaul, took immediate action against the American forces. Japanese aircraft flew south and arrived over the transports at noon. Mikawa's naval forces sailed as soon as they were formed. American ground fire and Wildcat fighters prevented the Japanese airmen from doing any substantial damage to the landing forces on the seventh and eighth. As a result of the air attacks, however, Admiral Fletcher requested permission from Admiral Ghormley (in Noumea) to withdraw his carriers. Citing his need to refuel and the loss of a fifth of his fighters, Fletcher gained permission to retire late on the afternoon of August 8. Because Fletcher decided to withdraw, Turner, Amphibious Force Commander, conferred with Vandegrift and also decided to pull out. He would leave early on the ninth.

The loss of air cover was the most critical problem which faced the marines, but nearly as important was the logistical chaos which developed at Red Beach. Lacking proper equipment to handle the cargo and adequate labor forces, the pioneers and sailors unloaded and stored the vital supplies around the small beach area as best they could.* Congestion resulted, presenting an inviting target to enemy gunners and fliers. The supplies eventually were moved within the marine perimeter defensive line.

About the time that Turner learned of Fletcher's plan to withdraw, he received information that Japanese naval forces were moving toward Guadalcanal from Rabaul. Turner deployed his warships to meet the Japanese threat; but that evening the crews of the picket destroyers and sentinel cruisers guarding the entrance to Sealark Channel near Savo Island failed to detect Mikawa's five heavy cruisers, two light cruisers, and one destroyer as they approached. Mikawa opened fire at 1:36 A.M. on August 9. In the next 32 minutes, his men taught the United States Navy a lesson in night surface combat, sinking four Allied heavy cruisers and one destroyer, killing 1,270 officers and men, and wounding an additional 709. The Battle of Savo Island was probably the worst defeat ever inflicted on the United States Navy in a fair fight. Fortunately for Vandegrift's forces, Mikawa, who lost none of his ships, did not attack the American transports.[18]

Turner continued to land supplies and troops until late afternoon on the ninth before withdrawing to Noumea. In his haste to depart, however, Turner left the marines without all their supplies and equipment—much of it was still in the holds of the ships—and without 1,400 men of the reserve regiment. With his departure, the ground forces were in serious trouble; having only a 37-day supply of food and four units of fire,† there was doubt in the minds of not a few men that they could survive.

Under this pressure, Vandegrift needed to accomplish two interrelated tasks quickly. First, he had to secure a perimeter around Lunga Point to repulse Japanese attacks; then he had to complete the enclosed airfield so that fighters could land at Guadalcanal to support his division. In the next weeks, his marines worked hard at both tasks. By the eighteenth, Henderson Field** was completed, and two days later, 31 Marine aircraft landed. Army and Navy airplanes arrived soon after. With fighters available, the chances for the Americans on Guadalcanal brightened materially.

While the marines were concerned with their immediate problems, Japanese air and naval forces bombarded their

---

*As the war progressed, shore party organization and operations improved with each amphibious landing, enabling supplies, equipment, and material to be moved quickly ashore with and behind the assault forces.

† A unit of fire was the amount of ammunition needed for an average day in combat.

** Named for Major Loften Henderson, a marine air leader who died at Midway.

Lunga Point, Guadalcanal

positions almost daily. The Japanese survivors assembled outside the American perimeter, but they did little to attract the attention of the invaders.

On August 13, Imperial General Headquarters, however, ordered the *Seventeenth Army* to retake Tulagi and Guadalcanal, while continuing the Port Moresby Operation. To provide additional resources to make this feasible, the *Ichiki Detachment* (2,000 men strong) was ordered south from Truk* to reinforce the units on Guadalcanal. Five hundred men from the *Yokosuka 5th Special Naval Landing Force* were also ordered to assist the Japanese garrison. The leading echelon of Colonel Kiyono Ichiki's detachment began landing at Taivu Point (east of the perimeter) on August 18, while the naval troops went ashore at Kokumbona Point (west of the perimeter) over 30 miles away.[19] (*See Atlas Map No. 17a.*)

On Guadalcanal, Vandegrift continued to strengthen his perimeter rather than attempting to destroy the remaining Japanese on the island. While he did patrol, raid, and launch small attacks, these actions were normally short and indecisive, serving only to locate the Japanese. On August 19, sensing that Japanese reinforcements were arriving, the general dispatched part of a company eastward to reconnoiter Koli Point. Around noon that day, the patrol killed some Japanese soldiers who were obviously not members of the original naval garrison; they also found maps which outlined the American positions around Henderson Field, indicating that the new Japanese units were planning an attack.

Irritated that he had been prematurely discovered, Ichiki decided to attack the marine perimeter as quickly as possible. (*Actions not shown.*) After moving them along the

coast, the colonel deployed his forces the next evening at the mouth of the Ilu River. At 3:10 A.M. on August 21, Ichiki attacked without preparatory fires. Driving through small arms and 37-mm cannister fire, Japanese infantrymen penetrated the American perimeter, but they were soon ejected. Ichiki immediately launched a second attack from the sea. This time he supported it with mortar and artillery fires. When the Japanese infantrymen assaulted through the breaker line into the main line of resistance, however, small arms and cannister fire decimated their ranks, and the attack collapsed.

Ichiki did not attack again, but remained in position to harass the Americans. That brought about his downfall. Shortly after daylight, American artillery fire began to fall on his position, while marine reserves moved around his inland flank to trap his troops against the sea. Once the marines closed the trap, fighter aircraft, tanks, and artillery fire chewed up the Japanese detachment. By 5:00 P.M., most of the 1,000-man force had been killed. The Battle of Tenaru was over.* The defeated Colonel Ichiki burned his regimental colors and committed *hara-kiri*.

Following this debacle, the Japanese Navy began convoying reinforcements to Guadalcanal. Rear Admiral Raizo Tanaka commanded the first groups of warships which brought in the new Japanese units. Coming at night to

*Actually the Ilu. Originally, the marines switched the names of the nearby streams.

Japanese Casualties After the Battle of the Tenaru (Ilu)

*Some sources say Guam.

avoid Allied air attacks, Tanaka would assemble his ships in the Shortland Islands (south of Bougainville) in the morning, sail to within 200 miles of Guadalcanal by 6:00 P.M., and then after dark run in toward his landing points to discharge troops and cargo. While the ships unloaded, his destroyers passed the time by bombarding the American installations around Henderson Field. Tanaka would retire and be out of range of Allied aircraft by dawn.[20] This operation was soon dubbed the "Tokyo Express" by the marines, and its route down through the parallel chain of the Solomon Islands was called "The Slot." The "Tokyo Express" ran frequently and quite efficiently down "The Slot" until early December, because until then the Japanese dominated the sea at night while the Americans had to be content with controlling it during the daylight hours.

Two days after the Battle of the Tenaru, Admiral Tanaka headed south with 1,500 men, the main elements of the *Ichiki Detachment* and the *Yokosuka 5th Special Naval Landing Force*. Admiral Kondo (*Second Fleet*), with three carriers from Admiral Nagumo's *Carrier Force* (now the *Third Fleet*) and a huge surface force, supported Tanaka's move. Kondo hoped to destroy any American carriers which engaged him.

In Noumea, Ghormley learned of the Japanese naval movements from Australian coastwatchers* in the northern Solomons, and ordered Fletcher to intercept the enemy force. At 9:05 A.M. on August 24, an American scout pilot spotted Kondo's ships off the eastern Solomons. Fletcher launched his aircraft at 1:45 P.M.; within a couple of hours his pilots inflicted fatal damage on the *Ryujo*. Nagumo immediately retaliated, sending the air groups from the *Shokaku* and *Zuikaku* aloft at 3:07 P.M. and 4:00 P.M. Nagumo's pilots bombed the *Enterprise*, but could not get through to the *Saratoga*.† The *Enterprise* survived, although she had to return to Noumea for repairs. In the last action of the Battle of the Eastern Solomons, American fliers badly damaged the Japanese seaplane carrier, *Chitose*. Unaffected by the carrier battle, Tanaka continued steaming southward with his transports. Early on the twenty-fifth he met disaster when American dive bombers and B-17s mauled his convoy, forcing him to withdraw. Many of the naval troops aboard were lost at sea.

In Rabaul and Tokyo, the loss of the *Ichiki Detachment* awakened the Japanese commanders to the danger posed by the new American beachhead. Accordingly, on August 29, Imperial General Headquarters changed priorities in the battle area and directed that emphasis be given to the recapturing of the Solomons; the Port Moresby operation was downgraded to a secondary task.[21] To insure that the American beachhead was destroyed, General Hyakutake ordered the remainder of the *Ichiki Detachment*, the *Kawaguchi Detachment*, and the *Aoba Detachment* to reinforce Guadalcanal.** The 6,000 new troops were really too few for the task. The Japanese leaders did not realize that the Americans had deployed a division on the island, because the quick withdrawal of the American fleet and the lack of immediate reinforcement seemed to imply that the Americans had sent ashore only a large reconnaissance force.

Major General Kiyotoke Kawaguchi decided to land on opposite sides of the marine perimeter (Tasimboko on the east; Kokumbona on the west) so that he could attack the American position from two directions. (*See Atlas Map No. 17a.*) He planned to launch a coordinated attack in which Rabaul-based aircraft and ships would bombard the marine positions to aid his ground assault. In early September, air attacks grew more and more ferocious, and his forces began to strike the American patrols outside their perimeter.

To attack the Lunga Point area, Kawaguchi ordered his battalions to strike from the west, south, and southeast. The main attack would go in against the ridgeline which covered the rear of the American position. (*See Atlas Map No. 17c.*) To get into position, he ordered his soldiers to cut their way through the jungle so that they would not be detected. Finally, just after 9:00 P.M. on September 12, the Japanese launched a two-battalion attack against the rear of the Lunga Point position, splitting the defensive position in two and entering Vandegrift's back door. In the desperate fight which followed, the marines beat off over 12 assaults and won the Battle of the Ridge. There were other uncoordinated and sporadic Japanese attacks at different positions. None, however, were as fierce and sustained as Kawaguchi's main effort. By the end of the battle, the Japanese force was tactically ineffective.

The American position began to improve on September 18, when Vandegrift's third organic regiment (4,262 men), ammunition, and additional aircraft arrived. Vandegrift now had cause to believe that he could close his perimeter. While the marines were pleased with the new development, the Navy licked its wounds. The reinforcement effort had

---

* The coastwatchers, mostly Australians, New Zealanders, or Britishers who had lived in the area before the war, constantly reported to Allied radio stations Japanese air and naval movements during the campaigns. They continued to do so in later campaigns. Coastwatchers were members of the Allied Intelligence Bureau. They were led by Commander Eric Feldt, Royal Australian Navy.

† On August 31, the Japanese submarine I-26 torpedoed the *Saratoga*, putting the carrier out of commission for three months. Admiral Fletcher, flying his flag on the *Saratoga*, was relieved; he later commanded the North Pacific Area under Nimitz.

** These units became the *Kawaguchi Force*.

Date	Battle
August 7, 1942	1st Marine Division seizes Guadalcanal and nearby islands.
August 8, 1942	Naval Battle of Savo Island.
August 21, 1942	Battle of the Tenaru (Ichiki defeated).
August 24, 1942	Naval Battle of the Eastern Solomons.
September 12–14, 1942	Battle of the Ridge (Kawaguchi defeated).
October 11–12, 1942	Naval Battle of Cape Esperance.
October 22–25, 1942	Japanese Counteroffensive (Hyakutake defeated).
October 26–27, 1942	Naval Battle of Santa Cruz Island.
November 12–15, 1942	Naval Battle of Guadalcanal.
November 30, 1942	Naval Battle of Tassafaronga.
December 17, 1942– February 8, 1943	General Patch's offensives.
February 8, 1943	Japanese complete withdrawal.

Major Battles During the Guadalcanal Campaign, 1942–1943

cost them the carrier *Wasp*, sunk on September 15. Like the Japanese, the Americans were learning that it was costly sailing to Guadalcanal.

Using the additional troops, Vandegrift now tried to expand his beachhead west to the Matanikau River. In late September, the Japanese easily blocked an advance, and in the process nearly trapped and annihilated a marine battalion. After extracting his units, the general attacked westward again when he discovered that the Japanese had brought in 150-mm howitzers, which could shell Henderson Field from the riverline. (Since his artillery could not neutralize the Japanese pieces, Vandegrift wanted to keep them out of range of his area.) This attack jumped off on October 8 and ran into a Japanese force which was also preparing an attack. In the tough fighting that followed, the marines gained the upper hand, but the threat of a new Japanese counteroffensive made Vandegrift pull his forces back into the perimeter after the river fight. It was fortunate that he did so.

On October 9, Lieutenant General Haruyoshi Hyakutake, the *Seventeenth Army* commander, landed on Guadalcanal to take charge of the next offensive against Henderson Field. The Japanese general was determined to break the American position with new units which were due to reinforce the remnants of the Guadalcanal garrison in early October. His main combat forces would be the *2nd*

Division and two battalions of the veteran *38th Division.*[22]

As the Japanese prepared for their next attack, Admiral Ghormley sent a task force under Admiral Turner to Guadalcanal to deliver the 164th Infantry Regiment of the Americal Division as a reinforcement for the marines. Rear Admiral Norman Scott escorted the troopships with his cruisers, while a carrier group (*Hornet*) and a battleship group stood nearby to help.

The movement of the Japanese and American forces to Guadalcanal triggered another naval action. Learning that the Japanese were moving a sizeable number of troops down "The Slot," Scott abandoned his escort mission and moved to intercept the Japanese vessels on October 11. At 11:46 P.M., he surprised the incoming Japanese ships. During the Battle of Cape Esperance—it could have been called the Battle of Mutual Reinforcement—Scott's ships crossed the Japanese "T," sank a cruiser and a destroyer, and killed Rear Admiral Arimoto Goto, veteran of the Coral Sea. One American destroyer went under in the fight. The Japanese, however, managed to land their reinforcements. Two days later, the 164th Infantry came ashore at Lunga Point.

The next few days proved trying ones for the Americans on Guadalcanal. On the thirteenth, Japanese bombers and 150-mm howitzers bombarded the Lunga Point area, and that night Japanese aircraft bombed Henderson Field. But, more critical from the American viewpoint, two Japanese battleships moved in and shelled the American positions for 90 awful minutes with their 14-inch batteries. Over 900 high explosive shells slammed into the perimeter, wrecking Henderson Field, destroying most of the stored gasoline, and damaging or destroying over half the aircraft. The following night, two heavy cruisers lobbed over 750 eight-inch shells at the same targets while Japanese bombers continued to pound the area. On the fifteenth, two Japanese regiments landed near Tassafaronga despite American air attacks. Admiral Nimitz called the situation critical.[23]

For his attack, Hyakutake would have 20,000 troops to move against the 23,000 weakened marines* and green soldiers who manned the American perimeter. He decided to move nine battalions inland to attack Bloody Ridge, while a 2,000-man force would remain near the mouth of the Matanikau River and launch a coordinated diversionary attack. (*See Atlas Map No. 17d.*) Twenty-five artillery pieces would support the main effort from the vicinity of the river mouth. Hyakutake was determined not to make the third Japanese attack another "bamboo-spear" affair.[24]

---

*Malaria, dengue fever, inadequate rations, heavy work, and great tension had taken a toll of the marines by this time. In fact, malaria caused more casualties than the Japanese. It might be added that during the campaign the Japanese suffered even more severely from such deleterients than did the Americans.

Inside the marine perimeter, Vandegrift shifted his forces to the west to meet the expected attack. Everywhere his troops improved their positions.

As Hyakutake moved to implement his plan, Admiral Kondo sortied from Truk once again with four carriers "to apprehend and annihilate any powerful forces in the Solomons area, as well as any reinforcement."[25] If everything went as planned in this coordinated effort, the Japanese Navy hoped to isolate the battlefield so that Hyakutake could wipe out the American beachhead.

The Japanese offensive, however, unravelled from the first. (*See Atlas Map No. 17d.*) Hyakutake's diversionary force attacked prematurely because the main force was continually delayed as it moved, single file, along a previously prepared trail in heavy rains. On October 23, the diversionary force commander sent nine medium tanks against the western corner of the marine position. Marine antitank gunners destroyed the tanks; artillerymen then fired behind the tanks to interdict the troops who were expected to follow the tanks—and decimated hundreds of Japanese infantrymen. The attack petered out.

Late the next afternoon, the main Japanese force finally moved into position to attack, but the *2nd Division* commander was not really prepared for the assault. His mortars and artillery were spread out along the jungle trail to the rear. If he assaulted without them, his troops would once again have to use light infantry weapons to breach the American positions on Bloody Ridge. Nevertheless, the attack was launched, just like those of predecessor Japanese units. In a bitter, all-night struggle, the Japanese infantrymen crashed into Lieutenant Colonel Eugene "Chesty" Puller's battalion, but could not break through. Army reinforcements arrived in time to fill the holes in Puller's lines, while the Japanese forces became disoriented and failed to launch all the assigned attacks. Puller's forces held. At dawn, the marines and soldiers still held Bloody Ridge.

On October 25, Hyakutake again attacked, but with little improvement in style or coordination. His losses were staggering. In the west, a Japanese force did succeed in overrunning a marine company early on the morning of the twenty-sixty, but the marines quickly restored the position. By dawn on that day, the largest Japanese counteroffensive of the Guadalcanal campaign was over. There would be no more. Hyakutake had failed, just as Kawaguchi and Ichiki had failed previously. Nearly half of his force on the island was not used.

During the land battle, Rear Admiral Thomas Kinkaid maneuvered with the *Enterprise* and *Hornet* air groups to attack Admiral Kondo's fleet off Santa Cruz Island. Early on October 26, the naval air forces engaged. In a series of vicious attacks, Japanese pilots bombed, crashed, and torpedoed the *Hornet*, damaging her fatally. They also scored hits on the *Enterprise* and a battleship, and sank a destroyer. American carrier pilots damaged the light carrier *Zuiho*, the big *Shokaku*, and two destroyers. The unlucky *Shokaku* had to limp northward again for a nine-month sojourn in the repair yard—just as she had had to do after the Battle of the Coral Sea. Kinkaid, moreover, held the edge over Kondo in one important statistic: he lost 74 planes while Kondo lost 100. It was a loss that the *Combined Fleet* could not afford.

Throughout the Guadalcanal campaign, American and Japanese leaders increasingly searched for reinforcements to throw into the fray, which became a contest for the initiative in the war. For the Americans, reinforcements had to come from forces scheduled for North Africa or England, or for those scheduled to fight in the Battle of the Atlantic. The choices embroiled Admiral King, General MacArthur, and General Millard Harmon (the Army commander in the south Pacific) in arguments with General Marshall over strategic priorities. Under constant pressure, the Army Chief of Staff allowed some reinforcements to trickle into the Pacific, but he refused to endorse the movement of massive air or ground reinforcements, believing that the Pacific had enough strength for its secondary role. General Henry Arnold, the Air Chief of Staff, staunchly supported his superior. The impasse was broken on October 24, following the Japanese counteroffensive on Guadalcanal, when President Roosevelt intervened in the discussion and directed the Chief of Staff to send what was needed to the Pacific to guarantee victory at Guadalcanal. Marshall then ordered the 43rd Infantry Division (a replacement for an Australian division kept in North Africa) and the 25th Infantry Division to the South Pacific Area.[26]

Like their American counterparts, Imperial General Headquarters had difficulty rounding up forces to counter the American attack. Generally the air and land forces came from quiet areas. The Japanese also had problems finding the shipping required to move the troops and equipment to the battle zone. Each ship used to support Guadalcanal reduced the tonnage of raw materials shipped to Japan. Not surprisingly, therefore, on November 16 Imperial General Headquarters began reorganizing its forces in the Solomons-New Guinea area. First, it established the *Eighth Area Army** (to be commanded by Lieutenant General Hitoshi Imamura of the *Sixteenth Army* in Java). Then it organized the *Eighteenth Army* and assigned it the task of continuing operations in New Guinea. *Seventeenth*

---

*An area army was the equivalent of an Allied army, not an Allied army group. The Japanese army was the equivalent of an Allied corps. There was no corps organization in the Japanese Army.

Army would continue to fight only in the Solomons. General Imamura was told to recapture the Guadalcanal area with the assistance of the *Combined Fleet.* The *38th Division* was diverted to the *Seventeenth Army* for the next offensive against the American beachhead in November. In December, four other divisions would be ordered south from Korea and China.[27]

In October, following the third defeat of the Army forces, Admiral Yamamoto took a direct interest in land operations. He sent a staff captain to Guadalcanal to talk with General Hyakutake before the *Eighth Area Army* had been activated.[28] Yamamoto wanted Hyakutake to give priority to Guadalcanal over the Port Moresby operation so that once and for all the objective in the Solomons could be achieved. Hyakutake agreed to the admiral's wishes. Moreover, Yamamoto proposed that during the next offensive the *Combined Fleet's* ships attack Henderson Field to destroy the airfield and its aircraft, after which the Army could mop up the shattered American force. Hyakutake also agreed to this plan.*

Early in November, Admiral Tanaka again began shepherding Japanese reinforcements into Guadalcanal via the "Tokyo Express" for the next action. His ships landed the first elements of the *38th Division* on the island on November 10; the main body would follow a few days later.

As the Japanese regrouped their forces, Admiral Nimitz decided to replace Ghormley with a more aggressive commander. With Admiral King's approval, he picked Vice Admiral William Halsey for the job. Halsey, enroute to the South Pacific when the decision was made, assumed the post of theater commander on October 18. From that time on, the Navy became more aggressive in the south Pacific Area.

In early November, while the Japanese were reinforcing, Halsey sent Turner to Guadalcanal with marine reinforcements and another regiment of the Americal Division. The day after the troops went ashore (November 11) Turner retired. His naval escort followed him a short way, and then turned back to intercept the Japanese transports and warships which coastwatchers reported were moving south once again toward Guadalcanal.

From November 12 to November 15, American naval forces clashed with Kondo's *Second Fleet* as it tried to force

its way through the narrow waters to attack Henderson Field and allow Tanaka to land the main body of the *38th Division.* In nearly three days of continuous naval action, Kondo could not achieve his goal, although he pummeled the Americans unmercifully for a good part of the time and sank 10 American warships, 7 of them in the opening engagement on the night of November 12. On the fourteenth, the Americans did immense damage to the Japanese transports, sinking six and damaging four more which were beached to land the *38th Division.* The battle ended with a battleship engagement, the first since Jutland. It was as majestic as it was grim. When the smoke cleared, the United States Navy held the sea.† The naval Battle of Guadalcanal was the decisive battle of the naval campaign. Following it, the Japanese never regained control of the sea or the air—control which was essential if they were to reinforce the garrison ashore and to attack the American perimeter.

Shortly after the battle, Vandegrift ordered his marines to advance to the west to take Kukumbona. As it developed,

† Rear Admirals Daniel Callaghan and Norman Scott died in this closely contested battle.

General Alexander Vandegrift as Commandant, USMC

*This action illustrates the confusing overlap of interests and jurisdiction between Army and Navy commanders at Rabaul and Admiral Yamamoto at Truk. Yamamoto was senior to the naval commander at Rabaul. There was no similar Army headquarters between the senior Army Commander at Rabaul and Imperial General Headquarters. At this time, moreover, the Imperial Navy had more interest in the Solomons than did the Army; hence, Yamamoto would not hesitate to step in to influence the situation. The Imperial Navy was charged with operations in the Pacific Area at the start of war.

General Hyakutake also launched a local offensive along the coast to protect his position. By November 21, neither general had gained much ground, and the forces settled down along a line from Mount Austen to Point Cruz on the coast. Ground fighting, as it had all along, continued sporadically.

Later in November, the "Tokyo Express" began once again to deliver troops and supplies to the Japanese forces. In another naval engagement, the Battle of Tassafaronga, Halsey's sailors attempted to intercept one of the express runs. The Americans stopped the delivery of troops, but the experienced Admiral Tanaka, a torpedo expert of the first rank, wreaked havoc with his destroyers: at the cost of one destroyer sunk and one damaged, he sank an American heavy cruiser and inflicted major damage on three more heavy cruisers. From that point on, however, the Japanese resupply runs were really ineffective. Each run could bring in rations for a couple of days, but this was not adequate. To complicate the effort further, the ships could not land the goods because they could not risk the delay in the face of dominant Allied air and naval forces. Therefore, they rolled barrels of supplies overboard, hoping that barges could tow them ashore or that the tide would carry them ashore. In addition, submarines were pressed into service as supply boats, truly a waste of these valuable craft.

Vandegrift's campaign ended on December 9, 1942, when Major General Alexander Patch, USA, assumed command of operations ashore. The 1st Marine Division began withdrawing to Australia the same day. Patch's Americal Division was soon reinforced by a regiment of the 25th Infantry Division and by the 2nd Marine Division, which assumed control of its units which had been at Guadalcanal from the beginning. With fresh troops, Patch launched his first offensive on December 17 to take the Mount Austen area, an initial objective of the 1st Marine Regiment on August 7.

With the arrival in January of the remainder of the 25th Infantry Division, Halsey activated XIV Corps and made Patch its commander. The general launched his first corps offensive on January 10, 1943 with two divisions abreast. Driving westward along the coast, he kept his right division pushing frontally while using his inland division to envelop. By late January, Patch was prepared to launch a final attack to trap and destroy the Japanese forces near Cape Esperance. (*See Atlas Map No. 17a.*)

Unknown to the American commander, representatives of Imperial General Headquarters had met with the Emperor on December 31 and decided to withdraw from Guadalcanal. The Japanese High Command then ordered *Seventeenth Army* to defend the Solomons from north of the "Isle of Death," and directed *Eighteenth Army* to reinvigorate its offensive against Port Moresby. On January 4, 1943, General Imamura received orders to withdraw from Guadalcanal in early February. During the first week of February he evacuated over 10,000 of his troops—the remnants of the 36,000 men who had been sent to the island after the American invasion.[29]

Moving along the coast, Patch's direct pressure force linked up at Cape Esperance on February 8 with the small encircling force which he had landed at Verahue on January 21. When Patch closed his pincers, the Japanese were gone. (*See Appendix 10.*)

The Guadalcanal campaign was not a scintillating example of modern warfare. At best, it was a series of hard-fought, attritive battles which sapped everyone's strength. It did, however, show the interdependency of air, land, and sea operations, because it demonstrated that an effective mix of the three distinct forces was needed to ensure victory. This would be true throughout the Pacific war, and would distinguish that war from all other wars. At the same time, the campaign illustrated the vital need for adequate logistical planning, readily available reserves, and the coordinated commitment of forces—all traditional principles of good operations.

From the point of view of some Japanese, the phlegmatic American victory at Guadalcanal was the decisive campaign of the war, because this campaign made them realize that Japan could not win the war against the growing combat power of the United States—especially if the Japanese continued to make so many mistakes. Many Japanese did not share this view. They could not deny, however, that the American victory stopped Japanese advances in the south

Guadalcanal

Pacific and secured the Allied line of communications to Australia. The Americans also gained an airfield complex, an invaluable anchorage, and a logistical base for their next thrust into the central Solomons. With a base at Guadalcanal and another in Papua, the Allies gained the necessary steppingstones to secure advanced fighter strips and isolate Rabaul.

To Secure Port Moresby

Victory in Papua ebbed and flowed with the tide of battle on Guadalcanal. From the first, the interrelationship between the two campaigns was clear and binding.* With each reverse on Guadalcanal, the Japanese changed their plans for Port Moresby; and in the Southwest Pacific Area, the Allies kept one eye cocked eastward as they developed plans for Papua.[30]

Nearly as important as the strategic interrelationship between Guadalcanal and Papua was the equal difficulty of the battlefields. The Papuan campaign was fought first in the high Kokoda Mountains of southeastern New Guinea, which form the island's lower spine, and at swampy Milne Bay at the southeast tip of the great island. The final battles were fought along the coastal strip near Buna and Gona, a swampy, rainy, jungled area, which encompassed some coconut plantations and was even more unhealthy than Guadalcanal—malaria, dengue, and skin infections flourished. In Papua, however, some small towns and reasonable trails and tracks allowed for movement over the Kokoda Mountains and along the coast. Other areas—mountains and swamps—were virtually impassable, even to trained infantry.

Shortly after landing in the Buna area on July 22, Lieutenant Colonel Hatsuo Tsukamoto led the infantry battalion and some supporting groops of the *Yokoyama Force* inland toward Wairopi and the Kokoda Trail. Five days later, Tsukamoto occupied Kokoda, after breaking through the small Australian force and its reinforcements. (*See Atlas Map No. 19a.*) There, Tsukamoto stopped to wait for the main body of the *South Seas Detachment* and to build up his supplies. Meanwhile, combat troops, support troops, and supplies poured into the beachhead in preparation for the build-up, the airfield construction, and the advance on Port Moresby. This continued until the 1st Marine Division landed on Guadalcanal. Then Imperial General

Headquarters began diverting available units to the Solomons.

In Australia, General MacArthur took immediate action to stem the Japanese advance. First, he ordered the Australian 7th Division to deploy two brigades to Port Moresby and a third to Milne Bay. Even though transportation was scarce, the general pushed these units forward; on August 19 he had 22,000 troops at Port Moresby and 9,458 more at Milne Bay. MacArthur next pressed for the completion of airfields in the Cape York Peninsula of northern Queensland so that his fighters and bombers could take the air war to the Japanese. By the end of August, three of the fields were ready; three more were completed in early September. Finally, MacArthur ordered Lieutenant General Sydney Rowell, commanding Australian I Corps and New Guinea Force, to hold the crest of the Owen Stanley Mountains, and then to retake Kokoda, the Buna-Gona area, and Salamaua and Lae. Furthermore, MacArthur told Rowell to maintain and reinforce KANGA Force, establish a special force at Milne Bay, and infiltrate units northwestward from Milne Bay along the Papuan coast to join the troops advancing to Kokoda.

The Japanese completely frustrated MacArthur by launching two offensives in late September. On the night of August 25, 1,500 naval landing troops came ashore at Milne Bay (in lieu of Samarai Island) to capture the new Allied airfields there; and the following day, Major General Tomitaro Horii attacked along the Kokoda Trail with his strong *South Seas Detachment* in an effort to take Port Moresby. At Milne Bay, the Japanese naval troops failed to dislodge the Australian infantry and the American engineers, and after Admiral Mikawa in Rabaul decided not to reinforce failure, the surviving troops withdrew. By September 5, the Australians could claim the first Allied ground victory in the Southwest Pacific Area. On the Kokoda Trail, however, the Australians fared less satisfactorily. There, General Horii—repeating the pattern of earlier Japanese operations in Malaya and Burma—fixed his outnumbered opponents with one regiment, then constantly flanked the Australians with his second regiment. By September 16, Horii had captured Ioribawa Ridge, barely 25 miles from Port Moresby. From that position, the Japanese could see the beach at Port Moresby. (*See Atlas Map No. 19a.*)

Horii's rapid advance worried MacArthur, who had not expected it. His intelligence officer, Colonel Charles Willoughby, had continually told him that the Japanese would not drive overland from Buna to take Port Moresby, but would develop airfields near the beachhead for attacks on Port Moresby and the Cape York Peninsula. As a result, MacArthur queried the Allied Land Forces on September 7 to see why the Australians were regularly withdrawing.

---

*This interrelationship of simultaneous campaigns would be a characteristic of the two-pronged drive from Papua and Guadalcanal to isolate Rabaul in 1943, and the two-pronged drive from the Southwest and Central Pacific Areas toward the Philippines in 1944.

When General Rowell reported his own situation accurately, MacArthur immediately deployed an additional Australian brigade to Port Moresby to release one there for employment on the Kokoda Trail. At the same time, the general planned to stop Horii's force by sending one American regimental combat team along a trail to the east of the Kokoda Trail to flank the Japanese force and force Horii to withdraw.

After the fact, we now know that MacArthur need not have had great concern about the *South Seas Detachment* taking his advanced base. His forces outnumbered the 5,000 Japanese, and Horii's troops were in bad physical condition. Lieutenant General George Kenney's Fifth Air Force fighters and attack bombers had virtually destroyed the Japanese supply lines; on September 17, the general had no food to issue to his troops on Ioribaiwa Ridge. Furthermore, as a result of the Battle of the Ridge on Guadalcanal (Kawaguchi's attack) and the defeat at Milne Bay, Imperial General Headquarters ordered *Eighteenth Army* to withdraw its forward forces from the Owen Stanleys and secure the beachhead at Buna-Gona. Offensive operations were to stop in Papua until the decision was reached in the Solomons.

Horii began withdrawing on September 24. For a time, the retrograde movement remained orderly, although it was marred by a lack of food which caused many Japanese troops to resort to cannibalism to survive.* The Australian 7th Division followed the withdrawing Japanese, and after many bitter fights recaptured Kokoda on November 2 and Wairopi on November 13. (*See Atlas Map No. 19b.*)

Just after the Australians began their counterattack along the Kokoda Trail, General MacArthur ordered Allied Land Forces to destroy the Japanese beachhead at Buna-Gona. While Australians continued along the Kokoda Trail to gain the line of the Kumusi River near Wairopi, an American regiment would be sent across the Owen Stanleys on the Kapa Kapa-Jaure track to seize the Kumusi River line south of Wairopi. A third force, an Allied one, would secure the Milne Bay-Cape Nelson region and nearby Goodenough Island. MacArthur wanted these forces to approach Buna-Gona in such a way that they could quickly withdraw in case the Japanese succeeded in the Solomons and once again went on the offensive in Papua. Moreover, the general wanted his units to consider their logistical preparations carefully before attacking. To improve his own theater logistics, MacArthur established a logistical command at Port Moresby to control supplies and transportation.

As soon as two regiments of the American 32nd Infantry Division† (Major General Forrest Harding, commanding)

---

*A Japanese officer wrote in mid-October that his troops were eating roots, and grass, and that some other units were eating the flesh of Australian soldiers.

† The 126th Infantry moved by sea to Port Moresby. The 128th Infantry, a sister unit, deployed by air. It was the first large-scale air-transported move of the war for American forces.

arrived in Papua, elements of the 126th Infantry began moving over the Owen Stanleys to Jaure. (*See Atlas Map No. 19b.*) They struggled against improbable odds as the mountainous terrain exhausted the green American troops. The men of the 128th Infantry found the coastal route nearly as difficult. The available overland trail proved nearly impossible, and only a jungle-trained Australian independent company succeeded in negotiating it. Without landing craft and without charts of the reef-filled waters, small luggers and even native outriggers had to be used to move troops and supplies along the coast. (*See Atlas Map No. 19c.*)

Cecil Abel, an old New Guinea hand and a Christian missionary, saved the remainder of the American troops from interminably battling the Papuan marshes and mountains when he provided information in mid-October that a grass airfield could be quickly cleared near Fasari, and from there troops could move over good trails to Buna. Additional reconnaissance showed that similar fields could be prepared quickly near Pongani by cutting and burning off the grass and small trees. Armed with this information, Generals Harding and Blamey asked MacArthur for permission to fly the remaining troops to the Pongani area; but MacArthur did not approve the request until Blamey assured him that there were adequate land routes for withdrawal and that the troops would be properly concentrated so that they could not be cut off by the Japanese. (*See Atlas Map No. 19c.*) By November 15, the troops of the 7th and 32nd Divisions were in position to strike Buna-Gona, and Goodenough Island was in Allied hands. As the Allies approached the beachhead, General Imamura arrived on November 18 to take command of the new *Eighth Area Army*. He was followed on November 25 by Lieutenant General Hatazo Adachi, commander of the new *Eighteenth Army*, who was to take charge of operations in Papua.

The Japanese beachhead on the northern coast of Papua was similar to the marine position on Guadalcanal, but the Japanese had been more thorough than the marines in erecting their defenses. For the most part they held the only high—and dry—ground in the swamp-infested area, and their positions were masterpieces of field engineering. Coconut log bunkers with adjoining firing positions covered all reasonable approaches, while interlocking fields of fire for automatic weapons crisscrossed every defensive area and covered each bunker. Jungle grass and shrubs grew on each bunker, making it blend totally with the surrounding locale.

As the Allies approached, 6,500 Japanese manned three main defensive areas: Gona village on the northwest near the Basabua anchorage; the Sanananda Track position about three and a half miles south of Sanananda and the Japanese supply base of Giruwa; and the elongated Buna Village-Buna Mission-Point Giropa-Cape Endaiadere position. (*See Atlas Map No. 19d.*) In the west, about 900 army troops of various units held Gona under Major Tsume Yamamoto. In the center, Colonal Yosuke Yokoyama, an engineer, had close to 2,500 troops along the Sanananda Track; 1,800 of them were stationed at the forward line of defense around the track junction under the command of the experienced Lieutenant Colonel Hatsuo Tsukamoto. In the east, naval troops under Captain Yoshitatsu Yasuda, IJN, held the Buna Village-Buna Mission area, while Colonel Hiroshi Yamamoto commanded the service, labor, anti-aircraft, and newly arrived infantry troops in the Cape Endaiadere position. There were about 2,500 men in the defenses between Buna and Cape Endaiadere position. There was no overall Japanese commander in Papua, because General Horii had drowned during the retreat to Buna. (*See Appendix 11.*)

Troops of Major General George Vasey's 7th Division and Major General Harding's 32nd Division advanced eagerly toward the Japanese positions, believing that they would meet only stragglers from the fight in the Owen Stanleys or service troops. They did not expect much of a fight. (*See Atlas Maps No. 19d and No. 19e.*) On November 19, they learned how sadly mistaken they had been. At Gona, the Australians lost 36 men in their first engagement. After regrouping, they attacked in battalion strength for three days (November 22 to 24); still there was no break-through, as two battalions suffered over 60 casualties each. By the twenty-fifth, these Australians were incapable of launching further attacks. (*See Atlas Map No. 19d.*)

The Australians advancing on the Sanananda Track fared little better. Tired and half starving, the Australians made contact on November 19, and attacked in force the next two days against Colonel Tsukamoto's outpost line. While the main attack failed to achieve much, Captain B.W.T. Catterns led his company to a position astride the track two miles behind the Japanese outposts. Exploiting this success, the Australians forced Tsukamoto to withdraw to his first defensive line at the track junction to the north. There the Australians stopped, exhausted. Catterns' company was down to 26 men; most companies were nearly as weak. Both sides reinforced. A new regiment (the American 126th Infantry from the 32nd Division) attacked on the twenty-second and gained a meager 350 yards. The Americans, who had bragged a little too much to the Australians, were forced to prove their mettle while their Allies watched for the next few days. Finally, on November 26, a company of the 126th Infantry slipped into a blocking position north of the track junction but south of the second Japanese defensive line. The Americans held firm in this position as the situation stagnated with the Japanese in firm control on the Sanananda Track.

General Harding's first attacks in the east brought his battalions close to their final objective, but none of his units penetrated the Japanese defenses. Attacking on three trails, which canalized their movements, as had been the case in the Australian zone, Harding's infantry hit and bounced off the Japanese defenses on November 19. The confident Americans were stunned by the stiff resistance. (*See Atlas Map No. 19e.*) South of the Buna Mission, the 2nd Battalion, 128th Infantry struck one of the strongest Japanese positions (the Triangle) on November 21. Reinforced by another battalion, the American task force (now the URBANA Force) tried again on the twenty-sixth to break the enemy position, but failed. Attacking the Triangle on the night of the twenty-sixth, URBANA Force failed again, although one company pushed through to the coast at Siwori Village, where it cut the Japanese line of communications between Buna and Sanananda.

East of Cape Endaiadere, Brigadier General Hanford MacNider (WARREN Force) attacked in strength along two routes on November 20 and 21. He gained nothing and sustained heavy casualties.* His route proved so treacherous as it approached the airfield below Cape Endaiadere that MacNider abandoned it as a route of attack. In the future, the general would have to attack along the coast.

By December 1, the Japanese had stopped the Allies everywhere. Casualties had been high—the 32nd Division took 492—Allied attacks had achieved little, and, most critical, the Allies faced a bitter, siege-like fight with inadequate weapons. Half starved, sick with fevers and diseases of the jungle, without quinine or atabrine for malaria, without adequate water purification tablets, the Australian and American soldiers faced a dispiriting campaign. In the bloodied National Guard regiments as well as in the decimated Australian battalions, morale began to ebb.[31]

General Harding recognized the problems and asked for reinforcements, tanks, and artillery, but he got virtually nothing. It was nearly impossible to find more American troops at the time—only the 41st Infantry Division remained in Australia—and the Fifth Air Force could not fly in much heavy equipment. The burden of supply fell on the Navy, but the Allied naval force commander would not send his ships into the restricted waters along the coast near Oro Bay where the Japanese had air and naval superiority. His fears were justified. Just before Harding had launched his first attacks, Japanese pilots sank the coastal luggers which were hauling meager supplies to Oro Bay, thus destroying the division's supply line for the moment.

The most surprising Allied deficiency in Papua was the lack of artillery. In late November, one 105-mm howitzer arrived by air. It was destined to be the only American light

---

*Company C, 128th Infantry lost 63 men in three days of combat. All four of its officers were lost. Two sergeants commanded the company on November 21. Both were killed within hours of each other. Such casualties were not uncommon in the fights during this period.

field piece used by the Allies throughout the period.*
Because it was the only weapon capable of reducing the
Japanese strongpoints—other artillery fire merely bounced
off the bunkers—the Allies tried to substitute bombing for
medium and heavy artillery, but inadequate control
procedures and inaccurate bombing techniques kept the
Allied pilots from really assisting the ground troops. In
many cases, Allied pilots bombed and strafed Allied and
Japanese troops with great impartiality.

Hearing that American infantrymen had broken and run
during Harding's initial attacks, MacArthur became incensed.
He called in Lieutenant General Robert Eichelberger, the
newly arrived American I Corps commander, and ordered
him to "take Buna or don't come back alive." MacArthur
knew his troops were green and poorly trained, but he
believed that aggressive leadership would make up for these
deficiencies. He also felt that Harding had failed to do the
required job, and accordingly told Eichelberger to relieve
Harding and any of his subordinates as necessary.[32]
MacArthur would not tolerate an American failure at Buna.

General Eichelberger moved up to the front immediately
to assess the situation. He found that Harding seemed to
work only from his command post, and that neither he nor
his regimental commanders knew what was going on at the
front. The general found discipline lacking in the forward
companies; furthermore, the soldiers there would not fire
their weapons because they did not want to stir up the
Japanese. Finding his West Point classmate reluctant to
make changes or accept his criticism, Eichelberger relieved
Harding and then began to clean house among the regimental
commanders. By December 4, Eichelberger, using selected
officers, had assumed complete control of the burden of
taking Buna.

Before Eichelberger could accomplish much in the
American zone, the Australians fought their way into Gona
on December 9. There the Japanese soldiers, many of
whom were wearing gas masks, had slept and fought for
days beside the decaying corpses of their comrades. Once
Gona was occupied, the Australians moved west to engage
the Japanese troops who had moved from the mouth of the
Kumusi River to the Amboga River, barely two miles away.
These Japanese included survivors from the Kokoda Trail
and soldiers of Major General Yamagata's *21st Independent
Mixed Brigade*, which had landed in the area because
Allied air attacks prevented a landing near Gona. The two
forces clashed immediately, and continued to do so until
late December. After Yamagata found that he could not
break through to relieve Gona, he sent his men by boat to
the Sanananda Area.

Relieved:
Lieutenant General Sydney Rowell, Australian I
Corps.
Major General Arthur Allen, Australian 7th
Division.
Major General Forrest Harding, American 32nd
Infantry Division.

Died/Killed:
Major General Tomitaro Horii, South Seas
Detachment.
Major General Kensaku Oda, South Seas
Detachment.

Wounded in Action:
Brigadier General Hanford MacNider, WARREN
Force.
Brigadier General Albert Waldron, American
32nd Division.
Brigadier General Clovis Byers, Commander,
32nd Division troops at the front.

Senior Officer Casualties in Papuan Campaign

During early December, fighting reached a stalemate on
the Sanananda Track. An Australian battalion established
another roadblock north of the first roadblock, but all other
Allied operations failed to crack the Japanese line.

At the same time, the Americans also failed to advance in
the Cape Endaiadere sector. At Buna on December 5,
however, Staff Sergeant Herman Bottcher, a Spanish Civil
War veteran, lifted the spirits of the Allies when he broke
through the Japanese defenses with his platoon and reached
the coast just east of Buna Village.† After more heavy
fighting, URBANA Force captured a deserted Buna Village
on December 14.

Eichelberger gradually improved the morale of the 32nd
Division. The general was always at the front pushing his
commanders to attack, while his staff worked to supply the
troops. Regardless of the dangers, he also demanded that
his men eat hot rations. His bravery and concern improved
morale and efficiency, but he also profited from the fact that
his soldiers had learned how to fight the determined
Japanese. While the Americans improved on the battlefield,
Eichelberger made sure that his 41st Division in Australia
was being trained for similar operations.[33]

The situation further improved for the 32nd Division
after General Sir Thomas Blamey, Allied Land Force
Commander and now the New Guinea Commander, sent
the 18th Australian Brigade with tanks to reinforce
WARREN Force on December 15. Brigadier George
Wootten, an Australian, took command of WARREN
Force and launched a tank-led attack on December 18. The
tanks did the trick. The Allies immediately broke through

---

*The Australians had some 25 pounders—approximately 3½ inch in
caliber—but these smaller, flatter-trajectory weapons were not effective
against bunkers.

† For his performance, Bottcher was awarded a Distinguished Service
Cross and given a battlefield commission to captain. He served with the
32nd Division until killed in action in the mountains of Leyte in late 1944.

Australian Tanks and Infantry of WARREN Force Close in on Cape Endaiadere, January 1943

along the coast to Cape Endaiadere, and on January 2, 1943, they made contact with URBANA Force at Giropa Point. (*See Appendix 12.*)

URBANA Force began to make headway against the Buna defenses after mid-December, when the Americans pushed up to Entrance Creek, flanking the Triangle. (*See Atlas Map No. 19f.*) New frontal attacks initially failed to crack the fortified area; but, with Eichelberger's vigorous encouragement, the regimental commander finally moved two companies across the creek north of the Triangle on the twenty-second. The next day, a single platoon miraculously broke through defenses and nearly reached the sea. Holding against counterattacks, the small group of Americans became the key to the Triangle. A regimental attack on December 25 failed to link up with the platoon, but two days later a company broke through to the platoon and established a vital corridor across the top of the Triangle. This move turned the Triangle, forcing Captain Yasuda to withdraw his forces to the Buna Mission. There was no slackening in bitterness in the final fight for the Mission. But, inevitably, the Japanese recognized their plight; caught between three advancing American columns, they withdrew as best they could. Captain Yasuda and Colonel Yamamoto committed *hara-kiri* before the Buna Mission fell on January 2, 1943.

The loss of Buna had not been unexpected in Rabaul or Tokyo, although it was a severe blow to Japanese plans for the future. Without reinforcements and without air and naval support, the Japanese defenders could not be expected

to do much more. All attempts to relieve or evacuate the garrison, however, were made too late to help the majority of the defenders.

With Buna reduced, the Allies turned their attention to the Sanananda Track, where Lieutenant Colonel Tsukamoto still held the Australians and Americans at bay. With a fresh, well-trained regiment from the 41st Infantry Division and Brigadier Wootten's 18th Brigade, the Allies soon neutralized Tsukamoto's defense at the track junction and then enveloped the second line of defense north of the roadblocks. On January 16, the Allies entered Sanananda. Final resistance in the area ended five days later, but not until about 2,100 Japanese had escaped and headed for Salamaua and Lae where Imperial General Headquarters hoped to build up strength for another advance into Papua.

The Papuan campaign had been brutal. While General MacArthur issued one of his dramatic and highly optimistic communiqués, which spoke of small losses, the Allies had paid a dear price for their new real estate and for the security of Port Moresby. In destroying perhaps 13,000 Japanese troops, the Australians had lost 2,165 dead, with 3,533 wounded, while the Americans lost 930 dead, with 1,918 wounded.* To make matters worse, malaria permanently disabled 2,334 American troops and probably a larger number of Australians. These casualties were greater than those on Guadalcanal, but in Papua the Allies were attacking most of the time.[34]

*Allied dead include missing in action.

Combat in Papua had shown how well a half-starved Japanese soldier could fight in prepared positions, and also how necessary it was to have trained troops with the proper tools of war to fight against such a determined opponent. Furthermore, it had made men believers in a strict malaria control program.

The Papuan campaign was quite unlike the Guadalcanal campaign in that it was a more orthodox land campaign in which ground forces predominated. However, the seeds of expanded air operations—particularly close air support and air supply—were planted. So were the seeds of expanded amphibious operations, which would move the bulk of MacArthur's supplies and nearly all of his maneuver forces around the theater. MacArthur's Navy, however, would not become a combat force similar to the ones which fought the naval engagements around Guadalcanal. For such actions the general would have to rely on his land-based airpower.

In other ways, the Papuan campaign did resemble the Guadalcanal campaign. There was the same critical need for sound logistical planning, readily available reserves, and the coordinated commitment of all forces. Furthermore, if ground troops were to be victorious on a jungle battlefield, the Papuan campaign revealed the necessity for careful integration of infantry, tank, engineer, and artillery forces— just as the strategic interdependence of air, land, and sea forces had been demonstrated earlier. For example, the infantry tank would develop into a nearly indispensable weapon in the Pacific War, but its employment demanded efficient infantry, engineer, artillery, and tank coordination. Papua also revealed a sticky problem—the need for close Allied cooperation. This problem was solved by MacArthur in his own imperious way. He totally dominated his Australian commanders, and gave the Americans command of all major operations as soon as American troops predominated in his force.

As the lessons of the Papuan campaign were being absorbed, the 41st Infantry Division—the first of the theater-trained American divisions—began to advance along the New Guinea coast against the Japanese at the mouth of the Kumusi River. Behind it, the Allies prepared to turn Buna, Dobodura, and Oro Bay into major logistical, training, and staging bases for the next battles. MacArthur now had his steppingstone in Papua to complement Halsey's at Guadalcanal.

Task Two loomed in the future. To accomplish it, MacArthur and Halsey would have to cooperate with one another. This would mean carefully timing their different but complementary moves, and orchestrating the employment of their air, land, and sea forces to isolate, divide, and destroy the Japanese between Guadalcanal and Papua and the bastion of Rabaul.

To Inflict Losses on the Japanese Forces: CARTWHEEL

Before the end of the Guadalcanal and Papuan campaigns, Allied leaders began considering future operations in the Pacific and the Far East. These were the subject of further discussion at the Casablanca Conference in January 1943, when the Combined Chiefs of Staff agreed in vague terms to continue operations against Japan throughout that year.[35] At Casablanca, the Chiefs gave the British the mission of attacking Burma, looked forward to the early seizure of Rabaul, and optimistically contemplated the drive of United States forces across the Pacific toward Truk and the Marianas.[36]

In Washington, Brisbane, and Noumea, also, American leaders were looking forward to new operations in 1943. Because of differing viewpoints, in March the Joint Chiefs of Staff invited representatives of MacArthur, Halsey, and Nimitz to Washington to discuss plans for the remainder of the year. Most of the discussion centered on MacArthur's ELKTON Plan and the resources which were needed to accomplish it. This plan envisioned the capture of Rabaul by two coordinated drives beginning in Papua and Guadalcanal (Task Two and Task Three of the Joint Chiefs of Staff directive of July 2, 1942). After heated debate, the Pacific representatives agreed that only Task Two could be accomplished in 1943, given the resources on hand and the reinforcements which could be provided. The capture of Rabaul would have to wait until 1944, or until more forces could be provided.

On March 23, the Joint Chiefs limited operations in 1943 to the original Task Two objectives. (*See Atlas Map No. 20.*) Accordingly, they ordered MacArthur to establish airfields in Kiriwina and Woodlark Islands in the Solomon Sea; to seize the Lae-Salamaua-Finschhafen-Madang area of New Guinea; to occupy western New Britain; and to seize and occupy the Solomons (including the southern portion of Bougainville). These operations were designed to prepare for the seizure of the entire Bismarck Archipelago. The Joint Chiefs left MacArthur in overall command, but they directed that Halsey retain tactical command of all forces employed in the Solomons, and that all elements of the Pacific Ocean Area forces not employed by Halsey would remain under Nimitz's control.* They left the timing of the operations to MacArthur and Halsey.[37]

---

*The argument over who would command broke down once again along Army and Navy lines. Admiral King finally gave in to the proposal Marshall originally made on December 1, 1942—probably to save his good working relationship with the Chief of Staff.

MacArthur immediately modified his ELKTON Plan to meet the requirements of the new directive and issued his ELKTON III Plan (code name: CARTWHEEL) on April 26, after conferring with Halsey.* On May 6, he followed with warning instructions to his commanders. The instructions read in part:

The general scheme of maneuver is to advance our bomber line towards Rabaul; first by improvement of presently occupied forward bases; secondly, by the occupation and implementation of air bases which can be secured without committing large forces; and then, by the seizure and implementation of successive hostile airdromes.

By destructive air attack soften up and gain air superiority over each attack objective along the two axes of advance. Neutralize with appropriate aviation supporting hostile air bases and destroy hostile naval forces and shipping within range. Prevent reinforcement or supply of objectives under attack. Move land forces forward, covered by air and naval forces, to seize and consolidate each successive objective. Displace aviation forward on to captured airdromes. Repeat this process to successive objectives, neutralizing by air action, or by air, land, and sea action, intermediate hostile installations which are not objectives of immediate attack.[38]

These instructions were the blueprint for MacArthur's offensives for the duration of the war. They would be tested in the actions which led to Rabaul so that following the capture of the Japanese bastion, MacArthur's forces could move rapidly on the Philippines. Like the Japanese, American leaders had recognized that fighter cover was a key ingredient to successful offensives in the vast Pacific. Unlike the Japanese, they had also recognized that air, land, and sea forces had to be balanced, interdependent, and under some sort of unified command and control at the working level.

Although MacArthur planned to start CARTWHEEL around June 1, he had to postpone it until the last day of the month because of delays in assembling troops for Kiriwina. (*See Atlas Map No. 20.*) Three major forces were prepared to carry out his strategic blueprint. General Blamey's New Guinea Force, primarily Australian, would reduce the Japanese positions in the Salamaua-Lae-Finschhafen-Madang area; Lieutenant General Walter Krueger's newly

formed ALAMO Force,† primarily American, would attack Woodlark, Kiriwina, and New Britain; and Admiral Halsey's United States Army, Marine Corps, and New Zealand divisions would attack New Georgia and then Bougainville in the Solomons.

Japanese Imperial General Headquarters and Japanese Army and Navy leaders in Rabaul had not been idle while the Allies were developing their new plans. Faced with defeat in the Solomons and Papua, the Japanese were still confident that they could hold the line in the central Solomons and in the Lae-Salamaua area of New Guinea. They believed also that eventually they could move overland again and attack Port Moresby.[39]

More importantly, because the Japanese knew that Rabaul would be a key objective for the Allies, they spared no effort to improve the defenses of that bastion. A secure Rabaul would protect Truk, the Philippines, and the Netherlands East Indies against attack from the south. The Army remained concerned with the New Guinea area, while the Imperial Navy concentrated its efforts on protecting the Solomons.

General Hitoshi Imamura, commanding *Eighth Area Army*, deployed his forces to defend New Guinea and Bougainville. He ordered part of the *51st Division* to Lae and Salamaua, and sent the *20th Division* to Madang, the *41st Division* to Wewak, and the *6th Division* to Bougainville. The small *Southeastern Detachment* went to New Georgia to bolster naval forces there. Although Imamura ordered most of his *6th Air Division* to New Guinea, he retained some air units at Rabaul. Lieutenant General Hyakutake commanded the Army forces (*Seventeenth Army*) in the Solomons, while Lieutenant General Adachi commanded those (*Eighteenth Army*) in New Guinea. (*See Atlas Map No. 20.*) Imamura did not have to worry about Netherlands New Guinea because Imperial General Headquarters ordered *Southern Army* (Field Marshal Count Terauchi) to defend the territory between Hollandia and the Vogelkop Peninsula.**

Imamura's naval colleague, Vice Admiral Jinichi Kusaka, commanded the coequal naval command in Rabaul, *Southeastern Area Fleet*, which was organized on November 18. The admiral, charged with the defense of the central Solomons, sent the *7th* and *8th Combined Special Naval*

---

† ALAMO Force was essentially Sixth Army. Apparently, MacArthur did not want American troops to serve under Australian command. For these operations General Blamey assumed direct command of New Guinea Force.

** On October 22, *Second Area Army* was ordered south from Manchuria to take command of defenses in western New Guinea and nearby areas. In March 1944, it took command of *Eighteenth Army* and *Fourth Air Army* in New Guinea.

---

* MacArthur's plans for the capture of Rabaul were all similar to his original 1942 propositions. His ELKTON I Plan (March 12, 1943), ELKTON II Plan (March 23, 1943), and his ELKTON III Plan (April 26, 1943) differed little in concept. They were strikingly similar to his original TULSA Two B Plan of August 21, 1942.

Landing Forces to Santa Isabel and New Georgia, respectively, to hold the area. He kept his *Eleventh Air Fleet* in Rabaul. Kusaka also commanded the *Eighth Fleet*, but it had few ships and would have to depend on reinforcements from Admiral Yamamoto if heavy naval action was anticipated. (*See Appendix 14.*)

During his tenure in Rabaul, General Imamura dealt directly with Imperial General Headquarters. Admiral Kusaka often did so also, but he was technically under the command of Admiral Yamamoto at Truk.

Unlike the Allies, the Japanese did not suspend operations for several months following Papua and Guadalcanal.* In late January of 1943, they tried to capture the base at Wau, New Guinea used by KANGA Force. They failed. After the battle for Wau ended, the Australians pushed the Japanese back towards Salamaua; by April, the Australian 3rd Division watched the Japanese garrison there and waited for the Allies to begin CARTWHEEL operations. (*See Atlas Map No. 20.*) Besides putting the Australians in an excellent position for the impending offensive in June, the battle of Wau triggered the Battle of the Bismarck Sea. (March 2 to 4, 1943.) In that battle, alerted and rehearsed Allied fliers attacked the convoy which was bringing the remainder of the *51st Division* into Lae to reinforce the area.† The Japanese lost 3,664 of the 6,912 troops embarked.[40]

During this interim period, the Japanese air forces were quite active. In the January 4, 1943 Central Agreement, which governed all Japanese actions in the Solomons and New Guinea, Imperial Headquarters had ordered its air forces to take the offensive against the Allies. As one result, in April, Admiral Yamamoto brought carrier squadrons from the *Third Fleet* to Rabaul in order to attack the nearby Allied bases. During Operation I-GO, Yamamoto's carrier pilots raided Guadalcanal (April 7), Oro Bay (April 11), Port Moresby (April 12), and Milne Bay (April 14). Although they claimed great success, it was illusory. Satisfied with his pilots' reported success, Yamamoto withdrew the carrier planes to Truk. (*See Atlas Map No. 20.*)

Operation I-GO was Yamamoto's last contribution to the Pacific War. After returning to Truk, he decided to visit his forces at Buin, Bougainville to congratulate them on the part they had played in Operation I-GO, and generally to improve morale in the area. When American cryptographers discovered his detailed itinerary, American commanders

decided to ambush the admiral's party. On April 18, 1943, Army P-38s from Guadalcanal intercepted and shot down two bombers carrying Admiral Yamamoto's group, killing the Commander-in-Chief of the *Combined Fleet.*

As the first months of 1943 passed, the Japanese forces awaited the inevitable Allied offensive in the southwest Pacific. By June, 123,000 troops, 390 operational aircraft, and a small fleet stood ready to meet the Allies.[41]

MacArthur's operations began on the night of June 30 when the 112th Cavalry Regiment and the 158th Infantry Regiment landed at Kiriwina and on the Woodlark Islands. This operation (CORONET) met no resistance, and within a short time engineers began building the airfields which would assist MacArthur and Halsey in dominating the Solomon Sea and attacking Rabaul. (*See Atlas Map No. 20.*)

At about the same time, Admiral Halsey landed his forces on Rendova Island and around the periphery of New Georgia to begin the campaign of New Georgia in the central Solomons. (*See Appendix 15.*) Halsey's main objective was the new Japanese airfield at Munda Point. (*See Atlas Map No. 21a.*) In this complicated maneuver (Operation TOENAILS) Halsey next established a beachhead near Munda Field on July 2 and 3, with most of the 43rd Infantry Division. The main battle for New Georgia began the next day, when the army commander ashore launched a two-regiment attack towards Munda Field.

The American offensive quickly bogged down because the commanders not only had underestimated the Japanese strength on the island, but also had misgauged their desire to hold New Georgia at all cost. As soon as the Americans

Admiral William Halsey

---

* On February 21, Admiral Halsey seized the unoccupied Russell Islands off Guadalcanal for new airbases. This minor action involved marines and troops from the 43rd Infantry Division.

† Skip bombing was employed effectively during this engagement by B-25 medium bombers and A-20 light bombers.

landed, General Imamura sent 4,000 troops to assist the 10,000 already on New Georgia. Most of these reached their destination, even though Allied naval forces tried to intercept them on July 6 (Naval Battle of Kolambangara). (*See Atlas Map No. 20.*) As a result of the Japanese resistance, the fight for New Georgia degenerated into a battle of attrition between two equal forces.*

When the 43rd Infantry Division looked as if it might be unequal to the task of taking Munda, Halsey ordered Major General Griswold, commanding XIV Corps, to take command of operations ashore. (*See Atlas Map No. 21a.*) He then sent the untried 37th Infantry Division and a regiment of the veteran 25th Infantry Division to assist the 43rd Division. Griswold's troops took Munda on August 5, after which he moved to clear the area north of the field and to secure the offshore islands of Rendova and Arundel.

Halsey decided not to invade nearby Kolombangara, because the approximately 10,000 Janapese troops there would have made such an operation another bloody battle. Instead, he ordered a regiment of the 25th Infantry Division to bypass the island and seize the weakly held Vella Lavella. The soldiers landed on August 15. There was little resistance. Final clearance was left to a brigade group of the New Zealand 3rd Division. (*See Atlas Map No. 21c.*)

By October, the Japanese knew they had lost the central Solomons, and began evacuating their cut-off garrisons. They did this successfully, even though American destroyers tried to prevent the withdrawal of the Vella Lavella garrison on the night of October 6 (Naval Battle of Vella Lavella). (*See Atlas Map No. 20.*)

Probably the most unique aspect of the New Georgia operation was the development of severe psychological problems among the troops of the 43rd Infantry Division. During their first night in the jungle, a number of men from one regiment became nervous and disoriented; they laid down heavy fire at imagined Japanese targets and caused great confusion. Thereafter, the men of that regiment never regained their composure, and many developed severe emotional disorders. Such "war neurosis" became a major medical problem. It was cured by rest, training, leadership, and informing the soldiers about their missions and the problems they would face.[42]

At the same time that the landings off New Guinea and in the central Solomons were taking place, MacArthur began his drive against Lae and Salamaua. (*See Appendix 16.*) He had planned a land attack against Salamaua to deceive the Japanese garrison in the coastal town. Then he expected to make an amphibious attack near Lae to take that port, while a parachute force dropped at Nadzab to block the Japanese retreat from Lae up the Markham Valley. This latter operation would also seize an existing airfield and secure the location for a new airfield complex. (*See Atlas Map No. 21c.*)

MacArthur's operations (POSTERN) proceeded as planned. First, a reinforced American battalion from the 41st Infantry Division landed at Nassau Bay on the night of June 29, and, after securing a beachhead, it joined the Australians near Salamaua on July 2. The Japanese forces defended the high ground near Salamaua tenaciously. It took the Australian-American force until September 12 to capture the town and its nearby airfield. Before Salamaua fell, Major General Wootten's Australian 9th Division landed near Lae (September 4 to 6). The American 503rd Parachute Infantry Regiment dropped at Nadzab on September 5 and immediately seized the airfield there. The Americans were soon joined by Australian engineers, who came overland from Wau, and by American engineers and Australian 7th Division troops, who were flown in from Port Moresby and other Papuan airfields. Once assembled, Major General Vasey's veteran infantry moved east and took Lae on September 16, aided by Wootten's 9th Division troops.

The Japanese garrison in Lae, including those who had escaped from Salamaua, retreated north over the difficult mountains of the Huon Peninsula toward Sio and Kiari, on the north coast of the peninsula. Many perished enroute; nearly all abandoned their heavy arms and equipment.

As soon as the Allies had secured the Lae-Nadzab area they began to build new airstrips to support attacks against Rabaul and New Britain. At the same time, MacArthur ordered Blamey to take Finschhafen as soon as possible, in order to prepare for the jump across the Vitiaz and Dampier Straits to New Britain. He also directed Blamey to send the 7th Division up the Markham Valley and into the Ramu Valley, towards the Japanese base at Bagadjim. (*See Atlas Map No. 21d.*)

By this time, the American Joint Chiefs of Staff had ordered MacArthur to neutralize Rabaul instead of capturing it. Marshall also proposed that CARTWHEEL Operations be extended to take positions farther north—Wewak, the Admiralties, and Kavieng. (*See Atlas Map No. 20.*) Moreover, he told MacArthur that his forces would go to the Philippines once CARTWHEEL ended.[43] Details were left unresolved.†

---

*It was in New Georgia that Private Rodger Young, 37th Infantry Division, won a posthumous award of the Medal of Honor. His exploits are celebrated in the popular infantry song, "The Ballad of Private Rodger Young."

†During May and August of 1943, two Allied conferences were convened. Following them, the Joint Chiefs of Staff developed the plans for two offensives in the Pacific—one in the Southwest Pacific Area and another in the Central Pacific Area. These plans are discussed in later chapters.

Meanwhile, faced with new Allied victories in New Guinea and the Solomons, as well as the loss of the Aleutians in May, Imperial General Headquarters feared a major American offensive in the central Pacific. This led to the establishment of a new defensive line in September. It ran from the Bonins to the Marianas, Carolines, and western New Guinea. (*See Atlas Map No. 22.*) Rabaul became an outpost, but one which was reinforced with a new army division and additional aircraft. As a result, General Imamura and Admiral Kusaka reshuffled their forces to hold Bougainville, to strengthen Madang and Wewak, to defend western New Britain, and to hold open a line of communications to New Guinea.[44]

General Wootten's forces landed near Finschhafen on September 22, and occupied the town on October 2. (*See Atlas Map 21d.*) The Japanese contested Wootten's advance, but after failing to dislodge the Australians, they retreated. Wootten followed and captured the Japanese base at Sio on January 15, 1944. The capture of Finschhafen gave MacArthur a valuable advanced airfield for the attack on New Britain.

In December, the 1st Marine Division and the 112th Cavalry Regiment landed on New Britain (Operation DEXTERITY). The marines' key objective was an airfield near Cape Gloucester, while the cavalrymen went ashore to capture the PT-Boat base at Arawe. As it turned out, DEXTERITY was unnecessary: the airfield proved unusable and the PT-Boat base was not needed.

Before the Southwest Pacific Area forces landed on New Britain, Halsey began his final moves in the Solomons. (*See Atlas Map No. 21b.*) First, on October 29, 1943 he invaded Treasury. He then sent a large raiding force to Choiseul Island (October 27 to November 4) to distract Hyakutake's attention from the difficult Cape Torokina area where Halsey planned to land.

When Halsey invaded Bougainville on November 1 there was minimum ground opposition, but such was not the case at sea or in the air. He had to beat off a Japanese naval attack on November 2 (Naval Battle of Empress Augusta Bay), and then had to deal with a series of intense Japanese air raids. (*See Atlas Map No. 20.*) In addition, Halsey sent his carrier aircraft against Rabaul to neutralize a large Japanese cruiser force, which Admiral Kondo had sent south from Truk to attack the beachhead.* The American carrier pilots heavily damaged the Japanese warships, ending the Japanese naval threat to Bougainville.

The 3rd Marine Division spearheaded Halsey's landing before the 37th Infantry Division, veterans of New Georgia,

come in on the marines' left flank in mid-November. (*See Atlas Map No. 21b.*) The marines took the brunt of the casualties in the first days, but once the beachhead had been secured and landing strips were started, Halsey replaced them with the Americal Division and eventually sent in Major General Griswold, XIV Corps commander, to control the forces on Bougainville. Griswold expanded the beachhead, emphasizing logistical matters in anticipation of enemy reaction, which came in the form of a strong Japanese counterattack in March 1944.

In New Guinea, on December 17, MacArthur ordered Krueger to take Saidor in order to split the *Eighteenth Army* in two and gain a new base for the attacks along the New Guinea coast and into the Admiralties. (*See Atlas Map No. 21d.*) Krueger hurriedly sent a regimental task force from the 32nd Infantry Division ashore on January 2, 1944, forcing 20,000 Japanese at Sio to begin a 200-mile retreat to Madang. Only 10,000 survived the ordeal.

By the end of January, Allied air power had nearly neutralized Rabaul. Constant raids had become more and more effective as fighters from airfields in Bougainville, from New Guinea, and from available carriers joined the attack on the Japanese bastion. In January alone, the Allies flew 2,888 sorties against Rabaul. Unexpectedly, Vice Admiral Spruance's carrier pilots administered the *coup de grace* to Japanese airpower at Rabaul when they destroyed 250 to 275 Japanese aircraft at Truk in a surprise raid on February 16 and 17.[45] After this disaster, Admiral Mineichi Koga, the new Commander-in-Chief of the *Combined Fleet*, withdrew all naval aircraft from Rabaul. Thereafter, Rabaul was no longer an offensive threat to the Allies. (*See Atlas Map No. 20.*)

With forces at Saidor, in western New Britain, and on Bougainville, MacArthur and Halsey were in a position in early 1944 to wrap up the extended CARTWHEEL operations. At all Allied headquarters, future objectives were discussed at length. On February 13, MacArthur approved the invasions of the Admiralties and Kavieng, establishing a target date of April 1. This was to be a major operation, supported by Admiral Nimitz's carrier forces.

Neither of the invasions was executed as planned. In a surprising move, MacArthur sent a reconnaissance-in-force into the Admiralty Islands on February 29, after Kenney had reported that the islands were deserted. (*See Atlas Map No. 20.*) They were not; but MacArthur, who went with the BREWER Reconnaissance Force of the 1st Cavalry Division (Brigadier General William Chase), ordered the force to hold what it had, and called for immediate reinforcements. The cavalrymen held, beating off many vicious Japanese attacks within the first three days. When the remainder of the division arrived, the

---

*This November 5 carrier strike was the first of six such strikes which the Americans launched against Rabaul and Kavieng from November 1943 to January 1944.

Americans began to clear the islands.[46]

MacArthur's move put "the cork in the bottle," and isolated Rabaul once and for all. It also captured Seadlor Harbor, which the Americans wanted to turn into a major fleet base for the advance to the Philippines. Moreover, the Admiralties gave the Allies new airfields from which B-24s could strike Truk.

By March 1, CARTWHEEL had succeeded, and the Japanese in the southwest Pacific were strategically defeated. Those who remained would be "mopped-up," contained, or ignored.* The route to the Philippines was open, and MacArthur was already thinking of his next step—the long jump to Hollandia, past the remainder of the Japanese *Eighteenth Army*.

After March 1944, the Allies in the Southwest Pacific Area tidied up their battlefields. (*See Atlas Map No. 21d.*) In New Guinea, the Australian 7th Division drove through the Ramu Valley and across the Finisterre Mountains to meet the Australian 5th Division, which marched along the coast from Saidor. Together, the Australian divisions captured Bagadjim (April 13), and, continuing north, soon took Madang (April 24) and advanced to Alexishafen (April 26). On Bougainville, Griswold's XIV Corps beat off Hyakutake's fierce counteroffensive (March 9 to 17), forcing the Japanese commander to revert to guerrilla warfare. (*See Atlas Map No. 21b.*) North of Bougainville, Halsey occupied Green Island (February 15), and then took undefended Emirau Island in the Saint Matthias Group (March 20). Major General Innis Swift's cavalrymen secured the Admiralties on May 18.

Patterns

During CARTWHEEL, the Allies had set a pattern which would be repeated in the great offensive of 1944 and 1945. Moving on exterior lines, they hit the overextended Japanese at weak spots; gained air superiority; seized existing airfields and ports, or places where such facilities could be built; and then moved forward again under the protection of land-based fighter aircraft. Strong Japanese positions were bypassed, if possible. As a result, 98,000 Japanese troops were left behind at Rabaul, the remnants of the *6th Division* were stranded on Bougainville, and many Japanese troops were cut off from their bases in New Guinea. The

Allies used joint and combined forces, in which the land, sea, and air elements of several nations and services were controlled by one commander in the theater or major area of operations. In most battles, they relied on heavy fire support from all available artillery, ships, and airplanes, rather than wasting human lives in desperate frontal attacks.

At the beginning of the war, these tactics could not have been used because the Allies had been fighting on a shoestring. However, their cause was advanced by the victories at Midway (June 4, 1942), El Alamein (November 14, 1942), and Stalingrad (February 2, 1943). Those successes allowed more and more ships, planes, troops, and supplies to be moved to the Pacific to support the war against Japan. America's tremendous industrial power was beginning to exert its force.

In the early operations in the Pacific, the Allies profited from Japanese mistakes and, it seemed, from the study of Japanese operations during the Centrifugal Offensive. The Japanese, however, seemed to ignore their own deficiencies. They never really unified their forces, but continued to send them into battle piecemeal. They also failed to realize the size of the Allied forces, and often missed golden opportunities to destroy small Allied units on land and sea. Stubborn and brave, the Japanese were superb warriors. Their courage and tenacity was truly incomprehensible; but fight as they did, they never were able to gain their commanders' strategical or tactical objectives after the Battle of the Coral Sea.

By early 1944, Japan had lost most of her fine naval air force (over 2,900 aircraft), a large number of warships (around 50), and a substantial number of firstline troops (approximately 100,000) as a result of the fighting in the South and Southwest Pacific Areas.[47] She had gained no strategic results worth mentioning—unless, of course, the jungle war could be considered successful because it had delayed an expected Allied counteroffensive for a year and a half. Even so, Japan could not exploit the situation by building up her air forces, improving her fleet, rebuilding her army, and increasing her merchant marine, because the losses in the southeast region were too severe.

1944 began auspiciously for the United States. She had already penetrated the central Pacific and had new carriers, freshly trained divisions, and growing air squadrons. With no defensive commitments, the Americans were about to shift over to offensive war, which would bring them quickly to the Philippines and shortly thereafter to Japan. The Australians and the New Zealanders would be left behind to clean out the jungle.

Midway had set up the jungle war; the jungle war, in turn, set up the rapid advances of MacArthur and Nimitz which would reach Leyte in October 1944.

---

*"Mop-up" was a contemporaneously used term which was intended to imply a relatively easy task of fixing and then eliminating bypassed Japanese forces. Troops from Australia and New Zealand, who were given the chore, resented the use of the term, and did not find the task easy.

Notes

[1]Mitsuo Fuchida and Masatake Okumiya, *Midway, The Battle That Doomed Japan* (New York, 1955), pp. 11-12 and John Toland, *The Rising Sun, The Decline and Fall of the Japanese Empire, 1936-1945* (New York, 1971), pp. 390-392.

[2]Toland, *The Rising Sun*, p. 391.

[3]This section is based upon: Louis Morton, *Strategy and Command: The First Two Years* (Washington, 1962), pp. 289-323; John Miller, Jr., *Guadalcanal: The First Offensive* (Washington, 1949), pp. 1-58; Samuel Eliot Morison, *Coral Sea, Midway and Submarine Actions, May 1942-August 1942* (Boston, 1967), pp. 252-277; and Frank O. Hough, Verle E. Ludwig, and Henry I. Shaw, Jr., *Pearl Harbor to Guadalcanal, History of U.S. Marine Corps Operations in World War II* (Washington, 1958), pp. 235-253.

[4]For Army matters, Morton, *Strategy and Command*, and Miller, *Guadalcanal*, were used. Their strategic comments are more complete than the other sources.

[5]Morison, *Coral Sea, Midway and Submarine Actions*, pp. 261-262; Miller *Guadalcanal*, pp. 20-21.

[6]For Marine Corps data see Hough, et. al., *Pearl Harbor to Guadalcanal*, pp. 235-253. Morison, *Coral Sea, Midway and Submarine Actions*, pp. 264-277, also covers this material.

[7]Hough, et. al., *Pearl Habor to Guadalcanal*, p. 252; Miller, *Guadalcanal*, p. 55.

[8]Fletcher's attitude is explained in Samuel Morison, *Coral Sea, Midway and Submarine Actions*, p.281 and in Hough, et. al., *Pearl Harbor to Guadalcanal*, p. 252.

[9]For American strengths see Hough, et. al., *Pearl Harbor to Guadalcanal*, p. 252. For Japanese strengths see Colonel Vincent J. Esposito (ed), *The West Point Atlas of American Wars*, (2 Vols.; New York, 1959), II, Map 133.

[10]This section is based on: Saburò Hayashi (in collaboration with Alvin D. Coox), *Kogun, The Japanese Army in the Pacific War*, (Quantico, Va, 1959), pp. 51-55; *Reports of General MacArthur*, Volume II-Part I, *Japanese Operations in the Southwest Pacific Area* (Washington, 1966), pp. 138-142; Samuel Milner, *Victory in Papua* (Washington, 1957), pp. 39-63; and *Reports of General MacArthur*, Volume I, *The Campaigns of MacArthur in the Pacific* (Washington, 1966), pp. 31-62.

[11]For Japanese details see: Hayashi and Coox, *Kogun*, pp. 51-55 and *Reports of MacArthur*, II-I, *Japanese Operations*, pp. 138-141.

[12]Milner, *Victory in Papua*, pp. 23-25; Dudley McCarthy, *South-West Pacific Area—First Year, Kokoda to Wau* (Canberra, 1962), p. 112. Australians have questioned how offensive-minded MacArthur was in March 1942 and whether Australian leaders were as passive-minded regarding continental defense as they believe MacArthur implied.

[13]For KANGA Force see: McCarthy, *Kokoda to Wau*, pp. 84-107 and *Reports of MacArthur*, I, *Campaigns of MacArthur*, pp. 49-50.

[14]Details of the actions in New Guinea are from Milner, *Victory in Papua*, pp. 39-63.

[15]Samuel Eliot Morison, *The Two-Ocean War, A Short History of the United States Navy in the Second World War* (New York, 1972), p. 143, gives the personal details on Admiral Crutchley.

[16]Richard Tregaskis, *Guadalcanal Diary* (New York, 1943), pp. 11 and 27.

[17]Unless otherwise indicated, this section is based primarily on Hough et. al., *Pearl Harbor to Guadalcanal*, pp. 253-274 (ground action) and Morison, *Two-Ocean War*, pp. 139-178 (naval action). Also see: Hayashi and Coox, *Kogun*, pp. 58-66; Miller, *Guadalcanal*, pp. 137-139, 227-231, and 336-350; *Reports of MacArthur*, II-I, *Japanese Operations*, pp. 146-149, 171-173, and 193-197; Samuel Eliot Morison, *The Struggle for Guadalcanal, August 1942-February 1943* (Boston, 1950); Toland, *The Rising Sun*, pp. 393-492 (this source was treated skeptically); Raizo Tanaka, "The Struggle for Guadalcanal," in United States Naval Institute, *The Japanese Navy in World War II* (Annapolis, 1969), pp. 52-73; and Morton, *Strategy and Command*, pp. 324-363.

[18]Morison, *Two-Ocean War*, pp. 142-148; Morison, *Struggle for Guadalcanal*, pp. 17-64; and Toshikazu Ohmae, "The Battle of Savo Island," in United States Naval Institute, *The Japanese Navy in World War II* (Annapolis, 1969), pp. 74-85.

[19]Hayashi and Coox, *Kogun*, pp. 58-59 gives order of battle information.

[20]For detailed information on the "Tokyo Express" see Tanaka, "Struggle for Guadalcanal," pp. 54-61.

[21]Hayashi and Coox, *Kogun*, p. 59.

[22]*Ibid.*, p. 60.

[23]See Morison, *Two-Ocean War*, p. 159, for Nimitz's comments.

[24]Tanaka, "Struggle for Guadalcanal," p. 56, comments on "bamboo-spear" tactics.

[25]Morison, *Struggle for Guadalcanal*, p. 198. See also Hough, et. al., *Pearl Harbor to Guadalcanal*, pp. 339; Morison, *Two-Ocean War*, pp. 160-161; and Tanaka, "Struggle for Guadalcanal," pp. 62-63 for comments on Japanese Army-Navy cooperation in the Battle of Santa Cruz Island.

[26]For discussions in Washington during the critical period on Guadalcanal, see Morton, *Strategy and Command*, pp. 324-351.

[27]For Japanese reorganization and reinforcements see Hayashi and Coox, *Kogun*, pp. 60-62.

[28]Hough, et. al., *Pearl Harbor to Guadalcanal*, pp. 345-347; John Deane Potter, *Yamamoto, The Man Who Menaced America* (New York, 1971), pp. 303-304.

[29]Hayashi and Coox, *Kogun*, pp. 62-65 cover the withdrawal from Guadalcanal.

[30]This section is based primarily on Milner, *Victory in Papua*, unless otherwise indicated. Also see: *Reports of MacArthur*, I, *Campaigns of MacArthur*, pp. 45-49; *Reports of MacArthur* II-I, *Japanese Operations*, pp. 124-207; McCarthy, *Kokoda to Wau*, pp. 384-533; Hugh Buggy, *Pacific Victory, A Short History of Australia's Part in the War Against Japan* (Canberra, n.d.), pp. 145-215; Robert L. Eichelberger, *Our Jungle Road to Tokyo* (New York, 1950), pp. 17-62; and Jay Luvaas (ed.), *Dear Miss Em, General Eichelberger's War in the Pacific, 1942-1945* (Westport, Connecticut, 1972), pp. 30-58.

[31]McCarthy, *Kokoda to Wau*, pp. 413, 500-501, speaks of irresolute Australian troops. See Milner, *Victory in Papua*, pp. 196-197, 208-211, and 228-229, and Eichelberger, *Our Jungle Road*, pp. 26-27.

[32]Milner, *Victory in Papua*, pp. 203-205; Eichelberger, *Our Jungle Road*, pp. 21-27; Luvaas, *Dear Miss Em*, pp. 35-40; and George C. Kenney, *General Kenney Reports, A Personal History of the Pacific War* (New York, 1949), pp. 156-158.

[33]Luvaas, *Dear Miss Em*, pp. 44-45. See letter from General

Eichelberger to Major General Horace Fuller, Commanding General, 41st Infantry Division.

[34]Casualty figures are mostly from Milner, *Victory in Papua*, pp. 364-368 and 370-374. They are generally the same as those given in McCarthy, *Kokoda to Wau*, pp. 527 and 531. Casualty statistics in Appendix 13 are from Milner.

[35]John Miller, Jr., *Cartwheel, The Reduction of Rabaul*, (Washington, 1959), p. 8. Morton, *Strategy and Command*, p. 383, differs slightly from Miller in his conclusions about what the Combined Chiefs of Staff agreed to.

[36]This section is based primarily on Miller, *Cartwheel*.

[37]Morton, *Strategy and Command*, p. 641. See: "Joint Chiefs of Staff Directive: Offensive Operations in the South and Southwest Pacific Areas During 1943, 28 March 1942."

[38]Miller, *Cartwheel*, p. 26, quoting from GHQ Warning Instructions 2, May 6, 1943.

[39]Morton, *Strategy and Command*, pp. 624-626. See paragraph 6, "Japanese Army-Navy Central Agreement Concerning the South Pacific Area Operations, With Supplement, 4 January 1943."

[40]For the Battle of the Bismarck Sea, see: Miller, *Cartwheel*, pp. 39-41; Samuel Eliot Morison, *Breaking the Bismarcks Barrier, 22 July 1942-1 May 1944* (Boston, 1968), pp. 54-65; Wesley Frank Craven and James Lea Cate (eds.), *The Army Air Forces in World War II*, Volume IV, *The Pacific: Guadalcanal to Saipan, August 1942 to July 1944* (Chicago, 1950), pp. 135-150; and Kenney, *General Kenney Reports*, pp. 197-206.

[41]Miller, *Cartwheel*, p. 47 lists Japanese strengths.

[42]Miller, *Cartwheel*, pp. 112-113, 120-122, and 140 discusses "war neuroses."

[43]Miller, *Cartwheel*, pp. 222-225 and Morton, *Strategy and Command*, pp. 471-472 cover the modification of CARTWHEEL and the authorization for MacArthur to go to the Philippines.

[44]Hayashi and Coox, *Kogun*, pp. 71-73; Miller, *Cartwheel*, pp. 212-214; and Morton, *Strategy and Command*, pp. 655-656 ("Japanese General Outline of the Future War Direction Policy, Adopted at the Imperial Conference, 30 September 1943") and pp. 657-660 ("Japanese Army-Navy Central Agreement Concerning the Central and South Pacific Operations, With Supplement, 30 September 1943").

[45]For the raid on Truk, see: Miller, *Cartwheel*, p. 312 and Samuel Eliot Morison, *Aleutians, Gilberts and Marshalls, June 1942-April 1944* (Boston, 1951), pp. 314-332.

[46]Miller, *Cartwheel*, pp. 312-350; interviews with Major General William C. Chase, USA, Ret., Colonel William E. Lobit, USA, Ret., Colonel (Doctor) John Hall, USA, Ret., and other members of the 1st Cavalry Division who fought in the Admiralties.

[47]Casualty figures are just estimates. Aircraft and ship figures are from United States Strategic Bombing Survey (Pacific), *The Campaigns of the Pacific War* (Washington, 1946), p. 160; troop casualties are from an interview of Lieutenant General H. Imamura, *Eighth Area Army* Commander, found in United States Strategic Bombing Survey (Pacific), *The Allied Campaign Against Rabaul* (Washington, 1946), p. 85, Item 208.

Atolls, Volcanoes, and Carriers: Nimitz Strikes

7

*I have at last come to the place where I will die.
I am pleased to think that I will die calmly in
the true samurai style.*

Unknown Japanese soldier on Saipan

In 1921, when Major Pete Ellis of the Marine Corps mapped out his plan for the conquest of Micronesia, little did he realize that the United States would muster the huge air, naval, and land forces necessary to eject the Japanese from their positions in the mandated islands of the central Pacific. Unlike the jungle war, the war in the central Pacific was one of plenty. When Admiral Nimitz began his first invasion, he lacked some combat shipping and some other essential items, but he was able to deploy eleven fast carriers and five new escort carriers—they carried over 800 aircraft—to support his assault forces. The United States had come a long way from the shoestring days of 1942 and 1943, when the Navy had only one or two operational fleet carriers in the Pacific. In addition, Nimitz could count on five Army divisions, one veteran marine division from the South Pacific Area, and a well-equipped Seventh Air Force to support his actions.

By 1944, the Japanese were not able to meet the American forces man-for-man, plane-for-plane, or even ship-for-ship, because the Allies in the South and Southwest Pacific Areas had destroyed much of the Japanese Navy, naval air force, and army air force, as well as many excellent ground units. To further complicate the situation, the Japanese still faced a difficult situation in China, where they had a million soldiers stationed and worried about the resurgent Soviet armed forces, which were beginning to chew up the German *Wehrmacht*. The Japanese, however, were still capable of powerful resistance. In the year-long campaign on the spits of coral and the tops of volcanoes which formed the tiny islands of Micronesia, they would make the United States pay dearly for all new victories.

The many tiny islands which formed the Gilberts, Marshalls, Carolines, and Marianas were quite unlike those in the South and Southwest Pacific Areas. Except for the Marianas, they were, for the most part, low pieces of ground surrounded by coral reefs, covered with large stands of coconut, and dotted with large, well-fortified concrete and log pillboxes and other defensive works. The islands were needed for the bases from which the Allies could intercept Japanese shipping and air routes across the Pacific, and from which they could attack the Philippines, China, and even Japan. (*See Atlas Maps No. 20 and 22.*)

The American drive across the central Pacific would be dominated by sweeping actions of the new carrier task forces of the Pacific Fleet and the bloody assaults of large amphibious forces upon a multitude of beaches. Admiral Ernest King had always wanted to conduct such air operations, because he felt they would bring decisive results and would employ the new ships and forces of the Pacific Fleet. The central Pacific was a naval battlefield, one which challenged the aggressive Chief of Naval Operations. In November 1943, after much urging by King, the United States Pacific Fleet, supported by all other arms and services, began the greatest sustained naval campaign in United States history.

"To Maintain and Extend Unremitting Pressure Against Japan"

Even before the fighting ended in Papua and Guadalcanal and before the Joint Chiefs of Staff issued their March 23,

1943 directive for continued operations toward Rabaul, American and British Chiefs of Staff began to consider new plans for an offensive in the Central Pacific Area. These plans were proposed by the Americans. The British members of the Combined Chiefs of Staff only acceded to them under some duress and after they found that the plans would not greatly interfere with their operations in Europe.[1]

The decision of the American Joint Chiefs to turn to the central Pacific as an area for a massive attack on the Japanese eastern flank was not unexpected. For years, Army and Navy officers had planned for such an eventuality in case Japan captured the Philippines. In many respects, the new plans merely updated war plan ORANGE, which had been discarded before war began. Plan ORANGE, however, never assumed that Australia would be a base and that the Japanese would be in the Solomons–New Guinea area; therefore, throughout the discussions urging a central Pacific offensive, the war at hand in the southwest Pacific complicated the final decision to attack through Micronesia.

When speaking at the Casablanca Conference on January 14, 1943, Admiral King had proposed that the Allies attack in the central Pacific once Rabaul was taken. He believed that the Allies should take Truk to eliminate that major Japanese base, seize the Marianas to gain the strategic key to the region, and then invade the Philippines to cut the Japanese line of communications to the Southern Resources Area.[2] The admiral and his colleagues further proposed that in 1943 the Allied forces facing Japan should be able to launch both offensives in Burma and offensives to capture Rabaul. The British Chiefs of Staff, however, were not prepared to support such an optimistic program and pared it down to one in which the Allies attacked toward Burma, Rabaul, and the Marshall Islands with the forces available in each area.

Following Casablanca, King instructed his staff to begin planning for the seizure of the Ellice and Gilbert Islands, and perhaps the Marshalls. He then queried Admirals Nimitz and Halsey for comments on a new central Pacific drive. Both admirals reported that any move on the new front would be inappropriate; all efforts should continue to be concentrated against Rabaul, the prime objective at that time. The next month, during the Pacific Military Conference, which was convened to decide on the next moves in the South and Southwest Pacific Areas, King again brought up the subject of a Central Pacific Area drive. After his naval subordinates and other naval staff officers opposed such a move, the Chief of Naval Operations dropped the subject.

General MacArthur would have argued against King's plan to make a major drive across the central Pacific, because he was devoted to the idea of returning to the Philippines by way of the northern coast of New Guinea.

He did agree with King, however, that the Philippines ought to be the decisive Allied objective in 1943 and that their recapture would be a blow to the Japanese economy. By the time of the Pacific Military Conference, MacArthur had already developed RENO I, his basic plan for the return to the Philippines, but he had not submitted it to the Joint Chiefs. Only his ELKTON plan was discussed by the Pacific planners.

While the two senior officers developed their ideas, different planning groups, working for the Joint Chiefs of Staff, were considering new long-range plans for the defeat of Japan. In April, the Joint United States Strategic Committee presented "The Strategic Plan for the Defeat of Japan" to the Joint Chiefs. This plan, when finally approved, would become the cornerstone of strategy in the Pacific for 1943 and 1944.[3]

The American planners assumed that the Allies would require the unconditional surrender of Japan, and that they might have to invade the Japanese home islands to achieve this extreme goal. Moreover, although they hoped that a sea blockade might cause the Japanese to surrender unconditionally, they believed that a devastating air offensive against the Japanese nation would be the best means to the desired end. To accomplish this, the Allies would need airbases near Japan. There were many possibilities. In the north, Siberia and the Kuriles could be used with Russian permission, but the Allies soon learned that Premier Joseph Stalin wanted no American aircraft on his soil. Formosa was also a possibility, but it did not have good port facilities; moreover, it was held by strong Japanese forces. The joint planners concluded that China would be the best site for bomber bases, and since logistics would play such a tremendous part in any air offensive, the bases had to be near a port which could be reached from the Pacific. Hong Kong served this purpose well. (*See Atlas Map No. 22.*)

How to get to Hong Kong at least cost and in minimum time was the initial problem. The planners decided that the key to Hong Kong was the control of the South China Sea. American forces would have to enter that sea through the Sulu and Celebes Seas, attacking from either their New Guinea bases or from newly–won positions in the Japanese mandated islands. British forces, after recapturing Burma, would open the Malacca Straits. To secure the South China Sea, the Americans would recapture the Philippines, while British forces moved into Indochina. Although the American staff officers liked the central Pacific route the best, they recommended to the Joint Chiefs that the forces in the southwest Pacific continue to advance so that the drives could be mutually supporting. Hong Kong was to be captured primarily by Chinese forces, which would be assisted by American units. After its capture, the Allies would develop airbases in the area and then begin an "overwhleming bombing offensive against Japan." Finally, the Allies would invade Japan.[4]

This plan seems a bit specious today because of the Japanese strength in the Philippines and around the South China Sea, and it is difficult to see how the American planners believed that they could advance successfully into a Japanese-dominated *cul-de-sac*–like the South China Sea.* In view of their anxiety over MacArthur moving with exposed flanks into the Philippines, the joint planners seemed to have ignored the greater dangers which the Allies would have faced in the South China Sea.

The planners, however, proposed one idea which had lasting value and which the Joint Chiefs accepted: the drive across the central Pacific. From this time forward, the officers in Washington decided to open a new front in the Pacific; and once the Combined Chiefs of Staff approved "The Strategic Plan for the Defeat of Japan" at the TRIDENT Conference in Washington in May 1943, the Joint Chiefs remained wedded to the central Pacific offensive for the duration of the war. However, they did not remain wedded to a fixed strategy. As a result, they would adapt their plans to take advantage of opportunities, such as the development of the B-29, and reverses, such as the delay of the Burma campaign. The Allies, therefore, would never go to Hong Kong, although the China strategy was not rejected until the Joint Chiefs decided to go to Luzon rather than Formosa.

Advocates of the advance across Micronesia had several reasons for believing that such an attack was superior to any launched from the Southwest Pacific Area. (*See Atlas Map No. 22.*) First, the United States could employ its growing naval forces in a huge area which was most suitable for naval warfare and against objectives sufficiently important to force the Japanese *Combined Fleet* to seek battle with a Pacific Fleet which would soon be superior in strength. Second, in March 1943, when no Allied advance had begun yet in the southwest Pacific, the Allies would attack on the shortest route to the Philippines, the one which hit the Japanese on their weakest flank and offered the chance for the quickest decision. Third, by striking the small atolls and islands, where the Japanese could station only small forces, the Allies could deploy smaller forces than were needed in the Solomons-New Guinea area. Fourth, the route was much less hazardous to the soldiers' health than the malaria-infested islands of the southwest Pacific. Lastly, if the Allies managed to destroy or neutralize the Japanese fleet, they could possibly strike directly at Japan without

having to go to the Philippines, the Netherlands East Indies, China, or even New Guinea.

On the other hand, MacArthur and his supporters, when told of the new plan, opposed the new front because it seemed like a diversion of resources. MacArthur had a large force in being which was soon to be fully engaged. To move it would demand too much time and shipping. Furthermore, MacArthur argued that the attack in the central Pacific would be a frontal one against isolated objectives; accordingly, it would require difficult beach assaults and huge naval forces, and would produce indecisive results and an immense number of casualties. The general also suggested that the Australians would not look favorably on the abandonment of their area. While he recognized that a drive in the central Pacific would assist his movements, MacArthur never felt that it was justified.[5]

With the benefits of hindsight and objectivity, it is now clear that the mutually supporting twin drives had more power to hurt the Japanese than did a single one. The dual effort would be similar to the twin drives which had been made toward Rabaul. Moreover, since they were both major efforts, neither really was a secondary attack. MacArthur would fight with the preponderance of ground and land-based air forces; Nimitz would fight with the preponderance of naval, marine, and naval air forces.

On May 8, 1943, the Combined Chiefs of Staff approved the American concept for the defeat of Japan. At the same time, the military chiefs approved operations to retake the Aleutians; † invade Burma; capture the Marshalls, the Carolines, the Bismarcks, the Solomons, and New Guinea; and continue air and submarine offensives against the Japanese line of communications so that the Allies could "maintain and extend unremitting pressure against Japan"[6] in 1943. This could be done because, for the first time in the war, the United States would have enough forces to employ in the Pacific theaters.

As soon as the TRIDENT Conference ended, the American planners began working on proposals for the invasion of the Marshall Islands, the first step toward the Celebes Sea.[7] They faced several problems. What objectives should be taken? How should the drive be coordinated with the one to Rabaul? And what troops were needed? By June 10, the Washington planners had decided that they needed a corps of two amphibiously trained divisions to take the Marshalls. Since there were only four available (three marine divisions in the South and Southwest Pacific Areas and the 7th Infantry Division in the Aleutians), the Joint

---

*At a Naval College war game in 1933, the American fleet (Blue Force) had pursued the Japanese fleet (Orange Force) into the South China Sea and was annihilated.

† The American 7th Infantry Division landed on Attu on May 11, 1943. Organized resistance ended on May 30. The division landed on Kiska on August 15. There was no resistance, because the Japanese had withdrawn their garrison on July 28. These operations secured the American northern flank.

Chiefs of Staff would have to take them from Halsey and MacArthur, who were about to launch CARTWHEEL. Before the problems were reconciled, however, the Joint Chiefs told Nimitz to invade the Marshalls on November 15. MacArthur was informed of the decision.

For the next month, the strategic planners worked out the solutions to their many Pacific problems. By July 20, the Joint Chiefs of Staff had made two important decisions. The Gilberts, not the Marshalls, would be invaded first. (*See Atlas Map No. 22.*) This was decided in part because the operation would take only one marine division instead of two, thus not jeopardizing MacArthur's planned invasion of New Britain. It was also based on the fact that Nimitz needed more aerial photographs of the Marshalls and wanted to seize the Gilberts as a base for taking them. While the joint planners were adjusting their views on the Marshalls, they also recommended that Rabaul be neutralized so that the Americans would not simply mimic the Japanese offensive in reverse, would not use up excess troops, and would not slow down their advance toward the Admiralties. The Joint Chiefs accepted this recommendation and ordered MacArthur to bypass Rabaul. Then, on July 21, they directed Nimitz to invade the Gilberts on November 15. His objectives were to improve the line of communications to Australia, to inflict losses on the Japanese, and to prepare to enter the Marshalls on January 1, 1944. To aid Nimitz, the Joint Chiefs assigned him Halsey's 2nd Marine Division.

The original objectives in the Gilberts were Tarawa and Nauru. But as planning and reconnaissance proceeded, Nimitz's staff soon recommended that the Nauru landing be scrapped because of the difficult terrain on the island and because its distance from Tarawa would cause a dispersal of the invasion force. Nimitz accepted his staff's advice. When he met with Admiral King on September 25, he persuaded the Chief of Naval Operations that Makin was a preferable objective to Nauru. With King's approval, the Joint Chiefs adjusted their plans. Tarawa and Makin would be the first objectives in the central Pacific drive. (*See Atlas Maps No. 20 and No. 22.*)

"To Hold Out as Long as Possible"

Makin, and to a greater extent, Tarawa, were focal points of Japanese defensive preparations in the Central Pacific Area in 1943.[8] The Japanese began to reinforce and improve their positions in the Gilberts long before they lost Guadalcanal and Papua, and many months before their

forces faced defeat in the Solomons and New Guinea. A catalyst for this preparation had been the raid conducted by Lieutenant Colonel Evans Carlson's 2nd Marine Raider Battalion on August 17 and 18, 1942. Carlson's men landed to distract the Japanese from the battle raging on Guadalcanal, as well as to destroy enemy troops and installations and to capture important documents and persons. The Japanese diverted no forces from Guadalcanal, but recognizing how weak their garrison was in the Gilberts, they deployed additional troops to clear, occupy, and develop the islands. They began building new airfields on Tarawa and Nauru, improved the seaplane anchorage at Makin, and began elaborate fortifications on the spit of coral called Betio, which was the largest island in Tarawa Atoll.[9] (*See Atlas Maps No. 20 and No. 23b.*)

By November 1943, the Japanese had made Betio a formidable position, one which bristled with field guns, howitzers, naval guns, large and small machineguns, and seven 37-mm-gun tanks. Concrete and coconut log bombproofs, a special ammunition railroad, connecting trenches, gun positions, and narrow-slitted pillboxes made the Japanese defenses even more formidable. So did the coral reef which surrounded Tarawa, the beach and water obstacles such as tetrahedrons, and the usual mines. Only the north coast defenses of Betio were incomplete in November 1943. Two special naval landing teams of 1,000 to 1,500 men each manned the defenses. Supporting troops brought the total combat strength of the atoll garrison up to about 3,000, although there were 4,836 men on the atoll, many of whom were Korean laborers. (*See Atlas Map No. 23b.*)

Makin was neither as well manned nor as well fortified as Tarawa. On the atoll, barely 100 miles north of Tarawa, the Japanese deployed some base force troops and had a fairly large group of Korean laborers. Prior to the invasion, 300 or so of the the 798 men there could be classified as combat troops. (*See Atlas Map No. 23a.*)

By May 1943, the Japanese High Command had established a new plan of defense (*Z* Plan). Under this plan, local commanders all along the defensive perimeter were expected to hold their positions by destroying invading forces at the shoreline, or, if that were impossible, by counterattacking constantly to delay or prevent the Allies from gaining their positions as bases. Added emphasis was given to the strengthening of positions from the Aleutians through Wake, the Marshalls, the Gilberts, and Truk to the Bismarcks.[10] The Allies soon invalidated Operation Z when they drove into the central Solomons and advanced into the Lae-Salamaua-Finschhafen area of New Guinea.* (*See Atlas Maps No. 19 and No. 20.*) As mentioned

---

*The *Z* Plan remained in effect until May 1944.

earlier, Imperial General Headquarters, with the approval of the Emperor, quickly revised Japanese war plans in September of 1943 so that henceforth only a line of absolute defense—running from the Kuriles south through the Marianas to western New Guinea and then along the Malay Barrier to Burma—would be held at all costs. (*See Atlas Map No. 22.*) This decision placed the Gilberts outside the essential Japanese defensive perimeter, but it did not mean that the Japanese wanted their forces to withdraw from areas outside the perimeter. Like their brethren in the southeast region, the Japanese naval troops of the *6th Base Force* in the Gilberts and Marshalls were expected to repulse the invaders or to fight to the last man. The Japanese needed time to build up their new defensive line, and the forces in the exposed outposts were expected to gain that time, regardless of the ultimate cost.[11]

At the same time that Imperial General Headquarters decided on a new strategy, civilian agencies in the Japanese Government recommended that new measures be taken to improve the Japanese position in the occupied areas of the Empire and to improve relations with the Soviet Union and Germany. With Italy's surrender in 1943, the growing success of the Russians on the Eastern Front, and the festering sore in China, the Japanese political and economic advisors proposed the following program:

1. Japan will strive to the utmost to prevent the outbreak of war with the Soviet Union, will take the initiative in improving Soviet-Japanese relations, and endeavor to mediate for peace between the Soviet Union and Germany at the proper opportunity.
2. Japan will maintain unremitting pressure against Chungking and will take the earliest possible opportunity to settle the Chinese problem....
3. Japan will take every possible measure to strengthen cooperation with Germany.
4. Japan will win the confidence of the nations and peoples of Greater East Asia and will guide them in order to receive and further encourage their cooperation with Japan's war efforts.
5. Resolute measures will be taken to build up the decisive military capability, especially air power, and a dauntless spirit to face the national crisis will be encouraged in order to bring the total national power into full play.
6. A propaganda effort against the enemy will be conducted under a consistent policy, and will be directed mainly toward the propagation of the Axis cause, diffusion of Japan's policy in Greater East Asia, demoralizing our major enemy, the United States, alienation of the United States, Britain, China, and the Soviet Union, and helping India achieve her independence.[12]

Japan's greatest fear was Soviet intervention in the war; she was prepared to do almost anything to prevent that act. She also hoped that by preaching anti-Colonialism she could gain the support of her conquered people. But the Japanese leaders knew that their failure to subdue China and their inability to win new victories in the Pacific damaged Japanese credibility in the eyes of the subject peoples.[13] Fair treatment, justice, anti-Colonialism, and mutual cooperation would have been better goals in 1942.

The Japanese High Command estimated that Japan would soon face an Allied force of 35 divisions, 4,000 aircraft, 12 aircraft carriers, 100 submarines, and many other surface ships. To meet this threat, the Japanese military wanted 55,000 aircraft in 1944; but Japanese industry, which had about a 17,000-plane annual capacity, could hardly be expected to meet that goal. The Japanese Army was still strong, although Imperial Headquarters would have to redeploy troops from Manchuria, China, and Japan to hold the Pacific. While the Japanese naval forces also were strong, the real weakness in the fleet was not the lack of ships but the lack of first class pilots. Japanese submarines, still plentiful, and deadly when used properly, were being diverted to supply missions which ultimately demoralized thé fighting crews. But, most important, the Japanese nation lacked the ships to transport industrial supplies, troops, and military equipment from point to point within the expanded Empire. Japanese shipping losses averaged 100,000 tons a month by mid-1943; in less than two years the Allies had sunk 1,745,000 tons (445 vessels) of merchant shipping while damaging an additional 2,109,800 tons (414 vessels). This total loss amounted to two thirds of Japanese prewar merchant tonnage (6,000,000). As a result of these staggering losses, Japanese industry was taxed to the limit as it tried to replace not only merchant ships but also warships, and particularly airplanes.[14]

By the time the Emperor approved the September 1943 recommendations, Imperial General Headquarters faced the nearly impossible task of defending the Japanese Empire. With dwindling combat forces, which were spread all over the Pacific and Far East, and were facing larger Allied forces, Japanese commanders would face defeat in detail* if they could not quickly deploy their forces from place to place using their interior routes of communications. (*See Atlas Map No. 22.*)

To a great extent, the success of the new Japanese strategy would depend on the *Combined Fleet* at Truk. While Admiral Koga's fleet was not as powerful as the one which had attacked Pearl Harbor and Midway, the admiral

---

*Defeat in detail results from having forces so widely dispersed that the enemy can mass against individual concentrations and defeat them one by one.

still had sufficient ships left to challenge any American invasion, and he was more than willing to use them. Unfortunately for Koga and the Japanese, Allied actions in the southeastern region would neutralize Japanese naval power before it could be used against Nimitz's invasion forces. (*See Atlas Map No. 20.*)

Key to the Japanese defense would be the Marianas, because they controlled the sea lanes which crisscrossed the western Pacific. Furthermore, the Japanese were able to stage their aircraft through the Marianas to the Philippines, the Netherlands East Indies, Truk, and eventually to Rabaul and New Guinea. If the Marianas fell, the crack in the absolute defensive perimeter would probably prove fatal. (*See Atlas Map No. 22.*)

Imperial General Headquarters did not insist that its subordinate commanders follow its instructions to the letter. As a result the build-up of positions in Micronesia was often haphazard. To make matters worse, while the Tarawa garrison built new defenses and an expensive airfield, more important points such as Saipan were not improved quickly enough. Even more importantly, Imperial General Headquarters continued to pay greater attention to the battle at hand in New Guinea and the Solomons; as one result of this fascination, Admiral Koga deployed critical air and naval forces to a lost strategic cause when he should have been watching his eastern flank.* (*See Atlas Map No. 20.*) There was no excuse for this since the Japanese recognized that a drive in the central Pacific would be more dangerous than one farther south, where, for the time being, it was possible to delay the Allies. With the advent of the new American offensive, the Japanese high commanders would face a crucial stage in the war which would decide the fate of their nation.[15]

Proving a Doctrine: Tarawa and Makin

Admiral Nimitz and his staff quickly worked out the detailed organization which would be used for the seizure of the Gilberts.† The admiral appointed his Chief of Staff, Vice Admiral Raymond Spruance, a veteran of Midway, to command the Central Pacific Force (Fifth Fleet). Spruance,

---

*The Japanese leaders believed that the Americans would not begin the drive across the central Pacific until they had more carriers.

†By this time Admiral Nimitz had attempted to make his headquarters a truly joint one. While Army and Navy officers were assigned to his joint staff, the admiral failed to set up a totally separate theater staff which was independent from his fleet staff or from the Army's Central Pacific Force staff. Officers from the two service staffs doubled as Nimitz's joint staff officers. At this time, General Richardson, USA, commanded all Army forces in the Central Pacific Area.

in turn, commanded four major task forces: a fast carrier force, an assault force, an amphibious corps, and a defense and shore-based air force. Rear Admiral Charles Pownall commanded the fast carriers, which included the veteran *Saratoga* and *Enterprise*, four brand new 27,100-ton Essex class carriers, and five new 11,000-ton light carriers. (*See Appendix 17.*) Also included were five new battleships. Rear Admiral Richmond Turner commanded the assault forces for the third time in the war. (Previously he had led them at Guadalcanal and New Georgia.) Turner, the designated officer in tactical command, controlled all amphibious shipping, the support forces (including several old battleships and six new Kaiser-build escort carriers), and the landing forces. The immediate commander of the landing forces was Major General Holland Smith, prewar expert in amphibious operations. Holland Smith controlled two other generals with the same last name: Major General Julian Smith, commanding the 2nd Marine Division, which was to assault Tarawa; and Major General Ralph Smith, commanding the 27th Infantry Division, elements of which were to take Makin.[14]

Once pre-invasion plans were made, all the units had sufficient time to rehearse and check their plans before they converged on the target area from all over the eastern and southern Pacific. Units paid special attention to logistical preparations because in amphibious assaults extra care had to be taken to insure that each unit was self-sufficient. Constant air, submarine, and photographic reconnaisance missions gave the American commanders an exact picture

The New Battleship USS *Washington*

of the Japanese defenses. In fact, on Tarawa, because photo intelligence specialists were able to locate and identify Japanese latrines, they were able to determine accurately the number of defenders who were ashore.[17] By the time Admiral Spruance ordered his force to the Gilberts, he had reasonably trained, equipped, and supplied his forces—at least in comparison to the naval task force that had invaded Guadalcanal.

Although Nimitz had been supporting Halsey in the South Pacific Area since the end of the early carrier raids and the decisive battle of Midway, his Central Pacific Area forces had not been idle elsewhere. As mentioned, Carlson's battalion had raided Makin during the Guadalcanal campaign. Next, the admiral had been involved with the operations in the north Pacific, where the Americans recovered first Attu and later Kiska from the Japanese in May 1943. (*See Atlas Map No. 22.*) From September 1 to October 6, 1943, the Pacific Fleet Commander had sent his fast carriers west to conduct a series of strikes against several Japanese outposts and also to assist Halsey in the South Pacific Area. Three carriers attacked Marcus Island (September 1), and then six carriers struck Tarawa and Makin Atolls (September 18 and 19) and Wake Island (October 5 and 6). These strikes were made primarily to train the new carrier groups; but, as one result, the Japanese withdrew their aircraft from Tarawa.[18] Just before the attack on the Gilberts, Nimitz sent two carrier groups (six carriers) south to assist Halsey, who immediately employed them to protect his forces, which had just landed on Bougainville. Carrier strikes against Rabaul between November 1 and 11 destroyed nearly two thirds of the naval aircraft which Admiral Koga had deployed there from his carriers at Truk; they also severely damaged the cruiser force that he sent south to attack the American beachhead. These carrier attacks so depleted Koga's air and naval power that he was unable to attack Spruance's Central Pacific Force in the Gilberts with his *Combined Fleet*.[19] (*See Atlas Map No. 20.*) In addition to these actions, small naval and air forces occupied Baker Island in the Ellice group from August 18 to 28. Baker offered the Seventh Air Force a new base from which to fly photo reconnaissance missions over the Gilberts.

In two other major operational areas, progress and innovation continued. American submarines prowled the central Pacific battlefield, sinking as many merchantmen and troopships as possible, thus adding to the problems of the Japanese armed forces throughout the Pacific and the Far East. Nearly as important, from an American point of view, the Navy adopted a new floating logistical base system which was built initially around Service Squadron 4. This innovation allowed the fleet to take with it tenders,

Fleet Admiral Chester Nimitz, 1945

repair ships, tugs, minesweepers, concrete fuel barges, general store barges, and special lighters. These auxiliaries carried a 30-day supply of food and medicine for 20,000, 3 units of antiaircraft fire, 10 units of aircraft bombs, one unit of fire for ground weapons, 15 days of fuel for the landing force, spare parts, and repair facilities needed for advanced operations.[20]

Admiral Spruance's force (200 ships, 27,600 combat troops, 7,600 garrison troops, 6,000 vehicles, and 117,000 tons of cargo) began moving toward the Gilberts around November 12. From the South Pacific Area, Rear Admiral Harry Hill led the South Attack Force (2nd Marine Division reinforced) toward Tarawa. In Hawaii, Rear Admiral Turner in the old battleship *Pennsylvania*, survivor of the Pearl Harbor attack and the old flagship of the Pacific Fleet, weighed anchor and led the North Attack Force toward Makin. (*See Atlas Map No. 20.*) As the transports moved out, the 11 fast carriers sortied on various missions. One group, built around the new *Yorktown*, struck the Marshalls to prevent Japanese aircraft there from interfering with the scheduled landings. Another group worked over Makin for two days, and then stood by to protect the amphibious forces. A third group pounded Tarawa for three days after coming up from Rabaul. The fourth group, also coming north from the south Pacific, neutralized Nauru in the Gilberts. Army bombers assisted the naval fliers by striking numerous targets throughout the Gilberts and the Marshalls from Baker and other nearby islands.

The Japanese spotted the incoming forces before the

Americans were able to land their first troops, but Japanese airmen could not damage even the slow LSTs which preceded the North Attack Force. On November 19, the invading forces sighted each other, and early the next morning both forces began sending their craft ashore.[21] (*See Atlas Map No. 20.*)

The first troops to land in the Gilberts were the men of the 165th Infantry Regiment. (*See Atlas Map No. 23a.*) Two battalions landed at 8:31 A.M. on the west end of Butaritari Island, the pork chop-shaped main island of Makin Atoll. Encountering little difficulty, the national guardsmen from New York drove due west toward the key Japanese positions in the center of the long stem of Butaritari, while two companies turned right and left to clear the short arms of the pork chop. By 10:55 A.M., the New Yorkers had marched through minimum resistance to the planned beach-head line, and had virtually secured all of the island west of the line.[22]

At 10:41 A.M., the regiment's remaining battalion landed from the lagoon on the north side of the island's stem in the area where the Japanese were expected to conduct their main defensive. Two companies formed the main attack, and they pushed directly across the 300-yard wide stem to reach the south coast, while at the same time small elements turned right and left to protect the flanks of the battalions. Little resistance was met until after the infantry-men reached the south coast and turned west, then east, to clear the Japanese out of their defensive position.

For the remainder of the day, most of the action took place in the sectors of the battalions advancing eastward from the first beachhead and the troops who maneuvered westward from the second beachhead. There were several small, but stiff, fire fights, which were often resolved by the tanks which had come ashore. In one fight, the Japanese killed the American regimental commander while he was trying to get tanks to move forward against a particularly difficult bunker. By 4:00 P.M., the Americans had linked up with each other in the west, and by the end of the day's fighting only one Japanese pocket of resistance remained. (*See Atlas Map No. 23a.*)

After the link-up, the men of the 165th Infantry bedded down for the night and prepared for the next day's operations, which they hoped would clear the entire island. On the twenty-first, the regiment destroyed the remaining enclave in the west and continued its drive toward the east. The main operations toward the east bogged down with little gain, but the following day the Americans advanced quickly when a special detachment was deployed to the adjacent island of Kuma to cut off the Japanese retreat. On the night of November 22, the Japanese tried to break out of their position, but the Americans held in place, even though they had failed to dig in and organize night perimeters. By noon on November 23, the Americans had secured Butaritari.

This action has been called "frustratingly slow" by General Holland Smith,* and most observers agree that the Army troops did not perform their mission with great speed or dash.[23] Many commentators, however, failed to remember that most green units—particularly national guard or militia formations—do poorly in their first fights, and all are terribly slow in accomplishing their missions, even when faced with small enemy garrisons.†

After the first waves of American infantry landed on Makin, the first marines landed at 9:10 A.M. on Beach Red 1 on the western end of Betio Island in the Tarawa Atoll. The marines suffered heavy casualties as they struggled to establish themselves ashore. Many were hit as they waded across the coral reef, which was nearly 500 yards off shore. Only the marines in the armored tractors** of the first wave reached the shore without having to disembark from their landing craft.[24] (*See Atlas Map No. 23b.*) Seven minutes later, the first battalion arrived at Beach Red 3; five minutes after that, the tractors of the third assault battalion crawled ashore at Beach Red 2.

Japanese resistance everywhere was heavy and deter-mined, even though the pre-invasion bombardment by aircraft and ships had managed to neutralize most of the

Betio: Beach Red 2 at Central Pier

*General Smith was a proud, provincial, and irascible marine, who made many unreasonable statements and became embroiled in feuds with the Navy and Army. He seldom complimented Army troops.

†This had been true on Guadalcanal and in Papua, and had included American and Australian units as well as Army and Marine Corps units.

**These lightly armored vehicles (LVTs) were developed before the war. (See Chapter 2.) Newer LVT(A)s were called amphibious tanks by the Army. They were used as fire assault vehicles in later landings. LVTs mounted protective machineguns. LVT(A)s had 37-mm cannons.

large caliber guns on the island. Japanese defenders shelled the approaching boats and tractors with bursting rounds and 37-mm antiboat guns, while machinegunners raked the beaches and the water between the beach and the coral reef. Marines took heavy casualties everywhere as they waded ashore and moved inland against the Japanese defenses, which were practically at the water line. Because of the bitter resistance, units became scrambled and confusion became the order of the day. There was also a good deal of confusion offshore, where ever since the operation had started, nothing had begun on time. Now, with the heavy casualties and disruption ashore, as well as the concurrent poor communications between ship and shore, the chaos worsened.

On Betio, Colonel David Shoup found a difficult situation and ordered his reserve ashore at Beach Red 2. (*See Atlas Map No. 23b.*) Shortly thereafter, Major General Julian Smith told Shoup that a battalion from the division reserve was prepared to land and assist his beleaguered troops. Shoup asked General Smith to send the battalion to Beach Red 3 where his troops seemed to be progressing according to schedule. After he released the battalion, General Smith had only one other battalion left in reserve, because his third regiment, the 6th Marines, was designated the V Amphibious Corps reserve.

Throughout the remainder of the first day, the marines held a precarious position on the beach, one which worried all commanders ashore and afloat. Units could not maneuver; all the men could do was push directly ahead. Some gains were made with the assistance of tanks, which had come ashore before noon, but the marines did most of their fighting with their light individual weapons. Without demolitions, flamethrowers, and close-in artillery or direct fire weapons support, the marines could bypass and isolate nearby pillboxes, but could not destroy them. Operations, therefore, were discouragingly slow. (*See Atlas Map No. 23b.*)

When darkness fell on November 20, Colonel Shoup's men held two small beachheads on Betio. The bulk of his force (four battalions) held a perimeter—barely 700 yards long and 300 yards deep—which encompassed part of the Japanese airfield and the adjoining portions of Beach Red 2 and Beach Red 3. A single battalion held the northwest corner of Betio at Beach Red 1 and along Beach Green on the western portion of the island. Off the reef, General Smith's remaining reserve battalion stayed in its boats, awaiting orders to land. (*See Atlas Map No. 23b.*) Fortunately for the Americans, the Japanese did not counterattack during the night; by not doing so they missed their best chance of destroying Colonel Shoup's battalions.

By the end of the second day, the marines had gained the upper hand on Betio by advancing all the way to the south coast of the island along Beach Green and by establishing a battalion perimeter on the central coast south of the Japanese airfield. Late in the afternoon the situation further improved when a battalion from the corps reserve (6th Marines) landed at Beach Green, while another battalion from the reserve secured adjacent Baikiri Island. At 5:10 P.M., Colonel Shoup announced that his troops were winning. Later that night, Colonel Merritt Edson, the division's chief of staff, assumed command ashore.

On November 22, the third day, Colonel Edson, the victor over Kawaguchi on Guadalcanal, directed the fresh battalion of the 6th Marines to attack along the south coast of the island to link up with the battalion south of the airfield, while one battalion in the Beach Red 3 area also attacked eastward. By the end of the day, Edson had a firm line across the island at the eastern edge of Beach Red 3, a position from which the Americans could overrun the island the following day. To the west, another corps reserve battalion landed, and marines prepared to move against the surviving Japanese pocket between Beach Red 1 and Beach Red 2. To aid in the next attacks, Edson deployed the marine artillery regiment to Baikiri Island. (*See Atlas Map 23b.*)

During the night of November 22, the surviving Japanese launched a series of piecemeal and uncoordinated attacks, which caused some heavy casualties but did not crack the marines' eastern line. These attacks unexpectedly exhausted the defenders; on the following day, the marines were able to overrun the eastern tail of Betio. The same day, two battalions, attacking from Beach Green and Beach Red 2, crushed the Japanese pocket in the west.

General Julian Smith, who had assumed command ashore on the twenty-second, declared Betio secure the following morning, although it was several more days before the marines killed or captured the last of the Japanese and Koreans on the island. Marines then landed at other islands in the Tarawa Atoll and went to four other atolls in the Gilberts, where they eliminated a few Japanese and secured the atolls for the base forces which landed soon thereafter. (*See Atlas Map No. 23b.*)

Bloody Tarawa cost the marines 3,301 casualties, 900 of whom died as a result of the fighting. But the Japanese paid an even higher price—all but 146 of their original 4,836-man garrison died.[25] These losses shocked the American people, and many asked whether such actions were necessary. General Holland Smith, stung by the heavy casualties, claimed after the war that Tarawa was a mistake, and that the Marshalls, not the Gilberts, should have been the strategic goal. No other high commander agreed.[26] Tarawa illustrated just how difficult amphibious assaults against well-defended shorelines would be, something that had always been recognized by those men who had developed the doctrine for such operations. Moreover, according to Marine Corps Headquarters:

> ... casualties to the assaulting troops at Tarawa amounted to 20 percent, a figure well within the calculated amount that can be sustained in a successful amphibious assault against a strongly defended enemy island, and actually less than those sustained during corresponding periods of initial assaults in several succeeding operations in which the Corps would participate.[27]

Tarawa demonstrated that amphibious assaults could work, but it also revealed deficiencies in technique. In future operations, naval gun batteries would have to fire destruction rather than neutralizing missions, and preliminary bombardment would have to be increased. Supporting fires and close air strikes would have to be scheduled to give the attacking troops protection right up to the time of landing, artillery would have to be placed on nearby islands to support the landing troops as quickly as possible, and more amphibian tractors would have to be used in the first waves to traverse the coral reefs which surround the atolls. These lessons, and many others—particularly ones involving ship-to-air, ship-to-shore, and infantry-tank communications—would be absorbed before the next assaults took place in the Marshalls.

During the battle ashore at Makin and Tarawa, Admiral Spruance's ships kept a wary eye on the Japanese air and naval forces in the Marshalls and in the local area. Carrier fighter pilots beat off several Japanese air strikes and executed the first carrier-launched, radar-controlled, night interception of the war.* Some Japanese bombers did get through, but they did no damage. The Japanese submarine *I-175* achieved a major success on November 23 when it sank the escort carrier *Liscomb Bay* off Makin, killing 644 of the crew, including her captain and admiral.[28] Because Admiral Koga at Truk could not deploy the full force of the *Combined Fleet* at this time, however, overall Japanese reactions were weak.

With the seizure of the Gilbert's, Spruance secured a major island group in the central Pacific which would provide excellent bomber and fighter bases for the advance into the Marshalls in January 1944. The securing of the Gilberts also shortened the line of communications to Australia and the Southwest Pacific Area. Tactically, the operation proved the soundness of amphibious assault doctrine, and provided information for the improvement of techniques which would be used again and again in the

Central Pacific Area. Most importantly, seizure of the Gilberts committed the United States strategically to the central Pacific offensive.

Surprise Moves: Kwajalein, Majuro, and Eniwetok

Concurrent with the Gilberts operation, the Joint Chiefs of Staff and Admiral Nimitz continued to plan for succeeding operations in the Central Pacific Area.[29] In December, the Chiefs met with their British counterparts at Cairo and Teheran (SEXTANT Conferences), where they developed the strategy for 1944. Meanwhile, Nimitz and his staff completed the major outlines for the attack on the Marshalls.

At the SEXTANT Conference, although the leaders of the Allied nations paid most attention to the forthcoming invasion of Europe, they also considered worldwide operations. It was during these critical discussions that the western Allies solidified their plans for the central Pacific drive in 1944, deciding on the following items: (*See Atlas Map No. 22.*)

1. An overall plan for the defeat of Japan was approved in principle. In it, the Allies decided that the main effort against Japan would be made in the Pacific, hoping that an invasion of the Japanese homeland would be unnecessary.
2. A schedule of operations was accepted, which included the seizure of the Marianas for the establishment of airbases from which the new, long-range B-29 Superfortresses could bomb Japan.
3. Southwest Pacific Area Forces would continue to drive up the coast of New Guinea toward the Vogelkop Peninsula.
4. Operations would be started to clear upper Burma, and by May 1, 1944, B-29s would begin bombing Japan from bases in China.
5. When planning future assaults against the Japanese, it could be assumed that the Soviet Union would eventually enter the war against Japan.[30]

As a result of these conferences, the Pacific emerged as a major theater of war, second only to Europe; the Mediterranean and Southeast Asian (China-Burma-India) theaters were relegated to secondary positions. Also, the mutually supporting drives across the Pacific became coequal, although the new central Pacific drive was considered the first among equals.

Nimitz profited from these decisions because more and more resources flowed into his theater and the Joint Chiefs showed more interest in his rapid advance to the Marianas.

---

*Rear Admiral Arthur Radford, commanding the *Enterprise* group, developed this technique. Unfortunately, in the first operation, Lieutenant Commander Edward "Butch" O'Hare, the Navy's first ace, was lost.

Even before the Gilberts operations began, Nimitz had contemplated the delayed move into the Marshalls, planning to strike deep into the island chain to seize the nerve center of Japanese defenses—Kwajalein Atoll. (*See Atlas Maps No. 20 and No. 22.*) This was a bold decision because Nimitz chose to bypass those easternmost atolls (Wotje, Maloelap, Mille, and Jaluit) which the Japanese had fortified and garrisoned with most of their aircraft in the island group.* (*See Atlas Map No. 20.*) Admiral Spruance, Admiral Turner, and General Holland Smith all opposed the theater commander, but Nimitz held firm and ordered his subordinates to plan to seize Kwajalein in January 1944. Spruance, however, was able to convince his boss to take one atoll in the eastern chain, Majuro, for a fleet base.[31] After Admiral Nimitz and his staff had worked out the general plans for the operation (FLINTLOCK), Spruance and his subordinates put to practice the lessons learned in seizing the Gilberts. Allocating larger air, naval, and land forces, they planned for intensive pre-invasion bombardment, extensive submarine reconnaissance, improvements in command ships, and the pre-positioning of field artillery on nearby islets. Spruance expected to land his forces at Kwajalein and Majuro atolls on January 31, 1944, following two days of intensive carrier strikes against all the Marshalls. Admiral Turner would again command the Joint Expeditionary Task Force (V Amphibious Force), and General Holland Smith (V Amphibious Corps) would command the Expeditionary Troops. This time, however, Smith would assume control of the landing forces once they were ashore.[32] The fast carriers, now organized as Task Force 58 under Rear Admiral Marc Mitscher, would support and cover the entire operation, while Land-Based Air, another of Spruance's principal commands, continued to pound the Japanese positions. In addition, the battleships, cruisers, and destroyers of the fleet would bombard the main objectives, starting on D-2.

The plan of maneuver was relatively simple. Spruance would approach Kwajalein Atoll from the northeast and deploy three major assault forces against the selected objectives. (*See Atlas Map No. 20.*) Rear Admiral Richard Conolly's Northern Attack Force would carry the untried 4th Marine Division (Major General Harry Schmidt) into the lagoon at the northern end of the atoll, where they would attack principally the adjoining islands of Roi and Namur, but also other adjacent islands. Admiral Turner would lead his Southern Attack Force off the coast of Kwajalein Island—the southernmost island in the atoll—where the

partially veteran 7th Infantry Division (Major General Charles Corlett), would assault several small islands and Kwajalein.† (*See Atlas Map No. 24.*)

Farther east, Rear Admiral Harry Hill, commanding the Majuro Attack Group, would send his composite Marine and Army force ashore at Majuro the day before the main assaults were made at Roi, Namur, and Kwajalein. (*See Atlas Map No. 20.*) The 22nd Marines, a separate regiment, and the bulk of the 106th Infantry of the 27th Infantry Division formed the corps reserve and remained afloat.

The landing units were well prepared for their tasks. At the Jungle Training Center in Hawaii, the Army troops learned to fight in fortified areas, improved their infantry-engineer and infantry-tank techniques, and learned how to employ flamethrowers. At Camp Pendleton, California, the marines practiced similar techniques. All the units absorbed the lessons learned in the Gilberts, participated in amphibious training exercises, and prepared for the tough fight ahead. In addition, more efficient shore parties were organized, including new signal units, which were needed to improve battle communications.

In the interlude between the end of the Gilberts Campaign and the invasion of the Marshalls, other actions took place in the central Pacific which affected the forthcoming operation. The Allies quickly built airbases in the Gilberts, and from them heavy B-24s and medium B-25s, escorted by P-39s and P-40s, neutralized the Japanese air centers at Mille (by January 10), Maloelap (by January 27), Jaluit (by January 29), and Wotje (by January 29). When Admiral Mitscher's fast carriers arrived, only the airfield at Roi was operational, because it was beyond effective range of the B-24s. (*See Atlas Maps No. 20 and No. 22.*)

In addition to their bombing missions, the land-based air squadrons photographed the Marshalls for the key commanders, while submariners helped to reconnoiter the landing beaches. Rear Admiral Pownall's fast carriers also raided Kwajalein and Wotje Atolls on December 4. (*See Atlas Map No. 20.*) Four days later, two carriers launched strikes against Nauru in the Gilberts. The carrier attacks in the Marshalls were not highly successful, but they did trigger a change in command and philosophy which affected the fleet operations for the remainder of the war.

Several characteristics had been common to previous carrier actions. They were commanded for the most part by non-aviators, like Fletcher, Kinkaid, Wilson, and Spruance. Then there was the tendency to employ the carriers in single task groups. Also, the flattops were used cautiously and

---

*Nimitz's planners originally desired to take these atolls along with Kwajalein.

†Two regimental combat teams of the 7th Infantry Division had seen combat in the Aleutians.

defensively.* While these characteristics were acceptable during the early carrier war, when the Japanese fleet was totally superior, the young air enthusiasts in the Navy objected to them. When the new carriers began to arrive in quantity in late 1943, the number of air admirals grew, and their influence began to be felt in the Pacific Fleet. The naval aviators wanted many things: an aviator in Nimitz's billet or at least as a deputy to Nimitz; air officers in tactical command of all carrier groups and task forces; the integration of battleships into carrier groups so that the great ships could protect the flattops with their antiaircraft batteries; the employment of multi-carrier task groups; and the aggressive use of the carriers.

One by one, the young air admirals got their way. Admiral Pownall's performance as the senior carrier group commander irritated the influential airmen in Nimitz's headquarters; following his rather conservative performance at Kwajalein in December, these men convinced Nimitz to replace him with the aggressive Marc Mitscher. About this time, a senior air admiral had just become Nimitz's Assistant Chief of Staff for plans. The way was also paved for the appointment of a naval aviator as the deputy to Nimitz after the seizure of the Marshalls. These changes, plus the recent organization of multi-carrier task groups, met many of the objections of the naval aviators. Still, these men could not convince Spruance to use his carriers offensively. That would take more time. Moreover, the naval aviators neither swayed Nimitz to replace Spruance with an air officer, nor forced Spruance to appoint their choice of air officers to his staff. Spruance, however, never meddled in the tactical handling of his carriers.[33]

The Japanese had also been busy during the interlude in operations. The Imperial Army sent reinforcements into the Marshalls to help bolster the Navy's defenses. The Navy had been pressing for the construction of defenses and airfields, and had constantly deployed more and more aircraft to its forward bases in the Marshalls—Mille, Maloelap, Jaluit, and Wotje. (See Atlas Maps No. 20 and No. 22.) Vice Admiral Masashi Kobayashi, commanding Fourth Fleet and charged with the defense of the Japanese mandates, did everything possible to insure that his outposts would delay the Americans. The Japanese commanders, however, did not anticipate the American landing at Kwajalein. (See Atlas Maps No. 20 and No. 24.) They believed that the next assaults would hit their eastern

bastions, probably Jaluit, Mille, or Wotje. At these positions, and throughout the islands, the Japanese planned to annihilate the Americans at the beach by offensive action. Therefore, they built defenses around the perimeter of the islands and emplaced extensive offshore beach obstacles on the seaward side of the islands in an effort to strengthen the natural obstacles of the coral reefs. (See Atlas Maps No. 24 and No. 24a.) After Tarawa, the Japanese began to improve their lagoon defenses because the Marines had attacked from the lagoon side of that coral spit. Because of the small, flat land areas in the various atolls, they did not build their defenses in depth, although bomb shelters in the rear of the beaches effectively deepened the positions. At all locations, the Japanese prepared to fight to the last man if the invaders could not be destroyed at the water's edge.

Unfortunately for the Japanese, their forces in the Marshalls—particularly at Kwajalein Atoll—were not strong enough to stop determined invasions by 54,000 assault troops backed by 297 ships (including 12 fast carriers and 8 escort carriers) and nearly 800 naval aircraft. There were about 345 combat-effective naval troops on Roi and Namur, along with 2,150 air force headquarters troops, 357 fleet laborers, and 700 other miscellaneous troops. (See Atlas Map No. 24a.) The small islands, the largest of which was only about 1,300 yards square, were reasonably well-fortified, but the fortifications were designed to prevent an assault from the sea. The airfield on Roi covered the entire island. On Kwajalein Island, there were 5,000 Japanese, only 1,820 of whom could be called combat effective. (See Atlas Map No. 24b.) Kwajalein is larger than either Roi or Namur, being about 4,500 yards long and 1,800 yards wide. The defenses on Kwajalein were hastily prepared, and although the best positions faced the sea, the Japanese troops had erected a two-strand barbed wire fence at the water's edge on the lagoon side. There were several small units on adjoining islands in the Kwajalein Atoll, but there were none on the other major objective, Majuro Atoll.

Admiral Mitscher's carrier air groups were the first American forces to see action in the Marshalls campaign. Striking on January 29, 1944, the naval airmen completely destroyed the remaining Japanese air forces in the area during the first of the two days of planned pre-invasion strikes. Since many of the Japanese pilots were from the Third Fleet's carriers, the Americans virtually destroyed the last trained carrier pilots of the Combined Fleet. In these early operations, Admiral Mitscher proved that carrier forces could enter a hostile area, gain and maintain aerial superiority, and remain in the area while an amphibious force landed and conducted its assigned campaign. From that time on, the carrier admirals felt that their ships could survive in any desired battle area.

---

*Ironically, these characteristics enabled two-nonrated admirals, Fletcher and Spruance, to win at Midway the most important carrier battle of the war. The two admirals also commanded the naval forces which defeated the Japanese carrier fleets at the Battle of the Coral Sea and the Battle of the Philippine Sea. Fletcher commanded in the first action; Spurance in the second.

Vice Admiral M. Kobayashi, Commander-in-Chief,
Fourth Fleet, Truk

Army Forces:

1st South Seas Detachment
1st Amphibious Brigade, A Detachment
2nd South Seas Detachment
3rd South Seas Garrison Detachment

Navy Forces:

6th Base Force (Rear Admiral M. Akiyama, Kwajalein)

51st Guard Force (Jaluit)
52d Guard Force (Maloelap)
53d Guard Force (Wotje)
61st Guard Force (Kwajalein)
66th Guard Force (Mille)
Elements, *Yokosuka 4th SNLF* (Kwajalein)

24th Flotilla (Rear Admiral Yamada, Kwajalein)

Japanese Combat Forces, Marshall Islands and Vicinity, January 1944

On January 31, the American forces began to land. These forces, however, did not attack the main objectives. Instead, they secured the several small islands adjacent to Roi, Namur, and Kwajalein. Taking these islands would allow the marines and the soldiers to pre-position their field artillery to support the main assaults, and would also secure the passages through the coral reef so that Admiral Turner's ships could enter the lagoon to support the invasions. The lagoon also provided a safe anchorage for the American vessels, one which protected them from prowling Japanese submarines. (*See Atlas Maps No. 22b and No. 22d.*)

Carriers at Sea

On D+1, the 4th Marine Division hit the beaches on the south shore of Roi and Namur, while the two regimental combat teams of the 7th Infantry Division landed on the west coast of Kwajalein. Both beaches were selected because the Japanese defenses there were the weakest. Reefs at both objectives, however, were a problem. Off Kwajalein they are precipitous and about 100 to 130 yards wide, while on the lagoon side of Roi and Namur they are somewhat larger, but more easily traversed. (*See Atlas Maps No. 24a and No. 24b.*) General Schmidt landed his division with two regiments abreast, and each regiment employed two battalion landing teams abreast. Colonel Louis Jones' 23rd Marines overran Roi by nightfall of the first day, but Colonel Franklin Hart's 24th Marines took an extra day to overrun Namur. There was little maneuvering—the marines landed and then drove straight across the islands to the north shore, which was only about 800-1000 yards away. General Schmidt lost 190 killed and 547 wounded, but he virtually annihilated the Japanese garrison, taking only 91 prisoners out of the 3,563 men on the islands.[34] (*See Atlas Map No. 24a.*)

There was some confusion during both days of the marine operations because of difficulties with the amphibious tractors, amphibious tanks, and landing craft. In fact, operations were delayed several times on February 1, and the marines did not land until 11:33 A.M. at Roi and 11:45 A.M. at Namur. Hart's troops landed piecemeal because the order to land was given before the regiment was properly assembled offshore. Once ashore, things went very smoothly, although Major General Holland Smith must have been chagrined to find that his untried marines also were trigger happy, shooting up the countryside at night, and were somewhat overcautious in their first attacks.

Major General Corlett's attack of Kwajalein was a model amphibious operation in which there were no hitches. (*See Atlas Map No. 24b.*) At 6:18 A.M., the battleships *Mississippi* and *Pennsylvania* opened fire on the objective area, soon being joined by another battleship, three cruisers, and eight destroyers. At one time the *Mississippi* closed to within 1,500 yards of the shore to fire her 14-inch main batteries. B24s, dive bombers, and fighters added their ordnance to the bombardment, and by 9:30 A.M. "the entire island looked as if it had been picked up to 20,000 feet and then dropped."[35]

At 9:00 A.M. the first waves of LVTs started for shore behind rocket-firing LCI gunboats. On the flanks, amphibian tanks and LCI gunboats fired guns and 4.5 inch rockets as the waves moved toward the beaches. Navy pilots made last minute strafing runs, and the artillery on nearby Carlson Island and the ships kept firing until two minutes before the first tractors landed at 9:30 A.M. Artillery kept firing until the landing craft were 35 yards out, and then shifted 200 yards inland. Right behind the first wave came the supporting ones at two minute intervals; by 10:15 A.M., the two assault battalions were ashore. There were few casualties.

Since he chose to land on the narrow flank of the island, General Corlett attacked with two regiments on line, battalions in column. On the first day (February 1), his lead battalions cleared the western third of Kwajalein with little difficulty and few casualties. On the second day, Corlett's troops took the middle third of Kwajalein, but bogged down on the lagoon side of the island when Japanese resistance stiffened. The third day turned out to be a brutal one for the 184th Infantry on the north, because it ran into an area of rubble, large concrete blockhouses, and pillboxes which had to be cleared point by point. By the end of the day, the Americans and the Japanese were intermixed along the front line, often inside each other's perimeters. Corlett reorganized his forces and renewed the attack on February 4; but he soon discovered that he had to clean up his front area before his attacking troops could move. When this was done, the 32nd Infantry on the south pinched out* the 184th Infantry, made about a half-turn to the left, and cleared the island by dark. (*See Atlas Map No. 24b.*) The infantrymen of the 7th Infantry Division suffered increased casualties on each succeeding day. All told, General Corlett lost 142

---

*One unit "pinches out" another unit by taking over the second unit's front and then continuing to advance alone with a larger frontage.

Infantry and a Tank Advance in the Marshalls— Probably Kwajalein

killed, 854 wounded, and 2 missing; his troops killed 4,938 Japanese and took 206 prisoners.

General Holland Smith once again complained about the slowness of the Army's attack, but his comments lacked substance since the 7th Infantry Division had attacked a much larger island, had met more troops, and had fought through more difficult areas than had the marines on Roi-Namur. The only problem revealed was defective tank-infantry liaison, caused primarily because the sea water shorted out the makeshift telephones placed on the rear deck of each tank. Control, communications, supply, artillery support, naval gunfire support, and air support had been excellent; and the ship-to-shore movement illustrated how well the Americans had perfected amphibious assault techniques. †

Majuro fell easily on January 31, and by February 7 the marines and soldiers had finished clearing all the other islands in the Kwajalein Atoll.[36] (*See Atlas Map No. 20.*)

Because the invasion had gone so well and the reserve troops had not been committed, Admiral Nimitz decided to strike westward immediately and take Eniwetok Atoll, 330 miles away in the western Marshalls. (*See Atlas Maps No. 20 and No. 22.*) Commanders adjusted their plans quickly, reviewed the available but incomplete aerial photographs of Eniwetok, and dispatched a small landing force composed of the relatively untrained and untried troops of the 22nd Marines and 106th Infantry Regiment to take the atoll. To insure that the impromtu invasion was not disrupted by the Japanese air and naval forces at Truk, Nimitz ordered a large carrier strike on the Japanese bastion on D-Day. (*See Atlas Map No. 20.*)

The Japanese has about 2,645 combat effective troops at Eniwetok Atoll when Rear Admiral Harry Hill put the first troops of the Eniwetok Expeditionary Force ashore on some of the smaller islands of the atoll on February 17. The following day, Colonel John Walker's 22nd Marine Regimental Combat Team secured Engebi Island, then assisted the 106th Infantry in taking Eniwetok Island (February 21), and finally captured Parry Island (February 22). Following these actions, Walker's marines cleared out the other unfortified islands of the Marshalls, with some assistance from the 111th Infantry, a separate Army regiment.

No attempt was made to invade the strong Japanese outposts at Jaluit, Maloelap, Mille, and Wotje. They were left to wither on the vine until the Japanese Empire collapsed. In the months to come, American air forces would constantly bomb these atolls to keep them neutralized.

---

† The 7th Infantry Division used a large number of amphibious trucks (DUKWs)for the first time in the Pacific. They proved invaluable for transporting troops, artillery, and supplies.

As the Expeditionary Force landed at Eniwetok Atoll, Admirals Spurance and Mitscher led an attack on Truk, some 669 miles away. On February 17 and 18, air and surface forces destroyed 250 to 275 aircraft, 137,091 tons of merchant shipping, and 15 warships of various kinds. The attack, which included the first low-level, carrier, bombing attack made at night, virtually neutralized Truk, and caused Admiral Koga to withdraw the remaining aircraft at Rabaul to replace his losses at Truk. Koga had withdrawn from his fleet base before the raid, and had taken most of the capital ships with him. Thereafter, he never brought his flag back into the Truk lagoon. Neither did his successors.[37] (*See Atlas Map No. 20.*)

The successful invasion of the Marshalls illustrated how well the air, land, and sea forces assigned to Admiral Spruance had absorbed the lessons of Makin and Tarawa. Amphibious techniques had been perfected; after the assault on the Marshalls, American landings would become more and more professional. If the Gilberts proved the soundness of a doctrine, the Marshalls proved the soundness of amphibious techniques. In addition, the actions in the Marshalls, as well as the spectacular strike on Truk, proved the contentions of the zealous naval airmen that

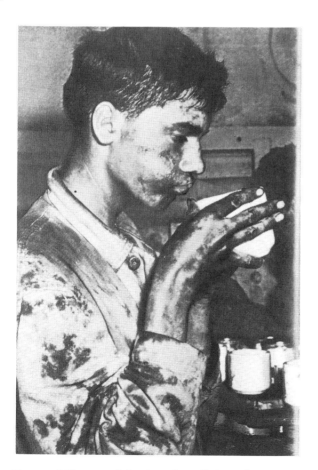

Teenaged Veteran of the Assault on Eniwetok

carriers had indeed replaced battleships as the capital ships of the fleet, and that the fast carrier groups were strong enough to go anywhere in the Pacific and survive, even if tied down to the support of an invasion. Carriers could operate within range of land-based air forces—at least in 1944, when Japanese air forces were a shell of their former selves.

With MacArthur's capture of the Admiralties and the resultant isolation of Rabaul, Nimitz no longer had to consider moving south to help Halsey invade New Ireland or to help MacArthur capture the Admiralties. He was free to attack westward from his position in Micronesia, with the knowledge that his north flank was secured, his south flank protected, and his rear completely under American control. With growing combat power, fleet bases at Majuro and Eniwetok, and a veteran force, Nimitz could either take Truk or go directly to the Marianas. (*See Atlas Map No. 22.*) Whatever he did, his next move would strike Japan's absolute defensive perimter, where he could expect an even more difficult fight.

Strategic Decision: The Marianas

The quick victory in the Marshalls reinforced the opinion of the joint Chiefs of Staff that the main drive against Japan should be made in the central Pacific.[38] The immediate problem, however, was where to go after the Marshalls. Most of the high commanders and service strategists had pondered the question for some time. There were two schools of thought: one urged that Truk be taken; the other advocated bypassing the Japanese bastion and striking directly into the Marianas. Admiral King had consistently argued that the Marianas were the keystone to the Pacific. His support grew even stronger as the months flew by, and in early 1943 he had pushed the Marianas into the tentative planning schedule for 1944 operations. Finally, after the Quebec Conference in August 1943, the admiral achieved his cherished goal when Air Force planners recommended that the islands be taken for airbases for the new B-29s. (*See Atlas Map No. 20.*) Originally, General Henry Arnold, the Army's air chief, wanted the B-29s to fly from China; but his staff eventually decided that the Chinese could not secure the airfields and that the logistical problems involved with running a major air campaign from China would be too taxing.[39] The seizure of the Marianas for B-29 bases fitted into the American plan for the defeat of Japan; that plan emphasized the prospect of a naval and air campaign which might bring Japan to her knees and preclude an amphibious invasion.

After these strategic ideas were ultimately approved by the Combined Chiefs of Staff, Admiral Nimitz prepared the first of his GRANITE Plans on December 27, 1943. GRANITE envisioned the seizure of Kwajalein (January 31), with a concurrent air attack on Truk (March 20), Eniwetok (May 1), Mortlock Island (July 1), Truk (August 15), and Saipan, Tinian, and Guam (November 15). If Truk could be bypassed, the Allied forces would invade the Palaus instead, and the time schedule would be rearranged slightly. (*See Atlas Maps No. 20 and No. 25.*)

At a January 1944 planning conference in Hawaii, which Nimitz called to coordinate Pacific operations, MacArthur's representatives argued against the Marianas invasion, suggesting instead that all the Allied resources be put into the drive northwestward in the Southwest Pacific Area. While Nimitz continued to support his plans for the Marianas, some of his own staff officers did not see the value of attacking the islands because they did not believe that airpower alone would defeat Japan. Furthermore, some of them believed that the attacks would be too costly and that the islands would not provide particularly good fleet bases.

Admiral King was upset by these discussions. His project, however, was saved by the quick victory in the Marshalls and the great success of the first carrier raid on Truk. With Truk nearly helpless, the Marianas became the logical objective for the next move in the central Pacific.

The entire subject was then considered by the strategic planners and the Joint Chiefs in Washington. On March 12, 1944, after much study and the usual amount of compromise between all parties concerned, the Joint Chiefs ordered Nimitz and MacArthur to do the following: (*See Atlas Maps No. 20, No. 22, and No. 25.*)

1. Cancel the Kavieng operation and complete the isolation of Rabaul with minimum forces.
2. Complete development of recently captured Manus in the Admiralty Islands as a major fleet and air base.
3. Occupy Hollandia, Netherlands New Guinea (target date: April 15).
4. Gain control of the Marianas-Carolines-Palau area by neutralizing Truk, occupying the southern Marianas (target date: June 15), and the Palaus (target date: September 15).
5. Occupy southern Mindanao (target date: November 15)
6. Occupy Formosa (target date: February 15, 1945) or Luzon (target date: February 15, 1945).[40]

The operations which Nimitz was tasked to mount were sizeable. In addition, he would have to support MacArthur's attacks on Hollandia and Mindanao with the Pacific Fleet.

The March directive set the stage for the attack into the Marianas.*

Nimitz's attack plan (Operation FORAGER) did not vary greatly from the ones developed previously for the attacks in the Gilberts or Marshalls. He placed all forces under Spruance, who in turn organized a Joint Expeditionary Force under the recently promoted Vice Admiral Turner. Turner further broke his forces down into two main elements: the Northern Landing Force which was to take Saipan and Tinian, and a Southern Landing Force which was to assault Guam. Turner retained command of the Northern Force, but assigned the other amphibious command to Rear Admiral Conolly. Coequal to Turner would be Lieutenant General Holland Smith, also newly promoted, who would command all the landing forces once they were ashore. Smith, like Turner, would personally direct the operations of V Amphibious Corps on Saipan and Tinian. Major General Roy Geiger, the commander of the I Marine Amphibious Corps on Bougainville, would command the III Amphibious Corps when it went ashore at Guam. Marc Mitscher, now a vice admiral and still commanding the fast carrier task force, would destroy the Japanese air forces in the area before the invasion, and then cover the entire operation. Vice Admiral Charles Lockwood's submarines,

---

*The decision to invade the Marianas opened a heated debate about the next important objective—Luzon or Formosa. This subject is covered in a later chapter.

Admiral Raymond Spruance, 1945

directly under Nimitz, would assist Spruance. (*See Appendix 20.*)

Admiral Spruance had 105,859 assault troops for the operation—66,779 for Saipan and Tinian and 39,080 for Guam. These men formed the 2nd, 3rd, and 4th Marine Divisions, the 27th and 77th Infantry Divisions, the 1st Marine Provisional Brigade, and the XXIV Army Corps Artillery. In addition, Spruance had 15 fast carriers, 14 escort carriers, 891 carrier aircraft, 14 battleships, 25 cruisers, and 152 destroyers to support the invasion. Some land-based bombers from the Central and Southwest Pacific Areas would assist by bombing Truk and the Palaus.[41] (*See Atlas Map No. 25.*)

The basic plan was straightforward. Prior to the initial invasion of Saipan, Mitscher would strike Truk again to neutralize that base; conduct a series of raids to destroy as much of the Japanese air forces as possible in the Marianas and Palaus; and then return to the Marianas on June 12, three days before the landings, to complete the destruction of the Japanese air forces there. His new battleships would begin the pre-invasion bombardment the next day, being joined by the old battleships, which would arrive on June 14. On June 15, after three days of continuous air and naval gunfire bombardment, the V Amphibious Corps would land the 2nd and 4th Marine Divisions abreast on the west coast of Saipan to gain a beachhead. (*See Atlas Maps No. 25 and No. 26a.*) The 2nd Marine Division, in the north, was to seize the first high ground, then the dominating Mount Tipo Pale and Mount Tapotchau in the central part of the island. The 4th Marine Division, in the south, was to secure a line 2,000 yards inland, then take Aslito airfield. One battalion would demonstrate off the northern coast to divert Japanese forces from the beachhead area. General Smith would keep the 27th Infantry Division afloat as a corps reserve. Once Saipan was captured, V Amphibious Corps would redeploy to seize Tinian to the southwest. (*See Atlas Map No. 26b.*) General Geiger would invade Guam three days after V Amphibious Corps landed in Saipan. Geiger planned to land his 3rd Marine Division and the 1st Provisional Marine Brigade on line on the west coast of Guam (*See Atlas Map No. 26c*), secure a beachhead line along the high ground dominating the landing areas, and seal off the Orote Peninsula with his separate brigade. General Geiger's reserve also would be the 27th Infantry Division.

Inherent in the plan for invading the Marianas was the hope that the operation would trigger a fleet engagement with the Japanese *Combined Fleet* in the western Pacific. In many ways, American naval thinking at this time was similar to Admiral Yamamoto's when he attacked Midway in 1942, and in many ways the antagonists' positions were the reverse of their 1942 positions. Even though the Pacific Fleet was definitely superior to the *Combined Fleet* now, another Midway could change that in exactly five minutes.

Admiral Soeumu Toyoda, commanding the *Combined Fleet*, was preparing for such a fleet engagement.* On May 3, 1944, he issued orders for the A-GO Operation in which the *Combined Fleet* would sortie to defeat the American fleet in the waters off the Palaus. (*See Atlas Map No. 25.*) While the Japanese considered that the Americans might attack the Marianas, they hoped that they would attack the Palaus first so that the naval battle would develop closer to their strong airbases and their meager fuel supplies. Operations around the Marianas would strain the *Combined Fleet* because of its lack of tankers and its shortage of fuel. (*See Appendix 18.*) In this anticipated action, the key Japanese force would be Vice Admiral Jisaburo Ozawa's *First Mobile Fleet*, which would be based at Tawi Tawi in the Sulu Archipelago.[42]

The Japanese knew that another American invasion was inevitable in the central Pacific, but for some reason the key commanders never recognized the signs of the forthcoming attack in the Marianas. Many Japanese naval officers believed that the Palaus or the Carolines would be the next American objective because of Mitscher's raid on the Palaus and MacArthur's seizure of Hollandia. Senior Japanese Army officers thought that the Marianas would be next, but they believed that the strike would come from New Guinea or that the Allies would launch a simultaneous invasion into the Carolines and Marianas from the Marshalls and New Guinea. As a result, Japanese garrisons were not alerted for the American assault into Saipan, even after Admiral Mitscher began his pre-invasion air strikes. In fact, just after the raids were over on June 11, the Japanese ground commander on Saipan ordered his infantry forces to build a new road to improve communications rather than deploying his troops to improve defensive positions.[43]

While not alert, the Japanese in the Marianas had an abundance of troops and generally excellent positions throughout the volcanic islands. On Saipan, they had 25,469 army troops and about 3,200 naval combat troops. On Tinian, the garrison was considerably smaller: 3,929 army and 4,110 navy personnel. There were 18,500 army and navy personnel on Guam. In rough terms, the Japanese had the equivalent of two divisions on Saipan, two thirds of one on Tinian, and one and one third on Guam. Altogether, they were a formidable force.[44]

---

*Admiral Toyoda replaced Admiral Koga on May 3, 1944. Koga had disappeared on March 31 while enroute to Davao by air. He had been enroute to his forward headquarters in Davao to direct operations against the expected major Allied thrust in western New Guinea.

In an attempt to enhance their chances of success, Imperial Japanese Headquarters organized new headquarters in the Pacific. Army forces were placed under the *Thirty-First Army*, commanded by Lieutenant General Hideyoshi Obata,* whose headquarters was on Saipan; his command was activated on February 18, 1944. Vice Admiral Chuichi Nagumo, the beached commander of Japan's carrier forces, was appointed the commander of the *Central Pacific Area Fleet* on March 10, 1944. (*See Atlas Map No. 25.*) Under Nagumo, whose headquarters was on Saipan also, Imperial Headquarters placed the nearly defunct land-based *Fourth Fleet*,† which was restricted to defending Truk and the eastern Carolines. The Japanese headquarters in Tokyo also technically placed General Obata's *Thirty-First Army* under Nagumo, but old traditions and ways did not die. Army commanders did not subordinate themselves to the Navy. As a result, the commanders on the ground, Nagumo and Obata, decided not to press the issue of unified command, relying instead on the senior commander assuming control on each island. Neither commander assumed responsibility for the entire area. This decision was totally unsatisfactory, considering the problems which the Japanese faced trying to coordinate their defensive efforts across the western Pacific.[45] (*See Appendix 19.*)

Still, the attempt at unified command shows that the Japanese were trying to solve their problems. Perhaps it would have been better to appoint an army officer to supreme command since the Army dominated the scene after the influx of so many new troops from Japan, China, and Manchuria. Previously, the Navy had nearly fought alone in the central Pacific with its own forces.

In Japan, the Army and Navy were also quarreling over strategic priorities in aircraft production and shipping protection. Consequently, the Emperor intervened. On February 10, 1944, at his bidding, the services compromised on aircraft allocations, splitting the available numbers in about half (27,000 each). No practical agreement was reached on the protection of shipping, even though in the first quarter of 1944 Japanese losses totalled close to one million tons. The Army, in fact, took matters into its own hands to protect its convoys after the Navy refused to support this vital program vigorously. As these matters were being discussed, General Tojo intervened, trying to unify Japan's war effort and keep military requirements from overriding national policy. Already Premier and War

Minister, Tojo also assumed the position of Chief of the Army General Staff on February 21. After taking this unprecedented step—a violation of the Meiji Constitution—he succeeded in improving coordination between the Army and the Navy and in better subordinating the Army's demands to national objectives.[46] General Obata's official subordination to Admiral Nagumo in the Marianas may have been a substantial outgrowth of Tojo's actions.

Prior to the actual invasion, several events occurred which influenced the forthcoming action. In February, American submarines began to sink an amazing number of troop ships which were enroute to the Marianas and other Japanese outposts. On February 29, for example, the submarines torpedoed the *Sakito Maru*, killing 1,392 of the 3,080 reinforcements aboard.[47] (Many of the Japanese soldiers on Saipan later proved to be stragglers who had been rescued at sea after they had lost all their equipment, including their own individual weapons.) Nearly as important were Admiral Mitscher's carrier strikes. The soft-spoken, aggressive carrier commander attacked the Marianas (February 22 to 23), the Palaus (March 30 to April 1), and Truk (April 29 to 30), after supporting MacArthur's landing at Hollandia a few days earlier; he then raided Wake and Marcus Islands (May 19 to 23) before beginning the pre-invasion strikes in the Marianas. Mitscher's pilots virtually neutralized the remaining Japanese air forces in the Central Pacific Area. (*See Atlas Map No. 25.*) The Japanese, however, continued to reinforce their air garrisons, and it was not until the afternoon of June 11 that Mitscher achieved aerial supremacy over the target area. Finally, while Nimitz was preparing the way for his invasion, MacArthur's advance up the New Guinea coast past Hollandia to Wakde-Sarmi (May 17 to 18), distracted the Japanese. (*See Atlas Map No. 25.*) As a result of his invasion of Biak on May 27, the Japanese *Combined Fleet* diverted many of its aircraft from the Marianas to western New Guinea, while some of its warships were sent south to destroy the invasion forces there (Operation *KON*) and to land reinforcements.[48] This distracted the Japanese Navy from the central Pacific, even though naval leaders believed at this time that the Americans would strike next into the Marianas or Carolines. Japanese fleet elements and transports sailed south three times, but each time they were recalled. (*See Atlas Map No. 25.*) As the third *KON* Operation began, Admiral Spruance landed his forces on Saipan. Admiral Toyoda immediately ordered the *A-GO* operation executed and Admiral Ozawa sortied with *First Mobile Fleet*. He was joined enroute by the *KON* forces. Spruance's unhampered landing owed much to MacArthur's distraction of the Japanese Fleet and to the loss in western

---

*General Obata was not at Saipan when the Americans landed. Consequently, he exercised no tactical command.

† The *Fourth Fleet*, organized on November 15, 1939, was primarily a base defense unit, not an orthodox combat fleet.

New Guinea of about eight percent of the land-based air forces in the Marianas.*

Following the pre-invasion air strikes and the naval gunfire bombardment, Smith's two marine divisions began to land on June 15 on Saipan, just a few days after General Eisenhower's armies landed at Normandy. (*See Atlas Map No. 26a.*) The Marshalls' landing pattern was repeated: LCI gunboats led the assault, cannon and machinegun-firing amphibian tanks followed, and then waves of amphibian tractors went ashore. The original plans called for the amphibian tanks to lead the assault inland, but they could not survive in the rough terrain or in the face of enemy fire. While all the battalions got ashore quickly, the landing was far from perfect. Units were intermixed, Japanese fire was intense, a large gap developed between the divisions, and casualties mounted steadily. By nightfall, the marines held a tenuous 10,000-yard-wide and 1,000-yard-deep beachhead, which was ripe for a determined counterattack. The Japanese launched such an attack that night, but the marines beat off the tank-led assaults with the help of naval gunfire illumination and 5-inch naval gunfire.

For five more days, the marines fought to secure their beachhead. By then, Holland Smith had landed the 27th Infantry Division and deployed it on the south flank of the 4th Marine Division. This caused Spruance to delay the invasion of Guam, because it deprived him of his only reserve division.

As the marines fought for the first difficult yards on the beaches of Saipan, American submarines reported the approach of the Japanese fleet from the southern Philippines. Faced with the threat of a naval attack and desiring to meet the Japanese fleet in decisive battle, Spruance deployed his fast carrier task forces westward on June 18, accompanied by some of Turner's warships, while that admiral retired with many of the vulnerable transports. The night before the first engagement, Spruance would not allow Mitscher to close with the Japanese because he feared that the enemy would slip around his fleet and strike the amphibious forces at Saipan. Instead, he held Mitscher in position to defend the beachhead, much to the carrier commander's irritation. *(See Atlas Map No. 25.)*

On June 19, Admiral Ozawa launched the first of four attacks. Over 430 Japanese aircraft—the familiar Zeros, Kates, and Vals—bored into the Fifth Fleet; but they did no real damage. The newer and greatly improved American naval fighter, the Grumman Hellcat, and the massive

Hellcats

antiaircraft batteries on the new battleships took their deadly toll of the intruders, shooting down 330 by the end of the five-hour "Great Marianas Turkey Shoot." The same day, American submarines sank two Japanese carriers: the veteran *Shokaku*, and the new 34,200-ton flagship of Admiral Ozawa, the *Taiho*. After these losses, Ozawa decided to withdraw, although he had about 100 aircraft left aboard his remaining carriers.

On June 20, Mitscher launched 216 aircraft in the late afternoon, after Ozawa's force was detected. His pilots sank another carrier (the 27,500-ton *Hiyo*), damaged four others, sank two oilers, and knocked 65 of the remaining Japanese planes out of the air. Mitscher lost 100 aircraft, most of which ran out of fuel or crashed trying to land at night. (Mitscher went so far as to turn on his searchlights to get his pilots home, but still many had to ditch. Over half of the crews were rescued the following day.) A cautious pursuit proved ineffective. Nevertheless, the Battle of the Philippine Sea—the greatest carrier battle of the war—sealed the fate of the Marianas. From then on, Spruance had complete air supremacy over the islands.[49] The admiral, however, was severely criticized for being too cautious.

Meanwhile, the marines and soldiers had captured Aslito Field and cut Saipan in two in the south, sealing the fate of the island but not ending Japanese resistance. (*See Atlas Map No. 26a.*) To destroy the main Japanese force, Smith turned his two marine divisions north on June 20, and then reinforced them with two regiments of the 27th Division. In this phase of operations, the Americans ran into well-defended cliff and cave positions, suffering heavy casualties.

---

*The Japanese planned to defend the Marianas primarily with the land-based *First Air Fleet*, while the *Combined Fleet* was designated to stop an invasion of the Palaus. Biak, however, drained off so much airpower that the *First Air Fleet* was nearly impotent. In this way, Biak was to the Marianas what Rabaul was to the Gilberts.

By July 9, after taking Mount Tipo Pale, Mount Tapotchau, Purple Heart Ridge, Death Valley, and the Kagman Peninsula, the Americans had reached the north coast of Saipan, ending the main battle. Mopping-up operations would continue, however, until August.

Just before the final American moves, General Yoshitsugu Saito (the commander of the *43rd Division* and the tactical commander of the forces on Saipan) issued a spiritual message to his troops, and then committed suicide. The unlucky Nagumo, certainly not the typical Japanese warrior, did likewise, far from the destroyers that he loved and the carriers which he did not really understand. The two commanders were joined by hundreds of Japanese men, women, and children who leaped off the cliffs near Marpi Point (*See Atlas Map No. 26a.*) onto the rocks below because they feared capture by the Americans. The most inexplicable act was one of a Japanese officer who beheaded a small group that was stranded on a spit of land off Saipan, resisting Americans who were trying to convince the survivors to surrender.[50]

Operations on Saipan confirmed lessons already learned earlier, but not yet completely absorbed, and also exacerbated old jealousies. It was illustrated once again that a long pre-invasion bombardment was preferable to a short one, and that the old battleships did a better bombardment job than the newer ones. Close air support could be improved—the pilots still bombed both sides impartially—and the amphibian tanks were unsuitable for land combat. Naval gunfire again proved especially good against seaside caves and for illumination. And, fortunately for the Americans, Japanese beach defense tactics were still inadequate.[51] The fighting also increased lingering bitterness between the Marine Corps and the Army, because although General Holland Smith relieved General Ralph Smith allegedly for not following orders, in actuality it was chiefly because the 27th Infantry Division did not meet his standards of rapid, aggressive attacks. The Smith versus Smith controversy reached the highest level of military command, but it was never resolved. Most Army officers associated with Holland Smith decided that they would never willingly serve with him again. In fairness to the marine general, the 27th Infantry Division was not one of the best in the theater. In fairness to the division, Holland Smith seemed to underestimate its difficulties in battle and did not always give it professionally competent orders in critical situations. In retrospect, Holland Smith's earlier criticism of the 27th Infantry Division on Makin (and also on Eniwetok) probably soured his judgment, and did nothing to improve the confidence of the soldiers in the marine commander. Smith was not Eichelberger. His impatience, publicly stated preference for marine troops, inefficient corps headquarters,

Lieutenant General Holland Smith

and penchant for criticizing others, did little to inspire his soldiers.[52]

As soon as the V Amphibious Corps could be withdrawn from the line, it was used to take Tinian. For that operation, Major General Julian Smith replaced Holland Smith as corps commander, although the senior Smith retained control of Expeditionary Troops. Julian Smith conducted the Tinian operation with every advantage: abundant photographic intelligence, captured Japanese plans, extensive prebombardment, artillery support from Saipan, overwhelming manpower, and a relatively easy shore-to-shore amphibious movement. Landing one behind the other on July 24, his two divisions completed the subjugation of Tinian eight days later. The great prize was the airfield complex. From it, the *Enola Gay* would carry the first atomic bomb to Japan. Many critics have called Tinian the perfect amphibious operation; with all its inherent advantages, it should have been.* (*See Atlas Map No. 26b.*)

Before Major General Roy Geiger could invade Guam, Nimitz had to assign the 77th Infantry Division to Spruance as a force reserve. Once the new force was allotted, and once the situation on Saipan showed that the Americans would win there, Spruance ordered the invasion to begin on July 21.

The errors which were made on Saipan were not repeated on Guam. The Americans insured that intelligence was excellent and that pre-invasion bombardment was long and

---

*At Tinian, for the first time in the war, airmen dropped napalm.

well conceived. After securing his beachhead, Geiger directed his forces inland to seize the high ground to the east, turned Brigadier Lemuel Shepherd's 1st Provisional Marine Brigade north to clear the Orote Peninsula, and launched a two-division drive—the marines on the left, the soldiers on the right—northwestward to clear the island. Guam fell on August 10, but the Japanese survivors on the island continued to resist until after the end of the war. (*See Atlas Map No. 26c.*) After the campaign, General Geiger applauded the performance of the soldiers of the 77th Infantry Division (an Organized Reserve division which drew most of its men from the vicinity of New York City), somewhat soothing the strained service relations which had developed in the Central Pacific Area.

While the techniques applied in the Marianas did not differ much from those employed in previous actions in the central Pacific, the islands themselves provided a different battleground, a cross between the coral atolls of the Marshalls and the jungled islands of the Solomons. Saipan and Guam are tough pieces of terrain—essentially tips of ocean volcanoes—dominated by rugged central mountains, covered with cane fields or rice paddies, and surrounded by coral reefs. They could not be taken by short assaults; rather they were large enough for two and three-division sustained ground campaigns, supported by naval and air forces. In many ways, the Japanese erred significantly by defending these islands at the beaches, where American firepower would obviously overwhelm them. Inland defenses, using the heavy terrain and arranged in depth, would have been much more difficult to capture. In fact, such defenses might have consumed so much American manpower, at a time when most reserves had to be sent to Europe, that they would have delayed the American advance westward to the Philippines or northward to Japan.* Unfortunately for Japan, her leaders adopted new defensive tactics too late in the war, employed them finally at Peleliu, Leyte, Luzon, Iwo Jima, and Okinawa. Even so, the Japanese exacted a high price for the Marianas—nearly 14,000 American casualties on Saipan, 7,000 on Guam, and 1,800 on Tinian.[53]

The loss of the Marianas led to the fall of the Japanese government of Hideki Tojo and his associates on July 18, 1944. From that time forward, most knowledgeable Japanese knew that their Empire was doomed. The supposedly impregnable inner defensive sphere had been cracked, and the once mighty *Combined Fleet* was a skeleton of its

previous self, without aircraft and good carrier pilots. Within a few months, Japan would have to resort to desperate efforts in an attempt to save herself. Meanwhile, her dedicated soldiers, sailors, and airmen would fight on as best they could. During those same months, the Americans would build the bases in the Marianas from which the first B-29s would bomb Japan on November 24, 1944.

Stepping Stones West: The Palaus

With the capture of the Marianas, Nimitz could go in two directions—either toward the Palaus and on to the Philippines, Formosa, and China, or directly north to the Volcano Islands, the Bonin Islands, Okinawa, and Japan. (*See Atlas Maps No. 22 and No. 27.*) While the planners and the Joint Chiefs considered these alternatives, Nimitz continued to work on the westward advance, the one outlined for him by the Joint Chiefs in March.[54] His major objectives were Yap and Ulithi in the western Carolines, and the Palaus.† The first two islands would isolate Truk completely; and Ulithi Atoll would also provide the Navy an excellent naval base, which would make it unnecessary for the fleet to return to the Marshalls for replenishment and maintenance. The Palaus would provide a steppingstone to the Philippines, while also protecting MacArthur's right flank as he entered the southern Philippines from Vogelkop Peninsula and Halmahera. In addition, Nimitz would gain control over the eastern approaches to the Philippines-Formosa-China coast area. (*See Atlas Map No. 27.*)

Admiral William Halsey was appointed to command the new drive (Operation STALEMATE). His Third Fleet staff replaced Spruance's Fifth Fleet staff, but the ships remained the same. For his advance, the former South Pacific Area commander would have a large landing force and a growing fleet. Halsey's amphibious commander from the South Pacific Area, Vice Admiral Wilkinson, would command the Joint Expeditionary Force, and Major General Julian Smith would command all the landing forces. Major General Roy Geiger would control the 1st Marine Division and the 81st Infantry Division (III Amphibious Corps) in the attack on the Palaus, and Major General John Hodge would command the 7th and 96th Infantry Divisions (XXIV Corps) in the invasion of Yap and Ulithi. The 77th Infantry Division, still fighting on Guam, was designated the floating reserve; the

---

*American manpower reserves in the Central and Southwest Pacific Areas were never plentiful, and really serious losses on a sustained basis would have been quite damaging. As seen later at Iwo Jima, the Marine Corps did not have abundant replacements; and on Luzon, some Army divisions were committed understrength. Europe absorbed the majority of the Army's reserves and replacements.

---

† The Palau group of islands are the westernmost group in the Caroline Islands. Also called the Pelews.

Vice Admiral Marc Mitscher

5th Marine Division would be the general reserve in Hawaii. Once again, Mitscher would command the carriers. Land-based air forces in the central and southwest Pacific would also support Halsey's operations. (*See Appendix 20.*)

Several developments changed Nimitz's original plans for Operation STALEMATE. First, the slow and difficult Marianas campaign, which drained off valuable troops and resources, forced the admiral to reduce his goals in the Palaus. Instead of planning to take the entire chain, Nimitz decided to drop the assault on the main island of Babelthaup (or Palau Island) and concentrate on Peleliu, its adjacent small islands, and Anguar, southwest of Peleliu. The next change came after Nimitz sent Halsey west to raid the Bonin Islands* (August 31 to September 2), Yap* (September 7 to 8), the Palaus* (September 8), and Mindanao (September 7 to 10). When his pilots found the southern Philippines weakly defended, Halsey diverted further strikes into the Visayas instead (September 12 to 14). (*See Atlas Map No. 27.*) Once again, the airmen met little resistance while destroying 300 aircraft. Based on these strikes,

*These islands had been earlier raided by Task Force 58: Yap, Palaus, and Ulithi (July 25 to 28), and the Bonins (August 4 to 5).

Halsey radioed Nimitz that the central Philippines were lightly held and recommended that all Central Pacific Area operations (Palaus, Yap, and Ulithi) and Southwest Pacific Area operations (Talaud Islands and Mindanao) be cancelled so that MacArthur could invade Leyte immediately. Nimitz reported Halsey's recommendations to MacArthur and to the Joint Chiefs of Staff, who were attending the OCTAGON Conference in Quebec. Within hours, the Joint Chiefs, with the concurrence of MacArthur and Nimitz, authorized the landing in Leyte for October and cancelled the Yap, Talaud, and Mindanao invasions. The Joint Chiefs also approved the diversion of Hodge's XXIV Corps and additional assault shipping to MacArthur.

Admiral Nimitz and General MacArthur both wanted the Palaus operations to go as planned. So did the Joint Chiefs, who felt that the area was vital to the control of the route to Luzon-Formosa-China area. With the marines practically at the beaches, the Joint Chiefs supported Nimitz's and MacArthur's recommendations. On September 15 the invasion began as scheduled, as did MacArthur's landing at Morotai.

Major General William Rupertus' 1st Marine Division had been assigned the mission of taking Peleliu, and Major General Paul Mueller's well-trained but inexperienced 81st Infantry Division had drawn the assignment for Angaur and Ulithi. (*See Atlas Map No. 27.*) Unfortunately, Rupertus overconfidently predicted a short campaign to his troops, and American intelligence officers did not detect that Peleliu was more heavily fortified than Tarawa, even though they knew that there were about 10,500 Japanese troops on the coral island. These included 6,300 combat troops—primarily the *2nd Infantry Regiment*. On Angaur, there were about 1,400 Japanese, most of whom were members of the *1st Battalion, 59th Infantry*. Ulithi was not expected to be defended. Originally under the command of the *Thirty-First Army* on Saipan, all these forces belonged to *Southern Army* at the time of the American invasion.[55] (*See Atlas Map No. 22.*)

When Rupertus' marines landed on Peleliu they got the shock of their lives, finding the Japanese in strength and in occupied positions (on the left flank) which were nearly impossible to attack. (*See Map, pg. 169.*) By the end of the first day (September 15), the general had committed all of his reserves except one battalion; and by September 21 the Japanese had stopped Rupertus' 1st Marines cold on the left flank. General Geiger forced Rupertus to accept an Army regiment from the 81st Infantry Division to reinforce his line, even though Rupertus did not want Army troops.[56] (The soldiers justified General Geiger's confidence in them and contributed much to the eventual victory on Peleliu.) The 1st Marines' problems, however, had not prevented the

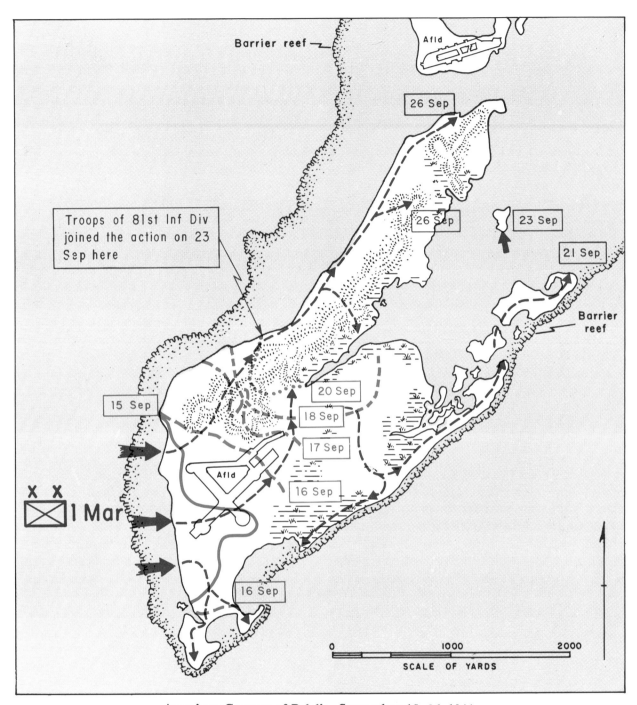

American Capture of Peleliu, September 15–26, 1944

5th and 7th Marines from securing most of the southern portion of the island, including the airfield. By the end of the month, Peleliu was under American control. Rupertus, however, still had to destroy the large Japanese forces which occupied the coral limestone caves and underground positions in the mountainous Umurborgol pocket in the center of the island. General Mueller's soldiers continued to fight until November 27, more than a month after the last marines had departed Peleliu.

Peleliu seemed to be a jinxed operation from the start. Many things went wrong in the planning, approach, and actual operation ashore. Perhaps overconfidence neutralized intelligent preparation, or perhaps the new naval commanders did not assimilate the lessons their predecessors had learned in the atoll war. More importantly, however, the Japanese for the first time in the Central Pacific Area, defended an island in-depth, and used the extraordinarily difficult coral formations of Peleliu to protect their troops from American firepower and to delay the American offensive. The Japanese abandoned their standard beach defense tactics and did not waste their men in bloody *banzai* charges. Instead, they fought cunningly and viciously to extract the highest price for their mandated island. For the Americans, Peleliu marked the first time that land-based marine aviators in the central Pacific flew the close support missions for the marine infantry; consequently, the support was the most effective so far in the Central Pacific Area.* Later, marine airmen would support their brother marines from escort carriers, a practice Holland Smith had advocated since Tarawa.[57]

Before Peleliu was secure, the infantrymen of the 81st Infantry Division seized Angaur during the period of September 17 to 20—mopping up continued until October 21—and occupied undefended Ulithi on September 23. (*See Atlas Map No. 27.*) Marines and soldiers also cleared out the small islands adjacent to Peleliu from which the Japanese shelled the troops on Peleliu.

The Palaus campaign was a costly one. (*See Appendix 21.*) The Marines sustained 6,526 casualties, the Army 3,275, and the Navy 663. Many officers and commentators believe that the islands should not have been taken, and they are probably right.[58] Admiral Halsey's bold recommendation to scrap the invasion was not accepted by the Joint Chiefs, Nimitz, or MacArthur. For good reasons, albeit conservative ones, they wanted to play things safe. Safety in this case cost a high price, even though the islands were ultimately quite useful as bases for the air forces which bombarded the Philippines for MacArthur. Peleliu took its place beside the bloody fights of the Pacific War (Tarawa and Saipan) and the sanguinary American assault on Omaha Beach in Normandy. It did not, however, gain the strategic results which those other amphibious assaults achieved.

The Next Steps

In just under a year, Admiral Nimitz's naval campaign completely overwhelmed the Japanese forces in Micronesia. During that time, the admiral's forces shattered the absolute defensive perimeter of the Japanese Empire and severely punished the Japanese *Combined Fleet*.

American actions in the theater were characterized by the use of overwhelming firepower, the avoidance where possible of strong Japanese positions (e.g., Truk), the constant demand for air supremacy over the battlefield, and the application of superior combat power at desired land objectives. Since marine units generally dominated the land war, and islands had to be taken by assault, the marines suffered the highest number of casualties and won an unenviable reputation for taking excessive losses. In many cases these could have been avoided. But if speed overrides deliberateness, if assaults must be made against defended positions, and if operations are not flawlessly executed, high casualties will be the inevitable result. With hindsight, it appears that Tarawa, Saipan, and Peleliu were too costly; but substitute operations in the Central Pacific Area might have been even more costly.*

The Japanese forces in Micronesia did everything possible to delay and punish the American forces, but in 1944 they simply had too little combat power to defeat their opponents. Lacking strong air forces and a unified command, and clinging to an unrealistic doctrine of beach defense, the Japanese commanders could not expect to win. Nevertheless, in the Marianas and the Palaus they did bring the American offensive to a temporary halt, and they applied tactics on Peleliu which would be repeated again on Iwo Jima, Okinawa, and in the Philippines.

Perhaps the greatest problem the Japanese faced was the proper utilization of their forces. In early 1944, they launched an offensive against Imphal, India, attacked in China to destroy American airbases, and at the same time tried to defend against Allied thrusts in the Central and Southwest Pacific Areas.[59] With a dwindling number of trained men, materiel, and air and naval forces, the Japanese High Command faced a difficult problem trying to decide where to use its combat power. Nowhere was this more evident than in the Pacific, where Imperial General Headquarters watched the drives of MacArthur and Nimitz approach the Philippines. (*See Atlas Maps No. 25 and No. 27.*) At no time did the Japanese commanders properly anticipate the next Allied move; therefore, MacArthur and Nimitz constantly surprised them during the year.

As defeat followed defeat, the Japanese leaders who replaced Tojo moved closer and closer to two alternatives: unconditional surrender or continued fanatical resistance. When the Allies took the next step into Leyte on October 20, 1944, the Japanese would continue to resist fanatically, but they would begin using a new tactic against Allied ships—especially against the aircraft carriers. Japanese naval pilots on Luzon would decide to crash their planes into the Allied ships because their squadrons could no longer conduct successful orthodox strikes. Thus was born the *Kamikaze Corps*—the "Divine Wind"—which would hopefully bring a stop to the Allied drive on Japan and her

---

*Until this time, most of the marine air units had operated in the South Pacific Area.

*One of MacArthur's objections to an advance across the central Pacific had been the probability of high casualties. His own operations in the Southwest Pacific Area resulted in far fewer casualties, except for Biak.

possessions, just as a divine wind had stopped Kublai Kahn centuries before. Born in desperation, *kamikazes* would exact a terrible toll in the coming months. Faced with the Allies' materiel abundance, the Japanese turned more and more to a war of spirit—the last and nearly inexhaustible resource of the nation of *samurai*.

Notes

[1]This section is based primarily on Louis Morton, *Strategy and Command, The First Two Years* (Washington, 1962), pp. 376-541 and 645-667. Also see: Louis Morton, "Japanese Policy and Strategy in Mid-War," in United States Naval Institute *Proceedings*, LXXXV (February 1959), 52-64; Philip A. Crowl and Edmund G. Love, *Seizure of the Gilberts and the Marshalls* (Washington, 1955), pp. 1-59; and Samuel Eliot Morison, *Aleutians, Gilberts and Marshalls, June 1942-April 1944* (Boston, 1951), pp. 69-120.

[2]For Admiral King's early strategical ideas see: Morton, *Strategy and Command*, pp. 437-441; and Crowl and Love, *Gilberts and Marshalls*, pp. 7-10.

[3]Morton, *Strategy and Command*, pp. 447-453 (development of strategic plans), and pp. 644-647 ("The Strategic Plan for the Defeat of Japan," approved by the Combined Chiefs of Staff, May 19, 1943). See also Crowl and Love, *Gilberts and Marshalls*, pp. 11-12 (Pacific Military Conference) and pp. 12-17 (Strategic Plan for the Defeat of Japan and the TRIDENT Conference).

[4]For the actual summary of the American plan see "Strategic Plan for the Defeat of Japan," in Morton, *Strategy and Command*, pp. 644-647. For the selection of Hong Kong as an objective, see Morton, *Strategy and Command*, pp. 446-451; Crowl and Love, *Gilberts and Marshalls*, p. 13; and Morison, *Aleutians, Gilberts and Marshalls*, pp. 80-81.

[5]For a discussion of the virtues of the two drives, see Crowl and Love, *Gilberts and Marshalls*, pp. 13-14, and Morton, *Strategy and Command*, pp. 443-444, 448-451.

[6]"Strategic Plan for Defeat of Japan," paragraph 2b. See Morton, *Strategy and Command*, p. 644.

[7]For planning on the Gilberts see: Crowl and Love, *Gilberts and Marshalls*, pp. 18-43; Morison, *Aleutians, Gilberts and Marshalls*, pp. 82-85; and Morton, *Strategy and Command*, pp. 461-472 and 521-527.

[8]This section is based on: Crowl and Love, *Gilberts and Marshalls*, pp. 60-74; Morton, *Strategy and Command*, pp. 543-558; Morton "Japanese Strategy in Mid-War," pp. 52-64; and Saburo Hayashi (in collaboration with Alvin D. Coox), *Kogun, The Japanese Army in the Pacific War* (Quantico, Va, 1959), pp. 71-78.

[9]Crowl and Love, *Gilberts and Marshalls*, pp. 60-66, and Morison, *Aleutians, Gilberts and Marshalls* cover the Makin Raid and its aftermath.

[10]Crowl and Love, *Gilberts and Marshalls*, p. 65, comment on the Z Operation Plan. The United States Strategic Bombing Survey (Pacific), *The Campaigns of the Pacific War* (Washington, 1964), pp. 6-7, gives greater detail and Crowl and Love p. 221, include Admiral Koga's "Combined Fleet Ultrasecret Operation Orders 73", dated March 8, 1944, which was the admiral's implementation of the Z Operation Plan.

[11]Morton, *Strategy and Command*, pp. 543-547 and pp. 655-656 ("Japanese General Outline of Future War Direction Policy," September 30, 1943); Morton, "Japanese Strategy in Mid-War," p. 58; and Hayashi and Coox, *Kogun*, pp. 72-73.

[12]Morton, "Japanese Strategy in Mid-War," pp. 62-63. For the impact of the political ideas cited, see "Japanese General outline of Future War Direction Policy," September 30, 1943 in Morton, *Strategy and Command*, pp. 655-656.

[13]Morton, "Japanese Strategy in Mid-War," pp. 59-62.

[14]Morton, "Japanese Strategy in Mid-War," pp. 56-57.

[15]Morton, "Japanese Strategy in Mid-War," p. 56, quoting from General Hikosahuro Hada, Deputy Chief of the Army General Staff.

[16]This section is based on: Morison, *Aleutians, Gilberts, and Marshalls*, pp. 69-120; Morton, *Strategy and Command*, pp. 473-501; Crowl and Love, *Gilberts and Marshalls*, pp. 18-165; and James R. Stockman, *The Battle of Tarawa* (Washington, 1947).

[17]Morison, *Aleutians, Gilberts, and Marshalls*, fn 5, p. 149.

[18]Crowl and Love, *Gilberts and Marshalls*, pp. 67-68, and Morison, *Aleutians, Gilberts and Marshalls*, pp. 92-93.

[19]John Miller, Jr., *Cartwheel: The Reduction of Rabaul* (Washington, 1959), pp. 251-255; and Samuel Eliot Morison, *Breaking the Bismarcks Barrier, July 1942-1 May 1944* (Boston, 1968), pp. 323-336, 346-347.

[20]Morison, *Aleutians, Gilberts and Marshalls*, p. 106 and pp. 100-113, covers the new logistical system.

[21]Morison, *Aleutians, Gilberts and Marshalls*, pp. 114-120, (Naval actions).

[22]Crowl and Love, *Gilberts and Marshalls*, pp. 75-126 (Action on Makin).

[23]Holland M. Smith and Percy Finch, *Coral and Brass* (New York, 1949), p. 125 is the harshest source of criticism. Morison, *Aleutians, Gilberts and Marshalls*, pp. 132-135, generally supports Holland Smith's criticism. Crowl and Love, *Gilberts and Marshalls*, pp. 125-129, the Army historians, criticize the Army actions in a more reasonable vein.

[24]Actions on Tarawa are from Stockman, *Tarawa*.

[25]For casualties on Tarawa, see Stockman, *Tarawa*, p. 72.

[26]Smith, *Coral and Brass*, p. 111 and pp. 132-134; Stockman, *Tarawa*, p. 65. Crowl and Love, *Gilberts and Marshalls*, p. 157, state:

> General [Holland] Smith was alone among high ranking officers to voice this opinion. [i.e., "Tarawa was a mistake."] Admirals King, Nimitz, Spruance, as well as General Julian Smith, were all in agreement that the capture of Tarawa and Makin was a necessary prelude to the invasion of the Marshalls.

[27]Stockman, *Tarawa*, p. 67.

[28]Morison, *Aleutians, Gilberts and Marshalls*, pp. 140-143.

[29]This section is based primarily on Crowl and Love, *Gilberts and Marshalls*, pp. 166-374.

[30]Morton, *Strategy and Command*, pp. 668-672, ("Overall Plan for the Defeat of Japan," approved in principle by the Combined Chiefs of Staff, December 2, 1943.) See also, Morton, p. 604 (Table 13) and pp. 673-674 ("Specific Operations for the Defeat of Japan, 1944, 3 December 1943.")

[31]Morison, *Aleutians, Gilberts and Marshalls*, pp. 201-208.

[32]Marine command problems are discussed in Crowl and Love, *Gilberts and Marshalls*, p. 170; Robert D. Heinl, Jr., and John A. Crown, *The Marshalls, Increasing the Tempo* (Washington, 1954), pp. 14-15; Frank O. Hough, Verle E. Ludwig, Henry I. Shaw, Jr., *Pearl Harbor to Guadalcanal, History of U.S. Marine Corps Operations in World War II*, Volume I (Washington, 1958), pp. 240-241 and 373-374.

[33]Clark G. Reynolds, *The Fast Carriers, The Forging of an Air Navy* (New York, 1968), pp. 28-33 (multi-carrier groups), pp. 88-96 (doctrine), and 111-128 (command), discusses carrier force development.

[34]For action at Roi-Namur, see Crowl and Love, *Gilberts and Marshalls*, pp. 304-332.

[35]For action at Kwajalein, see Crowl and Love, *Gilberts and Marshalls*, pp. 219-301. Quote is from p. 232.

[36]For action at Majuro and Eniwetok, see Crowl and Love, *Gilberts and Marshalls*, pp. 302-304, 333-369.

[37]Morison, *Aleutians, Gilberts and Marshalls*, pp. 315-332 (First Truk Raid).

[38]This section is based primarily on: Philip A. Crowl, *Campaign in the Marianas* (Washington, 1960), pp. 1-133, 191-202, 262-266, 269-284, 301-338, and 436-447; and Jeter A. Isely and Philip A. Crowl, *The U.S. Marines and Amphibious War, Its Theory and Its Practice in the Pacific* (Princeton, NJ, 1951), pp. 310-392.

[39]Crowl, *Marianas*, pp. 11-13.

[40]For strategic planning see Crowl, *Marianas*, pp. 13-20. The parts of the March 12, 1944 directive are outlined on pp. 19-20.

[41]Strength figures are from Crowl, *Marianas*, p. 36, and USSBS, *Campaigns of the Pacific War*, p. 234.

[42]For the A-GO Operation see: Crowl, *Marianas*, pp. 119-123; USSBS, *Campaigns of the Pacific War*, pp. 210-211 and 226-231 (Admiral Toyoda's "Combined Fleet Ultrasecret Operation Order No. 76," dated May 3, 1944); Robert Ross Smith, *The Approach to the Philippines* (Washington, 1953), pp. 346-350; and Masonori Ito with Roger Pineau, *The End of the Imperial Japanese Navy*. Translated by Andrew Y. Kuroda and Roger Pineau, (New York, 1962), pp. 96-99.

[43]Crowl, *Marianas*, pp. 69-73.

[44]Crowl, *Marianas*, pp. 65-69 (Saipan), 279 (Tinian), pp. 329-333 (Guam), and 453-454 (Summary), gives the Japanese order of battle.

[45]Crowl, *Marianas*, pp. 56-57; and Hayashi and Coox, *Kogun*, p. 77, pp. 79-81, and 84-85.

[46]Hayashi and Coox, *Kogun*, pp. 79-81.

[47]Crowl, *Marianas*, p. 59.

[48]For Operation KON, see: Smith, *Approach to the Philippines*, pp. 350-364, USSBS, *Campaigns of the Pacific War*, p. 181; Crowl, *Marianas*, pp. 120-121, Samuel Eliot Morison, *New Guinea and the Marianas, March 1944-August 1944* (Boston, 1953), pp. 118-132; and Ito and Pineau, *End of the Japanese Navy*, pp. 95-96.

[49]For the Battle of the Philippine Sea, see: USSBS, *Campaigns of the Pacific War*, pp. 213-215 and 214-272 (which includes "First Mobile Fleet Classified [Report] No. 1048" dated September 5, 1944, a report on the A-GO Operation, and other related Japanese documents); Ito and Pineau, *End of the Japanese Navy*, pp. 92-109; and Samuel Eliot Morison, *The Two-Ocean War, A Short History of the United States Navy in the Second World War* (New York, 1972), pp. 277-289.

[50]Crowl, *Marianas*, pp. 264-265; Robert Leckie, *Strong Men Armed, The United States Marines Against Japan* (New York, 1969), p. 358; Morison, *New Guinea and the Marianas*, p. 337; and Smith, *Coral and Brass*, p. 199, quoting a Japanese officer.

[51]Isely and Crowl, *Marines and Amphibious War*, pp. 325-326, and 329-335.

[52]For the Smith versus Smith controversy, see: Crowl, *Marianas*, pp. 191-201; Smith, *Coral and Brass*, pp. 168-180, and Edmund G. Love, *The 2th Infantry Division in World War II* (Washington, 1949), pp. 652-673.

[53]Crowl, *Marianas*, p. 446.

[54]This section is based on: Isely and Crowl, *Marines and Amphibious War*, pp. 392-422 and 428-431; Smith, *Approach to the Philippines*, pp. 450-456 and 459-463; USSBS, *Campaigns of the Pacific War*, pp. 273-275; Frank O. Hough, *The Assault on Peleliu* (Washington, 1950), pp. 1-20; and Samuel Eliot Morison, *Leyte, June 1944-January 1945* (Boston, 1958), pp. 12-18.

[55]Smith, *Approach to the Philippines*, pp. 461-462.

[56]Hough, *Peleliu*, pp. 105-106 and p. 109.

[57]Isely and Crowl, *Marines and Amphibious War*, pp. 416-422; Hough, *Peleliu*, p. 180; and Crowl and Love, *Gilberts and Marshalls*, p. 15.

[58]Smith, *Approach to the Philippines*, pp. 573-575 and Morison, *Two-Ocean War*, p. 360.

[59]Hayashi and Coox, *Kogun*, pp. 86-91 (China) and pp. 92-101 (Imphal).

"I Shall Return"   8

Life is as the weight of a feather compared to one's duty.

Japanese Proverb

No man ever dominated a theater of war more than Douglas MacArthur dominated the Southwest Pacific Theater in World War II. He was the drive spring and the center of major decision in the area. Moreover, he was consumed by a fierce desire and determination to return to the Philippines and avenge a humiliating defeat as well as liberate the Filipinos and thousands of Allied civilians, soldiers, sailors, and airmen from the Japanese occupation.

MacArthur's strategic thinking was best exemplified by his famous statement: "I shall return." Admiral King, in

General Douglas MacArthur

fact, sarcastically commented that the general seemed more interested in accomplishing his personal goal than in winning the war.[1] The admiral was in many ways quite right, but if he had been placed in command of the Pacific Fleet, he would probably have acted similarly. Given the nature of high commanders, MacArthur's attitude was not unusual—he was just a more dramatic figure than most, and as a result was not an easy subordinate to manage.

Douglas MacArthur, however, did not dominate the Joint Chiefs of Staff, who throughout the war remained committed to a worldwide coalition strategy and to the Navy's central Pacific drive. The Joint Chiefs did not give MacArthur an inkling that he would realize his ambition to return to the Philippines until Marshall told MacArthur that following the Rabaul operation he would get a chance to continue northwestward, and eventually would probably invade Mindanao. Moreover, it was not until March 1944 that the Joint Chiefs actually ordered MacArthur to invade Mindanao; and, as noted often, MacArthur was never allowed to make the main attack in the Pacific in his theater. During these months, MacArthur seemed to fear that his drive toward the Philippines would be curtailed if he were not successful and did not speed up his operations. To achieve his desired goal, the general had to keep moving forward quickly.

With the capture of the Admiralties, MacArthur gained the springboard from which he launched his most impressive campaigns: the 1300-mile offensive which took him from the Admiralties to Morotai in approximately six and a half months, the invasion of Leyte one month later, and the Philippine campaign of 1945. His campaign in the Philippines continued until the end of the war, and just before war ended he began sending Australian forces into Borneo. Japan surrendered, however, before MacArthur could begin his most challenging operation—the invasion of the Japanese home islands.

"The IGHQ is Disoriented Like Hempstrands"

Few Japanese war leaders had anticipated the need for large garrisons and new defensive lines inside their planned defensive perimeter of 1942. As we have seen, during the jungle and atoll wars Japan had to extemporize new lines of defense as the Allies cracked her perimeter at different places in the Pacific.[2] Accordingly, in early 1944, Imperial General Headquarters faced the difficult question of how to stop the Allied drive up the northern coast of New Guinea. Complicating matters was the fact that the planners had not counted on defensive war in this area, and, as a consequence, they did not even have combat troops deployed in the critical areas behind the forward battle lines. If the Allies should once again manage to pierce the defenses of General Adachi's *Eighteenth Army* or to envelop that army, there would be no ground forces to stop them from advancing rapidly to the southern Philippines. Even those islands and the Netherlands East Indies were not heavily defended, because after their quick victories in 1942 the Japanese leaders had evacuated most of their divisions to China, Manchuria, and Burma, leaving few occupation troops behind. In the last months of 1943, for example, there was only one division in the Indies, and one division and three brigades in the Philippines.

Imperial General Headquarters began to fill the military vacuum in western New Guinea and the Indies when it ordered two new headquarters (Lieutenant General Korechika Anami's *Second Area Army** and Lieutenant General Fesataro Teshima's *Second Army*) to move to the south on October 22, 1943. (*See Atlas Map No. 22.*) In November, General Anami, as the senior commander, assumed control of the two armies in the area: the *Nineteenth Army*, which had just recently taken over control of the eastern portion of the Indies, and the new *Second Army*. Initially he established his headquarters in Davao, but on April 25, 1944 he moved it south to Menado, Celebes. Anami was expected to control operations in Timor, Netherlands New Guinea, Ceram, Amboina, Halmahera, Morotai, and the islands in the Arafura Sea. Eventually, however, Imperial General Headquarters assigned him the remaining area of New Guinea east of Hollandia and the Palaus (after the fall of the Marianas). With these new areas came additional troops: rear echelon troops from General Imamura's *Eighth Area Army*; the *14th Division* (from the *Thirty-First Army*) in the Palaus; and General

Adachi's *Eighteenth Army* in Australian New Guinea, formerly a part of Imamura's *Eighth Area Army*. (*See Appendix 22.*)

All of this reorganization would be of little practical use unless Imperial General Headquarters deployed fresh infantry and air units to hold the forward positions. Five divisions moved southward in early 1944, but American submariners destroyed the bulk of one division when they sank most of its transports on the high seas. (*See Atlas Map No. 25.*) By early April, however, General Anami had seven divisions in the Indies and New Guinea. Three of these, including the one which was nearly decimated, were stationed in the Indies under *Nineteenth Army*. One more, the *36th*, had moved into the Biak-Wakde-Sarmi area of Netherlands New Guinea where it formed the bulk of General Teshima's *Second Army*. The battered *20th, 41st,* and *51st Divisions* of General Adachi's *Eighteenth Army* assembled in the Madang-Wewak area of Australian New Guinea. Two other divisions, the *32nd* and *35th*, had been ordered south to join the *Second Army*, but they would not be deployed before MacArthur advanced again[3]

While seven divisions seem like a large force, they could not defend the vast expanse of western New Guinea and the Indies. For instance, General Adachi's front line units at Madang were over 500 miles southeast of General Teshima's division, which occupied Biak and the Maffin Bay-Sarmi-Wakde Island area. When Teshima's other divisions arrived in late April, they would move to Sorong and Manokwari, but even then they would be over 150 miles from the closest garrisons. The divisions of the *Nineteenth Army* had equally large areas to defend: elements of the *5th Division* on the south coast of New Guinea were over 200 miles distant from the northern outposts. To make matters worse, no large combat unit was stationed at Hollandia, which was the essential base between Madang and Biak; only the division near Sarmi was in a position to cover this key location.[4]

The Japanese High Command, however, did not overlook Hollandia. In March 1944, just about the time that the American Joint Chiefs issued new instructions for prosecuting the war in the Pacific, Imperial General Headquarters ordered General Anami to develop and hold Hollandia as a base; to hold New Guinea west of Wewak; to develop new defensive positions in western New Guinea; and to defend the islands between the Vogelkop Peninsula and the Philippines.† (*See Atlas Map No. 22.*) General Anami immediately ordered General Adachi to withdraw from the Madang area to Wewak, where he was to concentrate the bulk of his army as fast as possible. Additionally, Anami

---

*A Japanese area army corresponded to an Allied army. A Japanese army corresponded to an Allied corps.

† The Japanese first began considering developing Hollandia as a base in September 1943, when they established their absolute defensive perimeter.

directed Adachi to send the cadre of one division to Hollandia. For some unknown reason, Adachi ignored these specific orders and chose to remain in position until late April. Only after Anami dispatched his chief of staff to see Adachi did troops of the *Eighteenth Army* begin moving westward toward Wewak and Hollandia.

While General Adachi's inexplicable tardiness hurt the Japanese cause, the emphasis placed by Imperial General Headquarters on defending the Vogelkop-Mindanao area also detracted from defensive preparations in western New Guinea and the displacement of more troops into the Hollandia area. The planners in Japan *did* want Hollandia developed as a base, but this was not to be at the expense of the northern area.[5] (*See Atlas Map No. 25.*) Thus, because Anami gave precedence to the Vogelkop-Mindanao sphere over Wewak and Hollandia, Adachi's three divisions around Madang and Teshima's single division in the Wakde-Sarmi-Biak area were the only forward units facing the anticipated Allied drive up the New Guinea coast—the great middle ground between them was unoccupied or virtually unprotected. Furthermore, by the time the Japanese High Command decided to build up Hollandia, the situation in the Pacific had deteriorated to such an extent that Hollandia could only serve as a forward outpost. The Japanese faced an insoluble dilemma: they did not really have the forces to deploy that far southward again, but at the same time they could not allow the Allies to gain new airfields from which they could interdict the Japanese line of communications to the Southern Resources Area. Even as Imperial General Headquarters drew back its planned main line of strategic resistance from the Wewak area to the Vogelkop-Arafura Sea-Halmahera area, it still wanted Hollandia developed as a forward outpost.

Two other matters made the Japanese position in western New Guinea more tenuous. First, most Japanese believed that the Allies would next attack between Madang and Wewak; second, the Japanese air commanders at Hollandia failed to secure their base properly. As a result, General Kenney's heavy B-24 bombers and B-25 and A-26 strafers, escorted for the first time by new long-ranged P-38s, decimated the Japanese squadrons at Hollandia during the period March 30 to April 3, 1944. In all, the Allied pilots destroyed nearly 300 Japanese aircraft.[6]

Following the disaster at Hollandia, Imperial General Headquarters relieved the local commanders at Hollandia, but it did not appoint a new overall commander to take charge of the area. Even more important, that headquarters placed General Anami under the direct command of General Count Hisaichi Terauchi (*Southern Army*)* in

Southern Army and *Kwantung Army* were the equivalent of army groups.

P-38 Lightning

Singapore. (*See Atlas Map No. 22.*) This move forced Terauchi to pay more attention to the critical developments in the Pacific rather than to the actions in Burma and China. At the same time, it placed all the Japanese army and army air forces facing MacArthur under one commander. Terauchi, however, did not control General Obata's *Thirty-First Army* in the central Pacific, although he had assumed direction of the forces in the Palaus by the time the Americans assaulted that island group.

The Imperial Japanese Navy could not assist Terauchi and Anami in the accomplishment of their missions unless it deployed units of the *Combined Fleet* to the critical areas. The *Combined Fleet*, however, was steadily losing its punch. By April, it had given up its base at Truk, had departed its temporary anchorage in the Palaus, and had started to move to new anchorages farther west. Terauchi's coequal naval force was *Southwest Area Fleet*, which included the *Ninth Fleet* and the *First, Second, Third*, and *Fourth Expeditionary Fleets. Ninth Fleet*, in turn, supported General Adachi's army, and the *Fourth Expeditionary Fleet* supported General Teshima's army. These naval units had few warships; for the most part they were land-based forces with small coastal-type vessels and landing craft.[7]

As the Japanese waited for the inevitable thrust along the New Guinea coast, Imperial General Headquarters hoped that its forces could stop the Allied drive so that a major counteroffensive could be launched with the fleet in mid-1944.[8] Japanese offensive schemes relied on a resurgent Japanese Air Force, but as has been seen time and time again, the Japanese carelessly lost hundreds of their aircraft during Allied raids on Rabaul, Truk, Wewak, and the Palaus. The new losses at Hollandia only added to a deteriorating air position. Realistically, then, the Japanese could only hope that in April 1944 their ground forces would stop some of the Allied invasions, or perhaps immobilize as many Allied units as possible along the New Guinea coast. Inevitably, however, as Japan grew more and more impotent at sea and in the air, her land forces had little chance to succeed. Moreover, any planned naval offensive in mid-1944 would be difficult to mount. Just as the Japanese leaders should have thought out the whole problem of defense in the Central Pacific Area and then executed an attainable plan, they similarly should have devised a more satisfactory solution to their defensive problem in the Southwest Pacific Area. As it was, their disordered forces and mutually unsupportable positions invited envelopment, isolation, and destruction.

The Long Jump: Hollandia

On March 5, 1944, General MacArthur radioed General Marshall in Washington:

> Recent seizure of a foothold in the Admiralties . . . presents an immediate opportunity for rapid exploitation along the north coast of New Guinea. To this end I propose to make the Hollandia area instead of Hansa Bay my next objective, capturing the airfields and base in that vicinity for further support of operations toward the Philippines.[9]

Seven days later the Joint Chiefs approved the operation for April 15.[10]

The press of events had pushed MacArthur into this decision. For months he had concentrated on Rabaul's isolation; then, hoping to speed up the war, he had proposed advancing to Hansa Bay (between Madang and Wewak), to Kavieng, and to the Admiralties. In January, the general's representatives had met in Hawaii with Admiral Nimitz' staff to discuss the carrier support needed for these actions and to consider other matters of Pacific strategy, namely the bypassing of Truk and the seizure of the Marianas. Both theater staffs recommended that Truk be ignored and that the Allies strike for the Palaus instead of the Marianas. (*See Atlas Map No. 22.*) Following this conference, MacArthur sent his chief of staff to Washington to argue for the concentration of effort in the Southwest Pacific Area. This upset King, who had no intention of allowing an emasculation of the central Pacific drive.

As these discussions developed in Washington, Nimitz' forces captured Eniwetok, and MacArthur's troops landed in the Admiralties. (*See Atlas Map No. 20.*) Since both operations were completed ahead of schedule, the Americans had an opportunity to speed up future actions in the Pacific.

Now Admiral Nimitz reversed his earlier opinion and recommended that his forces should advance to the Marianas. With conflicting advice from MacArthur and Nimitz and new opportunities for offensive action, the Joint Chiefs directed their own planners to restudy the schedule of operations for the remainder of 1944. While the joint planners worked on their estimates, General MacArthur learned that Admiral King was pressing for immediate action in the Central Pacific Area; this news triggered his message about Hollandia to General Marshall. Simultaneously, he alerted Lieutenant General Walter Kreuger to prepare for an attack there. In Washington, Major General Richard Sutherland, MacArthur's chief of staff, drew up the RENO IV plan to incorporate MacArthur's new suggestions, and on March 8 he submitted the plan to the Joint Chiefs.

Disagreeing with MacArthur's proposals, however, the joint planners once again recommended that the main effort be made in the Central Pacific Area. Marshall was not satisfied with their efforts, whereupon the Joint Chiefs assimilated the views from their planners, MacArthur, and Nimitz, and then issued a directive on March 12 which was an amalgam of all the views.* Of immediate concern to MacArthur were the cancellation of the Kavieng operation scheduled for April 1, the approval to occupy Hollandia, the instructions that Mindanao would be seized in November, and the directive to begin planning for the invasion of Luzon while Nimitz planned for the invasion of Formosa.[11]

The long leap to Hollandia was MacArthur's boldest plan since he proposed to attack Rabaul in 1942. Implementation of the plan, however, required the support of the carrier task forces of the Pacific Fleet. The Joint Chiefs, accordingly, directed Nimitz to provide such support with the understanding that the carriers would only be on station for three days. Prior to helping MacArthur, however, Admiral Mitscher was to sortie into the western Pacific and strike the Palaus and the central Carolines in order to help isolate the southern battlefield. In return, MacArthur's bombers would strike Central Pacific Area targets in preparation for Nimitz' invasion of the Marianas. (*See Atlas Map No. 25.*)

MacArthur planned to use most of two divisions to seize beachheads east and west of the objective area—the deep water harbor at Hollandia and the airfield complex just to the west near Lake Sentani. (*See Atlas Map No. 28.*) One of the divisions would land near the town of Hollandia while the other disembarked near the tiny village of Depapré,

---

*See Chapter 7, section entitled "Strategic Decision: Marianas," which covers the same material, but centers on the March 12 directive's impact on the Marianas operation.

some 25 miles farther west. The divisions would move inland simultaneously to converge on the airfields which lay in the lowland bowl formed by the Cyclops Mountains to the north, the Takari Hills to the west, and the largely unexplored mountains to the south. In addition to Mitscher's Task Force 58, General Kenney's Allied Air Forces and Admiral Kinkaid's Allied Naval Forces would support the landings. General Blamey's Australians would continue to attack northwestward along the New Guinea coast toward Madang and Wewak, keeping pressure on Adachi's *Eighteenth Army.*

Because of his tenuous air support, MacArthur was forced to add an additional objective to the original Hollandia plan. With limited fast carrier support, the general had to have bases forward of Nadzab from which his own land-based fighters could provide day-to-day cover over Hollandia. Many places were considered, but finally MacArthur decided to land at lightly-defended Aitape, 125 miles southeast of Hollandia, so that he could quickly capture the nearby Tadji airstrips. (*See Atlas Map No. 25.*) Engineers were expected to rehabilitate the Japanese fields within 48 hours so that Australian P-40s could fly into them and thereafter cover the Hollandia operation, regardless of how long carrier air forces from the central Pacific remained in the vicinity. A brigade-sized force would land at Aitape; it would then remain in the area to protect Hollandia from the Japanese *Eighteenth Army*, which was expected to move north against the new Allied beachheads. To support the Aitape landing, MacArthur directed that the eight escort carriers borrowed from the Pacific Fleet would remain in the area for the duration of their southern sojourn.[12]

In addition to his air problems, the general faced severe logistical problems.* The movement of 50,000 combat troops, 23,000 service troops, and 12,000 air force troops required more ships than had been used before, and more than were available in the Southwest Pacific Area. Therefore, MacArthur had to borrow assault shipping (transports and LSTs) from the South and Central Pacific Areas. Even then his shipping space was limited. In order to get all the required equipment and supplies to the beachheads, his commanders had to bulk combat load their vessels rather than palletize their supplies or stow them on vehicles. Moreover, merchant ships with civilian crews were pressed into service in the rear areas to release training forces for active operations; some of them were also in the Hollandia task force.[13] In addition to the shipping problems, the demand for rapidly rehabilitated air strips and new bases required that an unusually large number of engineer and service units be put ashore right behind the assaulting battalions.† Furthermore, restricted beaches at Humboldt and Tanahmerah Bays and poor road nets inland presaged difficulties in unloading supplies in the objective area. There were also more mundane supply problems which fell on subordinate commanders: a shortage of 2.36-inch bazooka rockets, lighters, beach sleds for the quick removal of supplies from beaches, and trucks. All these logistical problems were aggravated by the invasion of Europe (OVERLORD).

General MacArthur and his staff did not coordinate the tactical and logistical aspects of his major plans. The general normally tasked General Krueger, Sixth Army and ALAMO Force commander, with such coordination. For Hollandia he continued that policy. In turn, General Kreuger delegated the responsibility for the ground operations to his two task force commanders. Lieutenant General Robert Eichelberger, commanding I Corps, controlled the RECKLESS Task Force, which would seize Hollandia; Brigadier General Jens Doe, the assistant commander of the 41st Infantry Division, commanded the PERSECUTION Task Force, which would seize Aitape and the Tadji strips. (*See Appendix 23.*) Both of these officers would remain under the control of the naval amphibious force commanders (Rear Admiral Daniel Barbey at Hollandia and Captain Arthur Noble at Aitape) until their forces were

---

† MacArthur, in general, considered service troops so essential that in January 1945 he recommended that newly-formed combat units in the United States be converted into service units.

General Walter Krueger

---

*MacArthur reported to Marshall about this time that "Victory is dependent upon the solution of the logistic problem."

firmly established ashore. Major General William Gill's 32nd Infantry Division was designated ALAMO Force Reserve.

Krueger's final plans called for simultaneous assaults on Aitape and Hollandia. (*See Atlas Map No. 25.*) General Doe would land two battalions of his 163rd Regimental Combat Team on D-Day to seize the Tadji strips. The following day, he would send Colonel Merle Howe's 127th Infantry (32nd Infantry Division) ashore to assist in capturing Aitape town and to engage Japanese forces in the hinterlands. Routine air, artillery, and naval gunfire bombardments were planned in support of the landings.

Because there was little time for detailed reconnaissance of the invasion sites, the Allies had to select their beaches from aerial photographs. While this posed no real problem at Aitape, it did prove to be crucial at Hollandia. At Humboldt Bay, the beaches were small and shallow, but at Tanahmerah Bay they were almost unacceptable. They were so bad, in fact, that Admiral Barbey did not want to use Red Beach 1 at Depapré which was bordered by large coral reefs. (*See Atlas Map No. 28.*) Eichelberger agreed; but he eventually reversed his decision, as did Barbey, when the assault division commander, Major General Frederick Irving, said that he needed the beach to insure the quick seizure of the head of the road which ran to the airfields, and to provide for any contingency.

At Tanahmerah Bay, General Irving planned to land two regiments of his 24th Infantry Division abreast to secure the road network inland, take the town of Depapré, and then attack along the trail through the Takari Hills toward the airfield on the north side of Lake Sentani. (*See Atlas Map No. 28.*) The bulk of the two regiments would land on Red Beach 2, while one battalion would go ashore over the coral reefs at Red Beach 1, near Depapré. Simultaneously, General Horace Fuller, commanding the 41st Infantry Division, would seize a beachhead at Humboldt Bay; then his troops would drive inland on the Hollandia-Pim-Koejaboe Road to the airfields and a link-up with Irving's division. Fuller also would employ two regiments, but most of his battalions would land in column on White Beach 1.

Irving was designated to make the main attack because the Allied commanders believed that Tanahmerah Bay would be less heavily defended than Humboldt Bay. In this way, they hoped to achieve tactical surprise and then quickly capture the airfields. MacArthur, Krueger, Eichelberger and Barbey would accompany the Tanahmerah Bay task force.

One special situation developed at Hollandia which would be duplicated again at Leyte and Luzon. Neither MacArthur nor his naval commander, Vice Admiral Thomas Kinkaid, controlled Mitscher's Task Force 58. Mitscher was charged with supporting the operation as planned, but he was free to maneuver as he wished in case the Japanese fleet intervened.

After General Krueger completed his final plans, his subordinate commanders worked feverishly to prepare their units for the impending operation. In early April, the troops began loading on their transports; following rehearsals on April 8 to 10, the assault forces sailed for a scheduled rendezvous off the Admiralties on the twentieth. To deceive the Japanese as to the objectives, Admiral Kinkaid charted a circuitous route, initially moving north from the Admiralties before turning west for a direct run into Hollandia. Earlier, the Allies had taken other deceptive measures to convince General Adachi that Wewak was their objective. Dummy parachutists were dropped, empty life rafts were floated ashore, minor naval bombardments were conducted, and rumors were spread that Wewak would be attacked. Furthermore, Allied fighter pilots were restrained from striking the Hollandia area to prevent compromising MacArthur's plans.

By the time the 200 ships of the Allied task force arrived off Hollandia, General Kenney's airmen had all but eliminated the Japanese air strength in the area. They did this from March 30 to April 3, when Kenney sent his heavy bombers, strafers, and fighters against the Hollandia strips. Lulling the Japanese into a false sense of security with fruitless night raids, keeping his P-38s south of the area, and cratering their airstrips constantly, Kenney forced the Japanese to bunch their 300 airplanes on one or two strips and to relax their security precautions. When he finally ordered massive strikes, similar to those which he had used to neutralize Wewak and Rabaul, Kenney gained impressive results. In three days, his pilots destroyed nearly 300 aircraft, decimating the Japanese air forces in New Guinea for the duration of the campaign.[14] When Mitscher's Navy pilots arrived, there was not much for them to do, although they destroyed the Japanese aircraft at Wakde-Sarmi, flew close support missions, and protected the beachhead from air or sea attacks launched from Biak, the Vogelkop, and Amboina.

It was a rainy day when the RECKLESS Task Force arrived off Hollandia and Depapré. At 7:00 A.M., Fuller's troops landed near Hollandia, and nine minutes later Irving's units came ashore near Depapré. There was no serious opposition. The Japanese troops in both areas fled, although near White Beach 1 they had excellent beach defense positions. (*See Atlas Map No. 28.*)

Just after the lead units landed at Red Beach 2 (Depapré) they found that an impassable mangrove swamp, hitherto unknown, lay 30 yards behind the beach. Only dismounted troops could work their way through it. Since Red Beach 2 was the main division beach and bulk supplies were already moving ashore, Irving faced a trying situation. When he also discovered that there was no road from Red Beach 2 to Depapré, the general knew that he was landing in an isolated *cul-de-sac*. Therefore, he began diverting his additional waves to Red Beach 1 and transshipping landed supplies to Red Beach 1 by boat. When Eichelberger learned of the situation ashore, he decided to shift his main attack to the Hollandia area.

As Irving worked out his logistical problems at the beach, his lead battalion moved rapidly inland. Patrols left Red Beach 1, marched over grueling terrain, and by dark on April 22 entered Dazai. The next day, Irving's troops reached Sabron, but because of the difficult terrain they could not be adequately resupplied. General Irving thereupon directed other combat battalions to hand-carry supplies to the front. This helped somewhat, but his lead battalion remained in dire logistical straits until the twenty-sixth, when they broke through light Japanese opposition to reach the westernmost airfields around Sentani Lake. Behind them, engineers worked feverishly to improve the trail so that supplies could be trucked forward from the beaches.

As Irving's battalions reached the airstrip, Fuller's lead units reached the eastern strips. Fuller's drive inland had not been as difficult, because the road inland from Pim was better, and he had been able to execute small amphibious envelopments on Sentani Lake to by-pass expected enemy strongpoints. (*See Atlas Map No. 28.*) Japanese opposition was light and ineffective.

On April 26, Irving's and Fuller's lead units met between the airfields, completing the initial phase of the operation. Immediately thereafter, engineers moved in rapidly to begin working on the strips, while the infantrymen began mopping up around the area. The capture of the major objectives had been comparatively cheap—by June 6, when the Hollandia area was secured, the Americans had lost 124 killed, 28 missing, and 1,057 wounded. In contrast, the Japanese had lost 10,000 dead from their garrison of 11,000.[15] Most of the Japanese lost their lives trying to escape west to Sarmi.

As at Depapré and Hollandia, General Doe's PERSECU-TION Task Force achieved complete strategical and tactical surprise at Aitape. (*See Atlas Map No. 25.*) His lead battalions landed on April 22, secured the beachhead area, and then moved inland and secured the Tadji airstrips by 12:45 P.M. An hour later, Australian engineers began working on the airfields. The following morning, after his other regiment landed, Doe began pushing his forces into the countryside to destroy any Japanese forces there and to ferret out any large-scale movements against the Aitape area. On the April 24, the first Australian P-40s arrived.

There was no effective Japanese reaction to General Krueger's landing operations, although everyone expected that the Japanese air forces would try to interfere with the landings once they were discovered. One Japanese pilot did manage to sneak through on the night of April 23 and detonated a Japanese ammunition park at Humboldt Bay, killing 24 soldiers. In addition to the air attacks, the Japanese commander at Sarmi directed a small force south to assist the Hollandia garrison, but recalled it when the Allies landed near Sarmi. To the southeast, General Adachi decided to move 20,000 troops to attack the Allied beachhead, a move which would require several weeks. When he arrived in July, Adachi gave the Allies all they could handle (Battle of Driniumor River) in the Aitape area for some time. His attacks forced General Krueger to build up the PERSECUTION Task Force from two regiments to over two reinforced divisions. Even then, fighting continued, and MacArthur was forced to replace the Americans with Australian forces when he drove into the Philippines. Although the Allies had defeated Adachi's main thrust by August 10, 1944, killing over 10,000 Japanese, the fighting continued until the end of the war.[16] (*See Atlas Maps No. 25 and No. 27.*)

The success of the Hollandia operation so pleased MacArthur that on April 22 he proposed to his assembled commanders (Krueger, Eichelberger, Kinkaid, and Barbey) that he immediately attack the Wakde-Sarmi area and Biak with his uncommitted troops. Barbey wanted to go, but Eichelberger demurred because he believed it would be dangerous to continue the attack while there was the possibility of heavy Japanese resistance in the landing areas. Krueger did not commit himself. With such divided response, MacArthur decided to let the matter ride. His next operation would proceed as planned.[17]

Unfortunately for the Americans, Hollandia did not prove to be a good area for heavy bomber fields because the rains prevented rapid construction and the wet ground would not support the heavy bombers. Therefore, Kenney's bombers would not be able to support the advance of Nimitz into the Marianas unless new strips were captured quickly. Biak seemed to be the best alternate area for the heavy bombers. Hollandia, however, did become a major logistical center, and MacArthur, Krueger, and Eichelberger moved their forward headquarters there. Aitape proved as useful. From the Tadji strips, Allied fighters were able to fly into the Beelvink Bay area where they could support actions against Biak and other nearby Japanese locations. Furthermore, the forces at Aitape kept the Japanese *Eighteenth Army* away from Hollandia; at the same time, a number of new regiments gained their first combat experience in the area, something which served them well in the Philippines.

The long fighting around Aitape, however, tied down troops which MacArthur could have redeployed elsewhere. Still, the Hollandia and Aitape oprations speeded up the advance to the Philippines. The next moves were already planned. Within five months, MacArthur's troops would land at Morotai, after making smaller hops into Geelvink Bay and the Vogelkop Peninsula. (*See Atlas Maps No. 25 and No. 27.*)

The Short Jumps: Advance to Morotai

Until he finally reached the Philippines, General MacArthur would fight during the remainder of 1944 in Dutch territory— Netherlands New Guinea and Morotai.[18] His next main target was Biak in Geelvink Bay. (*See Atlas Map No. 25.*) Biak would give him a major bomber base to replace the one he had hoped to build at Hollandia; it would also serve to neutralize the Japanese positions in the Geelvink Bay area, and would provide fields for the advance of his own bomber and fighter lines toward Halmahera and the Palaus. Before he could land at Biak, however, MacArthur believed that he had to secure a subsidiary base at Sarmi and the Wakde Islands, just offshore from Sarmi. This base would allow his fighters and bombers to displace forward to cover the landing on Biak; it would also eliminate a dangerous Japanese flanking position. Moreover, the new operations would divert Japanese attention from the central Pacific.

Japanese commanders realized that MacArthur would probably attack both Wakde-Sarmi and Biak, and were reasonably well prepared to meet an invasion at either point. High ranking officers in the *Combined Fleet* also considered the problem of defending Biak, but faced with what they believed to be an imminent invasion in the Marianas or Palaus, they decided not to react to any attack on Biak. The *A-GO* Operation, which looked forward to a decisive battle with the Pacific Fleet near the Palaus, did not provide for a counterthreat toward Biak.*

During late April and early May, MacArthur and his subordinates completed their planning for Wakde and Sarmi. General Krueger, as was customary, coordinated the plans for the operation, and on April 30 he issued his field order to the landing force. MacArthur, however, decided against attacking the well-defended Sarmi position because the area was not suitable for heavy bomber fields. Accordingly, on May 10 he directed Krueger to concentrate

on Wakde and to substitute Biak for Sarmi. The ALAMO Force commander adjusted his plans, and eventually ordered General Doe's 163rd Regimental Combat Team (TORNADO Task Force) to land at Arawe on May 17. This landing was designed to secure the area for the redeployment of the landing force and to establish an artillery base for the bombardment of Wakde Island (actually the largest island of the group, correctly known as Insoemoar Island). Following that, Doe was to assault small, well-garrisoned Wakde Island on May 18, and clear the nearby islands as fast as possible. (*See Atlas Map No. 25.*) As soon as Wakde was secured, Krueger's assault shipping would return to Hollandia, pick up the remainder of General Fuller's 41st Infantry Division, and sail for Biak. Allied fighter and bomber squadrons were to displace forward as soon as the engineers could prepare the Wakde airstrip.[19]

The critical part of the Wakde-Sarmi plan was executed quickly and in good order, although the reinforced battalion which assaulted Wakde Island met stiff and determined resistance, reminiscent of some of the atoll landings in the central Pacific. Wakde fell on May 20. Engineers had begun improving the runways the day before, so that by the twenty-first, fighters were able to fly in. Wakde provided an unexpected bonus in that the strip could handle heavy bombers, which could support the upcoming invasion of the Marianas.

Operations continued in the Sarmi-Maffin Bay area until early September. By that time the main American forces were about to land at Morotai. With an adequate number of new divisions, MacArthur no longer had to worry about finishing one operation before starting another. Once his strategic objectives were secured, he pushed on as quickly as possible, leaving occupation forces behind to hold the captured areas and to destroy the surviving Japanese forces in the hinterland.[20]

The advances to Wakde and Sarmi illustrated MacArthur's style of warfare. That style obviously grew out of his early experiences in Papua, his observation of Halsey's operations in the South Pacific Area, his discussions with the Joint Chiefs of Staff, and probably his evaluation of earlier Japanese operations in the Philippines, Malaya, the Netherlands East Indies, and New Guinea. His essential objectives were key airfields and ports or places where such installations could be built. To get there he advanced under the cover of land-based fighters or, if possible, under the cover of carrier-based air forces. His amphibious forces normally assaulted or landed at lightly-held positions where they could either envelop or cut off and isolate well-defended Japanese positions, such as Rabaul or Wewak, without sustaining heavy casualties. Once established

---

*See Chapter 7, section entitled "Strategic Decision: The Marianas," for an earlier reference to the *A-GO* operation.

ashore, MacArthur advanced his land-based air cover, secured his coastal airfield-port enclave, and leaped onward toward the Philippines with his interdependent land, air, and sea forces. MacArthur repeated this pattern when he attacked Biak.

As the fighting continued near Aitape and Sarmi, General Fuller landed on the southeastern coast of Biak with one reinforced regimental combat team from his 41st Division (HURRICANE Task Force) on May 27. (*See Atlas Map No. 25.*) The Japanese did not contest his landing, but when Fuller's troops advanced westward to seize Mokmer airdrome they met a determined naval garrison and the excellent *22nd Infantry Regiment.* From prepared positions in coral-ridged mountains which overlooked the American objective, the 11,400 Japanese thwarted Fuller's drive toward the airfield, even though they were surprised by the American landing. The general asked for reinforcements and got an extra regiment, but even then he did not succeed in securing the vital air strip. MacArthur exerted pressure on Krueger because he needed the airfield so that Kenney could begin to support Nimitz. Krueger, in turn, began to push Fuller. On June 13, Fuller asked for another regiment, and the next day Krueger ordered Eichelberger forward from Hollandia to take charge of HURRICANE Task Force. Fuller, who was to keep his division, asked to be relieved.* Eichelberger, the fireman of Buna, soon got the troops moving, but not until he had been reinforced with another regiment and the marines had stormed ashore at Saipan. Finally, on August 20, Krueger was able to declare Biak cleared; by this time the island had become a rapidly developing air and naval base. The Allies, however, had paid a high price for Biak: 400 men killed, 2,000 wounded, 5 missing, and 7,234 non-battle casualties, including over 1,000 cases of scrub typhus and 423 troops hospitalized for psychoneurosis.[21]

In the meantime, the American invasion of Biak had spurred Japanese implementation of Operation KON.† On three occasions, elements of the Japanese *Combined Fleet* sailed for Biak to deliver reinforcements and to bombard the Allied positions. (*See Atlas Map No. 25.*) At the same time, the Japanese deployed most of the aircraft of the *First Air Fleet* south from the Marianas to western New Guinea and Halmahera to support the KON operation. While about 1,200 Japanese reinforcements did land on Biak during the period, Japanese warships did not accomplish their mission, and the Japanese naval pilots suffered heavy casualties. Consequently, only 20 percent of the *First Air Fleet* was available to meet the American thrust into the Marianas. Conversely, however, Nimitz' forces diverted the full force of the *Combined Fleet* from Biak, saving MacArthur some desperate days.[22]

Just after the Biak landings, General MacArthur reorganized his command to assimilate many of the forces which had previously been assigned to the South Pacific Area. He appointed General Kenney the commander of the Far Eastern Air Forces, which included Kenney's veteran Fifth Air Force and Admiral Halsey's yeoman Thirteenth Air Force. General Oscar Griswold's XIV Corps, comprising the American 25th, 37th, 40th, 43rd, and 93rd** Infantry Divisions, came under MacArthur's command. MacArthur immediately directed Griswold to secure the Allied air and naval bases in the Solomons and the Bismarcks, and ordered New Guinea Force to defend the Allied installations in New Guinea. Seventh Fleet got some additional units from Halsey's Third Fleet, but it still had no aircraft carriers. To prepare for future advances, MacArthur activated Eighth Army—its headquarters had recently arrived from the United States—and appointed General Eichelberger its commander. To handle civil affairs in the recaptured areas, the general continued his policy of turning back the areas to their civil administrators without resorting to intermediate military governments.[23]

Because the Biak operation took so long, the Allies captured tiny Owi Island nearby and turned it into a fighter base. Then MacArthur ordered Krueger to seize Noemfoor Island for another such base and to protect the Allied gains at Biak. Krueger began the Noemfoor (TABLETENNIS) operation on July 2 when he sent the 158th Regimental Combat Team (CYCLONE Task Force) ashore; he ended it on August 31, after most of the Japanese garrison had been destroyed or captured. Noemfoor was noted for the unusual jump casualties suffered by the 503rd Parachute Infantry Regimental Combat Team, for giving Allied fighters and bombers easier access to the Vogelkop area, and for the Japanese atrocities and acts of cannabalism that took place there.[24]

General MacArthur had hoped to jump from Hollandia to the Vogelkop Peninsula, but without carrier support he had been forced to make the smaller jumps just described in order to secure intermediate fighter and bomber bases. (*See Atlas Map No. 27.*) As the advance progressed, he was,

---

*Eichelberger did relieve his West Point classmate and long-time friend when Fuller would not withdraw his request for relief. This was the second time Eichelberger relieved a classmate during the war. Fuller became a Deputy Chief of Staff in Admiral Louis Mountbatten's Southeast Asia Command Headquarters.

†See Chapter 7, section entitled "Strategic Decision: The Marianas" for earlier reference to the Japanese reaction.

**The 93rd Infantry Division, the only black division in the theater, saw no combat. It was used strictly for logistical and security missions. The black combat troops served primarily as service troops in the theater.

accordingly, considering several sites for the next landings; he eventually settled upon the Sansapor-Mar region of the peninsula for a one-division landing in July. Such a move would bypass the enemy forces at Manokwari and would also place Allied units between that base and the next important Japanese base at Sorong. Interestingly, besides the tactical reasons for invading the area, most of the early discussion about sites on the Vogelkop had centered upon the capture of oil fields in the area. Once the tempo of the war speeded up, however, Allied planners realized that they would not be able to exploit these fields until the middle of 1946—a date by which most of them hoped that the war would be over.[25] Consequently, MacArthur attacked Vogelkop for intermediate bases only.

MacArthur directed Krueger to seize Sansapor (Operation GLOBETROTTER) and Mar on July 30, and on that date Krueger landed most of Major General Franklin Sibert's 6th Infantry Division (TYPHOON Task Force). Within two days, the American infantrymen had secured the area, and engineers moved in to build new bases. Small units also captured the offshore islands of Middleburg and Amsterdam on July 30. By September 3, two airfields (one at Mar and one on Middleburg Island) were operational, and fighters and medium bombers began flying missions to support the next jump to Morotai.

The Sansapor-Mar operation completed the last phase of MacArthur's New Guinea campaign, which had begun when his forces landed at Hollandia on April 22. (*See Atlas Map No. 25.*) In barely four months, MacArthur's men had advanced 1,000 miles. In so doing, they had isolated General Adachi's *Eighteenth Army*, surrounded General Teshima's *Second Army* with a ring of airbases, and destroyed Japanese Army air forces within the area as well as the bulk of the Japanese *First Air Fleet* aircraft. Except for Biak, the Allied forces had seized all objectives quickly and efficiently, although many extended fights developed after the strategic goals had been achieved.

MacArthur decided to invade Morotai in mid-July, again assigning the task to General Krueger. (*See Atlas Map No. 27.*) He had not always considered Morotai to be the desired objective in the area; but after studies showed that it was suitable for airbases and was more lightly defended than his original target (Halmahera), the general opted for the smaller island, which lies just north of Halmahera. The planned invasion had at least two strategic overtones: first, Morotai would provide the necessary airbases for the invasion of Mindanao; second, these bases would protect his left flank from Japanese air attacks as he advanced northward. At one time, MacArthur had envisioned the seizure of the islands in the Arafura Sea, also to assist in protecting that flank; but as the war progressed, he decided

against the seizure of these islands because his air forces alone could neutralize the Japanese air forces in the Arafura Sea. The move to Morotai had to be coordinated with Nimitz' offensive into the Palaus, which would secure MacArthur's right flank by destroying Japanese airbases there; the Palaus, too, would provide airfields for the advance into the Philippines. Because of reduced shipping and tenuous air support from Morotai-based fighters, MacArthur resurrected an old plan to seize the Talaud Islands north of Morotai, thereby providing the additional airbases needed for the advance to Mindanao. All of these details were worked out between Nimitz and MacArthur in July 1944, and by the end of the month the commanders had agreed upon the following sequence of operations (*See Atlas Map No. 27.*):

September 15: Simultaneous invasions of Morotai and the Palaus.
October 5: Seizure of Yap Island and Ulithi Atoll in the western Carolines.
October 15: Seizure of the Talaud Islands.
November 15: Landings at Saragani Bay in southern Mindanao.

To insure their mutual success, Nimitz and MacArthur further agreed to deploy their land-based air forces against targets which lay between their route of advance: Yap, Woleai, Truk, and Ponape. Nimitz would also send his fast carriers west to soften up the Palaus and raid the Philippines. The admiral would then send some of the carriers south to attack Japanese bases in the Celebes on September 15 and to stand by to assist the invasion of Morotai.[26]

Krueger sent Major General Charles Hall's XI Corps (TRADEWIND Task Force) ashore at Morotai on September 15, and by the next day Hall had secured his main objectives. Mopping up was completed by October 4. As planned, engineers moved in quickly to build the necessary airfields, and on October 4 MacArthur had one operational fighter field only 300 miles from the Philippines. From Morotai, fighters and medium bombers could reach Leyte; and from that island the Australians would eventually mount their 1945 offensives into Borneo.

Enroute to Morotai, General MacArthur was unaware of the results of Admiral Halsey's air raids into the Philippines and his subsequent recommendation against the invasion of Yap, the Talaud Islands, and Mindanao in favor of a direct assault into the central Philippines. When the Joint Chiefs of Staff queried MacArthur's Headquarters about his ability to attack Leyte, however, General Sutherland, MacArthur's chief of staff, replied that MacArthur could attack ahead of the original schedule. As soon as radio silence was lifted following the attack on Morotai, MacArthur confirmed Sutherland's decision. Thirty-five days later, MacArthur would land on Leyte, but during those days the general had much to accomplish. His tasks included canceling the invasion of Mindanao and the Talaud Islands; developing new plans; altering shipping allocations; assimilating the XXIV Corps and III Amphibious Force from the Central Pacific Area into his organization; and coordinating his operations with Admiral Halsey, who would command Third Fleet and the fast carrier task forces which would support the landings.[27]

While the higher commanders had been dealing with the most important actions, General Eichelberger was conducting his first operations as an army commander. His troops secured Asia and Mapia Islands between Vogelkop and Morotai. These small actions allowed the general to test Eighth Army under stress and to provide it with that combat experience which would be so valuable later.

MacArthur was rightfully proud of his advance from the Admiralties to Morotai. It had been fast, bold, imaginative; and it had covered a tremendous amount of ground. Furthermore, he had suffered relatively few casualties compared to the force which had fought the atoll war in the Central Pacific Area. (*See Appendix 24.*) From Hollandia to Morotai, for example, MacArthur suffered fewer casualties than the central Pacific forces suffered in the Palaus alone. Low casualties were only one characteristic of the rapid finale to the New Guinea campaign.

During the New Guinea campaign, many other forces assisted ALAMO Force and New Guinea Force in defeating the Japanese. Among these unsung contributors were Coastwatchers, Allied Intelligence Bureau agents, and guerrillas. In addition, ALAMO Scouts gathered valuable information for Sixth Army; and fighter aces, such as Richard Bong and Tommy McGuire, helped to destroy the Japanese air forces. Australian engineers, airmen, and sailors fought side-by-side with the Americans at every turn; and small PT boat crews raided the New Guinea coast as if it were the Spanish Main, destroying Japanese barge and coastal traffic. To these soldiers, sailors, airmen, and civilians, MacArthur and his major combat forces owed a share in the credit for their brilliant string of successes.[28]

Plans for Leyte: Musketeer and Sho 1

Unaware of the recent landings in the Palaus and at Morotai, Filipinos, prisoners of war, and internees in the occupied Philippines waited expectantly for the MacArthur moon, which would signal the end of the detested Japanese occupation. In Manila on September 21, while the Japanese practiced their antiaircraft gunnery, life went on as usual. Inside the University of Santo Tomas, interned children were at school; some of them, on the fifth floor of the Main Building, had a bird's-eye view of Manila and Manila Bay. Late in the morning, the hum of deep-throated aircraft engines, so different from the high-pitched Japanese engines, announced the arrival of strange aircraft over Manila. As the Japanese continued their gunnery practice, the small grey ships began to peel off from their large formations and dive toward the port area and the harbor. Explosions followed, and in a minute everyone realized that the little grey planes were American. The deduction was electric. Everywhere the internees ran to see what was happening, but no one had a better view of the raid than the kids on the roof of the Main Building. Teachers dismissed school quickly, and the children of Santo Tomas ran home to tell their parents and their friends about the sights they had seen.

It did not take long for the children to talk expertly of Grummans or for them to become knowledgeable about the number of planes lost in each succeeding raid. Somehow, everyone soon learned that these first planes came from American carriers. In the days and weeks that followed, the internees waited for the sequel to the raids, but it would be some time before they heard more encouraging news. They all knew, however, that the Americans would soon be landing in force to drive the Japanese from the Philippines.[29]

By the time Halsey's fliers attacked Luzon for the first time, American and Japanese planners had mapped out their strategies for the impending battle in the Philippines. On September 15, the Joint Chiefs of Staff had decided once and for all to invade Leyte on October 20, although they had not decided where to go after that. General MacArthur, however, had continually updated his RENO plan as he advanced toward the Philippines. By June 1944, the fifth and last edition of the plan proposed an advance into the southern Philippines, a subsequent landing on Leyte, and then an invasion of Luzon in order to gain bases either to support or mount an invasion of Formosa. In early July, after his staff coordinated RENO V with Admiral Nimitz' staff in Hawaii, MacArthur developed MUSKETEER I, his first detailed plan for the campaign in the Philippines, and one which was a logical extension of the more comprehensive RENO plan.

In MUSKETEER I, MacArthur planned to secure the Philippines in four phases with four different sets of operations called KING, LOVE, MIKE, and VICTOR. (*See Map, page 186.*) During his first actions (KING I and KING III), the general expected to seize portions of southern and western Mindanao to support his more

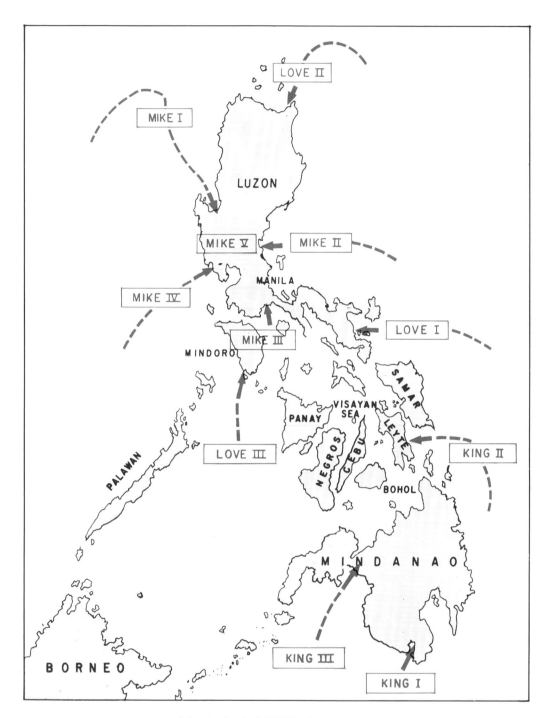

MacArthur's MUSKETEER I Plan

important invasion of Leyte on December 20, 1944 (KING II). Following the KING operations, MacArthur would begin his LOVE operations to gain favorable positions from which to invade central Luzon. During LOVE I, he would land forces on the Bicol Peninsula of Luzon; in LOVE II, he would send Australia's I Corps to Aparri, Luzon; then, in LOVE III, the general planned to use American paratroopers and infantrymen to secure airbases in southern Mindoro. Once these operations

succeeded, MacArthur expected to launch his main effort of the campaign on December 20, by sending the Sixth Army ashore at Lingayen Gulf to secure the Central Plain and Manila (MIKE I). Then, as necessary, additional forces would be landed at Dingalen Bay (MIKE II) and at Batangas (MIKE III) to assist the main attack, and at Zambales (MIKE IV) to cut off the Bataan Peninsula. During MIKE V, MacArthur planned to consolidate his gains on Luzon. By the time the last MIKE operation began, however, the general expected to have begun the VICTOR operations which were designed to clear the by-passed Japanese forces from the Visayas and Mindanao.*

Shortly after MUSKETEER I was developed, MacArthur flew to Hawaii to discuss Pacific operations with President Roosevelt, Admiral William Leahy, and Admiral Nimitz. About a month later, he published MUSKETEER II, which was basically the same as his earlier plan, although he deleted LOVE I (Bicol), MIKE III (Batangas), MIKE IV (Zambales), and MIKE V (Consolidation). Then, after learning of Halsey's recommendation to by-pass Mindanao, MacArthur immediately ordered General Krueger to execute KING II (Leyte) on October 20 and to cancel KING I and KING III (both on Mindanao). Finally, just before executing KING II, the theater commander developed MUSKETEER III, which focused on the cherished

*Note the similarity of the MIKE operations to the Japanese operations on Luzon in December 1941. (*See Atlas Map No. 9.*)

invasion of Luzon on December 20. In MUSKETEER III, MacArthur retained the MIKE I main assault at Lingayen and the preceding LOVE III seizure of southern Mindoro, while relegating LOVE II (Aparri) and MIKE II (Dingalen Bay) to contingent status. This last MUSKETEER plan would remain a hypothetical one, however, until the Joint Chiefs of Staff decided whether to invade Formosa or Luzon.[30]

By late 1944, General Krueger and his staff were old hands at amphibious operations, but KING II was far larger than any other landing they had mounted. Krueger's eventual plan, as always, was straightforward. (*See Map, this page.*) He would attack in four phases. In the first phase, small elements, primarily the newly organized 6th Ranger Infantry Battalion, would seize the islands at the mouth of Leyte Gulf, while minesweepers cleared the channel into the landing beaches. Then, in Phase II, the general would send two corps ashore simultaneously: Major General Franklin Sibert's X Corps on the north,

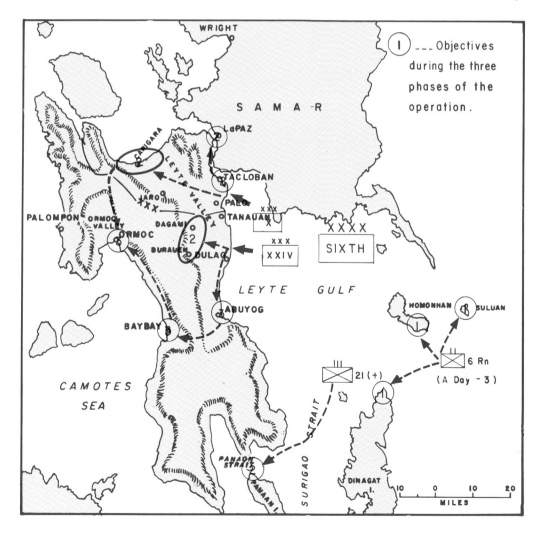

Krueger's Plan for the Conquest of Leyte

near Tacloban, and Major General John Hodge's XXIV Corps on the south, near Dulag. During this phase, Sibert's two divisions would secure the Tacloban area, seize the major airfield north of the town, cut the main coastal route, and attack northwestward toward Carigara; Hodge's corps would seize the airfields near Dulag and Burauen, then move inland, on order, from Abuyog to Baybay. Also during this phase, the reinforced 21st Infantry Regiment would seize the strait between Panaan and Leyte Islands and clear the southern part of Leyte. In Phase III, Krueger's two corps would link up at Ormoc, or in the Ormoc Valley; clear Leyte and the southwestern portion of adjacent Samar Island; and open Surigao Strait. In Phase IV, the general presumed he would be required to clear Samar and other nearby islands. Once ashore, Krueger also would have to construct airfields rapidly for Kenney's aircraft. To assist Sixth Army, MacArthur gave Krueger command of the Filipino guerrillas in the area, as well as the recently organized Army Support Command. In reserve were one regiment and two divisions.[31]

Admiral Thomas Kinkaid's reinforced Seventh Fleet would support the landing forces. (*See Appendix 25.*) Kinkaid's own amphibious forces, commanded by "Uncle Dan" Barbey, would work with the X Corps, while Vice Admiral Wilkinson, Halsey's long-time amphibious commander, would support XXIV Corps. Additional warships

from the Pacific Fleet, particularly Rear Admiral Jesse Oldendorf's six old battleships, would provide the pre-invasion bombardment. Eighteen escort carriers were part of Kinkaid's fleet for the invasion.

Admiral Halsey's Third Fleet would also be involved, but this great armada would not be controlled by Kinkaid or MacArthur. Literally in general support, to use artillery terms, Halsey was under Nimitz' command; as had been the case throughout the Pacific war, he was free to engage the Japanese fleet any time there was an opportunity to do so. To protect the invading forces, Nimitz ordered Halsey to raid Okinawa, Formosa, and Luzon prior to the landing on October 20.

Halsey's fast carriers and Kinkaid's escort carriers were needed to support the Leyte landings because General Kenney's fighters could not cover the area from bases in Morotai. His bombers could, however, and they were scheduled to bombard the southern and central Philippines, while his Australian squadrons, with some American help, attacked Japanese positions in the Netherlands East Indies. Furthermore, the Joint Chiefs ordered the B-29 squadrons in China to strike the Formosa area in support of the invasion.

As the plans developed and the troops and equipment assembled throughout the Pacific (*See Atlas Map No. 29*) for the largest action of the Pacific war to date, MacArthur faced several problems. His engineers warned him that Leyte would probably be unsuitable for airbases because of its unstable soil and the impending rainy and typhoon seasons. The general understood the problem, but he decided to go ahead in order to gain time and keep the Japanese off balance. There were also problems associated with the coordination of shipping. The vast number of staging areas and ports of embarkation made supervision difficult; more important, however, was the fact that Hodge's XXIV Corps was not loaded according to Southwest Pacific Area directives.* There was no time to reload the embarked corps, so MacArthur had to be content with its less flexible loading. Then there was the problem of attacking a friendly country. MacArthur warned his airmen, in particular, to avoid the destruction of nonmilitary targets and to keep civilian casualties to an absolute minimum. Moreover, the general did not want valuable ports reduced to rubble, as he planned to use them later.[32]

As the Allies rushed to complete their preparations, Blamey's Australians and Eichelberger's Americans began to take over the areas which Krueger evacuated in the

Vice Admiral Thomas Kinkaid

---

*XXIV Corps was combat-loaded for the invasion of Yap when it was diverted to MacArthur. Its accompanying shipping could also only support XXIV Corps, unlike the shipping used by MacArthur. At Leyte, XXIV Corps landed in LVTs designed for coral reefs.

southwest Pacific. At the same time, the Japanese, reeling from the rapid Allied advances in the Southwest and Central Pacific Areas and from the destruction of their naval and land air forces, were frantically preparing for the next Allied move.

Following the Battle of the Philippine Sea and the invasion of the Marianas, the Emperor summoned his field marshals and fleet admirals to query them on the future conduct of the war. These senior military men concluded that while it was advisable to regain Saipan, it would be difficult; they also believed that Japanese forces must continue to hamper American air operations mounted from the Marianas, that the inner Japanese defenses must be strengthened immediately, and that all Japanese air forces must be combined to conduct unified operations against the Allies. About a month later, on July 24, Imperial General Headquarters adopted a new "Plan for the Conduct of Future Operations," incorporating many of the earlier suggestions made to the Emperor. This document proposed that Japan:

1. Strengthen the defenses on the sea frontier which included the Philippines, Formosa, the Ryukyus, Japan, and the Kuriles.
2. Prepare to annihilate the Allies by concentrating air, naval, and land forces of the Empire to attack the Allies when they invaded any part of the sea frontier. (This led to the adoption of the *SHO* (Victory) operation plans.)
3. Pursue operations in China to overrun American bomber bases and to open up continental railroads to the south as an alternate line of communications to the Southern Resources Area.
4. Select sea routes to the south which lay near the China coast to ensure the protection of shipping.[33]

With new *SHO* Operations, the Japanese High Command hoped to gain a decisive victory over the Allies, no matter where they attacked. In effect, the Japanese outlined a mobile defense writ large. The Army would take the brunt of an attack until the Japanese could deploy their rebuilt air forces and the *Combined Fleet* against the Allied carriers and the vulnerable assault shipping in beachhead areas. *SHO-1*, the hypothesized decisive battle in the Philippines, was to be ready in August. *SHO-2*, the decisive battle at Formosa and in the Ryukyu's, would also be planned for August; *SHO-3*, the decisive battle in the home islands, and *SHO-4*, the decisive battle in Hokkaido, would be scheduled for October.[34]

The single most important ingredient of the *SHO* plans was the employment of massed land-based airpower, which the Japanese hoped would severely maul attacking fleets.

Then, under the cover of the land-based air, the weakened *Combined Fleet* would sortie to crush the assault shipping in and near beachhead areas. The plan was not really new. For months, Japanese leaders had tried to apply similar ones in the Pacific—the *Z* and the *A-GO* operations—although each had failed miserably. What was new were some of the tactics which would be implemented. Imperial General Headquarters ordered the air forces to hold their strength in safe areas until after the Allies landed. Once the Allies were ashore and were faced with the most vulnerable part of the amphibious assault, the Japanese air commanders were to hurl their squadrons at the invaders to destroy their cargo shipping and their carriers. No longer would the Japanese try to concentrate on just the carriers, because they had learned that such operations usually met quick defeat. In addition, Imperial General Headquarters changed the tactics of the land forces, ordering them to abandon plans to defeat the Allies at the beaches in favor of erecting defenses in-depth farther inland. The problem of unifying commands also was discussed, but only certain air units were put under single commanders. Cooperation still remained the standard procedure between Army and Navy commands.[35]

Before the high command issued its plan, it began to ship troops and airplanes to the threatened areas, especially to the Philippines. Those islands seemed more and more to be the likely targets for the Allied drive following the seizure of Peleliu and Morotai. Because of all the probable Allied alternatives, however, Imperial General Headquarters could not concentrate all of its forces at one spot. Nevertheless, by early October, the Japanese High Command had built up its Philippine garrison to nine divisions and four Independent Mixed Brigades, 545 land-based Army aircraft, and 426 more land-based naval aircraft. There were also many light naval craft in the area. (*See Atlas Map No. 29.*) Manila became the headquarters for the newly organized *Fourteenth Area Army* (Lieutenant General Tomoyuki Yamashita), the *Southwestern Area Fleet* (Vice Admiral Gunichi Mikawa), and the *Fourth Air Army* (Lieutenant General Kyoji Tominaga). The *5th Land Based Naval Air Force* (Vice Admiral Takajiro Onishi) was at Clark Field. At Davao, the high command established the headquarters of the reorganized *First Air Fleet*, and eventually placed it under *Southwestern Area Fleet*. In Manila, Field Marshal Terauchi also established the headquarters of his *Southern Army*, which controlled all land and Army air forces facing MacArthur. (*See Appendix 26.*) Scattered throughout Terauchi's area were other air force units, fairly large ground units, and the *Second Fleet*, commanded by Vice Admiral Takeo Kurita. Kurita's fleet formed the *First Striking Force* of the *Combined Fleet*, and it was training at

Lingga Roads off Sumatra, just south of Singapore. The remainder of the *Combined Fleet* stayed in Japan, where Admiral Ozawa was feverishly trying to train pilots for his carrier task forces of the *Third (Mobile) Fleet.* (*See Appendix 27.*)

Any recapitulation of Japanese strengths at the time is impressive, but a summary of deficiencies is even more important. First and foremost, because the fleet lacked oil it had to remain close to its supply points in the south. Second, the Japanese lacked trained pilots to man their carriers. Third, because of Allied submarine actions, Japanese food imports were dwindling, something which added to their problems in the Philippines, where food shortages upset the pro-American population. Then there were technical problems. The Japanese were just beginning to employ radar, but they needed time to train crews. Nor was the Zero any longer dominant in the skies; the Army's forked-tailed P-38, the Navy's stubby Hellcat, and the Marine gull-winged Corsair all were a match for it, even if they could not turn with the Japanese fighter or outclimb it. Attempts to devise new, decisive weapons brought few results. One innovation, a balloon bomb, certainly was not a major weapon. As a result of these technical deficiencies, a lack of airpower, and the growing number of threats to the Empire, the Japanese began to fall back on their long suit—spiritual strength.[36]

Spiritual strength, however, would not be enough to stop the growing power of the Allied forces. On Leyte, the scene of the next Allied invasion, only the reinforced *16th Division* stood in the way of the attacking forces. (*See Atlas Map No. 29.*) Unfortunately for the Japanese, the division did not have enough time to prepare its defenses; instead it had to work for an extended period of time building airfields for the squadrons which were to be the key to success in the *SHO-1* Operation. Construction of these fields had begun in May, when Imperial General Headquarters started to take an interest in the defense of the Philippines after years of neglect. Lacking adequate service units, the Japanese had to order combat troops to do the work.[37]

When General Yamashita arrived in Manila to take over *Fourteenth Area Army* on October 9, he inherited a complex and unsatisfactory situation. His forces were not sufficiently trained, equipped, or deployed to make a major stand against the Allies. Moreover, the defense plans were poor, and his staff was unfamiliar with the local conditions. Finally, his two higher headquarters were desirous of executing different plans with respect to Leyte. Field Marshal Terauchi wanted to meet the Allies where they landed and fight the decisive land battle there. Since everything pointed to an Allied attack on Leyte, Terauchi

wanted permission to prepare to defend Leyte in strength. Imperial General Headquarters, however, directed Yamashita to fight the decisive land battle on Luzon, even though it planned to fight the decisive air and sea battle near Leyte.[38]

As Yamashita pondered his situation, Kurita worked diligently near Lingga Roads to prepare for *SHO-1*, and Ozawa frantically tried to whip his pilots into shape in Japan. Both Kurita and Ozawa knew what they were to do if the Americans sailed into Leyte Gulf—*Combined Fleet* wanted Ozawa to sail south from Japan to drew the Allied carriers northward, while Kurita attacked the Leyte area with his *First Striking Force*. Kurita was expected to launch a pincers attack on the Allied invasion force: one part of his fleet would slip through San Bernadino Strait to drive into the beachhead, while the remainder of his ships would sail through Surigao Strait to attack the landing force in the rear. Kurita himself would lead the northern force, while Vice Admiral Shoji Nishimura would lead the southern one.[39]

As the summer days wore on in 1944, the Japanese commanders became more and more convinced that Mindanao or Leyte would be the next Allied objective, although they were not sure that the Allies would not make a bold move into Luzon (or even into Formosa or the Ryukyus). As each Japanese commander prepared feverishly for the next action, Admiral Halsey raided Mindanao and the Visayas in September, causing Imperial General Headquarters to order the implementation of *SHO-1*. When the Americans retired without following up the air raids, the embarrassed high command cancelled its earlier order and henceforth became reluctant to direct its field units to prepare for *SHO-1* without word of actual Allied invasion. As a result, the commanders in the field were unable to pressure the supreme headquarters into activating the plan ahead of time so that they could harness all their energy to its demands—even though the high command predicted that the Allies would probably attack in late October.[40]

In the upcoming battle, the Japanese would be strong enough to deny victory to the Allies if they did everything right and if the Allies made all the mistakes. If, however, the Japanese made their share of errors, they would have a hard time overcoming the expanded power of the United States Pacific Fleet and the forces of MacArthur. Still, on each side there was a similar ingredient for disaster—neither the attackers nor the defenders planned to fight under one command. Supreme command of the opposing forces rested in Imperial General Headquarters in Tokyo and with the Joint Chiefs of Staff in Washington.

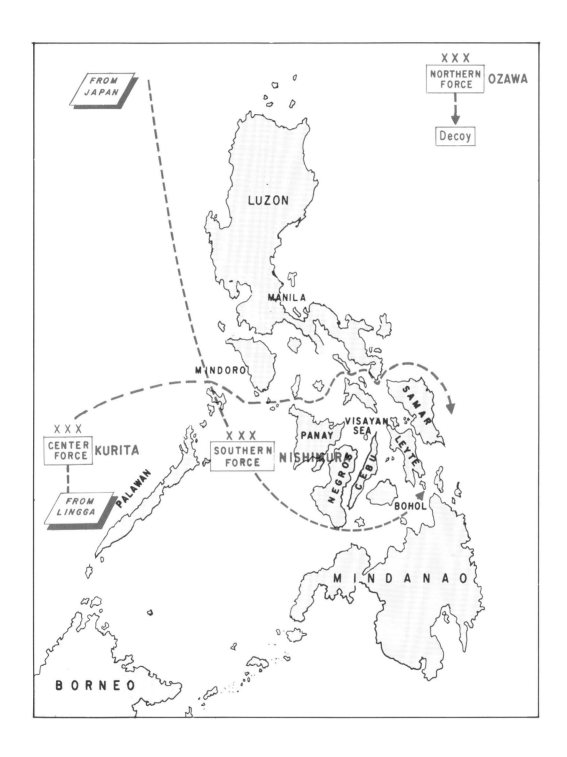

Japanese SHO-1 Plan

Decisive Battles: "Better Leyte Than Never"

Admiral Halsey's fast carriers opened the Leyte campaign by attacking Okinawa, Luzon, and Formosa during the period of October 10 to 14. His pilots raided Okinawa on the tenth, destroying over 100 Japanese aircraft and forcing the *Combined Fleet* to alert its land-based naval air forces to implement the *SHO-2* (Formosa) and then the *SHO-1* (Philippines) operations. (*See Map, page 191.*) The following day, Halsey's men made an insignificant raid on the Aparri area of Luzon; then, on the twelfth, the American naval airmen began an intense, three-day attack on Formosa in which the Japanese lost over 500 aircraft while the Americans lost about 90.[41]

The Formosa air battle had lasting strategic impact. First, the Americans killed many of the newly-trained carrier pilots who were rashly committed to reinforce the land-based naval air forces on Okinawa. This denuded Admiral Ozawa's carriers of their trained air groups. In addition, the Japanese airmen reported sinking so many American ships that their commanders proclaimed a major victory, one which they thought would delay an Allied invasion of the Philippines or would require the Allies to launch the invasion without the cover of fast carriers.*

*The Japanese claimed to have sunk 11 carriers, 2 battleships, and 3 cruisers. In fact, they crippled one cruiser, hit another, and bombed one carrier.

Lastly, by overreacting to the carrier attacks, the Japanese naval commanders lost the core of their air forces, which were the key to the successful execution of any *SHO* operation. Without airpower, the *Combined Fleet* and the Imperial Army could not stop the Allied offensive anywhere.[42]

Not quite a week after leaving their embarkation point, and only a few days after the Formosa air battle, Lieutenant Colonel Henry Mucci's 6th Rangers began landing on Suluan, Dinagat, and Homonhon Islands in the mouth of Leyte Gulf to initiate the invasion of the Philippines. (*See Atlas Map No. 30.*) Three days later, on October 20, General Krueger's two corps began landing against varied degrees of resistance. In the north, Major General Verne Mudge's 1st Cavalry Division seized the Tacloban area quickly, and Major General Frederick Irving's 24th Infantry Division worked its way inland toward Palo and the dominant hill mass nearby. In the XXIV Corps beachhead, Major General James Bradley's 96th Infantry Division, entering combat for the first time, met the stiffest opposition. By the end of the day, Bradley's regiments had only been able to move about a thousand yards inland. Farther south, Major General Archibald Arnold's 7th Infantry Division also met tough opposition, but managed to secure its initial objectives enroute to the airfields at Dulag. By this time, Imperial General Headquarters had ordered *SHO-1* executed.[43] (*See Atlas Map No. 29.*)

As Krueger's division attacked inland, the American submarines *Darter* and *Dace* reported the advance of Japanese fleet units toward the central Philippines. (*See*

Outgunned American Ships Use Smoke Screens for Concealment During the Battle off Samar, October 25, 1944

Appendix 27.) These new movements conformed generally to earlier plans, which envisioned Admiral Ozawa drawing the American fast carriers north while Admirals Kurita and Nishimura converged on the Leyte beachhead to destroy the vulnerable invasion forces. As Kurita's force passed Palawan enroute to the Sibuyan Sea, the American submarines *Dace* and *Darter* sank two cruisers, including the admiral's flagship, and then damaged a third cruiser. Two days later, Halsey's airmen attacked Kurita's heavy ships in the Sibuyan Sea (Battle of the Sibuyan Sea), sinking the super battleship *Musashi*, and damaging a heavy cruiser and several other warships. In the face of the American air attacks, Admiral Kurita reversed course. Meanwhile Japanese land-based airmen had nearly evened the score: one pilot bombed and sank the light carrier *Princeton*.

With the apparent Japanese threat reduced, Admiral Halsey turned his attention to the reports that the Japanese carriers had been sighted off northern Luzon. (*See Atlas Map No. 29.*) Immediately deciding to attack the baited fleet, he started north, but both failed to leave a force to guard San Bernadino Strait and to warn Admiral Kinkaid of his departure. Meanwhile, Kurita had reversed course once again and was steaming east. Like Halsey, however, he did not inform his subordinate, Admiral Nishimura, of his delay and the resultant change of plan. Nishimura consequently steamed toward Surigao Strait—he was the southern pincer—ahead of Kurita's northern pincer.

Admiral Kinkaid meanwhile had been preparing to meet the Japanese fleet, which had been reported moving into the Mindanao Sea enroute to Surigao Strait. He deployed Admiral Oldendorf's six old battleships across the top of the strait, and sent his PT boats and destroyers forward to engage. During the night of October 24 (Battle of Surigao Strait), Oldendorf annihilated Nishimura's force as his radar-controlled guns pounded the Japanese admiral's column when the old battleships capped the "T" during the melee. After that, Oldendorf's force prepared to meet the unexpected attack by Admiral Shima's *Second Striking Force*, which had come down from Japan and followed in Nishimura's wake. Shima, however, turned away before coming to close quarters. After a short pursuit, the battle ended; but Oldendorf, now short of armor-piercing ammunition, was unprepared to meet another Japanese onslaught immediately.

Unknown to Kinkaid and Oldendorf, Kurita had slipped through San Bernadino Strait and turned south early on October 25 to fulfill his mission of destroying the Allied shipping in the gulf. Halsey knew of this development, but did not believe that Kurita was capable of doing much after his previous beating. When the Americans finally realized what was happening, only Rear Admiral Clifton Sprague's Escort Carrier Group was in a position to stop Kurita's attack. Unfortunately, Sprague's thin-skinned carriers and light escort vessels were not strong enough to meet the Japanese admiral's battleships and heavy cruisers. The available American aircraft, however, would save the day.

The Battle off Samar began at 6:48 A.M., October 25, when Kurita opened fire on the surprised Americans. (*See Atlas Map No. 29.*) Sprague immediately began violent maneuvers to avoid destruction; he then managed to hide his small carriers in a nearby squall, while he radioed for help. Kurita, meanwhile, bored in, but allowed his captains to maneuver independently. At the same time, Sprague ordered his screen destroyers and then his destroyer escorts to attack; overhead, all available pilots harassed Kurita's ships. Kurita steamed on. His battleships and heavy cruisers began to wreak havoc—they sank two destroyers and one destroyer escort, hit the escort carrier *Kalinan Bay*, and sank the escort carrier *Gambier Bay*. The American pilots fought back, sinking two heavy Japanese cruisers. Just as it appeared that the Japanese would break through the American screen, Kurita ordered a withdrawal because he feared that he was moving into a trap. This controversial decision relieved the pressure on Kinkaid's forces, ending the surface Battle off Samar. Shortly thereafter, however, volunteer Japanese naval aviators began the first organized *kamikaze* raids of the war. They crashed five escort carriers before noon, sinking one, the *St. Lo*.

Farther north, Halsey had been steaming at top speed to meet the Japanese carriers which had successfully drawn him away from the beachhead area. (*See Atlas Map No. 29.*) When his pilots finally engaged on October 25 they found carriers without aircraft; but in the ensuing fight they did manage to sink the *Zuikaku*—the sole surviving Pearl Harbor Attack carrier—three smaller flattops, and a destroyer. The able and experienced Admiral Ozawa, however, maneuvered his plane-less fleet with skill and daring throughout the engagement, and his newly armed battleships and cruisers fired the most intense antiaircraft barrages of the war. Ozawa's chief of staff later commented that the American carrier pilots fought poorly, although they had the numbers present to overwhelm the vulnerable ships of Ozawa's fleet. The Battle off Cape Engaño pulled Halsey away from the Leyte beachhead, and Halsey's critics have dubbed it the "Battle of Bull's Run." MacArthur, however, never criticized his old comrade-in-arms, although Admiral Kinkaid severely attacked Halsey for leaving him uncovered and unwarned off Leyte.

The four major fights which took place at sea during the period of October 23 to 25—known as the Battle for Leyte

Gulf—destroyed the combat power of the *Combined Fleet.* Never again would it sortie to meet the Allies. The last months of the war would find its major surviving ships anchored in homeland ports or dispersed in the southern waters where they could do no harm. Leyte Gulf, the largest naval battle in history—it involved 282 ships, hundreds of airplanes, and over 187,000 sailors—was the most decisive sea action of the war. It set the stage for the decisive land battle on Leyte, and for the rapid development of Japan's new weapon—the *kamikaze.*[44]

United States	Japan
1 Light Carrier (CVL)	1 Fleet carrier (CV)
2 Escort carriers (CVE)	3 Light carriers (CVL)
2 Destroyers (DD)	3 Battleships (BB)
1 Destroyer escort (DDE)	6 Heavy cruisers (CD)
	4 Light cruisers (CL)
	11 Destroyers (DD)

Ship Losses in the Battle For Leyte Gulf

With the defeat of the Japanese naval surface forces, MacArthur could proceed with the war ashore. In the succeeding weeks he saw Krueger's forces accomplish their planned missions on the east coast, secure the line of inland airfields near Dagami and Burauen, and then push against the Japanese positions in the central mountains. In the north, the 1st Cavalry Division and the 24th Infantry Division secured Carigara by November 2 (*See Atlas Map No. 30A*); in the center, the 7th Infantry Division drove south to Abuyog and crossed the island to Baybay by the same date. None of these moves was easy: the Japanese fought stubbornly at several strong positions and had to be rooted out of their mountain positions man-by-man. With the capture of Baybay and Carigara, however, Krueger gained excellent positions from which to move on the key port of Ormoc, through which the Japanese had been reinforcing Leyte. (*See Atlas Map No. 30.*)

By November 2, Yamashita had landed new formations to reinforce the *16th Division*, after Imperial General Headquarters finally accepted Field Marshal Terauchi's advice and declared Leyte to be the zone of decisive action for the Japanese Army in the Philippines. Yamashita opposed this decision, but once it was confirmed he began shifting his forces southward as ordered. Before the campaign was over, he had sent three divisions and several brigades, regiments, and battalions to Leyte, including the crack *1st Division*, which was reported to be one of the four

best in the Japanese Army. (*See Atlas Map No. 30.*) The Japanese lost a cruiser, 8 destroyers, 5 naval transports, 5 cargo ships, and 6 other craft, eventually transporting 30,000 soldiers and 10,000 tons of supplies to Leyte.[45]

Without adequate airbases on Leyte—construction was delayed because of the heavy rains and the resultant soaked ground—MacArthur could not stop the first Japanese reinforcements. (*See Atlas Maps No. 30 and 30B.*) Consequently, General Sosaku Suzuki, the *Thirty-Fifth Army* commander and the senior officer on Leyte, delayed Krueger's operations at key places. In the mountains at the north end of the Ormoc Valley, his *1st Division* made the Americans fight for every yard of ground. Eventually Krueger deployed the best part of three divisions to clear the entrance to the valley near Limon before his troops finally broke through the Japanese defenses to take the town on November 24.

As the American forces moved south from Carigara they formed the right arm of General Krueger's double envelopment. To the south, the 7th Infantry Division, moving north toward Ormoc, and the 77th Infantry Division, which arrived from Guam and which Krueger landed near Ormoc on December 7, formed the left arm. (*See Atlas Map No. 30B.*) By December 21, the forward troops of the 77th Infantry Division had made contact with the lead elements of the 1st Cavalry Division, which had come south from Limon, thus securing the Ormoc Valley. Following this, the 32nd Infantry and 1st Cavalry Divisions turned right to

Infantry on Leyte

clear the western portion of Leyte, while elements of the 77th seized Palompon on the west coast by amphibious assault.

During the entire period, the 96th Infantry Division and reinforcing units such as the 11th Airborne Division and the 112th Cavalry Regimental Combat Team, advanced slowly through the central mountains toward the west. While the major battles on the ground were taking place in central and northern Leyte, troops of the 1st Cavalry Division moved onto Samar, elements of two divisions secured southern Leyte, and the 6th Rangers and Filipino guerrillas pacified the islands in Leyte Gulf.[46]

The land battle on Leyte was as decisive as the sea battle, for it was on this jungled island that MacArthur's divisions destroyed Yamashita's capacity to wage decisive warfare on Luzon. In effect, MacArthur won the Philippines at Leyte. Yamashita, forced to squander valuable divisions on Leyte, would not be able to repulse or seriously hamper the invasion of Luzon. Moreover, since the Japanese had continued to fling all available air units at the Americans on Leyte, the Americans slowly but surely neutralized orthodox Japanese air squadrons before they left Leyte for Luzon.

Branch	Killed	Wounded
Infantry	2,380 (82.42%)	7,749 (78.61%)
Engineer	132 (4.58%)	762 (7.73%)
Medical	100 (3.47%)	375 (3.80%)
Field Artillery	96 (3.33%)	328 (3.33%)

**Selected Sixth Army Battle Casualties
During Leyte Campaign
October 20–December 25, 1944**

By December 25, General Krueger had completed the major part of the Leyte campaign, although mopping up would continue for months. Krueger did not remain to complete that action, however, because he had already landed Sixth Army forces on Mindoro (LOVE III) on December 15 to establish airbases which could support the coming invasion of Luzon. Simultaneously, he was preparing to land at Lingayen Gulf (MIKE I) on January 9, 1945. On December 26, MacArthur ordered General Eichelberger to clear Leyte with Eighth Army forces so that Krueger could prepare to assault Luzon with his Sixth Army. About the same time, Yamashita abandoned Japanese forces on Leyte to their fate, and began to concentrate on defending Luzon.[47]

Leyte, however, was not an unqualified American success. MacArthur's engineers had been right—Leyte did not

Rainy Season on Leyte

provide a suitable area for airfields because of its water-logged terrain. Consequently, the Japanese were able to reinforce their garrison, thus delaying the planned invasion of Luzon from December 20 to January 9, and requiring MacArthur to build up Sixth Army to over seven full divisions and several separate regiments. Many of these units saw hard fighting and were understrength when committed to Luzon. (*See Appendix 28, Casualties.*)* Still, these deficiencies did not override the strategic significance of Leyte: Halsey had destroyed the *Combined Fleet's* remaining power; Halsey and Kenney's airmen had decimated the Japanese air forces; and Krueger's divisions had ground up the Japanese *Thirty-Fifth Army*. Furthermore, MacArthur's move into the island split the Philippines in two, setting up Sixth Army's northern invasion of Mindoro and Luzon, and Eighth Army's eventual maneuvers to the west and south. When all the Philippines fell, the Allies similarly would split the Japanese Empire in two. From the archipelago, MacArthur would drive into Borneo, while Nimitz would attack north from the Marianas toward Iwo Jima and Okinawa. Moreover, Allied heavy bombers would gain a new base area from which they could raid the Japanese positions in the Indies, China, and the Ryukyus; and the Allies would recapture ports valuable for staging future attacks in the western Pacific.

MacArthur's return excited the long-suffering Filipinos, who soon spread the good news over the "Bamboo Telegraph." Within a few hours, a public address announcer calmly advised the internees in the University of Santo Tomas that the long-delayed rice ration for October had finally arrived—"better Leyte than never."[48]

*The "Battle of the Bulge" in Europe (December 1944) siphoned off nearly all available infantry replacements and caused General Marshall to send the last of his mobilized divisions to Europe.

Continental War: Luzon

Three weeks before the Leyte invasion, the Joint Chiefs of Staff ordered MacArthur to invade Luzon and directed Admiral Nimitz to take Iwo Jima and Okinawa.* This decision settled an old argument: Luzon would be invaded rather than Formosa.[49]

General MacArthur, as was to be expected, had always supported an invasion of Luzon. The general felt that the United States was honor-bound to retake all of the Philippines, but he also felt that Luzon was a better strategic objective than Formosa. From Luzon, the Allies could cut the Japanese line of communications to the south and establish bases from which they could invade Formosa. In MacArthur's opinion, he could take Luzon more cheaply, quickly, and with fewer forces than Nimitz could take Formosa.

On the other hand, Admiral King believed that Formosa was a sounder strategic objective than Luzon. King felt that holding the island would ease the invasion of Luzon, that the Allies could not gain their coveted base on the China coast until they had taken Formosa, and that an invasion of Luzon would delay the attack of Formosa and the more decisive area farther north. If the Joint Chiefs decided to ignore Formosa, the Chief of Naval Operations recommended that the Allies attack Japan next, rather than go to Luzon. In the Pacific, Admiral King had only one lukewarm supporter in the person of Admiral Nimitz. MacArthur would not accept his stand, nor would Halsey, who wanted to go to Luzon and then to Okinawa. Even Nimitz' staff officers did not support King's Formosa plan.

While Nimitz supported his chief's strategy, he unwittingly helped to kill King's proposal when he submitted his plan for the invasion of Formosa. Nimitz recommended that his forces take only southern Formosa while simultaneously landing at Amoy on the China coast. Such a move would require more combat troops to take and defend two beachheads and more service troops to support the additional ground forces; and it would not provide airbases closer to

Japan than Luzon. Quite logically, therefore, since additional combat troops would not be available until the war ended in Germany, service troops were even more scarce than combat troops, and the airbases were so far away, Nimitz' plan offered no advantages over MacArthur's Luzon proposal.

As the Army planners in Washington considered Nimitz' plan they became more and more uninterested in Formosa. Deficiencies in combat and service troops, the lack of shipping, and two other crucial developments influenced their final recommendations. One development concerned MacArthur. Once the Joint Chiefs approved the Leyte landing for October 20, the general said that he could invade Luzon on December 20, nearly two months earlier than the Joint Chiefs had considered invading either Formosa or Luzon.† On the heels of this announcement, General Joseph Stilwell reported that the Chinese Army was unable to hold or recapture the airfields in China which were used by the Fourteenth Air Force. Because supplying these airfields was the main reason that the joint planners had recommended that the Allies secure a port on the Chinese coast in the first place, Stilwell's message effectively nullified the need for landing on the China coast. When all considerations had been evaluated, the Army planners in Washington rejected Nimitz' plan.

Admiral King, however, tried one last time to stop MacArthur's move to Luzon. He said that the general's operation would tie up the fast carriers for six weeks in order to protect the beachhead, secure the reinforcement convoys, and neutralize the Japanese air forces on Formosa and Luzon. General MacArthur, with his goal in sight, was ready with a counter. He immediately promised that he would need the fast carriers to cover his landings only; thereafter, he would only need some escort carriers to assist him until Kenney's land-based squadrons were operational on Luzon. Then, as if this were not enough, Nimitz submitted a new plan which ignored Formosa. Now the admiral proposed to attack Iwo Jima in late January 1945, and invade Okinawa on March 1. King, opposed once again by his naval commanders in the Pacific, finally capitulated and agreed to invade Luzon.

Once the directive came from Washington, MacArthur wasted little time preparing plans.[50] Enroute to Leyte, he directed General Krueger to prepare for the invasion of Mindoro (December 5) and Luzon (December 20) and to coordinate the air, land, and naval plans. But precious time was lost when the long and bitter fight on Leyte, the

---

* During the Roosevelt-MacArthur-Nimitz Conference in Hawaii on July 26 and 27, 1944, the subject of Luzon and Formosa had come up along with the revived proposal to bypass the Philippines entirely and invade Formosa. Previously, on March 12, 1944, the Joint Chiefs of Staff had ordered MacArthur to prepare plans to invade Mindanao. MacArthur, of course, argued for the invasion of the Philippines and, particularly, for the invasion of Luzon over Formosa. At this time, Nimitz supported MacArthur's plans for the invasion of Mindanao or the Visayas, but favored Formosa over Luzon. MacArthur and his supporters indicate that President Roosevelt approved of MacArthur's plan to invade the Philippines, although there is no record of such a decision being made. Also implied is an approval to invade Luzon instead of Formosa. On September 15, the Joint Chiefs of Staff ordered MacArthur to invade Leyte; on October 3, they ordered him to invade Luzon.

† He also said that he would gain his strategic objective—the Central Plains and Manila—within four to six weeks after landing. Following this schedule, MacArthur would complete his vital Luzon campaign before Formosa was ever invaded.

attendant inability to build the needed airbases, and a shortage of assault shipping forced MacArthur to postpone the invasion of Mindoro until December 15 and the invasion of Luzon to January 9. Moreover, the general realized that Mindoro had become more important in the scheme of events, because without adequate airbases in the central Philippines he needed bases on Mindoro in order to invade Luzon as planned.

Following MacArthur's guidance, Krueger planned to invade southwestern Mindoro expressly to seize one airfield and build others. Since there were only a few Japanese on the island, for the assault the Sixth Army commander organized a small task force built around the 19th Infantry Regimental Combat Team (24th Infantry Division) and the separate 503rd Parachute Infantry Regimental Combat Team. Because he was short of service troops, Krueger deployed 1,200 combat troops from the 77th Infantry Division to unload the assault shipping during the landing. While the American commanders did not foresee any problems taking the island, they did know that they were advancing into an area where Japanese air forces stationed throughout the Philippines could attack their convoys easily.

After the naval task force left Leyte for Mindoro, it ran into a hornet's nest of *kamikazes* on the afternoon of December 13. (*See Atlas Map No. 31.*) One Japanese pilot in a black plane crashed the cruiser *Nashville* during the first attacks, and by the end of the campaign Japanese fliers had sunk five Liberty ships and five LSTs, in addition to damaging the *Nashville* and several smaller warships. Besides these air raids, the Japanese tried to attack the Allied force with a small surface group on the night of December 26, but American airmen drove off this force, sinking one destroyer in the process.

On Mindoro, the American regiments took their objectives on December 15 with little difficulty, because the Japanese garrison fled into the hills when the naval bombardment started. Five days later, Kenney sent a fighter group to Mindoro, while American and Australian engineers continued to work on additional airstrips. Following the main landings, small forces captured nearby islands (*See Atlas Map No. 31*), and higher commanders connived to convince the Japanese that the Allies would land next on southern Luzon. To deceive them, the Allies occupied Marinduque Island, moved troops to northeastern Mindoro, dropped dummy parachutists, swept harbors in southern Luzon, and intensified guerrilla operations near tentative landing areas.[51]

The Allied landing on Mindoro surprised Yamashita as well as other members of the Japanese hierarchy who had expected that the Allies would invade either Negros or Panay, where they could gain developed airbases.[52] Just before the Mindoro landing, however, Yamashita had contemplated a move toward Panay or Negros, and he also had requested once again that the reinforcement of Leyte be stopped so that he could better prepare for the defense of Luzon. Following the Mindoro landing, moreover, Yamashita showed no interest in executing a counter-landing, but continued to plan the defense of Luzon. On December 19, following the visit of his chief of staff to Manila, Marshall Terauchi finally agreed to let Yamashita fight the battle as he saw best. Imperial General Headquarters then told the Emperor that *SHO-1* had been expanded to include all of the Philippines, instead of just Leyte.

General Yamashita was perhaps the Japanese Army's finest tactician and most able field commander. Faced with a grave situation, the general knew that he could not meet the Allies on their own terms because he could not command the air over any battlefield and thus could not fight in open terrain where Allied air forces could decimate his units. After concluding that he could not challenge Allied armor also, Yamashita decided that his area army would:

> . . . secure the vital northern Luzon area with its main strength, and the mountainous regions east of Manila and west of Clark Field with elements of its forces. The forces in each of these areas will coordinate their operations with the objective of containing the American forces on Luzon and destroying [their] fighting strength, and at the same time will prepare for protracted resistance on an independent, self-sufficient basis.[53]

Yamashita rejected holding the Bataan Peninsula because it was a *cul-de-sac*. (*See Atlas Map No. 32.*) Furthermore, he could not hope to support and feed his troops there because the Allies could easily employ their awesome firepower against the peninsula.[54] Yamashita ordered his 262,000 men to occupy the Zambales Mountains west of Clark Field, instead of Bataan, thereby denying the airbase to the invaders; to move into the mountains east of Manila, where long-range artillery could shell the capital and the Japanese could hold the reservoirs and filter plants which controlled Manila's water supply; and to withdraw into the northern mountains, which controlled the Cagayan Valley, the second most important rice-growing area on Luzon. In the north, Yamashita planned to hold the line from near Rosario to San Jose, Balete Pass, and Baler Bay as long as possible so that his troops could collect the rice in the Cagayan Valley. He did not want to hold Manila. According to his plan, once the Americans landed and the naval troops in Manila finally came under his control, they were to evacuate the city and join the army forces east of Manila.

As it turned out, however, the naval commander in Manila later would decide to defend the city to the bitter end, in order to protect the naval facilities in the city.[55]

By early January, 1945, Yamashita was deploying his forces as planned. (*See Atlas Map No. 32.*) West of Clark Field, Major General Rikichi Tsukada commanded the *KEMBU Group* of 30,000; east of Manila, Lieutenant General Shizuo Yokoyama commanded 80,000 men of the *SHIMBU Group*; and in the north, Yamashita commanded the bulk of his own *Fourteenth Area Army* (the *SHOBU Group*), a force of 152,000.[56] His deployment, however, was not complete, and he kept moving supplies and units into the mountain redoubts as fast as he could. (*See Appendix 29.*) Nevertheless, by January 9 Yamashita did have sufficient forces in position to impede the Allied invasion, hold the Baguio and Clark Field areas for some time, and threaten any march toward Manila. With seven divisions, an independent mixed brigade, a raiding group, and a large number of air and naval troops, he would try to better the American performance on Bataan.

MacArthur's plan for Luzon employed most of the forces he had used at Leyte. Supported by the aggressive Halsey's Third Fleet operating east of Luzon, MacArthur's troops would move to the objective area aboard the ships of Kinkaid's Luzon Attack Force. Kinkaid's Seventh Fleet, reinforced by escort carriers and other warships from the central Pacific, would secure the attack convoys as they moved from Leyte Gulf to Lingayen Gulf. In the air, Kenney's squadrons would cover the invasion forces, while simultaneously attacking Japanese targets in southern Luzon. Furthermore, B-29s from China and the Marianas would bomb ports in Formosa and aircraft depots in Japan to assist the invasion forces. Lastly, Halsey would enter the South China Sea to block any Japanese force sortieing from Singapore and strike lucrative targets in the area. (As it turned out, this attack shocked the Japanese, improved Chinese morale, and deceived the Japanese as to the direction of MacArthur's attack.)[57]

The delay of the invasion of Luzon to January 9 forced Nimitz to postpone his invasions of Iwo Jima and Okinawa because of the need to divert fast carriers, escort carriers, and much assault shipping to MacArthur. Even upon their return, Nimitz would not be able to redeploy these naval forces at once because he would have to rest weary crews and perform maintenance on warships. Furthermore, time would be required to load the waiting invasion forces on transports. Consequently, Admiral Nimitz rescheduled the assault on Iwo Jima for February 15, and the one on Okinawa for April 1.

In the southwest Pacific, MacArthur's own operations would soon become more complicated. After moving Krueger's Sixth Army to Luzon, the general would have to deploy the Eighth Army to assist Krueger momentarily before turning Eichelberger southward to clear the Visayas and Mindanao and open the road to the Indies. Simultaneously, he would have to move his American divisions forward from New Guinea and points south so that he could operate effectively in the Philippines, meanwhile turning over the bypassed areas to the Australians. Finally, the general would bring Australian units forward to begin the invasion of Borneo. Every one of these interrelated moves had to be coordinated with the others in order to insure the proper utilization of limited ground, air, and sea forces.

General Krueger developed his plans as soon as MacArthur issued firm instructions to him on October 12. Deciding not to land on the east coast of Lingayen Gulf, as the Japanese had done in 1941, Krueger opted for the poorer southern beaches in an attempt to surprise the Japanese and avoid their prepared positions on the east side of the gulf. (*See Atlas Map No. 33.*) He planned to land with two corps abreast (Major General Innis Swift's I Corps on the left and Major General Oscar Griswold's XIV Corps on the right) on S-Day. Two days later, he would land the 158th Infantry Regimental Combat Team to the left of I Corps, and by that date he would have the bulk of his ready reserve (the 25th Infantry Division, 13th Armored Group, and 6th Ranger Infantry Battalion) either ashore or landing. Other forces—including the 11th Airborne Division on Leyte, four back-up divisions (the 1st Cavalry, 32nd Infantry, 33rd Infantry, and 41st Infantry) and the 112th Cavalry Regimental Combat Team—would be available in January or February, as needed. (Some of these would be committed later under Eighth Army command to assist Krueger.) After landing, Krueger planned a three-phase attack to seize the Central Plains and Manila. During Phase I, he would secure his beachhead and begin building air and logistical bases within it. In Phase II, he would fight his way across the Agno River. In Phase III, he would destroy the Japanese in the Central Plains and capture the Philippine capital.[58]

As the Allied ships moved north to mount the largest amphibious invasion of the Pacific war, the senior officers knew that they were moving into a dangerous area. Any doubts about the ability of the Japanese to conduct a vigorous defense were soon dissipated when fearsome *kamikazes* on Luzon unleashed a devastating attack on Admiral Kinkaid's ships between January 4 and 12. On the fourth, the suicide pilots mortally damaged the escort carrier *Ommaney Bay*. The next day they crashed the cruisers *Louisville* and *HMAS Australia*, two escort carriers, four other ships, and an LCI gunboat. On the sixth, the terror continued as *kamikazes* hit the battleship *New*

Mexico, killing her skipper, Lieutenant General Herbert Lumsden (Winston Churchill's representative to MacArthur's headquarters), and killing and wounding over 100 more officers and men. Fifteen other ships were hit the same day—the unlucky *Australia* took her third *kamikaze*—and soon everyone realized they were in a real fight. For three more nerve-wracking days, the Japanese suicide pilots bored in on the Allied vessels, scoring hits on several LSTs and crashing into the *Australia* three more times.

As a result of these attacks, Admiral Oldendorf, leading the van, recommended that the invasion plan be reconsidered, and Admiral Kinkaid requested that Halsey cover the landings with his fast carriers. MacArthur decided differently. He continued to advance, but asked the Joint Chiefs to send B-29s against Formosa and asked Halsey to pound the same island with his carrier air groups. On the tenth, the suicide air attacks subsided, but suicide boats began attacking the ships in Lingayen Gulf. During these new attacks, the Japanese sank two LCIs and damaged four LSTs.[59]

Type of Ship	Sunk	Damaged Heavily	Damaged Lightly	Total
Battleships		3	1	4
Heavy Cruisers		2	1	3
Light Cruisers		3	1	4
Escort Carriers	1	4	2	7
Destroyers	1	4	11	16
Liberty Ships	6	4	2	12
LSTs	6	1	4	11
All other ships	10	9	15	34
Total	**24**	**30**	**37**	**91**

Kamikaze Attacks at Mindoro and Luzon Landings December 13, 1944–January 13, 1945

On January 9, General Krueger's four divisions landed quickly, met little opposition, and secured the army beachhead line by dark. (*See Atlas Map No. 33.*) Following the landing, the general deployed his corps for a coordinated advance toward the Agno River, beginning the only continental-style war waged in the Pacific area. Seven days later he held a 60-mile long front, which stretched from Damortis on the left to Binalonan and Aguilar in the center to Sual on the right. During this time, only Swift's I Corps had met truly determined resistance because it ran into the southern positions of Yamashita's *SHOBU Group*.

On January 12, MacArthur became concerned about Krueger's slow advance and urged him to move more quickly toward Manila. Krueger initially demurred because of the danger to his left flank, but a week later he sent

Griswold's XIV Corps southward to take Clark Field, while echeloning Sixth Army to the left to protect the northeastern flank. Griswold's troops marched south, meeting little opposition until they approached Bamban and neared Clark Field. (*See Atlas Map No. 33.*) At both places the Japanese defended stubbornly, but by January 28, Griswold's veterans had captured Clark Field, gaining the first strategic prize on Luzon for MacArthur. Meanwhile, in the I Corps' zone, General Swift's infantrymen continued to meet stiffer resistance as they attacked Yamashita's defenses.[60]

During this period, Krueger learned that the Japanese still held several hundred Allied prisoners in a camp near Cabanatuan, 25 miles in front of his forward units. The general immediately ordered the 6th Rangers to rescue the inmates; four days later, the rangers, assisted by ALAMO Scouts and Filipino guerrillas, brought the prisoners of war back within American lines.[61]

By the time the prisoners reached friendly lines, several important developments had taken place on Luzon. (*See Atlas Map No. 33.*) Griswold had captured Fort Stotsenberg and had patrols in Calumpit, barely 25 miles north of Manila.* To assist Griswold, MacArthur had landed Major General Charles Hall's XI Corps on the west coast of Zambales Province on January 29 to cut off a possible Japanese retreat into Bataan and to threaten the rear and flank of the *KEMBU Group* facing Griswold. (MIKE VII).† Additionally, MacArthur ordered Eichelberger to execute a reconnaissance-in-force at Nasugbu on January 31 (MIKE VI), with the idea of using Major General Joseph Swing's 11th Airborne Division to contain the Japanese forces south of Manila.** Eichelberger, however, would turn the landing into a full-scale drive on Manila, setting up a double envelopment of the city. Furthermore, the day before the paratroopers went ashore, MacArthur made a personal reconnaissance of Griswold's area along Highway 3 and told General Krueger afterwards that Major General Robert Beightler's 37th Infantry Division lacked drive and initiative, as was evidenced by its slow movement. MacArthur's actions spurred Krueger to issue new orders for a quickened advance to Manila, one which would send the recently arrived 1st Cavalry Division down Highway 5 to the east, while the 37th Division continued south on Highway 3.[62]

---

*As a soldier in the 12th Infantry, Krueger had fought in this area during the Philippine Insurrection, nearly 45 years earlier. At that time he had served under the command of Major General Arthur MacArthur, Douglas' father.

†Previously planned as MIKE III in MUSKETEER I–III. Ordered executed on January 14, 1945.

**Not a part of the original MUSKETEER Plans. Discussed first in November 1944; ordered executed on January 15, 1945.

Before Krueger could begin his two-pronged attack, MacArthur visited the cavalry division and told Major General Verne Mudge to "Go to Manila. Go around the Nips, bounce off the Nips, but go to Manila. Free the internees in Santo Tomas. Take Malacañan Palace and the Legislative Building."[63] Within 48 hours, Mudge's troopers bolted for the Philippine capital.

As the first days of February dawned, MacArthur watched his divisions converge on Manila. (*See Atlas Map No. 33.*) In the north, Brigadier General William Chase led the mounted columns of the 5th and 8th Cavalry southward, having as his objective the liberation of Santo Tomas. Farther west and south, the dismounted 37th Infantry Division moved slowly down Highway 3, delayed at every stream by blown bridges; at the same time, from Olongapo, Major General Henry Jones' 38th Infantry Division struggled eastward to join Beightler's troops, but could not overcome the strong Japanese defenses along Zip Zag Pass on Highway 7. South of Manila, MacArthur watched Swing jump his 511th Parachute Infantry Regimental Combat Team onto Tagaytay Ridge, on the north rim of Lake Taal. Thereafter, the paratroopers advanced north rapidly along Highway 17 toward the *Genko Line* and Nichols Field, with a "spearhead tipped with brass" (Swing and Eichelberger).[64]

MacArthur's favorites, the cavalrymen, entered Manila on the evening of February 3, after driving 100 miles through lightly held Japanese territory.* A few hours later, a medium tank, "Battlin' Basic," smashed through the front gates of Santo Tomas, beginning the liberation of the largest internment camp in the islands. Shortly thereafter the children of Santo Tomas surrounded their new heroes to beg, borrow, or steal a cavalryman or any part of his person or gear to show off to their parents. Later, in their shanties, families began to cook their few hoarded rations to celebrate their good fortune.[65]

But the joy in Santo Tomas was short-lived.† Within hours, Manila became a battleground. For the next month, Mudge's cavalrymen, Beightler's infantrymen, and Swing's paratroopers and glidermen had a real fight on their hands. It raged from house to house, in the City Hall and in the Post Office, on Wack Wack golf course and in Rizal baseball stadium, against the Genko Line, at Nichols Field and in Fort McKinley, and finally against Intramuros (the ancient Walled City), which stood nearly impregnable on the south

Infantry Advances on Luzon

bank of the Pasig River. Facing point-blank fire of infantry weapons, advancing against fire from depressed antiaircraft guns and naval guns,** and crossing roads and streets laced with naval mines, the ground soldiers destroyed each Japanese unit where it stood. Finally, on March 3, 1945, Griswold announced that his corps had overcome all organized resistance in rubble-strewn Manila.[66]

With the capture of his main strategic objective on Luzon, General MacArthur decided to clear Manila Bay so that he would use Manila as a port before defeating Yamashita's troops in the mountains. To do this he had to secure Bataan and capture Corregidor. Krueger's troops did just that in mid-February. (*See Atlas Map No. 34.*) First, the rejuvenated 38th Infantry Division, now commanded by Major General Chase, took Zig Zag Pass, moved quickly into the Bataan Peninsula, and then seized Mariveles across from Corregidor on February 15. The next day, elements of the same division assaulted the south shore of the rocky fortress while Colonel George Jones's 503rd Parachute Infantry Regimental Combat Team jumped onto Corregidor. Jones's paratroopers surprised the Japanese garrison, and, with the help of the infantrymen from Bataan, secured the island in 12 days. The capture of Corregidor opened Manila Bay, but the badly damaged port

---

*Many cavalry officers knew this area well because they had served at Fort Stotsenberg before the war.

† For several days, Santo Tomas was a major American position inside the city, and therefore the Japanese shelled the camp repeatedly, causing heavy military and civilian casualties.

**One infantry company commander who faced Japanese naval gunfire at Nichols Field allegedly reported: "Tell Halsey to quit looking for the Jap Fleet. It's dug in on Nichols Field."

could not be used until early April. To make the bay more secure, General Chase's troops had to clear Caballo Island, Carabao Island (Fort Frank), and El Fraile (Fort Drum) in March and April.[67]

About the time that the paratroopers jumped onto Corregidor, United States Marines assaulted Iwo Jima, and elements of the 11th Airborne Division, assisted by Filipino guerrillas, liberated over 2,300 internees from the Los Banos Internment Camp during a daring parachute-ground-amphibious raid.[68] Shortly thereafter, General Krueger began moving his corps against Yamashita's isolated strongholds, while General Eichelberger began executing the VICTORY operations in the Visayas.

The remaining campaigning in the mountains of Luzon was difficult, severely taxing the American infantrymen who had to dig the determined Japanese out of caves and pillboxes as they advanced into each redoubt area. (*See Atlas Map No. 34.*) To maintain his attacks, Krueger deployed more and more troops until he had used eight infantry divisions, the 1st Cavalry Division, the 11th Airborne Division, three separate regimental combat teams, and a large number of organized guerrilla regiments in the various areas of Luzon. The bulk of these (four divisions and an equivalent guerrilla division) fought under General Swift (I Corps) and slowly battered their way north to decimate and surround General Yamashita's *SHOBU Group*. Three more were fully employed, first against the *SHIMBU Group* east and northeast of Manila, and later in the southern part of Luzon. Against the *SHIMBU Group*, General Griswold's soldiers (XIV Corps), and then General Hall's (XI Corps), found the fighting just as tough, but since they faced fewer Japanese soldiers than in the north, and because these Japanese were dying of starvation, the Americans overcame the last organized Japanese resistance in the area by the end of May. Griswold's and Hall's troops fought around Clark Field for some time, but the combat in that area against the remainder of the *KEMBU Group* was not as touch or as costly as in the other areas, because Griswold's attacks in January had badly chewed up the *KEMBU Group*.*

By July 1, when Krueger turned over operations on Luzon to Eichelberger, Sixth Army had cleared out most of Luzon except for the 50,000 Japanese surrounded in the rugged mountains a few miles northeast of Baguio, the summer capital of the Philippines. (*See Atlas Map No. 34.*)

Infantry in Northern Luzon

Strategically, Krueger had long since won the battle of Luzon for MacArthur; nevertheless, Yamashita had conducted a tough, protracted campaign which tied down many American divisions and caused a great number of casualties. With his unbelievably brave soldiers, adequate weapons, and a reasonable amount of food, Yamashita had waged an excellent delaying action, and by the end of the war he still engaged two American divisions and about a division of guerrillas. To accomplish this, the Japanese commander had sacrificed 172,765 of his 232,000 men in the *SHOBU, SHIMBU, and KEMBU Groups*; in the overall campaign, he had lost 205,535 of his original garrison of 275,685. On the other hand, Sixth Army and Eighth Army suffered a total of 37,870 casualties, 8,310 of whom were killed in action, died of wounds or disease, or were missing in action. In addition, many hundreds of Filipino guerrilla soldiers and several thousand Filipino civilians died as a result of military action.[69] On the surface, Yamashita conducted a more effective defensive campaign on Luzon in 1945 than MacArthur had conducted in 1941 and 1942. It is probably fair, however, to conclude that both did the best with what they had.[70]

---

*During these various operations the Japanese killed Major General Edwin Patrick, commander of the 6th Infantry Division, when he was visiting the front lines, and Brigadier General James Dalton, the Assistant Division commander of the 25th Infantry Division, near Balete Pass. They also seriously wounded Major General Verne Mudge of the 1st Cavalry Division, who pushed his luck once too often at the front in southern Luzon.

MacArthur's Final Campaigns: The Visayas, Mindanao, and Borneo

General Robert Eichelberger, a proud and capable soldier, fondly reminisced about the success of his Eighth Army in the Philippines whenever he discussed his operations after the war. He had every reason to be proud of his soldiers. (*See Appendix 30.*) During the period of February to July 1945, Eichelberger's troops made 52 different landings: the execution of MIKE VII (Zambales) and MIKE VI (Nasugbu) on Luzon; the clearance of the Visayan Island Passages which stretched from San Bernadino Strait to Lubang Island between Luzon and Mindoro; and the completion of the VICTOR operations which cleared Palawan, Panay, Negros, Cebu, Bohol, the Sulu Archipelago, and the second most important island in the Philippines, Mindanao. (*See Atlas Map No. 35.*)

On these islands, Eichelberger's troops, often assisted by Filipino guerrillas,* fought stubborn Japanese who normally retreated into the central mountains of each island to conduct prolonged defenses. After many quick and efficient landings, Eichelberger found that his units often got bogged down in tough fights against determined Japanese, who chose to fight to the last man and who would not give up until Japan surrendered.[71]

Eichelberger's VICTOR operations were masterful actions which were very similar to General Imamura's operations in 1941 and 1942, when the *Sixteenth Army* moved into the Indies during the Japanese centrifugal offensive. (*See Atlas Map No. 10.*) One interesting difference was the American development of river boat operations in Mindanao, probably the only such actions in the Pacific war.[73]

Following the VICTOR operations, which opened the invasion route into the Netherlands East Indies via Borneo, MacArthur launched the OBOE operations, his last major effort of the war. (*See Atlas Map No. 35.*) These operations, conducted by Lieutenant General Leslie Morshead's Australian I Corps and supported by Allied air and naval forces, began in May 1945. For months, the Australian

Lieutenant General Robert L. Eichelberger in the Combat Zone

First Army, successor to New Guinea Force, had been battling the bypassed Japanese in the Solomons, on New Britain, and near Wewak.† While not pleased with their role as mop-up troops, the Australians were not completely enthusiastic about the new OBOE operations because they were trying to reduce their forces and were not at all convinced that the operations were necessary. Still, even though they knew that the war was nearly over—Germany surrendered on May 8, the United States Marines had captured Iwo Jima, and Admiral Nimitz' forces had the Okinawa situation well in hand—the Australians showed considerable dash and fortitude as they landed at Tarakan Island (May 1), Brunei Bay (June 10), and Balikpapen (July 1). They quickly took their objectives, all of which were important oil centers.[74]

---

*The contributions of the Filipino guerrillas to the success of all Allied campaigns in the Philippines, although not discussed in any detail in this text, cannot be overlooked. At the same time, those contributions should not be romanticized. It is impossible to measure in concrete terms how guerrilla units influenced the outcome of the campaigns. These units assisted American forces on each island, often sustaining heavy casualties; and their efforts saved many American lives. Given their limited armament, guerrilla units lacked staying power in a stiff fight, but most of them served to the limits of their capabilities. Some units were good; others were not. Those which pursued political goals or were led by men with delusions of grandeur, usually caused more trouble than 'they were worth.[72]

†The last time Australian forces had participated in a Southwest Pacific Area offensive operation was in April 1944, when they took Madang and Alexishaffen in New Guinea.

Operation	Planned Date	Description
OBOE I	April 23	Landing at Tarakan Island by a brigade group of 6th Division. Executed May 1.
OBOE II	May 18	Landing at Balikpapen by the 9th Division. Eventually the 7th Division conducted the action on June 10.
OBOE III	May 28	Landing at Bandjermasin by a brigade group of 9th Division. Cancelled.
OBOE IV	June 27	Main attack of I Corps against Suribaya, Java, occupation of Java, and seizure of Lombok Strait area. Cancelled.
OBOE V		Consolidation of the remainder of the Netherlands East Indies. Cancelled.
OBOE VI		Occupation of the remainder of Borneo. Became Brunei Bay operation, conducted by the 9th Division (−) beginning July 1.

Planned Operations of the Australian I Corps, 1945

As was his custom, MacArthur visited the Australians in Borneo, but by this time the general was little interested in these actions. He was awaiting and planning a bigger event—the invasion of Japan (DOWNFALL). For a while, however, the new General-of-the-Army would have to content himself with overseeing mop-up operations in the Philippines and points south, and with finishing the Borneo operations. Meanwhile, he planned operations OLYMPIC and CORONET* and assumed command of all United States Army forces in the Pacific.

The Philippine campaign was MacArthur's last major undertaking of World War II. His next major invasion would not occur until he surprised and then destroyed the North Korean Army by landing at Inchon during the Korean War. By that time, the general would be the modern *shogun* of Japan, and his trusted subordinates (Krueger, Kenney, Kinkaid, and Eichelberger), his admired comrade Halsey, and the reliable Nimitz would have retired. When MacArthur finally returned to the United States and civilian life in 1951 after 33 years of service† as a general officer, his reputation as a major commander would rest upon Bataan, Buna, the Admiralties, Hollandia, Leyte, and the Philippine campaign—all fitting precursors to Inchon, which capped the list.

*DOWNFALL was the code name for the general invasion of Japan. OLYMPIC (the invasion of Kyushu) and CORONET (the invasion of Honshu) were the names of specific operations. (*See Atlas Map No. 50.*)

†MacArthur had been promoted to brigadier general while a brigade commander in the 42nd (Rainbow) Division during World War I.

Notes

[1]Daniel E. Barbey, *MacArthur's Amphibious Navy, Seventh Amphibious Force Operations 1943-1945* (Annapolis, 1969), p. 183.

[2]This section is based primarily on: Saburo Hayashi (in collaboration with Alvin D. Coox), *Kogun, the Japanese Army in the Pacific War* (Quantico, 1959), pp. 76-78 and 102-105; *Reports of General MacArthur*, Volume II-Part I, *Japanese Operations in the Southwest Pacific Area* (Washington, 1967), compiled from Japanese Demobilization Bureaux Records, pp. 248-265; and Robert Ross Smith, *The Approach to the Philippines* (Washington, 1953), pp. 84-102.

[3]Hayashi and Coox, *Kogun*, pp. 76-78; and Smith, *Approach to the Philippines*, pp. 86-95.

[4]*Reports of MacArthur*, II-I, *Japanese Operations*, p. 255 (Plate 64).

[5]Japanese strategy is best discussed in *Reports of MacArthur*, II-I, *Japanese Operations*, pp. 250-261; and Smith, *Approach to the Philippines*, pp. 91-92 and 95-99.

[6]For information on the air raid on Hollandia see: George C. Kenney, *General Kenney Reports, A Personal History of the Pacific War* (New York, 1949), pp. 373-374 and 379-381; Wesley Frank Craven and James Lea Cate (eds.), *The Army Air Forces in World War II*, Volume IV, *The Pacific—Guadalcanal to Saipan, August 1942 to July 1944* (Chicago, 1950), pp. 591-596; and Smith, *Approach to the Philippines*, pp. 49-51.

[7]Masanori Ito with Roger Pineau, *The End of the Imperial Japanese Navy*, translated by Andrew Y. Kuroda and Roger Pineau, (Chicago, 1962), pp. 110-116; and Smith, *Approach to the Philippines*, pp. 90, 93-95.

[8]For the planned Japanese counteroffensive in 1944 see: Smith, *Approach to the Philippines*, p. 88; Louis Morton, *Strategy and Command, The First Two Years* (Washington, 1962), p. 659 (Paragraph II, Supplement to the "Japanese Army-Navy Central Agreement Concerning the Central and South Pacific Operations, 30 September 1943"); and *Reports of MacArthur*, II-I, *Japanese Operations*, pp. 250-251 (differs somewhat from the Central Agreement cited in Morton).

[9]*Reports of General MacArthur*, Volume I, *The Campaigns of MacArthur in the Pacific* (Washington, 1966), p. 142.

[10]This section is based primarily on: Smith, *Approach to the Philippines*, pp. 13-205. Other important sources are: *Reports of MacArthur*, I, *Campaigns of MacArthur*, pp. 142-148; *Reports of MacArthur*, II-I, *Japanese Operations*, pp. 250-276; Barbey, *MacArthur's Amphibious Navy*, pp. 158-184; Kenney, *Kenney Reports*, pp. 369-389; Walter Krueger, *From Down Under to Nippon, The Story of the Sixth Army in World War II* (Washington, 1953), pp. 56-78; Robert Eichelberger, *Our Jungle Road to Tokyo* (New York, 1950), pp. 100-112; Jay Luvaas (ed.), *Dear Miss Em, General Eichelberger's War in the Pacific, 1942-1945* (Westport, Connecticut, 1972), pp. 103-121; and Maurice Matloff, *Strategic Planning for Coalition Warfare, 1943-1944* (Washington, 1959), pp. 451-465.

[11]The strategic developments are covered best in Matloff, *Strategic Planning, 1943-1944*, pp. 43-44 and 451-465. See also Philip A. Crowl, *Campaign in the Marianas* (Washington, 1960), pp. 12-20; and Smith, *Approach to the Philippines*, pp. 1-12.

[12]For plans of Hollandia and Aitape see: Smith, *Approach to the Philippines*, pp. 13-52; *Reports of MacArthur*, I, *Campaigns of MacArthur*, pp. 142-145; Barbey, *MacArthur's Amphibious Navy*, pp. 158-167; Krueger, *Down Under to Nippon*, pp. 56-64; Craven and Cate, *Guadalcanal to Saipan*, p. 584; and Eichelberger, *Jungle Road*, pp. 100-105.

[13]Smith, *Approach to the Philippines*, pp. 35-40; and Barbey, *MacArthur's Amphibious Navy*, pp. 187-188 talk about shipping problems.

[14]For air operations see note 6.

[15]For Hollandia operations see: Smith, *Approach to the Philippines*, pp. 53-83; Krueger, *Down Under to Nippon*, pp. 63-69; and Eichelberger, *Jungle Road*, pp. 105-112. Casualty figures are from Smith, *Approach to the Philippines*, pp. 83 and 102.

[16]For Aitape operations see: Smith, *Approach to the Philippines*, pp. 102-205; *Reports of MacArthur*, I, *Campaigns of MacArthur*, pp. 145, 156-160; *Reports of MacArthur*, II-I, *Japanese Operations*, pp. 261-265 and 297-302; and Krueger, *Down Under to Nippon*, pp. 69-74.

[17]The impromptu strategic conference is reported in Barbey, *MacArthur's Amphibious Navy*, p. 173.

[18]This section is based upon: Krueger, *Down Under to Nippon*, pp. 79-132; *Reports of MacArthur*, I, *Campaigns of MacArthur*, pp. 149-165; Smith, *Approach to the Philippines*, pp. 206-231 (Wakde), 280-305 (Biak), 346-364 (*KON* Operation), 397-424 (Noemfoor), 425-449 (Vogelkop) and 450-479 (Morotai); Barbey, *MacArthur's Amphibious Navy*, pp. 185-228; and United States Strategic Bombing Survey (Pacific), *Campaigns of the Pacific War* (Washington, 1946), pp. 180-182.

[19]For Wakde-Sarmi see: Krueger, *Down Under to Nippon*, pp. 79-85 and 346-350; Smith, *Approach to the Philippines*, pp. 200-212.

[20]*Reports of MacArthur*, I, *Campaigns of MacArthur*, p. 150.

[21]For Biak see: Eichelberger, *Jungle Road*, pp. 135-154; Luvaas, *Dear Miss Em*, pp. 125-143; Smith, *Approach to the Philippines*, pp. 280-396; Krueger, *Down Under to Nippon*, pp. 93-105; *Reports of MacArthur*, II-I, *Japanese Operations*, pp. 283-297; and Harold Riegelman, *Caves of Biak, An American Officer's Experiences in the Southwest Pacific* (New York, 1955), pp. 135-155.

[22]For the *KON Operation* see: Smith, *Approach to the Philippines*, pp. 346-364; USSBS, *Campaigns of the Pacific*, p. 181; Samuel Eliot Morison, *New Guinea and the Marianas, March 1944-August 1944* (Boston, 1953), pp. 118-132, 168 and 220-221; and *Reports of MacArthur*, II-I, *Japanese Operations*, pp. 117-133, 287-292.

[23]*Reports of MacArthur*, I, *Campaigns of MacArthur*, pp. 149-150.

[24]For Noemfoor see: Smith, *Approach to the Philippines*, pp. 421-422 (atrocities and such); and Krueger, *Down Under to Nippon*, pp. 103-113.

[25]For the Vogelkop operations see: Krueger, *Down Under to Nippon*, pp. 114-121; Smith, *Approach to the Philippines*, pp. 425-428 (oil situation); and *Reports of MacArthur*, I, *Campaigns of MacArthur*, pp. 159-160.

[26]For Morotai operations see: Smith, *Approach to the Philippines*, pp. 450-456; *Reports of MacArthur*, I, *Campaigns of MacArthur*, pp. 174-178; and Krueger, *Down Under to Nippon*, pp. 122-132.

[27]Sutherland's acceptance of the Leyte invasion and MacArthur's

confirmation are found in: Samuel Eliot Morison, *Leyte, June 1944-January 1945* (Boston, 1958), pp. 12-18; and M. Hamlin Cannon, *Leyte, The Return to the Philippines* (Washington, 1954), pp. 8-9.

[28]For some information about these various units and individuals see: William F. Heavy, *Down Ramp! The Story of the Army Amphibian Engineers* (Washington, 1947); Allison Inc, *Allied Intelligence Bureau* (New York, 1958) (intelligence/espionage operations); Eric A. Feldt, *The Coastwatchers* (New York, 1946) (intelligence/espionage/guerrilla operations); Kenney, *Kenney Reports*, pp. 4-12, 362-365, 393-394 (Bong) and 315, 440-441, 495-498 (McGuire); Krueger, *Down Under to Nippon* pp. 29, 49, 108, and 117 (ALAMO Scouts); Morison *New Guinea and the Marianas*, pp. 15-24 (submarines); and *Reports of MacArthur*, I, *Campaigns of MacArthur*, p. 164 (PT Boats).

[29]Author's personal knowledge.

[30]This section on American planning for the Philippines is based upon: *Reports of MacArthur*, I, *Campaigns of MacArthur*, pp. 166-198; Wesley Frank Craven and James Lea Cate (eds), *The United Army Air Forces in World War II*, Volume V, *The Pacific-Matterhorn to Nagasaki, June 1944-August 1945* (Chicago, 1953), pp. 282-285; Matloff, *Strategic Planning, 1943-1944*, pp. 479-487; and Cannon, *Leyte*, pp. 1-9, and 21-39.

[31]Krueger, *Down Under to Nippon*, pp. 148-153 and Sixth United States Army *Report of the Leyte Operation, 17 October 1944-25 December 1944* (APO 201, 1945) pp. 17-25, 91-93 ("General Headquarters, Southwest Pacific Area, Operations Instructions Number 70, 21 September 1944") and 93-95 ("Field Order 25, Headquarters Sixth Army, 23 September 1944").

[32]For the warning of engineers see: Cannon, *Leyte*, pp. 35-36; and Stanley L. Falk, *Decision at Leyte* (New York, 1966), pp. 67-68. For restrictions on non-military targets see: *Reports of MacArthur*, I, *Campaigns of MacArthur*, pp. 191-192.

[33]Hayashi and Coox, *Kogun*, pp. 114-116 (Paraphrase).

[34]For Japanese planning of the SHO Operations see: Cannon, *Leyte*, pp. 85-102; Hayashi and Coox, *Kogun*, pp. 108-109, 113-118; Ito and Pineau, *End of the Imperial Japanese Navy*, pp. 110-120; *Reports of MacArthur*, II-I, *Japanese Operations*, pp. 304-342 and 353-363; Morison, *Leyte*, pp. 65-73; and Falk, *Decision at Leyte*, pp. 41-56.

[35]Hayashi and Coox, *Kogun*, pp. 84-85 and 117 briefly cover the problem of unified command in the Japanese forces in 1944. See also: Falk, *Decision at Leyte*, pp. 73-74; and Shigeru Fukudome, "The Battle off Formosa," in *The Japanese Navy in World War II* (Annapolis, 1969), p. 101.

[36]Hayashi and Coox, *Kogun*, p. 118; Ito and Pineau, *End of the Imperial Japanese Navy*, pp. 113-114 and 118-120; and *Reports of MacArthur*, II-I, *Japanese Operations*, p. 311.

[37]Falk, *Decision at Leyte*, pp. 51 and 70-71; and *Reports of MacArthur*, II-I, *Japanese Operations*, pp. 316-318.

[38]*Reports of MacArthur*, II-I, *Japanese Operations*, pp. 356-357; and Falk, *Leyte*, pp. 47-48 and 54-55.

[39]The original Japanese attack plan is quoted in part in *Reports of MacArthur*, II-I, *Japanese Operations*, p. 330 (See paragraphs 2a and 2b, "Outline of Operations, Combined Fleet Top Secret Operations Order No. 85, 8 August 1944"). Most discussions of the *SHO-I* plan give the final version which was not issued until October 18. See also Ito and Pineau, *End of the Japanese Navy*, p. 116.

[40]Falk, *Decision at Leyte*, pp. 51-52.

[41]This section is based on Falk, *Decision at Leyte*, pp. 91-93; Cannon, *Leyte*, pp. 54-102 and 361-370; USSBS, *Campaigns of the Pacific*, pp. 280-287 and 295-318; Ito and Pineau, *End of the Japanese Navy*, pp. 110-183; Hayashi and Coox, *Kogun*, pp. 120-129; Krueger, *Down Under to Nippon*, pp. 141-196; *Reports of MacArthur*, I, *Campaigns of MacArthur*, pp. 196-241; and *Reports of General MacArthur*, Volume II-Part II, *Japanese Operations in the Southwest Pacific Area* (Washington, 1967), Compiled from Japanese Demobilization Bureaux Records, pp. 365-433.

[42]For the Formosa Air Battle see: Fukudome, "Battle Off Formosa," pp. 100-105; Morison, *Leyte*, pp. 87-109; and Falk, *Decision at Leyte*, pp. 57-64.

[43]Krueger, *Down Under to Nippon*, pp. 156-163; *Reports of MacArthur*, I, *Campaigns of MacArthur*, pp. 196-241; and Samuel Eliot Morison, *The Two-Ocean War, A Short History of the United States Navy in the Second World War* (New York, 1972), pp. 366-370.

[44]The summary of the Battle for Leyte Gulf comes from: Tomihi Kyoanagi, "The Battle of Leyte Gulf," in *The Japanese Navy in World War II*, pp. 106-115; Rikihei Inoguchi and Tadashi Nakajima, "The Kamikaze Attack Corps," in *The Japanese Navy in World War II*, pp. 116-127; Morison, *Two-Ocean War*, pp. 370-398; Falk, *Decision at Leyte*, 125-251; and USSBS, *Campaigns of the Pacific*, pp. 283-286. Other sources include: Ito and Pineau, *End of the Japanese Navy*, p. 121; *Reports of MacArthur*, II-II, *Japanese Operations*, pp. 365-367 and 381-405; Hanson Baldwin, "The Greatest Sea Fight-Leyte Gulf," in *Battles Won and Lost, Great Campaigns of World War II* (New York, 1969), pp. 326-369 (narrative) and 587-607 (detailed footnotes—including remarks by Halsey and Kinkaid).

[45]The Japanese reinforcement program is discussed in: Cannon, *Leyte*, pp. 99-102; *Reports of MacArthur*, II-II, *Japanese Operations*, pp. 405-409, 435, and 438; Falk, *Decision at Leyte*, pp. 220-225; and USSBS, *Campaigns of the Pacific*, pp. 287 (figures).

[46]Krueger, *Down Under to Nippon*, pp. 168-188; and Sixth Army, *Report of the Leyte Campaign*, pp. 45-83.

[47]Krueger, *Down Under to Nippon*, p. 186; Hayashi and Coox, *Kogun*, p. 126; and *Reports of MacArthur*, II-II, *Japanese Operations*, pp. 432-433.

[48]Author's personal knowledge.

[49]The Luzon-Formosa argument is best covered by Robert Ross Smith, *Triumph in the Philippines* (Washington, 1963), pp. 3-17, or in his earlier work, which is virtually the same—Robert Ross Smith, "Luzon Versus Formosa," in Kent Roberts Greenfield (ed.), *Command Decisions*, (Washington, 1960), pp. 461-477.

[50]This section is based primarily on Krueger, *Down Under to Nippon*, pp. 199-200 and 211-213; *Reports of MacArthur*, I, *Campaigns of MacArthur*, pp. 242-325; Smith, *Triumph in the Philippines*, pp. 18-103, 212-248, 306-313, 340-358, 361-366, 418-422, 572-579, and 651-658; and Morison, *Two-Ocean War*, pp. 402-410.

[51]For Mindoro planning and operations see: Krueger, *Down Under to Nippon*, pp. 199-207; Morison, *Two-Ocean War*, pp. 402-404; Barbey, *MacArthur's Amphibious Navy*, pp. 284-288; and Smith, *Triumph in the Philippines*, pp. 43-54.

[52]*Reports of MacArthur*, I, *Campaigns of MacArthur*, p. 251; *Reports of MacArthur*, II-II, *Japanese Operations*, pp. 445-446;

and Hayashi and Coox, *Kogun*, p. 128.

[53]*Reports of MacArthur*, II-II, *Japanese Operations*, p. 451 (from Paragraph 1, "Operational Policy Outline for Luzon, 19 December 1944," which is quoted in some detail).

[54]Yamashita's ideas about Bataan are found in Smith, *Triumph in the Philippines*, pp. 94 and 311.

[55]Smith, *Triumph in the Philippines*, pp. 92, 97, and 240-244.

[56]Smith, *Triumph in the Philippines*, pp. 92 and 94-97; and *Reports of Macarthur*, II-II, *Japanese Operations*, p. 464 (Plate 110).

[57]MacArthur's plans are discussed in detail in Smith, *Triumph in the Philippines*, pp. 32-38. See also *Reports of MacArthur*, I, *Campaigns of MacArthur*, pp. 242-256. For MacArthur's order see: Sixth United States Army, *Report of the Luzon Campaign, 9 January 1945-30 June 1945* (APO 201, 1945) Volume I, pp. 109-111 ("General Headquarters, Southwest Pacific Area, Operations Instruction Number 73, 12 October 1944").

[58]Krueger, *Down Under to Nippon*, pp. 211-213 and 218-219. See also Sixth Army, *Report of the Luzon Campaign*, Volume I, pp. 117-120 ("Field Order Number 34, Sixth Army, 20 November 1944").

[59]Morison, *Two-Ocean War*, pp. 404-410; Smith, *Triumph in the Philippines*, pp. 60-67; and *Reports of MacArthur*, I, *Campaigns of MacArthur*, pp. 256-259 discuss the *kamikaze* attacks. Barbey, *MacArthur's Amphibious Navy*, pp. 287-288, discusses the psychological impact of the attacks on the crews.

[60]For the initial actions ashore see Krueger, *Down Under to Nippon*, pp. 223-234.

[61]John H. Bradley, "From the Dark Side of the Moon: Raiding by Ground Forces in the Southwest Pacific During the Second World War," (unpublished MA Thesis, Rice University, 1970), pp. 186-221, covers the Cabanatuan raid.

[62]Krueger, *Down Under to Nippon*, pp. 235-245, and *Report of the Commanding General, Eighth Army, on the Nasugbu and Bataan Operations, MIKE SIX and MIKE SEVEN* (n.p., 1945), Foreword, pp. 8-10, and 75.

[63]B.C. Wright, *The 1st Cavalry Division in World War II* (Tokyo, 1945), p. 126.

[64]Smith, *Triumph in the Philippines*, pp. 211-236; Krueger, *Down Under to Nippon*, pp. 239-245; and Eichelberger, *Jungle Road*, pp. 181-199.

[65]Wright, *1st Cavalry Division*, pp. 125-134, and author's personal knowledge.

[66]For a complete view of Griswold's corps operations see: *After Action Report, XIV Corps, M-1 Operations* (APO 453, 1945).

[67]For Bataan and the clearance of Manila Bay see: Smith, *Triumph in the Philippines*, pp. 309-357 and 361-366; and *The 38th Infantry Division, "Avengers of Bataan,"* (n.p., n.d.), pp. 5-32.

[68]Bradley, "Dark Side of the Moon," pp. 221-245, covers the Los Baños raid.

[69]Smith, *Triumph in the Philippines*, pp. 361-579. Casualty figures are found on pp. 692-694. For the survey of the last actions on Luzon see Krueger, *Down Under to Nippon*, pp. 253-320; and *Reports of MacArthur*, I, *Campaigns of MacArthur*, pp. 280-294.

[70]Louis Morton, "The Decision to Withdraw to Bataan," *Command Decisions*, pp. 169-172. In the pages cited, Robert Ross Smith, not Morton, raises the question of who did the better job on Luzon—MacArthur in 1941-1942 or Yamashita in 1945.

[71]Eichelberger, *Jungle Road*, pp. 200-232; Luvaas, *Dear Miss Em*, pp. 222-276; Barbey, *MacArthur's Amphibious Navy*, pp. 304-320; and *Reports of MacArthur*, I, *Campaigns of MacArthur*, pp. 327-362, summarize the Visayan and Mindanao campaigns. Also useful are the several reports of Eichelberger on the actions.

[72]For a straightforward account of Filipino guerrilla activities under Sixth Army in northern Luzon, see Krueger, *Down Under to Nippon*, pp. 300-318. Also of value is Russell Volckmann, *We Remained, Three Years Behind Enemy Lines in the Philippines* (New York, 1954), pp. 193-220; and Smith, *Triumph in the Philippines*, p. 657-658. More elaborate tributes to the guerrillas are found in *Reports of MacArthur*, I, *Campaigns of MacArthur*, pp. 295-325.

[73]Smith, *Triumph in the Philippines*, pp. 625-626, briefly covers operations on the Mindanao River.

[74]For Australian planning, opinion, and attitudes toward Borneo see Gavin Long, *The Final Campaigns* (Canberra, 1963), pp. 31-54, 48-49, and 388-389. For Australian irritation at mopping-up operations see pp. 608-616—"General Blamey's Appreciation of May 1945." For a brief summary of the actual operations see *Reports of MacArthur*, I, *Campaigns of MacArthur* I, pp. 371-383.

China-Burma- 9
India: The War
for East Asia

The nation which indulges toward another an habitual hatred or an habitual fondness is in some degree a slave. It is a slave to its animosity or to its affection, either of which is sufficient to lead it away from its duty and its interests.

George Washington's Farewell Address

After World War I the United States was strongly isolationist. Its leaders remembered George Washington's caveat regarding entry into entangling alliances, and supported it as one of the foundations of American foreign policy. But another precept was that the purpose of foreign policy was the defense of moral principle, even in distant lands, rather than self-defense of one's national interest. In extension, the United States felt a strong moral commitment to China. We made ourselves mentor and protector of that country. Our missionaries went to China to enlighten the Chinese and show them how to build for themselves a democratic society such as we enjoyed. We looked upon the Chinese as our wards; we cherished Chiang Kai-shek, the leader of the Chinese and a convert to Christianity, as one of us; and we were also swayed by the eloquence and charm of his wife, an Americanized graduate of Wellesley College. This ingenuous attachment that we felt to the China represented by Chiang and Madame Chiang was to have a profound effect on American foreign policy in Asia from the 1930s to the present.[1]

The Closing of the Door

The Republic of China had grown in the late 1920s and early 1930s and appeared to be coalescing into a unified state. The economy had progressed, and peace and stability gradually spread as the Nationalist Government, controlled by the Kuomintang Party under Generalissimo Chiang Kai-shek, slowly brought the war lords to heel and attracted more Chinese to its banner. Although Japan had taken over Manchuria in 1931, Chiang focused his attention on unifying that part of China under his control. (*See Atlas Map No. 36.*) By 1937, the Chinese Communists were the only major dissidents. Possessing their own small army, they were compressed into the far northwest section of China. Generalissimo Chiang was stoutly opposed to them, whittling away their territory by numerous expeditions. Left alone, he might eventually have defeated Mao Tse-tung's Communists.[2]

But Japanese imperialists, as well as Chinese Communists, posed a problem for Chiang. As the resources of the Nationalist Government did not allow him to deal with both simultaneously, the Generalissimo had attempted to crush the Communists, while opposing Japan by diplomacy alone. Chinese public opinion, however, was outraged by the Japanese, and in December 1936 a group of Chinese had kidnapped the Generalissimo. They then insisted that he lead both Nationalists and Communists in a United Front which would oppose the Japanese. Chiang had won his freedom by agreeing. The next Japanese provocation meant large-scale hostilities.[3]

To consolidate its control of China and to resist Japanese territorial encroachments in China, the Nationalist Government had attempted to build a modern army. For military assistance and hardware, the Kuomintang turned to Germany, Italy, and Russia —not to the United States, whose Army in the 1930s was unimpressive. By 1937, the German Military Mission had brought about 30 divisions, all loyal to the Generalissimo, to a level of efficiency never before realized in China.[4]

By western standards, the better Chinese divisions,

including the German-trained divisions, were mediocre. All together, these divisions numbered about 40; but they were understrength, lacked heavy equipment, and were widely dispersed. The remaining several hundred "divisions" were poorly armed and trained bands loyal only to their local commanders. The greatest asset of the Chinese Army was the toughness and bravery of the peasant soldier. Its greatest liability was the inability of the war-lord commanders to see their soldiers as anything more than pawns in the unending political struggles. Quite clearly, since China had not yet emerged from the feudal era, the tapping of her vast national resources for a unified effort would be a monumental task.[5]

In terms of formal structure and by his 1936 agreement, Chiang Kai-shek commanded the coalition army—the Generalissimo's 30 divisions, Chinese Communist divisions, and the war lords' "divisions." He maintained control through political appointees who had been placed in positions of consequence. Loyalty to the Generalissimo, rather than battlefield success, was the *sine qua non* of a brilliant military career. The Chinese Army was deployed over 12 war areas corresponding to provincial boundaries. In the rear of each war area were a few of the Generalissimo's loyal divisions to insure the fealty of the war-area commanders. The war-area commander's divisions were his property; this property—a military and political asset— was not expendable, for replacements would not be forthcoming. This decentralized system had two major drawbacks: the dispersion of better troops precluded concentrating forces at decisive points, and 12 war-area commanders with both military and political power resulted in the creation of semi-autonomous satraps. The latter drawback put a premium on the Generalissimo's political ability to keep the war-area commanders loyal.[6]

The China stalemate exploded in July 1937, when the Japanese Kwangtung Army escalated the East Asian War by staging an incident at the Marco Polo Bridge. That incident ultimately led to the capture of Peking and an expedition to Shanghai and the Chinese capital of Nanking. (*See Atlas Map No. 37.*) Chiang's German-trained divisions, supported by the war lord's militia, fought bravely but ineffectively. While battering most of Chiang's best divisions, however, the Japanese failed to destroy his government.* The fighting was watched and studied by Colonel Joseph

W. Stilwell, the U.S. Military Attaché to China from 1935 to 1939.[7]

As Chinese forces fell back into the interior and the Chinese Government retreated to Chungking on the upper Yangtze, the Chinese and sympathetic observers released accounts to the western world, claiming that the Chinese had lost because they lacked modern weapons. Neither the German Military Mission nor Stilwell agreed with the press releases. According to their reports, the Chinese committed basic military errors: neglect of fundamental principles of strategy and tactics, indifference to intelligence, poor command and staff procedures, and failure to maintain the equipment they had.[8]

Exploiting China's weakness, imperialistic Japan became increasingly involved in ever expanding military operations in China. In an attempt to resolve the "China Incident," however, Japan was unwittingly drawing the United States into the war for East Asia—and away from her traditional isolationism. A brief collision between the United States and Japan—the sinking of the U.S. gunboat *Panay* and three Standard Oil tankers on the Yangtze River on December 12, 1937—added fuel to America's sense of moral outrage. This incident had a profound impact on President Roosevelt, who began to convert moral opposition to material opposition. He sought a way to aid China. As a first step, the President publicized Japanese atrocities in the U.S. press, causing a shift in public sentiment toward the support of China. This was followed by limited financial aid to the Nationalist Government.[9]

By 1939, unable to obtain a quick victory in China in two years, Japan had initiated a strategy of strangulation, employing minimum forces to control the seaports and overland routes into China and mounting occasional "rice offensives" to gather food for her army. (*See Atlas Map No. 38.*) Since the overland routes through Indochina, Burma, and Russia still remained open, the Generalissimo sought foreign aid before the Japanese blockade was complete. As war in Europe after September 1939 made it unlikely that European powers friendly to China could provide assistance, the Chinese Government approached the United States, which was sympathetic, but was not prepared to intervene in the Sino-Japanese conflict. In appraising the possibility of war with Japan, however, American planners recognized the advantage of having

---

*The best Chinese division was no match for its Japanese counterpart. Both were organized on the triangular concept (three regiments in a division; three battalions in a regiment; three companies in a battalion); but the similarities ended there. The Japanese division had an authorized strength of 15,000 as compared to 10,000 for the Chinese division. Moreover, a Chinese division was seldom up to strength, normally averaging 6,000 to 7,000; during a campaign these figures dwindled, as the Chinese had no replacement system. Although both Japanese and Chinese

divisions were authorized all the arms and services needed to make them self-sufficient combat teams, the Japanese received their authorizations while the Chinese did not. For example, the Chinese division had only a rudimentary supply system, none of the authorized artillery, and was woefully understrength in heavy weapons. Many other factors, such as competent leadership and troop motivation, tended to increase further the disparity in combat power between a Japanese and a Chinese division. At best, one Japanese division might roughly equal three Chinese divisions.

China's manpower and geographic position in friendly hands. The U.S. response was to continue financial loans. [10]

In September 1940, Japan became a member of the Axis and forced the Vichy Government into granting her the right to occupy northern Indochina. This left the Burma Road as China's only remaining transportation link to the western powers. Russia's preoccupation in the West and ideological affinity with the Chinese Communists had dried up the Russian link. Anxious lest the Japanese cut the Burma Road, in October 1940, the Generalissimo again asked the United States for economic aid: $30 million worth of ground force material (enough to equip 30 divisions), and 500 U.S. aircraft to be manned by American volunteers. Extension of a $100 million credit on December 1, 1940 became the first step toward providing military aid for China. Of this sum, $25 million could be used to purchase arms. As this amount was insufficient to finance the air program and equip 30 divisions, the Chinese chose to build up their air strength. [11]

The passage of the Lend-Lease Act on March 31, 1941 placed the United States in a better position to support China. All Chinese requests were considered in the light of the availability of material and of the already formulated policy of assisting the primary Allied effort against Germany while containing Japanese expansion. Scattered through these Chinese requests were indications of the strategy behind them, which suggested that airpower would protect China's airfields and cities and their approaches. With these secure, the Chinese Army could be revitalized and ultimately assume the offensive. The Chinese lend-lease program, which the U.S. finally sponsored, provided for equipping 30 Chinese divisions, establishing a 500-plane air force, and maintaining a line of communications to China. [12]

The most immediate help came from the "Flying Tigers," or the American Volunteer Group (AVG). As an air program was emerging from the Chinese 500-plane proposal by the early spring of 1941, the United States agreed to supply, maintain, and operate the American Volunteer Group requested by Chiang in October 1940. Colonel Claire Chennault, an American citizen who had become a colonel in the Chinese Air Force after his retirement from the U.S. Army Air Corps in 1937, was commander of the AVG. By the summer of 1941, 101 American pilots arrived in China under a one-year contract; one hundred P-40s were obtained from the British. The AVG was part of the Chinese Air Force, and until the United States entered the war, it had no official connection with the U.S. Army Air Force. (On March 4, 1942, Chennault agreed to serve under Stilwell and further consented to the induction of the AVG into American service. The AVG fought in the First Burma campaign, and in July 1942 became the China Air Task Force under Chennault's command.) [13]

The concept of giving China lend-lease aid was approved because, at this time in Washington, there existed both a myth and a hope about China. An ardent Sinophile faction asserted that the Chinese were courageously and completely resisting the Japanese and needed only weapons to drive the Japanese into the sea. The armed services were too well informed to share that belief, but they hoped that a revitalized and reformed Chinese Army might cause the Japanese enough concern to bar further expansion southward. As the myth and the hope converged, lend-lease aid to China gathered support in high places. [14]

Past experience with China suggested to members of the War, Treasury, and State Departments that a U.S. military mission should be sent to China to advise and assist the Chinese in procuring and using lend-lease materiel. Significantly, this mission (American Military Mission to China —AMMISCA), which was headed by Brigadier General John Magruder, was not authorized to conduct staff talks with the Chinese on Sino-American cooperation in the event that America was drawn into the Asian and Pacific wars. Such talks would have helped fill a gap in prewar planning. AMMISCA, concerning itself with effective application of lend-lease aid, reported that the Chinese Army was not actively engaged with the Japanese. Both the myth and the hope were disputed by reality. In fairness to Chiang, however, it must be recognized that the force the Japanese had in China was superior to his own force. A comparison of the relative strengths of the antagonists seems to have dictated that the Chinese employ a Fabian strategy. [15]

But the Japanese comprised only one of Chiang's many problems. An equally dangerous enemy was the Chinese Red Army. Chiang had been on the verge of destroying the Communist forces of Mao Tse-tung and Chu Teh in the fall of 1936. Planning a final extermination campaign in early 1937 to destroy his only remaining adversary, he had had to defer these plans when forced into creating a United Front with the Communists. Although the sincerity on both sides may be doubted, the Communists initially kept their side of the bargain by gaining a propaganda victory over the Japanese at Ping–Sing Pass in September 1937. (*See Atlas Map No. 36.*) This engagement, however, ended the Communists' contribution to the United Front. Chiang soon learned that Mao and his Communists in Yenan were deliberately conserving their strength and holding back a good part of the force that might have been directed against the Japanese in order to prepare for the eventual clash with the Nationalists. Mao's principal activity seemed to be the assiduous spreading of the seeds of Communism. In order to counter this Communist policy, the Generalissimo began committing Nationalist forces to blockade Mao's base in Shensi in late 1939. Eventually, some 150,000 to 200,000 of Chiang's most reliable troops were diverted to his other war—the Civil War.[16]

Meanwhile, Japanese aspirations inexorably soared. In April 1941, Japan signed a Neutrality Pact with Russia. Prior to this treaty, only two powers confronted the island empire in China—the Soviet Union and the United States. Now Japan's traditional enemy was diplomatically eliminated, leaving only one non-Asian obstacle to Japan's goal. Moreover, the beginning of the Russo-German War two months later reinforced treaty terms and effectively foreclosed any threat of Russian intervention. Although the Japanese Foreign Minister proposed attacking Russia, War Minister Hideki Tojo felt that there was no point in helping Germany, and that Japan should turn south to take advantage of this new Allied crisis. Accordingly, on July 24, with a view toward influencing Thailand and completing the blockade of China, Japan occupied southern Indochina, precipitating the crisis that led to Pearl Harbor. Among American demands was an insistence that Japan withdraw from all her recently acquired Chinese territory except Manchukuo; among Japanese demands was one that called for an end to American aid to China.[17]

One can find numerous reasons for the Japanese-American clash, but no reason is more important than American aid to China. The United States sought a proxy to contest Japan, and Chiang served that purpose. But the Generalissimo also sought a surrogate. Wanting someone to fight the Japanese for him, he actively sought assistance, especially American-sponsored airpower. Unfortunately, the proud and frustrated Japanese military leadership also sought a surrogate. They needed both an explanation for 100,000 dead and a reason for their failure to subdue an "inferior" China. Their surrogate, their reason for failure in China, their barrier to success, became the "Arsenal of Democracy," the United States.[18]

When the Japanese attacked Pearl Harbor, China, Great Britain, the Netherlands, and the United States found themselves allies. Cooperation was essential if their joint effort were to be effective. The United States had engaged in strategic planning with the British and Dutch, but other than a commitment to equip a modern Chinese Army and Air Force, no arrangements for a unified effort had been made with the Chinese. Logic indicated the necessity of a satisfactory working relationship with China and an understanding of what the Chinese would do with their lend-lease supplies. For her part, China was interested in playing the role of a great power beside her new allies.[19]

The ARCADIA Conference in December 1941 addressed

the problem of the Asian war. Applying the principle of unified command, the Allies created ABDACOM (American-British-Dutch-Australian Command) to direct operations in southeast Asia. The arrangement, however, did not include China within the scheme of unified command, because it was agreed that the Chinese would never consent to any portion of their country being placed under foreign control. (*See Atlas Map No. 39.*) Therefore, the Combined Chiefs of Staff (CCS) suggested establishing a China Theater under the Generalissimo, who, as Supreme Commander, China Theater, would not be subordinate to the Chiefs, an Anglo-American staff. Though an Allied commander, the Generalissimo was responsible only to himself, making him unique among those who held similar posts. Moreover, as Chiang was not responsible to the CCS, he could not be expected to endorse the Germany-first strategy. As for the remainder of the Asian continent, India and Burma fell within the British area of strategic direction; both were placed, after ABDACOM's dissolution, under General Headquarters, India.[20]

The Chinese asked Roosevelt to send a high-ranking American officer to be chief of the Generalissimo's joint (or Allied) staff. The President was anxious to honor this request in order to reassure the Chinese. Moreover, General Marshall believed that if the Chinese were properly led, trained, and equipped, they would be the equal of soldiers anywhere. If they actively and effectively opposed the Japanese, this would enhance the strategic defensive in Asia until Germany was subdued. Marshall's first choice was Lieutenant General Hugh A. Drum, but Drum showed no enthusiasm for the job, partly because he had expected the European command, and partly because he had not been told that Chiang would take an American as his Chief of Staff for China Theater. Consequently, Lieutenant General Joseph W. Stilwell was selected for the job.[21]

Marshall and Stilwell had served together at the Infantry School and in China. The Chief of Staff had a high regard for Stilwell's skill as a tactician and a trainer of troops, and his star had risen with Marshall's. Born in 1883, Stilwell was no longer young, but he was energetic and tireless. As military attaché in China he had examined the mechanism of the Chinese Army, and had also studied the Sino-Japanese campaign of 1937 and 1938. Marshall knew that Stilwell was no diplomat, but the mission that Stilwell was offered demanded a great many other qualities. The situation in Burma appeared grim in early 1942. The Japanese seemed unstoppable, and the British and Chinese were at odds. Therefore a skilled field commander from a third ally might be acceptable to both countries as a solution to the command problem. Additionally, Marshall was interested in a reform of the Chinese Army. Stilwell met the necessary criteria. He was a gifted field commander and trainer of troops, with the added qualification of being thoroughly acquainted with China and the Chinese military establishment.[22] Stilwell's personal assessment was from a different perspective. The Chinese "remember me," he noted, "as a small-fry colonel that they kicked around."[23] If Stilwell's prestige and personal influence were to become a factor, his mission would be difficult. The suitability of Stilwell's appointment may well be debated.

When Stilwell met Roosevelt for an interview prior to his departure, he wrote in his diary, "Events are forcing all concerned to see the vital importance of Burma. We must get the airline [over the Hump] going at once, and also build both the back-country roads [the Ledo and Imphal Roads]."[24] The loss of Malaya in February opened the Indian Ocean and Bay of Bengal to Japanese exploitation, and the Japanese drive across the Tenasserim area threatened Rangoon. Once Rangoon fell, the last land link to China was gone. To exacerbate matters, all Chinese ports were controlled by the Japanese. If China were to be kept in the war, an air line of communications over the Himalayas (The Hump) had to be opened, and a new land route across northern Burma had to be hacked through the jungles and mountains. (*See Atlas Map No. 40.*) An American force would be required. Initially, Stilwell had an air task force, the nucleus of the Tenth Air Force, and a logistical element (Services of Supply in China, Burma, India [CBI]).[25]

The War Department ordered Stilwell to increase the effectiveness of U.S. aid to China and to assist in improving the combat efficiency of the Chinese Army. Despairing of reform in the Chinese Army, Magruder had supported lend-lease aid for primarily political reasons: it would keep the Generalissimo in power, it would prevent the end of China's passive resistance, and it would hold open the possibility of using Chinese bases to bomb Japan. As far as their Army was concerned, the Chinese apparently intended no offensive action which would dissipate the political value of their troops. Consequently, both the desire and the ability to reform the Army were minimal. China's pet strategic antidote was airpower.[26]

With the departure of Stilwell and his staff for Chungking in February 1942, the United States took another major step toward aiding China. The beginning of a plan to resolve the difficulty inherent in Sino-American cooperation had been devised, although the problems involved were yet to be completely known, let alone solved. Reports from China had revealed the major problem: how could the Chinese be induced to pull their weight in the global struggle? Stilwell's task would be difficult and would require the full support of the U.S. Government if he were to succeed.[27]

Upon his arrival in China, Stilwell began building what

was to become his theater headquarters. For this task he initially used personnel from AMMISCA and personnel newly arriving in the CBI. In order to perform his mission, Stilwell was given four posts: Joint Chief of Staff to the Supreme Commander, China Theater; Commanding General of U.S. forces in CBI; U.S. representative on an Allied military council in Chungking; and representative of the President for lend-lease affairs. Building a new organization was only part of Stilwell's task; of greater importance was the resolution of command relationships and responsibilities. (*See Appendix 31.*)

China's share in the First Burma campaign pointed out some of Stilwell's command problems. As Burma lay on the border between the Middle Eastern and Pacific spheres of responsibility, any Allied operation in Burma would be based on two separate areas of strategic direction. Because Chiang was accountable to no one, and was thus a free agent to order Stilwell and General Ho Ying-chin (Chief of Staff of the Chinese Army) accordingly, the Generalissimo was beyond control of the CCS whose task it was to reconcile national differences. Thus, Stilwell was torn between two loyalties if the interests of the CCS and China diverged; and when the United States and China disagreed, Stilwell was automatically placed in a dilemma. This predicament not only complicated military operations, but promised to make the second part of Stilwell's mission—the reform of the Chinese Army—most difficult.[28]

When Stilwell arrived in China, the Generalissimo sent him to Burma to command the Chinese forces there. His efforts were rendered futile by the lack of coordination in the Chinese effort. This period, however, was beneficial in that it gave him a glimpse of the local scene. As the Japanese juggernaut rolled through Burma, Stilwell developed his plans for the future. (*See Map 11 and Chapter 4 for details of the campaign.*) Since Japanese occupation of Burma would isolate China from lend-lease stores accumulating in India, Stilwell proposed moving 100,000 Chinese soldiers to India to equip them with lend-lease materiel and train them into an effective combat force from which an improved Chinese Army could grow. The Generalissimo agreed to the plan "in general." In May 1942, as the British troops withdrew through the Chin Hills to Imphal, Stilwell led a party out farther north through Homalin; most of the Chinese Fifth Army retreated through the Hukawng Valley to Ledo while the Sixty-Sixth Army retired into China.[29]

At the end of May 1942, the Japanese held most of Burma. They had completely isolated China by land, and were in a position to isolate her by air. From Burma they could launch attacks into China or India as they chose: they could bomb Calcutta and other Bengali cities, the focal point of the Indian war effort against Japan; or they could attack into western China. The one bright spot was Stilwell's safe arrival on Indian soil on May 15. American legend now had a new figure: "Vinegar Joe" Stilwell, the sharp-tongued, indomitable, gruff-voiced, kind-hearted old soldier who could survive any jungle. Stilwell offered no excuses, painted no soothing picture of a brilliant withdrawal, and acidly articulated his oft-quoted "hell of a beating" epigram.[30]

False Starts

After walking out of Burma, Stilwell's difficult mission began. As the Chinese did not give him a staff, Stilwell set to work with an interpreter and a stenographer. As Chief of Staff, China Theater, he proposed to build an elite Chinese force, equipped by lend-lease, to retake all Burma and reopen communications with China. Once this had been done and an effective Chinese Army had been created, a powerful air offensive could be launched against the Japanese homeland. Chiang had tentatively agreed to the elite Chinese force, and Stilwell asked the War Department to send him one or more U.S. divisions for use in Allied operations to retake Burma. Marshall replied that U.S. troops were not available; but, recognizing the need to reopen the Burma Road, the Chief of Staff concurred in this portion of the operation. Because India and Burma were under British strategic direction, reopening the Burma Road, Marshall stated, would have to be primarily a British effort. At this time, Great Britain was facing a crisis in North Africa. Moreover, in southeast Asia, Churchill was more interested in Singapore than in Burma and China, which he thought was not a world power on the same level as Great Britain, the United States, or Russia. Global priorities and differences between the Allies were working against Stilwell's efforts in the CBI.[31]

To the Generalissimo, Stilwell recommended reform of the Chinese Army as the priority task. In a lengthy report to Chiang, he enumerated the Army's weaknesses: dispersion of available equipment among the 300-odd divisions, lack of competent leadership at the higher echelons, logistical deficiencies, and an ambiguous system of command. In conclusion, he recommended that 30 divisions be brought up to strength, purged of the inefficient, and placed under a single commander. Madame Chiang, noting that this was what the German advisers had told the Generalissimo, made counterassertions: first, lend-lease equipment had to be brought in; then attention could be directed to training troops. As Barbara Tuckman observes, Stilwell was learning

Generalissimo and Madame Chiang Kai-shek With Lieutenant General Stilwell in the Spring of 1942

that "the Chinese from necessity had made manipulation of the strong by the weak into a fine art . . . Chiang played every strategem and every maneuver."[32] Prospects of reforming the Chinese Army dimmed as Chiang chose to evade Stilwell's proposals.[33]

Sino-American difficulties had been brewing for months, largely because of three important matters which were vexing the Chinese. First, Chiang was offended by the rejection of his bid for membership in the CCS. Also, the Chinese had been led to expect more lend-lease aid than they could receive. Finally, several aviation projects for China were slow in materializing. Denial of CCS membership was a major irritant, for that body controlled lend-lease allocation. Further complicating the matter of aid was the fact that the quantity of lend-lease aid sent to China was dependent upon the amount of tonnage which could be flown over the Hump; although the United States had promised 3,500 tons a month, the monthly average through July 1942 was below 100 tons. To the Generalissimo, it appeared that the United States was not honoring its part of the agreement with China. Since it was diplomatically inadvisable to blame Stilwell's superiors, Chinese disappointments, predictably, were charged to Stilwell as though he were a free agent.[34]

Then, in June 1942, an incident occurred which triggered the long personal struggle between Chiang and Stilwell. The crisis in North Africa led President Roosevelt to withdraw aircraft from the Tenth Air Force, which was tasked with supporting Stilwell and Chiang. The aircraft were needed to bolster the British, who were desperately striving to stop Rommel's drive on Alexandria. The diversion of the Tenth Air Force to Egypt was merely another in a long series of irritations and disappointments, but it boomeranged on Stilwell, who found himself suddenly confronted with a Chinese ultimatum—the famous Three Demands. Frustrated, Chiang demanded three U.S. divisions for Burma, a 500-plane air force in China, and 5,000 tons a month flown over the Hump. If these demands were not met, he threatened to negotiate a separate peace with Japan. Clearly, global priorities precluded satisfaction of the Three Demands; all the resources America could spare were going to the embattled British at Cairo and the Russians at Stalingrad. Three U.S. divisions were not available, plane production lagged behind commitments, and the Hump route had all the C-47 transport aircraft the United States could provide. Although a cool reaction in Washington caused Chiang to back off, the frustrated Chinese leader placed the blame on Stilwell. Irreparable damage had been done to Stilwell's relations with the Generalissimo.[35]

While the diplomatic crisis was being resolved, Stilwell tried to get on with his mission. He developed a joint American, British, and Chinese plan to retake all of Burma (Operation ANAKIM) and reopen the major land route through Rangoon and along the Burma Road for substantial quantities of U.S. aid. In order to accomplish his mission of reforming the Chinese Army, however, Stilwell still needed leverage. He asked that U.S. aid be committed only in return for positive Chinese action. The President vetoed this request. Stilwell warned that China would coast, letting others fight the war; China wanted to finish the war with her arsenals stocked and her armies well-equipped—by implication, to resolve internal problems during the postwar period. Although Stilwell's analysis was not far from the truth, Roosevelt would not relent.[36]

Turning his attention to planning the air war in the China Theater, Stilwell developed an air war plan in September 1942. Chennault's China Air Task Force (CATF), which Stilwell commanded through the Tenth Air Force, was charged with protecting the Hump route, the Chinese Air Force, Chungking, and the Yangtze Valley. Chennault favored a more aggressive approach, although the amount of tonnage coming over the Hump was insufficient for such operations. At this time, Stilwell recognized that the Chinese wanted CATF —the Generalissimo's surrogate—strengthened to a point where it could alone fight and defeat the Japanese. Chinese desires matched Chennault's ambitions, and it was clear that Chennault and Stilwell were on the verge of becoming rivals. Such an approach, however, would consume all

Hump tonnage, pre-empting Stilwell's plans for revitalizing 30 Chinese divisions. Thus, while Stilwell focused on a land line of communications and army reform, Chennault, who had won Chiang's confidence as leader of the AVG, was developing his proposals for the defeat of Japan with a small air force.[37]

Continuing his planning aimed at seizing the initiative, Stilwell next proceeded to create a U.S. theater of operations in CBI. On July 2, 1942, the Generalissimo had given Stilwell command of the Chinese forces in India, and his command now included these forces, formed into two divisions (X-force), as well as a growing Tenth Air Force and Services of Supply (SOS). (*See Appendix 32.*) The magnitude of Stilwell's task, the increasing size of his command, and the geographic extent of his area of operations inevitably required expansion of Stilwell's organization— originally a task force—into a theater of operations. The unreliable nature of communications and transport and the fact that the two major portions of Stilwell's theater were under two different supreme commanders, Chiang and General Archibald Wavell (British Commander-in-Chief, India), however, forced a considerable amount of decentralization. Consequently, Stilwell established his principal headquarters in Chungking and a branch office in New Delhi, the site of the British headquarters in India.[38]

While the Tenth Air Force spend most of 1942 building up its forces and deploying toward Burma, the SOS was completely committed. The latter organization not only supported the U.S forces in CBI and X-force but also handled Chinese lend-lease. Numerous logistical problems complicated the task of SOS: a world-wide Allied shipping shortage; a four-month round-trip voyage from U.S. ports; overcrowded or threatened Indian ports, which forced SOS to use Karachi until late 1942 when operations were shifted to Calcutta; and an inadequate transportation net in India. (*See Atlas Map No. 40.*) Concerning lend-lease aid, however, SOS was merely an administrative agent. Stilwell, nevertheless, did control one aspect of this system in that he set priorities for dispatch of cargo by U.S. aircraft. To Stilwell, this meant that Chinese Army reform, beginning with the revitalization of 30 Chinese divisions, took priority over Chennault's requirements.[39]

Meanwhile, the Chinese divisions which had escaped from Burma to India, designated X-ray force or X-force, were being brought back to strength and trained at Ramgarh in Bihar Province. In providing training to individual officers and men, American personnel found that great ingenuity was needed to overcome the language barrier, the concept of face, and the indifference of the Chinese to time. Once interpreters were trained, the American instructor, with his Chinese interpreter, overcame the language problem.

Ramgarh Training Center

Teaching through interpreters, however, took three times as long as teaching where no language barrier existed. The concept of face made it difficult to train senior officers with their juniors, and all officers with enlisted men. Overcoming preconceived notions fostered by seven years of passive defense was also hard. The Chinese, vastly experienced in war as they had known it, did not willingly accept suggestions from men who, as the Chinese pointed out, had never heard a shot fired in anger. The time problem was handled by constant coordination through liaison officers. A new phase began after Chinese officers and men of the 22nd and 38th Divisions had finished about six weeks of basic training; then the Chinese units were reassembled to conduct their own training with American aid and guidance. The basic principle was to help the Chinese help themselves. As a result of the success at Ramgarh—the campaign in Burma would clearly demonstrate the progress made there in upgrading X-force—American-manned training centers were established in China in early 1943 as another step in accomplishing Stilwell's mission to reform the Chinese Army. Starting with 30 divisions, Stilwell just might manage to revitalize the Chinese Army.[40]

The precondition for attempting Stilwell's plan for the reconquest of Burma was resolution of the diplomatic crisis. On August 1, 1942, the President promised almost 500 aircraft for the China Theater, plus more aircraft to fly the Hump in early 1943; but he regretted that American divisions could not be sent, thus failing to meet one of Chiang's three demands. Stilwell now secured conditional Chinese agreement to his plan to retake Burma (ANAKIM). His proposals fitted in well with Wavell's for a similar

operation, and both men went forward with plans and preparations. (*See Atlas Map No. 41.*) Wavell, as Supreme Allied Commander, India, assigned Stilwell and his Chinese divisions in India to the Hukawng Valley of north Burma. A road from India to China (the Ledo Road) was being build there, and Stilwell agreed to assume responsibility for it.[41]

Burma is a country of alternating north-south mountain ranges and river valleys covered with a tropical forest. In 1942, it was a curiously isolated land. The Himalaya Mountains divide India, Burma, and China, and only a few jungle trails linked Burma with India and Thailand. Practically all commerce with the outside world funneled through Rangoon, which beleagured China had also depended on as the port for American lend-lease supplies that reached her via the Burma Road. The prerequisite for military operations was breaching these mountain and jungle ramparts. Climatic conditions further limited operations to the dry season (October through mid-May); monsoon rains dampened all activities during the remaining four months. Another complicating factor was the sheer physical problem of exerting effort in a subtropical climate where disease, especially malaria, was endemic. A final constraint was logistical support; the Assam line of communications from the Allied port of Calcutta to both British and American forces was hopelessly inadequate. (*See Atlas Map No. 40.*) An India-based offensive into Burma was not especially enticing.[42]

In spite of Wavells' initial proposal and guarded optimism, the British soon indicated a reluctance to mount operations into Burma. The war in the European and Mediterranean Theaters had taken a turn for the worse. In North Africa,

Rommel seemed unbeatable; and the rapid German advance toward the Don at the southern end of the Russian front had created a threat to both Iraq and Persia. British resources in India were diverted from Burma to deal with these threats. Complicating matters, Mahatma Gandhi's Congress Party chose mid-1942 to initiate a civil disobedience campaign in order to pressure Great Britain into granting India her independence. In June, violence erupted, diverting more British troops from Burma. Thus, by the end of August 1942, Wavell felt that sufficient resources would not be available for major offensive operations before the 1943 monsoons, although he finally agreed to a limited campaign to take Akyab.

The Chinese, too, found many reasons for postponing the reconquest of Burma. The Generalissimo wanted the British to dominate the Bay of Bengal, occupy the Andaman Islands, and seize Rangoon as a prelude to challenging the Japanese in Burma. Chiang reasoned that this would cut Japanese sea communications to Rangoon, increasing their vulnerability in Burma. The British understood, but they did not have the naval resources to implement his proposal.[43]

The Chinese were also slow in concentrating 30 divisions in Yunnan (designated Yunnan force or Y-force) to form the eastern pincer in the converging attack into Burma. Bringing this number of divisions loyal to the Generalissimo to one province would affect the entire structure of domestic politics. Chiang's control in the remaining 11 provinces would be weakened, and the war-area commander in Yunnan was not anxious to have Chiang's divisions innundate his province. (*See Atlas Map No. 36.*) The problem of forming Y-force for the Burma offensive, therefore, became yet another very important facet of the crux of the antagonism between Stilwell and the Generalissimo. As Yunnan was the obvious place to begin Chinese Army reform in China, revitalization was to start with Y-force. Chiang was reluctant to send his divisions to Yunnan; he was also reluctant to send war-area commanders' divisions, which were of doubtful loyalty, to Yunnan to be trained, armed, and equipped by the Americans, lest some day they be turned against him. The problem of where and how to begin Chinese Army reform was one part of the web in which Chiang was caught.[44]

The other part was how to fight the Japanese. The Generalissimo did not wish to risk loyal divisions in costly battles against the Japanese. Yet Y-force was to fight the Japanese in Burma. If Y-force was formed from divisions loyal to Chiang, they would be revitalized first—a potential plus—but they would also be committed against the Japanese—a potential political disaster. The Generalissimo was in a quandry. He wanted and vitally needed American help; but that help was not needed as much for use against the Japanese as for the survival of his Nationalist regime. Yet the Americans, specifically Stilwell, did not offer aid on this basis. Stilwell's mission was to help China do her share in defeating the Japanese. Stilwell was a soldier with a military mission. Known with reason as "Vinegar Joe," he was a determined, unyielding man with high standards of performance and integrity. He had little tolerance for what he viewed as Chiang's obstructive machinations, elusiveness, and apparent indifference. Because he made no attempt to ingratiate himself with someone he did not respect, Stilwell's relationship with Chiang turned increasingly bitter.

Chiang, however, still held a trump card. Stilwell could be ignored if the Generalissimo could persuade his benefactor, President Roosevelt, to accept an alternative solution to fighting the East Asian War. Roosevelt obviously had a vested interest in China, and viewed China's role in the Asian struggle from a political as well as a military viewpoint. All Chiang needed now was a rationale to avoid committing Chinese forces. He found it in a plan submitted by Stilwell's opportunistic subordinate, Chennault.[45]

In the fall of 1942, General Chennault placed before the Chinese, British, and Stilwell's superiors his claim that with 105 fighters, 30 medium bombers, and 12 heavy bombers, he could defeat the Japanese in China. Chennault felt that a great deal could be accomplished through airpower; but he was also miffed by being made subordinate to other airmen, especially Brigadier General Clayton L. Bissell, Tenth Air Force Commander, who did not have Chennault's combat record. His aspirations for aggressive air operations had thus far been stymied by Stilwell's China air plan and Hump-resource allocation. As the AVG and CATF had done a great deal with meager resources, Chennault claimed that airpower could do the job if adequate support were provided. To avoid having his plan rejected by his superiors, Bissell and Stilwell, he went directly to Chiang.[46] Accepting Chennault's plan, the Generalissimo called a halt to operations scheduled for the spring of 1943. He insisted that the solution to China's military problems lay in the United States sending more and more airpower to China, rather than in anything the Chinese might do for themselves. The stormy issue lay now directly at Roosevelt's doorstep. Inevitably, the President would have to choose between supporting Stilwell and Marshall, with their insistence on coercing the Generalissimo to reform his army and fight the Japanese, and Chennault, whose plan permitted Roosevelt to be in full accord with Chiang's wishes.[47]

Meanwhile, Wavell had launched the Second Burma campaign, his Akyab offensive, in October 1942. He had planned a joint amphibious and land assault, but the forces designated for the amphibious assault and its landing craft were delayed by extended operations in Madagascar.* Wavell decided to continue with the ground attack; when his troops had advanced close to Akyab, he expected to conduct a short-range amphibious attack. The Japanese, however, had reinforced the Arakan area and, early in March 1943, they managed to halt the Allied land advance too far north of the port to make the modified amphibious attack feasible. They then launched a counteroffensive, and by the beginning of the monsoons in May they had recaptured Maungdaw. (*See Atlas Map No. 41.*) Although Wavell's effort had failed, it brought to light defects, primarily tactical, in the rapidly expanding Anglo-Indian Army. These were corrected, and by the end of 1943 the Anglo-Indian divisions had reached a level of training that made them equal to the Japanese.[48]

Well to the north of the Arakan area, in central Burma, the unorthodox Brigadier Orde C. Wingate led an experimental foray into Burma from February to June 1943. Wingate had been sent to Burma at Wavell's request. He had served in Palestine and Ethiopia, where he acquired a profound knowledge of guerrilla warfare and an ability to apply the principles of war to novel situations. Studying the First Burma campaign, he perceived the counter to the Japanese tactical system. Japanese encirclement tactics were normally directed against their enemies' line of communications, upon which they threw up roadblocks. Carrying supplies in their packs, relying on animal transport, and being trained to move swiftly through the jungle, they were not road-bound like the Allied divisions. Since the latter were dependent on motor transport, roadblocks were a fatal hazard to Indian troops.[49]

Wingate proposed to strip units of all nonessential equipment, organize into small columns with a base of fire and a maneuvering element, and resupply entirely by air. Such units would have good jungle mobility and would not be hindered by roadblocks. The mission of these units, Wingate suggested, should be to precipitate disorganization behind Japanese lines, which could then be exploited by pressure from regular infantry divisions. Wingate had originally intended to support Chiang's advance in the spring campaign by operating around Myitkyina and Lashio.[50]

After the Generalissimo's withdrawal from the Spring 1943 operation, Wingate asked for a chance to test his theories against the Japanese. In February 1943, the Chindits, some 3,000 strong, crossed the Chindwin River. Supplied by air, they penetrated deep into Burma without meeting much opposition, and damaged the railway south of Indaw. Wingate then crossed the Irrawaddy into an area with many roads and trails, thereby enabling the Japanese to surround his force, which had to disperse to get back as best it could. By early June, 2,200 men were able to exfiltrate to Assam or China. This incursion had little immediate strategic value, but it gave a considerable morale boost to Great Britain and India.[51]

The Chindits had gained valuable experience in the art of making deep penetrations into enemy territory. They had done no damage to the Japanese that bombers could not have done more cheaply, but great results were to issue from Wingate's foray. On the Allied side, commanders recognized that troops supplied by air could move in strength in Japanese rear areas. Its greatest effect, however, was that it led the Japanese to conclude that the hills on India's borders, previously felt to be impenetrable, were not a barrier, and that India could be invaded. They failed to note that armies in the jungle could be supplied by air. Consequently, the Japanese began planning their own spring campaign into Assam for 1944, a campaign that would prove fatal.[52]

Strategic Direction

One defends when his strength is inadequate; he attacks when it is abundant.[53]

Sun Tzu

American interest in China was founded on more than just moral grounds. Roosevelt, looking forward to the postwar world, wanted a strong China as the dominant and stabilizing power in east Asia after Japan's defeat. The goal of the American military establishment was more immediate; it wanted a strong China which would help defeat Japan. Although these goals were not necessarily compatible, Roosevelt and his military advisers could agree on one point: the collapse, surrender, or collaboration of the Chungking Government would destroy America's military and political aims in east Asia. This was the reasoning that dictated the campaign to supply, invigorate, and mobilize China, and to re-open the land link through Burma.[54]

---

*Indicative of relative priorities and limitations in resources, operations in Madagascar pre-empted operations in Burma. The Madagascar campaign, initiated in March 1942 to seize and hold the Vichy French naval and airbase at the northern tip of the island in order to protect the vital lines of communication in the Indian Ocean, started well and appeared certain of quick success. But, although the French asked for terms, they dragged out negotiations, and the British were forced to withdraw resources previously promised to Wavell for the Burma campaign in order to force the French to capitulate.

Although meager resources had permitted only limited activity during the dry season of 1942 to 1943, a large-scale offensive in Burma was high on the agenda of the Casablanca Conference in January 1943. Before China's masses could help defeat Japan, the Allies needed to re-establish land communications with China; effective Chinese armies could not be armed and maintained with the limited Hump tonnage. The CCS decided that plans and preparations should be made for the reconquest of all of Burma (Operation ANAKIM) with a target of November 1943; but the final decision to attack would be deferred until the next Allied conference. Then, inasmuch as China had not be represented at Casablanca, a delegation was sent to Chungking to win the Generalissimo's approval. He gave it in February.[55]

Following Casablanca, American military planners developed a strategic outline for the Pacific which was designed to be presented at the next Allied conference. They felt that if Japan's sea lanes in the Far East were severed and if her vital centers (industry and the will to resist) were destroyed by an air offensive, Japan might capitulate before an invasion became necessary. China was the preferred base for the strategic air offensive; but to support this offensive logistically, a port on China's coast, preferably Hong Kong, would have to be opened. This, then, became the tentative objective for the dual drive across the Pacific. But how were these drives related to operations in CBI? Accepting British reluctance to retake all of Burma, the planners limited their goal for 1943 to the taking only of north Burma. A land link between India and China (the Ledo and Burma Roads) could then be established. With a land line of communications, the Chinese Army

could be supplied with the material resources they needed to hold the airbases in eastern China (*See Atlas Map No. 40.*) that were necessary for the air offensive against Japan. Naturally, the priority claim on resources would go to Stilwell for upgrading the Chinese Army and the campaign in north Burma. This conflicted with the plan that Chenault had recommended to Chiang in the fall of 1942, which required that priority be given to airpower.[56]

The controversy as to whether an air effort in China Theater should precede or follow major reforms in the Chinese Army came before the President in March 1943. The results of Army reform would not be apparent before 1944, while Chennault was already claiming significant achievements. The Generalissimo was satisfied with his Army as it was. Furthermore, he promised Roosevelt that Chinese forces could protect Chennault's airfields if the Japanese reacted with an offensive against them. Although Stilwell disagreed with both Chennault and Chiang, the President decided to support his ally's desires. Airpower won out. In order to implement this decision, CATF became the Fourteenth Air Force in March 1943, and was to be built up to 500 aircraft; to support air operations, Hump tonnage was to be built up to 10,000 tons a month. Chennault was given first priority on all supplies flown to China, and finally gained his independence from Tenth Air Force control. Additionally, Chennault became Chief of Staff, Chinese Air Force, thus formally obtaining direct access to the Generalissimo. Cautioning Stilwell against hindering Chennault or angering the Generalissimo, Marshall gave him orders to support Chennault's operations and to allow Chennault free rein to see what he could do.

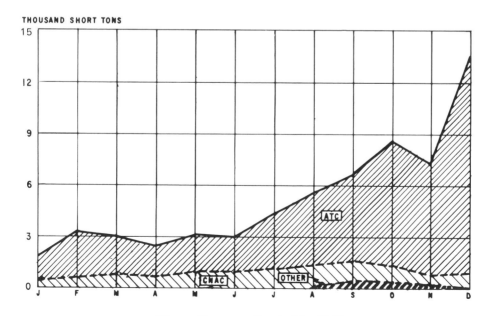

Hump Tonnage Carried in 1943

Henceforth, preparations in China proceeded in two separate and often conflicting areas. Chennault worked to increase his air force and fly more missions; Stilwell sought to reform the Chinese Army and prepare for a campaign in Burma. Preparations for a greater air effort and the campaign in north Burma each required Hump tonnage, a fact which increased the existing friction between Stilwell and Chennault.[57]

Politically, the President's decision promoted Sino-American unity, but glossed over grave military flaws. Marshall had argued that the timing of Chennault's plan was wrong, warning that as soon as Chennault's efforts stung the Japanese, they would react by attacking Chennault's airfields. Such an attack would have to be met by the Chinese Army, which was still untrained, unreformed, and without lend-lease equipment. Marshall pointed out that logistically even an enlarged Hump route was inadequate; a land line through north Burma was the only feasible alternative. Finally, lines of communication in China from Yunnan airfields to Chennault's bases in eastern China were inadequate and highly vulnerable to enemy interdiction. Although there were no easy solutions to these problems, the myth of airpower and political aspiration took flight from the logistical and military realities of the situation. As with the TORCH decision in July 1942, the President overrode the proposals of his military advisers.[58]

Shortly thereafter, the Americans presented their strategic plan for the defeat of Japan to the CCS at the TRIDENT Conference (May 1943). As expected, the CBI portion was the thorny issue. The British wanted to avoid fighting in the jungles of Burma, and would have been content just to augment the air route to China. Favoring the indirect approach, they proposed seizing Sumatra and Singapore as an alternative. Churchill, however, finally agreed to the reconquest of north Burma by British and Chinese forces (a modified ANAKIM). But Chiang, who made his desires known through his representative in Washington, wanted a full-blown ANAKIM—the reconquest of all of Burma. Both the British and Chinese readily agreed to Chennault's air offensive. Chiang's request for operations in both north and south Burma was not satisfied; he could be pleased, however, with the decision to give priority to Chennault. Most disappointed were Marshall and Stilwell. The TRIDENT decisions were reaffirmed in August of 1943 at QUADRANT. It was clear that the Americans (oriented on China) and the British (focused on Singapore) still differed in their ultimate aims.[59]

The decision to limit operations to north Burma elevated the Ledo Road to a new level of importance as a potential line of communications to China. Competing with it was the Hump route, which was constantly being expanded. The expansion of the air route meant that engineer resources had to be shifted from road building to airfield construction. Additionally, it soon became apparent that Allied logistical resources in Asia could not support both ground and air operations on the scale called for by TRIDENT and the President's decision. By August 1943, Chennault was handicapped because adequate supplies were not reaching him; Stilwell was handicapped because Chennault's priority, although not large enough to support major air operations, was large enough to obstruct preparations for ground operations by Y-force, assuming the Chinese wished to make them.[60]

Without Chinese participation in the reconquest of north Burma, these operations appeared to be impossible; yet the President's decision confirmed and strengthened Chiang in his unwillingness to take the offensive in either China or Burma. It was a dilemma that would have to be solved if the blockade of China were to be broken. Moreover, Stilwell could do little to accomplish his mission to increase the effectiveness of aid to China and to assist in improving the combat efficiency of the Chinese Army. Stilwell's Commander-in-Chief showed scant interest in his mission, yet it remained unchanged. As the President had rejected all suggestions that the Chinese be required to do anything in return for U.S. aid, only Chiang ultimately determined what was done in the China Theater.[61]

Dissatisfaction with the conduct of the war in southeast Asia and realization that the Allied effort in Asia needed more logistical support finally caused the Allies to create the Southeast Asia Command (SEAC) in August 1943, with Vice Admiral Lord Louis Mountbatten as Supreme Commander. Henceforth, operations in Burma would no longer be run by Headquarters, India, which was always more oriented toward the Middle East. Lieutenant General Brehon B. Somervell, commander of U.S. Army Service Forces, planned a major logistical effort for CBI. If Mountbatten's superiors gave him the resources to succeed in his new post, the retaking of Burma and reopening of the land link to China would make possible a greatly increased flow of weapons to the Chinese Army, as well as supplies to Chennault. That, in turn, would be a long step toward opening a port on the China coast, the tentative objective for MacArthur and Nimitz.

Somervell and Mountbatten travelled to Chungking in October 1943 to brief the Generalissimo on SEAC. When they arrived, Stilwell's enemies were on the verge of having Chiang ask for Stilwell's recall, but Somervell's diplomacy and Madame Chiang's support persuaded the Generalissimo to keep Stilwell as his Chief of Staff, although no staff had yet been created. This reconciliation and the creation of SEAC seemed to augur well for the Allied war effort in

Asia. Stilwell, however, felt that he could do nothing more to improve the combat efficiency of the Chinese Army. His military mission to China was at an end. Henceforth, he concentrated on his duties as a U.S. theater commander, which included aiding China, and as Deputy Supreme Commander, SEAC. It was time to get on with the east Asian war.[62]

The tempo of the dual thrust in the Pacific, and the Allied effort in Europe, however, were beginning to have a profound impact on the war against Japan. The European war could terminate as early as October 1944, and the Allies hoped to defeat Japan 12 months later. Operations in Burma and China were lagging, while Nimitz and MacArthur were beginning to pick up momentum. It now appeared entirely possible that the war in the Pacific could end before the Allies conquered Burma or engaged large Japanese armies in China. Stalin also said that Russia would enter the Asian war three months after the Russo-German war was ended. The military importance of China began to pale. Roosevelt was determined, however, to have China treated as a great power, coequal with Great Britain, the United States, and Russia.[63]

In November 1943, Roosevelt and Chiang met Churchill at Cairo (SEXTANT) and agreed to the operations in north Burma. When Chiang insisted that an attack be made to capture the Andaman Islands (BUCCANEER) simultaneously, he was told by Roosevelt that the British would conduct the operation, although Churchill naturally objected. The critical commodity was landing craft, which were in demand for both OVERLORD and several Mediterranean schemes. Churchill and Roosevelt then met Stalin at Teheran, where the latter again promised to enter the east Asian war, but insisted that no landing craft be diverted from Europe. He supported the decision to invade southern France (ANVIL), which committed any landing craft which might have been used for BUCCANEER. As Chiang's agreement to use Y-force was contingent on BUCCANEER, he reneged on his commitment in north Burma.

The war was on the verge of passing China by. The relative importance of each theater had been determined. The Pacific thrust was definitely the main effort against Japan; Burma and China ranked behind all other theaters. Additionally, the CCS at this point recognized the importance of the Marianas as a launching platform for B-29s, the long-range, heavy bomber which was to pound Japan into submission.[64]

Because the Andaman Island operation was precluded by global priorities, Roosevelt offered Chiang the option of delaying the north Burma operation until the fall of 1944, when landing craft would be available. Seeing resources

again denied CBI, a bitterly disappointed Chiang accepted Roosevelt's offer. Chiang's willingness to accept this delay was a key in the sequence of frustrated efforts that also began to overtax American patience. American military planners realized that it was simply too late to bring China's manpower actively into the war. The mission assigned to Stilwell, through no fault of his own, was no longer possible. Lowering their sights, the Allies still wanted to open the Burma Road, but only to have another option if the Pacific offensives stalled. American air planners continued to express interest in China as a B-29 base, but this interest would eventually dwindle. Of even greater importance, Chiang's most ardent supporter, Roosevelt, now began to have doubts about China. From both a military and a political view, a watershed that divided Sino-American relations had been reached.[65]

The Burma Campaign Begins

He who is prudent and lies in wait for an enemy who is not, will be victorious.[66]

Sun Tzu

Ironically, as China's importance in the global conflict receded, Mountbatten began the decisive campaign in Burma. In his implementation of the decision to clear north Burma and re-establish a land link with China, the SEAC commander had planned four operations: a thrust by X-force from Ledo toward Myitkyina, an advance by British-Indian forces across the Chindwin toward Indaw, an attack toward Akyab by the XV Corps, and a deep penetration by Wingate's Chindits to aid Stilwell's advance. (*See Atlas Map No. 41.*) The Chinese contribution, until it was scrubbed after SEXTANT, was to be an attack by Y-force across the Salween River. To support the India-based offensives, the problem of improving the Assam line of communications to an acceptable standard was approached with vigor and determination.[67]

The mistakes of the First Burma campaign were analyzed and digested. Just as Stilwell was making great progress upgrading X-force, the main field army in Burma (the Anglo-Indian Army) was being revitalized after its disastrous defeat in 1942. The man responsible for the difficult task of rebuilding this shattered force was Lieutenant General (later 1st Viscount) William Slim, one of the truly great commanders of World War II. He trained his soldiers to fight in the jungle; he prepared them for Japanese encircle-

Lieutenant General William Slim

ment tactics; and in the process he restored troop confidence and morale. This was accomplished primarily through small unit patrolling and carefully planned minor offensives. Once Indian and British soldiers knew that they could defeat Japanese soldiers, high morale replaced despair. The weapon was ready; two ill-prepared divisions had been replaced by the finely tuned IV Corps and XV Corps of the Fourteenth Army.[68]

Because a shortage of assault shipping precluded the more quickly decisive amphibious landing in south Burma, Mountbatten had to begin the three-pronged invasion out of India. The odds for an Allied victory were slender because the Japanese had not been idle; the Burma Area Army had been reinforced to a strength of eight divisions. If the Fourteenth Army could seriously weaken the Japanese Army before plunging into Burma, however, the whole picture would change. The only way this could be done was to entice the enemy into a major battle under circumstances favorable to the Fourteenth Army and thereby smash three or four Japanese divisions. Fortuitously, Slim had his Varro in the impetuous Japanese commanders of the *Fifteenth Army* (Lieutenant General Renya Mutaguchi) and *Burma Area Army* (Lieutenant General Masakazu Kawabe); his Cannae, however, would come about with the opening moves taking place on the flanks.[69]

In November 1943, with the end of the monsoon, the Indian XV Corps began the Akyab offensive on the southern flank. The XV Corps was approaching the strong defensive positions in Arakan covering Maungdaw when the Japanese launched the first of two expected offensives on February 4, 1944. The *55th Division* passed approximately 5,000 men behind the leading Indian divisions, cutting their line of communications. (*See Atlas Map No. 41.*) Supplied by air, these divisions stood firm, and reserves brought forward by

air repulsed the Japanese with heavy losses. Airpower gave the British superior strategic mobility and countered the usual Japanese tactic of cutting the Indians' supply line. This battle was the turning point of the Third Burma campaign. For the first time, an Allied force had met, held, and decisively defeated a major Japanese attack. The victory had an electric effect on the Fourteenth Army, as the legend of Japanese invincibility in the jungle was smashed. The pattern for victory was set. Exploiting its success in Arakan, the XV Corps drove the Japanese out of all their main defenses covering Akyab by May 1944.[70]

Like the southern flank in Arakan, the northern flank in the Hukawng Valley was a subsidiary operation to Slim's main effort around Imphal. Yet from a political and global military view, it was the main front in CBI, The reason for conducting the Third Burma campaign was to break the blockade of China by opening the Ledo-Burma Road. Stilwell's attack began in October 1943 from Ledo to Myitkyina. Supporting the two Chinese divisions of X-force—it would be redesignated Northern Combat Area Command (NCAC) in February 1944—was a Chinese tank group armed with light tanks. NCAC was opposed by the *18th Division*, which could expect little help because of the decisive struggle planned for the central front against Fourteenth Army. As insurance, Wingate's Special Force was used to cut communications to the enemy's northern front.[71]

Sixty years old and nearly blind, Stilwell took personal command of X-force—a decision subject to criticism. In December, as X-force commander, Stilwell was a corps commander within the SEAC structure of which he was Deputy Supreme Allied Commander. In order to coordinate Slim's and Stilwell's activities, Mountbatten proposed that both serve under General Sir George Giffard, commander of the ground forces of SEAC (11th Army Group). But Stilwell, a known Anglophobe and Deputy Commander of SEAC, refused to serve under Giffard, whom he despised. The command problem was solved when Stilwell offered to serve under Slim until X-force reached Kamaing, giving Slim operational control of a third corps-sized unit. (*See Appendix 33.*) The command structure in CBI resembled a Chinese puzzle.[72]

On orders from the Generalissimo, the Chinese divisions did not press forward as fast as they might, but progress was made thanks to Merrill's Marauders. (*See Atlas Map No. 41.*) Wingate's activities had spurred the JCS into improvising the 5307th Composite Unit (Provisional) for service in Burma; it soon became known as Merrill's Marauders, after the commander Brigadier General Frank D. Merrill. Stilwell used this force in a series of wide enveloping movements to get in the rear of the *18th Division*. By the

**General Stilwell and General Merrill Confer
at Merrill's Headquarters**

end of March, the Hukawng Valley had been cleared, and entry into the Mogaung Valley was assured. In late April, the Marauders, reinforced by some Chinese regiments, began to move across the mountains and then south against Myitkyina. Surprising the Japanese by an advance from the north, this force captured Myitkyina airfield on May 17, 1944, but the Japanese waged a fierce fight for the town itself for 11 more weeks.[73]

Stilwell's advance was also assisted by the members of a powerful tribe in north Burma, who offered great potential as scouts, guides, and irregulars. They were organized in 1942 by Detachment 101 of the Office of Strategic Services, commanded by Captain William R. Peers; the force was known as the Kachin Rangers. Using a mixed personnel of Kachins, Burmese, and Americans, the Rangers performed a wide variety of missions: an intelligence net was set up behind Japanese lines in north Burma; guerrilla forces were organized around a cadre of trained Americans and Kachins to attack Japanese lines of communication and harass small units; and espionage and counterespionage operations were conducted. When the Third Burma campaign opened, this force was several hundred strong and steadily expanded its operations. It eventually organized four battalions and began fighting as regular troops. Although the Rangers ultimately cleared a portion of central Burma, their greatest contribution was in assisting the advance of Stilwell and later Sultan, Stilwell's successor.

To the south of NCAC, three brigades of Special Force—Wingate's renamed Chindits, enlarged to six brigades—were moved into Burma by land an air. By the end of March 1944, approximately 12,000 men, supplied entirely by air, had been established around Indaw and had blocked the southern approaches to Myitkyina, effectively cutting the communications of the enemy forces facing Stilwell. (*See Atlas Map No. 41.*) Although the Japanese made repeated unsuccessful attempts to break the block, by early April it was apparent that newly arrived Japanese divisions might overwhelm the block. Also, the monsoon season was approaching, limiting air supply of Special Force at Indaw. Accordingly, it was ordered to move north at the end of April, establish a new block at Mogaung, and come under Stilwell's command in mid-May.[74]

Although Special Force established its new block south of Mogaung on May 7, it was forced to withdraw with heavy losses on May 25, leaving the Japanese free to reinforce Myitkyina, or the area around Mogaung, and thereby block the approach to Myitkyina of Stilwell's main force. They did not move quickly enough to do either. NCAC took Kamaing on June 16 and Mogaung on June 26. Stilwell was thus able to use the road to Myitkyina. Now reinforced by three more Chinese divisions, NCAC finally occupied the town on August 3. Thereafter, operations ceased until the end of the rains. The capture of Myitkyina was of immense value, for once the airfields had been constructed and a pipeline built to them from Ledo, the air ferry could operate into China without flying across the Hump.[75] Stilwell wrote three weeks later, "It was a bitch of a flight. . . . FIRST SUSTAINED OFFENSIVE IN CHINESE HISTORY AGAINST A FIRST-CLASS ENEMY."[76]

Stilwell could be proud that his efforts to build an effective, albeit small, Chinese force had borne fruit. The Chinese fought well against the skilled and determined *18th Division*. Stilwell deserved high praise for his feat; but credit must also be given to Slim's IV Corps, which was fighting the first phase of the decisive engagement of the campaign around Imphal. The numerical superiority of NCAC was achieved because the main Japanese forces were held locked in the vital Imphal battle, and any reinforcements that could be scraped together were fed into that furnace.

Slim had taken the measure of his foe, and a great encounter loomed over the Imphal region. Both sides were ready to fight to the finish. In Slim's view, the logistical and geographical problems of invading Burma to find and fight the Japanese made such a venture at best a gamble—unless the IV Corps could wear down the Japanese strength before the invasion. Fighting a defensive battle in Arakan had paved the way to victory on that front; a similar battle on the Imphal plain was equally promising, and the Japanese seemed willing. Slim planned to withdraw with IV Corps before the enemy attack, persuading the Japanese that it was in retreat. The Japanese would follow over the wild country between the Chindwin River and the Imphal Plain.

There, at Imphal, the IV Corps would turn on the Japanese, who would by then be overextended and with an execrable line of communications behind them. The Japanese could be isolated by airpower while British reinforcements massed for the counterblow. As Slim completed planning his classic defensive-offensive, the Japanese gave every indication of a willingness to cooperate in this mutual endeavor.[77]

The Japanese Varro, Kawabe, viewed the Arakan fighting as subsidiary, its purpose being to absorb Allied reserves. On the northern flank, he economized forces and traded space for time; here he could afford to yield ground, because if he won in the center, the north would automatically fall to him. Mutaguchi, bold to a fault, launched his *Fifteenth Army* on the second Japanese offensive in early March 1944; its objective was the destruction of the British IV Corps in Assam. (*See Atlas Map No. 41.*) Assuming that the key British bases at Imphal and Kohima would be taken in three weeks, the Japanese provided only shoestring logistical support for their combat forces, a disastrous mistake.[78]

In accordance with prearranged plans, Slim withdrew his IV Corps back to prepared positions, covering the Imphal plain as soon as the enemy crossed the Chindwin. When Mutaguchi's troops cut the Imphal road on March 29, the IV Corps was isolated from India. With the attack and encirclement of Kohima (April 4 to 8), the Japanese drew to within 30 unobstructed miles of the Assam line of communications to Ledo. The Japanese attack was stronger than anticipated, but Mutaguchi could not sustain it. The indomitable English and Indian soldiers persisted. Slim reinforced Imphal with a division flown in from Arakan; the Indian XXXIII Corps was also placed under Slim's command and concentrated at Dimapur.[79] The Japanese

Lieutenant General R. Mutaguchi

had exhausted their resources. By now, the Allies had gained air superiority over Burma, and, supplied by air, the IV Corps was able to hold its position around Imphal and begin its counteroffensive in May. The XXXIII Corps, after relieving the Kohima garrison, attacked southward. (*See Atlas Map No. 42.*) By the end of June, the two corps had linked up, and the Imphal road was reopened. By July 1, sickness, hunger, and battle casualties had permanently crippled the *Fifteenth Army*; as the monsoon season worsened, Japanese units retreated to the Chindwin in considerable disorder. Slim, determined to exploit the situation, unleashed a relentless pursuit through the monsoon rains. The initiative had changed hands; after two and one half years, the Allies were the dominant force in Burma. The first phase of the decisive battle over, Slim began maneuvering his forces for the second and final phase—annihilation.[80]

When the Third Burma campaign had begun in late 1943, the Allies had command of the air, an important prerequisite of victory. The rapid growth of Anglo-American airpower, based in India, made possible a campaign of a type not seen before—a campaign in which the customary Japanese tactic of encirclement was devastatingly countered. Anglo-American control of the air denied the Japanese strategic mobility, isolating and crippling their offensives against the British. The Allies, on the other hand, could fly a division to the scene of action. Perhaps more important, the Japanese tactic of encirclement was no longer the menace it had once been. Development of effective air-ground coordination made possible resupply of forward units entirely by air, unrestricted air reconnaissance, and effective close air support to blast machinegun nests and entrenchments. Bombers, fighters, and transports soared overhead endlessly, succoring and supporting the Allied advance.[81]

Lieutenant General M. Kawabe

Air Supply Drops Were a Key to Success in Burma Operations

As the victims, the Japanese commented: "The Allies were able to carry out their operations freely and unhindered whereas Japanese without air supplies and with their only means of supply—ground transport—cut off, were in a paralyzed state. . . . The difference in ground-air cooperation between the Japanese Army and the Allies was the difference between victory and defeat."[82]

Equally important in the successes in north Burma and Manipur State were the logistical triumphs. The major improvement was on the Assam line of communications, whose control was assumed by an Anglo-American military panel. American service troops occupied key positions at Calcutta and on the Bengal and Assam Railway. Increased tonnage along the Indian part of the line of communications came at an opportune time as the tempo of operations quickened in CBI.[83]

China Explodes

The harpoon hit the little bugger right in the solar plexus, and went right through him. It was a clean hit, but beyond turning green and losing the power of speech, he did not bat an eye.[84]

Lieutenant General Joseph W. Stilwell

In China, the picture remained one of problems and unfulfilled projects. Although the military situation had hardly changed since 1939, internal conditions declined into a state of increasing chaos. Inflation sapped the country's economy, foreign trade had stopped, railways had almost come to a standstill, other communications had broken down, food production was falling, and Chiang's government seemed to be disintegrating, its authority flouted in large parts of the country. The conspicuous necessity for reform within the Nationalist Government—and its equally conspicuous absence—alienated many Americans who failed to appreciate Chiang's problems. The Nationalists seemed incapable of energizing China's resources for war.[85]

Conditions were ideal for Chinese Communist exploitation. Proclaiming to be agrarian reformers and staunchly anti-Japanese while covertly undermining the Nationalist Government and extending their influence in northern China, the Chinese Communists seemed—to some Americans—a possible alternative to the "decadent" Nationalists. To the Generalissimo, they were treacherous enemies who could not be ignored. The United Front had long since dissolved. Chiang had to divert scarce resources to his most important front, the Communist front. This not only thinly spread the Generalissimo's resources, but also exasperated his American ally; extraordinary efforts were being made to supply Nationalist forces, while a substantial portion of those forces were being deployed, not against the Japanese, but against other Chinese.[86]

On his second front in eastern China, Chiang continued to follow a Fabian strategy against the Japanese, who still controlled most of the key communications centers. Primarily to confiscate crops and grain, the Japanese conducted sporadic operations of no great importance. In some areas there had been no fighting for years—supposedly, the opposing commanders reached mutually profitable understandings. While the Nationalists, as well as the Communists, occasionally fought the Japanese, both withheld forces to block the other. Chiang, however, was at a greater disadvantage, for his best troops (the X- and Y-forces) were committed to the Burma front. Chiang simply did not have the resources to oppose his adversaries actively on three fronts. Thus far, Japanese passivity had enabled the Generalissimo to maintain a fragile equilibrium.[87]

Although Chiang's problems may have been insoluble, a wiser selection of priorities might have made a difference. When confronted with the choice of increased airpower or the reform of the Army, the Generalissimo had chosen the former. Consequently, the one American combat force in China, Chennault's Fourteenth Air Force, was carrying the burden of the war against the Japanese with a growing air offensive. The trade-off was an unimproved Chinese Army. Stilwell had wanted to revitalize 30 Chinese divisions (Y-force) to reconquer north Burma, but the Chinese were slow in concentrating and organizing this force at a time when Chennault's Hump priority denied them equipment. To oppose the Japanese in east China, Stilwell wanted to revitalize a second group of 30 Chinese divisions (Zulu force or Z-force) in the Kweilin area (*See Atlas Map No. 38.*); but by spring 1944, little had been accomplished regarding this concentration either. These delays can be explained in part as a means of bargaining for lend-lease supplies, and in part as attributable to Chinese politics. Nevertheless, a more vigorous effort to reform the army—the Stilwell approach—might have paid dividends in terms of making more resources available to Chiang in the spring of 1944, when Chennault's air offensive threatened to galvanize the Japanese into action. Time was running out as the Generalissimo's options were disappearing.

By threatening to withdraw aid for the re-equipping of his armies, the Americans at last obtained the Generalissimo's consent to an offensive across the Salween in May 1944 by Y-force. After the conferences at Cairo and Teheran in December 1943, Roosevelt's attitude toward China had changed. The Generalissimo's withdrawal from the north Burma operation after Cairo; the Soviet promise to enter the east Asian war; and the contrast between Stilwell's defeat of the Japanese *18th Division* with two Chinese divisions—he was later reinforced with three more divisions—and the Generalissimo's reluctance to engage one weakened Japanese division with 12 Chinese divisions, all affected the President's appraisal of Chiang Kai-shek as a soldier and an ally. His messages to Chiang grew steadily harsher in tone, culminating in a threat to cut off lend-lease unless China played a more active role in breaking the blockade. After two years, it seemed that Roosevelt finally had bought Stilwell's approach.[88]

In May 1944, just before the monsoon rains began, Y-force crossed the Salween toward Burma. (*See Atlas Map No. 41.*) This force, commanded by General Wei Lihuang, was a Chinese army in the China Theater under Chinese leadership, even though Americans provided liaison teams down to regimental level to advise and assist with logistical support. The 12-division force was opposed by the Japanese *56th Division.* Wei's objectives were Tengchung and Lungling. If they could be taken, Wei's forces and Stilwell's five crack Chinese divisions would be very close to meeting, thereby breaking the blockade of China and shattering the Japanese position in north Burma. Not only would the logistical situation be greatly improved, but Stilwell's five divisions could move to east China to help stem the Japanese offensive which had gotten underway in April. All this was not to be. The Chinese advance bogged down, and even though Lungling was taken, it was quickly lost to a Japanese counterattack. By the end of June 1944, Wei was mired down before Tengchung and Lungling, while in east China the Japanese seemed to be moving at will.[89]

By committing his strategic reserve to the Salween campaign, Chiang had been forced to gamble on continued Japanese inactivity in east China. He had lost. Ironically, airpower had been too effective. Japanese Imperial General Headquarters was concerned about the potential menace of B-29 raids to Japan and the Fourteenth Air Force's attacks on the lines of communication of the *China Expeditionary Army*. (*See Atlas Map No. 43.*) Both these problems could be resolved by taking the east China air fields (Operation ICHIGO), the current bases for Chennault's tactical aircraft and potential bases for the B-29s. The Japanese launched ICHIGO in April 1944, thus bringing the China stalemate to an end.[90]

As May melted into June, Japanese actions made it unmistakably clear that ICHIGO was not just another foray, but a major effort. The Generalissimo and Chennault began asking for help in the form of more resources. Stilwell did what he could, but the problem was deep-rooted—the Chinese Army was unreformed, and airpower alone could not stop the Japanese. To the JCS, the solution was obvious. On July 1, 1944, in a memorandum to the President, they presented their argument:

> The time has come, in our opinion, when all military power and resources remaining to China must be entrusted to one individual capable of directing that effort in a fruitful way against the Japanese. There is no one in the Chinese Government or armed forces capable of coordinating the Chinese military effort in such a way as to meet the Japanese threat. During this war, there has been only one man who has been able to get Chinese forces to fight against the Japanese in an effective way. That man is General Stilwell.[91]

The President concurred and attempted to persuade Chiang to accept Stilwell as his field commander, even though he was known to be *persona non grata* to the Generalissimo. China's situation was desperate, and it demanded desperate remedies. As an expression of American gratitude for the victories in north Burma, as a sign of the President's confidence in him, and as recognition of the great responsibilities which were confidently expected to soon be his, Stilwell was promoted to full general on August 1, 1944, a rank he then shared with only Generals Marshall, MacArthur, Eisenhower, and Arnold.[92]

During August, the Generalissimo postponed a final decision on command in China. Events along the Salween did not suggest that there would be any speedy relief for China by a victory on that front, and in east China the Japanese offensive was temporarily stalled by a valiant defense of Hengyang. While the city was under siege, Stilwell was warned that the Chinese commanders in that area, who were suspected of disloyalty and thus denied arms by Chiang, were contemplating revolt. Under the protracted stresses of war and occupation, Chinese leaders were reverting to a pattern of warlord-separatism. The Chungking Government seemed on the brink of disintegration at a time when the defeat of Japan in the Pacific was virtually assured. Although disaffected Chinese made overtures for American support, Stilwell adhered to his policy of not intervening in Chinese domestic politics, and refused. The crisis abated in late August with the General-issimo still maintaining tenuous control of China. But although Chiang survived, American confidence in Chung-king was rapidly ebbing.[93]

As this internal crisis passed, a setback in early September on the Burma Road made the Generalissimo threaten to withdraw his Y-force from the north Burma campaign. Ironically, the Japanese Salween counteroffensive was halted on September 14, its objective having been merely to relieve pressure on the *56th Division.* Moreover, the monsoon was about to lift, and full-scale renewal of the Allied offensive in north Burma was scheduled to begin in a few weeks.[94] The crisis point had come in Sino-American relations. When word of Chiang's decision to withdraw Y-force reached President Roosevelt at the OCTAGON Conference in Quebec, he approved a reply which was sent to Stilwell for delivery. On September 19, 1944, Stilwell delivered the President's note to the Generalissimo:

> The only thing you can now do in an attempt to prevent the Jap from achieving his objectives in China is to reinforce your Salween armies immediately and press their offensive, while at once placing General Stilwell in unrestricted command of all your forces.[95]

It was an ultimatum. Believing that Stilwell had deliberately engineered this confrontation, Chiang publicly declined to appoint Stilwell as field commander of the Chinese forces and asked for Stilwell's recall on October 2. Stilwell noted in his diary: "Reasons given by GMO. Incompetent, non co-op, lack of respect, . . . unwarranted diversion of mu-nitions and men to Burma. Responsibility for disaster in South China."[96] Stilwell had become Chiang's scapegoat.

President Roosevelt had to choose between Stilwell and the Generalissimo. It was a difficult decision, for Stilwell had gained the President's respect and admiration; yet Stilwell and Chiang were incompatible, and the United States was committed to Chiang's China. On October 18, 1944, Roosevent decided that Stilwell would be recalled at once. When word of the President's decision reached Chungking, the Generalissimo's victory was an accomplished fact, though not of the dimensions he had hoped. Stilwell was now on orders to leave CBI, but there was no American to take responsibility for what might happen in China, and the Generalissimo was told that there would be no American sent to command the Chinese Army in China. Moreover, Roosevelt's attitude toward Chiang grew less accommo-dating. Not three months after Chiang forced Stilwell's recall, the President met with Churchill and Stalin at Yalta. There the attitude the President adopted toward Chinese territory and interests suggests that the Generalissimo's triumph of October 1944 was one of the steps that led to the Manchurian partition of February 1945. Stilwell had not been recalled in disgrace.

When Stilwell left CBI Theater, the situation in China appeared grim, but the projects begun by Stilwell in the dark days of 1942 were nearing fruition. The fast-approaching completion of these projects would give his successors re-sources far beyond any that Stilwell ever had. He had created in the Chinese Army in India a force of five divisions that compared very favorably with any in the Japanese Army. What seemed to be a lack of Chinese interest limited Chinese Army reform in China proper, but even there progress had been made. Training centers were established, and the Y- and Z-forces had been exposed to American training. The Third Burma campaign had been successfully waged and was near completion. Inevitably, the Japanese would be driven south; their blockade of China was doomed. The line-of-communications projects under Stil-well's command were also close to completion. The problems along the Assam line were only a memory; its capacity had increased from 5,117 tons in May 1943 to 124,499 tons in October 1944. The air link had also increased dramatically from 3,706 tons in all of 1942 to 35,131 tons in October 1944. The Ledo Road to Myitkyina was nearly complete, and the pipeline was complete. The stage was now set for the next act in China's wartime drama, the act in which the blockade would be broken. Thanks to Stilwell, his successors in 1945 would have the means to carry on the work he had almost single-handedly begun in 1942 in compliance with Marshall's orders: "Support China."[97]

The Tide Turns

> *Now an army may be likened to water, for just as the flowing water avoids the heights and hastens to the lowlands, so an army avoids strength and strikes weakness.*[98]
>
> *Sun Tzu*

After a hiatus of nine months, the next great Allied conference (OCTAGON) convened in September 1944 at

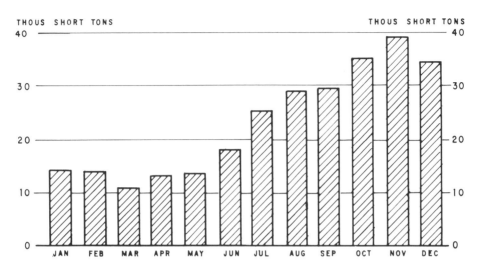

Tonnage Shipped by Air from India to China, 1944

Quebec. With success in all theaters except China, discussion of political rather than military issues took priority. At the previous conferences the British had been reluctant to support operations in Burma, but the smashing defeats inflicted on the Japanese in the spring of 1944 along the Indo-Burmese border and in north Burma were steadily altering the points of view among British and Americans. Mountbatten recommended exploiting Slim's success. The British Chiefs of Staff went further, advocating an airborne and amphibious assault on Rangoon. Although national objectives differed—the United States was interested in reopening communications to China, while Great Britain wanted to take Singapore—the Allies agreed to the reconquest of Burma, rather than just north Burma. Into this situation of full agreement between British and Americans to retake Burma, Chiang injected the previously mentioned desire to withdraw Y-force from the Salween campaign, thus upsetting CCS strategy for Burma. The patience of Chiang's primary backer, Roosevelt, now reached a limit. Shortly after OCTAGON, the American Chiefs of Staff, analyzing the situation in China, decided to invade Luzon rather than Formosa; the Americans no longer planned to establish a lodgment on China's coast, bringing China's usefulness to the Grand Alliance into serious question.[99]

At OCTAGON, the CCS agreed to define the overall objective in the war against Japan as the attainment of Japan's unconditional surrender to be gained by lowering Japanese will to resist. One means of achieving this was through strategic bombing. In September 1943, the Army Air Force planners had suggested bombing Japan into submission with B-29s based in India and staged through Chinese bases. Because of the vulnerability of the east China fields, Cheng-tu in west China was selected as the staging base. (*See Atlas Map No. 43.*) This decision had

been approved by the CCS at QUADRANT and reaffirmed at SEXTANT, although the Marianas then appeared to offer better bases.[100]

In early June 1944, the B-29s of the XX Bomber Command, Twentieth Air Force, initiated the strategic bombing offensive against Japan from airfields at Cheng-tu. Their operations, as well as those of Chennault's airmen, however, were tremendously handicapped by the fact that all supplies, including aviation gas, had to be flown in over the Hump. As the B-29s were used to bomb Japan rather than China, they had little impact on Chiang's desperate attempts to stop ICHIGO, while consuming Hump tonnage which Chennault and the Chinese Army urgently needed. Then came the seizure of the Marianas in July 1944 and the availability of the considerably better bases for the B-29's; these bases were easier to support logistically, and allowed deeper penetration into Japan than did the Cheng-tu bases. Not surprisingly, therefore, in December 1944, Stilwell's successor in China asked that the B-29s be withdrawn. Accordingly, by early 1945 the focal point of the strategic air offensive against Japan had shifted to the Marianas. Although sound logistical and military reasons supported this shift, it appeared to signify the end of China's usefulness to the Grand Alliance. Time was running out for Chiang.[101]

The war in east Asia, however, had not yet been decided. Stilwell's former command was divided into the China Theater and the India-Burma Theater, which remained part of SEAC. (*See Appendix 34.*) Lieutenant General Daniel I. Sultan, Stilwell's deputy theater commander, assumed command in India-Burma with the missions of breaking China's blockade and supporting China Theater; and Major General Albert C. Wedemeyer, Deputy Chief of Staff, SEAC, replaced Stilwell as Chief of Staff to the

Major General Claire L. Chennault (left) Welcomes General Albert C. Wedemeyer to China Theater, 1944

Generalissimo with the missions of creating conditions for more effective employment of U.S resources in China and assisting the Chinese in playing a more active role in the war.[102]

Wedemeyer's most immediate task was stemming the Japanese offensive in east China. Seeing ICHIGO as a threat to Kunming and to the Hump and Ledo Road (renamed the Stilwell Road by Chiang) terminus in China, he advised the Generalissimo to move additional divisions to the Kweilin-Liuchow area to blunt the enemy attack. Wedemeyer assisted in this movement by ordering an airlift to transport Chiang's highly-touted divisions to the critical spot from the northwest, where they had been watching the Communists in Sian. But when these forces, as well as those divisions from the Salween front, melted away before the Japanese, Wedemeyer was forced to recall two divisions from the X-force in Burma. Both the withdrawal of two divisions from Burma and the request for transport aircraft to facilitate troop movements met with initial resistance from SEAC, but success in Burma against weakening Japanese resistance removed SEAC's objections. The two divisions arrived in late December 1944 and early January 1945. (*See Atlas Map No. 43.*) As the Chinese forces (known as the ALPHA force) began to concentrate for the defense of Kunming, the Japanese drive on Kweiyang began to run out of steam and was finally halted by the two divisions from Burma, logistical problems, and Imperial General Headquarters in December 1944. The threat to east China had passed, but in the process the Japanese had inflicted grievous wounds on the Chinese Nationalist armies, the Chungking Government, and Sino-American relations.[103]

Although the Chinese licked their wounds, Mountbatten's troops were exploiting Slim's brilliant victory at Imphal. (*See Atlas Map No. 42.*) Meanwhile, the northern and southern forces (NCAC and the XV Corps) awaited the end of the monsoon.* Fourteenth Army (now the IV and XXXIII Corps) mercilessly pursued the Japanese throughout the monsoon. Although appalling climatic conditions turned roads and tracks into porridge, numerous bridgeheads were established across the Chindwin by the first week in December 1944, putting Slim into position for the second phase of the decisive battle—destruction of the Japanese Army in Burma. On his north flank, Sultan and Wei Li-huang were tasked to open the Burma Road; on his south flank, XV Corps was directed to aid Slim's advance by driving down the Arakan coast and capturing airfields from which supplies could be rapidly flown to the Fourteenth Army. The stage was set for *Burma Area Army's* Armageddon.[104]

In northern Burma, Sultan advanced southward on October 15, 1944 with a force which consisted of an American brigade (including Merrills' Marauders), the MARS Task Force, a British division, and five Chinese divisions. Occupying Bhamo on December 15, he linked up

*To enable Slim to concentrate his attention on the vital central front, Giffard had removed both the XV Corps and the Arakan front from Slim's command. The command situation was further unscrambled in November when Allied Land Forces South-East Asia (ALFSEA), which superceded 11th Army Group, took command of the XV Corps, the Fourteenth Army, and NCAC (*See Appendix 33.*).

Jungle Road During 1944 Monsoon

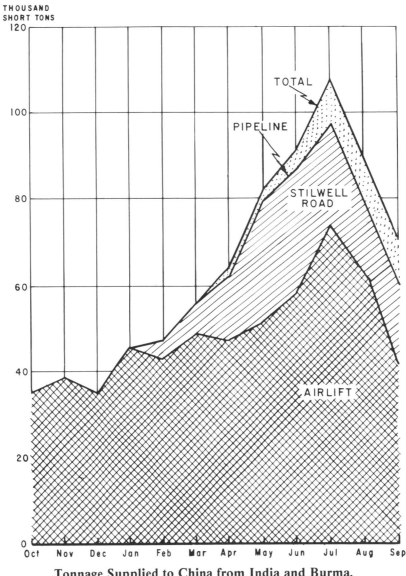

THOUSAND
SHORT TONS

**Tonnage Supplied to China from India and Burma,
October 1944–September 1945***

with the Yunnan armies on the old Burma Road on January 20, 1945. The road from Ledo to China was now clear, and the first convoys from India reached Kunming on February 4. Work was immediately begun on extending the Ledo-Myitkyina oil pipeline to Kunming. Continuing southward, Sultan's forces occupied Lashio on March 7. Meanwhile, using Myitkyina as a staging area, the Air Transport Command began doubling its monthly air deliveries to China. With an increased air supply and a road and pipeline from India, the blockade of China was over.[105]

The offensive in Arakan began on December 12, 1944. On January 4, 1945, the XV Corps occupied Akyab, which the Japanese had abandoned two days earlier. (*See Atlas Map No. 42.*) During February, the XV Corps seized Ramree Island by amphibious assault. Reluctantly, it suspended major operations, since with the occupation of

Akyab and Ramree the goals of the campaign had been achieved. Airfields were rapidly built to make air supply of the Fourteenth Army possible for its decisive blow.[106]

Slim had hoped that the Japanese would make a stand in the open country north of Mandalay, where British armor could operate effectively. Instead the new Japanese commander in Burma, Lieutenant General Hoyotaro Kimura, decided to defend farther south, along the line, Mandalay-Lashio. Any British assault on Mandalay would, therefore, first have to force a crossing of the broad Irrawaddy River. Kimura believed that by catching the Fourteenth Army

*The graphs used in this chapter which depict tonnages delivered to China are based upon depictions in Charles Romanus and Riley Sunderland, *China-Burma-India Theater: Stilwell's Command Problems.* (Washington, 1956) and Romanus and Sunderland, *China-Burma-India: Time Runs Out in CBI.* (Washington, 1958).

astride the river at the end of a long and tenuous supply line, he could inflict a severe defeat similar to that the Japanese themselves had suffered at Imphal. Success against the British would then leave him free to concentrate against Sultan and Wei Li-huang with every prospect of success. Although theoretically sound, his plan ignored the supply and combat capabilities of the Allied air forces, the now superior jungle craft of British troops, the amazing feats of logistical improvisation which Allied staffs could achieve on short notice, and Slim.[107]

Showing great flexibility of mind and supported by his dedicated staff, Slim recast his plan in record time. The XXXIII Corps was to move directly south against Mandalay, thus drawing Kimura's attention and divisions into the Mandalay area. (*See Atlas Map No. 42.*) Meanwhile, the IV Corps, moving secretly south through the jungle hills west of that city, would suddenly appear at Pakokku, seize a crossing, and strike promptly and violently at Meiktila, a key Japanese base on Kimura's line of communications. If Meiktila fell to the British while Kimura was engaged around Mandalay, he would be compelled to detach large forces to clear his vital supply line. Kimura's forces would then be caught between the anvil of the IV Corps and the hammer blows of the XXXIII Corps from the north.[108]

By February 1, 1945, the Fourteenth Army, which was supplied almost entirely by air, had closed up to the Irrawaddy from a point 40 miles north of Mandalay to Pakokku, 140 miles downstream. With the supply situation under control, Slim began crossing the Irrawaddy in mid-February. The IV Corps captured Meiktila on March 3, cutting the Japanese supply line. In a desperate attempt to stave off final defeat, Kimura concentrated his remaining forces in Burma and launched an offensive to recapture Meiktila; this last ditch effort to regain the town failed, and Mandalay meanwhile fell (March 20) to XXXIII Corps. This offensive was the last Japanese one in Burma. In fighting the decisive battle, Slim provided a classic example of the strategic envelopment.[109]

Time was running out for the Japanese in Burma, as Kimura was thrown back with very heavy losses and with his armies losing all cohesion. Quickly regrouping, Slim resumed the pursuit to Rangoon, his main force following the axis of the Rangoon-Mandalay railroad while a secondary effort moved down the Irrawaddy. (*See Atlas Map No. 44.*) It was a race with the coming monsoon season and against Kimura's attempts to rebuild his defenses. Led by armor and supplied largely by air, the British forces quickly gained momentum. A Japanese attempt to concentrate at Toungoo was broken up by Karen tribesmen under British officers. Kimura's concentration for a final stand at Pegu

was overrun on May 1, just as the monsoon rains began. To ensure that Rangoon was occupied before the full fury of the monsoon broke, the XV Corps launched the long awaited airborne-amphibious assault on May 2; the city, which had been left undefended, was entered without opposition a day later. The campaign for the reoccupation of Burma was now over, except for mopping-up operations, as those Japanese isolated in western Burma tried to break out. There were no more major operations in Burma prior to the Japanese capitulation on August 15.[110]

The War for East Asia

In time of war you have to take your allies as you find them.[111]
Lieutenant General Joseph W. Stilwell

In China, the sun was setting on Japan's imperial aspiration, but not without a final convulsion. During early 1945, the Japanese had continued to consolidate their position in southeastern China, clearing the Canton–Hengyang railroad in February. (*See Atlas Map No. 45.*) Meanwhile, Army leaders in China were arguing for an offensive against Chungking, believing that one more push—they had almost been successful at Kweiyang in November 1944—would either force the Nationalists to a separate peace or render them impotent. Imperial General Headquarters, however, vetoed all plans for an operation into China's hinterlands for good reasons. American successes in the Pacific, combined with the threat of a landing on the China coast, compelled the Japanese to redeploy the Army to the coastal region of south and central China. First, however, there were two final operations in central China—one in March to seize the Allied air base at Laohokow, and one in April against Chihkiang. The Laohokow operation was successful, but the April operation failed because of combined Fourteenth Air Force-Chinese resistance and the need to redeploy troops to Manchuria to meet a growing Russian threat. These were the last large-scale Japanese offensives in China. During the summer of 1945, the Emperor's forces moved into central and northern China to defend against the expected Soviet attack and an anticipated American landing around the Shantung Peninsula.[112]

Although the Chihkiang campaign was of little operational consequence, militarily it was important because the Japanese thrust was turned back by an improved, essentially Chinese Army: ALPHA force. Army reform was finally beginning to pay dividends. Thanks to operations in Burma, resources were no longer the problem they had been in 1942 and 1944; and Chiang, his back driven to the wall during ICHIGO and his airpower thesis destroyed, now supported the reforms. But the most important element was Wedemeyer. His tact and diplomacy enabled him to establish an easy working relationship with the Generalissimo. Chiang was able to consider Wedemeyer's proposals on their merits. Equally important, Wedemeyer's advice and assistance in stopping ICHIGO was instrumental in winning Chiang's confidence. Under these circumstances, Wedemeyer's advice for reforming the Army fell on receptive ears.[113]

A precondition for reform was resuscitation of the American advisory effort in China. When Stilwell left China to join X-force in November 1943, he had lost hope in Chinese Army reform. Although the Y- and Z-forces had been exposed to American training in the centers that Stilwell had established in China, the impact was minimal, and China became a military backwater. Stilwell turned his attention to Burma, where he fought a magnificent campaign against the Japanese. The trade-off, however, was stagnation in China; when Stilwell lost interest in China, the military assistance program he initiated atrophied. While lack of command emphasis was one part of the problem, cynicism was the other part. Stilwell's subordinates in China soon adopted his skeptical attitude toward the Chinese, and Wedemeyer arrived to find the climate among Americans permeated with lethargy and skepticism. Being able to devote his complete attention to China—Stilwell was never able to to this—Wedemeyer breathed new life into the moribund advisory effort.[114]

Wedemeyer started by instituting joint American-Chinese staffs at all major echelons. Wedemeyer and General Chen Cheng, the Minister of Defense, ran the staff, and each staff section was jointly run by Chinese and American officers. The success of this staff created a spirit of friendly cooperation at the top level, and this spirit soon began to filter down to the lowest echelon. Reorganization of combat forces was the next task. Like Stilwell, Wedemeyer recommended the qualitative approach; whereas Stilwell wanted initially to upgrade 30 divisions, Wedemeyer suggested that 39 divisions (ALPHA force) be trained and equipped by the United States. In order to assure support for this force, the Generalissimo consented to appoint an American, Major General Gilbert X. Cheves, as commanding general of ALPHA force's services of supply.[115]

Finally, Wedemeyer assigned American advisory groups to each Chinese division. (*See Appendix 35.*) The senior member of each group served as the military adviser to the Chinese unit commander. If the Chinese commander disagreed with his American counterpart, the Chinese commander exercised his own judgment. Using American channels, however, the American adviser could notify the next higher American adviser that his Chinese counterpart had overruled him. If necessary, the differences in judgment could ultimately come to the attention of Wedemeyer and the Generalissimo for a final decision. In addition to giving the American advisers with Chinese divisions the ability to influence their counterparts, this parallel chain of command served to keep the Joint American-Chinese staff informed when Chinese channels were slow in reporting the situation.[116]

By the spring of 1945, China finally seemed to be responding to American proddings. In retrospect, this raises questions of the Chinese contribution to the war effort. Could the Chinese have done more? The Japanese were able to gain all their objectives in Asia by 1942 because both the United States and China were unprepared for war, and Great Britain was almost totally absorbed in the Anglo-German war. During 1942 and 1943, there was little activity on either side as the Japanese consolidated their gains and organized their defense, and the Allies gathered strength, overcame serious logistical problems, initiated an air offensive, and kept China in the war by air supply. What contribution could the Chinese have made during this preparatory period? Chiang was faced with many difficult problems, not the least of which were logistical and political. Yet by fighting the Generalissimo's war for him with the Fourteenth Air Force, the United States neither compelled him to upgrade the Chinese Army nor to reorder his logistical priorities accordingly. Chiang was given a way of escape, and he took it. Should the Allies, as Stilwell advocated, have forced Chiang to do more by using lend-lease as a bargaining lever? Chiang seemingly had the option of coming to terms with the Japanese; but considering Japan's imperialistic aspirations and China's internal strife, it is highly debatable that this was a viable option. Perhaps, ironically, Japan could have helped the Allied cause by staging a major offensive in China in the period of 1942 to 1943. This might have had a catalytic effect, spurring the Generalissimo into action earlier in the war.

During 1944 and 1945, the Allies launched an offensive to recapture Burma and break the blockade of China. Chiang's contribution, the Salween campaign, was minimal, but he was confronted with problems in China in the form of ICHIGO and the Chinese Communists. When Roosevelt finally applied pressure on Chiang to appoint Stilwell to the command of Chinese forces, he was unsuccessful; nevertheless, the Generalissimo weathered the storm in China, and the offensive in Burma succeeded. The pressure was off; but the relief came as a result of the American offensives in the Central Pacific and Southwest Pacific

Areas, not as a result of Japanese defeat in Asia. Yet, the Japanese Army had maintained over one million men in China. Was Chiang's contribution worthwhile? Did the United States accomplish its purpose in east Asia by supporting China?[117]

By June 1945, it was obvious that Japan had lost her war. The American offensives in the Pacific had penetrated Japan's inner ring. The Americans now had forward bases for an invasion of Japan, the Japanese Navy was a memory, and the remaining Japanese airpower was destroying itself in *kamikaze* attacks. Stalin, victorious in Europe, shifted Russian divisions to Asia in keeping with his Yalta commitments as well as in fulfillment of his imperial aspirations. Since Japanese forces in Manchuria, the one-time crack Kwantung Army, had steadily declined in strength and quality due to transfer of veteran units during the war, it was necessary to reinforce them with divisions from southern China. This withdrawal was followed up—but apparently little troubled—by the Chinese. At the same time, the Fourteenth and Tenth Air Forces harassed the Japanese by interdicting their transportation net and shipping. No decisive action took place in this area, however, before the end of the war.[118]

After atomic bombs fell on Hiroshima and Nagasaki on August 6 and 9, 1945, Japan opened peace negotiations. She surrendered on August 14. Russia declared war on Japan on August 8. The next day, the Russians launched their main attack into Manchuria from the west, supported by attacks from the north. (*See Atlas Map No. 45.*) Using masses of armor and motorized units, the Russians swept across the Manchurian plains against defeated Japanese forces which lacked modern armor and effective antitank weapons and could offer only token resistance. Although the war ended officially on August 15, the Russians continued their advance for five more days. By this time,

they were close to their objective—Mukden in Manchuria —and had landed a force on the northeast coast of Korea; they had also occupied Sakhalin. The Russians then declared that after years of ineffective American fumbling among the Pacific islands, the Red Army had delivered the decisive blow which defeated Japan.[119]

When Japan surrendered, 39 Chinese divisions had American equipment, and American logisticians were beginning to create a Chinese service of supply capable of supporting that number of divisions in combat. Only 16, however, had completed training, and there was no pool of trained replacements. The effort to upgrade the Chinese Army was comprehensive, but it was just beginning to gather momentum. If the Nationalist Government was to command and support this force in battle, time to complete the work was needed. Considerable Chinese interest and cooperation was now forthcoming, and adequate American resources were on hand or in sight. The critical commodity was time. If Japan had fought on long enough and well enough, that, paradoxically, might have bought Chiang the time he needed—and could have been the salvation of his government.[120]

When peace was restored, however, Chiang had run out of time. Wedemeyer was told to support the Nationalists unless they engaged in civil war. He requested five American divisions to assist the overextended Nationalists in disarming the Japanese in Manchuria, but the American rush to demobilize precluded such a move. Meanwhile, the Communists, with Japanese weapons left them by the Russians, reverted to guerrilla warfare. Civil war and then the Cold War replaced World War II, as conflict continued in China. The first phase, for control of China, was won by the Communists in 1949, when Chiang fled to Formosa, thus ending a civil war which had been going on intermittently for 37 years, and of which World War II was only a part.[121]

Notes

[1]Louis J. Halle, *The Cold War as History* (New York, 1967), pp. 191–194.

[2]Charles F. Romanus and Riley Sunderland, *China-Burma-India Theater: Stilwell's Mission to China* (Washington, 1953), p. 5.

[3]*Ibid.*, p. 5.

[4]*Ibid.*, p. 6.

[5]*Ibid.*, p. 33.

[6]*Ibid.*, pp. 33-36.

[7]Brigadier General Vincent J. Esposito (ed.), *The West Point Atlas of American Wars* (2 Vols.; New York, 1959), II, Section 2, 111; Barbara W. Tuchman, *Stilwell and the American Experience in China, 1911-45* (New York, 1971), pp. 107-155.

[8]Romanus and Sunderland, *Stilwell's Mission to China*, p. 6; Tuchman, *Stilwell*, pp. 107-255.

[9]Jim R. Paschall, "U.S. Aid to China, 1932–1940" (Unpublished M.A. Thesis, Duke University, 1971), p. 49.

[10]Saburo Hayashi (with Alvin D. Coox), *Kogun, The Japanese Army in the Pacific War* (Quantico, 1959), p. 13; Theodore Ropp, *War in the Modern World* (New York, 1962), p. 359; Esposito, *West Point Atlas,* II, Section 2, 112.

[11]F.F. Liu, *A Military History of Modern China, 1924-1949* (Princeton, 1956), p. 208; Romanus and Sunderland, *Stilwell's Mission to China*, pp. 9-12; Hayashi and Coox, *Kogun*, p. 18.

[12]Liu, *Military History of Modern China*, p. 176; Romanus and Sunderland, *Stilwell's Mission to China*, pp. 12-14.

[13]Romanus and Sunderland, *Stilwell's Mission to China*, pp. 17-19.

[14]*Ibid.*, p. 23.

[15]Liu, *Military History of Modern China*, p. 197; Romanus and Sunderland, *Stilwell's Mission to China*, p. 29.

[16]Liu, *Military History of Modern China*, pp. 200-206.

[17]Hayashi and Coox, *Kogun*, pp. 19-21; Ropp, *War*, p. 363.

[18]Paschall, "U.S. Aid to China," p. 92.

[19]Romanus and Sunderland, *Stilwell's Mission to China*, p. 50.

[20]*Ibid.*, pp. 61-62.

[21]Liu, *Military History of Modern China*, p. 177; Romanus and Sunderland, *Stilwell's Mission to China*, p. 66; Ropp, *War*, p. 382.

[22]Liu, *Military History of Modern China*, pp. 177-180; Romanus and Sunderland, *Stilwell's Mission to China*, pp. 70-71; Tuchman, *Stilwell*, pp. 293-297.

[23]Joseph W. Stilwell, *The Stilwell Papers* (New York, 1948), p. 19.

[24]*Ibid.*, p. 38.

[25]Romanus and Sunderland, *Stilwell's Mission to China*, pp. 78-79.

[26]*Ibid.*, pp. 79-83.

[27]*Ibid.*, p. 80.

[28]Liang Chin-tung, *General Stilwell in China, 1942-1944; The Full Story* (New York, 1972), pp. 2, 23-24; Romanus and Sunderland, *Stilwell's Mission to China*, pp. 86-90.

[29]Esposito, *West Point Atlas*, II, Section 2, 127; Romanus and Sunderland, *Stilwell's Mission to China*, pp. 125-136.

[30]Romanus and Sunderland, *Stilwell's Mission to China*, pp. 143-148.

[31]Romanus and Sunderland, *Stilwell's Mission to China*, pp. 151-152; Ropp, *War*, p. 382.

[32]Tuchman, *Stilwell*, p. 6.

[33]Chin-tung, *Stilwell in China*, p. 51. Romanus and Sunderland, *Stilwell's Mission to China*, pp. 152-157.

[34]Stilwell, *Papers*, p. 118; Chin-tung, *Stilwell in China*, pp. 54-59.

[35]Stilwell, *Papers*, p. 118.

[36]Albert C. Wedemeyer, *Wedemeyer Reports!* (New York, 1958), p. 282; Romanus and Sunderland, *Stilwell's Mission to China*, pp. 169-187.

[37]Romanus and Sunderland, *Stilwell's Mission to China*, pp. 187-190.

[38]*Ibid.*, pp. 191-221.

[39]*Ibid.*, pp. 198-212.

[40]Field Marshal The Viscount Sir William Slim, *Defeat into Victory* (New York, 1961), pp. 64-65; Liu, *Military History of Modern China*, pp. 184-191; Romanus and Sunderland, *Stilwell's Mission to China*, pp. 219-220, 290-292.

[41]S. Woodburn Kirby, *The War Against Japan*, Vol. II, *India's Most Dangerous Hour* (London, 1958), pp. 235-236; Romanus and Sunderland, *Stilwell's Mission to China*, pp. 224-229.

[42]Esposito, *West Point Atlas*, II, Section 2, 127.

[43]Kirby, *Most Dangerous Hour*, pp. 237-249; Romanus and Sunderland, *Stilwell's Mission to China*, p. 261.

[44]Tuchman, *Stilwell*, p. 4.

[45]Romanus and Sunderland, *Stilwell's Mission to China*, pp. 250-251.

[46]Chin-tung, *Stilwell in China*, p. 7; Romanus and Sunderland, *Stilwell's Mission to China*, pp. 251-261.

[47]Romanus and Sunderland, *Stilwell's Mission to China*, p. 261.

[48]Kirby, *Most Dangerous Hour*, pp. 133-144; Slim, *Defeat into Victory*, pp. 147-161.

[49]Kirby, *Most Dangerous Hour*, pp. 243-244; Romanus and Sunderland, *Stilwell's Mission to China*, p. 303; Slim, *Defeat into Victory*, pp. 29, 119.

[50]Romanus and Sunderland, *Stilwell's Mission to China*, p. 303; Slim, *Defeat into Victory*, p. 163.

[51]S. Woodburn Kirby, "War in Eastern Asia," in *A Concise History of World War II*, Ed. by Vincent J. Esposito (New York, 1964), p. 304.

[52]Romanus and Sunderland, *Stilwell's Mission to China*, p. 304.

[53]Sun Tzu, *The Art of War*, translated with an introduction by Samuel B. Griffiths (London, 1971), p. 85.

[54]Tuchman, *Stilwell*, p. 6.

[55]Romanus and Sunderland, *Stilwell's Mission to China*, pp. 269-276.

[56]Michael Howard, *Grand Strategy*, Vol. IV, *August 1942-September 1943* (London, 1972), pp. 248-251; Romanus and Sunderland, *Stilwell's Mission to China*, pp. 177-280.

[57]Romanus and Sunderland, *Stilwell's Mission to China*, pp. 278-286, 313-322.

[58]*Ibid.*, pp. 278-310.

[59]Howard, *Grand Strategy*, pp. 399-405, 437-447, 571-574;

Romanus and Sunderland, *Stilwell's Mission to China*, pp. 341-353; Ropp, *War*, p. 383.

[60]Romanus and Sunderland, *Stilwell's Mission to China*, pp. 341-353.

[61]*Ibid.*, pp. 354-388.

[62]*Ibid.*, p. 389.

[63]Charles F. Romanus and Riley Sunderland, *China-Burma-India Theater: Stilwell's Command Problems* (Washington, 1956), p. 49.

[64]Chin-tung, *Stilwell in China*, p. 9; Romanus and Sunderland, *Stilwell's Command Problems*, pp. 256-259; Wedemeyer, *Wedemeyer Reports!*, pp. 256-257.

[65]Romanus and Sunderland, *Stilwell's Command Problems*, pp. 80-82.

[66]Sun Tzu, *Art of War*, p. 83.

[67]Esposito, *West Point Atlas*, II, Section 2, 142; Slim, *Defeat into Victory*, pp. 170-172.

[68]Slim, *Defeat into Victory*, pp. 115-121; 142-143, 168-196.

[69]*Ibid.*, pp. 214-232.

[70]Kirby, "Eastern Asia," p. 306; Romanus and Sunderland, *Stilwell's Command Problems*, pp. 165-169; Slim, *Defeat into Victory*, pp. 233-247.

[71]Romanus and Sunderland, *Stilwell's Command Problems*, pp. 36-37; Slim, *Defeat into Victory*, p. 251.

[72]S. Woodburn Kirby, *The War Against Japan*, Vol. III, *The Decisive Battles* (London, 1961), pp. 45-47; Tuchman, *Stilwell*, pp. 541-542.

[73]Esposito, *West Point Atlas*, II, Section 2, 142; Romanus and Sunderland, *Stilwell's Command Problems*, pp. 119-220; Ropp, *War*, p. 384.

[74]Hayashi and Coox, *Kogun*, p. 98; Kirby, "Eastern Asia," p. 307.

[75]Romanus and Sunderland, *Stilwell's Command Problems*, pp. 226-256.

[76]Stilwell, *Papers*, p. 313.

[77]Slim, *Defeat into Victory*, p. 281; Romanus and Sunderland, *Stilwell's Command Problems*, p. 172.

[78]Esposito, *West Point Atlas*, II, Section 2, 142.

[79]Hayashi and Coox, *Kogun*, pp. 93-100; Slim, *Defeat into Victory*, pp. 285-344.

[80]Slim, *Defeat into Victory*, pp. 315-346.

[81]Hayashi and Coox, *Kogun*, pp. 100-101; Romanus and Sunderland, *Stilwell's Command Problems*, pp. 83-116.

[82]Romanus and Sunderland, *Stilwell's Command Problems*, p. 90.

[83]*Ibid.*, pp. 188-293.

[84]Stilwell, *Papers*, p. 333.

[85]Halle, *Cold War*, pp. 196-198; Liu, *Military History of Modern China*, pp. 202-205.

[86]Halle, *Cold War*, pp. 196-198; Wedemeyer, *Wedemeyer Reports!*, p. 287.

[87]Esposito, *West Point Atlas*, II, Section 2, 149; Kirby, "Eastern Asia," pp. 307-309; Liu, *Military History of Modern China*, pp. 221-225.

[88]Romanus and Sunderland, *Stilwell's Command Problems*, pp. 297-328.

[89]Kirby, "Eastern Asia," p. 307; Hayashi and Coox, *Kogun*, p. 98; Romanus and Sunderland, *Stilwell's Command Problems*, pp. 329-360.

[90]Hayashi and Coox, *Kogun*, pp. 89-91; Romanus and Sunderland, *Stilwell's Command Problems*, pp. 316-326.

[91]Romanus and Sunderland, *Stilwell's Command Problems*, p. 382.

[92]*Ibid.*, pp. 359-389.

[93]*Ibid.*, pp. 389-398.

[94]*Ibid.*, pp. 399-442.

[95]*Ibid.*, ,p. 446.

[96]Ropp, *War*, p. 384.

[97]Romanus and Sunderland, *Stilwell's Command Problems*, pp. 471-472.

[98]Sun Tzu, *Art of War*, p. 101.

[99]Kent R. Greenfield (ed.), *Command Decisions* (Washington, 1960), pp. 461-477; Charles F. Romanus and Riley Sunderland, *China-Burma-India: Time Runs Out in CBI* (Washington, 1959), pp. 81-85.

[100]Wesley F. Craven and James L. Cate, *The Army Air Forces in World War II*, Vol V, *The Pacific: Matterhorn to Nagasaki, June 1944-August 1945* (Chicago, 1953), pp. 3-32.

[101]Romanus and Sunderland, *Times Runs Out*, pp. 26, 161-162.

[102]Romanus and Sunderland, *Time Runs Out*, pp. 6-15, 46-75; Wedemeyer, *Wedemeyer Reports!*, pp. 270-271.

[103]Esposito, *West Point Atlas*, II, Section 2, 141, 152; Kirby, "Eastern Asia," p. 309; Romanus and Sunderland, *Time Runs Out*, pp. 56-64, 142-170; Wedemeyer, *Wedemeyer Reports!*, pp. 290-293, 328-330.

[104]Slim, *Defeat into Victory*, pp. 347-369.

[105]Kirby, "Eastern Asia," p. 310; Romanus and Sunderland, *Time Runs Out*, pp. 89-141, 183-205; Wedemeyer, *Wedemeyer Reports!*, pp. 298-301.

[106]Esposito, *West Point Atlas*, II, Section 2, 151; Kirby, "Eastern Asia," pp. 309-310.

[107]Slim, *Defeat into Victory*, pp. 373-390.

[108]*Ibid.*, pp. 394-475.

[109]Kirby, "Eastern Asia," pp. 310-311; Slim, *Defeat into Victory*, pp. 394-475.

[110]Romanus and Sunderland, *Time Runs Out*, pp. 226-230, 325-329; Slim, *Defeat into Victory*, pp. 479-534.

[111]Stilwell, *Papers*, p. 320.

[112]Hayashi and Coox, *Kogun*, pp. 145-150; Romanus and Sunderland, *Time Runs Out*, pp. 170-179.

[113]Liu, *Military History of Modern China*, p. 192; Wedemeyer, *Wedemeyer Reports!*, p. 282; Romanus and Sunderland, *Time Runs Out*, pp. 231-290.

[114]Wedemeyer, *Wedemeyer Reports!*, pp. 294-295.

[115]Liu, *Military History of Modern China*, pp. 193-195; Wedemeyer, *Wedemeyer Reports!*, pp. 296-297.

[116]Wedemeyer, *Wedemeyer Reports!*, p. 297.

[117]Hayashi and Coox, *Kogun*, p. 150.

[118]Halle, *Cold War*, pp. 92-97; Hayashi and Coox, *Kogun*, pp. 169-172; Romanus and Sunderland, *Time Runs Out*, pp. 330-367, 386-388; Ropp, *War*, pp. 384-385.

[119]Esposito, *West Point Atlas*, II, Section 2, 152; Hayashi and Coox, *Kogun*, pp. 173-175; Kirby, "Eastern Asia," p. 311.

[120]Romanus and Sunderland, *Time Runs Out*, pp. 368-386.

[121]Halle, *Cold War*, pp. 98, 197-201; Ropp, *War*, p. 385.

Allied Victory: Toward a Newer Order in the Far East

10

There is no substitute for victory.

Douglas MacArthur

Shortly after daybreak on February 19, 1945, the assault elements of the 4th and 5th Marine Divisions began loading into the amphibious tractors which would carry them on to the soft, volcanic-ash beaches of Iwo Jima at 9:00 A.M. (*See Atlas Map No. 46.*) That tiny island in the Bonin-Volcano Islands* would become the site of the most heroic battle fought by the Marine Corps during the Second World War.[1] While each marine knew that the fight would be a tough one, none realized that for five terrible weeks the three divisions of Major General Harry Schmidt's V Amphibious Corps would battle the 20,000 Japanese ashore from hole to hole and cave to cave in a sanguinary effort to wrest the volcanic spit from the Japanese Empire. In the battle, all but a handful of the Japanese defenders would die, while 5,885 marines would be killed or would die of their wounds, and 17,272 more would be wounded in action—in all over 33 percent of the landing force.[2] By March 26, Iwo Jima, which would be immortalized by the dramatic flag raising on Mount Suribachi, would replace Peleliu and Tarawa as the marines' bloodiest battle of the Pacific war.

Admiral Nimitz planned the landing on the island as soon as he received instructions on October 3 to support MacArthur's move into Luzon, take an island in the Bonin-Volcano Island Group, and then advance to Okinawa. The United States needed Iwo Jima for forward airbases so that fighters could escort the B-29s to Japan and so that crippled

B-29s could have a safe way station enroute home from their targets; furthermore, the island had to be denied to the Japanese, because they, too, wanted it as a forward fighter base. While there were other nearby islands which were not as well fortified, Iwo Jima was the only one on which engineers could build airfields.

The Japanese began to fortify the island after the loss of Saipan in July 1944. By early 1945, Lieutenant General Tadamichi Kuribayashi, commanding a reinforced division and naval garrison troops, had prepared Iwo Jima for a prolonged defense. Kuribayashi decided to hold the high ground at either end of the island rather than defend the beaches; this would enable his troops to catch the Americans in enfilade fire after they had landed. Moreover, the Japanese commander had his men build elaborate underground defensive positions, which were impervious to heavy bombing and even to direct naval gunfire. He expected his men to die defending Iwo and to inflict casualties on the Americans at a ratio of 10:1.

Because of these preparations and the size of his garrison, General Kuribayashi conducted an excellent defense and virtually decimated the 24 infantry battalions of the three marine divisions (*See Atlas Map No. 47.*) which assaulted his island bastion.† Kuribayashi's men fought with the usual dedication of Japanese soldiers and sailors; but, in the end, the marines defeated them with a mixture of shell, flame, explosives, and uncommon valor.

With the capture of Iwo Jima the air campaign against Japan grew in intensity, reaching staggering proportions in mid-April when Major General Curtis LeMay's B-29s

---

*The Bonins are actually a group of islands in the Volcano Island group. In World War II, however, the name Bonins was applied to the Volcano Island group.

† The average casualty figure for the battalions was 687 killed, died, and wounded. The 3rd Battalion, 9th Marines suffered the least casualties—508; the 1st Battalion, 26th Marines suffered the most—1,025. A line battalion normally had between 750 and 1,000 men assigned. To further illustrate the intensity of the fight, 566 marines were killed and 1,755 wounded on February 19. This roughly approximated two of the eight battalions which landed that day.

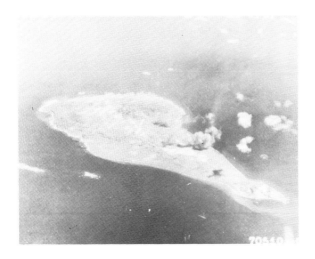

Iwo Jima
(Mount Suribachi is in Lower Right)

began low-level, night, fire-bomb raids on major Japanese cities. During the ensuing months, 24,761 airmen landed crippled bombers on Iwo Jima; at the same time, Army P-51 Mustangs* and the admirable Navy Hellcats protected the bombers on the raids on Japan, saving countless other crews from interception and destruction.[3]

In early 1945, it was obvious to both the Japanese and the Allies that the final stage of the war in the Pacific was at hand. Three Allied forces (Admiral Mountbatten's in Burma, General MacArthur's in the southwest Pacific, and Admiral Nimitz's in the central Pacific) had punctured the Japanese defensive perimeter, thereby destroying the continuity of Japan's defensive system and cutting Japan off from the vital resources in the Netherlands East Indies. (*See Atlas Map No. 46.*) In addition to the land campaigns, Allied submarines had sunk a major portion of the Japanese merchant marine; Allied submarines, carriers, and surface forces had decimated the Imperial Japanese Navy; and Allied air forces had gutted the Japanese land and naval air forces, except for those husbanded in the Japanese home islands. To make matters worse, carrier aircraft, as well as B-29s, now were striking Japan with increasing success; and on the horizon loomed the armies of the Soviet Union, which the Japanese feared would eventually strike into Manchuria, the last remaining enclave of Japanese power. Finally, the "China Incident" remained unsolved. The Japanese, however, knew nothing about a potential, cataclysmic threat—the atomic bomb.

The last moves on the Pacific chessboard centered on

Okinawa and Japan, and they resembled the actions of a champion facing a beginner at the end of a game. The Allies held a number of powerful pieces, which could move quickly and safely to any decisive spot; the Japanese had one or two such pieces, which they desperately sacrificed to gain a momentary victory, leaving only a row of devoted pawns to succor and protect their Emperor. Fortunately, after losing their last powerful pieces in the fight for Okinawa, the Japanese capitulated before their Emperor and his pawns were overwhelmed, thus ending Japan's "New Order" in the Far East.

Blowtorches, Corkscrews, and Kamikazes: Okinawa

Admiral Nimitz shifted his attention to Okinawa during September 1944, when the Joint Chiefs of Staff were considering the question of invading Formosa or Luzon.[4] When the Joint Chiefs decided in favor of Luzon, partly as a result of Nimitz' new interest in Okinawa but also because of the opposition of most of his subordinate commanders to Formosa, the admiral was able to dust off his Formosa (CAUSEWAY) plans and adapt many of them for use at Okinawa (ICEBERG). Since most amphibious operations had been quite similar and many of the key commanders were the same, this saved planning time for everyone concerned.[5]

Nimitz designated his most experienced commanders to conduct the largest invasion of the Pacific war. (*See Appendix 36.*) He appointed conservative and meticulous Raymond Spruance as overall commander of the Central Pacific Task Forces, and grizzled Marc Mitscher to command the American carrier task force. (*See Atlas Map No. 47.*) Vice Admiral Sir Bernard Rawlings, RN, would command the newly-arrived British carrier forces.† Neither Admiral King nor General Marshall really wanted British participation in the war because of the short range of their ships and the possibility that the British would try to influence American operations in the Pacific unduly. Nevertheless, the British carriers, all sporting nearly *kamikaze*-proof steel decks,** would be a welcome asset in the campaign.[6] Along with Mitscher, Spruance had the profane Richmond Turner, who would command the sailors of the Joint Expeditionary force, which was to prepare the

---

*The Americans developed the P-51 Mustang and the British improved the engine. In all-around performance, this fighter plane, which saw service in the latter part of the war, was superior to other Allied and Axis pursuit aircraft.

†One British carrier, HMS *Victorious,* had served in the Pacific with the *Saratoga* from March to August 1943. She had been loaned to the Pacific Fleet because of the loss of the *Wasp* and *Hornet.*

**American carriers had wooden decks.

Fleet Carriers	Displacement (tons)	Speed (in knots)	Number of Aircraft
HMS Formidable* (Joined May 23)	25,500	31	54
HMS Illustrious (Detached May 1)	25,500	31	54
HMS Indefatigable*	26,000	31½	72
HMS Indomitable*	25,500	31	54
HMS Victorious*	25,500	31	54

*Hit by *kamikazes* during Okinawan campaign.

British Fleet Carriers

way for the assault, land five divisions in the Ryukyus, and then support them ashore. Once ashore, Lieutenant General Simon Bolivar Buckner would take command of the two Marine and four Army divisions assigned to Tenth Army. Buckner, an Army general who had commanded in Alaska earlier in the war and who was involved in reviewing the Smith versus Smith controversy on Saipan, was the first Army officer to command a major amphibious operation in Nimitz' realm. For some unknown reason the proto-marine, Holland Smith, the commander of the Fleet Marine Force in the Pacific, was not designated to command Tenth Army, probably because of the greater size of the Army contingent and the previous unpleasantness between Smith and the Army.

General Buckner's invasion plans were quite orthodox. (*See Atlas Maps No. 47 and No. 48b.*) He planned to

Lieutenant General Simon Bolivar Buckner

achieve his assigned objectives in three phases, the first of which would begin six days before the main invasion of Okinawa Island. On that date, Major General Andrew Bruce's 77th Infantry Division was to seize several of the Kerama Islands west of Okinawa for fleet and seaplane bases for the Navy; thereafter, it would secure Keise Shima Island, from which 155-mm guns would then support the main landings. Buckner's main attack would begin on April 1, when Major General Roy Geiger's III Amphibious Corps and Major General John Hodge's XXIV Corps would land abreast on the west coast of Okinawa at the Hagushi Beach, while the 2nd Marine Division conducted a full-scale demonstration off the east coast near Minatoga. After both corps crossed the island and split the Japanese defenses, Buckner planned to send Hodge to clear southern Okinawa, while Geiger held fast in the north. Once Hodge completed his assignment, Buckner would begin his second phase by sending both corps north to capture the remainder of Okinawa, the anticipated center of Japanese defenses. The last part of the second phase of the operations would consist of the seizure of Ie Shima island, which the Americans wanted for airbases. Following these actions, General Buckner would begin the last phase—the destruction of the Japanese forces on the other islands around Okinawa and the development of bases on them. Also during this phase V Amphibious Corps would take Miyako Island in the Sakishima Island Group, between Okinawa and Formosa.

Because of Okinawa's close proximity to Japan (*See Atlas Map No. 47*), all the senior American commanders anticipated that the Japanese would fight desperately to hold the island, just as they had done previously everywhere else. This time, however, the Americans believed that the Japanese would be able to employ more aircraft and perhaps the remainder of their Navy from home bases. As a result, Admiral Nimitz planned to use all the forces at his command to pin the Japanese forces in position, secure his communications, neutralize airbases in Japan, bombard Okinawa, interdict shipping from Japan to Okinawa, and, most importantly, gain local air superiority over Okinawa. (*See Appendix 37.*) To assist Nimitz, the Joint Chiefs ordered MacArthur to send his bombers north to strike targets on Formosa, while the bombers from the Twentieth Air Force in China and the Marianas (commanded by General Henry Arnold, the Army Air Force Chief of Staff) were directed to attack strategic targets in Formosa, Japan, and Okinawa.

Okinawa and the nearby islands were needed as the major base area for the invasion of Japan. On them, engineers and construction troops would build eight airfields and one seaplane base, and would develop a major advanced fleet base. They would also rehabilitate Naha port. This was an ambitious task, considering that the Rykukyus were 6,000 miles away from the United States and that logistic planners had to consider a 120-day lead time for ordering and delivering supplies. Therefore, most of the important equipment and key construction supplies had to be shipped to Okinawa with the invasion force. As in many previous operations, once ashore, the American engineers would be required to build bases while troops fought nearby to expand the beachhead.

While the command structure, the assault plan, the various forces employed, and the mission of base construction were not new to the invading forces, there were some new wrinkles added for this campaign. First and foremost, the troops were probably the best equipped of the war. For example, Hodge's XXIV Corps was completely re-equipped when it was pulled out of the fighting on Leyte to embark for Okinawa, much to the satisfaction of General Eichelberger's Eighth Army soldiers who inherited the discarded equipment, which was better than anything they had.[7] Second, the invasion troops received new items of equipment: flamethrower tanks, 57-mm and 75-mm recoilless rifles, variable time (VT) artillery fuzes, sniper-scopes, and new sound-locating sets for counterbattery fire. Third, General Buckner planned to wage a vigorous psychological campaign to weaken the will of the Japanese to resist, and to placate the Okinawans so that they would not react hostilely to the invasion. Lastly, Buckner attached several military government units to his combat forces to control, feed, and care for approximately 300,000 Okinawan civilians who would soon be homeless and without food or medicines.

Imperial General Headquarters could not employ as many forces in battle in the Pacific as could the United States and her Allies. (*See Appendix 37.*) But even in the bleak days of early 1945, the Japanese High Command began activating forces for the eventual defense of the homeland while it shifted forces from China and Japan to vital areas such as French Indochina, Formosa, and Okinawa.[8] For the most part, the Japanese planners realistically analyzed Allied intentions after the landings in the Philippines. They made several assumptions: the next Allied attacks would strike Okinawa, the Bonins, or Formosa; the Soviet Union would attack in Manchuria as soon as Stalin found a good opportunity to do so; and ultimately the Allies would invade Japan. At the same time, however, the Japanese planners were too optimistic, believing that air operations alone could stop the Allies by breaking up the invasion forces at the beachheads. Moreover, the majority of the aggressive Japanese military leaders gave unwarranted weight to the moral superiority and spirit of their troops, without remembering that they had failed to stop the Allies

to date. Nevertheless, this optimism was complemented by a deep pessimism about the overall Japanese situation, which had grown steadily worse since 1942. With dwindling stocks of food, salt, oil, iron ore, and lumber; continual defeats everywhere except in China; mounting anti-war sentiment at home; and the growing material and physical strength of the Allies, many Japanese leaders saw clearly that the weakened Japanese armed forces could not stop landings on the Bonins, Formosa, and Okinawa, or even repel landings on the Japanese main islands. The pessimists could easily drive themselves into a deep depression by considering the probability of the Soviet Union's entry into the war following the collapse of Hitler's Germany, and the inevitability of redeployment of American armies and air forces from Europe to the Pacific.

Following the landings on Leyte, Imperial General Headquarters began planning for a decisive battle around Japan in 1945. Of necessity, the activities of Marshal Terauchi's *Southern Army* were relegated to secondary importance. Nevertheless, as late as January 27, 1945, Imperial General Headquarters told Terauchi to secure the strategic areas in Burma, the Philippines, Sumatra, Malaya, Thailand, and French Indochina to hinder the American advance toward China and Japan. (*See Atlas Map No. 46.*)

Throughout the southern region, however, the Japanese position was deteriorating. General Slim's troops were reconquering Burma as the pro-Japanese Indian and Burmese National Armies collapsed; General MacArthur's forces surged onto Luzon and then into the remainder of the Philippines; and British naval air forces began to strike Sumatra from the Indian Ocean. Even to previously stable, Vichy-controlled French Indochina the Japanese deployed two divisions and considered interning the French Army units there because they were concerned about General Charles DeGaulle's return to power in liberated France. Moreover, they feared that the Allies would invade Indochina from the Philippines in the near future. With the landing on Iwo Jima, the Allied threat to the Japanese home islands became more obvious. To deal with all of these dangerous developments, Imperial General Headquarters abolished unnecessary headquarters in the southern region and decided not to reinforce *Southern Army*. Then it pragmatically deployed new units from China, Korea, and Japan to Formosa, the Manchurian border facing the Soviet Union, and Okinawa.

On February 3, Imperial General Headquarters ordered its forces to "crush American attempts to advance air and seabases toward Formosa and Okinawa," but it stopped short of implementing its previous SHO-2 plan.[9] In the new order, the Japanese High Command planned to unify and coordinate all the air forces to strengthen the defense of

Japan, and formally endorsed and emphasized the use of special attack (*tokko* or suicide) units. The Japanese leaders, realizing that air operations were the key to their planned defense, prepared to use orthodox and *kamikaze* squadrons to destroy any new beachheads. Even at this stage of the war, however, the high command insisted on the use of ground counterattacks at the beaches to repel the invaders, although commanders on Iwo Jima and Okinawa thought differently.

The Japanese had not been able to respond strongly to the invasion of Iwo Jima because the island was too far away, but the American landing clearly indicated that the next Allied objective would be Okinawa, a place where the Japanese could offer stiff resistance because they could employ their husbanded air groups against the invading forces.

Elongated Okinawa, the main island in the Ryukyus, is not as large or rugged as Leyte or Luzon, but it is an ideal place for a strong defensive stand. (*See Atlas Map No. 48a.*) The most difficult terrain is in the north, but in the south a series of limestone escarpments, honeycombed with hundreds of natural caves, provided the Japanese with a remarkably strong position for a prolonged battle of attrition. It was there that Lieutenant General Mitsuru Ushijima, commanding the *Thirty-Second Army*, decided to deploy the majority of his forces.[10] An officer who was as well respected as General Kuribayashi, the Iwo Jima commander, Ushijima thoroughly understood his situation and his mission. Ignoring advice from Japan to plan counterattacks at the beaches, Ushijima emulated Kuribayashi on Iwo Jima and Yamashita on Luzon; he decided to yield the offensive to the Allies because he could not compete with their mobility, firepower, and airpower. Moreover, he believed that he could delay the Allies best by forcing them to attack his deep, prepared positions.

To accomplish his delaying mission, Ushijima carefully positioned his forces to gain maximum utilization of the terrain. He created a strong outpost line with one brigade of the *62nd Division* across the narrow neck of Okinawa from Chaton to Toguchi; behind this line, he deployed the remainder of the division from Uchitomari to Tsuwa, in what was the first line of resistance in his defensive belt. (*See Atlas Map No. 48a.*) Farther back, the general had his troops build and occupy a series of concentric defensive positions around Shuri, the ancient capital of Okinawa, while to the southeast he deployed the *24th Division* to guard the beaches near Minatoga and southern Okinawa. To the east, he stationed the *44th Independent Mixed Brigade* in the Chinen Peninsula to assist the *24th Division* in repelling landings on the Minatoga beaches. Ushijima anticipated that the main Allied forces would land across

the Minatoga beaches.[11] Naval troops were stationed on the Osoku Peninsula below Naha. Smaller units were sent north to defend the Motobu Peninsula and Ie Shima Island, and some Okinawa Home Guard (*Boeitai*) units were assigned to cover the large Hagushi beaches at the western center of the island. Since these units were not strong enough to impede a major attack, their mission was to delay an invader and destroy airfields on Ie Shima as well as the two east of the Hagushi Beaches.

Crew-served weapons to support the defending forces were carefully apportioned and sited. To add strength to his meticulously sited positions on the formidable terrain, Ushimjima assigned his abundant automatic weapons units to the front line formations and had his subordinates emplace these weapons to dominate all approaches into the defensive positions. Japanese strongpoints were mutually supporting and were built on the forward and reverse slopes of the key hills. Furthermore, the general organized all his artillery under one command,* but could not afford to mass his numerous weapons in one area because of the probability of Allied air and artillery attacks. He therefore scattered the artillery throughout the area, hiding it in caves and other underground positions. By the time he had finished making his dispositions, Ushimjima had the strongest fortified position in the Pacific.

To assist the garrison on Okinawa, the Imperial Japanese Navy stationed over 300 suicide (*kaiten*) boats in the Kerama Islands, and also planned to send the giant battleship *Yamato* (twin to the *Musashi*, which was sunk near Leyte) southward to strike the invasion force when it arrived off of Okinawa. This, too, would be a suicide mission—a decoy for the air attacks which would simultaneously rip into the Allied ships supporting the landing forces.[12] In these air attacks, *kamikaze* pilots from the Army and the Navy hoped to cripple the supporting fleet in 10 scheduled attacks.† As the days of the last winter of the Second World War gradually slipped away, signs began to appear that the defenders of Okinawa were soon to be tested.

When Admiral Mitscher's carrier groups attacked the Kyushu airfields, the Inland Sea, Kure, and Kobe (*See*

---

*This was the first time this had been done by the Japanese in the Pacific war. Allied observers constantly criticized the Japanese for their piecemeal and ineffective use of artillery. On Okinawa, the Japanese stilled such criticisms.

†By this time, the *kamikaze* pilots were not all volunteers. Admiral Toyoda, commanding the remains of the once mighty Combined Fleet, began ordering his pilots to perform such attacks, and thereafter morale dropped significantly in many naval air units. Still, many Japanese pilots cheerfully engaged in these desperate assaults, continuing to do so until the end of the war.

Franklin Under Attack

Atlas Map No. 47) on March 18 and 19,* the senior Japanese commanders concluded that the Allies would by-pass Formosa to invade Okinawa. Subsequent Allied actions soon confirmed this judgment.

On March 22, American minesweepers began sweeping the approaches to the Kerama Islands and Okinawa, and three days later, on Palm Sunday, "frogmen" from the fleet's underwater demolition teams started inspecting landing beaches in the Keramas. The following day, General Bruce's 77th Infantry Division landed at several spots in the islands; by the twenty-ninth, the veterans of Guam and the amphibious end run to Ormoc on Leyte had completed 15 different amphibious landings, securing the Keramas for naval and seaplane bases. On the thirty-first, XXIV Corps artillerymen landed on Keise Shima and emplaced their 155-mm guns.

Shortly after the initial operations began, Rear Admiral Morton Deyo's ships opened up a seven-day preparatory bombardment of the landing beaches and specified inland targets on Okinawa. At first, Deyo's gunners had to fire from long distances, but once the minesweepers cleared the coastline, they were able to saturate their targets from close ranges. From positions farther offshore, Admiral Mitscher's carrier pilots simultaneously attacked targets which the naval gunners could not hit, while protecting the growing fleet from Japanese air attack. Southwest of Okinawa, Admiral Rawling's British carrier air groups attacked the Sakishima Islands (*See Atlas Map No. 47*) to reduce Japanese air attacks from bases there.[13]

Snug in their underground shelters, the Japanese waited for the expected landings which began early on Easter Sunday—coincidentally, April Fool's Day. The soldiers

*The Japanese air squadrons reacted violently to these attacks, heavily damaging two fleet carriers (the *Franklin* [724 KIA, 265 WIA] and the *Wasp* [101 KIA, 269 WIA]), lightly damaging the *Intrepid*, the *Yorktown*, and the *Enterprise*, and hitting one destroyer. The Japanese lost 161 aircraft out of 193 employed. These losses delayed Japanese air attacks on the fleet at Okinawa until April 6.

and marines of the Tenth Army, expecting to meet bitter resistance during the familiar run to the beaches even though the supporting ships and artillery had plastered the beaches with over 100,000 shells, reached shore easily around 8:30 A.M. (*See Atlas Map No. 48b.*) Within two hours, XXIV Corps soldiers had overrun Kadena airfield; an hour later, III Amphibious Corps marines overran Yontan airfield. As the leading units pushed farther inland, reserves and service troops landed, and everywhere the Americans wondered where the Japanese were. Okinawa had unexpectedly turned out to be another Luzon, rather than a Tarawa or Saipan.[14]

To the southeast of the island, Rear Admiral Jerauld Wright's Demonstration Group had a harder time of it because Japanese *kamikazes* crashed two LSTs and a transport, killing a number of marines and sailors. Even with these casualties, the 2nd Division marines demonstrated toward the Minatoga beaches, turning back just about the time the troops landed in the west.[15]

By the end of L-Day, General Buckner had four divisions ashore—from north to south, the 6th Marine, 1st Marine, 7th Infantry, and 96th Infantry—and was preparing to continue his attack inland the following day. His engineers had even repaired the captured airfields sufficiently for emergency landings, and his service troops began unloading assault supplies. Only offshore had the Japanese managed to hurt the Americans. There they crashed the battleship *West Virginia* and two other ships, in addition to those in the Demonstration Group.

On April 2, 7th Infantry Division troops reached the east coast of Okinawa, cutting the island in two, and the next day the adjacent 1st Marine Division followed suit. (*See Atlas Map No. 48b.*) While these center units met little organized resistance, the flank divisions began to hit small, strong Japanese positions as they advanced toward their objectives.

As General Hodge turned his corps southward on April 3, his soldiers encountered increasing resistance. American planners had not anticipated this, believing that the main Japanese positions would be in the north. During the next three days, however, the soldiers of the 7th and 96th Infantry Divisions disproved such predictions, as they fought their way through the outguards of Ushimjima's defenses and struck the "iron resistance" that was soon to become the trademark of the *Thirty-Second Army*. By April 8, the troops of the two attacking divisions had reached a rough line stretching from Uchitomari on the west to Kaniku in the center, and on to an area between Tsuwa and Ouki on the east. Ahead lay the main defenses of Shuri. (*See Atlas Map No. 48b.*) The first major position to be attacked would be the Kakazu area in the western zone.

Meanwhile, in the north, General Geiger's troops met

tough outposts in the Yontan Zan mountain complex northeast of Yontan airfield; but once the marines of the 6th Division broke through them they met only stragglers retreating toward the Motobu Peninsula. (*See Atlas Map No. 48b.*) This unexpected development led General Buckner to cancel his plans for Phase I and to lift all restrictions from the offensive operations of III Amphibious Corps. As a result, Geiger pushed his 6th Division forward, and on April 7 the marines occupied Nago and Taira, successfully isolating the Motobu Peninsula. (*See Atlas Map No. 48b.*) They finally dominated that peninsula by April 18 after much close-in fighting in the Yae-Take mountain complex. For several weeks thereafter, marines and soldiers conducted counterguerrilla operations in northern Okinawa.

Just as Hodge's troops began to hit real opposition and Geiger's troops approached Motobu Peninsula, Admiral Toyoda launched the first of 10 planned *kamikaze* attacks against Allied forces at Okinawa.* Coupled with the air attack, Vice Admiral Seiichi Ito, commanding the *Surface Special Attack Force* (the *Yamato* and her escorts), sortied from the Inland Sea to attack the invasion forces. The *Yamato*, fueled for a one-way voyage, sailed without air cover to serve as the decoy for the attacking air squadrons. Toyoda sent 699 aircraft—355 of them *kamikazes*—

*The TEN-GO (Heaven) Air Operation.

Major General Roy Geiger

against Spruance's and Buckner's forces on April 6 and 7; in the two days his airmen heavily damaged or sank ships in and around Okinawa and the Kerama Islands. These included the fleet carrier *Hancock* (72 killed, 82 wounded) and the battleship *Maryland* (16 killed and 37 wounded). Fortunately for the ships at Okinawa, the *kamikazes* concentrated on the destroyers on picket duty—ones like the *Bush*, which suicide pilots crashed three times. When the attacks subsided, Spruance's sailors knew that they had been in a vicious fight, but they probably did not realize that they would have to beat off nine more major attacks and many more smaller ones before they left Okinawa.[16]

The cruise of the *Yamato* proved to be a slaughter of the first magnitude, analgous to the sinking of the *Repulse* and the *Prince of Wales* off Malaya in 1941. Mitscher's pilots found the great battleship on April 7, and in a few hours they sent her under with all but 269 of her crew of 2,767. As the *Yamato's* mighty 18.1-inch main batteries disappeared—they had never been fired in naval combat—the age of the battleship came to an end.[17]

With the exception of the marines' operations in the north, the eventual battle on Ie Shima* (April 16 to 21), and landings on other small islands around Okinawa, the pattern of the Okinawa campaign was fully developed by the time that Hodge's corps hit the main Shuri defenses on April 9. From then on, American infantrymen and tankers would batter themselves against formidable Japanese positions, gaining at the best only a few yards each day, while at sea and around the new air and naval bases Allied sailors and airmen would fight off the dangerous Japanese air attacks.

From April 9 to 12, General Bradley's 96th Infantry Division troops, who had been tested on Leyte, tried to take the high ground near Kakazu, one of the strongest Japanese positions. They were repulsed, with high casualties. (*See Atlas Map No. 49a.*) In the center of the XXIV Corps line, Bradley's battalions and the right flank units of General Archibald Arnold's 7th Infantry Division also failed to make any real headway. Arnold's men, attacking the heavily fortified town of Ouki, had no better luck. Hodge had to make new plans to regain offensive momentum following these reverses.

As the American divisions approached his main defenses, General Ushimjima, at the urging of his aggressive chief of staff, Lieutenant General Isamu Cho, and the young Imperial General Staff officers on his staff, decided to launch an all-out attack to split the invaders in half and seize the key town of Kishaba in the center of the American rear

*Ernie Pyle, probably the most famous American war correspondent of World War II and a veteran of many of Europe's battlefields, was killed at Ie Shima.

area. (*See Atlas Maps No. 49a and No. 48b.*) Ushijima's chief of operations, Colonel Hiromichi Yahara, argued against such an attack, knowing that it had little chance of success. Unfortunately, Ushijima followed Cho's advice. Thus, on the night of April 12, following the announcement of President Roosevelt's death, four of Ushijima's battalions infiltrated the American positions all along his front, as his artillery pounded the American defenses. (*See Atlas Map No. 49a.*) While some Japanese assault units nearly reached Ginowan that night and the following one, Hodge's troops and naval gunfire decimated the attacking battalions. Colonel Yahara's worst fears had been well founded; the offensive failed.

After the abortive attack, the Japanese licked their wounds, reorganized their battered units, and began to improve their defenses, while Hodge prepared to attack with three divisions on April 19. Hodge wanted to seize the valley and the highway which stretched across Okinawa from Naha on the west to Yonabaru on the east (*See Atlas Map No. 49a*), but he did not know that his forces would strike into the very heart of Ushijima's intricate defenses. Nevertheless, realizing that his men were in for a tough fight, Hodge did everything possible to insure success. He planned for a massive air, artillery, and naval-gunfire preparation; he quickly sent 1,200 replacements to his two divisions; and he deployed Major General George Griner's recently assigned 27th Infantry Division (originally the floating reserve for Tenth Army) into the line on the right of the 96th Infantry Division. The success of Hodge's attack greatly depended on Griner's fresh troops. Griner directed his right regiment to cross Machinato Inlet secretly during the night of April 18 to seize that part of the Uraseo-Mura

Escarpment* in its zone before dawn. Griner's left regiment was to attack from its initial position on the north side of Kakazu Ridge the next morning to clear Kakazu town and capture the crest of the Escarpment in its zone. Hodge ordered his two other division commanders to seize Shuri, Yonabaru, and the portions of the Naha-Yonabaru road which fell within their zones. (*See Atlas Map No. 49a.*)

Each of Hodge's divisions would assault positions that were held by a force the approximate size of a reinforced battalion, but these positions were incredibly strong. The Japanese troops had all the advantages of underground cover; extraordinarily good observation and fields of fire; dominating terrain; pre-registered artillery, mortar, and machinegun fires; emplaced minefields; and ingenious reverse-slope defenses in unpatterned terrain, which could break up the continuity of any attack. All across the line, the Japanese occupied commanding terrain, none of which was more difficult to assault than the Urasoe-Mura Escarpment, which rises from the East China Sea and gains height toward the southeast, ultimately forming an abrupt 215-foot northern palisade. (*See Atlas Map No. 49a.*)

General Griner's right regiment moved out late on the afternoon of April 18, and during the night successfully pushed forward to the northwest end of the Uraseo-Mura Escarpment. In the morning, 650 Navy and Marine Corps planes, 27 battalions of artillery, 6 battleships, 6 cruisers, and 6 destroyers pummelled the Japanese defensive areas in support of the three-division attack. The effort was to no avail; the 4,000 Japanese in the *62nd Division* came out of their underground positions and stopped the American

---

*Key terrain is identified on appropriate maps by special numbers.

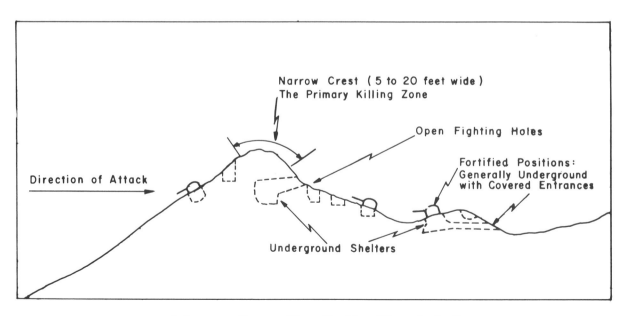

A Japanese Reverse Slope Position (Hypothetical)

divisions in the low ground between the opposing lines. In one area around Kakazu (*See Atlas Map No. 49a*), the Americans lost 20 tanks in vicious fighting in which the Japanese hurled themselves and satchel charges on the armored vehicles. Hodge lost 720 men, killed and wounded.[18]

American casualties grew markedly in the week that followed the opening attacks against the outer ring of the Shuri defenses. Infantrymen and tankers along the front lines could not really maneuver in the rugged terrain; therefore they began to use a mixture of "blowtorches" (flamethrowers) and "corkscrews" (explosives) to rout the Japanese from their pillboxes, blockhouses, and subterranean emplacements. At the same time, artillerymen and supporting tankers did their best to destroy the Japanese positions with direct and indirect fires. Regardless of the supporting fires, however, it was the blowtorches and corkscrews of the assaulting forces which ultimately killed the defenders in the small-unit battles.

From west to east, the Japanese died in place to stop the American infantry divisions. Around Gusukuma, one American regiment took eight days to clean out a hilly area called Item Pocket. (*See Atlas Map No. 49a.*) Just east of Item, one battalion of Griner's 27th Infantry Division suffered 50 killed and 43 wounded on April 20 as it spearheaded the fight for two pinacles on the Urasoe-Mura Escarpment. Altogether that day, Griner lost 506 men, the greatest single day's loss on Okinaw.[19] Farther east, Griner's troops repeatedly attacked the deadly Kakazu Pocket, which, though by-passed, still continued to thwart American moves all around it. At the same time, the 96th and 7th Infantry Divisions launched grueling assaults in their zones. Bradley's 96th fought to take Nishibaru and Tombstone Ridges quickly, but his battalions struggled four days before coming close to taking their objectives. Arnold's 7th Infantry Division took about the same time to overcome the Japanese battalion which stubbornly defended Hill 178, Ouki Hill, and Skyline Ridge in the eastern part of XXIV Corps' zone.

As American casualties rose, so did those of the Japanese. Under the steady battering Ushijima saw the Americans annihilate his best units and begin to crack his line. After committing some of his reserves to the line, the Japanese commander finally decided to withdraw to his next defensive ring on the night of April 23 under the cover of a heavy artillery bombardment. Hodge's troops did not notice Ushijima's withdrawal until the next day, when to their surprise they found most of the Japanese positions unoccupied. Gratefully, they moved forward to occupy the abandoned defenses. (*See Atlas Map No. 49a.*) There, for the first time, they saw the evidence of their successful fight—hastily prepared mass graves and cordwood-stacks of Japanese bodies awaiting burial. The fight was far from over, however. The slow advance southward presaged an even slower one, as Ushijima pulled back toward the core of his mountain defenses near Shuri and fed reserves from his *44th Independent Mixed Brigade* and *24th Division* into line.

By this time, the American commanders knew that they were involved in a costly battle, and were considering ways to quickly end it. General Bruce, who had executed the end run at Ormoc and had previously urged one at Saipan, recommended that a landing be made at Minatoga, but General Buckner vetoed any such move because the beach could not handle the supplies needed for a division and because the enveloping force would land in a well defended zone. (*See Atlas Map No. 49a*) The possibility of an amphibious assault to the rear of the Japanese lines made the Tenth Army staff consider the use of the two marine divisions on Okinawa and the 2nd Marine Division which had returned to Saipan. At this time, however, none of these divisions were available for employment. Nimitz, some days before, had directed Buckner to keep III Amphibious Corps free to land at Miyako Island during the last phase of ICEBERG in place of V Amphibious Corps, which had been severely mauled at Iwo Jima. A few days later, Nimitz decided to postpone the Miyako landings, and released III Amphibious Corps to Tenth Army. However, even with three additional divisions, all amphibiously trained, Buckner decided against an amphibious envelopment, relying instead on a slow, safe, frontal push toward Shuri. Buckner based his decision partly on the fact that his three Army divisions needed immediate relief after over three weeks of desperate fighting. With this in mind, the Tenth Army commander ordered the 1st Marine and 77th Infantry Divisions south immediately. As soon as an army division could relieve the 6th Marine Division of its mop-up in northern Okinawa, Buckner planned to send that division into the line.[20]

General Hodge did not wait for new divisions, however, before ordering a general (frontal) attack on April 26 against the second ring of the Shuri defensive area. As the 1st Marine and 77th Infantry Divisions moved into the XXIV Corps area, Hodge's tired divisions once again began assaulting Japanese emplacements along the line from Gasukuma to the Urasoe-Mura Escarpment to Kochi and Kochi Ridge. (*See Atlas Map No. 49a*) In the western sector, Griner's exhausted 27th Infantry Division, the unit which Holland Smith had castigated on Makin and Saipan, was overextended; after a few small battles it could go no farther. On April 30, after Major General Pedro de Valle's 1st Marine Division relieved the soldiers, one marine regiment immediately jumped off in the attack. The marines struck the fresh troops of the *44th Independent Mixed*

Brigade, who stopped them with heavy casualties. Several other attempts brought small gains with additional high casualties.

In the center, General Bradley's 96th Division nearly cracked through the reverse-slope defenses of the decimated *62nd Division* along the Maeda Escarpment on April 29, but Ushijima moved in reserves from the newly deployed *24th Division* on his east flank to hold Maeda at all costs. On April 29, when the 77th Division replaced the 96th, Bruce's troops began a bloody, close-in, demolition battle with the determined Japanese; but as the Americans advanced, the local Japanese commanders launched vicious counterattacks to recover lost ground. This pattern of close attacks followed by immediate counterattacks involving hand-to-hand combat typified the fighting in the Shuri defensive area. In this close battle, which caused heavy casualties on both sides, tanks were often the key to success.

On the eastern flank, Arnold's 7th Infantry Division had also been totally unsuccessful. (*See Atlas Map No. 49a.*) The fresh *24th Division* repelled all of its assaults on Kochi Ridge. Nothing, in fact, went right for the troops of the 7th in the last days of April; friend and foe alike managed to kill and wound them.*

The situation on Okinawa changed radically on May 4, when against the advice of Colonel Yahara, but with the encouragement of the fiery General Cho, Ushijima launched a division-sized counteroffensive designed to destroy XXIV Corps.[21] For this attack, Ushijima used the fresh *24th Division*, other Army troops, tanks, and all available artillery, which was pulled out of the caves to support the powerful assaults. † Furthermore, he attacked on the day that air groups in Japan launched the fifth massive bombing and *kamikaze* attack on Okinawa-based shipping.

After moving into position under the cover of darkness, the *24th Division* jumped off early on May 4 from the vicinity of Kochi Ridge and points east, while engineer units tried to envelop both American flanks amphibiously. (*See Atlas Map No. 49a*) After pounding the 7th Infantry Division, the Japanese broke through along that division's boundary with the 77th Infantry Division, advancing about 2,000 yards into the center of Hodge's corps area. Ushijima's troops did everything possible to drive on, but once Allied aircraft, artillery, and tanks engaged the Japanese, the small attacking force was unable to destroy the larger

American force. By midnight on the fifth, Ushijima's soldiers had shot their bolt; retreat followed. The ill-advised attack destroyed 5,000 Japanese troops, gutted the *24th Division*, and decimated Ushijima's only tank regiment, thus opening the way for the successful destruction of the Shuri defenses in the next three weeks. During this period, one of Bruce's regiments fought an isolated battle for the Maeda Escarpment, which it captured on May 6 after extraordinarily bitter fighting (*See Atlas Map No. 49a*) In the west, General de Valle's marines also were attacking. Both these actions cost more battle casualties than the Japanese counteroffensive, proving once again the soundness of Colonel Yahara's recommendations for conservative, determined defense in the face of superior Allied firepower.

The Japanese air offensive on May 3 and 4 was more successful than the land attack. Bombers and *kamikazes* sank or damaged 17 ships, including an escort carrier. They killed or wounded 628 sailors.[22]

General Buckner took direct command of operations in southern Okinawa on May 7, when Geiger's III Amphibious Corps joined Hodge's XXIV Corps on line. Two days later, Buckner ordered a coordinated attack to begin on May 11. In actuality, the four divisions made a frontal attack, although some reports indicate that the general planned to execute a close, double envelopment of the Japanese line with his flank divisions while his two center divisions pushed against the main Shuri defenses. (*See Atlas Map No. 49b.*)

In the west, Major General Lemuel Shephard's 6th Marine Division, which had carried the earlier fight in northern Okinawa, spent most of its time and effort trying to overcome the Japanese forces occupying three mutually reinforcing hill positions (Sugar Loaf, Horseshoe Hill, and Crescent Hill) near the town of Asato. After 10 days, the marines finally seized Sugar Loaf, but they could not take the other positions because the Japanese on Shuri heights, barely 1,500 yards east, could fire on them with impunity. During this period the marines suffered 2,662 casualties and 1,289 cases of battle fatigue.[23]

Flame Thrower Being Used Against Japanese-Occupied Cave on Okinawa

---

*The 17th Infantry Regiment, 7th Infantry Division suffered 60 casualties from friendly fire during the period of April 26 to 30. Twenty-five were killed and wounded when a carrier-based aircraft strafed the regiment on April 30.

† The heavy artillery bombardment caused many cases of combat fatigue among the U.S. Army troops. Japanese artillery included 320-mm spigot mortars.

	All Non-Battle April 1–June 30	Neuro Psychiatric Only April 1–May 30
XXIV Corps		
7th Infantry Division	4,825	7,762
27th Infantry Division	1,969	(4 Army Divisions)
77th Infantry Division	2,100	
96th Infantry Division	2,817	
III Amphibious Corps		
1st Marine Division	5,101	6,315
6th Marine Division	4,489	(2 Marine Divisions)
Total Tenth Army	26,211	14,077

American Non-Battle Casualties on Okinawa, April–June 1945

General de Valle's 1st Marine Division began its attack toward Shuri Heights, but did not gain its objective by the time the 6th Marine Division had occupied Sugar Loaf to the west. De Valle's marines, however, should not be criticized for the slowness of their attack; the Japanese positions were simply too strong and too well-manned to permit a quick advance. In fact, the terrain itself was nearly overwhelming. In one area, the Japanese had built their positions into the face of an unscalable 200 foot cliff; in another they had build emplacements in tombs. Even with air support, naval gunfire, artillery, tanks, flamethrowers, and napalm, De Valle's marines could only advance a few yards at a time. In the 10-day period, however, they did seize Dakeshi and Dakeshi Ridge and move forward another 1,000 yards to the ridgelines and draws which led to Shuri Heights from the west. As usual the cost was high: the 7th Marine Regiment alone, winner of a Presidential Unit Citation for its action, lost over 1,000 dead and wounded.

Adjacent to the 1st Marine Division, General Bruce's 77th Infantry Division tried to take the eastern sector of the Shuri defensive area. The Japanese stopped the soldiers short of their objective, battering them time and time again at well-defended pieces of high ground on which they had constructed exceptionally fine reverse-slope defenses. By May 21, Bruce's troops had pushed ahead 1,500 yards in the right of the zone and 500 yards in the left, and were less than 500 yards from Shuri in many places.

On Tenth Army's eastern flank, General Bradley's 96th Infantry Division, after replacing the 7th Infantry Division following a 10 day rest, began its attack along both sides of the valley leading to Shuri on May 11. (*See Atlas Map No. 49b.*) One regiment fought alongside the 77th Infantry Division to capture adjacent ridges and hill masses in front of Shuri, while another seized the eastern slopes of Conical Hill, near the coastal town of Yonabaru. The Conical Hill slugfest, a turning point in the battle for Shuri, created the

first rupture in the Japanese defensive line. Promptly, Hodge pushed Arnold's rested 7th Infantry Division through the coastal valley into southern Okinawa.

By May 21, General Buckner had five divisions in line and was finally in a position to close in on Shuri. Then heavy rains intervened, bogging down all his divisions and making further advances up the mountain slopes nearly impossibly. Still, the general had no choice but to drive his troops forward. They did the best they could for seven days, but made no important gains against the Shuri defenses. The combination of the Japanese, the rain, and the mud was too overwhelming.

During this period, there were several other important developments. General Buckner assumed command of all Okinawa forces on May 17, coming under the direct command of Admiral Spurance. Ten days later, Admiral Halsey replaced Spruance. More importantly, the Japanese airmen continued to attack the Okinawa area, concentrating on the Allied naval vessels, the new airfields on Ie Shima, and the refurbished and improved Kadena and Yontan fields. (*See Atlas Map No. 48a.*) Bombers and *kamikazes* constantly hindered Allied activities, causing substantial casualties both on ships and on shore. Furthermore, in a daring raid on May 25, the Japanese from the *Giretsu (Heroic) Airborne Unit* tried to seize Yontan airfield by air assault. Although most of the planes crashed, 10 Japanese soldiers did land safely. The Japanese destroyed 7 aircraft, damaged 26 more, and ignited 70,000 gallons of gasoline before they were killed.[24]

While the rains* stopped the 1st Marine, 77th Infantry, and 96th Infantry Divisions from successfully attacking the rugged objectives in their zones, the two flank divisions did advance, beginning a double development of the Shuri

---

*An American staff officer reported that "Those on the forward slopes of the hills slid down; those on the reverse slopes slid back. Otherwise no change."[25]

Date of Attack	Number of Planes
April 6–7	355
April 12–13	185
April 15–16	165
April 27–28	115
May 3–4 (w/counteroffensive)	125
May 10–11	150
May 24–25	165
May 27–28	110
June 3–7	50
June 21–22	45

The Ten Kamikaze Attacks (Operation TEN-GO), April–June 1945

position. (*See Atlas Map No. 49b.*) Shephard's marines entered Naha on May 27, and then attacked eastward successfully, gaining the high ground running southwest from Shuri toward Kokuba on May 30. In the east, Arnold's 7th Infantry Division drove into Yonabaru, turned west, and attacked along the Yonabaru-Kokuba valley, threatening to isolate Ushjima's *Thirty-Second Army*. The Japanese, however, stopped the American advance, prevented a possible link-up between the soldiers and the marines, and kept open a route of withdrawal to the southern tip of Okinawa.

Unknown to the Americans, the Japanese were withdrawing south through the open corridor at this critical time because Ushijima had decided on May 21 to prolong the campaign by moving to new positions farther south, rather than to hold Shuri to the last man. (*See Atlas Map No. 49b.*) Quickly and artfully, the Japanese developed their plans; on May 22, the first units moved south, and four days later the main combat units marched out. The senior American commanders never fully realized that the remnants of *Thirty-Second Army*—by this time at least 50,000 Japanese had died on Okinawa—had withdrawn by May 30, even though their leading units began to break through the usually tough Japanese defenses at about the same time. Consequently the Americans faced another prolonged fight after they destroyed the Japanese covering forces.

For many of the soldiers and marines of Tenth Army who had tried for two months to destroy the Japanese bastion around Shuri, it seemed that the area would never fall. When it did, the battle for Okinawa did not end, although final victory was only a few days off. More bitter combat took place as the Americans moved into the Oroku Peninsula and the Yuza-Dake mountain redoubt in southern Okinawa. Finally, around June 18, General Ushijima's decimated *Thirty-Second Army* began to collapse, becoming an undisciplined mob as it did so. Thereafter, the Americans either hunted down the Japanese survivors or

tried to talk them into surrendering. Over 7,000 Japanese soldiers eventually capitulated before mopping-up operations ceased on June 30.

Neither the victorious nor the vanquished commander lived to see the end of the Okinawa campaign. On June 18, while visiting the outpost of the 8th Marine Regiment, 2nd Marine Division, probably his favorite marine regiment, General Buckner was mortally wounded.* Barely four days later, General Ushijima, recently promoted to full general, left his cave after having dinner and drinks with his staff; then, in the last minutes of darkness before dawn, he committed *hara-kiri,* disemboweling himself with his sword. Next to him, General Cho, his chief of staff, did the same.[26]

Ushijima's skillful defense of Okinawa and the desperate and continued attacks of the Japanese air forces made the Okinawa campaign the most costly Allied operation of the Pacific war. There were 12,281 men killed. Each service and organization shouldered the losses in different ways. The Navy had the most killed (4,907); the Army's XXIV Corps absorbed the greater amount of the ground casualties (4,412 killed, 17,689 wounded); the 6th Marine Division sustained the most battle casualties of any division (8,326); and the 1st Marine Division had the most non-battle casualties among the divisions (5,101). Materiel losses were also significant. The Americans lost 763 planes (458 in combat), more than 230 tanks in the XXIV Corps zone alone, and 36 ships (26 by *kamikaze* attacks.) Additionally, the Japanese damaged 368 American ships (164 by *kamikazes*) as well as 4 of the 5 fast British carriers involved in the operation. Japanese losses were disproportionally larger—over 110,000 Japanese died, and 4,155 aircraft were lost, 1,900 of which were *kamikazes*.[27]

When General Joseph Stilwell arrived to take command of Tenth Army from Lieutenant General Roy Geiger, who was the interim and recently promoted commander, construction troops were working feverishly to turn Okinawa into a huge base to support the air bombardment and eventual invasion of Japan. In addition, Stilwell found himself the military governor of the Ryukyus, and thus responsible for the care of the refugees in the area. Neither Stilwell, nor his commanders, nor his troops, however, realized in June 1945 that they had fought their last battle, although they certainly must have hoped that the end of the war was just around the corner. Few knew that General MacArthur in the Philippines, the commander of all United States Army troops in the Pacific since May 25 and the designated commander for the invasion of Japan (Operation

---

*On June 19, Brigadier General Claudius Easley, Assistant Division Commander, 96th Infantry Division, was killed by machinegun fire, the second American general to die in action on Okinawa.

DOWNFALL), was planning to use Tenth Army* for the invasion of Kyushu on November 1, 1945 (Operation OLYMPIC), and for the invasion of Honshu (Operation CORNONET) on March 1, 1946. Few veterans of Okinawa would have wanted to attack the Japanese on their home islands after their recent experience; more *kamikazes*, corkscrews, and blowtorches might have been too much.

Massacre at Sea: Devastation on Land

As the fighting raged on Okinawa, American submarines continued their long and successful war of attrition against Japanese ships, while American B-29 bombers pounded the Japanese home islands from the new bases in the Marianas. The submarine campaign, the first Allied offensive campaign of the war, was, however, waning because the submariners, primarily Americans, had nearly run out of targets after three years of war.[28] After destroying over a million tons of merchant shipping in 1943, and nearly double that amount in 1944, the submariners more and more found themselves performing noncombative missions: reconnoitering the Japanese home islands; inserting additional agents into the Netherlands East Indies and French Indochina; standing picket duty around the fleet off Okinawa; and prowling the bomber routes to rescue downed pilots. At the same time, the American bombing campaign against Japan intensified, first pummelling and then burning out many of Japan's major cities and the heart of Japanese heavy industry.

Both the submarine and bombing campaigns attacked the industrial and logistical fabric of Japan, destroying her ability to import food and raw materials, to manufacture weapons of war, and to maintain her war base. Each in turn directly affected the morale of the Japanese people. The submarines slowly cut off Japanese food imports and other commodities needed for normal living (e.g., oil), while the B-29s drove thousands from their homes, businesses, and factories, forcing them to abandon the cities and move into the countryside. Consequently, the two campaigns had as much of a part in bringing Japan to surrender in August 1945 as did the drives of Mountbatten, MacArthur, and Nimitz against the overextended Japanese defensive perimeter.[†]

The submarine campaign bore early fruit. By November 1943, Allied submariners had reduced the number of Japanese cargo ships to below the starting tonnage of December 1941; thereafter, they continued to sink Japanese ships at an ever increasing rate. Inadvertently, however, the submariners did not severely damage the Japanese tanker fleet, which continued to grow until reaching its peak tonnage in January 1944. Not until April 1945 did the submariners reduce the tanker tonnage to below the starting

*Ultimately, Tenth Army was dropped from the troop list. (*See Atlas Map No. 50.*)

[†] General Hideki Tojo said three factors defeated Japan: the destruction of her merchant marine; fast carrier operations; and the Allied "leapfrog" strategy.

Month and Year	Tonnage	
	Merchant Ships (minus tankers)	Oil Tankers
Beginning Strength December 7, 1941	5,421,143	575,464
May 1942	5,591,077[1]	607,329
December 1943	5,252,201[2]	686,498
June 1943	4,763,634	772,670[3]
December 1943	4,170,825	863,593
June 1944	3,353,961	835,358[4]
December 1944	1,978,572[5]	868,947
April 1945	1,902,734	562,136[6]
August 15, 1945	1,547,418	26,948

[1] Peak strength tonnage for merchantmen during war.
[2] Merchantmen tonnage dropped below starting figure in November and remained there for duration of war.
[3] United States placed Japanese tankers fourth on priority list.
[4] Tankers reached their peak tonnage of 873,070 in January 1944; then nearly regained that in October 1944 with 872,333 tons.
[5] 1944 was the key year in the war for the Japanese merchant fleet. During the year it lost over 2,000,000 tons of shipping.
[6] Tanker tonnage dropped below starting figure and remained there for the duration of the war.

Decline of the Japanese Merchant Marine

| Year and Month | By Allied Submarines[11] | | Total | |
	Number of Ships	Tonnage	Number of Ships	Tonnage
1941				
December	6	31,693	12	56,060
1942				
January	7	28,351	17	73,795
February	5	15,975	9	33,248
March	7	26,183	15	78,159
April	5	26,886	7	36,684
May[1]	20	86,110	22	96,565
June[2]	6	20,021	8	32,379
July	8	39,356	12	67,528
August[3]	17½	76,652	20	92,331
September	11	39,389	12	46,579
October	25	118,920	37	164,827
November	8	35,358	27	158,992
December	14	48,271	21	71,787
1943				
January	18	80,572	28	122,590
February	10½	54,276	19	93,175
March[4]	26	109,447	38	150,573
April	19	105,345	27	131,782
May	29	122,319	35	131,440
June	25	101,581	28	109,115
July	20	82,784	25	90,507
August	19	80,799	23	98,828
September	38	157,002	47	197,906
October	27	119,623	38	145,594
November[5]	44½	231,683	68	314,790
December	32	121,531	61	207,129
1944				
January	50	240,840	87	339,651
February[6]	54	256,797	115	519,559
March	26	106,529	61	225,766
April	23	95,242	37	129,846
May	63½	264,713	69	277,222
June[7]	48	195,020	75	285,204
July	48	212,907	63	241,652
August	49	245,348	65	294,099
September	47	181,363	121	424,149
October[8]	68½	328,843	134	514,945
November	53½	220,476	97	391,408
December	18	103,836	45	191,876
1945				
January[9]	22	93,796	125	425,505
February	15	55,746	29	87,464
March	23½	70,727	73	186,118
April[10]	18	60,696	51	101,702
May	17	32,394	116	211,536
June	43	92,267	108	196,180
July	12	27,408	111	235,830
August	4	14,559	26	59,425

[1] Battle of the Coral Sea.
[2] Battle of Midway.
[3] Seven Naval Battles of the Solomons.
[4] Battle of the Bismarck Sea.
[5] Invasion of the Gilberts.
[6] First Strike on Truk.
[7] Invasion of the Marianas and Battle of the Philippine Sea.
[8] Invasion of Leyte.
[9] Invasion of Luzon and carrier strike into East China Sea.
[10] Invasion of Okinawa.
[11] United States submarines made approximately 98 percent of the sinkings.
      British and Australian submarines made the rest. The ½ ship designation indicates a sinking made with another attacking agent.

Japanese Merchant Ship Losses[29]

figure of December 1941.[30] Considering that American naval leaders knew that Japan was an oil-poor nation, an earlier concentration of effort on Japanese tankers probably would have brought great results by the end of 1943. Still, the Japanese were unable to supply themselves adequately with oil by the middle of 1944, when, as mentioned, the *Combined Fleet* moved to Tawi Tawi and then to Singapore to be nearer its oil sources.[31]

Besides sinking approximately 60 percent of all the Japanese merchantment and tankers (1,178 of 2,117) destroyed by the Allies, Allied submariners sank nearly a third of all the Japanese warships (214 of 686) which saw action during the war.[32] Quite naturally, carriers became and remained the first priority target in 1943 when Vice Admiral Charles Lockwood, commanding Submarines, Pacific Fleet, ordered his men to concentrate on those important vessels. Ultimately, American submariners destroyed ten carriers, the most important of which probably were the veteran *Shokaku*, the spanking new *Taiho* (sunk during the Battle of the Philippine Sea), and the 62,000 ton, steel and concrete-decked, "unsinkable aircraft carrier" *Shinano* (sunk during her maiden voyage in November 1944).[33] The loss of these large fleet carriers, along with great losses in newly-trained carrier pilots, destroyed any chance that the Imperial Navy had to reconstruct a strong carrier striking force.* Probably more important to the American submariners than the sinking of the carriers, however, were their many victories against the light cruisers, destroyers, and submarines of the *Combined Fleet*. These ships were their natural enemies at sea, and the submariners particularly relished their role as destroyer killers. By the end of the war they had sunk 39 of their arch enemies.[34]

The submariners also aided the soldiers and marines who were advancing across the central Pacific and along the coast of New Guinea in 1944. In this role they torpedoed troop ships which were bringing reinforcements to the Marianas and to the Halmahera-western New Guinea area. Time and again the Japanese lost battalions, regiments, and, on occasion, nearly a division, all of which would have hardened their defenses had they not been destroyed. In the case of Saipan, such reinforcements might have stopped the American invasion.[35]

Most of the heavy action during the submarine campaign took place in the Central Pacific Area, where Admiral Lockwood's submarines ranged from their base in Hawaii (later Guam) to the coasts of Japan, China, and the Philippines. From Freemantle, Australia (later Luzon), however, Rear Admiral Ralph Christie's Southwest Pacific Area submarines also attacked the Japanese merchant fleet, primarily in the Celebes, Java, and East China Seas. Moreover, Christie's submariners performed many unusual duties. They inserted and extracted numerous intelligence, espionage, and guerrilla agents into the many islands of the area; they rescued Allied nationals, pilots, and, on occasion, local native leaders; and, because in 1942 they received the least amount of torpedoes during the year-long torpedo shortage, they laid a great number of mines throughout their combat area. In the Southwest Pacific Area, the submariners also maintained the line of communications and supply to the Philippines from the time of Wainwright's surrender until MacArthur's return.[36]

Performing one other important task during the war, submariners reconnoitered the landing beaches throughout the Pacific, or carried landing parties to the desired areas to make physical inspections of landing sites. Such actions, especially around the reef-bounded coral atolls of the central Pacific, proved invaluable when coordinated with aerial photography.[37]

For some unexplained reason, the Japanese naval leaders never chose to counteract the Allied submarine offensives during the war, thus allowing the daredevil American skippers to take a heavy toll of their merchant and fighting ships. The Japanese only organized a convoy escort force in late 1943, but even then they did not put much emphasis on it.[38] Furthermore, they made no great effort to gain and install radar and sonar devices to alert them of impending attacks or to enable locating the American boats. Even when the Japanese trapped an attacking submarine they did not attack it well, using poor depth charges and seldom staying in the area to confirm their kills. Consequently, they failed to destroy many American boats while at the same time claiming greater successes than they achieved. Considering that the Imperial Navy had learned its lessons from the Royal Navy, the legacies of the U-Boat campaigns of World War I and World War II against the British Isles should have made a deeper impression on the commanders of the *Combined Fleet*. Certainly the Japanese could have warded off many of the Allied underwater attacks. Additionally, they could have destroyed more Allied submarines if they had put some effort into even a mediocre anti-submarine campaign. The Allies profited from this inexcusable failure.

When the submarine campaign reached its zenith in 1944, American submariners fought with new, wakeless, electric torpedoes. With new radar many skippers chose to attack at night only, foregoing daylight raids entirely. Furthermore, to improve their offensive capability, after September 1943 American submariners began to operate

---

*In all fairness, the American sinkings of these ten carriers were not as important as the aerial sinkings at Midway and the steady loss of pilots. The Japanese submariners hurt the American cause more in the early carrier war, when they torpedoed and damaged the *Saratoga* (January 11, 1942), sank the *Yorktown* (June 7, 1942), torpedoed and seriously damaged the *Saratoga* again (August 31), and then sank the *Wasp* (September 15, 1942) and *Hornet* (October 26, 1942).

in wolfpacks in those areas close to the Chinese and Japanese coasts where the Japanese ships sailed once their routes across the central Pacific had been blocked.[39]

In many ways, the submarine war was a war of statistics, and any evaluation of it requires a study of what the Allied submariners actually did to the Japanese nation.[40] A tabulation shows how drastically imports of staples declined:

Commodity	1940	1943	1945 (through July)
Rice	1,694,000	1,135,800	151,200
Coal	7,001,000	5,181,000	548,000
Iron Ore	6,073,000	4,298,000	341,000
Salt	1,728,300	1,425,100	386,900

Decline in Japanese Imports, 1940–1945 (in metric tons)

While some of this decline can be attributed to air and other naval action, most of the credit must go to the submariners who destroyed the highest percentage of the shipping which brought these bulk supplies into Japan. Obviously the Allied submariners, primarily Americans, did an extraordinary job. This feat was even more amazing when one considers that American prewar naval doctrine emphasized that the United States submarine forces would concentrate on orthodox missions, such as attacking warships and scouting for the fleet. With good, long-ranged boats on hand, however, the American submariners were equipped to conduct unrestricted submarine warfare throughout the Pacific when the Japanese attacked Pearl Harbor. When the Chief of Naval Operations gave the word to begin on December 7, they did so with a vengeance.[41]

The cost, however, was high. American submariners lost approximately 18 percent of their force during the war.* This loss—six submariners lost their lives for every "blackshoe" sailor who died—was a staggering statistic for 2 percent of the naval service. These high casualties, however, surely were justified by the great results achieved by the submariners: the massacre of the Japanese merchant fleet and the resultant economic stangulation of Japan. By 1945, the submariners had virtually blockaded Japan.[42] By that same time, the American strategic air forces were beginning to devastate the Japanese home islands.

Five days before the *USS Archerfish* sent four torpedoes into the unsinkable *Shinano* off Tokyo Bay, Brigadier General Emmett "Rosie" O'Donnell, the officer who had led the first flight of B-17s to Luzon in 1941, climbed into

the *Dauntless Dottie*, a B-29, to lead the first air attack (SAN ANTONIO I) on Japan from the Marianas.[43] (*See Atlas Map No. 47.*) Although he left on the mission with 110 of the new, long-ranged, heavy bombers, O'Donnell bombed the target (Nakajima's Musashino aircraft plant on the edge of the crowded northwestern suburbs of Tokyo) with only 24 bombers. Enroute, 17 of his ships aborted, 6 could not bomb because of mechanical troubles, and 64 others missed the prescribed target because of the weather.[44] Fortunately, Japanese interceptors destroyed only one B-29 —and that by ramming—while Japanese antiaircraft guns proved to be inaccurate.†

General O'Donnell's mission brought the Strategic Air Forces into the Pacific war with a big bang. Earlier, some B-29s from India had made raids against Kyushu and Manchuria from a forward staging base in China near Cheng-tu. The logistical problems associated with an incredibly long line of communications and the Japanese offensive against the staging area, however, prevented that campaign from being an overwhelming success. As a result, in support of Nimitz and MacArthur B-29s had attacked other areas: the oil refinery at Palembang, Sumatra; Burma, Malaya, Thailand, and French Indochina; and, most importantly, Formosa. When Nimitz finally secured the Marianas, the air planners in Washington, who had previously urged that the Marianas be taken for bases for the B-29s, deployed their new squadrons to Saipan as quickly as possible in order to get on with the strategic air attack against Japan.

To insure that the Combined Chiefs of Staff did not gain strategic control of the new B-29s, the American Joint Chiefs organized an unusual command—the Twentieth Air Force—to direct the operations of the Superfortresses when they deployed against Japan. General Arnold, acting as the Joint Chief's executive agent, commanded the strategic air force. After the Twentieth Air Force was officially established, Arnold fought to keep all the B-29s under his direction because he did not wish MacArthur, or worse, Nimitz, to gain control over any part of this new air armada. When the B-29s came into the Pacific, however, Arnold, who remained with his headquarters in Washington, appointed Lieutenant General Millard Harmon, previously Admiral Halsey's Army commander in the South Pacific Area, to be his deputy commander. About the same time, Harmon became the commander of all Army Air Forces in the Pacific Ocean Areas; shortly thereafter Nimitz made him the commander of Pacific Ocean Areas Strategic Air

*The Japanese lost 128 submarines in action. The United States lost 41 to 44 submarines in the Pacific and 2 in the Atlantic, had 4 stranded, and lost 2 more operationally (52 total). The Germans lost 781 U-boats.

†Iwo Jima was a release point for the planes on the return flight. There they broke formation and flew to Saipan individually. Air-sea rescue operations saved one full crew on this strike. The importance of both Iwo Jima and air-sea rescue actions to the B-29s cannot be overemphasized.

Forces, which included all land-based air units in the admiral's domain. Because of Harmon's subordination to Nimitz, Arnold refused to allow Harmon to have operational control over the bombers because that essentially would have placed the B-29s under Nimitz. Consequently, Harmon found himself in everyone's chain of command, but deprived of real command of the B-29s. For nearly all of the remaining years of the war, Arnold would direct B-29 operations from Washington. After MacArthur assumed command of all Army and Army Air Force elements in the Pacific and Nimitz took charge of all naval forces, General Carl Spaatz's United States Army Strategic Air Forces (Eighth and Twentieth Air Forces) replaced Twentieth Air Force. But under the reorganization, Spaatz still remained an independent commander, subordinate only to the Joint Chiefs.[45]

Major General Heywood Hansell, commanding the XXI Bomber Command, began B-29 operations out of the Marianas in November 1944. The airplane had been specifically designed for high-altitude, long-range, daylight, precision bombing, and that was the way it was used for the remainder of 1944 and in the first months of 1945. Many problems were encountered in the early Superfortress operations which prevented the achievement of quick and decisive results. Because jet engines are more simple than piston types, even by present day standards, the B-29 was quite a complex aircraft. It had new fuel injection engines, which had many advantages, but were more vulnerable to engine fires than were the old carburetor types. It was the first of the pressurized aircraft, and that complicated operational, logistical, and maintenance problems. Because the round trip to Japan from the Marianas was in the neighborhood of 3,000 miles, there was a substantial strain on the aircraft and airmen alike. Operations at extremely high altitudes presented new meteorlogical problems, such as the jet stream. These winds often were well in excess of 100 knots, and they severely complicated bomb-aiming, navigation, and fuel management problems. It was difficult to implement the principle of mass, because hardly 300 airplanes were available during the fall of 1944, and many of these were necessarily down for maintenance on any given day. But General Arnold was impatient for results.

Following O'Donnell's initial attack, Hansell continued to send his bombers on daylight, high-altitude, precision attacks against his highest priority target, the Japanese aircraft industry.* Because of green crews and bad weather —heavy cloud cover constantly obscured the targets— Hansell's attacks failed to hurt the Japanese aircraft industry badly until January 19, 1945, when 62 of his

*Target priorities were: (1) engine plants, (2) assembly plants, and (3) major overhaul and repair facilities.

bombers struck a plant near the village of Akashi on the Inland Sea. This attack cut the plant's production by 90 percent. In addition to these doctrinal precision attacks, reminiscent of the first American strategic bombing raids in Europe, Hansell experimented with incendiary attacks at the urging of Twentieth Air Force headquarters in Washington.[46]

As it turned out, however, Arnold had become irritated over Hansell's lack of success and decided to replace his former chief planner and one-time protegé with Major General Curtis LeMay, the "driving operator," who had won his reputation in Europe, and then commanded the XX Bomber Command in India. LeMay took control of the XXI Bomber Command on January 20; but, as happened so often with others during the Pacific war, he had no more success with his first missions than had his predecessor. To make matters worse, B-29 losses continued to mount (5.7 percent in January), as Japanese interceptor pilots aggressively attacked the growing bomber flotillas. While LeMay ordered more precision strikes, he also ordered test incendiary raids as suggested once again by Twentieth Air Force headquarters in Washington.[47]

On February 19, Arnold sent LeMay new target instructions which designated incendiary testing as the second priority mission for B-29s. The first remained aircraft engine plants and the third became aircraft assembly plants. Based upon this new directive and in recognition of reports of bad weather, which would hinder his scheduled precision bombing attacks, LeMay decided to launch a 231-plane, area, firebomb attack on Tokyo on February 25. The raid proved the value of firebombing, especially when compared with precision attacks to date, particularly the eight attacks on the Musashino plant in Tokyo which had failed to do much damage.

LeMay, who had sent B-29s on a December 18 fire raid on Hankow, China, carefully studied the results of the incendiary attacks on Japan with his staff officers. After considering the advantages and disadvantages associated with night and daylight attacks, precision and area bombardment, aircraft protection and bomb loads, high and low-level raids, Japanese air and antiaircraft defenses, the general decided to send his bombers on a low-level, mass, night raid against Tokyo on March 9. Rejecting all the American strategic air doctrine of the day, by risking his giant bombers in an untried tactic, and by disarming the B-29s in order to carry more bombs, the general took a calculated risk which could have destroyed XXI Bomber Command as an effective force—and coincidentally ruined his career. Such was not to be the case. In the first minutes of the March 10 raid, the majority of the 334 B-29s which had left the Marianas began bombing Tokyo from 5,000 to 10,000 feet. The three-hour attack, directed against home industries and feeder plants near Tokyo's industrial heart and launched to support forthcoming operations against Okinawa, was a terrifying success. According to Japanese records, LeMay's bombers destroyed 267,171 buildings (about a fourth of Tokyo's total), killed 83,793, wounded 40,918, and burned out the homes of over one million other people. It was the most destructive attack of the war, and one which deeply shocked the Japanese people.[48]

The low-level fire attacks revolutionized American air tactics. (*See Atlas Map No. 51.*) In the days and months to follow, LeMay sent his air squadrons against Japan's largest cities (Tokyo, Nagoya, Osaka, Kobe, Kawasaki, and Yawata); and on June 16 he shifted his awesome fire attacks to the medium-sized cities, where other important segments of Japan's aircraft industry and many major industrial plants were located. The general believed that by driving his pilots and crews to the utmost to keep the pressure on Japan, his attacks could force the Japanese to surrender without the anticipated invasion of the home islands. While crew shortages and the support of the Okinawa operation—mainly attacks on known or suspected *kamikaze* bases—diluted his efforts, LeMay was still able to keep "unremitting pressure" on Japan. Airpower, the force which the joint planners had hoped would bring about Japan's capitulation when they originally drew up the first "Strategic Plan for the Defeat of Japan" in 1943, seemed to be on the verge of fulfilling its great promise.[49]

But for all the frightfulness of Japan's final agony, one's conclusions on the effectiveness of the strategic bombing campaign probably must remain ambiguous. It is true that absenteeism was on the rise in Japanese industry during the closing months of the war, and there is evidence that the morale of Japanese soldiers was being hurt by reports of the bombing attacks on their homeland. It is also true that production had fallen off radically. Finally, the invasion so feared was not necessary, and the air opposition to the bombing, even in daylight, was becoming weaker and weaker. But it is difficult to separate the result of the bombing from those of the naval blockade. Japanese industry was already starving for raw materials when the B-29s began their attacks, and the submarines had already seriously injured Japanese morale by radically reducing the caloric intake of the population before the Superforts burned down homes and drove the people out of the cities.[50]

By the end of June 1945, American bombers were flying over Japan with little difficulty, bombing what they liked, when and where they liked. In July, LeMay began dropping leaflets warning the people of his next targets. The Japanese had tried to disperse what was left of their industry and were rapidly preparing to meet the inevitable invasion, although many leaders believed that the nation must seek peace at any price. The B-29 campaign must be credited for much of

this thinking and for the consequent drop in Japanese national morale.[51] No nation as small and as highly populated as Japan could sustain itself in the face of constant fire-bombing, especially when such attacks continued with an increased naval and air blockade (the latter with aerial-sown mines) and the threat of a major invasion. The time was right for peace.

"If You Plan to Accept These Terms, You Had Better Be Prepared to Commit Hara-Kiri!"

Peace did not come easily to Japan. Although all indicators of national morale, food supplies, industrial output, and the general conduct of the war gave even the most militaristic Japanese cause to believe that the war was lost, the key military leaders clung desperately to the hope that Japan could fight one more climatic battle.[52] That battle might not win the war, but at least it would give the Japanese a chance for a negotiated peace. Furthermore, since the battle would be fought on the sacred soil of Yamato, the military leaders, particularly the incumbent War Minister, General Korechika Anami (formerly the commander of the Second Area Army in the Halmaheras), believed that the nation could fight its best battle of the war. There would be no need for a Navy because only the Allies would be faced with a long line of sea communications. The remnants of the Navy, coupled with the air forces of both the Army and the Navy, would attack the invaders conventionally and with hoarded numbers of *tokko* (special attack) forces, including the dreaded *kamikazes*. As the enemy approached, some 10,000 aircraft, nearly three quarters of which would be *kamikazes*, would engage the invaders from 200 miles out, all the way into the beachheads. Then suicide boats, human torpedoes, and other suicidal devices would be sent to destroy the Allies as they approached the landing beaches. Once they were ashore, the undefeated 2,350,000-man Imperial Japanese Army planned to attack the Allied divisions at the beaches and, with a three to one advantage in manpower, to push them into the sea. If that failed, the militia and people of Japan were expected to carry on guerrilla warfare to defeat the Allies.[53]

As had been the case throughout the war, the *samurai*-inclined leaders of Japan elevated the importance of spirit above that of steel, and believed sincerely that properly motivated Japanese soldiers and sailors could stop or at least cripple the Allied invasion.[54] It did not seem to matter that the Japanese lacked munitions, or that many soldiers or airmen were virtually untrained. It also did not seem to matter that the Imperial Japanese Army was now filled with the poorest physical specimens in the nation, men who were often the dregs of society, men who had grown more and more atrocious in the conduct of affairs with their civilian brethern, thus alienating much of the population. Incredibly, even the indescribable devastation of Japan and an imminent famine did not dampen the spirits of the Japanese military commanders; nor, moreover, did it improve their judgment, as they faced the probablilty of an impending invasion. Anything seemed better than unconditional surrender.[55]

Thus, the Japanese High Command, led by the most militant service—the Army—prepared to meet the Allied attack with an abundance of spirit and a lack of physical means. Throughout 1945, the Imperial General Headquarters had constantly adjusted its plans for the final battles, which it expected to fight, first on Kyushu and then on Honshu. After publishing its plan for *KETSU-GO*, the decisive defense of the homeland, on April 8, 1945, Imperial General Headquarters tried desperately to prepare for its execution. In late July, publicly confident, the Japanese High Command planned to defend the homeland with two general armies whose battle core was made up of 2 armored divisions, 58 infantry divisions, and 25 brigades. Their foe was estimated to be 60 Allied divisions. (*See Atlas Map No. 50.*) Behind the armies stood an official militia of 28,000,000 and the dreaded *kamikazes*.[56]

While Imperial General Headquarters developed its defensive plans, several prominent Japanese statesmen had been working behind the scenes for peace. As early as the summer of 1943, a small number of the respected *jushin* (former Prime Ministers and Presidents of the Privy Council) had tried to force the Tojo Government out of office as a step toward peace.[57] The fall of Saipan in June 1944 finally brought the fall of the Tojo clique and allowed the peace advocates among the *jushin* to place a member of their group, retired Admiral Mitsumasa Yonai, in the new cabinet. As the Deputy Prime Minister and the Navy Minister, Yonai became the man of moderation in the new Government. However, he could not publicly advocate peace. At the same time, Marquis Koichi Kido, Lord Keeper of the Privy Seal and the Emperor's closest advisor, began talking about peace with Prince Fumimaro Konoye, Tojo's predecessor as prime minister. Konoye and some of the *jushin* hoped to be able to terminate the war by Imperial decree and blame the defeat on Tojo. Throughout these discussions and those that followed, however, the civilian as well as the military leaders rejected the idea of unconditional surrender. To the military services, surrender was not only personally abhorent, but also violated all the codes

of the *samurai* and the armed forces, and would have impinged on the national policy by destroying the position of the Emperor.

Nothing came of these peace discussions until the Emperor asked to see the *jushin* following the American landing on Luzon in January 1945. During individual visits by each of the *jushin* in February, the Emperor apparently endorsed the ideas of the peace advocates among the group. During these talks, Prince Konoye recommended that the war be ended quickly to prevent a Communist-inspired revolt of the young officers.[58] Shortly thereafter, the new Prince Minister, General Kuniaki Koiso, proposed to negotiate a separate peace with China so as to free Japan's hands on the Asian continent. His suggestion was rejected.

Finally, on April 5, just after the Allies invaded Okinawa, General Koiso resigned as Prime Minister and recommended the formation of an Imperial General Headquarters Cabinet—one in which the prime minister would also be a member of the military high command. Marquis Kido and some of the *jushin*, however, quickly maneuvered to form a more peace-oriented cabinet. First, the peace group of the *jushin* pushed forward one of their rank—the 78-year old retired Admiral, Baron Kantaro Suzuki, a respected warrior with no known connections to their faction and a man whom the Emperor trusted. Second, Kido persuaded the aged Suzuki to accept the prime ministership. Baron Suzuki then made several wise choices for his cabinet. He selected Shigenori Togo as Foreign Minister, and persuaded Admiral Yonai to remain as Navy Minister against Yonai's own wishes. In the days ahead, these three would form the peace group inside the Cabinet—and much more importantly, inside the Supreme War Direction Council as well. The Army unknowingly added to the strength of the Cabinet and to the possibility of peace when it proposed that General Anami be the War Minister. In the critical days ahead, Anami would hold the Army in line by refusing to resign in crisis, and would allow Suzuki to gain peace, while at the same time steadfastly upholding the Army's desire to fight on.[59]

Prime Minister	**War Minister**
Admiral Baron Kantaro Suzuki	General Korechika Anami
Foreign Minister	**Chief of the Army General Staff**
Shigenori Togo	General Yoshijiro Umezu
Navy Minister	**Chief of the Navy General Staff**
Admiral Mitsumasa Yonai	Admiral Soemu Toyoda

The Supreme War Direction Council, April 1945

The Army, however, fearing that the Suzuki cabinet would at once seek peace, had laid down three conditions before helping to form the new Government. These required the new Government to fight to the finish, to unify the Army and Navy, and to take measures to insure victory in the battle of Japan. Suzuki's maiden radio speech emphasized the continued hard line of the military toward the prosecution of the war, pleasing the Japanese military services but annoying the Japanese peacemakers and disappointing the Allied listeners.[60] Still, many Japanese militarists remained suspicious of Suzuki and his government.

Immediately after the inauguration of the new government on April 8, Foreign Minister Togo moved into the foreground as the most active peace advocate. He called on the Emperor on April 21 and suggested that it was time to explore an end to the war. The Emperor said that he wanted the war ended quickly. Nearly simultaneously, Togo asked the Soviet Union to pledge its continued neutrality—the Soviet Government had notified Japan that it would terminate its Neutrality Pact which would expire in 1946— but the Soviets gave an evasive reply. Togo deferred further initiatives with the Soviets after this rebuff, but following Germany's unconditional surrender on May 8, Togo explained the development to the Emperor and once again the Emperor apparently said that he favored peace. The German collapse allowed Togo to propose that the Supreme War Direction Council, the most powerful body in Japan, begin considering new initiatives with the Soviet Union as a step toward possibly discussing peace. During the talks, Premier Suzuki unexpectedly proposed to his five colleagues that Japan seek mediation for a general peace through the Soviet Union. When the military officers did not object, Togo asked one of the *jushin* to open talks with the Soviet Ambassador in Japan (Jacob Malik) to stabilize relations between the two countries. Mediation, however, was not brought up in the first talks. As a result of the decision to consider mediation, the Japanese stopped budding efforts to seek an end to the war through the Governments of Switzerland or Sweden.[61]

Peace moves took a step rearward in early June when the Supreme War Direction Council, after reviewing the war situation, decided to endorse a belligerent "Basic Policy for the Future Duration of the War," reiterating previous declarations "to prosecute the war to the end to protect the Imperial Homeland."[62] After the Cabinet approved the policy on June 7, the Supreme War Council presented it to the Emperor the next day. The Emperor, as was the custom, said nothing, and the policy was adopted formally. Following the Imperial conference, however, Marquis Kido advised the Emperor to end the war, and suggested that an Imperial envoy be sent to the Soviet Union to seek mediation. The Emperor, now thoroughly alarmed by the truculent policy of the Government, approved Kido's

suggestions. With the Emperor's backing, Kido began contacting the key Japanese leaders about his plan. Suzuki, Togo, and Yonai agreed to support mediation through the Soviet Union. On June 18, after some delay, Kido talked with Anami, but Anami was noncommittal toward negotiations.[63]

The same day, however, Premier Suzuki called a meeting of the Supreme War Direction Council to discuss peace. The Council decided that Japan would have to fight as long as the Allies insisted on unconditional surrender, but it agreed to seek peace on acceptable terms through the mediation of the Soviet Union. The results of the meeting reached Kido and the Emperor; four days later, Kido arranged for the Council to meet again with the Emperor. At this meeting the Emperor took a decisive step by personally urging the Council members to end the war by diplomatic means.[64]

The Japanese leaders, however, did not act quickly or directly enough to end the war in either June or July. In fact, during all dealings with Soviet representatives in Japan and Moscow, the Japanese diplomats did not even bring up the proposition of mediation until July 25. Most of the diplomatic maneuvering centered on gaining Soviet approval of improved relations with Japan and trying to determine the mood of the Soviets. On July 11, Togo finally advised his ambassador in Moscow about the new Japanese ideas for peace, but he sent no concrete proposals. Furthermore, Togo told his representative that unconditional surrender would be unacceptable. Even the messages which Togo wanted transmitted to the Soviets spoke only of the Emperor's wish to restore peace and the dispatch of a special envoy to the Soviet Government. The Japanese Ambassador delivered these messages to the Soviet Deputy Foreign Minister on July 13, but Soviet Foreign Minister Molotov left with Stalin for the Potsdam Conference the next day without replying to the Japanese request. Consequently, Togo feared that the Soviets would discuss these proposals with the Americans and British, thereby prejudicing the Japanese-Soviet moves.[65]

On July 18, Molotov's deputy told the Japanese Ambassador in Moscow that the Japanese proposals were too vague and that the Soviet Government needed more details concerning the visit and mission of the Emperor's envoy. A week later, Togo instructed the Ambassador to tell the Soviets that Japan wished to seek an end to the war through the Soviet Union's good offices, and that the special envoy would bring concrete terms.[66] Two days after this message reached Moscow, the United States, Great Britain, and China published the Potsdam Declaration (July 26) which outlined their terms for peace with Japan. This proclamation shocked the Japanese leaders, who no longer could consider mediation. Now they would have to face the abhorent possibility of unconditional surrender.

While the Japanese leaders struggled to solve their staggering problems before the Potsdam Proclamation, American leaders continued to plan for the invasion of Japan because there seemed to be little chance that Japan would surrender unconditionally without a final desperate struggle. By late June, General MacArthur and Admiral Nimitz were preparing their forces for the impending invasion of Japan (Operation DOWNFALL). (*See Atlas Map No. 50.*) Following the May 25 directive of the Joint Chiefs of Staff, MacArthur planned to send the bulk of his Pacific divisions against the southern island of Kyushu on November 1 (Operation OLYMPIC) in order to seize airbases to support the decisive invasion of Honshu (Operation CORONET) on March 1, 1946. MacArthur directed General Walter Krueger, commanding Sixth Army, to conduct Operation OLYMPIC. The general gave Krueger I, V Amphibious, and XI Corps (six infantry, one cavalry, and three marine divisions) for the invasion, and IX Corps (two divisions) as a floating reserve. Another division would function as an advance attack force. Two others (one airborne) were to be follow-up units. MacArthur designated Lieutenant General Robert Eichelberger's Eighth Army, made up of XIII and XIV Corps (seven infantry and two armored divisions), and General Courtney Hodge's veteran First Army from Europe, consisting of III Amphibious and XXIV Corps (three marine divisions and three infantry divisions), to handle Operation CORONET. American infantry divisions (some coming from Europe or the United States) and American marine divisions would take Honshu; but if the situation warranted it, Australia, Canadian, British, and French divisions could be employed in later stages of the campaign.[67]

The invasion of Japan would be the largest amphibious operation of the war. By avoiding peripheral operations on the Asian mainland and by not relying on Japan to succumb only to an air bombardment or a naval blockade, Operation DOWNFALL would bring the war directly to Japan. Some American officials estimated that the attackers could suffer as high as a half a million or a million casualties. For this reason alone, many opposed the invasion; and, as was stated in the original 1943 Strategic Plan for the Defeat of Japan, they felt that the invasion should take place only if it proved necessary.[68]

General Marshall, however, thought the invasion would be necessary. So did General MacArthur. Admiral Leahy and Admiral King disagreed, believing that a naval blockade and air attacks would suffice. General Arnold's representative favored the landing because he had learned the inadequacy of an unsupported air campaign. The high-level American leaders did agree, though, that preparations for the campaign would have to proceed in case Japan did not capitulate for other reasons, and on June 18, President Truman confirmed that the Joint Chiefs should prepare for OLYMPIC, even though CORONET might be unnecessary.[69]

To assist the invasion, the Joint Chiefs long had advocated, as had MacArthur, the employment of the Soviet forces against Manchuria. Stalin had generously offered his forces in 1943, but he had never given the Joint Chiefs any concrete proposals until the Yalta Conference in February 1945. By then, the United States probably could have successfully attacked Japan alone. Indeed, Acting Secretary of State, Joseph Grew, suggested that the United States should recommend that the Soviets not attack as planned, thereby precluding the cession of Japanese territory to Stalin as payment for his intervention. Secretary of War Henry Stimson noted, however, that with the growth of Soviet power, the Soviets would do as they pleased in the area. Consequently, he believed that it was impractical to suggest to the Soviet leaders that their planned attack into Manchuria was no longer needed. As things stood in the summer of 1945, the Soviets would probably attack the Japanese as agreed, approximately 90 days after the surrender of Germany—or around August 8.

Unknown to MacArthur and Nimitz, two other developments were taking place in the United States which had the potential to affect the outcome of the war. First, certain members of the State Department, primarily Grew, the American Ambassador in Japan when the was had begun, hoped that President Harry Truman would notify Japan that the United States would accept terms for capitulation short of unconditional surrender. Grew believed that if the President announced that Japan could surrender without losing her Imperial dynasty, the Japanese peace faction might be able to lead the country to peace. Grew knew Baron Suzuki to be a moderate and believed that his government might be able to make this momentous decision.[70] While Grew did not get his way, Truman did decide to issue a proclamation during the next Allied conference at Potsdam. The second development—the construction of an atomic bomb—would become as important. Originally proposed by Albert Einstein to President Roosevelt in 1939, the atomic bomb had been worked on in great secrecy during the war. By December 30, 1944, Major General Leslie Groves, the Commanding General of the secret Manhattan Project, stated that the United States would have such a bomb in the late summer of 1945. As predicted, the atomic bomb reached the testing phase in mid-summer, just as the President and his advisors departed for the Potsdam Conference. If all went well, the awesome bomb could be used against Japan.*

---

*The bomb had originally been designed for use against Germany.

Because this new bomb could revolutionize warfare, President Truman organized a special Interim Committee to evaluate its use carefully. On June 1, this group of civilian government officials and scientists recommended that the bomb be used as soon as possible against a dual military and civilian target—and without a specific warning about the nature of the weapon. Just after this decision was made, many scientists who had worked on the project objected to its use. The scientific panel of the Interim Committee evaluated their objections, but concluded that the bomb should be used. After the bomb was tested successfully, many scientists again objected to its use unless "a convincing warning had been given [to Japan] that a refusal to surrender would be followed by the use of a new weapon."[71] Their petition probably did not reach either Secretary Stimson, who headed the Interim Committee and approved of the use of the bomb, or President Truman.

As Truman embarked with his staff for the Potsdam meeting with Stalin and Churchill, he knew that he could exercise three different options to end the war against Japan. He could allow the invasion of Kyushu to proceed as planned in November; he could offer terms short of unconditional surrender to entice the Japanese Government to capitulate; or he could try to shock the Japanese into ending the war by employing the atomic bomb against the military targets in Japan when the bomb became available.[72]

At Potsdam on July 16, the President learned that the bomb had been successfully testing in New Mexico, and talked immediately with Churchill about the success. Six days later, Truman met with the Joint Chiefs to discuss the bomb's use. Marshall approved of its use. Arnold hesitated and said that conventional bombing could bring about Japan's capitulation. Admiral Leahy, the senior member of the Joint Chiefs, apparently expressed a reluctance to use the awesome weapon because of ethical considerations. Later in the day, Truman asked Churchill for his opinion. The Prime Minister said that the bomb should be used to end the war as soon as possible. Truman then decided to employ the atomic weapon.[73]

During a meeting on July 24, Trumen mentioned the explosion of the bomb to Stalin quite casually, because he neither knew how to handle the matter nor how much he wanted to tell the Soviet leader about the bomb's development. Stalin said he hoped it would be used against Japan. A few days later, Clement Atlee, the newly elected Prime Minister of Great Britain, arrived and accepted Churchill's decision to approve the use of the bomb.[74]

Having decided to employ the atomic bomb, the President further decided to publish the previously prepared Potsdam Declaration to Japan (once Chiang Kai-shek approved it) in order to give the Japanese one more chance to capitulate

before the first bomb dropped. Prior to the issuance of the declaration, Secretary Stimson urged President Truman to include a statement that the Imperial dynasty could continue. Stimson advised that the Japanese acceptance might revolve around this single point. The final document, however, did not mention the Imperial dynasty. It was a blunt, hard proposal which included the following comments:

> . . .
>   (5) Following are our terms. We will not deviate from them. There are no alternatives. We shall brook no delay.
>
> . . .
> (13) We call upon the government of Japan to proclaim now the unconditional surrender of all Japanese armed forces, and to provide proper and adequate assurances of their good faith in such action. The alternative for Japan is prompt and utter destruction.[75]

With the publication of this document on July 26, Truman had exercised one of his three options. The Japanese had to respond quickly before he exercised another option. They had only a few days. On the same day, the *USS Indianapolis** delivered the fissionable material for the first operational atomic bomb to the waiting air group at Tinian in the Marianas.

Early the next morning, the Japanese picked up the text of the Potsdam Declaration. The Foreign Office immediately noted that the Soviet Government was not a party to the declaration, that unconditional surrender referred to the armed forces only, and that the declaration stated "terms." Togo advised that nothing be done until the Soviets replied to the earlier Japanese initiative for mediation. Furthermore, Suzuki accepted Togo's advice and told the cabinet that he would "kill it with silence." With the exception of Admiral Yonai, however, the military members urged Suzuki to take a stronger stand and to reject the declaration outright.[76]

The Japanese reactions began a modern tragedy which nearly ended in Japan committing national suicide. Relying too much on the Soviet Union, which had been moving troops toward Siberia for months and was on the verge of declaring war on Japan, and ignoring the demanding tone of the declaration, the Japanese leaders decided to wait when there was no time to wait. To make matters worse, their own deliberate, involved system of decision making would bring the process of seeking peace to an even slower pace.

---

*The *USS Indianapolis* was mysteriously sunk in one of the last combat actions of the war.

On July 28, General Anami, General Umezu, and Admiral Toyoda pressured Prime Minister Suzuki into making a strong public pronouncement against the declaration while Togo was absent from this meeting of members of the Supreme War Direction Council. At 3:00 P.M., therefore, the aged Prime Minister announced that:

> I believe that the Joint Proclamation by the three countries is nothing but a rehash of the Cairo Declaration. As for the Government, it does not find any important value in it, and there is no other recourse but to ignore it entirely and resolutely fight for the successful conclusion of this war.[77]

Suzuki's unfortunate statement served only to push Truman closer to directing that the atomic bomb be used.

That same day, at Potsdam, Stalin talked to Truman for a second time about the Japanese request for mediation, and told the American President that he would reject the Japanese overture. Truman thanked Stalin for his action. Stalin did not, however, immediately transmit his rejection to the Japanese.[78]

Two days later, the *New York Times* announced in a banner headline: JAPAN OFFICIALLY TURNS DOWN ALLIED SURRENDER ULTIMATUM. The comment summed up the official feeling in the American Government and highlighted a key concept which the Japanese had missed—the Potsdam Declaration was an ultimatum, not a negotiable document. The same day in Tokyo, peace groups urged Marquis Kido to press for acceptance of the declaration without further delay, but the Government took no further action. Togo, meanwhile, waited hopefully for the Soviets to reply to his July 25 message regarding the Imperial envoy. As could be expected, General Anami, General Umezu, and Admiral Toyoda continued to oppose the declaration.[79]

The Japanese tragedy approached its apogee in the first days of August, because President Truman had approved orders to drop the bomb after August 3 unless he countermanded the orders. Truman planned to take such action only if the Japanese accepted the Potsdam Declaration. On August 2 the Allied leaders left Potsdam. In Tokyo, Togo continued to press the Japanese Ambassador in Moscow for an answer from the Soviets, while the military leaders continued to object to the acceptance of the declaration.

Little occurred during the next few days except that the American bomber group on Tinian began to prepare for the special mission against one of four Japanese cities: Hiroshima, Nagasaki, Niigata, or Kokura. The Japanese Government remained silent, so final preparations for the special mission continued. Finally, early on the morning of August 6, Colonel Paul Tibbetts lifted his B-29, the *Enola*

The *Enola Gay*

Gay, into the Pacific sky from Tinian and turned north for Hiroshima. Aboard he carried the "Thin Man," the first operational atomic bomb. About six hours later, Japanese early-warning radar picked up Tibbetts' flight as three weather planes circled the city; however, the Japanese sounded an "all clear." Just a few minutes later, Japanese spotters reported two B-29s flying toward Hiroshima. Furthermore, they reported that the aircraft looked like reconnaissance ships.

At 8:11 A.M., Colonel Tibbetts began his approach to his target at 31,600 feet and 328 miles per hour. Below, the citizens of Hiroshima were beginning their day's work. Shortly thereafter the "Thin Man" fell free, and the bomber raced for safety. At approximately 2,000 feet above Hiroshima, the bomb exploded. Within seconds, it destroyed the central part of the city. Fires broke out everywhere. Thousands died instantly from the blast and the heat, and a peculiar mushroom cloud formed above the city. President Truman had exercised his most awesome option to gain a quick victory. In doing so, he had ushered in a new age of warfare.[80]

Truman heard about the successful strike while enroute home from Potsdam on the *USS Augusta*. Shortly thereafter a news release, explaining that an atomic bomb had been used against Japan, was issued in his name. The release was even more threatening than the Potsdam Declaration:

> It was to spare the Japanese people from utter destruction that the ultimatum of 26 July was issued at Potsdam. Their leaders promptly rejected that ultimatum. If they do not now accept our terms, they may expect a rain of ruin from the air, the like of which has never been seen on this earth.[81]

Later that day, when the President arrived in Washington, he authorized the use of the second bomb.

On August 7, Japanese radio intercept stations picked up

The "Thin Man" at Hiroshima

even though it did stun the Army leaders more, perhaps, than did the first atomic bomb.[82]

Finally, on August 9 the Supreme War Direction Council met to discuss the action which Japan should take. During its meeting the second atomic bomb struck Nagasaki. Even this did not bring rapid results. The military officers, led by General Anami, objected to the provisions of the Potsdam Declaration. Particularly annoying to them was the fact that the Allies did not mention what they were going to do about the Emperor, and, moreover, that they intended to occupy Japan, disarm and demobilize the Japanese armed forces, and prosecute Japanese war criminals. The key stumbling block was the fate of the Emperor. For him, the Army would fight. Anami urged continued resistance because he felt that the Japanese could repel the invasion and inflict so many casualties that the United States would negotiate terms for the end of the war rather than continue to fight. The tough *samurai* stated unequivocally: "We cannot pretend to claim that victory is certain, but it is far too early to say that the war is lost."[83] After much bitter debate, the council deadlocked 3-3 over accepting the Potsdam terms. Suzuki, Togo, and Yonai voted for immediate peace; Anami, Umuzu, and Toyoda were for continuing the war.

While Anami's intransigence might seem totally incomprehensible, he had reason for it. He could not move too fast or his hot-headed subordinates might stir up a revolt or begin an old cycle of assassinations reminiscent of the 1930s. At the same time, just by remaining in the Government and not resigning, the War Minister prevented the collapse of the Government as it crawled toward peace. If he resigned, it probably would have been impossible to get the Army or Navy to appoint new War and Navy Ministers to a peace cabinet, thus depriving Japan of a government in a time of terrible crisis. Therefore, Anami's truculence might have been planned; the general may have been following an ancient Japanese custom of role playing (*haragei*) to insure that the Government functioned and yet that the Army did not revolt. The feeling in the Army was so high against capitulation that Anami's own brother-in-law, an Army lieutenant colonel, could warn Anami "if you plan to accept these terms, you had better be prepared to commit *hara-kiri*." Whatever Anami was doing, he was playing a dangerous game.[84]

the announcement of the atomic attack. Togo immediately informed the Cabinet of the contents and then told the Emperor of the developments. With Premier Suzuki's approval, Togo advised the Emperor that the Potsdam Declaration must be accepted to prevent more damage. The Emperor agreed, but unfortunately Suzuki could not get the Supreme War Direction Council to consider the matter.

In Japan, no one took immediate action. The Army leaders seemingly ignored the bomb and tried desperately to treat it as a routine matter. Suzuki, Togo, and Kido apparently were convinced that it was time to capitulate, but they seemed incapable of securing the Cabinet or Supreme War Direction Council approval of such action. Kido and Togo did speak to the Emperor again, and both heard him urge immediate peace. Still they could not translate the Emperor's desires into action.

Meanwhile, other events presaged more problems for the Japanese leaders. The air group on Tinian prepared to move up the scheduled second atomic strike from August 11 to the ninth because of predicted bad weather. In Moscow, on the eighth, Molotov called in the Japanese Ambassador for what the latter hoped was an answer to the Japanese request for mediation. Instead, Molotov handed the Japanese Ambassador a note stating that as of August 9 the Soviet Union would consider itself at war with Japan. The Soviet declaration of war, dreaded by the Japanese Army for years, still did not force the Government to act,

Following the meeting of the Supreme War Direction Council on August 9, Prime Minister Suzuki arranged for the group to meet with the Emperor in his bunker at 2:00 A.M. the next morning. After asking the various officials to discuss their positions on the Potsdam Declaration for the Emperor, Suzuki suddenly asked the Emperor to decide whether or not to accept the Potsdam Declaration, as the Council members remained deadlocked at 3-3. This unexpected break with tradition finally settled the matter of peace or war. The Emperor announced that he wanted peace; the councilmen obediently bowed to his will. After this meeting the Japanese Cabinet approved the Emperor's decision. Following this necessary ratification, the Foreign Office dispatched messages (7:00 A.M., August 10, Tokyo time) to the Allies through Sweden and Switzerland, announcing that Japan accepted the Potsdam Declaration " . . . with the understanding that the said declaration does not compromise any demand which prejudices the prerogatives of His Majesty as Sovereign Ruler."[85]

Because of the Japanese qualification, the end was still not in sight. President Truman received the message, but he did not stop conventional air attacks against Japan. On the eleventh, Secretary of State James Byrnes replied for the United States and the Allies. He stated, in part, that the Emperor would be subject to direction by the Supreme Commander of the Allied Powers.[86]

Byrnes' reply touched off the last governmental crisis in Japan. For four days, Suzuki, Togo, Yonai, Anami, Umezu, and Toyoda debated their course of action. Finally, the six leaders met once again with the Emperor. Replaying the scenario of August 10, Suzuki asked the Emperor to decide whether or not to accept the declaration, with the added proviso that the Emperor would be subjected to direction by the Allied Supreme Commander. The Emperor announced that he did not feel that his position was threatened by the new statement, and that he still desired peace. Furthermore, he stated that he would be willing to announce his decision to the nation. The councilmen accepted the Imperial decision, as did the Cabinet. Following these actions, Japanese officials worked feverishly to prepare an Imperial Rescript announcing the surrender to the nation. Directly after its approval by the Supreme War Direction Council, the Emperor recorded the Imperial Rescript for broadcast the next day—August 15. Before the Imperial Rescript was prepared, however, the Japanese Government announced its acceptance of the latest Allied proposition. The United States took the message to mean that Japan had fully surrendered.[87]

When the Allies made preparations to accept the surrender of the Japanese forces throughout the Pacific and Asia, (*See Atlas Map No. 52*) Japan entered into her "longest day": August 14 to 15. During these hours, some Army officers revolted, killed the commander of the *1st Imperial Guards Division*, and forged orders for the deployment of the division around the Emperor's palace. They thus set the stage for a *coup d'etat* which would snatch the Emperor from the evil men who advised him and would abrogate the surrender. The *coup* failed because General Anami and a key subordinate did not join it, but it did create the specter of a revolt, something which Japanese leaders had feared ever since they had begun the search for peace over a year before.[88]

At noon on August 15, shortly after the arrest of the ringleaders of the Army revolt, a Japanese radio announcer asked his people to stand respectfully before their radios. Following the strains of the national anthem, the Japanese people heard the voice of their Emperor for the first time as he read the Imperial Rescript:

> . . . We have ordered Our Government to communicate to the Governments of the United States, Great Britain, China, and the Soviet Union that our Empire accepts the provisions of their Joint Declaration. . . .[89]

The Emperor's announcement stunnned the Japanese people. But with it peace came to the nation of *samurai* before Japan committed suicide in the face of an atomic age. That age temporarily negated the power of the *samurai's* sword and dagger and the "bamboo spear" philosophy, which had nearly brought the nation to ruin.

The man who was probably the most responsible for peace, however, did not hear his Emperor's announcement. To atone for his failures to the Army and his Emperor, General Anami had committed *hara-kiri* a few hours earlier.[90] By his act, Anami played out his role in true *samurai* fashion, gaining the respect of all his associates.

A Blue-Eyed Shogun

On August 30, 1945, Lieutenant General Robert Eichelberger arrived at Atsugi airbase near Yokohama to command the elements of the 11th Airborne Division, which had begun landing in newly surrendered Japan two days earlier.[91] Things were tense everywhere because the Americans did not know how the Japanese would react to their arrival. In fact, Atsugi had been a home base for *kamikaze* pilots; many of these men, influenced by fanatical commanders like their founder, Vice Admiral Takijiro Onishi, had been ordered to remove the propellers from all fighters at the base to avoid any compromising incidents.

Eichelberger was particularly concerned about security in the area because General MacArthur, the newly appointed Supreme Commander of the Allied Powers, planned to arrive at Atsugi two hours later. With barely a division in the airhead, Eichelberger really did not have sufficient troops to protect MacArthur if anything went wrong. He had to rely on the Imperial Japanese Army and the Japanese police.

At about 2:00 P.M., MacArthur's silvery C-54, *Bataan*, landed at Atsugi right on schedule. Shortly thereafter, the general stepped out into the bright sunlight, paused at the top of the flight ladder for photographs, and descended to meet Eichelberger and the other waiting officials. MacArthur spoke briefly with Eichelberger. Then he entered the car which the Japanese had provided and began the drive to his headquarters in the new Grand Hotel in Yokohama.

Preceded by truckloads of American paratroopers, MacArthur and his party travelled slowly toward Yokohama. Along the way, two divisions of Japanese troops stood guard. They turned their backs toward the Supreme Commander, just as they always had for the Emperor. It was a fitting display for the new blue-eyed *shogun*—the American general who would bring a newer order to the nation of *samurai*.

Notes

[1]This section on Iwo Jima is based on Jeter A. Isely and Philip A. Crowl, The *U.S. Marines and Amphibious Warefare* (Princeton, N.J., 1951), pp. 432-530. Also see Whitman S. Bartley, *Iwo Jima: Amphibious Epic* (Washington, 1954).

[2]Bartley, *Iwo Jima*, p. 231, and Isely and Crowl, *U.S. Marines*, pp. 453 and 482 (footnote).

[3]Bartley, *Iwo Jima*, p. 210 (B-29 statistics), and Martin Caiden, *Zero Fighter* (New York, 1973), p. 143 (Hellcat and Mustang fighters).

[4]This section on Okinawa is based primarily on Roy E. Appleman, et. al., *Okinawa: The Last Battle* (Washington, 1948) and Benis M. Frank, *Okinawa: Capstone to Victory* (New York, 1970). Appleman's is the more substantive work. He concentrates on Army operations. Frank highlights marine actions. Consulted also was Charles S. Nichols, Jr. and Henry I. Shaw, Jr., *Okinawa: Victory in the Pacific* (Washington, 1955).

[5]For planning about Okinawa see Appleman, *Okinawa*, pp. 1-7 and 17-43 and Samuel Eliot Morison, *Victory in the Pacific, 1945* (Boston, 1960), pp. 81-92. For the Luzon versus Formosa argument see either Robert Ross Smith, "Luzon Versus Formosa", in Kent Roberts Greenfield (ed.), *Command Decisions* (Washington, 1960), pp. 461-477, or Robert Ross Smith, *Triumph in the Philippines* (Washington, 1963), pp. 3-17.

[6]For comments on the British carriers see Maurice Matloff, *Strategic Planning for Coalition Warfare, 1942-1944* (Washington, 1959), p. 528 and Morison, *Victory*, p. 89 and pp. 102-107.

[7]Robert L. Eichelberger, *Our Jungle Road to Tokyo* (New York, 1950), p. 183. Also, Conversation on July 3, 1974 with Colonel Thomas E. Griess, who served in the 96th Infantry Division of the XXIV Corps on Leyte and Okinawa.

[8]Saburo Hayashi (In collaboration with Alvin D. Coox), *Kogun, The Japanese Army in the Pacific War* (Quantico, VA, 1959), pp. 133-136 and 138-141, cover the Japanese planning discussed.

[9]Hayashi and Coox, *Kogun*, p. 140.

[10]Appleman, *Okinawa*, pp. 7-17 (terrain) and 92-94 (selection of defensive positions).

[11]Frank, *Okinawa*, p. 22, states that Ushijima believed that the Allies would land at Minatoga. Appleman, *Okinawa*, p. 95, disagrees. He states Ushijima planned for a main landing at Hagushi.

[12]For the Japanese defensive plans see: Appleman, *Okinawa*, pp. 84-102; Hayashi and Coox, *Kogun*, pp. 138-141; Frank, *Okinawa*, pp. 14-24; Morison, *Victory*, pp. 199-209; and Masanori Ito with Roger Pineau, *The End of the Imperial Japanese Navy*, translated by Andrew Y. Kuroda and Roger Pineau (New York, 1962), pp. 184-187.

[13]Morison, *Victory*, pp. 94-102 and 109-139, covers the approach of the naval task force and preliminary operations. See also: Appleman, *Okinawa*, pp. 44-67 and 96; and Hayashi and Coox, *Kogun*, p. 141.

[14]Appleman, *Victory*, pp. 68-84. The remaining narrative about ground action on Okinawa is based on Appleman.

[15]For information about the marine demonstration see: Richard W. Johnston, *Follow Me!: The Story of the Second Marine Division in World War II* (New York, 1948), pp. 261-263; and Frank, *Okinawa*, p. 53.

[16]For the *kamikaze* attacks see: Morison, *Victory*, pp. 181-198, 221-230, 234-239, 251-262 and 267-272; and Hanson W. Baldwin, *Battles Won and Lost, Great Campaigns of World War II* (New York, 1968), pp. 461-478.

[17]For the cruise of the *Yamato* see: Mitsuru Yoshida, 'The Sinking of the *Yamato*," in United States Naval Institute, *The Japanese Navy in World War II* (Annapolis, 1969), pp. 138-147; Ito and Pineau, *End of the Japanese Navy*, pp. 188-190; Morison, *Victory*, pp. 199-209; and Appleman, *Okinawa*, p. 99.

[18]Appleman, *Okinawa*, pp. 102-137 (approach to Shuri) and 184-207 (attack of April 19).

[19]Appleman, *Okinawa*, p. 238.

[20]Appleman, *Okinawa*, pp. 258-264 (Buckner's decision).

[21]For the Japanese counteroffensive see: Appleman, *Okinawa*, pp. 283-310; and Frank, *Okinawa*, pp. 98-103.

[22]Appleman, *Okinawa*, p. 296 (May 3-4 air attacks). See also Morison, *Victory*, pp. 251-256.

[23]Appleman, *Okinawa*, pp. 310-323. Marine casualties are listed on p. 323.

[24]Hayashi and Coox, *Kogun*, p. 143, and Appleman, *Okinawa*, pp. 361-362, cover the *Giretsu* operation.

[25]Appleman, *Okinawa*, p. 370, quoting from 96th Infantry Division sources.

[26]Frank, *Okinawa*, pp. 149, 153-154, and 156-157; Johnston, *Follow Me!*, pp. 270-273; Appleman, *Okinawa*, pp. 470-471; and Morison, *Victory*, pp. 275-276.

[27]For casualties see: Appleman, *Okinawa*, pp. 489-490 (Tables 2 and 3); Morison, *Victory*, p. 233; and United States Strategic Bombing Survey (Pacific), *The Campaigns of the Pacific War* (Washington, 1946), pp. 326 and 331.

[28]This section is based primarily on Theodore Roscoe, *United States Submarine Operations in World War II* (Annapolis, 1949) and Samuel Eliot Morison, *The Two Ocean War, A Short History of the United States Navy in the Second World War* (Boston, 1972), pp. 416-433.

[29]The United States Strategic Bombing Survey, *The War Against Japanese Transportation, 1941-1945* (Washington, 1947), p. 47 (Figure 44).

[30]USSBS, *War Against Japanese Transportation*, p. 75 (peak tonnages).

[31]Ito and Pineau, *End of the Japanese Navy*, pp. 96 and 114.

[32]Morison, *Two Ocean War*, p. 431.

[33]Ito and Pineau, *End of the Japanese Navy*, pp. 26-29.

[34]Morison, *Two Ocean War*, p. 431.

[35]Samuel Eliot Morison, *New Guinea and the Marianas, March 1944-August 1944* (Boston, 1953), pp. 17, 20-21, 23, and 167-168; Robert Ross Smith, *The Approach to the Philippines* (Washington, 1953), pp. 232-233.

[36]Morison, *Two Ocean War*, p. 431.

[37]Philip A. Crowl and Edmund G. Love, *Seizure of the Gilberts and the Marianas* (Washington, 1955), pp. 27, 31-33, and 61-62 (Carlson's Makin Raid); Samuel Eliot Morison, *Aleutians, Gilberts and Marshalls, June 1942-April 1944* (Boston, 1951), pp. 97-98 and 222; and Roscoe, *Submarine Operations*, pp. 93-94.

[38]Japanese naval reactions are covered briefly in Morison, *Two-Ocean War*, pp. 419-420 and Hayashi and Coox, *Kogun*, pp. 81-84.

[39]Roscoe, *Submarine Operations*, pp. 170-172 (radars), pp. 240 (wolfpacks) and 262-263 (radars); and Morison, *Two Ocean*

War, pp. 425-432.

[40]Roscoe, *Submarine Operations*, p. 523.

[41]Ernest Andrade, Jr., "Submarine Policy in the United States Navy, 1919-1941," *Military Affairs* (April 1971), pp. 50-55.

[42]Samuel Eliot Morison, *Leyte, June 1944-January 1945* (Boston, 1958), p. 414 (footnote 19); and Roscoe, *Submarine Operations*, pp. 493-494.

[43]This section is based primarily on Wesley Frank Craven and James Lea Cate (eds.), *The Army Air Forces in World War II*, Volume V, *The Pacific: Matterhorn to Nagasaki, June 1944 to August 1945* (Chicago, 1953), pp. xii-xxvi, 507-576, 608-675. See pp. 554-559 for SAN ANTONIO I.

[44]Craven and Cate, *Matterhorn to Nagasaki*, pp. xv-xvi.

[45]Craven and Cate, *Matterhorn to Nagasaki*, pp. xvii-xviii, 33-41, 525-536, and 676-689.

[46]Craven and Cate, *Matterhorn to Nagasaki*, pp. 553-567. This section covers SAN ANTONIO II. For the January 19 raid see pp. 565-567.

[47]Craven and Cate, *Matterhorn to Nagasaki*, pp. 566-568, covers Hansell's relief and LeMay's first actions.

[48]Craven and Cate, *Matterhorn to Nagasaki*, pp. 142-144 (Hankow), 572-574 (Tokyo, February 25), and 611-618 (Tokyo, March 9-10). See also Alvin D. Coox, *Japan: The Final Agony* (New York, 1970), pp. 23-29.

[49]Craven and Cate, *Matterhorn to Nagasaki*, pp. xx, 614-627 (first raids) and 635-644; Louis Morton, *Strategy and Command: The First Two Years* (Washington, 1962), pp. 644-647. (Joint Chiefs of Staff Memorandum: Strategic Plan for the Defeat of Japan); and Coox, *Final Agony*, pp. 30-41.

[50]Craven and Cate, *Matterhorn to Nagasaki*, pp. 752-756.

[51]The United States Strategic Bombing Survey, *The Effects of Strategic Bombing on Japanese Morale* (Washington, 1947), pp. 1-9. See also quotes of Prince Konoye and Prime Minister Suzuki in Craven and Cate, *Matterhorn to Nagasaki*, p. 756.

[52]This section is based primarily on: Herbert Feis, *Japan Subdued, The Atomic Bomb and the End of the War in the Pacific* (Princeton, 1961); Craven and Cate, *Matterhorn to Nagasaki*, pp. 703-733; Hayashi and Coox, *Kogun*, pp. 151-182; Coox, *Final Agony*, pp. 61-154; Thomas M. Coffey, *Imperial Tragedy, Japan in World War II, The First Days and the Last* (New York, 1970), pp. 341-692; The Pacific War Research Society (Compiler), *Japan's Longest Day* (New York, 1972); Marius B. Jensen (ed.), *Japan's Longest Day* (Cambridge, Mass, 1971); Harry S. Truman, *Memoirs by Harry S. Truman*, Volume I, *Year of Decisions*. (New York, 1955), pp. 414-439; *Reports of General MacArthur*, Volume I, *The Campaigns of MacArthur in the Pacific* (Washington, 1966), prepared by his general staff, pp. 387-447; *Reports of General MacArthur*, Volume II-Part II, *Japanese Operations in the Southwest Pacific Area* (Washington, 1967), compiled from Japanese Demobilization Bureau Records, pp. 669-759.

[53]Coox, *Final Agony*, pp. 61-89; Hayashi and Coox, *Kogun*, pp. 151-168, 180-181; *Reports of MacArthur*, II-II, *Japanese Operations*, pp. 601-607 (KETSUGO Operational plans) and 609-611 (Tactics and Techniques); and Pacific War Research Society, *Longest Day*, pp. 9, 17, 19 and 24 (some of Anami's opinions).

[54]Hayashi and Coox, *Kogun*, p. 151 and pp. 178-179, discuss the impact of spirit. Also see Coox, *Final Agony*, pp. 71-77.

[55]Coox, *Final Agony*, pp. 61-93. See in particular pp. 81, 84, 86-88. Also see Feis, *Japan Subdued*, pp. 64-65, 74, and 168-173.

[56]Coox, *Final Agony*, pp. 77-85, 90-91 and 93; *Reports of MacArthur*, II-II, *Japanese Operations*, pp. 601-607; and Hayashi and Coox, *Kogun*, pp. 159-167.

[57]The early peace moves are described in *Reports of MacArthur*, II-II, *Japanese Operations*, pp. 669-680.

[58]Coox, *Final Agony*, pp. 101-102.

[59]Coox, *Final Agony*, pp. 103-105, and *Reports of MacArthur*, II-II, *Japanese Operations*, pp. 673-680, covers the formation of the Suzuki Cabinet. General Anami's key role is evident in all discussions of the surrender. Professor Alvin D. Coox believes Anami essentially played the most important role in the Japanese Cabinet ("Conversations with Alvin D. Coox, July 1973, San Diego, California.") Also see Saburo Hayashi, "General Anami and the End of the War," in Jensen, *Japan's Longest Day*, pp. 79-89.

[60]*Reports of MacArthur*, II-II, *Japanese Operations*, pp. 677-678 and Coox, *Final Agony*, pp. 105-106.

[61]Coox, *Final Agony*, pp. 106-107, and *Reports of MacArthur*, II-II, *Japanese Operations*, pp. 680-685.

[62]*Reports of MacArthur*, II-II, *Japanese Operations*, p. 687.

[63]*Reports of MacArthur*, II-II, *Japanese Operations*, pp. 685-696.

[64]The Imperial initiative on June 22 is explained in *Reports of MacArthur*, II-II, *Japanese Operations*, pp. 696-697. The background is discussed in pp. 692-696. Also see Coox, *Final Agony*, pp. 108-109.

[65]Feis, *Japan Subdued*, pp. 54-57; *Reports of MacArthur*, II-II, *Japanese Operations*, pp. 697-700; and Coox, *Final Agony*, pp. 109-113.

[66]Feis, *Japan Subdued*, pp. 68-69 and 92.

[67]*Reports of MacArthur*, I, *Campaigns of MacArthur*, pp. 385-401, 407-414, and 423-430.

[68]Feis, *Japan Subdued*, p. 12, and Truman, *Year of Decisions*, p. 417.

[69]Feis, *Japan Subdued*, pp. 5-11. Louis Morton "Soviet Intervention in the War With Japan," *Foreign Affairs*, XL (July 1962), pp. 653-662, presents a more detailed background to Soviet intervention.

[70]For Grew's proposition and its effect see: Feis, *Japan Subdued*, pp. 15-27; and Truman, *Year of Decisions*, pp. 416-417.

[71]Feis, *Japan Subdued*, p. 63. For other comments on the Interim Committee and the objectors to the bomb see: *Ibid.*, pp. 31-45; Truman, *Year of Decisions*, p. 419; Henry L. Stimson "The Decision to Use the Atomic Bomb" in Gordon B. Turner (ed.), *A History of Military Affairs in Western Society Since the Eighteenth Century* (New York, 1953), pp. 631-633; and Louis Morton, "The Decision to Use the Atomic Bomb", in Kent Roberts Greenfield (ed.), *Command Decisions* (Washington, 1950), pp. 494-500.

[72]The three options are a major theme in Feis, *Japan Subdued*, pp. 3-47.

[73]Feis, *Japan Subdued*, p. 76; Truman, *Year of Decisions*, p. 419; and Craven and Cate, *Matterhorn to Nagasaki*, pp. 713-714, and plate between pp. 712 and 713 (letter from President Harry S. Truman to Professor James L. Cate, dated January 12, 1953.

[74]Feis, *Japan Subdued*, p. 102 (footnote 91) (Atlee's com-

ments), and pp. 65-66 and 88-91 (notification of Stalin); Truman, *Year of Decisions*, p. 416.

[75]Jensen, *Japan's Longest Day*, pp. 1-3, contains the Potsdam Declaration. Quotes are from paragraphs (5) and (13).

[76]Feis, *Japan Subdued*, pp. 95-96, and Coox, *Final Agony*, pp. 114-117.

[77]Feis, *Japan Subdued*, p. 97, quoting from the United States Department of State, *Potsdam Papers*, Document 1258.

[78]Feis, *Japan Subdued*, p. 98.

[79]Feis, *Japan Subdued*, pp. 99-104.

[80]The first atomic attack is described best by Craven and Cate, *Matterhorn to Nagasaki*, pp. 716-717. Also see Feis, *Japan Subdued*, pp. 109-110. Target selection is discussed in both sources: Craven and Cate, pp. 710-711, and Feis, pp. 73-74.

[81]Truman, *Year of Decisions*, p. 422.

[82]For actions on August 7-8 see: Feis, *Japan Subdued*, pp. 113-114; Craven and Cate, *Matterhorn to Nagasaki*, pp. 718-720; Pacific War Research Society, *Longest Day*, pp. 14-15; *Reports of MacArthur*, II-II, *Japanese Operations*, pp. 706-709; and Coffey, *Imperial Tragedy*, pp. 390-400; 418-422, and 430-437.

[83]Pacific War Research Society, *Longest Day*, p. 19. Also see *Ibid*., pp. 15-21; Feis, *Japan Subdued*, pp. 118-119; and Coffey, *Imperial Tragedy*, pp. 438-448, and 452-457, for the details of the meetings on August 9.

[84]Coffey, *Imperial Tragedy*, p. 534.

[85]Jensen, *Japan's Longest Day*, pp. 3-4, contains the Japanese message to Secretary Byrnes, dated August 10, 1945. Quote is on p. 3. For details of Imperial Conference see: Coffey, *Imperial Tragedy*, pp. 461-476, and 479-482; and Coox, *Final Agony*, pp. 120-123.

[86]For Byrnes' complete reply see Jensen, *Japan's Longest Day*, p. 4.

[87]Feis, *Japan Subdued*, pp. 120-123, and Coox, *Final Agony*, pp. 124-132.

[88]This dramatic day is described excellently in Pacific War Research Society, *Longest Day*, pp. 52-232.

[89]The Imperial Rescript is reproduced in *Reports of MacArthur*, II-II, *Japanese Operations*, p. 729 (Plate 167). Also see Pacific War Research Society, *Longest Day*, pp. 231-323.

[90]Pacific War Research Society, *Longest Day*, pp. 186-188, 198-203, 210-211, and 219; Coffey, *Imperial Tragedy*, pp. 644-649, 653-655, and 674-677.

[91]This section is based on: Eichelberger, *Jungle Road*, pp. 259-263; *Reports of MacArthur*, I, *Campaigns of MacArthur*, pp. 452-453; and Courtney Whitney, *MacArthur, His Rendezvous with History* (New York, 1956), pp. 211-215.

Appendix 1
Japanese Order of Battle, Southern Regions, 1941

SOUTHERN ARMY (General Count H. Terauchi in Saigon)

Fourteenth Army (PI)
(Lieutenant General M. Homma)

16th Division
48th Division
65th Independent Mixed Brigade

Fifteenth Army (Burma)
(Lieutenant General S. Iida)

33rd Division
55th Division (−)

Sixteenth Army (NEI—Java)
(Lieutenant General H. Imamura)

2nd Division
38th Division (after Hong Kong
    operation)
56th Independent Mixed Brigade

Twenty-Fifth Army (Malaya)
(Lieutenant General T. Yamashita)

Imperial Guard Division
5th Division
18th Division

21st Division
(Lieutenant General H. Tanaka)

Army Troops

21st Independent Mixed Brigade
4th Independent Mixed Brigade
21st Independent Air Unit

3rd Air Group*
(Lieutenant General M. Sugawara)

4 fighter regiments
3 light bomber regiments
3 heavy bomber regiments
1 reconnaissance regiment

5th Air Group†
(Lieutenant General E. Obata)

2 fighter regiments
3 light bomber regiments
2 heavy bomber regiments
1 reconnaissance regiment

SOUTHERN FORCE, IMPERIAL JAPANESE NAVY (Vice Admiral N. Kondo)

Second Fleet
(Vice Admiral N. Kondo)

A battle/support fleet

Third Fleet
(Vice Admiral I. Takahashi)

An amphibious fleet

*Supporting Twenty-Fifth Army
† Supporting Fourteenth Army

Appendix 2

Conclusions of the Joint Congressional Committee Investigating the Pearl Harbor Attack

1. Operational and intelligence work requires centralization of authority and clear-cut allocation of responsibility.

2. Supervisory officials cannot safely take anything for granted in the alerting of subordinates.

3. Any doubt as to whether outposts should be given information should always be resolved in favor of supplying the information.

4. The delegation of authority or the issuance of orders entails the duty of inspection to determine that the official mandate is properly exercised.

5. The implementation of official orders must be followed with closest supervision.

6. The maintenance of alertness to responsibility must be insured through repetition.

7. Complacency and procrastination are out of place where sudden and decisive action are of the essence.

8. The coordination and proper evaluation of intelligence in times of stress must be insured by continuity of service and centralization of responsibility in competent officials.

9. The unapproachable or superior attitude of officials is fatal; there should never be any hesitancy in asking for clarification of instructions or in seeking advice on matters that are in doubt.

10. There is no substitute for imagination and resourcefulness on the part of supervisory and intelligence officials.

11. Communications must be characterized by clarity, forthrightness, and appropriateness.

12. There is great danger in careless paraphrase of information received, and every effort should be made to insure that the paraphrased material reflects the true meaning and significance of the original.

13. Procedures must be sufficiently flexible to meet the exigencies of unusual situations.

14. Restrictions of highly confidential information to a minimum number of officials, while often necessary, should not be carried to the point of prejudicing the work of the organization.

15. There is great danger of being blinded by the self-evident.

16. Officials should at all times give subordinates the benefit of significant information.

17. An official who neglects to familiarize himself in detail with his organization should forfeit his responsibility.

18. Failure can be avoided in the long run only by preparation for any eventuality.

19. Officials, on a personal basis, should never countermand an official instruction.

20. Personal or official jealousy will wreck any organization.

21. Personal friendship, without more, should never be accepted in lieu of liaison or confused therewith where the latter is necessary to the proper functioning of two or more agencies.

22. No considerations should be permitted as excuse for failure to perform a fundamental task.

23. Superiors must at all times keep their subordinates adequately informed and, conversely, subordinates should keep their superiors informed.

24. The administrative organization of any establishment must be designed to locate failures and to assess responsibility.

25. In a well-balanced organization there is close correlation of responsibility and authority.

Appendix 3

Japanese Order of Battle, Netherlands, East Indies, 1942

SOUTHERN FORCE (Vice Admiral N. Kondo)

Western Force
(Vice Admiral J. Ozawa)

Objectives:
Palembang
Western Java

Center Force
(Vice Admiral I. Takahashi)

Objectives:
Tarakan
Balipapen
Bandjermasin
Eastern Java

Eastern Force
(Vice Admiral I. Takahashi)

Objectives:
Menado
Kendari
Amboina
Makassar
Timor
Bali
Eastern Java

Eleventh Air Fleet (land-based)
(Vice Admiral N. Tsukahara)

21st Air Flotilla (108 aircraft)
Two light carriers, and three seaplane carriers. On occasion, the
  First Air Fleet supported
  operation.
23rd Air Flotilla (200 aircraft)

Sixteenth Army with Attached Special Naval Landing Forces
(Lieutenant General H. Imamura)

Palembang*

229th Infantry Regiment
Misc. paratroopers

Tarakan

Sakaguchi Detachment †
Kure 2nd SNLF

Menado

Sasebo Combined SNLF
Yokosuka 1st SNLF

*The Imperial Guards Division occupied northern Sumatra at a later date.

†The Sakaguchi Detachment was also known as the 56th Regimental Group, which was built around the 146th Infantry Regiment.

Balipapen

Sakaguchi Detachment

Bandjermasin

Sakaguchi Detachment (ELMS)

Kendari

Sasebo Combined SNLF

Amboina

228th Infantry Regiment
Kure 1st SNLF

Makassar

Sasebo Combined SNLF

Timor

228th Infantry Regiment
Yokosuka 3rd SNLF

Bali

Elements, 48th Division

Western Java

230th Infantry Regiment
2nd Division

Eastern Java*

Sakaguchi Detachment

Eastern Java*

48th Division

3rd Air Division

About 150 to 354 aircraft were
assigned.

*Center and Eastern Forces were regrouped and combined for the invasion of Java.

Appendix 4
Japanese Order of Battle at Coral Sea, May 5-8, 1942

TASK FORCE "MO"

Vice Admiral S. Inouye
CINC, Fourth Fleet, in a light cruiser at Rabaul

CARRIER STRIKING FORCE

Vice Admiral T. Takagi

2 carriers (*Shokaku* and *Zuikaku*)
 (123 aircraft)
2 heavy cruisers
6 destroyers
1 oiler

INVASION FORCES

Rear Admiral A. Goto

Tulagi Invasion Group
(Rear Admiral K. Shima)

1 transport
2 destroyers
9 miscellaneous small craft

Port Moresby Invasion Group
(Rear Admiral S. Kajioka)

11 transports
1 light cruiser
6 destroyers
2 oilers
1 repair ship
5 miscellaneous small craft

Support Group
(Rear Admiral K. Marumo)

Covering Group
(Rear Admiral A. Goto)

1 seaplane carrier (*Kamikawa Maru*)
  (12 seaplanes)
2 light cruisers
3 gunboats

1 light carrier (*Shoho*)
  (21 aircraft)
4 heavy cruisers
1 destroyer

OTHER FORCES

Submarine Force
(Captain N. Ishizaka)

7 submarines

Land-Based Naval Air Force
(Rear Admiral S. Yamada, Rabaul)

181 miscellaneous aircraft

Appendix 5

United States Order of Battle at Coral Sea, May 5-8, 1942

TASK FORCE 17
(Rear Admiral F. J. Fletcher in *Yorktown*)

Task Group 17.5 Carrier Group
(Rear Admiral A. Fitch in *Lexington*)

2 carriers (*Lexington* and *Yorktown*)
(141 aircraft)

Task Group 17.2 Attack Group
(Rear Admiral T. Kinkaid)

2 heavy cruisers
1 light cruiser
5 destroyers

Task Group 17.3 Support Group
(Rear Admiral J. Crace, RN)

2 heavy cruisers
3 light cruisers
5 destroyers

Task Group 17.6 Fueling Group

2 oilers
2 destroyers

Task Group 17.9 Search Group
(Commander G. DeBaun, Noumea)

12 Catalina patrol bombers

OTHER UNITS

Task Force 42: Eastern Australian Submarine Group
(Rear Admiral F. Rockwell)

11 submarines

SWPA Allied Air Forces

(Lieutenant General G. Brett in Australia)

482 miscellaneous aircraft
(most out of range)

Appendix 6

Simplified Japanese Order of Battle at Midway, June 3-6, 1942

COMBINED FLEET: Admiral I. Yamamoto in *Yamato*

Main Force (First Fleet)
(Admiral I. Yamamoto in *Yamato*)

7 battleships
2 light cruisers
21 destroyers
1 light carrier (*Hosho*) (8 aircraft)
2 seaplane carriers (*Chiyoda* and *Nisshin*) (no aircraft; carried midget submarines)

First Carrier Striking Force (First Air Fleet)
(Vice Admiral C. Nagumo in *Akagi*)

4 fleet carriers (*Akagi, Kaga, Hiryu,* and *Soryu*) (261 aircraft)
2 battleships
2 heavy cruisers
1 light cruiser
11 destroyers

Midway Invasion Force (Second Fleet)
(Vice Admiral N. Kondo in *Atago*)

2 battleships
8 heavy cruisers
2 light cruisers
11 destroyers
1 light carrier (*Zuiho*) (24 aircraft)
2 seaplane carriers (*Chitose* and *Kamikawa Maru*)
   (24 float fighters and 8 scout planes)
3 destroyer-transports

12 transports
4 minesweepers
3 submarine chasers
1 supply ship
2 cargo ships
1 patrol boat

Northern (Aleutians) Force (Fifth Fleet)
(Vice Admiral M. Hosogaya in *Nachi*)

8 heavy cruisers
1 carrier (*Junyo*) (45 aircraft)
1 light carrier (*Ryujo*) (37 aircraft)
2 light cruisers
1 auxiliary cruiser

12 destroyers
3 transports
1 minelayer
3 minesweepers
5 submarines

Advanced (Submarine) Force (Sixth Fleet)
(Vice Admiral T. Komatsu in *Katori*)

1 light cruiser
2 submarine tenders

15 submarines

Appendix 7

United States Order of Battle at Midway, June 3-6, 1942

UNITED STATES PACIFIC FLEET: Admiral Chester Nimitz in Hawaii

Carrier Striking Force: Rear Admiral F. J. Fletcher

Task Force 17
(Rear Admiral F. J. Fletcher in *Yorktown*)

1 carrier (*Yorktown*) (75 aircraft)
2 cruisers
6 destroyers

Task Force 16
(Rear Admiral R. Spruance in *Enterprise*)

2 carriers (*Enterprise* and *Hornet*) (158 aircraft)
6 cruisers
9 destroyers
4 oilers

Submarines: Rear Admiral R. English at Pearl Harbor

19 submarines

Shore-based Air, Midway

32 PBY Catalinas
19 B-17s
6 Avenger torpedo bombers
16 Dauntless dive bombers

Other Miscellaneous Ships, Vicinity Midway

10 PT boats
2 oilers
3 destroyers
1 sweeper

Shore-based Air, Midway

11 Vindicator dive bombers
20 Brewster Buffalo fighters
7 Wildcat fighters
4 B-26 Marauders

Task Force 8 (Aleutians)
(Rear Admiral R. Theobald in *Nashville*)

2 heavy cruisers
3 light cruisers
13 destroyers
6 submarines
3 tenders
24 miscellaneous craft
176 land-based aircraft

Other Miscellaneous Ships, Vicinity Midway

2 seaplane tenders
4 converted tuna boats
4 patrol craft

Appendix 8

Allied Organization for Guadalcanal and Papua Operations, August 1942

SOUTH PACIFIC AREA (Guadalcanal)

Commander, South Pacific Area (and South Pacific Force, Pacific Fleet)
(Vice Admiral R. Ghormley, USN)

Expeditionary Force: (Task Force 61)
(Vice Admiral F. J. Fletcher, USN)

Air Support Force: (Task Group 61.1) Rear Admiral L. Noyes, USN

South Pacific Amphibious Force: (Task Force 62)
(Rear Admiral R. Turner, USN)

Including 1st Marine Division (Reinforced): Major General A. Vandegrift, USMC

Land-based Air, South Pacific Force: (Task Force 63)
(Rear Admiral J. McCain, USN)

SOUTHWEST PACIFIC AREA, GENERAL HEADQUARTERS (Papua)

Supreme Commander: General Douglas MacArthur, USA

*Chief of Staff: Major General R. Sutherland, USA
*Asst Chief of Staff, G-1: Colonel C. Stivers, USA
*Asst Chief of Staff, G-2: Colonel C. Willoughby, USA
  Asst Chief of Staff, G-3: Brigadier General S. Chamberlain, USA
  Asst Chief of Staff, G-4: Colonel L. Whitlock, USA

Commander Allied Land Forces: General Sir Thomas Blamey, AIF (April 18, 1942)
Commander Allied Air Forces: Lieutenant General G. Kenney, USA (August 4, 1942)
Commander Allied Naval Forces: Vice Admiral A. Carpender, USN (July 1942)

*Served in Philippines with MacArthur (also known as "the Bataan Gang")

Appendix 9

Original Japanese Army Order of Battle for Advance on Port Moresby, July 1942

Yokoyama Force
(Colonel Y. Yokoyama, Commander, 15th Independent Engineer Regiment)

1st Battalion, 144th Infantry (Lieutenant Colonel H. Tsukamoto)
15th Independent Engineer Regiment
Detachment, 10th Independent Engineer Regiment
Company, Sasebo 5th Special Naval Landing Force
Mountain artillery, antiaircraft artillery, labor, support, service, and administrative troops

South Seas Detachment
(Major General T. Horii)

144th Infantry Regiment, Reinforced (55th Division)

Yazawa Detachment
(Colonel K. Yazawa, Commander, 41st Infantry Regiment)

41st Infantry Regiment (5th Division)

Kawaguchi Detachment
(Major General K. Kawaguchi)

124th Infantry Regiment, Reinforced

AOBA Detachment (Army Reserve)

4th Infantry Regiment, Reinforced (2nd Division)

Appendix 10

Estimated Ground Casualties and Major Naval Losses, Guadalcanal Campaign, 1942-1943

GROUND FORCES

Approximate Total US Army and Marine Corps Forces Employed: 60,000

	Killed	Wounded
1st Marine Division	774	1962
Americal Division	334	850
2nd Marine Division	268	932
25th Infantry Division	216	439
Totals	1,592	4,283

Approximate Total Japanese Army and Naval Troops Employed: 36,000 (of 43,000 dispatched)

Killed or missing	14,800
Died of disease	9,000
Lost at sea	4,346
POWs	1,000
Evacuated	9,000-11,000

NAVAL FORCES (Ships Sunk and Personnel Lost)

	US Pacific Fleet	Combined Fleet
Carriers (CV)	*2	0
Light Carriers (CVL)	0	†1
Other Carriers (AV)	0	1
Battleships (BB)	0	2
Heavy Cruisers (CA)	6	3
Light Cruisers (CL)	2	1
Destroyers (DD)	14	11
Submarines (SS)	0	6

Personnel losses have never been tabulated for either Navy. American naval casualties exceeded the losses of the American ground forces. Japanese naval casualties were probably equal to those of the American Navy but less than those of the Japanese Army.

*Hornet and Wasp
†Ryujo

Appendix 11

Major Japanese Combat Forces for Defense of Papua Beachhead, 1942-1943

Gona

(Major T. Yamamoto, Commander, Army Roadbuilding Unit)

Army Roadbuilding Unit
Service troops and walking wounded

Sanananda

(Colonel Y. Yokoyama, Commander, 15th Independent Engineer Regiment)

41st Infantry Regiment (−)
1st Battalion, 144th Infantry Regiment (−) (Lieutenant Colonel H. Tsukamoto)
15th Independent Engineer Regiment (−)
Artillery, antiaircraft artillery, cavalry, and naval construction troops

Buna

(Captain Y. Yasuda, IJN, Commander, Naval Troops and Airfield)

Sasebo 5th Special Naval Landing Force (−)
Yokosuka 5th Special Naval Landing Force (−)
Army engineer and service troops, and naval laborers

Cape Endaiadere

(Colonel H. Yamamoto, Commander, 144th Infantry Regiment)

300 replacements, 144th Infantry Regiment
3d Battalion, 229th Infantry Regiment (38th Division)
Artillery, antiaircraft artillery, and support troops

Major Reinforcements:

500 replacements, 144th Infantry Regiment (November 21). From Rabaul to Sanananda.

500 survivors, 41st Infantry Regiment (November 29). From Kumusi River area to Sanananda.

21st Independent Mixed Brigade (December 26-31). From Rabaul to Kumusi River area to Sanananda.

Appendix 12
Major Allied Combat Forces in Papua

Australian Forces

I Corps: Lieutenant General S. Rowell; relieved September 28, 1942 by Lieutenant General E. Herring

    7th Infantry Division: Major General A. Allen: relieved October 28, 1944 by Major General G. Vasey
      18th Brigade (Brigadier G. Wootten)
      21st Brigade
      25th Brigade

    7th Infantry Brigade
    14th Infantry Brigade
    16th Infantry Brigade
    30th Infantry Brigade
    2/7 Armored Regiment
    2/7 Cavalry Regiment (dismounted)
    2/6 Independent Company

United States Army

I Corps: Lieutenant General R. Eichelberger

    32nd Infantry Division: Major General E. Harding; relieved in December by Brigadier General A. Waldron; and then Lieutenant General R. Eichelberger*

      126th Infantry Regiment
      127th Infantry Regiment
      128th Infantry Regiment

    41st Infantry Division (−): Major General H. Fuller

    163d Infantry Regiment (Colonel J. Doe)

*Eichelberger assumed command of the troops after he lost the last of his subordinate general officers. Three had been wounded in action by this time.

Appendix 13

Approximate Allied Casualties, Papuan Campaign, 1942-1943

Battle Losses*	KIA	DOW	DOC	MIA	WIA
American Forces:	687	160	17	66	1,918
Australian Forces:	1,731	306	128	n/a	3,533
Totals:	2,418	466	135	66	5,451

Disease Losses

American Forces (entire campaign): 14,464 troops committed

Cases of Malaria (32nd Infantry Division)	5,358
Total, all causes	8,659

Australian Forces (through 1942): 18,000-20,000 troops committed

Cases of Malaria	9,249
Cases of dysentery	3,643
Cases of dengue fever	1,186
Total all causes	15,575

Regimental Attrition

126th Infantry, 32nd Infantry Division

Strength, mid-November:	3,171
Strength, January 22, 1943:	611

*KIA (killed in action); DOW (died of wounds); DOC (died, other causes); MIA (missing in action); and WIA (wounded in action).

Appendix 14

Major Japanese Forces Opposing Drives in South and Southwest Pacific Areas

Eighth Area Army:

(Lieutenant General H. Imamura [Rabaul])

Seventeenth Army: Lieutenant General H. Hyakutake (Shortlands)

  6th Division
  Miscellaneous Units

Eighteenth Army: Lieutenant General H. Adachi (Madang)

  20th Division (Madang)
  41st Division (Wewak)
  51st Division (Lae area)

New Britain Troops

  17th Division
  38th Division
  65th Brigade
  8th Tank Regiment

Fourth Air Army (established July 28, 1943): Lieutenant General K. Teramoto (New Guinea)

  6th Air Division
  7th Air Division (arrived July 1943)

Southeast Area Fleet:

(Vice Admiral J. Kusaka [Rabaul])

  Fourth Air Fleet: (Wewak)

  Eleventh Air Fleet: Vice Admiral J. Kusaka (Rabaul)

  Eighth Fleet: Vice Admiral G. Mikawa (Shortlands)

    Southeastern (Army) Detachment (New Georgia)
    7th Combined Special Naval Landing Force (Santa Isabel)
    8th Combined Special Naval Landing Force (New Georgia)
    Base Forces

Appendix 15
Major Allied Forces, South Pacific Area: Operation Cartwheel

General Douglas MacArthur, USA—Strategic Direction
Admiral William Halsey, USN—Tactical Commander

Naval Forces
(Admiral W. Halsey, USN)

Third Fleet: Admiral W. Halsey, USN

Elements, Royal New Zealand Navy

Amphibious Forces
(Rear Admiral T. Wilkinson, USN)

I Amphibious Corps: Lieutenant General A. Vandegrift, USMC/Major General R. Geiger, USMC

2nd Marine Division
3rd Marine Division
1st Marine Raider Regiment
1st Marine Parachute Regiment

Ground Forces
(Lieutenant General M. Harmon, USA)

XIV Corps: Major General O. Griswold, USA

Americal Division
25th Infantry Division
37th Infantry Division
43rd Infantry Division

3rd New Zealand Division
Other New Zealand Units

Air Forces
(Vice Admiral A. Fitch, USN)

Thirteenth Air Force: Major General N. Twining, USA

Navy Air Units

Marine Air Units

New Zealand Air Units

Appendix 16

Major Allied Forces, Southwest Pacific Area: Operation Cartwheel

General Douglas MacArthur, Commander-in-Chief

Allied Land Forces
(General Sir Thomas Blamey, AIF)

New Guinea Force: General Sir Thomas Blamey, AIF

3rd Australian Division
5th Australian Division
7th Australian Division
9th Australian Division

Elements, 41st Infantry Division
503rd Parachute Infantry Regiment

Alamo Force
(Lieutenant General W. Krueger, USA)

1st Cavalry Division
1st Marine Division (operational control)
Elements, 32d Infantry Division
112th Cavalry Regiment (from SOPA)
158th Infantry Regiment (separate)

Allied Air Forces
(Lieutenant General G. Kenney, USA)

Fifth Air Force: Lieutenant General G. Kenney, USA

Royal Australian Air Force Command: Air Vice Marshal W. Bostock, RAAF

Allied Naval Forces
(Vice Admiral A. Carpender, USN/Vice Admiral T. Kinkaid, USN)

Seventh Fleet: Vice Admiral A. Carpender, USN/Vice Admiral T. Kinkaid, USN
VII Amphibious Force: Rear Admiral D. Barbey, USN
Elements, Royal Australian Navy
Elements, Royal Netherlands Navy

Appendix 17

American Fast Carriers Utilized in Central Pacific Area: 1943-1944

Name*	Date Commissioned	Displacement (in tons)	Speed (in knots)	Aircraft Carried
LEXINGTON CLASS		33,000	33.9	90
CV-3 *Saratoga*	1927			
YORKTOWN CLASS		19,800	32.5	81-85
CV-6 *Enterprise*	1938			
ESSEX CLASS		27,100	33.0	80 (+)
CV-9 *Essex*	1942			
CV-10 *Yorktown*	1943			
CV-11 *Intrepid* †	1943			
CV-12 *Hornet*	1943			
CV-16 *Lexington* †	1944			
CV-17 *Bunker Hill*	1944			
CV-18 *Wasp*	1944			
INDEPENDENCE CLASS **		11,000	31.0	45
CV-22 *Independence*	1943			
CV-23 *Princeton*	1943			
CV-24 *Belleau Wood*	1943			
CV-25 *Cowpens*	1943			
CV-26 *Monterrey*	1943			
CV-27 *Langley*	1943			
CV-28 *Cabot*	1943			
CVL-30 *San Jacinto*	1943			

*No fast carrier was sunk during this period. The CVE *Liscome Bay* was sunk off Makin.

† Damaged during the period.

**Independence Class carriers normally were called CVLs but initially were designated CVs.

Appendix 18

Major Japanese Forces Opposing Drive in Central Pacific Area, June 1944

Combined Fleet*
(Admiral S. Toyoda, Inland Sea)

First Mobile Fleet: Vice Admiral J. Ozawa, Tawitawi

Second Fleet (formerly the Scouting Fleet): Vice Admiral T. Kurita, Halmahera and vicinity

Third Fleet (formerly First Air Fleet, still the carrier fleet): Vice Admiral J. Ozawa, Tawitawi

First Air Fleet (land-based air): Vice Admiral K. Kakuta, Tinian

Central Pacific Area Fleet: Vice Admiral C. Nagumo, Saipan

Fourth Fleet (the Mandates Fleet): Vice Admiral C. Hara, Saipan

Sixth Fleet (Submarine Fleet): Vice Admiral T. Takagi, Saipan

Thirty First Army
(Lieutenant General H. Obata, Saipan)

29th Division
43rd Division
Several separate brigades, regiments, battalions

*The Combined Fleet and all the listed numbered fleets (not air) were previously stationed at Truk.

Appendix 19

Major Japanese Combat Forces in the Marianas, June 1944

**Vice Admiral C. Nagumo, Commander-in-Chief,
Central Pacific Area Fleet, Saipan**

Saipan
(Lieutenant General Y. Saito)*

Thirty-First Army (Lieutenant General H. Obata)†

  43rd Division (Lieutenant General Y. Saito)*
  47th Independent Mixed Brigade
  3rd Battalion, 9th Independent Mixed Brigade
  1st Battalion, 18th Infantry Regiment

5th Base Force (Rear Admiral T. Tsujimura)**

  55th Naval Guard Force
  Yokoska 1st Special Naval Landing Force
  Elements, 41st Naval Guard Force

Tinian
(Colonel I. Ogata)

  50th Infantry Regiment (Colonel Ogata)††
  1st Battalion, 135th Infantry Regiment††
  56th Naval Guard Force**

Guam
(Lieutenant General H. Takashura)

  29th Division (Lieutenant General H. Takashura)††
  48th Independent Mixed Brigade ††
  10th Independent Mixed Brigade
  54th Naval Guard Force**

*Exercised actual tactical command on Saipan until his suicide.

† Although the senior army officer assigned to Saipan, he was absent during the battle. He was later killed on Guam.

**Part of Central Pacific Area Fleet.

†† Part of Thirty First Army.

Appendix 20

Major Allied Forces Committed, Central Pacific Area Drive, 1943-1944

Admiral Chester Nimitz, Commander-in-Chief, Hawaii

United States Navy
(Admiral C. Nimitz, Hawaii)

Fifth Fleet (Third Fleet): Vice Admiral R. Spruance*
  (Admiral W. Halsey)

  V Amphibious Force (III Amphibious Force): Rear Admiral K. Turner (Vice Admiral T. Wilkinson)
  Fast Carrier Striking Force, Task Force 58 (Task Force 38): Rear Admiral M. Mitscher (Vice Admiral M. Mitscher)
  Defense Forces and Land-based Air: Rear Admiral J. Hoover

Submarines, Pacific Fleet: Vice Admiral C. Lockwood, Hawaii

United States Marine Corps

V Amphibious Corps: Lieutenant General H. Smith

III Amphibious Corps (Originally I Marine Amphibious Corps): Major General R. Geiger

1st Marine Division †	4th Marine Division
2nd Marine Division	1st Marine Provisional Brigade
3rd Marine Division	

United States Army
(Lieutenant General R. Richardson, Hawaii)

Seventh Air Force: Major General J. Hale

XXIV Corps: Major General J. Hodge**

7th Infantry Division	81st Infantry Division
27th Infantry Division	111th Infantry Regiment (separate)
77th Infantry Division	

*The fleet headquarters changed, but the ships remained the same. When Spruance commanded, the force was Fifth Fleet; when Halsey commanded, it was Third Fleet. The same was true for the III and V Amphibious Forces. Mitscher, however, still commanded the Fast Carrier Striking Force under both Spruance and Halsey.

† The Marine Divisions and Provisional Brigade were assigned to either Amphibious Corps as needed.

**Hodge's XXIV Corps Headquarters was never committed. His XXIV Corps Artillery and his assigned divisions fought under Naval or Marine Corps commanders. Ranks shown are highest ranks held.

Appendix 21
Battle Losses, Palaus Campaign, 1944

United States Forces	KIA	WIA	TOTAL
1st Marine Division	1252	5274	6526
81st Infantry Division	540	2735	3275
US Navy	158	505	663
			Total 10,464

Japanese Forces			
Peleliu	11,000(+)		11,000(+)
Anguar, other islands	2,600		2,600
			Total 13,600

Regimental Attrition, 1st Marine Division (KIA, WIA, MIA):

1st Marines	1749
5th Marines	1378
7th Marines	1497
Total	4624

Appendix 22

Major Japanese Forces Opposing Allied Approach to the Philippines in Southwest Pacific Area, April 1944

Southern Army
(General Count H. Terauchi [Singapore])

Second Area Army: Lieutenant General K. Anami (Davao/Menado, Celebes)

Second Army: Lieutenant General F. Teshima (Manokwari)

32nd Division (arrived late April)
35th Division (arrived late April)
36th Division

Eighteenth Army: Lieutenant General H. Adachi (Madang)*

20th Division
41st Division
51st Division

Nineteenth Army: (Amboina)

5th Division
46th Division
48th Division

Fourth Air Army: (Menado, Celebes)*

Nearly defunct

Fourteenth Army: Lieutenant General S. Kuroda (Manila)

1 division
4 independent mixed brigades

*Originally part of General Imamura's *Eighth Area Army* (see Appendix 14).

Sixteenth Army: (western Netherlands East Indies)

   2 independent mixed brigades (probable)

Southwest Area Fleet (Suribaya, Java)

   Ninth Fleet, including the 17th Base Force (Hollandia)
   First Expeditionary Fleet
   Second Expeditionary Fleet
   Third Expeditionary Fleet
   Fourth Expeditionary Fleet (Airborne)

Appendix 23
Allied Organization for Attack on Hollandia

General Douglas MacArthur, Supreme Commander, SWPA

SEVENTH FLEET
(Vice Admiral T. Kinkaid)

    Task Force 77 Attack Force: Rear Admiral D. Barbey

        Task Group 77.1 Western Attack Group (Tanahmerah Bay): Rear Admiral D. Barbey

        Task Group 77.2 Center Attack Group (Humboldt Bay): Rear Admiral W. Fechteler

        Task Group 77.3 Eastern Attack Group (Aitape): Captain A. Noble

        Task Group 77.4 First Reinforcement Group: Captain E. Thompson

        Task Group 77.5 Second Reinforcement Group: Captain J. McGovern

    Task Force 78 Escort Carrier Groups: Rear Admiral V. Ragsdale

        Task Group 78.1 Carrier Division 22: Rear Admiral V. Ragsdale

        Task Group 78.2 Carrier Division 24: Rear Admiral R. Davison

    Task Force 74 Covering Force "A": Rear Admiral V. Crutchley, RN

    Task Force 75 Covering Force "B": Rear Admiral R. Verkey

    Task Force 73 Aircraft Seventh Fleet: Commodore T. Combs

Admiral Chester Nimitz, Supreme Commander, POA, In Support

Task Force 58 Fast Carrier Task Force: Vice Admiral M. Mitscher

Task Groups 58.1, 58.2, 58.3, and 58.4 (Carrier Task Groups One, Two, Three and Four)

Task Group 58.7 BATTLE LINE: Vice Admiral W. Lee

Appendix 24

American Casualties During the Approach to the Philippines

| | | Killed | | | Wounded | |
	USA	USN	USMC	USA	USN	USMC
Hollandia	155	4		1,060	7	
Aitape	450			2,550		
Wakde-Sarmi	415	3		1,500	10	
Biak	435	36		2,360	83	
Noemfoor	70			345	3	
Sansapor	15			45		
Morotai	30	15		85	18	
Palaus	540	158	1,250	2,735	505	5,275
Asia-Mapia	20			45		
Ulithi	5			10		

COMPARATIVE CASUALTIES

	Killed	Wounded
Southwest Pacific Area from Hollandia to Morotai	1,648	8,112
Central Pacific Area Invasion of the Palaus only	1,948	8,515

Appendix 25
Allied Organization for Attack on Leyte

General Douglas MacArthur, Supreme Commander, SWPA

Seventh Fleet and Central Philippines Attack Force
(Vice Admiral T. Kinkaid)

Task Force 78 Northern Attack Force: Rear Admiral D. Barbey

Embarking X Corps

Task Group 78.1 Palo Alto Attack Group
Task Group 78.2 San Ricardo Attack Group
Fire Support Unit North
Task Group 78.4 Dinagat Attack Group
Task Group 78.6 Reinforcement Group One
Task Group 78.7 Reinforcement Group Two
Task Group 78.8 Reinforcement Group Three

Task Force 79 Southern Attack Force: Vice Admiral T. Wilkinson

Embarking XXIV Corps

Task Group 79.1 Attack Group "ABLE"
Task Group 79.3 Transport Group "ABLE"
Task Group 79.5 LST Flotilla 16
Task Group 79.2 Attack Group "BAKER"
Task Group 79.4 Transport Group "BAKER"
Fire Support Unit South

Task Group 77.4 Escort Carrier Group: Rear Admiral T. Sprague

16 CVEs
Destroyers

Task Group 77.3 Close Covering Group: Rear Admiral J. Oldendorf

Task Group 77.5 Minesweeping and Hydrographic Group: Commander W. Loud, RAN

Task Group 77.6 Beach Demolition Group: Lieutenant Commander C. Morgan

Task Group 73.7 Seaplane Tenders, San Pedro Bay:

Task Group 70.1 Motor Torpedo Boat Squadrons Seventh Fleet: Commander S. Bowling

Task Group 77.77 Service Force Seventh Fleet Units Participating: Rear Admiral R. Glover

Admiral Chester Nimitz, Supreme Commander, POA, In Support

Third Fleet
(Admiral W. Halsey)

Task Force 38 Fast Carrier Force: Vice Admiral M. Mitscher

Task Group 38.1 Task Group One: 2 CVs, 2 CVLs
Task Group 38.2 Task Group Two: 3 CVs, 2 CVLs
Task Group 38.3 Task Group Three: 2 CVs, 2 CVLs
Task Group 38.4 Task Group Four: 2 CVs, 2 CVLs
Task Group 30.8 At Sea Logistics Group Third Fleet:

Task Force 17 Supporting Submarines Pacific Fleet: Vice Admiral C. Lockwood

Task Group 71.1 Supporting Submarines Seventh Fleet: Rear Admiral R. Christie

Appendix 26
Major Japanese Army Forces in Southern Area, September 1944

Southern Army
(Field Marshal H. Terauchi, Manila/Saigon)

Fourteenth Area Army: Lieutenant General T. Yamashita, Manila

8th Division (Luzon)
26th Division (Luzon)
103rd Division (Luzon)
105th Division (Luzon)
2nd Armored Division (Luzon)
55th Independent Mixed Brigade (Army Reserve, Luzon)
58th Independent Mixed Brigade (Luzon)
61st Independent Mixed Brigade (Luzon)
33rd Infantry Regiment (Army Reserve, Luzon)

Thirty-Fifth Army: Lieutenant General S. Suzuki, Cebu

16th Division (Leyte)
30th Division (Mindanao)
100th Division (Mindanao)
102nd Division (Palawan and Visayas)
54th Independent Mixed Brigade (Mindanao)

Fourth Air Army: Lieutenant General K. Tominaga, Manila

545 aircraft

Burma Area Army:

10 divisions
2 brigades

Seventh Area Army: (Malaya, Sumatra, Java)

   2 divisions
   9 brigades

Second Area Army: (Halmahera, Celebes, western New Guinea, and eastern Netherlands East Indies)

   6 divisions
   2 brigades

Thailand and Indo-China Garrison Armies:

   1 division
   2 brigades

Appendix 27

Major Japanese and Allied Naval Forces at the Battle for Leyte Gulf

Combined Fleet
(Admiral S. Toyoda, Japan [temporary duty Formosa])

Task Force Main Body (Third Fleet): Vice Admiral J. Ozawa, Japan*

3rd Carrier Division
4th Carrier Division
Cruisers and destroyers

First Striking Force: (Second Fleet): Vice Admiral T. Kurita, Lingga Roads †

Battleships, cruisers, and destroyers

Southwest Area Force (Fleet): Vice Admiral G. Mikawa, Manila

Second Striking Force (Fifth Fleet): Vice Admiral K. Shima, Japan**

Fifth Base Air Force (First Air Fleet): Vice Admiral T. Onishi, Clark Field, Luzon and Mindanao††

Sixth Base Force (Second Air Fleet): Vice Admiral S. Fukudome, deployed from Formosa to Clark Field, Luzon

Advance Submarine Force (Sixth Fleet): Vice Admiral S. Miwa, Japan

Pacific Fleet and Pacific Ocean Areas Forces
(Admiral Chester Nimitz, Hawaii)

*Also known as First Mobile Fleet, Mobile Fleet, or Northern Force. It was the decoy fleet.

† Split to become FORCE "A" or CENTER FORCE (Kurita) and FORCE "C" or VAN of SOUTHERN FORCE (Nishimura).

**Became the REAR of SOUTHERN FORCE.

†† Japanese naval air forces are difficult to pin down at this time. Each source presents a slightly different view of the command structure.

Third Fleet: Admiral W. Halsey

Fast Carrier Task Force (TF 38): Vice Admiral M. Mitscher

    Carrier Group (TG 38.1): Vice Admiral J. McCain
    Carrier Group (TG 38.2): Rear Admiral G. Brogan
    Carrier Group (TG 38.3): Rear Admiral F. Sherman
    Carrier Group (TG 38.4): Rear Admiral R. Davison

Miscellaneous Units

Southwest Pacific Area Forces
(General Douglas MacArthur, Leyte)

Seventh Fleet and Allied Naval Forces, SWPA: Vice Admiral T. Kinkaid

Central Philippines Attack Force (TF 77.7): Vice Admiral T. Kinkaid

    Northern Attack Force (TF 78): Rear Admiral D. Barbey
    Southern Attack Force (TF 79): Vice Admiral T. Wilkinson
    Closing Covering Group (TG 77.3): Rear Admiral J. Oldendorf
    Escort Carrier Group (TG 77.4): Rear Admiral T. Sprague

        "Taffy 1": Rear Admiral T. Sprague
        "Taffy 2": Rear Admiral F. Stump
        "Taffy 3": Rear Admiral C. Sprague

    Minesweeping and Hydrographic Group (TG 77.5): Commander W. Loud, RAN
    Beach Demolition Group (TG 77.6): Lt Cmdr C. Morgan
    Service Group (TG 77.77): Rear Admiral R. Glover

Appendix 28

United States Army Casualties, Leyte Campaign, October 20, 1944-May 1945

Organization	Killed	Wounded
Sixth Army Troops	141	813
Eighth Army Troops	61	340
X Corps		
Americal Division (+)	162	566
24th Infantry Division	544	1784
32nd Infantry Division	450	1491
38th Infantry Division	68	171
1st Cavalry Division	203	726
11th Airborne Division	168	352
1st Filipino Division*	14	38
108th Regimental Combat Team	14	39
112th Regimental Combat Team	32	128
Corps Troops	15	89
XXIV Corps		
7th Infantry Division	584	2179
77th Infantry Division	499	1723
96th Infantry Division	469	1189
Corps Troops	80	363

*A guerrilla force.

Appendix 29
Japanese Forces on Luzon, January 11, 1945

Fourteenth Area Army
(Lieutenant General T. Yamashita, Commanding)

Shobu Group: Lieutenant General T. Yamashita (Baguio)*

2nd Tank Division (—)
10th Division (—)
19th Division (—)
23rd Division (—)
103rd Division (—)
58th Independent Mixed Brigade
Tsuda Detachment (11th Infantry Regiment (—), Reinforced)
Elements, Fourth Air Army †

Shimbu Group: Lieutenant General S. Yokoyama

8th Division (—)
105th Division
Manila Naval Defense Force (bulk of the 31st Naval Special Base Force) (16,000)**
Elements, Fourth Air Army

Kembu Group: Major General R. Tsukada

1st Raiding Group (2nd Glider Infantry Regiment)
2nd Mobile Infantry Regiment (—), 2nd Tank Division
39th Infantry Regiment (—), 10th Division
Naval combat and service troops (15,000)
Elements, Fourth Air Army

Shobu was also the code name for Fourteenth Area Army.

† Marshall Terauchi placed the Fourth Air Army under Yamashita's command on January 1, 1945.

**By local agreement, all naval forces came under Yamashita's command once fighting began on Luzon.

Appendix 30

Eighth United States Army Operations in the Philippines, 1944-1945

Initial Actions in Support of Sixth Army on Luzon

MIKE VII	January 29	Landing of XI Corps (38th Infantry Division) at Zambales
MIKE VI	January 31	Landing of the 11th Airborne Division (+) at Nasugbu

Clearing of the Visayan Passages

	December 26, 1944	Landings of the Americal, 24th, and 40th Infantry Divisions from Lubang Island to the San Bernadino Strait area

The Victor Operations (Sequence of Initial Landings)

VICTOR III	February 28	Landing of the 186th Infantry RCT (41st Infantry Division) on Palawan
VICTOR IV	March 10	Phase I: Landing of the 41st Infantry Division (−) on Mindanao
VICTOR II	March 18	Landing of the 40th Infantry Division on Panay. Followed by landings on Negros Occidental.
VICTOR V	March 26	Landing of the Americal Division on Cebu. Followed by landings on Behol and Negros Oriental.
VICTOR II	April 17	Landings of X Corps (24th and 31st Infantry Divisions) on Mindanao

Other Operations

	December 26, 1944	Occupation and mop-up of Leyte; replaced Sixth Army
	January 1	Occupation and mop-up of Mindoro; replaced Sixth Army
	July 1	Occupation and mop-up of Luzon; replaced Sixth Army

Appendix 31
Division of Allied Command Responsibilities in Southeast Asia, March–April 1942

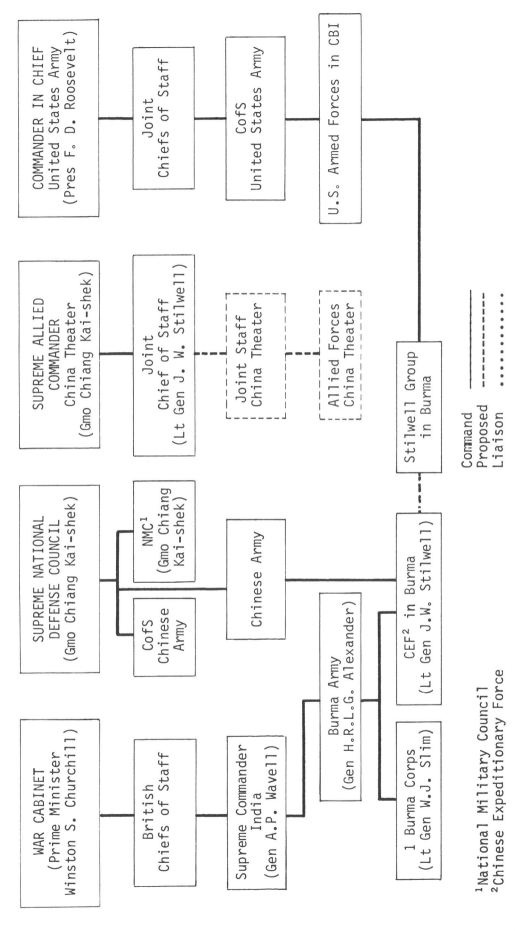

Command —————
Proposed - - - - - - -
Liaison ··········

[1]National Military Council
[2]Chinese Expeditionary Force

Source: Romanus and Sunderland, *Stilwell's Mission to China*, p. 88.

Appendix 32
Organization of U.S. Army Forces in China-Burma-India, December 1942

U.S. Army Forces, CBI:
(Lt Gen J. W. Stilwell)

Ramgarh Training Center (Brig Gen F. McCabe)

Infantry Section
Artillery Section
Language Section

Services of Supply (Maj Gen R. A. Wheeler)

Base Sections

Karachi
Calcutta
Ledo

Advance Section

Kunming

Tenth Air Force (Brig Gen C. L. Bissell)

India Air Task Force
China Air Task Force (Brig Gen C. L. Chennault)
India-China Ferry Command

Appendix 33
The Allied Chain of Command, Southeast Asia, December 1943–June 1944

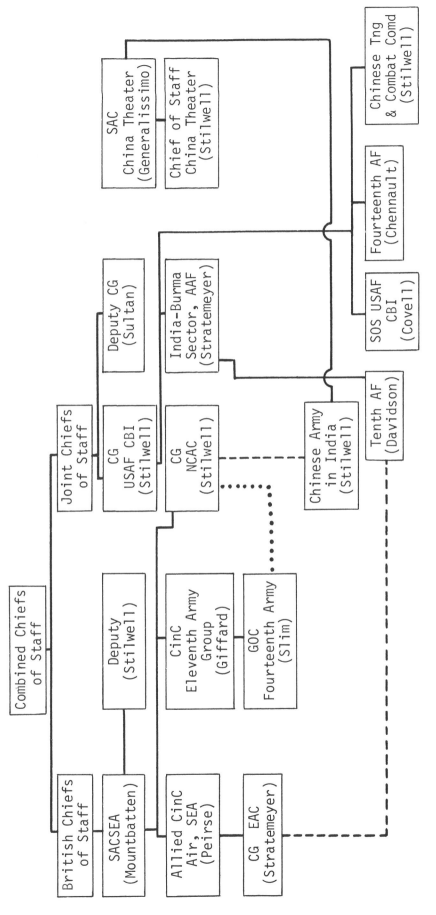

Source: Romanus & Sunderland, *Stilwell's Command Problems*, p. 6.

Appendix 34

The Allied Chain of Command, Southeast Asia, November 1944

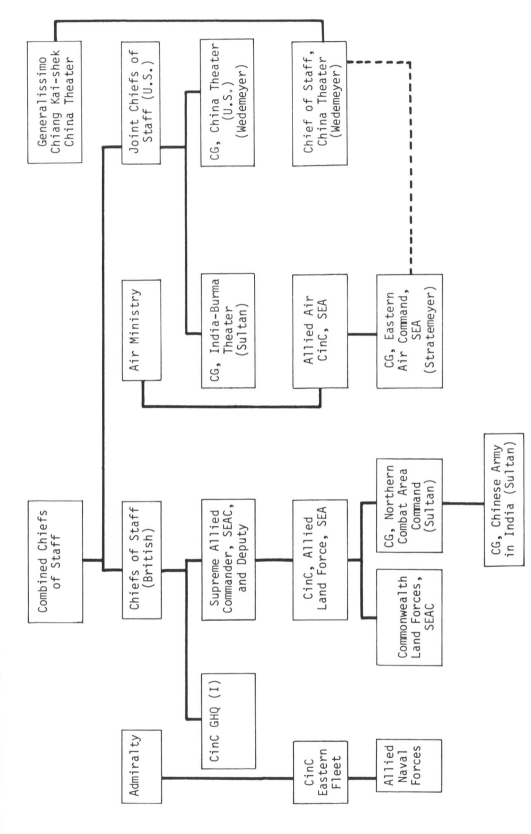

Source: Romanus & Sunderland, *Time Runs Out in CBI*, p. 30.

Appendix 35
American-Chinese Liaison System, 1944-1945

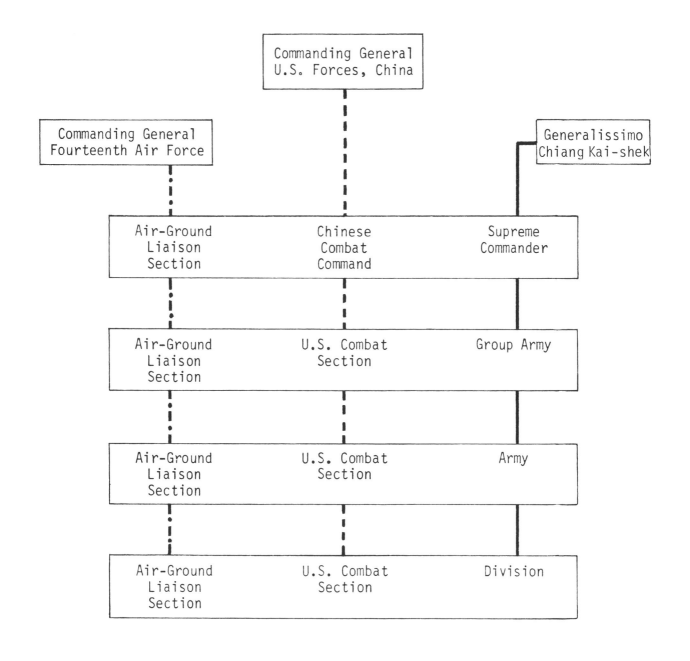

Source: Romanus and Sunderland, *Time Runs Out in CBI*, p. 263.

Appendix 36
Organization for Invasion of Okinawa

Admiral Chester Nimitz, Supreme Commander, POA

Central Pacific Task Force (Fifth Fleet)
(Admiral R. Spruance)

Covering Forces and Special Groups (Task Force 50):

Fast Carrier Task Force (Task Force 58): Vice Admiral M. Mitscher
British Carrier Task Force (Task Force 57): Vice Admiral Sir B. Rawlings, RN

Joint Expeditionary Force (Task Force 51): Vice Admiral R. Turner

Expeditionary Troops (Task Force 56 and Tenth Army): Lieutenant General S. Buckner, USA
Northern Attack Force (Task Force 53 Landing III Amphibious Corps): Rear Admiral L. Reifsnyder
Southern Attack Force (Task Force 55 Landing XXIV Corps): Rear Admiral J. Hall
Demonstration Group (with the 2nd Marine Division embarked): Rear Admiral J. Wright
Amphibious Support Force (Task Force 52): Rear Admiral W. Blandy
Western Islands Attack Group (Landing 77th Infantry Division): Rear Admiral I. Kiland
Gunfire and Covering Group (Task Force 54): Rear Admiral M. Deyo

North Pacific Force: Vice Admiral F. J. Fletcher

South Pacific Force: Vice Admiral N. Calhoun

Air Force, Pacific Fleet: Vice Admiral G. Murray

Service Force, Pacific Fleet: Rear Admiral W. Smith

Submarine Force, Pacific Fleet: Vice Admiral C. Lockwood

US Army Forces, Pacific Ocean Areas: Lieutenant General R. Richardson, USA

Strategic Air Forces, Pacific Ocean Areas: Major General W. Hale, USA

Forward Area, Central Pacific Force: Vice Admiral J. Hoover

Gilberts-Marshalls Force: Rear Admiral W. Harrill

Appendix 37

American and Japanese Forces Employed in Okinawa Campaign

United States	Japan

United States

Tenth Army:
Lieutenant General S. Buckner, USA

Army Troops:

20th Armor Group
713th Armored Flame Thrower
Battalion

XXIV Corps:
Major General J. Hodge, USA

7th Infantry Division (+)
27th Infantry Division (+)
77th Infantry Division (+)
96th Infantry Division (+)
Corps Artillery

III Amphibious Corps:
Major General R. Geiger, USMC

1st Marine Division (+)
6th Marine Division (+)
8th Marine Regiment, 2nd Marine Division (+)
Corps Artillery

Tactical Air Force:
Major General E. Mulcahy, USMC

Japan

Thirty-Second Army:
Lieutenant General M. Ushijima, IJA

Infantry Units: (38,310)

24th Division
62nd Division
44th Independent Mixed Brigade
1st-3rd Independent Battalions
26th-29th Independent Battalions
Miscellaneous Special Units

Armor, Artillery, and Automatic Weapons Units:
(11,476)

27th Tank Regiment
5th Artillery Command
Other Units

Shipping and Engineer Units: (4,465)

Air Force Ground Units: (6,936)

Line of Communications Troops: (7,333)

Naval Units: (3,500)

Miscellaneous Units: (3,359)

Okinawa Home Guard (*Boeitai*): (20,000)

Marine Air Wing 2
VII Bomber Command, USAAF
301st Fighter Wing, USAAF

COMPARATIVE STRENGTHS, APRIL 1, 1945

United States Forces: 182,821

Japanese Forces: 97,000 (approx.)
  (including *Boeitai*)

Selected Bibliography

General

Andrade, Ernest J. Jr., "Submarine Policy in the United States Navy, 1919-1941," *Military Affairs,* XXXII (April 1971), 50-53. An important article which deals ably with the development of submarine types and unrestricted submarine warfare.

Benedict, Ruth. *The Chrysanthemum and the Sword, Patterns of Japanese Culture.* Boston, 1946. Best social history and evaluation of the Japanese warrior available. Important for anyone attempting to understand the Japanese soldier, sailor, or airman (all warriors) in World War II.

Blakeney, Ben Bruce. "The Japanese High Command," *Military Affairs*, IX (Summer 1945), 95-101. This, and its companion piece in the next issue of *Military Affairs*, presents the best explanation of the Japanese command system available in article form.

Coffey, Thomas M. *Imperial Tragedy, Japan in World War II, The First Days and the Last.* New York, 1970. A worthwhile book which covers political actions in Japan.

Coox, Alvin D. *Japan, The Final Agony.* New York, 1970. An intriguing story about the final days of the Japanese Empire by the leading American historian of the Japanese Army in World War II.

Falk, Stanley L. *Bataan: The March of Death.* New York, 1962. Balanced account of a dreadful event which needs to be read by anyone interested in the attitudes of the Japanese Army.

Feis, Herbert. *The China Tangle.* Princeton, New Jersey, 1953. Careful coverage of the China problem.

_____. *Japan Subdued, The Atomic Bomb and the End of the War in the Pacific.* Princeton, New Jersey, 1961. A detailed and comprehensive book about diplomacy and the end of the war against Japan. Most useful.

_____. *The Road to Pearl Harbor, The Coming of the War Between the United States and Japan.* Princeton, New Jersey, 1950. A comprehensive summary of the events leading to war.

Greenfield, Kent Roberts (ed.). *Command Decisions.* Washington, 1950. This anthology contains an exceptional number of incisive and important articles concerning the Pacific war. Those dealing with the Admiralties, Luzon, and the atomic bomb are particularly interesting and valuable.

Harriman, W. Averell and Elie Abel. *Special Envoy to Churchill and Stalin, 1941-1946.* New York, 1975. Good coverage of Russian-American relations as they involved Far Eastern affairs and hostilities against Japan.

Hayashi, Saburo (in collaboration with Alvin D. Coox). *Kogun, The Japanese Army in the Pacific War.* Quantico, Virginia, 1959. The best single volume about the Japanese Army in the Pacific war. Difficult, disorganized, but essential. Coox's footnotes and biographical sketches are truly invaluable.

Headquarters, United States Army Forces, Far East, and Eighth United States Army Military History Section, Japanese Research Division. "Japanese Night Combat," May 10, 1955. A detailed and authoritative summary of Japanese tactics, day and night.

Inoguchi, Rikichei and Tadashi Nakajima. *The Divine Wind.* Annapolis, Maryland, 1958. Japanese history of the *Kamikaze* Force.

Isely, Peter A. and Philip A. Crowl. *The U.S. Marines and Amphibious War, Its Theory, and Its Practice in the Pacific.* Princeton, 1951. By far the best book about the Marines in the Pacific. The only single volume on the subject. Scholarly, balanced, and comprehensive.

Jensen, Marius B. (ed.). *Japan's Longest Day.* Cambridge, 1971. A fine recounting of the final hours which led to the surrender of Japan.

Kittredge, T.B. "United States Defense Policy and Strategy, 1941," *U.S. News and World Report*, December 3, 1954. A comprehensive article about the stated subject and its impact on Pearl Harbor.

Langer, William and L. and S. Everett Gleason. *The Undeclared War, 1940-1941.* New York, 1953. Probably still the definitive account of how the United States stumbled into war with Japan.

Mitchell, Donald W. *A History of Russian and Soviet Sea Power.* New York, 1974. Contains a good description of the brief Russian naval offensive against Japan in 1945.

Morton, Louis. "The Japanese Decision for War," *The United States Naval Institute Proceedings.* LXXX (December 1954), 1325-1335. A fine article.

Ogburn, Charlton, Jr. *The Marauders.* New York, 1959. A gripping account of "Merrill's Marauders."

Okumiya, Masataki and Jiro Horikoshi. *Zero.* New York, 1956.

A general account of the Pacific war from the Japanese viewpoint, with emphasis on air operations from 1937 to 1945.

Polmar, Norman, et. al. *Aircraft Carriers, A Graphic History of Carrier Aviation and Its Influence on World Events*. Garden City, New York, 1969. A comprehensive work about carriers and carrier aviation.

Potter, E.B. and Chester W. Nimitz. *Sea Power: A Naval History*. Englewood Cliffs, New Jersey, 1960. A basic text, written for midshipmen at Annapolis.

Reischauer, Edwin O. *Japan, Past and Present*. New York, 1969. An excellent summary of Japan's history by the foremost American historian of Japan.

Rhoer, Edward Van Der. *Deadly Magic*. New York, 1978. An account of how the Japanese code systems were broken and the results—by one of the Navy officers involved.

Romanus, Charles F. and Riley Sunderland. *Stilwell's Command Problems*. Washington, 1956.

_____. *Stilwell's Mission to China*. Washington, 1956.

_____. *Time Runs Out in CBI*. Washington, 1959. These three excellent U.S. Army official histories are indispensable to an understanding of the American involvement in the war in China and Burma.

Roscoe, Theodore. *United States Submarine Operations in World-War II*. Annapolis, 1949. The most comprehensive work available about American submarine operations in the Pacific.

Stimson, Henry L. "The Decision to Use the Atomic Bomb," in Gorden B. Turner (ed.). *A History of Military Affairs in Western Society Since the Eighteenth Century*. New York, 1953. A key decision maker's observations about one of the most critical decisions of the Pacific war.

Taylor, George E. and Franz H. Michael. *The Far East in the Modern World*. New York, 1956. A good basic source book about the political background of the modern nations in the Far East prior to World War II.

Toland, John. *The Rising Sun, the Decline and Fall of the Japanese Empire, 1936-1945*. New York, 1971. A popular work which covers the war from an essentially Japanese point of view and deals primarily with the early part of the war. Heavily anecdotal.

Sakai, Saburo and Martin Caidin. *Samurai!* New York, 1958. An account of the Japanese Naval Air Force in World War II by a surviving fighter pilot.

Sherman, Frederick C. *Combat Command: The American Aircraft Carriers in the Pacific War*. New York, 1950. A straightforward account.

The Pacific War Research Society (Compiler). *Japan's Longest Day*. New York, 1972. A detailed work by Japanese scholars which explores and explains the actions which finally brought Japan to surrender. Compelling, it gives an excellent insight into the minds and emotions of the Japanese and their leaders after three years of hard war.

United States Congress, Joint Committee on the Investigation of the Pearl Harbor Attack. *Pearl Harbor Attack Hearings*. Selected volumes. An overwhelming collection of information, letters, documents, and orders about the attack on Pearl Harbor. Valuable and informative.

United States Naval Institute. *The Japanese Navy in World War II*. Annapolis, 1969. An unusually excellent anthology of critical articles about the Japanese Navy. Useful and illuminating.

United States War Department. *War Department Technical Manual TM E30-480, Handbook on Japanese Military Forces*. Washington, 1944. The most complete source book about the Japanese armed forces. Useful.

Watson, Mark S. *Chief of Staff, Prewar Plans and Preparations*. Washington, 1950. Excellent U.S. Army official history dealing with prewar strategy.

Weigley, Russell F. *History of the United States Army*. New York, 1967. Useful institutional history of the Army, which covers the interwar years adequately.

Battles and Campaigns

Appleman, Roy E. et. al. *Okinawa: The Last Battle*. Washington, 1948. A first-class account of the bitter Okinawa campaign. A U.S. Army official history.

Bartley, Whitman S. *Iwo Jima: Amphibious Epic*. Washington, 1954. A straightforward and useful U.S. Marine Corps official monograph.

Bradley, John H. "From the Dark Side of the Moon: Raiding by Ground Forces in the Southwest Pacific Area During the Second World War." Unpublished MA Thesis, 1970. A study of American raiding actions in the theater, emphasizing raids on the prisoner-of-war camp at Cabanatuan and the internment camp at Los Banos in the Philippines.

Butler, J.R.M. *Grand Strategy*, Vol 2, Part 2. London, 1964. The official British history, portraying an ally's view of the strategy for prosecuting the war against Japan.

Cannon, M. Hamlin. *Leyte, The Return of the Philippines*. Washington, 1954. A U.S. Army official history.

Congdon, Don (ed.). *Combat, Pacific Theater, World War II*. New York, 1958. Outstanding collection of excerpted histories about special parts of the Pacific war.

_____. *Combat, The War With Japan*. New York, 1962. Outstanding collection of excerpted histories about special parts of the Pacific war.

Craven, Wesley Frank and James Lea Cate (eds.). *The Army Air Forces in World War II*. Volumes I, IV and V. Chicago, 1948-1953. These volumes present information about the development, organization, training, and employment of the Army Air Forces in World War II. The coverage of the Pacific and Asia, and especially the atomic weapons, is excellent.

Crowl, Philip A. *Campaign in the Marianas*. Washington, 1960. A U.S. Army official history of a difficult campaign which involved heated controversies between the Army and the Marine Corps.

_____ and Edmund G. Love. *Seizure of the Gilberts and Marshalls*. Washington, 1955. An excellent official history of the predominantly naval campaign.

Ehrman, John. *Grand Strategy*. Vol. V. London, 1956. The official British history, portraying an ally's view of the strategy for prosecuting the war against Japan.

Esposito, Vincent J. (ed.). *The West Point Atlas of American Wars*. 2 Vols. New York, 1959. Volume II, Section 2, covers the Pacific war. Terse, factual account with fine supporting maps.

Falk, Stanley L. *Decision at Leyte*. New York, 1966. A highly readable and comprehensive book about the air, naval, and land campaign at Leyte; good coverage of Japanese plans and actions.

Fuchida, Mitsuo and Masatake Okumiya. *Midway, The Battle That Doomed Japan, The Japanese Navy's Story*. New York, 1955. The finest single volume about the Imperial Japanese Navy through the Battle of Midway.

Hough, Frank O. *The Assault on Peleliu*. Washington, 1950. A U.S. Marine Corps official monograph. The battle for Peleliu shocked the Marine Corps badly. This honest account tells why.

Hough, Frank, Verle E. Ludwig, and Henry I. Shaw, Jr. *Pearl Harbor to Guadalcanal, History of U.S. Marine Corps Operations in World War II*. Washington, 1958. Excellent U.S. Marine Corps official history of prewar years and early combat actions in the Pacific war.

Huston, James A. *Out of the Blue: U.S. Army Airborne Operations in World War II*. West Lafayette, Indiana, 1972. Includes coverage of airborne operations in the Philippines, New Guinea, and Burma.

Kirby, S. Woodburn, et. al. *The War Against Japan*. 5 Vols. London, 1957. Kirby's volumes about the British Army in Burma and throughout the Asian and Pacific theaters of war are excellent histories. More tactical than the American histories, these works deal often with small units operating over extended periods and distances.

Long, Gavin. *The Final Campaigns*. Canberra, 1963. An Australian Army official history which covers many of the difficult operations in bypassed New Guinea and the Solomons as well as operations in Borneo. Excellent coverage of small unit actions.

Lord, Walter. *Day of Infamy*. New York, 1965. A valuable popular history about the attack on Pearl Harbor.

_____. *Incredible Victory*. New York, 1967. An unusually good popular history about the Battle of Midway.

McCarthy, Dudley. *South-West Pacific Area—First Year, Kokoda to Wau*. Canberra, 1956. An official Australian Army history which contains excellent accounts of small unit actions in the theater.

Matloff, Maurice and Edwin M. Snell. *Strategic Planning for Coalition Warfare*. Washington, 1953. Outstanding U.S. Army official history about American strategy.

Meretskov, K.A. Trans. David Fidlon. *Serving the People*. Moscow, 1971. Meretskov took part in the Russian offensive against Japan, which he describes according to Communist doctrine.

Merrifield, Robert B. "Japan's Amphibious Bid," *Marine Corps Gazette*, XXXVIII (May 1954), 40-47. A good summary of Japanese actions which serves as a basis for a comparison with American amphibious actions later in the war.

Merrill, James M. *Target Tokyo, The Halsey-Doolittle Raid*. New York, 1964. A popular account of one of the most important single actions of the Pacific war.

Middlebrook, Martin and Patrick Mahoney. *Battleship: The Sinking of the Prince of Wales and the Repulse*. New York, 1979. An exhaustive study of that early British naval disaster off Malaya.

Miller, John Jr. *Cartwheel, The Reduction of Rabaul*. Washington, 1959. An excellent narrative of American operations against Rabaul. An official U.S. Army history.

_____. *Guadalcanal: The First Offensive*. Washington, 1949.

Excellent official U.S. Army history about the Guadalcanal campaign.

Milner, Samuel. *Victory in Papua*. Washington, 1957. An outstanding U.S. Army official history. Especially valuable for the account about Buna and the leadership problems involved in that campaign.

Morison, Samuel Eliot. *The Two-Ocean War, A Short History of the United States Navy in the Second World War*. New York, 1972. This small volume serves as a useful summary of Morison's many volumes about the war and as an entry point to that extensive historical series.

_____. *The Rising Sun in the Pacific, 1931-April 1942*. Boston, 1948. Valuable account about the background of the opposing navies in the Pacific and the attack on Pearl Harbor.

_____. *Coral Sea, Midway and Submarine Actions, May 1942-August 1942*. Boston, 1967. Valuable account of early American naval actions.

_____. *The Struggle for Guadalcanal, August 1942-February 1943*. Boston, 1950. Excellent history of the naval actions which were so crucial to the campaign for Guadalcanal.

_____. *Breaking the Bismarcks Barrier, 22 July 1942-1 May 1944*. Boston, 1968. The naval story. Enhances Miller's *Cartwheel, The Reduction of Rabaul*.

_____. *Aleutians, Gilberts and Marshalls, June 1942-April 1944*. Boston, 1951. The naval campaign in the Central Pacific Area is the central theme.

_____. *New Guinea and the Marianas, March 1944-August 1944*. Boston, 1953. Good source for naval support of Hollandia operation and the Battle of the Philippine Sea.

_____. *Leyte, June 1944-January 1945*. Boston, 1958. Especially useful for the detailed account of the Battle for Leyte Gulf and the start of *kamikaze* warfare.

_____. *Victory in the Pacific, 1945*. Boston, 1960. Valuable for the description of the naval battle off Okinawa and for a final view of American submarine operations.

Morton, Louis. *Strategy and Command: The First Two Years*. Washington, 1962. An invaluable strategic summary of the first two years of war in the Pacific. Unfortunately, there is no similar book covering the final years of war. A U.S. Army official history.

_____. *The Fall of the Philippines*. Washington, 1953. A masterful account of a stunning American defeat. Clear, detailed, and dispassionate. A U.S. Army official history.

Nichols, Charles E. Jr., and Henry I. Shaw, Jr. *Okinawa: Victory in the Pacific*. Washington, 1955. A U.S. Marine Corps official history which complements Appleman.

Prange, Gordon W. *At Dawn We Slept: The Untold Story of Pearl Harbor*. New York, 1981. Probably the best documented, most comprehensive account of the U.S. debacle at Pearl Harbor.

_____. *Miracle at Midway*. New York, 1982. A comprehensive account of the pivotal naval battle.

Reports of General MacArthur. Volume I: *The Campaigns of MacArthur in the Pacific*. Washington, 1966. An excellent source, the best single volume history of the war in the Southwest Pacific Theater. Very pro-MacArthur; very pro-American.

Reports of General MacArthur. Volume II: *Japanese Operations in the Southwest Pacific Area*. 2 Vols. Washington, 1966. A very detailed history of Japanese operations in MacArthur's theater. Valuable for the text, the detailed footnotes, the excellent maps, and the translations of a great number of Japanese military and political documents.

Reports of the Commanding General, Eighth Army. 8 Vols. 1945. Excellent mimeographed reports of Eighth Army's operations on Luzon, in the Visayas, and on Mindanao.

Sixth United States Army. *Report of the Leyte Operation, 17 October 1944-25 December 1944.* APO 201, 1945. Good source for orders and summaries of the Leyte campaign.

_____. *Report of the Luzon Campaign, 9 January 1945-30 June 1945.* APO 201, 1945. A useful source of orders, documents, and summaries of actions concerning Luzon.

Smith, Robert Ross. *The Approach to the Philippines.* Washington, 1953. One of the largest and most detailed of the U.S. Army official histories. It covers everything from the Admiralties to Leyte and relates to the Central Pacific Area fairly well.

_____. *Triumph in the Philippines.* Washington, 1963. Detailed account of the campaigns in the Philippines following Leyte with emphasis on Krueger's campaign on Luzon and Eichelberger's campaigns in the Visayas and on Mindanao.

Stockman, James R. *The Battle for Tarawa.* Washington, 1947. A Marine Corps monograph. Short, clear, and useful. Excellent maps.

Smyth, Sir John. *Before the Dawn.* London, 1957. An account of the first days of the war in Burma.

Tsuji, Masanobu. Translated by Margaret Lake. *Singapore. The Japanese Version.* New York, 1961. This is Tsuji's version, and it tells more about Tsuji and the mentality of Japanese extremists than it does about the actual campaign.

The United States Strategic Bombing Survey. *The Effects of Atomic Bombs on Hiroshima and Nagasaki.* Washington, 1946.

_____. *The Effects of Strategic Bombing on Japanese Morale.* Washington, 1947. An interesting and useful study.

The United States Strategic Bombing Survey (Pacific). *Campaigns of the Pacific War.* Washington, 1946. An invaluable summary of all key actions in the Pacific war, containing excellent documents, many orders, and detailed statistics.

_____. *The Allied Campaign Against Rabaul.* Washington, 1946. Excellent monographic study of the campaign.

_____. *The War Against Japanese Transportation, 1941-1945.* Washington, 1947. Excellent monographic study of the subject.

Wigmore, Lionel. *The Japanese Thrust.* Canberra, 1957. One of the official Australian Army histories. Excellent. A must for the Australian side of the war.

Wright, B.C. *The 1st Cavalry Division in World War II.* Tokyo, 1945. An unusually good divisional history of one of the divisions which served in the Southwest Pacific Area. Good material on the Admiralties, Leyte, and Luzon.

Wohlstetter, Roberta. *Pearl Harbor, Warning and Decision.* Stanford, 1962. A scholarly study of Pearl Harbor which should be used in conjunction with more popular works.

Personalities

Barbey, Daniel E. *MacArthur's Amphibious Navy, Seventh Amphibious Force Operations, 1943-1945.* Annapolis, 1969. Valuable history written by MacArthur's chief amphibious commander.

Browne, Courtney. *Tojo: The Last Banzai.* New York, 1972. One of the only biographies of Tojo available.

Buell, Thomas B. *The Quiet Warrior.* Boston, 1974. An understanding and perceptive account of the life of Spruance, one of the important leaders in the Pacific war.

Chynoweth, Bradford G. "Visayan Castaways." Unpublished manuscript, 1950. An unusually honest and realistic story of an American commander's disheartening experiences in the central Philippines from 1941 to 1942.

Eichelberger, Robert L. *Our Jungle Road to Tokyo.* New York, 1950. A colorful account of the Pacific war from a corps and army commander's point of view.

Frank, Bemis M. *Halsey.* New York, 1974. A straightforward account of the career of America's most pugnacious World War II admiral.

James, D. Clayton. *The Years of MacArthur.* 2 volumes. Boston, 1970 and 1973. The best and most comprehensive biography of MacArthur. The two volumes cover the period from 1880 to 1945.

Kenney, George C. *General Kenney Reports, A Personal History of the Pacific War.* New York, 1949. The only available air memoir which deals intimately with the pilots and their actions throughout the Southwest Pacific Area.

Krueger, Walter. *From Down Under to Nippon, The Story of Sixth Army in World War II.* Washington, 1953. MacArthur's primary army commander's story. It is virtually the official history of Sixth Army.

Luvaas, Jay (ed.). *Dear Miss Em, General Eichelberger's War in the Pacific, 1942-1945.* Westport, 1972. A very colorful account of General Eichelberger's war. It is as much a study of MacArthur as it is of Eichelberger.

Percival, A.E. *The War in Malaya.* London, 1949. The defeated commander's record of the worst British defeat since Yorktown.

Potter, E.B. *Nimitz.* Annapolis, 1976. The most authoratative biography of Nimitz.

Potter, John Dean. *A Soldier Must Hang, The Biography of an Oriental General.* London, 1963. A biography of Yamashita.

_____. *Yamamoto, The Man Who Menaced America.* New York, 1971. One of the only biographies of Yamamoto available.

Slim, Sir William. *Defeat into Victory.* New York, 1961. The best autobiography of a general in World War II, and an outstanding source for evaluations of the British and Japanese soldiers in Burma.

Smith, Holland M. and Percy Finch. *Coral and Brass.* New York, 1949. An intemperate American marine's memoirs. Much good information, but better insights into the mind and soul of Smith and the Marine Corps.

Stilwell, Joseph W. *The Stilwell Papers.* New York, 1948. If not the most balanced account of world events and the war in Asia, easily the most colorful, controversial, and honest. Exemplary study of Stilwell. Many fine insights; much anger.

Taylor, Theodore. *The Magnificant Mitscher.* New York, 1954. The story of the U.S. Navy's outstanding carrier commander, emphasizing his Pacific operations.

Tuchman, Barbara. *Stilwell and the American Experience in China, 1911-1945.* New York, 1972. A popular work which covers the campaign in Burma.

Wainwright, Jonathan M. *General Wainwright's Story.* Garden City, New York, 1946. Wainwright's view of the American defeat in the Philippines.

Index